Mastering the Art
of French Cooking:
Volume II

Mastering the Art of French Cooking is, as the *Daily Telegraph* has said, a book that 'no serious cook can afford to be without', bringing as it does, the advice and expertise of the master-chef to the enthusiastic amateur. Julia Child and Simone Beck are both Chevaliers de la Confèrie du Tastevin and they collaborated with Louisette Bertholle on the first volume of *Mastering the Art of French Cooking*. In 1951 the authors, who have each studied under a number of eminent French chefs, together with Louisette Bertholle, started a cooking school in Paris, L'École des Trois Gourmandes, which has since become famous. Julia Child has also published *The French Chef Cookbook* and *From Julia Child's Kitchen* (also published by Penguin).

This volume covers soups, baking, meats, poultry, charcuterie, vegetables and desserts in detail. The superb recipes are accompanied by step-by-step instructions and there are many excellent illustrations which clarify the most complicated-sounding process. Writing about this volume the *Guardian* said, 'the authors are world famous, and enjoy the respect of distinguished cooks everywhere. Very thorough and exhaustive', the *Lady* called it 'an essential handbook for the ambitious cook', and *House and Garden* commented, 'for the truly dedicated cook there could be no more authoritative and reassuring guides'.

JULIA CHILD
AND SIMONE BECK

Mastering the Art of French Cooking

VOLUME II

ILLUSTRATED BY SIDONIE CORYN

*(Based on photographs by Paul Child, who also
contributed 36 of his own drawings)*

PENGUIN BOOKS

Penguin Books Ltd, Harmondsworth, Middlesex, England
Viking Penguin Inc., 40 West 23rd Street, New York, New York 10010, U.S.A.
Penguin Books Australia Ltd, Ringwood, Victoria, Australia
Penguin Books Canada Limited, 2801 John Street, Markham, Ontario, Canada L3R 1B4
Penguin Books (N.Z.) Ltd, 182–190 Wairau Road, Auckland 10, New Zealand

First published in the U.S.A. by Alfred A. Knopf, Inc. 1970
Published in Great Britain by Michael Joseph 1977
Published in Penguin Books 1978
Reprinted 1979, 1981, 1982, 1987

Made and printed in Great Britain by
Richard Clay Ltd, Bungay, Suffolk

To

ALFRED KNOPF

who is as much an appreciator of good writing,
type faces, layout, and paper as he is of fresh
foie gras, *truite au bleu*, and Meursault Les
Perrières. In short, he is the ideal publisher for
this kind of book, just as he is the ideal dinner
guest for those who have mastered the art of
French cooking

Contents

NOTES

* This symbol preceding a recipe title indicates that variations follow.

(†) Wherever you see this symbol in the body of recipe texts you may prepare the dish ahead of time up to that point, then complete the recipe later.

The references to Volume I are to the Penguin edition.

Illustrations

The illustrations are by Sidonie Coryn, based on photographs
  by Paul Child
The technical drawings, on pages 48–58, 243,
  261–3, 276–7, 280–81, 296, 313–17, 415, 468 and 470,
  are by Paul Child.

Foreword

Mastering any art is a continuing process, and that explains *Mastering the Art of French Cooking*, Volume II, which came about in the following way. When the idea of our first book was forming in the early 1950s, we were so naïve as to propose not only to ourselves but also to an indulgent publisher, who invested 250 dollars in the project, a complete one-volume treatise covering the whole of *la cuisine française*. After labouring for six years it was clear that our detailed method of approach called for a multi-volume study; we therefore sent our publisher 800 pages of manuscript on French sauces and French poultry. This early outpouring was quickly rejected as unpublishable, although it covered every conceivable sauce and every imaginable poultry detail, including such marginal esoterica as advice on what to do if you have a bloodless *canard* for the duck press – we shall not reveal the solution other than to say it involved a quick trip to the slaughterhouse. That first publishing rebuff, cruel as it was, shook us into a more rational and realistic approach. Meanwhile, we had opened our cooking school in Paris, L'École des Trois Gourmandes, first located in a rooftop kitchen on the rue de l'Université and later in the comfortable apartment of Louisette, the third member of our team. Now married to Henri de Nalèche, and living in the beautiful hunting country near Bourges, La Sologne, Louisette did not collaborate with us on Volume II. It was through her inspiration, however, that we three started both the first book and the school together.

The cooking school catapulted us into almost all areas of French cooking, because you cannot teach the subject and not include the standard dishes that everyone has heard about – *quiche lorraine*, onion soup, *bœuf bourguignon*, *coq au vin*, *sole bonne femme*, *mousse au chocolat*, and *soufflé Grand Marnier* – to name a very familiar handful. Thus Volume I in its final form was the natural result of our teaching. It also goes into the fundamental techniques of *la cuisine bourgeoise*, meaning expert

French home-style cooking – how to make the flour and butter *roux* for the *sauce velouté*, how to beat egg whites and fold them into the soufflé to get the maximum puff, how to sauté the meat so that it will brown, and the mushrooms so they will not exude their juice, how to peel and seed the tomato, boil the beans, peel the asparagus and fold the omelette. Volume I, is, in fact, a long introduction to French cooking and anyone who has mastered it has covered most of the primary methods and recipes.

Volume II is a continuation. But rather than continuing on every front, we have selected seven subjects, and having so long ago rejected complete treatises, we have pursued each only in the directions that we felt were most useful or interesting. We wanted to add to the repertoire of informal vegetable soups, for example, and these take up a large part of the first chapter. We felt the need for a fine lobster bisque; this gave rise to a study of lobster cutting, and in turn led us to crabs, which are not adequately explored in most recipes (the whole matter of crab tomalley is almost never mentioned, yet it is every bit as precious as lobster tomalley). Then, although we adore *bouillabaisse* (which is in Volume I), there are other French fish stews that make marvellous one-dish meals, so we have added a *marmite*, a *matelote*, and a *bourride*. Thus the soup chapter is an enlargement in breadth.

Meat, poultry, and vegetables we have attacked in depth, following the same system of theme and variations used in Volume I, but taking it perhaps even further. *Poulet poché au vin blanc*, starting on page 343, is a prime example. Ordinary pieces of frying chicken are poached in white wine and aromatic vegetables, making a deliciously non-fattening dish that you can serve informally as it is, with boiled rice and a green vegetable. Nothing could be simpler, yet you can take this same chicken out of the peasant kitchen, as it were, and serve it at the château. You can transform it into an elegant aspic or *chaud-froid* or turn its poaching liquid into a creamy *velouté* and create a *gratin* of chicken Mornay, a splendid dish for a buffet supper. With egg yolks and cream the original chicken dish becomes a Belgian *waterzooi*, with garlic mayonnaise it is a chicken *bourride*, and with slightly different vegetable flavours but the same cooking methods it is a *bouillabaisse* of chicken. Thus, starting with one master technique, you are putting your cooking vocabulary to use the way it should be used, and if you are just beginning to cook, this is an exercise in recognition. You will begin to relate the sauce you used for the casserole of chicken to the *velouté* you made for the *coquilles Saint-Jacques* in another recipe, as well as to the *velouté* base you made for a cream of crab soup; the flavours are different, the proportions are not identical, especially for the soup, but the basic method is the same. You will recognize that sauce when you run into it again in some other guise. Again, if you are new to it, and have finally conquered your fear of scrambling the egg yolks as you stir them over the burner for that lovely custard sauce, *crème anglaise*, you will be nonchalant about heating egg yolks in the sauce for a *bourride* – or vice versa: you know what to expect, you have been there before, and, in effect, you are beginning to feel like a cook. For the experienced, we hope these ideas will start you off on further ventures in other categories.

Beef stews, veal chops and steaks, and veal stews take the same type of tour, our object being to show what you can do with reasonably priced meats for family meals as well as for entertaining. On the other hand, the luxurious fillet of beef also has its series of transformations. It is roasted whole, baked in a cloak of mushrooms *duxelles* and wine, as well as being, in another recipe, cut into slices and stuffed before roasting. Finally, in an original version of Beef Wellington, it is sliced, stuffed, and baked in a special type of *brioche* crust. An expensive roast of veal undergoes a group of variations, as does a whole roasting chicken, which finally appears with a boned breast and a corseting of pastry.

We hope you will enjoy the vegetable chapter as much as we do, because we have had fun with these recipes. Although there are a few of the classics, like *pommes Anna* and *pommes duchesse*, most of the recipes are originals that we have been working on for a number of years until we felt they were ripe for you and this volume. The chapter starts with broccoli, which we have treated freely *à la française* although it is almost unknown in France; we love its colour, its flavour, and its year-round availability. We also love aubergines, not only for their beauty as a vegetable object, but also for their adaptability, and versatility; we have grilled them, sautéed them in *persillade*, creamed them, souffléed them, served them hot, cold, stuffed, and wished we had room to do more. A lovely recipe for pumpkin-in-pumpkin introduces a group of unusual courgette dishes stemming from sautéed chunks of it to an original clutch of grated courgette treatments. Spinach, chard, and turnips all have representation, as do several versions of sautéed potatoes. There are stuffed onions, stuffed cabbage, stuffed courgettes, and cold stuffed artichoke hearts. Again, most of the vegetable chapter is built on themes and variations, and is designed to engender the flow of your creative juices.

Two entirely new categories are the chapters on breads and pastry doughs and on *charcuterie*. One is not really dining *à la française* without proper French bread to mop up the sauce on one's plate, or a fine *terrine* or *pâté en croûte* to start the meal, *boudins blancs* for New Year's Eve or for the turkey stuffing, a symmetrically baked, close-grained, beautifully textured sandwich bread for hors d'œuvre, truffled sausages to bake in pastry, *brioches* and croissants for breakfast – in fact, all such items which we, here, consider luxuries but which are everyday staples bought in *boulangeries, pâtisseries*, and *charcuteries* all over France.

Until our editor, in her gentle but compelling way, suggested that we really owed it to our readers to include a recipe for French bread, we had no plans at all to tackle it. Two years and some 284 pounds of flour later, we had tried out all the home-style recipes for French bread we could find, we had two professional French textbooks on baking, we had learned many things about yeasts and doughs, yet our best effort, which was a type of peasant sour-dough loaf, still had little to do with real French bread. Then we met Professor Calvel of the École Française de Meunerie in Paris, and it was like the sun in all his glory suddenly breaking through the shades of gloom. Fortunately those two years on the wrong road had been useful, because as soon as Professor Calvel started in, we knew what he was talking about, even though every step in the bread-making process was entirely different from anything we had heard of, read of, or seen. His dough was soft and sticky; he let it rise slowly twice, to triple its original volume – the dough must ripen to develop its natural flavour and proper texture. Forming the dough into its long-loaf or round-loaf shapes was a fascinating process, and so logical; slashing the top of the risen loaves before sliding them into the oven was another special procedure.

This was a tremendously exciting day for us, as you can imagine. We now knew we could succeed, because we had seen and felt with our own hands so clearly where we had failed. We rushed home and went to work again while Professor Calvel's teaching was vividly with us. There remained the problem of working out the formula with American plain bleached flour instead of the softer French unbleached flour. There was also the matter of adapting the home oven by some simple means into a simulated baker's oven, with a hot surface for the bread to bake on, and some kind of effective steam contraption. Although you can produce a presentable loaf without these two professional oven requirements, you will not get quite the high rise or quite the crust. Paul Child and his usual Yankee ingenuity solved the hot baking surface by sliding a sheet of asbestos cement on to the oven rack to heat up with the oven; he created a great burst of steam by placing a pan of water in the bottom of the oven, and dropping a red-hot brick into it. The flour problem solved itself; although our *maître* loathes bleached flours, we found, thank heaven, that the familiar brands of plain bleached flour worked remarkably well.

Pastry dough, *pâte brisée* and *pâte feuilletée*, also go hand in hand with cooking and eating traditions in France. While packaged dough mixes and frozen adaptations can certainly serve in emergencies, it is part of your training as a cook that you be able to turn out at least the dough for a pastry shell as a matter of course. It is actually, we think, when you have made the dough for your first *quiche* or tart, and have been complimented enthusiastically and specifically on the crust, that you begin to feel you are stepping out of the kindergarten and into a more advanced class of cooking. If you have had troubles or qualms, therefore, about hand-made dough, try the recipe on page 156, using an electric mixer; it works quickly and beautifully. Again, if you have hesitated to tackle the traditional flan ring lined with dough and weighted down with foil and beans, try the upside-down cake tin method illustrated on pages 158–61, which is an easy way to make pastry shells. Furthermore, the egg formula in the recipe (page 157) makes a deliciously crisp, tender, buttery crust.

As soon as you feel confident with pie-crust dough, we urge you to take on the larger and more fascinating challenge of *pâte feuilletée*. This is the French puffing dough, which consists of hundreds of very thin layers of flour paste separated by hundreds of layers of butter; it rises in the oven to several times its original height, to form *vol-au-vent* and patty shells, puffed entrées like the cheese tart on page 205, as well as the biscuits on pages 621–7, and the tarts and desserts starting on page 593. Properly made, it is flakily tender, and a delight to both tongue and palate. Although few French home cooks make puff pastry, since they can buy freshly baked *feuilletées* at their local *pâtisseries*, it is something that you, as a cook, will find tremendously useful all the rest of your kitchen life. We have spent years on puff pastry ourselves, wanting to make sure that the recipe in this book would be as good with American flour as it is with French flour – the trouble with American plain flour being that it has a higher gluten content than French flour, and that makes differences all along the line. We worked out combinations of unbleached pastry flour and plain flour, we have tried instant-blending flour, and we have finally settled on a mixture of ordinary plain flour and cake flour as being the most sensible. Although it takes a little longer to work with, it produces a beautifully tender, high-rising dough that is even more impressive, we think, than its French counterpart. The illustrated recipe for simple puff pastry starting on page 166 is easy to follow, and we suggest your first creation be either that cheese tart mentioned above or the jam tart on page 600. Both of them are quick to form, yet give a very handsome effect to start you off in a whirl of success.

Our forefathers did the kind of cooking in Chapter 5, *Charcuterie*, if they lived on a farm and made their own sausages and cured their own pork. Few French householders, again, attempt any of this today, because they can buy all kinds of sausages *chez le charcutier*, as well as salted pork, preserved goose, sausage in *brioche*, moulds of parslied ham, fresh liver *pâté, terrines*, and all the other marvellous concoctions that embellish French gastronomical life. The particularly wonderful taste of these creations is derived from the fact that they are freshly made, on the premises. We, who want to partake of the same pleasures, must make our own. And for anyone who enjoys cooking, producing *charcuterie*, like making bread and pastry, is a deeply satisfying occupation. You will be amazed, if you have never tried your own before, how rewarding just a home-made sausage patty can be; it is only freshly ground pork mixed with salt and spices, but it tastes the way one dreams sausage meat should taste. The large *saucissons à cuire*, starting on page 390, will make you think of France, as will the *jambon persillé*. When you want a real *cassoulet*, you can make the real *confit d'oie*, and have enough preserved goose left in the crock for many more meals. The difficult Christmas present or the gifts to hostesses need bother you no more – bring along one of your own *pâtés en croûte*.

The final chapter contains favourite desserts and cakes that we have been testing out on our guinea pigs – our students and families – for a number of years. The frozen desserts, so useful for all of us who need attractive finales that we may complete well in advance, are made without benefit of the ice-cream freezer; they vary in complexity from quickly made fruit sorbets to an elegant chocolate mousse dressed in meringues, and a flaming French baked Alaska, *la surprise du Vésuve*. We also give you a group of original fruit desserts, custards, and a liqueur-soaked French shortcake, a number of handsome desserts made with puff pastry, and a selection of *petits fours*. Among the eight cakes at the end of the chapter are a fine French honey bread, *pain d'épices*, a walnut cake, a beautiful meringue-nut layer cake called variously *Le Succès, Le Progrès*, or *La Dacquoise*, and two chocolate cakes. It will be for you to judge whether we have achieved the ultimate in chocolate with *La Charlotte Africaine* or with *Le Glorieux*, or whether that perennial cake winner made of chocolate and almonds, *La Reine de Saba*, in Volume I, still retains the title.

In all of our recipes, and especially in those for desserts and cakes, we have taken full advantage of modern mechanical aids wherever we have found them effective. While Volume I reflects France in the 1950s and the old traditions of French cooking, Volume II, like France herself, has stepped into contemporary life. We must admit, in Volume I, to a rather holy and Victorian feeling about the virtues of sweat and elbow grease – that only paths of thorns lead to glory, *il faut souffrir pour être belle* and all that. However, we are teachers; we want people to learn. And if we make it hard to cook through snobbish insistence on always beating egg whites by hand in a copper bowl, for instance, or always mixing pastries by hand (*il faut mettre la main dans la pâte*), when it is the hot hand that makes all the trouble, we know we have already lost a great part of our audience. We have therefore developed our own methods for machine-beaten egg whites, page 685, for machine-made cakes, pages 627–57, and there are directions for doing all the pastries and doughs by machine as well as by hand. Because machines make cooking so much easier, and because recipes that take tedious effort by hand – like *quenelles*, mousses, and meringues – can be done in minutes by machine, we urge you to provide yourself with the best you can afford, and refer you to the illustrated suggestions on pages 685–8.

We have so far said hardly a word about the illustrations, which are, to our mind, the glory of Volume II. We can speak of them without a hint of modesty because they are the result of a remarkable feat of teamwork between Paul Child, our action photographer, and Sidonie Coryn, our illustrator. Because of their tireless expertise we have been able to picture step-by-step operations that to our knowledge have never been adequately illustrated before; we now feel confident that this combined visual and verbal presentation makes absolutely clear the most complicated-sounding process. For French bread alone there are thirty-four drawings, showing the procedure from the start: mixing the dough, kneading it, how it looks when risen, how to deflate it, and the intricacies of forming the dough into various loaf shapes. Fillet of beef is pictured in such detail that you can buy a whole one and trim it yourself. With an illustrated guide before you, you can bone out the breast of a chicken, trim and tie a saddle of lamb, or cut up a lobster. Puff pastry and croissants are illustrated every step of the way, as are *brioches* and *bouchées*. You can see how to form upside-down pastry shells, how to stuff a whole cabbage leaf by leaf, and if you have never done or even seen a *pâté en croûte* in your life, you can be assured of success, because you have twelve drawings to show you every necessary move.

Without the team of Child and Coryn such coverage would have been impossible. Paul Child, ready at a moment's notice, was there to make careful, detailed, perfect photographs of any step of any recipe at any time during the day or night. Occasionally, when on-the-spot drawings served better than photographs, he contributed his talents to such techniques as the art of cutting up lobsters and crabs, carving a saddle of lamb, or depicting the bone structure of a breast of veal, and he was happy to draw the tricky arrangement of an aubergine dish that our words alone had confused. The major load of illustrating fell, of course, to Sidonie Coryn – her 458 drawings for this book are an almost incredible achievement. From grapefruit knives and cake pans to the step-by-step illustrations for a *Pithiviers* and *Dacquoise*, from electric mixers and garlic presses to the intricacies of a *poularde en soutien-gorge*, she has skilfully and stylishly drawn the essence of Paul Child's photographs, eliminating non-essentials and putting the right emphasis on the points of crucial interest.

We have little else to add to this leisurely meander. Words of advice, such as 'Do read the recipes before you start in to cook', 'Be sure your oven thermostat is accurate', and other sage admonitions are in the foreword to Volume I. We shall therefore only repeat the hope that you will keep your knives sharp and that, above all, you will have a good time.

Best wishes and *bon appetit*!

J. C. and S. B.

Acknowledgements

Our friends, students, families, and husbands have continued to act graciously and courageously as guinea pigs throughout the accumulation of years since Volume I began and Volume II came to its fruition; we owe them very special thanks. Again the U.S. Department of Agriculture has been a wonderful source of assistance, as has the U.S. Bureau of Fisheries, especially its Boston Branch. We are also grateful to the National Livestock and Meat Board for technical advice on many occasions, and we are deeply indebted to R. A. Seelig of the United Fresh Fruit and Vegetable Association, whose bulletins and letters have taught us so many things we never knew before. Gladys Christopherson has been our faithful and cheerful manuscript typer, putting neatly on to paper the scrawls and spots of working copy; we thank her every finger. Avis DeVoto, still acting as foster mother, wet nurse, guide, and mentor, has also taken on the copy editing for our side, as well as the position of indexer-in-chief; our admiration and gratitude can only be expressed by her weight in fresh truffles. Paul Child, tireless photographer at a moment's notice, pinch-hitting illustrator, clever turner of phrases when the well is dry – we can only continue to love him and to feed him well. We have also our peerless editor, Judith Jones, to thank most sincerely and affectionately; her conception of the book has produced what you now hold in your hands.

1. Soups from the Garden – Bisques and Soups from the Sea

There is hardly a man alive who does not adore soup, particularly when it is home-made. Hot soup on a cold day, cold soup on a hot day, and the smell of soup simmering in the kitchen are fundamental, undoubtedly even atavistic, pleasures and solaces that give a special kind of satisfaction.

Although many of us think immediately of French onion soup when we put France and soups together in our minds, informal vegetable combinations are more typical of that best of all cuisines – the cooking one finds in French homes and small family-style restaurants. Leek and potato soup (*potage Parmentier*), and its numerous variations in Volume I, is the most typical of all, but there are many other vegetable combinations, including spinach, cucumbers, green peppers, celery, peas and pea pods, even aubergine, that are interesting, unusual, easy to make, and delicious to serve. In many of these soups the vegetables are simmered in water rather than meat or poultry stock because water does not disguise the natural taste of a subtle vegetable like asparagus, for example. We shall begin with a group of these, follow with an opulent series of bisques and other shellfish soups, and end with three hearty fish stews, each one a meal in itself.

A NOTE ON PURÉEING

Most soups need puréeing at some point in the cooking, and we think the best puréeing instrument is the French 'Mouli' food mill with interchangeable discs illustrated in Appendix Two, page 682. It is very efficient even with somewhat tough items like asparagus stems; it also performs the important function of holding back stringy fibres that you would otherwise have to sieve out. To use a food mill, set it over a large bowl and pour the soup from your saucepan through the food mill to strain liquid from solids, and pour the liquid back into the saucepan. Purée the solid ingredients, adding some of the liquid now and then to ease their passage; scrape any adhering purée off the bottom of the machine and into the bowl, then pour contents of bowl into saucepan. (Some electric mixers come with food mill or puréeing attachments that work very well.)

If you prefer the electric blender, pour most of the liquid off the solids and into a bowl; ladle a cup or so of the solids and a cup of the liquid into the blender jar. Purée by turning the machine on and off every second or two to avoid that too-smooth effect of baby food, since you will usually want the soup to have some texture. Then, if you are doing a fibrous vegetable like asparagus butts or pea pods, strain all of the soup through a sieve just fine enough to hold back the fibres. A little experimentation and always an analytical sampling of the soup yourself will tell you what you need to do.

SOUP THICKENERS – LIAISONS

Puréed soups need a binder or liaison, which thickens the soup liquid enough so that the puréed ingredients remain in suspension rather than sinking to the bottom of the bowl. The simplest liaison is a starch of some sort, like grated potatoes, puréed rice, farina, or tapioca. Other soups, usually called *veloutés*, are thickened with a flour-and-butter *roux*. A more elegant liaison is raw egg yolks, which, when beaten into and heated with the soup, thickens it lightly. All of these liaisons are more or less interchangeable, and which one to use depends on what effect and taste you want to achieve.

ENRICHMENTS – AND *CRÈME FRAÎCHE*

Butter, cream, and, again, egg yolks, alone or in combination, are stirred into many soups just before serving. They give a final smoothness and delicacy of taste. You can omit them if you wish, or use just a small amount.

Sour cream, if you prefer less butter fat, may often be substituted for double cream. But *crème fraîche* is the perfect soup enrichment: mix 2 parts double cream with 1 part sour cream, let it thicken at room temperature (5–6 hours), and refrigerate (keeps 10 days).

LEFT-OVERS, TINNED SOUPS, AND
IMPROVISATIONS

When you are the cook in the family, plan your vegetables ahead so that you will have left-overs for soup; it will save you a great deal of time, and make you feel remarkably clever besides. Extra rice, pasta, and creamed or mashed potatoes are always needed as thickeners, while onions and mushrooms can always be added for flavour. Left-over cauliflower, for instance, can be combined with watercress to make the delicious soup on page 35; spinach is the main ingredient for the *velouté florentine* on page 30; white beans or aubergine go into the *soupe à la Victorine* on page 46. Save also any extra bits of sauce or meat juices; these often provide that extra depth of taste and personality you are searching for. For example, a few tablespoons of left-over sauce from a chicken fricassee would be delicious in the cream of celery soup on page 25; you could certainly stir hollandaise instead of butter into the *potage aux champignons* on page 33; and some juices saved from the roast would enhance any onion soup. Finally, save any left-over soup; you can add it to a new one, or use it to give a home-made touch to tinned soups.

Green Soups from Green Vegetables

Potage, Crème d'Asperges Vertes
[Cream of Fresh Green Asparagus Soup]
At the peak of the asparagus season, when you can bear not to eat it whole, here is a marvellous soup to catch all the essence of that beautiful vegetable.

[*For 4 to 6 people*]

1. The onion flavouring

1 medium sliced onion
2 oz. butter
A 5-pt heavy-bottomed stainless saucepan with cover

While you are preparing the asparagus, cook the onions slowly in the butter for 8 to 10 minutes, until tender but not browned. Set aside.

2. Preparing the asparagus

About 2 lb. fresh green asparagus (24 to 28 spears 8 ins. by ¾ in.)

Slice ¼ inch off the butt of each asparagus. Peel the skin from the butt ends up to where the green begins, and remove scales. Wash thoroughly in warm water. Cut the tops 3 inches long and set aside. Cut the lower part of the asparagus stalks into ¾-inch crosswise pieces.

3. Blanching the asparagus

2½ pts water
2 tsp. salt
A 5-pt saucepan
A salad or vegetable basket or 2 slotted spoons

Bring the water and salt to a rapid boil, add the asparagus stalks and boil slowly, uncovered, for 5 minutes. Remove and drain, reserving the water, and stir the stalks into the cooked onions; cover and cook slowly for 5 minutes. Meanwhile bring the water back to the boil, add the reserved asparagus tops and boil slowly, uncovered, for 6 to 8 minutes or until just tender. Remove immediately and drain. Set aside, reserving water for the soup base.

4. The soup base

4 tbl. flour
The asparagus blanching water
½ pt or so of milk if needed

After the stalks and onions have stewed together for 5 minutes, uncover the pan, stir in the flour to mix thoroughly, and cook slowly, stirring, for 1 minute. Remove from heat and blend in half a cup of the hot blanching water; gradually stir in the rest, being sure not to add any sand that may be at the bottom of the pan. Simmer slowly, partially covered, for about 25 minutes or until the stalks are very tender. If soup seems too thick, thin out with milk.

5. Finishing the soup

The blanched asparagus tops
A food mill with medium disc (or an electric blender and sieve)
A 5-pt bowl
About ¼ pt double cream
2 or 3 egg yolks
A wire whisk
Salt and white pepper to taste

Line up the blanched asparagus tops and cut the tip ends into ¼-inch crosswise slices; reserve as a garnish. Purée the rest of the tops and the soup base into a bowl. (Pass soup through sieve to remove any fibres, if you have used a blender.) Pour the cream into the saucepan, blend in the egg yolks with a wire whisk; by driblets, beat in ½ pint of the hot soup. Pour in the rest of the soup, and the sliced tip ends.

(†) May be cooked ahead to this point; set aside uncovered until cool, then cover and refrigerate.

1 to 2 oz. soft butter

Shortly before serving, set over moderate heat and stir slowly with a wooden spoon, reaching all over the bottom of the pan until soup comes almost to the simmer. Remove from heat, carefully correct seasoning, and stir in the enrichment butter a small piece at a time. Serve immediately.

Cold Asparagus Soup

Omit the final butter enrichment and oversalt slightly. Stir several times as the soup cools, then cover and chill. Blend in more cream, if you wish, just before serving.

Using Frozen Asparagus

Frozen asparagus can never achieve the magic of fresh asparagus, but you can still turn out an excellent soup. Follow the master recipe, making the changes in each step as indicated.

Step 1

Increase the sliced onions to 3 medium ones in this step, or use a combination of onions and leeks

Step 2

A 10-oz. package frozen cut green asparagus
A 10-oz. package whole frozen green asparagus spears

Use the cut asparagus to replace the stalks and the whole
spears to replace the tops.

Step 3

¾ pt chicken stock
Optional: big pinch of monosodium glutamate

Substitute ¾ pint of chicken stock for ¾ pint of the water
called for in this step, and a little monosodium glutamate will
probably be useful. Drop the cut asparagus into the boiling
liquid for a minute or two, merely to defrost it, then add to
the onions. Boil the whole spears until just tender.

Steps 4 and 5

Follow master recipe.

Fresh White European Asparagus

European asparagus is either all white or tinged with mauve or
green near the tip, depending on the variety. Since the peel is
often slightly bitter as well as being much tougher than that
of all-green asparagus, peeling is essential. Peel each spear
$\frac{1}{16}$ of an inch deep up to the tender part near the tip. After
boiling the stalks, taste the cooking liquid; if it is bitter, discard it and use fresh boiling water for cooking the tops. Although the soup would normally be a pale cream colour, you
may turn it green by puréeing into it a cup of blanched chard
or spinach leaves.

Soupe Belle Potagère
[Pea-pod Soup]

You can make an excellent green pea soup using both pods
and peas. Next time you are shelling them, and have crackling
fresh pods, keep out the greenest and best of the lot, wrap

them in a plastic bag, and refrigerate for a soup the next day. A cup of shelled peas would be nice, too, but frozen ones will do for the garnish.

[*For 4 to 6 people*]

1. The onion flavouring

1 large leek and 1 onion, sliced, or use onions only
1½ oz. butter
A heavy-bottomed, 5-pt stainless or enamelled saucepan with cover

Cook the leeks and/or onions slowly in the butter for 8 to 10 minutes, until tender but not browned. Set aside.

2. The pea-pod soup base

1 lb. fresh green peas with very crisp pods

Pulling off and discarding stems and tips from the pea pods, shell the peas and set aside – you should have about 1 cup. Wash pods and chop roughly into 1-inch pieces. Stir the chopped pods into the leeks and onions, cover and cook slowly for 10 minutes.

3 tbl. flour
1½ pts hot water
1½ tsp. salt
1 large potato, peeled and sliced

Blend the flour into the pea pods and cook, stirring, for 1 minute. Remove from heat, gradually blend in ½ pint of the hot water, then stir in the rest along with the salt and sliced potato. Simmer, partially covered, for about 20 minutes or until vegetables are tender.

3. The peas

1 cup fresh peas (or a 10-oz. package of frozen peas)
A heavy-bottomed 3-pt saucepan with cover
¾ pt water for fresh peas; ¼ pt for frozen peas
1 large sliced spring onion or shallot
6 to 8 large outside lettuce leaves, chopped
½ oz. butter
¼ tsp. salt

If using fresh peas, boil them in the covered saucepan with the water, spring onion, lettuce, and other ingredients for 10 to 15 minutes or until peas are just tender, adding 2 to 3 tablespoons more water, if liquid evaporates entirely before peas are done; uncover and set aside. If using frozen peas, cook the same way but with only ¼ pint water, and boil only long enough for the peas to be tender.

4. Finishing the soup

A food mill set over a bowl (or an electric blender and sieve)
½ pt or so of milk if needed
Salt, white pepper, and sugar to taste
4 tbl. or more of double cream or sour cream

Purée the peas, then the soup base. If you are using a blender, sieve the soup base after puréeing to remove pea-pod fibres. Return to saucepan, bring to simmer, and thin out with milk if soup seems too thick. Taste carefully for seasoning, and add pinches of sugar to taste, which will help bring out the flavour. Stir in the cream.

(†) Set aside uncovered until cool, then cover and refrigerate.

1 to 2 oz. soft butter

Reheat to simmer just before serving. Check seasoning again, remove from heat, and stir in the butter a small piece at a time. Serve immediately.

Cold Pea-pod Soup

Omit the final butter enrichment and oversalt slightly. Stir several times as the soup cools, then cover and chill. Blend in more cream, if you wish, just before serving.

*Potage à la Florentine
[Cream of Spinach Soup]

Fresh and frozen spinach do almost equally well in this elegant soup of spinach simmered with rice and enriched with cream and egg yolks. Since it is good hot or cold, you may use the same system for a soup of green herbs, as you will see in the variations following.

[*For 4 to 6 people*]

1. The soup base

1 sliced onion
1 oz. butter
A heavy-bottomed stainless or enamelled pan with cover

Cook the onions slowly in the butter for 8 to 10 minutes, until tender but not browned.

1½ to 2 lb. fresh spinach (or a 10-oz. package frozen spinach)

For fresh spinach, trim, wash thoroughly, and chop roughly. For frozen spinach, thaw in a large bowl of cold water, drain and squeeze dry. Stir spinach into onions; cover and cook over low heat for 5 minutes, stirring occasionally to prevent spinach from scorching.

2 pts liquid (light chicken stock, or tinned chicken broth and water)
3 oz. plain raw white rice
Pinch nutmeg
Salt and pepper to taste
A food mill or electric blender
Chicken stock or milk if needed

Add the liquid to the spinach, bring to the boil, and stir in the rice. Season with the nutmeg, salt, and pepper. Simmer partially covered for 20 minutes or until rice is tender. Purée, bring again to the simmer and thin out, if too thick, with more liquid. Remove from heat.

2. Finishing the soup

A 3-pt bowl
A wire whisk
¼ pt double cream
2 egg yolks

Blend the cream and egg yolks in the bowl with the wire whisk; by driblets, beat in ¾ pint of the hot soup. Pour back into the saucepan.

(†) May be cooked ahead to this point. Set aside uncovered until cool, then cover and refrigerate.

Salt, pepper, and lemon juice
1 to 2 oz. soft butter

Shortly before serving, set over moderate heat and stir slowly with a wooden spoon, reaching all over the bottom of the pan until soup comes almost to the simmer. Remove from heat, carefully correct seasoning, adding lemon juice if you wish; stir in the enrichment butter a teaspoon at a time. Serve immediately.

Cold Spinach Soup

Omit the final butter enrichment, and oversalt slightly. Stir several times as the soup cools, then cover and chill. Blend in more cream if you wish, just before serving, or top each serving with a spoonful of sour cream.

Potage aux Herbes Panachées
[Green Herb Soup]

For those green-fingered wonders who grow their own herbs, here is a way to show off your tarragon, chervil, flat-leaved, pungent Italian parsley, shallots, spring onions, and chives. For those of us who wish to simulate the possession of a herb garden, the supermarket combination is leeks or onions, watercress, parsley, and dried tarragon.

1. The soup base

About ½ lb. onion flavouring (chopped shallots, spring onions, onions and/or leeks)
1½ oz. butter
Either (for herb gardeners): a large bunch of parsley including tender stems; a handful of chervil; a branch of tarragon leaves; chives
Or (for supermarket shoppers): a bunch each of parsley and watercress, including tender stems, and ½ tsp. dried tarragon
1 tbl. flour
1¼ pts hot water
3 oz. plain raw white rice
1 tsp. salt

Following the system for the preceding spinach soup, cook the onion flavouring in butter until tender. Chop greens roughly, stir into onion flavouring and cook 1 to 2 minutes or until wilted. Then add the flour and cook 1 minute, stirring. Remove from heat, beat in the hot water, and bring to the boil. Sprinkle in the rice and the salt. Simmer 25 minutes, then purée.

2. Finishing the soup

About 1 pt milk
More salt and tarragon, if needed
White pepper to taste
A small saucepan
3 to 4 oz. minced fresh herbs (same combination as in step 1)
½ oz. butter
4 tbl. double cream
2 egg yolks
1 to 2 oz. soft butter

Bring soup base to the simmer; thin out to desired consistency with milk. Season carefully. In a separate saucepan, stir the minced herbs and butter over moderate heat for several minutes until herbs are wilted. Remove from heat and let cool a moment, then stir in the cream; blend in the egg yolks with a wire whisk, and gradually dribble in ¾ pint of the hot soup base. Pour back into the saucepan. Just before serving, stir over moderate heat until soup comes almost to the simmer, correct seasoning again, remove from heat and stir in the butter.

Cold Green Herb Soup

See directions for the preceding spinach soup.

Vegetable *Veloutés*

*Potage aux Champignons, Île de France
[Cream of Mushroom Soup II]

Cream of mushroom soup appeals to almost everyone, even to those who claim they hate mushrooms. This is a very simple version compared with the full-dress recipe in Volume I. Here puréed raw mushrooms simmer in an onion-flavoured soup base, and if you have only a handful of stems rather than the 5 to 12 ounces of fresh mushrooms specified, you will still have a delicious soup.

[*For 4 to 6 people*]

1. The *velouté* soup base

1 finely minced onion
2 oz. butter
A 5-pt heavy-bottomed stainless or enamelled saucepan with cover
A wooden spoon
3 tbl. flour
¾ pt hot water
A wire whisk
1½ pts milk
2 tsp. salt
Pinch white pepper
Big pinch tarragon

Cook the onions slowly in the butter for 8 to 10 minutes, until tender but not browned. Add the flour and cook, stirring, for 1 minute. Remove from heat and blend in a few tablespoons of the hot water with a wire whisk. Gradually beat in the rest of the hot water, then the milk, seasonings, and tarragon. Bring to the simmer, stirring with wire whisk; simmer very slowly for several minutes while preparing the mushrooms.

2. The mushrooms

5 to 12 oz. fresh whole mushrooms or just the mushroom stems
A food mill with grating disc (large holes), an electric blender, or a large knife.

Trim and wash the mushrooms. If you are using a food mill with grating disc, chop the mushrooms roughly and grate directly into the soup base. If using a blender, chop roughly, and blend 1 or 2 ounces at a time with an equal amount of soup base, flicking switch on and off rapidly to avoid too fine a purée. Otherwise chop the mushrooms into ⅛-inch pieces with a knife, and add to soup.

3. Finishing the soup

More milk if needed, or light chicken stock
¼ pt or more double cream
Salt, white pepper, and drops of lemon juice

Simmer the soup, partially covered, for 25 minutes. Add more liquid if soup seems too thick, then stir in the cream. Carefully correct seasoning, adding drops of lemon juice if you feel they are needed.

(†) May be completed to this point. Set aside uncovered until cool, then cover and refrigerate.

1 to 2 oz. soft butter
2 to 3 tbl. minced fresh tarragon and/or parsley

Bring soup to simmer again just before serving. Remove from heat and stir in first the butter, a small piece at a time, then the herbs. Serve immediately.

A more elaborate garnish

Omit all or most of the cream and butter enrichments if you wish. Ladle the hot soup into bowls, drop a spoonful of sour cream in each and top with minced herbs, or with sliced or fluted mushroom caps previously simmered in water, butter, and lemon juice (Volume I, page 548).

Cold Mushroom Soup

Omit the final butter enrichment, and oversalt slightly. Stir several times as the soup cools, then cover and chill. Blend in more cream, if you wish, just before serving.

VARIATIONS

The following recipes are both for 4 to 6 people. They may be served either hot or cold, as for the mushroom soup.

Potage de la Fontaine Dureau
[Cream of Cauliflower and Watercress Soup]
This is a delicious and unusual, as well as a pretty, soup.

1. The *velouté* base

6 oz. sliced leeks and/or onions
2 oz. butter
3 tbl. flour
2½ pts liquid (hot water, or part hot water and part milk)
2 tsp. salt
Pinch white pepper

Following the master recipe for mushroom soup, cook the onions in the butter until tender, stir in the flour and cook 1 minute, blend in the liquid, add the seasoning, then simmer slowly while preparing the vegetables.

2. The vegetables; finishing the soup

A 6- to 7-in. head of cauliflower (1¼ to 1½ lb.)
A large pan of boiling salted water
1 bunch watercress
¼ pt or more double cream
1 to 2 oz. soft butter

Break cauliflower into flowerets and peel central stem; retain any tender leaves. Drop flowerets and stem (not leaves) into the boiling water, bring rapidly back to the boil; boil uncovered for 2 minutes. Drain, add to soup base, and simmer 15 minutes. Meanwhile, discard any wilted leaves and stems from watercress, wash cress and chop roughly. After cauliflower has simmered 15 minutes, add the cress and reserved cauliflower leaves. Simmer 10 minutes more: purée. Add the cream, and correct seasoning. Reheat only just before serving, to preserve the watercress green, then remove from heat and stir in the butter enrichment.

Potage Crème aux Oignons, Soubise
[Cream of Onion Soup]

This is a soup for onion lovers, and a pleasant change from the usual brown onion soup. The little touch of curry and a bit of wine give it special flavour, while the addition of rice turns it into a *soubise*.

1. The onion-*velouté* soup base

1 to 1½ lb. sliced onions
2 oz. butter
1 tsp. curry powder
2 tbl. flour
¾ pt hot water
¾ pt chicken stock or tinned chicken broth
Scant ¼ pt dry white wine or 6 tbl. dry white French vermouth
3 oz. plain white rice
1 bay leaf
Salt and white pepper to taste

Following the master recipe for mushroom soup, cook the onions in the butter until tender but not browned. Add curry and cook 1 minute more, then add flour and cook 2 minutes without browning. Remove from heat, beat in the hot water, then the chicken stock and the wine. Bring to simmer and sprinkle in the rice; add bay leaf, and season to taste. Simmer 30 minutes. Purée.

2. Finishing the soup

About 1 pt milk
¼ pt or more double cream
1 to 2 oz. soft butter
2 to 3 tbl. fresh minced chervil or parsley

Bring soup to the simmer. Thin out to desired consistency with milk, stir in the cream, and carefully correct seasoning. Reheat again to simmer just before serving; remove from heat and stir in the butter, then the herbs.

A Potato-based Soup

Potage Célestine

[Celery Soup with Potatoes, Leeks, and Rice]
This is leek and potato soup with a celery twist, and is equally good hot or cold.

[*For 6 people*]

1. The leeks and celery

The white part of 2 medium leeks, sliced; or 2 large onions, sliced
6 large celery stalks, sliced
¼ tsp. salt
1½ oz. butter
A heavy-bottomed 5-pt stainless or enamelled saucepan with cover
1½ pts light chicken stock, or tinned chicken broth and water
3 oz. plain white rice

Cook the vegetables slowly with the salt and butter in the covered saucepan until tender but not browned – about 10 minutes. Add the liquid, bring to the boil, stir in the rice, and simmer uncovered for 25 minutes.

2. The potatoes

3 or 4 medium baking potatoes, peeled and chopped
¾ pt water
½ tsp. salt
Another heavy 5-pt saucepan
A food mill with medium disc, a potato ricer, or an electric blender
¾ pt milk heated in a small pan
A wire whisk and a wooden spoon

Meanwhile, boil the potatoes with the water and salt. When tender, drain their cooking water into the leeks and celery. If you are using a food mill or ricer, purée the potatoes, return to saucepan, and beat in the milk to make a smooth, white cream. If you are using a blender, purée the potatoes with a cup of the milk, pour into saucepan, and beat in the rest of the milk.

3. Finishing the soup; herb-butter and croûton garnish

⅛ tsp. sugar (to bring out the flavour)
Salt and white pepper

Purée the leek and celery mixture with its liquid into the potato cream. Blend well with wire whisk and bring to the simmer; beat in sugar and seasonings to taste.

(†) Set aside uncovered until shortly before serving.

2 to 3 oz. soft butter
3 tbl. minced fresh chervil or tarragon; or minced fresh parsley and
   ¼ tsp. crumbled dried tarragon

A heated soup tureen, or a bowl and soup cups
Croûtons (see directions below)

Bring the soup to the simmer. Mash the butter and herbs in the soup tureen (or in the bowl, and divide among your soup cups). Blend the hot soup into the herb butter, sprinkle the croûtons on top, and serve immediately.

Cold Celery Soup

Omit the butter enrichment and the croûtons; oversalt soup slightly. Mash the herbs with 4 tablespoons double cream or sour cream, stir into the soup, and chill. Stir in more chilled cream, if you wish, before serving, and decorate with fresh minced herbs or parsley.

Croûtons
[Small Cubes of Bread Sautéed in Butter]

Stale, white bread
A baking sheet
A frying pan, preferably the non-stick kind
Clarified butter (butter melted, skimmed, and poured off milky
    residue in bottom of pan)

Preheat oven to 325°F., Mark 3. Remove crusts and, if un-sliced, cut bread into ¼-inch slices. Then cut into ¼-inch strips; cut strips crosswise to make ¼-inch cubes. Spread cubes on baking sheet and dry out in middle level of oven for 10 to 15 minutes, until outside is dry but not browning; this will prevent bread from absorbing too much butter when sautéed. Film pan with a ⅛-inch layer of clarified butter, set over moderate heat until it bubbles; add just enough bread cubes to make 1 layer. Sauté, shaking and tossing pan by handle, until cubes are a light golden brown, adding a little more butter if necessary to keep bread from burning. Let cool on paper towels.

(†) May be cooked in advance. May also be frozen, then thawed and crisped for a few minutes in a 375°F., Mark 5 oven.

Soups with a Farina Thickening

Rather than thickening soups with flour, rice, or potatoes, you may use *semoule de blé*, semolina, also known as farina or cream of wheat. This makes a pleasant change and also imparts its own subtle taste and texture.

*Potage aux Concombres
[Cream of Cucumber Soup]

The only thing to say about this soup is that it is perfectly delicious; it is especially good cold, but then it is also especially good hot.

[For 4 to 6 people]

1. The cucumbers

1½ lb. cucumbers (3, about 8 ins. long)

Peel the cucumbers. Cut 18 to 24 paper-thin slices and reserve in a bowl for later. Cut the rest of the cucumbers into ½-inch chunks.

2. The soup

3 oz. minced shallots, or a combination of shallots, spring onions, and/or onions
1½ oz. butter
A heavy-bottomed stainless or enamelled saucepan with cover
2½ pts liquid: light chicken stock, or tinned broth and water
1½ tsp. wine vinegar
¾ tsp. dried dill or tarragon
4 tbl. quick-cooking farina (cream of wheat) breakfast cereal
A food mill with medium disc, or an electric blender
More liquid if necessary
Salt and white pepper

Cook the shallots, spring onions, or onions slowly in the butter for several minutes until tender but not browned. Add the cucumber chunks, chicken broth, vinegar, and herbs. Bring to the boil, then stir in the farina. Simmer, partially covered, for

20 to 25 minutes. Purée, and return the soup to the pan. Thin out with more liquid if necessary; season carefully with salt and pepper.

(†) May be prepared in advance to this point.

½ pt sour cream
Soup bowls
1 to 2 tbl. minced fresh dill, tarragon or parsley

Bring to simmer just before serving, and beat in ¼ pint of the sour cream. Ladle into soup bowls, place a dollop of sour cream in each bowl, float slices of cucumber on top of cream, and decorate with a sprinkling of herbs.

Cold Cucumber Soup

After stirring in the ¼ pint sour cream, oversalt slightly and let cool uncovered, stirring occasionally. Then cover and chill. Ladle into chilled soup cups, adding a big spoonful of sour cream to each cup; float cucumber slices on top of the cream and decorate with herbs.

Potage aux Courgettes
[Cream of Courgette Soup]

You may substitute courgettes for cucumbers in the preceding soups, but do not peel them. Cut off stem and tip, scrub with a vegetable brush, and proceed exactly as for the cucumber soup. Decorate with herbs, however, rather than with courgette slices.

Potage Untel
[Green Turnip Soup]

This is one of those soups with a marvellous and unusual flavour that is difficult to decipher unless you are told the combination. Then the tastes of turnip and greens disclose themselves. You may not find any green leaves attached to your turnips unless they grow near by and it is turnip season, which is winter or early spring. Spinach leaves do nicely, however.

1. The turnips

1½ lb. fresh white turnips, peeled and quartered
1½ oz. butter
1 tsp. salt
1 tsp. sugar
½ to ¾ pt water
A heavy-bottomed 5-pt stainless or enamelled saucepan with cover

Boil the turnips slowly with the butter, seasonings, and water in a covered saucepan for 15 to 20 minutes, or until tender when pierced with a knife. Uncover, raise heat, and boil to evaporate liquid; toss turnips in the butter which remains for 2 minutes.

2. The greens

Either: ¾ lb. tender fresh turnip greens and fresh spinach;
Or: 10-oz. package of fresh spinach;
Or: 10-oz. package frozen spinach thawed in cold water and squeezed dry
1 oz. butter
A 10-in. stainless or enamelled frying pan
2 wooden spoons
½ tsp. salt
¼ tsp. sugar

Meanwhile, discard any wilted leaves from fresh greens and spinach, wash thoroughly and drain well. Heat butter in a frying pan to bubbling, over moderately high heat. Add greens and spinach, turn and toss with the 2 wooden spoons; sprinkle with salt and sugar and continue tossing for 2 to 3 minutes until greens are limp and fairly tender.

3. The soup

A food mill with medium disc, or an electric blender
1½ pts liquid: light chicken stock, or tinned broth and water
3 tbl. quick-cooking farina (cream of wheat) breakfast cereal
½ to ¾ pt milk
Salt and pepper
1 to 2 tbl. lemon juice

Purée the 2 vegetables together and bring to simmer in turnip-cooking pan with the broth. Sprinkle in the farina and simmer

5 to 6 minutes until farina is tender. Thin out to desired consistency with milk; season carefully with salt, pepper, and lemon juice.

(†) May be prepared in advance to this point.

1 to 2 oz. soft butter

Bring again to simmer just before serving; remove from heat and stir in the butter a teaspoon at a time.

Alternate Enrichments; Cold Soup

You may wish to enrich the soup with sour cream instead of butter, as for the preceding cucumber soup, or with cream and egg yolks as in the spinach soup on page 30. In any case, you may also serve it cold as suggested in both recipes.

Three Peasant Soups

Potage Magali
[Mediterranean Tomato Soup with Rice]

Typically Mediterranean, with its onions, tomatoes, garlic, saffron, and native herbs, this fragrant soup is even named after the Provençal heroine of many an operetta. It is best when tomatoes are at the season's peak, but the hot-house type can be pepped up with a bit of tomato paste.

[*For 4 to 6 people*]

1. The soup base

6 oz. thinly sliced leeks and onions, or onions only
3 tbl. olive oil
A heavy-bottomed 5-pt stainless or enamelled saucepan with cover
1½ lb. fresh, ripe, red tomatoes
4 large cloves garlic, minced or mashed
1½ to 2 pts liquid: light chicken stock, or tinned broth and water

2 oz. plain, raw, white rice
The following tied in washed cheesecloth:
6 parsley sprigs, 1 bay leaf, ¼ tsp. thyme, 4 fennel seeds, and, if available,
  6 large fresh basil leaves
A large pinch of saffron threads
Salt and pepper

Cook the leeks and onions slowly in the oil until tender but
not browned. Meanwhile, peel and halve the tomatoes,
squeeze out seeds and reserve juice. Chop tomato pulp roughly
and stir into the cooked leeks and onions. Add the garlic and
stir over moderate heat for 3 minutes. Then add the tomato
juice and liquid, bring to the boil, and sprinkle in the rice. Add
the herbs and saffron; season to taste with salt and pepper.
Simmer, partially covered, for 30 minutes.

2. Finishing the soup

If necessary: pinches of sugar
1 tsp. or more tomato paste
Salt and pepper

Carefully taste for seasoning, adding pinches of sugar to bring
out flavour and counteract acidity, and small amounts of
tomato paste if needed for colour and taste. Remove herb
bouquet.

(†) May be prepared ahead to this point.

2 or more tbl. minced fresh basil, chervil, or parsley

Serve either hot or chilled, sprinkled with fresh herbs.

Soupe Catalane aux Poivrons
[Catalonian Pepper and Leek Soup]
Another Mediterranean soup uses the same principles as the
preceding *potage Magali*, and the same general ingredients. Here
the character comes from sweet peppers rather than tomatoes,
a touch of ham or salt pork, and a typically regional final
liaison of egg yolks and olive oil.

[*For 4 to 6 people*]

1. The soup base

2½ to 3 oz. lightly smoked ham or lean salt pork, cut into ¼-in. dice
2 tbl. olive oil
A heavy-bottomed 5-pt stainless or enamelled saucepan with cover
1 lb. onions, diced
1 lb. leeks, thinly sliced (or more onions)
2 large red or green bell peppers, diced
4 large cloves garlic, minced or mashed
1 tbl. flour
1½ pts hot water
1 to 1½ pts light beef stock, or tinned chicken broth
2 oz. pasta (rice- or pepper-corn-shaped, or broken vermicelli), or plain
     white rice
A large pinch of saffron threads
¼ tsp. savory
Salt and pepper

Sauté the ham or salt pork in the oil over moderate heat until
it barely begins to brown, then stir in the onions and leeks.
Cook slowly several minutes until fairly tender but not
browned; stir in the peppers and garlic, and cook again for 3
to 4 minutes without browning. Finally sprinkle in the flour,
stirring for 1 minute, and remove from heat. Blend in the hot
water gradually, stir in the stock or broth, and bring to the
simmer; skim off any surface scum for a minute or two, then
stir in the pasta or rice. Add the saffron and savory, season to
taste, and simmer partially covered for 20 minutes. Carefully
correct seasoning.

(†) May be prepared ahead to this point; let it cool uncovered.
Bring again to the simmer just before serving. You may also
make the egg-yolk and oil enrichment in advance and store it
in a covered jar.

2. Finishing the soup

2 egg yolks
A wire whisk
A soup tureen or large mixing bowl
4 tbl. olive oil
A ladle

Beat the egg yolks in the bottom of the tureen or bowl until
thick and sticky; by droplets, beat in the olive oil exactly as

though you were making a thick mayonnaise. Stirring it, dribble in the hot soup until you have added ¾ pint; gradually stir in the rest. Serve immediately.

*Soupe à la Victorine

[Purée of White Bean Soup, with Aubergine and Tomato Garnish]

This meal-in-itself will fill up the family on a cold day, especially if you include pork or sausage with the beans. The aubergine and tomato garnish makes a lively and unusual touch to an otherwise traditional bean purée.

[*For 4 to 6 people*]

1. Soaking the beans: 1 hour

1½ pts of water
A 5-pt saucepan with cover
3 oz. dry white beans

Bring the water to a rapid boil, drop in the beans, and bring water rapidly back to the boil again; boil uncovered for exactly 2 minutes. Remove from heat, cover pan, and let soak for exactly 1 hour. Meanwhile, you may prepare all the rest of the ingredients for the soup.

2. The soup base: 1½ hours of simmering

1 lb. leeks and onions, sliced, or onions only
3 tbl. olive oil or 1½ oz. butter
An 8-in. enamelled, stainless, or non-stick frying pan
2 bay leaves
½ tsp. thyme
½ tsp. sage
Optional: ½ lb. lean side pork (fresh unsmoked bacon), or fresh
    fat-and-lean pork butt (shoulder), or Italian or Polish sausage
1½ tsp. salt
⅛ tsp. peppercorns
A food mill or an electric blender

Cook the leeks and onions slowly in the oil or butter until tender and translucent; raise heat slightly and cook for a few minutes more until very lightly browned. As soon as the beans have had their 1-hour soak, scrape the vegetables into them, and add the rest of the ingredients for the soup base (if using sausage rather than pork, add only for last 30 to 40 minutes of cooking). Bring to the simmer, partially cover the pan, and cook slowly for about 1½ hours or until beans are tender. Set pork or sausage aside for final step, purée the soup, and return to the pan.

(†) May be prepared ahead, set aside uncovered until cool.

3. The aubergine and tomato garnish

A firm, shiny, 1-lb. aubergine (about 8 in. long and 3½ in. at widest diameter)
A 3-pt glazed or stainless mixing bowl
1½ tsp. salt
1 lb. fresh, firm, ripe, red tomatoes (4 to 5 medium), peeled, seeded, and juiced
2 to 3 tbl. olive oil
The 8-in. frying pan again
4 large cloves garlic, minced or mashed
A cover for the frying pan

Peel the aubergine and cut into ½-inch dice. Toss in the bowl with the salt and let stand at least 20 minutes. Meanwhile, prepare the tomatoes and cut pulp into ½-inch squares; strain and reserve juice. When aubergine has stood its 20 minutes, drain and dry on paper towels. Heat the oil in the pan and sauté the aubergine, tossing it, to brown very lightly. Then toss with the tomato pulp and garlic, add the juice from the tomatoes, and cover the pan. Simmer slowly for 10 to 15 minutes until aubergine is tender but still holds its shape. Set aside.

(†) May be prepared ahead; let cool uncovered.

4. Finishing the soup

About 1 pt chicken stock or tinned broth
3 tbl. minced fresh green herbs: basil, parsley, and chives (or parsley only and dried basil or oregano to taste)

About 15 minutes before serving, bring the soup base to the simmer and thin out to desired consistency with chicken stock or broth. Cut the pork or sausage into slices ⅜ inch thick and add to the soup along with the aubergine and tomato. Simmer 3 to 4 minutes to blend flavours. Carefully correct seasoning, stir in the herbs, and serve.

Fennel and Tomato Garnish

Sliced fresh fennel cooked until just tender and then simmered for a moment with diced tomatoes and herbs makes an attractive alternative to the aubergine. Soak the beans and simmer the soup base as described in the preceding recipe; prepare the garnish as follows.

1 large fennel bulb, thinly sliced
2 tbl. olive oil or 1 oz. butter
2 oz. minced shallots or spring onions
2 large cloves garlic, minced or mashed
1 lb. tomatoes, peeled, seeded, juiced, and diced
Salt and pepper

Cook the fennel slowly in the oil or butter in a covered frying pan for 8 to 10 minutes, or until just tender but not browned. Add the shallots or spring onions, garlic, and tomatoes; toss with fennel, cover frying pan and cook for a few minutes until tomatoes have rendered the rest of their juice. Uncover, raise heat slightly and cook for a few minutes more to evaporate the juice. Season to taste. Set aside until you are ready to serve, then add to the soup as directed in the master recipe, step 4.

Le Potiron tout Rond
[Pumpkin Soup Baked in a Pumpkin]
This amusing presentation may be prepared either as a soup or a vegetable; the recipe for it is on page 476, in Chapter 6.

Shellfish Soups · *Bisques*

A bisque is a rich, thick, highly seasoned soup of puréed shellfish. Undoubtedly the bisque came into being because it is an easy as well as an elegant way to eat small crustaceans with complicated constructions like crayfish and crabs, and it is a wonderful solution for the chests and legs of lobsters.

This is the kind of recipe to pick for a group of friends who enjoy cooking together, since a bisque is not tricky to make – it just takes a long time. To get the true flavour, the raw shellfish are cut up and sautéed in their shells before being simmered with wine and aromatic ingredients. The meat is then removed from the shells; some of it is saved for a garnish while the rest is puréed. Finally, to extract every remaining bit of flavour and colour from the shells, they are puréed with butter, and everything is combined into a splendid soup.

We shall begin with illustrated directions on how to cut up lobsters and crabs, and follow with lobster bisque and its other shellfish variations.

Lobsters

BUYING LOBSTERS

A live lobster should be lively: it spreads its claws, arches its back, and flaps its tail noisily against the underside of its chest when you pick it up. To do so you must grab it with your thumb and index finger at its shoulder just behind the claw joints. You can keep live lobsters in the refrigerator at around 37°F. for a day or two in a heavy paper bag pierced with air holes, but you should cook them as soon as possible.

When you are picking shop bought boiled lobsters, look closely at their tails, which should curl up against the underside of the chests and spring back into place when straightened. A limp tail indicates that the lobster was moribund before cooking. Be sure also, in buying boiled lobster, that it smells absolutely sweet and fresh. Freshly boiled, cooled, and wrapped lobsters will keep for two to three days in the refrigerator at around 37°F. You may even wrap airtight and freeze a boiled lobster in its shell for several weeks.

To tell the sex of a lobster, look at the last pair of swimmerets on the under side, where chest meets tail. If they are

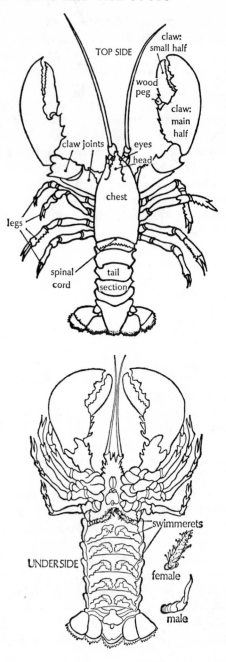

soft and hairy, the lobster is female; if they are hard, pointed, and hairless, the lobster is male.

ON DEALING WITH LIVE LOBSTERS

A number of the best French lobster recipes, including *homard à l'américaine* and *bisque de homard*, call for the sautéing of cut-up raw lobster. This means you must buy live lobster and either have it cut up for you and cook it immediately, or do the cutting yourself. The serious cook really must face up to the task personally. We suggest the following method. Run very hot water into a large pan or bowl. Place the lobster under side up on your cutting board; covering head and claws with a folded towel, hold lobster firmly down against the board with your left hand. Using a sharp knife or lobster shears, cut straight down $\frac{1}{2}$ inch into the belly of the lobster, at the point where tail and chest join, thus severing the spinal cord and killing the lobster instantly. Then, to paralyse all muscle spasms, plunge the lobster head first into the very hot water for 5 minutes, or until lobster is limp. Remove from water and cut as directed.

HOW TO CUT UP RAW LOBSTER

Furnish yourself with sharp-pointed lobster scissors or kitchen scissors, a large knife, a cutting board with groove to catch juices or a board set on a tray, a bowl to pour juices into, and another bowl for the lobster tomalley. You now want to split the lobster in two lengthwise, as follows. Turn the lobster top side up. With scissors, cut through centre of shell from end of tail up to but not through eyes in centre of head. Turn lobster over and again with scissors cut through shell from end of tail to within $\frac{1}{2}$ inch of tip of head. Then with your knife cut completely through the under side of the lobster lengthwise, following scissor cuts, from $\frac{1}{2}$ inch below tip of head down through tail, thus splitting lobster neatly in two except at the head. Finally grasp lobster in both hands where claw joints meet chest, and break the shell apart at the head to open it up.

Nestled in the head on one side of the lobster or the other is a pouch an inch long and $\frac{3}{4}$ inch in diameter which is the stomach

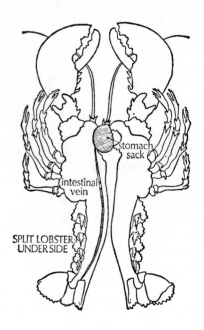

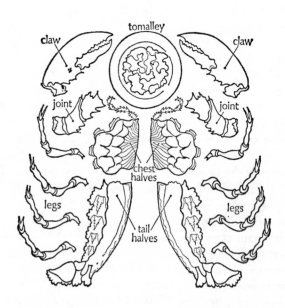

sack. Locate the sack with your fingers, twist it out, and discard it. (If you have cut sack in two while splitting the lobster, no harm is done; remove the two halves.) Pull out and discard the intestinal vein, a thin, flexible translucent or blackish tube that runs from the area of the stomach sack down through the tail meat. The greenish, and sometimes almost blackish, soft matter lying in the chest cavity is the tomalley; scoop it out into a small bowl. If your lobster is female, there will usually be some orange-red roe as well; add this to the tomalley.

With a knife or scissors, separate the two tail sections from the chests. Cut the legs and the claw joints from the chests, and cut claws from ends of joints. Crack claws in one or two places with a sharp whack of the knife. Drain juices into a bowl and reserve them, along with the tomalley. The lobster is now ready for sautéing.

HOW TO REMOVE THE MEAT FROM COOKED LOBSTERS

Split and open boiled lobster exactly as described in the preceding directions for raw lobster. Discard stomach sack and intestinal vein. Scoop tomalley from inside the chest sections into a bowl. After lifting meat out of tail sections, you want to remove meat from claws, claw joints, chest sections, and legs. With scissors, cut the claw joints from the chests, and separate each claw from its joint. Cut through shell on each side of joints, lift off shell, and remove meat.

The first step in removing the meat from the claws is to bend the small, hinged half rather slowly but firmly back on itself, towards the bottom of the claw (A); this will withdraw its cartilage from inside the meat of the main half of the claw. Dig the point of meat out of this small shell with a nut pick or the point of your scissors. Again with scissors, cut a window out of the main claw shell (B) and remove the whole piece of claw meat with your fingers.

Pull chest section from its outside shell (C). Note that there are spongy, hairy strips attached to outside side of chest at leg joints; these are gills. Pull off and discard them. Scrape out and

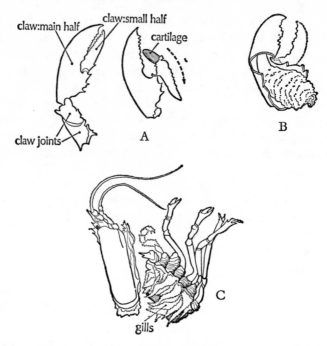

add to the tomalley any coagulated white matter clinging to the inside of the shell. Cut or twist off legs where they join the chest. Dig out meat from inside side of chest, going in between

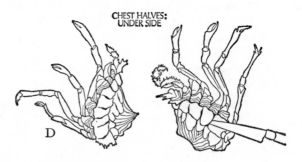

cartilaginous matter with the point of a knife (D). This is never a fast operation, but the small amount of meat you extract is the sweetest and tenderest of all. To remove the meat from the legs, sever them at each of their joints. Place on a

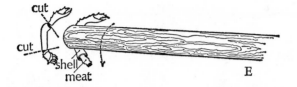

board and squeeze the meat out of each piece by rolling a pin (pestle or broom handle) over it (E). You will not get much, but again the meat is sweet, tender, and worth the time spent on extraction.

Crabs

HOW TO CLEAN AND CUT UP RAW CRABS FOR CRAB BISQUE

Stone crabs, rock crabs, and sand crabs, blue crabs, and their ilk and size are especially good for bisques because they are otherwise somewhat complicated to eat. If you are at the seashore you can gather them yourself, or ask lobstermen please not to throw them out, as they often do, but to save all

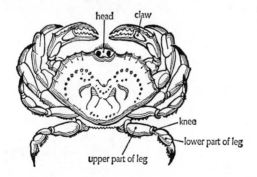

crabs for you. However you obtain them, they must be alive. Just before you are ready to clean and cut them, place them upside down in a large bowl or stoppered sink and cover with very hot water. As soon as air bubbles cease to rise, in a minute or two, the crabs will be limp and ready to work on. Your object in cleaning and cutting is to remove the main body, or chest–leg–claw portions of each crab, from the hard shell, called the carapace, and to collect the tomalley, which is the creamy substance in the chest cavity and carapace.

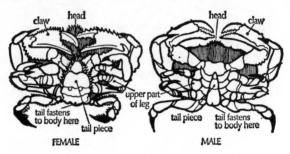

FEMALE   MALE

Turn crabs upside down. Note that female crabs have a wider tail flap than male crabs and the female's is usually edged with hair. Lift point of flap away from chest (A), then grasp flap close to the body of the crab and with a rather slow

point of flap lifted away from chest

twisting movement, pull it horizontally free from the end of the crab. The intestinal vein should draw out of the body at the same time.

Break off claw-joint sections where they join the body. To remove the leg–chest section, hold carapace firmly in your left hand and grasp all the legs close to the body in your right hand (B). Rock leg–chest portion back and forth and it will come loose from the carapace; pull it free. Both chest and interior of carapace should smell fresh and appetizing; your nose is the best judge.

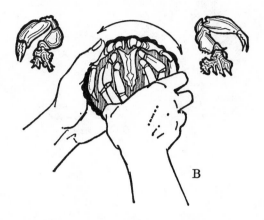

On either side of the chest, where it fitted into the shell, are feathery, spongy strips, which are the gills; pull off and discard them. Scrape the creamy tomalley out of the chest with your fingers and a spoon handle; place in a sieve set over a bowl.

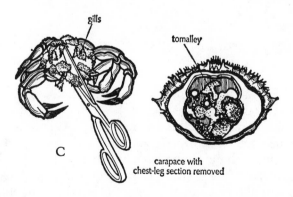

With a vegetable brush, scrub shell on underside of chest and around the legs under a stream of cold water; scrub the claw-joint pieces also. Finally cut the chest in half lengthwise as shown (c). (Trim off any mossy bits of shell with a knife or scissors.)

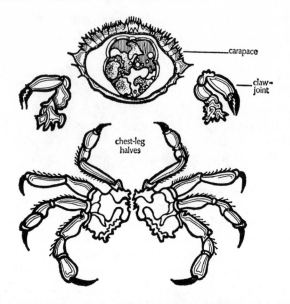

You now have prepared for cooking the chest–leg sections, which are cut in two, and the claw-joint sections. The other edible portion of the crab is the rest of the tomalley, which is in the carapace.

Crab tomalley

The greenish, brownish, and sometimes orange creamy matter left in the carapace is also called tomalley. It, along with the juices in the shell, constitutes some of the best parts of the crab.* Pour the juices through the sieve containing the chest tomalley; scoop soft matter out of the shell with your fingers, and into the sieve. When all the crabs are done, pour accumulated liquid into a separate container and reserve. Rub the tomalley through the sieve with a wooden spoon, scrape it off bottom of sieve into a bowl; reserve for step 7, page 63 (the lobster bisque recipe can also be used for crab, see page 64), where it will simmer with the crab-meat garnish. (After puréeing, the raw tomalley will become a rather dark green, which then becomes dark red when cooked.)

* When a whole crab is boiled, the tomalley turns greenish and orange while the liquid usually becomes white.

HOW TO REMOVE THE MEAT FROM COOKED CRABS

Provide yourself with a board and wooden mallet or wooden object of some sort for cracking the shells, and a grapefruit knife for extracting the meat. For a bisque made from small crabs, do not bother to delve too thoroughly because it will take all day; remove only what meat you easily can, and the shell debris will be simmered again anyway to extract all remaining flavour. Begin by twisting the legs from the chest sections, then break each leg off at the knee by bending it back upon itself at the joint, thus drawing the cartilage out of the upper leg meat. For a bisque, chop lower legs into $\frac{1}{4}$-inch pieces, and reserve for shellfish butter; otherwise discard them. To remove meat from upper legs, as well as from claws and joints, crack shell sharply but lightly with mallet, being careful not to shatter the shell into the meat. Then dig out what meat you easily can with the point of your grapefruit knife. To remove meat from chests, dig out what you can from the holes left by the legs, then from the other side, being careful not to include bits of shell or cartilage.

*Bisque de Homard à l'Américaine
[Lobster Bisque]

Considering the price of lobsters and the puréed nature of a bisque, we think it is a waste to use whole lobster here. We therefore suggest only the chests and the legs for the bisque, and the tails, claws, and tomalley for a splendid main dish, such as the *homard à l'américaine* described in Volume I. In fact, you could well combine the two, starting them out together, since both follow much the same pattern. Serve the main dish one night, and the bisque a day or two later. That is up to you, however, and we shall content ourselves with the chests and legs from 3 or 4 lobsters for the following recipe. As in most dishes of this type, you can expand or contract the ingredients to a certain extent without upsetting the balance of tastes, and you need not be disturbed if you have a little more or a little less of anything that is called for.

A NOTE ON TECHNIQUES AND EQUIPMENT

In the old days you would have needed a 6-quart marble mortar, a large wooden pestle, a 12-inch tamis sieve, a tortoise-shell scraper, and either a flock of kitchen minions or the strength of a Japanese wrestler to produce a proper bisque. Today's electric blender eliminates these colourful require-ments, but there are still multiple simmerings, strainings, and puréeings, as well as numerous bowls, sieves, and spoons that you will need. Do not wash anything off until the soup is done because you will be using the same utensils repeatedly and you don't want any marvellous titbits of flavour losing themselves down the drain.

[*For 6 to 8 people – about 3 pints*]

1. Preliminaries

6 oz. *mirepoix* (equal parts finely diced onions, carrots, and celery)
$\frac{3}{4}$ oz. butter
A heavy, 5-pt stainless or enamelled saucepan with cover
3 to 4 medium tomatoes peeled, seeded, juiced, and diced
The chest parts with the shells and the legs from 3 or 4 fresh, raw, $1\frac{1}{4}$- to $1\frac{1}{2}$-lb. lobsters

Cook the *mirepoix* slowly in the butter, in the saucepan, for 6 to 8 minutes, or until vegetables are tender but not browned. Meanwhile, prepare the tomatoes. Cut lobster chests in half lengthwise. (Illustrated directions for cutting lobster are on pages 51–3).

2. Sautéing the lobster

2 or more tbl. olive oil or cooking oil
A heavy, 10- to 12-in. non-stick or enamelled casserole (or chicken fryer or deep frying pan)
Cooking tongs

Film the bottom of the casserole with $\frac{1}{16}$ inch of oil; set over moderately high heat until oil is very hot but not smoking. Add the lobster chests cut side down and the legs. Do not crowd pan: sauté in 2 batches if all will not fit easily in one layer. Toss and turn frequently until shells are a deep red (4 to 5 minutes in all). Colour is important here, as it is the shells that tint the soup.

3. Simmering the lobster and removing the meat

Salt and pepper
6 tbl. cognac
Either: generous $\frac{1}{2}$ pt dry white wine;
Or: scant $\frac{1}{2}$ pt dry white vermouth
2 tbl. fresh tarragon or 1 tbl. dried tarragon
1 bay leaf
The *mirepoix* and tomatoes from step 1
1 clove garlic, mashed
Large pinch of cayenne pepper
A cover for the casserole

When the lobster is sautéed, lower heat slightly, salt and pepper the lobster, and pour on the cognac. Ignite by shaking pan vigorously or tilting it into heat source, or use a lighted match. When flames have died down, pour on the wine, mix in the tarragon, and add the bay leaf and other ingredients. Cover casserole, and simmer slowly for 20 minutes.

(†) May be simmered a day in advance; let cool uncovered, then cover and refrigerate (or freeze).

2 medium-sized bowls
A food mill with medium disc, or a sieve and a wooden spoon
An electric blender

(Before proceeding, you may wish to start the rice in the next step, so that it will be done by the time you are through here.) Remove the pieces of lobster from their cooking sauce and extract the meat from the shells following illustrated directions, pages 53–5. You will have about 1 cup; place in one of the bowls. Purée the cooking sauce through food mill or sieve into the other bowl, and scrape into jar of blender; reserve for step 5. Chop shells into $\frac{1}{2}$-inch pieces and reserve in a bowl for step 6.

4. Simmering the rice

$1\frac{1}{4}$ pts fish stock
$\frac{3}{4}$ pt beef stock or tinned beef bouillon
The saucepan from step 1, in which the *mirepoix* cooked
2 oz. plain, raw, white rice

Bring the fish stock and the beef stock or bouillon to boil in the saucepan; sprinkle in the rice. Stir up once, and simmer for 20 minutes. Set aside for step 5.

5. Puréeing rice and lobster meat

The saucepan of boiled rice
A large, fine-meshed sieve set over a 5-pt bowl
A rubber spatula
Half the lobster meat
The blender jar containing the puréed lobster cooking sauce

Drain rice through sieve, reserving its cooking liquid in the bowl. Scrape rice and the half portion of lobster meat into the blender. Purée, adding a little of the cooking liquid from the rice if mixture is too thick for easy blending in the machine. Scrape the purée out of the blender and into the rice saucepan.

6. Shellfish butter for final enrichment: lobster butter

3 oz. butter
The casserole in which the lobster cooked
The bowl of chopped lobster shells
The electric blender
The sieve from step 5
A wooden spoon
A rubber spatula
A small bowl to hold the butter

Heat butter to bubbling in casserole, stir in the chest and leg shells, and sauté for 2 to 3 minutes, tossing and turning, to heat thoroughly. Immediately scrape into blender and purée, flicking switch on and off and scraping shells down into blades as necessary. Scrape purée into sieve, and mash vigorously with spoon to extract as much butter as possible. Scrape all butter off bottom of sieve with rubber spatula and pack into bowl. Set aside for steps 7 and 8.

The bowl of rice cooking liquid from the rice from step 5
The saucepan containing the puréed rice and lobster from step 5

To extract all remaining flavour from blender jar, shells, and sieve, pour rice-cooking liquid into the casserole in which you just sautéed the shells. Heat to the simmer and pour liquid into blender to rinse it, then pour liquid back into casserole. Scrape shell debris from sieve into casserole, and swish sieve about in the hot rice cooking liquid to dislodge all debris. Simmer 3 to 4 minutes; strain liquid through the sieve and into the saucepan of puréed rice and lobster.

7. The lobster garnish

1 oz. of the lobster butter from step 6
A small frying pan
The remaining lobster meat from step 3
Salt and pepper
2 tbl. cognac or dry white vermouth

Heat the butter to bubbling in the frying pan; stir in the lobster meat, and sprinkle with salt and pepper. Sauté over moderate heat for 2 minutes, tossing and turning. Pour on the cognac or vermouth, and cook for a moment until liquid has evaporated. Scrape the lobster into the saucepan containing the rest of the soup mixture from step 6, and you are finally almost ready to serve.

(†) Recipe may be completed to this point; let cool uncovered, then cover and refrigerate or freeze.

8. Final flavouring and serving

If needed: more fish stock or bouillon
Salt, pepper, cayenne, and tarragon
$\frac{1}{4}$ to $\frac{1}{2}$ pt double cream
The remaining lobster butter from step 6
2 to 3 tbl. minced fresh chervil, tarragon, or parsley
Croûtons (diced bread sautéed in butter, page 39); or Melba toast, page 126; or your own French bread, page 89

Shortly before serving, bring the bisque to the simmer. It should be quite thick, but if it needs thinning stir in a little stock or bouillon. Carefully correct seasoning. Just before serving, stir in the cream, then remove from heat and stir in the lobster butter, a tablespoon at a time. Pour the bisque into a hot tureen or soup cups, and decorate with fresh herbs. Pass the croûtons, Melba toast, or bread separately.

VARIATIONS

Because all of the other shellfish bisques follow almost the same pattern as lobster bisque, you can really substitute prawn, shrimp, crab, or crayfish for lobster in the master recipe every time you see the word 'lobster'. To account for the very slight differences in method, here is a paragraph of special instructions for each.

Bisque de Crevettes
[Shrimp or Prawn Bisque]

You must have shrimps or prawns in the shell for this recipe because the shells give the bisque its characteristic colour and flavour. It is of prime importance, therefore, that you use only the freshest smelling and finest quality of shrimps or prawns, whether they are live and whole or frozen, raw, and headless. If they are whole, meaning with head and shell, simply wash and drain before sautéing them; if frozen, thaw in cold water until you can separate them, then sauté. Since they need only 5 minutes of simmering, cook the tomatoes and other ingredients called for in step 3 for 10 minutes before adding the shellfish; after their simmer, let them cool 10 minutes in the cooking sauce before draining and peeling them. Use the shells and several whole, cooked shrimps or prawns for the shellfish butter in step 6, and if the shrimps or prawns are very large, slice in half lengthwise those you are reserving for the garnish in step 7. You will need $1\frac{1}{4}$ to $1\frac{1}{2}$ pounds of raw shellfish for 3 pints of bisque (enough for 6 to 8 people).

Bisque de Crabes
[Crab Bisque]

Crab bisque is even more one of love's labours than lobster bisque, but it is so marvellously rich and deeply flavoured that if you pick the right guests your reward will be in watching their pleasure, as well as relishing your own. Clean and cut the crabs as illustrated on pages 55–8, then substitute crab for lobster in the master recipe, starting on page 59, with the following slight modifications. Because crab pieces will bulk larger than lobster chests, you will need two big casseroles for the sautéing in step 2, but may combine all together for the simmering in step 3. You will not have enough liquid to cover all of the crab pieces in this step, and should toss the pieces several times during the 20 minutes of cooking; do not forget to add the liquid from the carapaces and the tomalley to simmer here, along with everything else. Note that it is only the chopped-up lower legs that go into the shellfish butter in step 6, but add as well all the debris from the chests, claws, and upper legs to simmer at the end of the step, allowing a good 10 minutes of cooking to extract every bit of flavour. For 3 pints of wonderful soup, you will need 6 to 8 live crabs measuring 3 to 4 inches across the top of the shell.

Bisque d'Écrevisses
[Crayfish Bisque]

Fresh-water crayfish, crawfish, or *écrevisses*, as they are variously called, are miniature lobster-like crustaceans 4 to 5 inches long. With the few minor differences noted here, substitute the word 'crayfish' for the word 'lobster' in the master recipe starting on page 59. To clean live crayfish, drop them head first in a basin of very hot water and leave for 2 to 3 minutes or until bubbles cease to rise. After draining them, pull out the central flap at the base of the tail to draw out along with it the intestinal tube. (This action of removing the intestine is called *châtrer* in French recipes.) Sauté and simmer the crayfish whole as directed in the master recipe, but they need only 10 minutes of cooking in step 3. To shell them, remove the tail meat only, and use all of it for the garnish in step 7; the chests and shell debris go into the butter, step 6. If you wish to be very *haute cuisine*, have a dozen extra crayfish and make a small amount of a simple fish mousse, using the raw tail meat. Then remove chest–leg sections (but not claws and feelers) from covering shell, and fill the shells with the mousse. Poach 5 minutes in stock or bouillon before floating them in the bisque at serving time. You should have 24 to 30 live crayfish for 3 pints of soup plus 12 or so extra if you are doing the mousse.

Two Scallop Soups with a Crab or Lobster Variation

Scallops are so easy to come by, fresh or frozen, that we feel they should have their place in the soup repertoire. Although scallops are rarely so used in France, they are delicious as the unique fish in a *bouillabaisse* or *bourride*, and they make a marvellous *velouté* or cream soup.

Les Saint-Jacques en Bouillabaisse
[*Bouillabaisse* of Scallops]

This heady Mediterranean brew of leeks, onions, garlic, tomatoes, and herbs plus scallops can be a complete meal when served with plenty of fresh French bread and followed by fruit and cheese.

[*Serving 4 as a main course, 6 as a soup course*]

1. The soup base

$\frac{3}{4}$ lb. finely sliced leeks and onions, or onions only
4 tbl. olive oil
A heavy-bottomed stainless or enamelled 5-pt saucepan with cover
2 large cloves garlic, minced or mashed
4 medium tomatoes peeled, seeded, juiced, and diced
$1\frac{1}{2}$ pts white-wine fish stock
The juice from the tomatoes
2 large pinches saffron threads
The following tied in washed cheesecloth: 6 parsley sprigs, 1 bay leaf, $\frac{1}{4}$ tsp. thyme, $\frac{1}{2}$ tsp. basil, 4 fennel seeds, and a 2-in. piece of dried orange peel or $\frac{1}{4}$ tsp. bottled dried peel
Salt and pepper

Cook the leeks and onions slowly with the oil in the covered saucepan for 5 to 6 minutes until tender but not browned. Add garlic and tomatoes, raise heat slightly, and cook 3 to 4 minutes more. Add the rest of the ingredients, bring to the boil, and simmer partially covered for 30 minutes. Carefully taste for seasoning, adding salt and pepper as needed.

2. Preparing the scallops

1 lb. bay or sea scallops, fresh or frozen
A large bowl and sieve

Soak the scallops in cold water for 2 or 3 minutes if fresh, until completely defrosted if frozen. Lift out and drain, looking over each for sand; wash again if necessary. Leave bay scallops whole. Cut sea scallops into ⅜-inch chunks.

3. Finishing the soup

The soup base
The scallops
2 to 3 tbl. coarsely chopped fresh parsley
French bread
Optional: a bowl of freshly grated Parmesan cheese

Bring the soup base to a rapid boil, add the scallops, bring to the boil again and boil slowly uncovered for 3 minutes. Check seasoning again. Serve either from a warm tureen or in soup cups or plates, and decorate with parsley. Pass the bread and optional cheese separately.

(†) Soup may be cooked several hours before serving. Let cool uncovered, then cover and refrigerate. Bring to a full boil for 2 or 3 seconds before serving. Note that a full boil is necessary to redistribute the olive oil into the liquid.

Other Ideas

For a more nourishing soup, you can add ½ pound of diced potatoes or a handful of pasta to the soup base 10 minutes before the end of its simmering. You could enrich the soup with an egg yolk and oil liaison, as for the *soupe aux poivrons* on page 44, or with a *rouille*, as for the *bouillabaisse* in Volume I, page 70. See also the recipe for *bourride* with its *aïoli* enrichment on page 80.

*Velouté de Saint-Jacques

[Cream of Scallop Soup – hot or cold]

This deliciously creamy soup is a cousin of the Breton *mouclades*, mussel soup, and you may serve it either hot or cold.

[*For 4 to 6 people*]

1. The *court bouillon*

1½ pts liquid: ¾ pt dry white wine or ½ pt dry white vermouth plus
   water
½ lb. onions, thinly sliced
2 carrots, thinly sliced
¼ tsp. each: fennel seeds, thyme, and curry powder
4 peppercorns
1 clove garlic, mashed
½ bay leaf
6 parsley sprigs
1½ tsp. salt
A heavy-bottomed stainless or enamelled saucepan with cover
A sieve set over a bowl

Simmer the ingredients for the *court bouillon* in the partially
covered saucepan for 20 minutes. Strain, pressing liquid out of
ingredients, and return the *court bouillon* liquid to the pan.

2. Cooking the scallops

1 lb. scallops, fresh or frozen

Soak the scallops in cold water for 2 or 3 minutes if fresh, until
completely defrosted if frozen. Lift out and drain, looking
over each for sand; wash again if necessary. Cut into ¼-inch
dice. Bring the *court bouillon* to a boil, add scallops, bring again
to just under the boiling point, and simmer uncovered for 3
minutes. Drain the liquid into the bowl, leaving scallops in
sieve. Rinse and dry the saucepan.

3. The *velouté* soup base

1½ oz. butter
4 tbl. flour
A wooden spatula or spoon
The *court bouillon*
A wire whisk
About ¾ pt milk
About ¼ pt double cream
2 egg yolks
The scallops
Salt and white pepper

Melt the butter in the saucepan, stir in the flour, and cook
slowly for 2 minutes without browning. Remove from heat

and let cool a moment, then pour in all the warm *court bouillon* at once, beating vigorously with a wire whisk to blend thoroughly. Bring to the boil for 2 to 3 minutes, stirring to reach all over bottom of pan. Thin with milk as necessary; soup should not be too thick, since the egg yolks to come will also thicken it. Remove from heat. Pour the cream, reserving a spoonful, into the bowl, blend in the egg yolks with a wire whisk, and gradually dribble in about ¾ pint of the hot soup, beating. Return mixture to the pan and stir in the scallops. Carefully correct seasoning.

(†) Soup may be prepared to this point several hours in advance. Clean off sides of pan with a rubber spatula and float a spoonful of cream on the surface to prevent a skin from forming. When cool, cover and refrigerate.

4. Finishing the soup, and serving

1½ to 2 oz. soft butter
2 to 3 tbl. minced fresh parsley, chervil, or chives

Shortly before serving, set soup over moderate heat and stir continually with a wooden spoon until soup comes to just below the simmer. Remove from heat and stir in the butter, a tablespoon at a time. Serve in a warm tureen or soup cups, and decorate with the minced herbs.

To Serve Cold

Omit the final butter enrichment, and oversalt slightly. Clean off sides of pan with a rubber spatula and float a spoonful of cream on the surface. When cool, cover and refrigerate. Blend in more cream, if you wish, just before serving.

Velouté de Crustacés
[Cream of Shellfish Soup]
For tinned crab, and cooked or frozen crab or lobster meat.

Although the best shellfish soups are made, like the bisques, from fresh, raw shellfish in the shell, because every bit of the flavour goes into the soup, you can produce an excellent result with the cooked meat alone, plus a fish stock. This is a useful type of recipe for those times when you want something special on the spur of the moment. The technique here is almost the same as for the preceding scallop soup, but there is no *court bouillon*. (*Note:* This recipe works especially well with freshly cooked crab or lobster meat, as well as with the frozen meat or with tinned crab. We have not found tinned lobster to be at all successful.)

[*For 4 people*]

1. Preparing and flavouring the shellfish meat

7 to 8 oz. tinned crab meat, or cooked or frozen crab or lobster meat
A large sieve and bowl
1 oz. butter
An 8-in. enamelled or stainless frying pan
1 tbl. minced shallots or spring onions
$\frac{1}{8}$ tsp. tarragon
Salt and pepper
Either: $\frac{1}{4}$ pt dry white wine;
Or: 8 tbl. dry white French vermouth

Commercially tinned or frozen shellfish meat is usually packed with a preservative, which should be washed off. Therefore soak the meat in cold water for several minutes (or until completely thawed). Pick it over carefully to remove all bits of tendon, particularly if you are using crab meat. Drain thoroughly. Melt butter in pan, stir in shallots or spring onions, then the shellfish meat. Season with the tarragon, salt, and pepper and sauté over moderate heat for 2 to 3 minutes so that butter and flavourings will penetrate meat. Add wine or vermouth, boil rapidly to reduce liquid by half, and set aside.

2. The *velouté* soup base

1 medium onion, very finely minced
2 oz. butter
A 5-pt heavy-bottomed stainless or enamelled saucepan with cover
3 tbl. flour
$1\frac{1}{4}$ pts fish stock brought to the simmer in a small saucepan
About 1 pt milk
The shellfish meat
Salt and pepper to taste

About ¼ pt double cream
2 egg yolks

Cook the onions slowly in the butter until tender but not browned. Stir in the flour and cook for 2 minutes. Remove from heat, and beat in the hot liquid. Simmer partially covered for 20 minutes, thinning out as necessary with milk. Add the shellfish meat, simmer 2 to 3 minutes to blend flavours, thinning out again with milk if necessary. Correct seasoning. Pour the cream, reserving a spoonful, into shellfish pan, blend in the egg yolks, then about ¾ pint of hot soup added by driblets. Pour back into the soup.

(†) May be prepared ahead to this point, as directed in preceding recipe.

3. Finishing the soup and serving
Follow directions in preceding recipe.

French Fish Stews and Soups

Bouillabaisse is not the only French fish soup. From that same Mediterranean coast comes the *bourride* – thick, rich, and reeking of garlic, while from the opposite corner of France comes the *marmite dieppoise*, with its mussels, sole, cream, and eggs. Inland France has its own special fish soups too, called *matelotes*, *meurettes*, and *pauchouses*, made from fresh-water fish. These are all hearty dishes with big chunks of fish, and easily suffice as the main course of an informal lunch or supper.

FISH TO USE
For this type of recipe the fish should be fairly firm-fleshed so that it will keep its shape while it cooks. Whether fresh or frozen, it must smell as fresh as a breeze from the open sea or the primeval forest. You cannot, of course, duplicate a freshwater soup from Burgundy with fish from the Atlantic, but we do not think the fish itself is all that important: it is the rest

of the ingredients and the general method that give each dish its special character. Here are some suggestions for both ocean fish and fresh-water fish with their French translations or equivalents.

Ocean fish

Cod (*cabillaud, morue fraîche*); conger eel (*congre, fiélas*); angler-fish, monkfish (*lotte de mer, baudroie*); haddock (*églefin*); halibut (*flétan,* rare in France); sea bass (*bar, loup*); whiting, hake (*merlu, merlan,* or *colin*); various rockfish, if you are a fisherman.

Fresh-water fish

Bass and perch (*perche*); carp (*carpe*); eel (*anguille*); pike (*brochet*); trout (*truite*); small carp-like fishes (*tanche, barbeau, barbillon* are typical, and frequently mentioned in French recipes).

Scallops

Though rarely used for soups in France, scallops are delicious used in any of the following recipes, alone or in combination with other fish.

PREPARING FISH FOR COOKING

Small fish (6 to 8 inches) for stews and soups are cleaned and scaled, and left whole. Larger fish, after cleaning and scaling, are cut into slices $\frac{3}{4}$ to 1 inch thick. Very large fish are cut into thick fillets or steaks, and then into serving pieces about 3 by 4 inches in diameter. Bones and skin are usually not removed, but you may remove them if you wish. As soon as you have prepared the fish, wrap and refrigerate it until you are ready to cook. Make fish stock out of scraps, heads, skin, and so forth (Volume I).

Matelotes, Meurettes, Pauchouses
[Burgundy Fish Stew with Wine, Onions, *Lardons,* and Mushrooms]

You might call this dish the fisherman's *coq au vin,* fish sim-mered in wine with onions, pork bits, and mushrooms, and the wine becomes the sauce. Even those who are not enthusiastic fish eaters usually love this recipe and although it is supposed to be made with fresh-water fish or eels alone, we have used ocean fish like halibut, haddock, or scallops with complete success. As usual with French regional recipes, you can have endless arguments as to whether a *matelote* is cooked with red wine or white, or if it is only the *pauchouse* (spelled *pôchouse* by some) that simmers in white wine, and only the *meurette* that has *lardons* of pork, or vice versa, including a garnish of poached eggs and truffles for some versions. We shall not enter into the argument at all except to say that a fish-stock base to the sauce is essential, or your *matelote/meurette/pauchouse* will lack the savour and character it must have.

If this is a main course, you may wish to add a side dish of boiled potatoes to eat with the stew, as well as plenty of French bread. Serve either a strong dry white wine or a red, preferably Burgundy, to match whichever wine cooked with the fish. A green salad or cold vegetable vinaigrette could follow the stew, and then cheese and fruit or a dessert.

[*For 4 to 6 people*]

1. The sauce base

¼ lb. fresh fat-and-lean pork belly or butt, or a chunk of salt pork, or bacon
A 6-pt flameproof casserole or saucepan
1 tbl. pork fat or cooking oil
Either: 1 lb. onions, sliced;
Or: 1 onion, sliced, and 24 to 30 braised onions to be added at end of cooking
2 tbl. flour

Cut pork into *lardons* 1 inch long and ¼ inch thick. If you are using salt pork or bacon, drop into 3 pints of water, simmer 10 minutes, drain, rinse, and dry in paper towels. Cook with the pork fat or oil over moderately low heat for 4 to 5 minutes, stirring frequently, until pork is very lightly browned. Then stir in the sliced onions, cover pan, and cook slowly for about 5 minutes until onions are tender. Raise heat and brown very lightly. Sprinkle on the flour and stir over moderately high heat to cook and brown the flour for 2 minutes. Remove from heat.

¾ pt either red wine such as Côtes-du-Rhône, or dry white wine such as
  Côtes-du-Rhône or Pinot Blanc, or ½ pt dry white French vermouth
¾ pt fish stock
Big pinch pepper
1 bay leaf
2 allspice berries
½ tsp. thyme
1 clove garlic, mashed
Salt

Gradually stir in the liquids to blend smoothly with the flour.
Add the herbs and garlic and bring to the simmer. Salt lightly
to taste. Simmer half an hour. Liquid should be lightly thickened; thin out with a little more wine or stock if necessary.
Carefully correct seasoning.

(†) May be cooked in advance; when cool, cover and refrigerate.

2. Optional additions: to be prepared in advance of final cooking

1 lb. fresh mushrooms, quartered and sautéed in butter
8 to 12 canapés (triangles of crustless home-made-type white bread
  sautéed in clarified butter)

The mushrooms may be sautéed and set aside in a covered
dish; they will simmer in the sauce just before serving. Reheat the canapés in the oven for several minutes before serving.

3. Finishing the stew and serving

Either: 2 to 2½ lb. fish from the list on page 72, one or several varieties,
  prepared as described;
Or: scallops only
More stock if needed

Twenty minutes before you wish to serve, bring the sauce
base to the boil and add the fish. Pour on more liquid if necessary, so fish is just covered. Rapidly bring back to the boil and
boil slowly 8 to 10 minutes (3 to 4 minutes only for scallops)
until fish is done; flesh comes easily from bone, or will just
flake – do not overcook.

A hot serving dish
The optional braised onions and sautéed mushrooms
Parsley sprigs or minced fresh parsley
The optional canapés

Arrange fish on hot dish, cover, and keep warm. Skim off any surface fat and rapidly boil down sauce, if necessary, to concentrate its flavour or to thicken it. Add optional braised onions and/or mushrooms and simmer for ·a moment to blend flavours. Carefully correct seasoning. Spoon sauce and vegetables over fish, decorate with parsley and optional canapés, and serve immediately.

(†) If you find you cannot serve immediately, return fish to pan after sauce has been finished and optional vegetables added. Remove from heat, and just before serving reheat to the simmer, basting fish with sauce until hot through.

Marmite aux Fruits de Mer
Marmite Dieppoise
Chaudrée Normande
[Normandy-style Fish Stew with Sole, Shellfish, and White-wine Sauce]

When you order *marmite dieppoise* in Dieppe on the Normandy coast or at Prunier's in Paris, you are served an elegant combination of Channel sole, turbot, red mullet, mussels, shrimps, scallops, and *langoustines*, those small, lobster-like prawns, all steaming together in an abundant, deliciously winey-smelling, ivory-coloured sauce. It will cost you quite a number of francs, since *marmite dieppoise* is definitely in the luxury category.

You may serve the *marmite* as a first course, although we suggest it as the main attraction of the meal. You could start with a *pâté* or a *saucisson en brioche*, follow with asparagus or artichokes vinaigrette, and it would be fully in the Normandy tradition to end with an apple dessert such as the individual soufflés on page 570, or the *tarte aux pommes* on page 597. With the *marmite* itself, serve a fine white Burgundy, Graves, or Gewürtztraminer.

FISH TALK

Although you may use any of the choices listed on pages 71–2, you will have a combination more like the original with the equivalent of a fillet of sole, two 2-inch pieces of halibut, 4 to 6 prawns, scallops, and/or mussels, and ⅓ of a lobster per person, for the first serving, and half the amount for seconds. Whatever you have chosen, be sure each piece of fish smells absolutely fresh; pay particular attention to the prawns if frozen, because they can overpower everything else unless of unquestionable quality. A well-flavoured fish stock is essential here; if you cannot get bones and trimmings from fresh sole, buy an extra pound or so of fish.

[*For 6 people as a main course, 10 to 12 as a soup course*]

1. Preliminaries: may be done several hours in advance
(*a*) *Preparing the fish* (*see also preceding paragraph*):

1½ lb. skinless and boneless sole, plaice, or flounder fillets
1 to 1½ lb. scallops
1 to 1½ lb. raw prawns, medium size, and in the shell if possible
1 to 1½ lb. halibut steaks, 1 in. thick
Waxed paper
A bowl large enough to hold all the fish

Wash and drain all the fish. Trim sole or flounder fillets if necessary; cut in half crosswise. If scallops are large, cut into ½-inch pieces. Peel the prawns, reserving peel and also heads if you have whole fresh prawns. Remove skin and bones from halibut, cut fish into pieces roughly 2 inches in diameter, and reserve bones and trimmings. Place each type of fish on waxed paper and pack into bowl in the order listed; cover and refrigerate. Refrigerate trimmings and reserve for the fish stock.

Decoration note: You may wish to save some whole cooked prawns, lobster claws, or mussels to decorate each serving; we leave this to you.

(*b*) *Optional fresh mussels:*

2 quarts fresh mussels
¼ pt dry white wine or dry white French vermouth

Scrub and soak the mussels, and steam them open in the wine as described in Volume I. Reserve 12 pairs of shells for garnish.

Place mussels in a small bowl and moisten with a little of the cooking liquid; decant rest of liquid into another bowl, being sure to include no sand.

(c) *The lobsters:*

You may use 8 to 12 ounces of cooked lobster meat rather than fresh lobsters; thaw if frozen, then warm in butter, wine, and seasonings, page 70, before adding to the *marmite* in the next step.

2 live lobsters, $1\frac{1}{4}$ to $1\frac{1}{2}$ lb. each
A sieve set over a 2-pt bowl or small saucepan
2 to 3 tbl. olive oil or cooking oil
The *marmite* (a heavy-bottomed, 10-pt enamelled or stainless casserole, with cover)
1 lb. white of leek and onions (or onions only), sliced
$\frac{1}{4}$ lb. each of carrots and celery, sliced
2 bay leaves
$\frac{1}{2}$ tsp. thyme
8 to 10 parsley stems and/or roots (not the leaves)
Salt (none if using mussel liquid)
$\frac{3}{4}$ pt dry white wine or $\frac{1}{2}$ pt dry white French vermouth
2 oz. soft butter
3 egg yolks
$\frac{1}{4}$ pt double cream

Split the lobsters in half lengthwise, discard stomach sacks in head and intestinal veins, scoop green matter and roe into sieve, and chop lobster into pieces (illustrated on page 52). Film *marmite* with $\frac{1}{8}$ inch of oil, heat to very hot but not smoking, and sauté lobster for 3 to 4 minutes, turning frequently until lobster shells are bright red. Remove to a side dish. Lower heat, stir vegetables and herbs into pan, and sauté 8 to 10 minutes until tender but not browned. Season lobster lightly with salt, return to *marmite*, add wine, cover, and simmer slowly for 20 minutes. Then lift out lobster pieces, remove the meat and reserve it in a bowl; chop shells and return to *marmite*. At some convenient time, add soft butter to lobster green matter and rub butter with green matter through sieve into bowl; beat in the egg yolks and cream, and set aside or refrigerate. (Rinse sieve in lobster-cooking liquid to get all the flavour possible.)

(d) The fish stock (for 2½ to 3 pints):

Either: 2 to 3 lb. bones, heads, trimmings, and shells from the fresh fish
    you are using;
Or: an extra lb. of fish
Either: ¾ pt dry white wine;
Or: ½ pt dry white French vermouth (half the amount of either if you
    are using mussel cooking liquid)
The optional mussel cooking liquid and/or necessary cold water
2 tsp. salt (none if using mussel liquid)

Add all ingredients to the lobster-cooking *marmite*, bring to
simmer, skim, and simmer partially covered for 40 minutes.
Strain liquid into a bowl and discard residue. Wash out
marmite and return liquid to it; you should have 2½ to 3 pints
of deliciously flavoured brew. Boil down to concentrate
flavour and volume if necessary; carefully correct seasoning.

2. Final cooking and serving: about 30 minutes
(a) Cooking the fish:

The fish stock in its *marmite*
2 oz. butter
A heavy-bottomed 5-pt enamelled or stainless saucepan
1½ oz. flour
A wooden spoon, a wire whisk, a perforated skimmer, and a ladle
The bowl of prepared and refrigerated fish
The cooked lobster meat and optional mussels
More fish stock, white wine, or boiling water if needed
A large soup tureen or bowl-shaped platter set over a pan of almost
    simmering water

Bring the fish stock to the boil. During this time melt the
butter in the saucepan, blend in the flour, and cook slowly,
stirring, until butter and flour foam together for 2 minutes
without browning at all. Set this *roux* aside: it is for the sauce,
next step. When stock is boiling, add the halibut (or other
firm-fleshed fish); bring liquid rapidly to the simmer and
simmer 5 minutes. Then add the sole, scallops, and prawns,
pressing them down into the liquid. If really necessary, add a
little more liquid: ingredients should be almost covered.
Bring again rapidly to the simmer for 2 minutes, then add the
cooked lobster meat and optional cooked mussels. Bring

again to simmer for 1 minute and remove from heat. Lift fish out and arrange in tureen; cover loosely. (Some of the fish, like sole, may have flaked apart; lift only what you easily can into the tureen.)

(b) *The sauce:*

The flour-and-butter *roux* and cooking liquid from preceding step
More stock or cream if needed
The lobster green-matter, cream, and yolk mixture
Salt, white pepper, Cayenne pepper, and lemon juice

Reheat *roux* if necessary, remove from heat, and whisking it with a wire whisk, gradually ladle into it by driblets ¾ pint of hot cooking stock. When perfectly smooth, set over moderately high heat and rapidly beat in 1½ to 2 pints more stock. Simmer, stirring, for 2 minutes: sauce should be a little thicker than a fairly heavy cream soup. Boil down rapidly, stirring, if too thin; beat in a little more stock if too thick. Then, and again by driblets, beat ¾ pint of hot sauce into the lobster green-matter mixture, heating it gradually to prevent it from curdling. Gradually beat it back into the hot sauce, and set sauce over moderate heat. Stir slowly with a wooden spoon, reaching all over bottom of pan until sauce thickens and comes almost to the simmer. If sauce seems too thick, stir in a little more cream or stock. Taste very carefully for seasoning, adding salt, pepper, drops of lemon juice, and so forth if you feel them necessary. Proceed immediately to the next step.

(c) *Serving:*

The optional fish decorations, such as whole prawns, lobster shells, mussels, etc.
2 to 3 tbl. minced fresh parsley and/or chervil
Warm soup plates
12 to 18 canapés (triangles of crustless home-made-type white bread sautéed in clarified butter)

Gently fold the hot sauce into the warm fish in the tureen. Float optional fish decorations on top and sprinkle the herbs over all. Serve as soon as possible, ladling the stew into hot plates and adding a canapé or two to each portion. This is eaten with large soup spoon, knife, and fork.

(†) May be completed a day before, serving in the *marmite* instead of a tureen. When cold, cover and refrigerate; heat slowly to below the simmer before serving. Like a good New England chowder or lobster stew, it gains in flavour when made in advance.

Bourride
[Provençal Fish Stew with *Aïoli* – Garlic Mayonnaise]

This marvellous fish stew from Provence is for garlic lovers only, as the big chunks of fish are cooked in a broth that is then enriched with egg yolks and a mayonnaise into which at least 1 large clove of garlic per person has been puréed. Like *bouillabaisse*, the fish is served on a platter and the enriched broth in a tureen, but both are eaten together in soup plates. This is such a rich dish we suggest you serve it for lunch, and you will want nothing else but perhaps a bit of green salad and fresh fruit. You will need a strong, dry white wine, such as a Côtes-du-Rhône or Pinot Blanc.

[*For 6 to 8 people as a main course*]

1. Preliminaries: may be done several hours before final cooking
(*a*) *The fish:*

3 to 4 lb. assorted lean, firm-fleshed white fish, such as those suggested on pages 71–2

Prepare the fish as described, cutting it into chunks or steaks about 3 inches in diameter and 1 to $1\frac{1}{2}$ inches thick. Refrigerate until cooking time.

(*b*) *The cooking broth:*

$\frac{1}{2}$ lb. each of onions, carrots, and white of leek (or additional onion), sliced
3 to 4 tbl. olive oil
A heavy-bottomed 10-pt flameproof casserole
2 medium tomatoes, chopped
Either: 3 to 4 pts fish trimmings, bones, heads;
Or: about 1 lb. fish
$4\frac{1}{2}$ pts water

¾ pt dry white wine or ½ pt dry white French vermouth
2 bay leaves
¼ tsp. each of thyme, fennel, and dried orange peel
2 large cloves of garlic, unpeeled, halved
2 large pinches saffron flowers
1½ tbl. salt

Cook the vegetables in oil over low heat for 8 to 10 minutes, until tender but not browned. Add the tomatoes and cook 2 minutes, then add all the rest of the ingredients. Bring to the simmer, skimming occasionally, and simmer partially covered for 40 minutes. Strain into a bowl, wash out casserole, and return the stock to it. Correct seasoning, adding salt if necessary.

(†) If prepared in advance, cover when cool and refrigerate.

(c) *The* aïoli:

Crumbs from 1 slice, ⅜ in. thick, of home-made-type stale unsweetened white bread
Wine vinegar
A heavy 4-pt mixing bowl or a mortar
A wooden pestle, masher, or heavy ladle (for pounding)
6 to 8 cloves garlic and garlic press
½ tsp. salt
6 egg yolks (2 now, the rest later)
¾ to 1¼ pts olive oil
A large wire whisk
White or Cayenne pepper

Moisten crumbs with a tablespoon or two of vinegar and pound to a paste in the bowl. Purée garlic through press into the paste and continue pounding several minutes until absolutely smooth. Add salt and 2 of the egg yolks and pound until mixture is very thick and sticky. Then begin pounding and stirring in oil by droplets until sauce is thick and heavy. Thin out with drops of vinegar and begin beating in oil, a teaspoonful at a time, with whisk. Sauce should be heavy enough to hold its shape in a spoon. Season to taste. (Note that a more detailed recipe on *aïoli* and on mayonnaise in general is in Volume I.)

A 1-pt serving bowl
Plastic wrap
A covered jar if needed

Scrape half the sauce into serving bowl, cover airtight, and set aside for dining room. Beat the 4 remaining egg yolks into the rest of the sauce; cover airtight. (If doing in advance, transfer to a smaller container and cover.) This second half is to be combined with the stew just before serving.

2. Cooking and serving

(a) Cooking the fish:

The cooking broth
The prepared fish
A large perforated skimmer
A serving platter set over a pan of almost simmering water, and a cover
2 to 3 tbl. coarsely chopped parsley

About 15 minutes before serving, bring cooking broth to a rolling boil and add the fish, pushing it down into the broth, which should barely cover it. (Add a little boiling water if necessary.) Boil slowly, uncovered, for 6 to 10 minutes, depending on thickness of fish (2 to 3 minutes only for scallops); it is done when springy rather than squashy to the touch – do not overcook. As soon as fish is done, arrange on platter, moisten with a little of the cooking broth, decorate with parsley, and cover to keep it warm.

(b) Combining cooking broth and aïoli:

The egg-yolk enriched *aïoli* in a 5-pt bowl
A large wire whisk, a ladle, and a wooden spoon
A 1-pt serving bowl
Salt and white pepper
A warm soup tureen

Whisking *aïoli* with wire whisk, gradually dribble in several ladlesful of hot cooking broth until about a pint has gone in. (Ladle a ½ pint or so of broth also into serving bowl and keep warm.) Pour *aïoli* mixture back into casserole with rest of cooking stock and set over moderate heat. Stir continually and rather slowly with wooden spoon until broth slowly thickens enough to coat the spoon – 4 to 5 minutes – being careful that liquid does not come to simmer and scramble the egg yolks. Carefully correct seasoning; broth will be a beautiful, smooth, richly aromatic yellow-ivory colour. Pour it into the tureen and serve immediately.

(c) *Serving:*

12 or more slices of hot French bread, ¾ in. thick
Wide soup plates
The reserved plain broth
The hot fish on its platter, and the tureen
The reserved *aïoli* mayonnaise

For each serving, place 2 slices of bread in a soup plate and moisten with a spoonful of plain broth. Arrange chunks of fish over the bread and ladle over it the *aïoli* broth from the tureen. Each guest adds a spoonful of *aïoli* mayonnaise, and eats the *bourride* with soup spoon and fork.

2. Baking: Breads, *Brioches*, Croissants, and Pastries

Yeast Doughs · *Les Pâtes Levées*

The average French household does no yeast baking at all except for *babas*, *savarins*, and an occasional *brioche*. It certainly does no bread making, and there is no need to because every neighbourhood has its own *boulangerie* serving freshly baked bread every day of the week but one, usually Monday, when the *boulanger* takes his day off. Thus you cannot even find a bread tin in a French household supply store, and there are no French recipes for home-made bread. All of the recipes here, therefore, are those used by professionals whose techniques we have worked out for the home baker, using standard ingredients and household equipment.

Whether you are a home or a professional baker, you will find that time is really the key to successful bread making. Just as it takes time for cheese to ripen and wine to age, it takes time for yeast to do its full work in a dough. The function of yeast is not only to push the dough up but, equally important, to develop its flavour and its texture. Yeast feeds and multiplies on the starch in the flour. Flour also contains gluten, and it is the gluten that allows the dough to rise and stay risen in the oven because gluten molecules become gluey when moistened and join together in an elastic web throughout the dough. Then, while the yeast cells are feeding and multiplying on the starch, their voracious activity forms tiny pockets of gas that push up the surrounding mesh of gluten, making the dough rise. At the same time the gluten itself, if given time, goes through a slow ripening process that gives the dough flavour, cohesion, and elasticity. These important developments in the gluten must take place if a very simple dough, such as that for plain French bread, is to turn into something splendidly satisfying to eat. Thus, rather than trying to speed things up by using lots of yeast and a warm rising temperature, you want to provide time for ripening by slowing everything down with a minimum of yeast, a tepid temperature, and several risings. Many reasons are given for the doleful state of much contemporary bread both here and in France: it is not baked in wood-fired ovens; both the flour and water are full of chemicals; it is machine-kneaded; and so forth. The villain in the bread basket is speed: the yeast has not been given the time it needs to accomplish its triple function of developing flavour and texture as well as volume.

YEAST

Yeast is a living organism, but it is inactive or dormant when you buy it, either as a fresh cake or as dry yeast in a sealed envelope. Fresh cake yeast must be a uniformly creamy grey with no spots of discoloration, and is perishable; it will keep only about a week under refrigeration but for several weeks when wrapped airtight and frozen. Dry-active yeast should be stored in a cool, dry place, or in the refrigerator or freezer; use it before the expiration date stamped on the envelope. Either type of yeast may be used, but both must be completely liquefied before the yeast is ready to become active. Although you can mix it, as it is, into the dry ingredients and blend in warm water, we prefer the almost as rapid but visually positive method of liquefying it separately.

Proving yeast

When you know your yeast is fresh, you need have no doubts about its capacities. If you think it may be stale do not hesitate to make it prove itself by dissolving it in the warm water called for in your recipe; stir in also a tablespoon of flour and a pinch of sugar. It is active and ready to use if it begins to foam and to increase in volume in about 8 minutes: the yeast cells, spurred on by the sugar, are feeding on the flour.

DOUGH TEXTURE, VOLUME OF RISE, TEMPERATURE

Anyone used to English bread making will be surprised to find that the doughs for all of the following recipes are light, soft, and sticky when first made because the dough is to triple rather than double in volume during its first and usually its second rise: this is the period during which it develops its flavour and texture. Rather than rising in a warm place of around 85°F., which would cause it to ferment and acquire an unpleasant yeasty-sour taste, it must rise in the low 70s if you can possibly manage it, or at an even lower temperature if you wish to delay the process.

THE WEATHER

We therefore suggest that you do not attempt your first bread-making spree in a hot kitchen. When you are used to doughs and know how they should look, smell, and feel, you can adjust your procedures to the weather, letting the dough rise part of the time in the refrigerator, for instance, or deflating it when partially risen and letting it push itself up several times. Rainy or humid weather and steamy rooms also have their adverse affect, making dough unduly sticky, even sweaty; pick a dry day and a dry room, then, for your first venture. In other words, make everything as easy as possible for yourself.

TIMING AND DELAYED ACTION

Although it will take you a minimum of 7 hours from start to finish for most of these recipes, that does not mean that you are hovering over your dough for 7 straight hours. During almost all of this time the dough is sitting quietly by itself, rising in one form or another. Because you can slow down the rise by lowering the temperature, you may set it in the refrigerator or the freezer when you have to go out, and continue when you return. Thus, although you cannot successfully speed things up, you can otherwise fit bread making into almost any pattern that suits your schedule. Each of the recipes indicates various stopping points, and a delayed-action chart is on pages 104–5, at the end of the French bread recipe.

MACHINE VERSUS HAND MIXING

A heavy-duty table-model electric beater with a dough hook works very well for mixing and kneading dough, and can be adapted nicely to the French processes. Notes are at the end of each section.

Plain French Bread · *Pain Français*

A fine loaf of plain French bread, the long crackly kind a Frenchman tucks under his arm as he hurries home to the family lunch, has a very special quality. Its inside is patterned with holes almost like Swiss cheese, and when you tear off a piece it wants to come sideways; it has body, chewability, and tastes and smells of the grain. Plain French bread contains only flour, water, salt, and yeast, because that is the law in France. The method, however, is up to each individual baker. Until the 1800s and before commercial yeast was known, all bread was made with a *levain*, meaning dough left over from the previous batch; the procedure involved numerous risings and mixings to develop sufficient yeast cells for the day's quota of bread. Later a brewer's-yeast-and-flour batter was developed that simplified the process, but it was not until the 1870s that the kind of yeast we use today was manufactured in France. Since then the making of French bread has undergone many changes, some of which, notably the accelerated mechanical kneading and fast-rising systems used by some bakers, have had a disastrous effect on quality. Again, this is a question of trying to save time at the expense of taste and texture, because excellent bread may be made using modern ingredients, equipment, and methods.

We have had the great good fortune of being able to work with Professor R. Calvel, of the École Française de Meunerie, a trade school established in Paris to teach the profession of milling and baking to students and bakers from all over France. The science of bread making and the teaching of its art are the life work of Professor Calvel, and thanks to his enthusiastic help, which set us on the right track, we think we have developed as professional a system for the home baker as anyone could hope for. You will be amazed at how very different the process is from anything you have done before, from the mixing and rising to the very special method of forming the dough into loaves.

FLOUR

I shall not complicate the bread recipe by specifying other than 'strong plain flour', but if you can find a pure unbleached white flour with a gluten strength of 8 to 9 per cent, your loaf will more nearly resemble a good French loaf. It is a question of looking around, trying the health food stores, or asking your local baker to part with a few pounds of his own bread flour. The subject, however, is a complicated one, and I refer you to the masterful discussion of flour in Elizabeth David's *English Bread and Yeast Cookery*.

BAKERS' OVENS VERSUS HOME OVENS

Bakers' ovens are so constructed that one slides the formed bread dough from a wooden paddle right on to the hot, firebrick oven floor, and a steam-injection system humidifies the oven for the first few minutes of baking. Steam allows the yeast to work a little longer in the dough and this, combined with a hot baking surface, produces an extra push of volume. In addition, steam coagulating the starch on the surface of the dough gives the crust its characteristic brown colour. Although you can produce a good loaf of French bread without steam or a hot baking surface, you will get a larger and handsomer loaf when you simulate professional conditions. We give both systems – the master recipe, which requires no special equipment, and the simulated baker's oven system, which is described and illustrated on pages 108–12.

EQUIPMENT NEEDED FOR MAKING FRENCH BREAD

Unless you plan to go into the more elaborate simulation of a baker's oven, you need no unusual equipment for the following recipe. Here are the requirements, some of which may sound odd but will explain themselves when you read the recipe:

A 6- or 7-pint mixing bowl with fairly vertical rather than outward-slanting sides; a kneading surface of some sort, $1\frac{1}{2}$ to 2 square feet; a rubber spatula and either a metal scraper or a stiff wide metal spatula; 1 or 2 unwrinkled canvas pastry cloths or stiff linen towels upon which the dough may rise; a stiff piece of cardboard or plywood, 18 to 20 inches long and 6 to 8 inches wide, for unmoulding dough from canvas to baking sheet; finely ground cornmeal, or pasta pulverized in an electric blender, to sprinkle on unmoulding board so as to prevent dough from sticking; the largest baking sheet that will fit into your oven; a razor blade for slashing the top of the dough; a soft pastry brush or fine-spray atomizer for moistening dough before and during baking; a room thermometer to verify rising-temperature.

*Pain Français

[Plain French Bread]

Count on a minimum of $6\frac{1}{2}$ to 7 hours from the time you start the dough to the time it is ready for the oven, and half an hour for baking. While you cannot take less time, you may take as much more time as you wish by using the delayed-action techniques described at the end of the recipe.

[*For 1 pound of flour, producing: 3 long loaves*, baguettes, *24 by 2 inches, or* bâtards, *16 by 3 inches; or 6 short loaves*, ficelles, *12 to 16 by 2 inches; or 3 round loaves*, boules, *7 to 8 inches in diameter; or 12 round or oval rolls*, petits pains; *or 1 large round or oval loaf*, pain de ménage *or* miche; pain boulot]

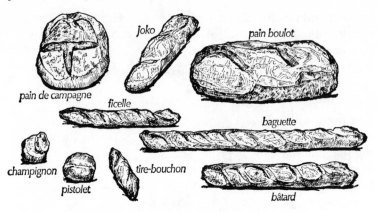

pain de campagne

joko

pain boulot

ficelle

baguette

champignon

pistolet

tire-bouchon

bâtard

1. The dough mixture (*le fraisage* or *frasage*)

Note: List of equipment needed is in paragraph preceding this recipe.

½ oz. fresh yeast or ¼ oz. dry-active yeast
4 tbl. warm water (not over 100°F.) in a measure
About 1 lb. strong plain flour
2¼ tsp. salt
½ pt tepid water (70 to 74°F.)

Stir the yeast in the warm water and let liquefy completely while measuring flour into mixing bowl. When yeast has liquefied, pour it into the flour along with the salt and the rest of the water.

Stir and cut the liquids into the flour with a rubber spatula, pressing firmly to form a dough, and making sure that all bits

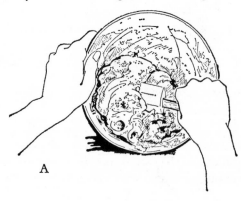

A

of flour and unmassed pieces are gathered in (A). Turn dough out on to kneading surface, scraping bowl clean. Dough will be soft and sticky. Let it rest for 2 to 3 minutes while you wash and dry the bowl.

2. Kneading (*pétrissage*)

The flour will have absorbed the liquid during this short rest, and the dough will have a little more cohesion for the kneading that is about to begin. Use one hand only for kneading and keep the other clean to hold a pastry scraper, to dip out extra flour, to answer the telephone, and so forth. Your object in kneading is to render the dough perfectly smooth and to work it sufficiently so that all the gluten molecules are moistened and joined together into an interlocking web. You cannot see this happen, of course, but you can feel it because the dough will become elastic and will retract into shape when you push it out.

Start kneading by lifting the near edge of the dough, using a pastry scraper or stiff wide spatula to help you if necessary, and flipping dough over on to itself (B). Scrape the dough off

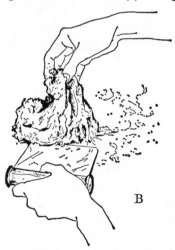

B

the surface and slap it down; lift edge and flip it over again, repeating the movement rapidly. In 2 to 3 minutes the dough should have enough body so that you can give it a quick for-

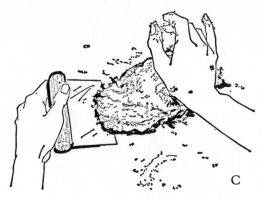

C

ward push with the heel of your hand as you flip it over (c). Continue to knead rapidly and vigorously in this way. If it remains too sticky, knead in a sprinkling of flour. (Whole kneading process will take 5 to 10 minutes, depending on how vigorous and expert you become.)

Shortly after this point, the dough should have developed enough elasticity so that it draws back into shape when pushed, indicating that the gluten molecules have united and are under tension like a thin web of rubber; the dough should also begin to clean itself off the kneading surface, although it will stick to your fingers if you hold a pinch for more than a second or two. Let it rest for 3 to 4 minutes. Knead again for a minute: the surface should now look smooth; the dough will be less sticky but it will still remain soft. It is now ready for its first rise.

3. First rising (*pointage premier temps*): 3 to 5 hours at around 70°F.

The dough is to rise to $3\frac{1}{2}$ times its original volume. Place the dough in the clean mixing bowl (note that the bowl should have fairly upright sides; if they are too outward slanting, the dough will have difficulty rising). Slip bowl into a large plastic bag or cover with plastic, and top with a folded bath towel. Set on a wooden surface (marble or stone are too cold) or on a folded towel or pillow, and let rise free from draughts any place where the temperature is around 70°F; if the room is too hot, set bowl in water and keep renewing water to maintain it at around 70°F. Dough should take at least 3 hours to rise; if the temperature is lower, it will simply take longer.

(†) *Delayed action:* See chart at end of recipe.

When fully risen, the dough will be humped into a slight dome, showing that the yeast is still active; it will be light and spongy when pressed. There will usually be some big bubbly blisters on the surface, and if you are using a glass bowl you will see bubbles through the glass.

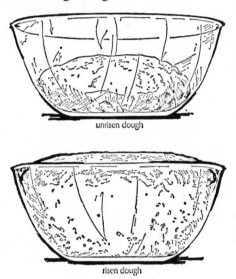

unrisen dough

risen dough

4. Deflating and second rising (*rupture; pointage deuxième temps*): 1½ to 2 hours at around 70°F.

The dough is now ready to be deflated, which will release the yeast-engendered gases and redistribute the yeast cells so that the dough will rise again and continue the fermentation process.

With a rubber spatula dislodge dough from inside of bowl (D) and turn out on to a lightly floured surface, scraping the bowl clean. If dough seems damp and sweaty, sprinkle with a tablespoon of flour. Lightly flour the palms of your hands and flatten the dough firmly but not too roughly into a

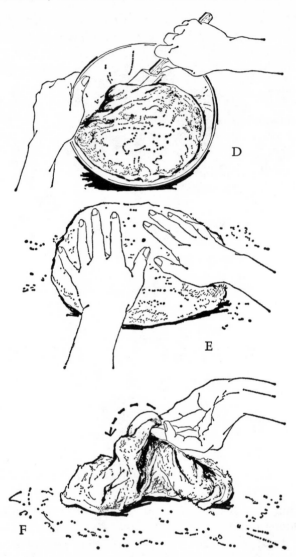

circle (E), deflating any gas bubbles by pinching them. Lift a corner of the near side and flip it down on to the far side (F). Do the same with the left side, then the right side. Finally lift the near side and tuck it just under the edge of the far side. The mass of dough will look like a rounded cushion.

Slip the sides of your hands under the dough and return it to the bowl. Cover and let rise again, this time to not quite triple, but again until it is dome-shaped and light and spongy when touched.

(†) *Delayed action:* See chart at end of recipe.

5. Cutting and resting dough before forming loaves

Loosen dough all around inside of bowl and turn out on to a lightly floured surface. Because of its two long rises, the dough will have much more body. If it seems damp and sweaty, sprinkle lightly with flour.

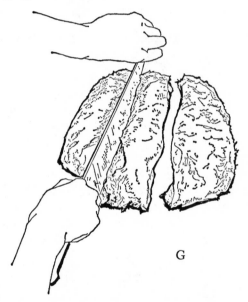

G

Making clean, sure cuts with a large knife or a scraper, divide dough into 3 equal pieces for long loaves (G), or whatever is specified for other shapes and sizes. After you have cut each piece, lift one end and flip it over on to the opposite end to fold the dough in two (H); place dough at far side of kneading surface. Cover loosely with a sheet of plastic and let rest for 5 minutes before forming. This relaxes the gluten enough for shaping, but not long enough for the dough to begin rising again.

H

While the dough is resting, prepare the rising surface: smooth the canvas or linen towelling on a large tray or baking sheet, and rub flour thoroughly into the entire surface of the cloth to prevent the dough from sticking.

6. Forming loaves (*la tourne; la mise en forme des pâtons*)

Because French bread stands free in the oven and is not baked in a tin, it has to be formed in such a way that the tension of the coagulated gluten cloak on the surface will hold the dough in shape. Following are illustrated directions for the familiar long loaf – the *bâtard* (baked size 16 by 3 inches); other shapes are described and illustrated at the end of the recipe. *Baguettes* are much too long for home ovens.

After the 3 pieces of dough have rested 5 minutes, form one piece at a time, keeping the remaining ones covered.

Working rapidly, turn the dough upside down on a lightly floured kneading surface and pat it firmly but not too roughly into an 8- to 10-inch oval with the lightly

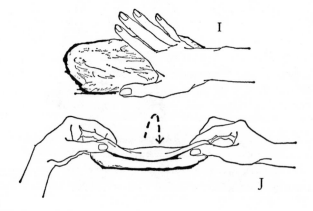

I

J

floured palms of your hands (I). Deflate any gas bubbles in
the dough by pinching them. Fold the dough in half lengthwise by bringing the far edge down over the near edge (J).
Being sure that the working surface is always very lightly
floured so the dough will not stick and tear, which would
break the lightly coagulated gluten cloak that is being formed,
seal the edges of the dough together, your hands extended,
thumbs out at right angles and touching (K). Roll the dough
a quarter turn forwards so the seal is on top (L). Flatten the
dough again into an oval with the palms of your hands (M).

Press a trench along the central length of the oval with the
side of one hand (N). Fold in half again lengthwise (O). This
time seal the edges together with the heel of one hand (P), and

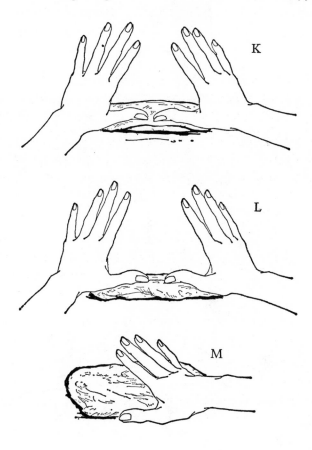

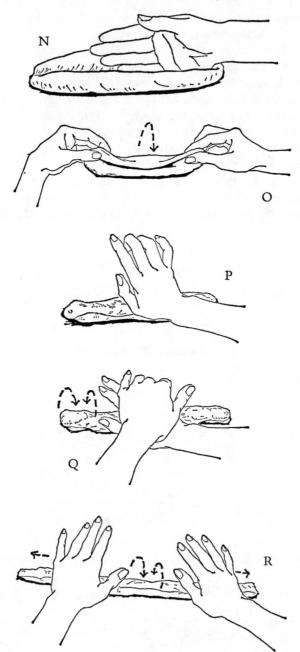

roll the dough a quarter turn towards you so the seal is on the bottom. Now, by rolling the dough back and forth with the palms of your hands, you will lengthen it into a sausage shape. Start in the middle, placing your right palm on the dough, and your left palm on top of your right hand (Q). Roll dough forwards and backwards rapidly, gradually sliding your hands towards the two ends as the dough lengthens (R).

Deflate any gas blisters on the surface by pinching them. Repeat the rolling movement rapidly several times until the dough is 16 inches long, or whatever length will fit on your baking sheet. During the extension rolls, keep circumference of dough as even as possible and try to start each roll with sealed side of dough down, twisting the rope of dough to straighten the line of seal as necessary. If seal disappears, as it sometimes does with plain flour, do not worry.

Place the shaped piece of dough, sealed side up, at one side of the flour-rubbed canvas, leaving a free end of canvas 3 to 4 inches wide (S). (The top will crust slightly as the dough rises;

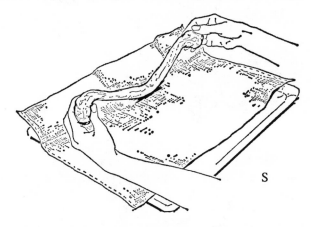

S

it is turned over for baking so the soft, smooth underside will be uppermost.) Pinch a ridge $2\frac{1}{2}$ to 3 inches high in the canvas to make a trough, and a place for the next piece (T). Cover dough with plastic while you are forming the rest of the loaves.

After all the pieces of dough are in place, brace the two sides of the canvas with long rolling pins (U), baking tins, or books,

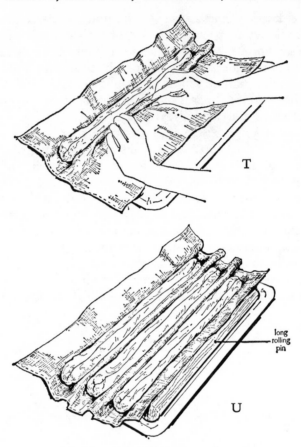

if the dough seems very soft and wants to spread out. Cover the dough loosely with a flour-rubbed dish cloth or canvas, and a sheet of plastic. Proceed immediately to the final rising, next step.

7. Final rise (*l'apprêt*): $1\frac{1}{2}$ to $2\frac{1}{2}$ hours at around 70°F.

The covered dough is now to rise to almost triple in volume; look carefully at its pre-risen size so that you will be able to judge correctly. It will be light and swollen when risen, but will feel still a little springy when pressed.

It is important that the final rise take place where it is dry; if your kitchen is damp, hot, and steamy, let the bread rise in another room or dough will stick to canvas and you will have difficulty getting it off and on to the baking sheet. It will turn into bread in the oven whatever happens, but you will have an easier time and a better loaf if you aim for ideal conditions.

Preheat oven to 450°F., Mark 8, 30 minutes before estimated baking time.

(†) *Delayed action:* See chart at end of recipe.

8. Unmoulding risen dough on to baking sheet (*le démoulage*)

The 3 pieces of risen dough are now to be unmoulded from the canvas and arranged upside down on the baking sheet. The reason for this reversal is that the present top of the dough has crusted over during its rise; the smooth, soft underside should be uppermost in the oven so that the dough can expand and allow the loaf its final puff of volume. For the unmoulding you will need a non-sticking intermediate surface such as a stiff piece of cardboard or plywood sprinkled with cornmeal or pulverized pasta.

Remove rolling pins or braces. Place the long side of the board at one side of the dough; pull the edge of the canvas to

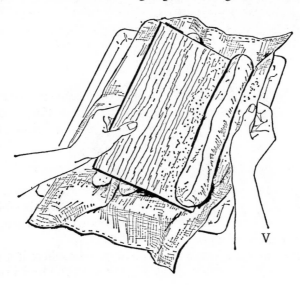

V

flatten it; then raise and flip the dough softly upside down on to the board (v).

Dough is now lying along one edge of the unmoulding board: rest this edge on the right side of a lightly buttered baking sheet. Gently dislodge dough on to baking sheet, keeping same side of dough uppermost: this is the soft smooth side, which was underneath while dough rose on canvas. If necessary, run sides of hands lightly down the length of the dough to straighten it. Unmould the next piece of dough the same way, placing it to the left of the first, leaving a 3-inch space. Unmould the final piece near the left side of the sheet.

9. Slashing top of the dough (*la coupe*)

The top of each piece of dough is now to be slashed in several places. This opens the covering cloak of gluten and allows a bulge of dough underneath to swell up through the cuts during the first 10 minutes of baking, making decorative patterns in the crust. These are done with a blade that cuts almost horizontally into the dough to a depth of less than half an inch. Start the cut at the middle of the blade, drawing towards you in a swift, clean sweep. This is not quite as easy as

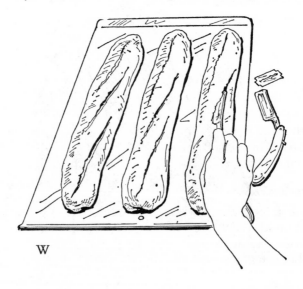

W

it sounds, and you will probably make ragged cuts at first; never mind, you will improve with practice. Use an ordinary razor blade and slide one side of it into a cork for safety; or buy a barber's straight razor at a cutlery store.

For a 16- to 18-inch loaf make 3 slashes. Note that those at the 2 ends go straight down the loaf but are slightly off centre, while the middle slash is at a slight angle between the two. Make the first cut at the far end, then the middle cut, and finally the third. Remember that the blade should lie almost parallel to the surface of the dough (w).

10. Baking: about 25 minutes; oven preheated to 450°F., Mark 8

As soon as the dough has been slashed, moisten the surface either by painting with a soft brush dipped in cold water, or with a fine-spray atomizer, and slide baking sheet on to rack in upper third of preheated oven. Rapidly paint or spray dough with cold water after 3 minutes, again in 3 minutes, and a final time 3 minutes later. Moistening the dough at this point helps the crust to brown and allows the yeast action to continue in the dough a little longer. The bread should be done in about 25 minutes; the crust will be crisp, and the bread will make a hollow sound when thumped.

If you want the crust to shine, paint lightly with a brush dipped in cold water as soon as you slide baking sheet out of oven.

11. Cooling: 2 to 3 hours

Cool the bread on a rack or set it upright in a basket or large bowl so that air can circulate freely around each piece. Although bread is always exciting to eat fresh from the oven, it will have a much better taste when the inside is thoroughly cool and has composed itself.

12. Storing French bread

Because it contains no fats or preservatives of any kind, French bread is at its best when eaten the day it is baked. It will keep for a day or two longer, wrapped airtight and refrigerated, but it will keep best if you freeze it – let the loaves cool first, then wrap airtight. To thaw, unwrap and place on a baking sheet in a cold oven; heat the oven to 400°F., Mark 6. In about 20 minutes the crust will be hot and crisp, and the bread thawed. The French, of course, never heat French bread except possibly on Monday, the baker's holiday, when the bread is a day old.

13. Canvas housekeeping
After each bread session, if you have used canvas, brush it thoroughly to remove all traces of flour and hang it out to dry before putting away. Otherwise the canvas could become mouldy and ruin your next batch of dough.

DELAYED ACTION: STARTING AND STOPPING
THE DOUGH PROCESS

As noted in the master recipe, there are numerous points at which you can slow down the action or stop it altogether, by setting the dough in a colder place, or refrigerating or freezing it. Exact timings for any of these delaying procedures are impossible to give because so much depends on what has taken place during the slow-down, how cold the dough is when it starts to rise again, and so forth. All you need to remember is that you are in complete control: you can always push down a partially risen dough; you can slow the action with cold; you can speed it with warmth. You will work out your own systems and the following chart will help you:

Delayed-Action Chart

TO DELAY THE FIRST RISING, SET DOUGH IN A COLDER PLACE

For approximately 5–6 hours of rise, set dough at 65°F.
For approximately 7–8 hours of rise, set dough at 55°F.
For approximately 9–10 hours of rise, set dough in refrigerator.

TO STOP ACTION ALTOGETHER AFTER FIRST OR SECOND RISE

Deflate, wrap airtight, and freeze. *Limit:* A week to 10 days, probably more for plain French bread dough, and risky after 10 days for doughs with butter and eggs. (We shall not venture farther upon this uncertain limb.)

TO DELAY SECOND RISING

(a) Set dough in a colder place.
(b) Set a plate on top of dough and a 5-pound weight; refrigerate.

TO DELAY OR FREEZE AFTER DOUGH IS FORMED

(a) Set dough in a colder place.
(b) Form dough on lightly oiled sheet; cover airtight and refrigerate or freeze, but note preceding time limit.

TO START ACTION AFTER THAWING

(a) Thaw overnight in refrigerator; complete the rise at room temperature.
(b) Set at 80°F., until thawed; complete the rise at room temperature.

OTHER FORMS FOR FRENCH BREAD

Long Thin Loaves
[Ficelles]

Cut the original dough, step 5, page 95, into 5 or 6 pieces and form as illustrated in the recipe, but making thinner sausage shapes about ½ inch in diameter (baked size: 12 to 16 by 1½ inches). When they have risen, slash as illustrated, step 9.

Oval Rolls
[Petits Pains, Tire-bouchons]

Cut the dough into 10 or 12 pieces and form like *bâtards*, but you will probably not have to lengthen them at all after the two foldings and sealings. When they have risen, make either 2 parallel slashes, or a single slash going from one end to the other.

Round Loaves
[Pain de Ménage, Miches, Boules]

When you want bread for sandwiches or for toast, a big round loaf is attractive. The object here is to force the cloak of coagulated gluten to hold the ball of dough in shape: the first movement will make a cushion; the second will seal and round the ball, establishing surface tension. To begin the process, after the risen dough has been cut and has rested 5 minutes, step 5, page 95, place it on a lightly floured surface.

Lift the left side of the dough with the side of your left hand and bring it down almost to the other side (A). Scoop up that side and push it back almost to the left side (B). Revolve dough a quarter turn clockwise and repeat the movement eight to ten times. This movement gradually smooths the bottom of the dough and establishes the necessary surface tension; think of the surface of the dough as if it were a fine sheet of rubber you were stretching in every direction.

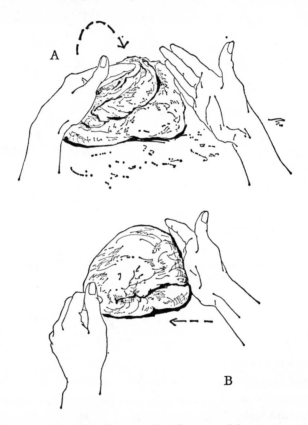

Then turn the dough smooth side up and begin rotating it between the palms of your hands, tucking a bit of the dough under the ball as you rotate it (c). In a dozen turns you should have a neatly shaped ball with a little pucker of dough, *la clé*, underneath where the edges have all joined together.

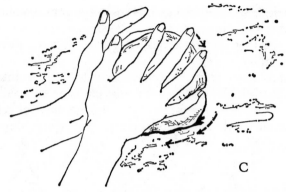

C

Place the dough pucker side up on flour-rubbed canvas; seal
the pucker by pinching with your fingers. Flour lightly, cover
loosely, and let rise to almost triple its size. After unmoulding
upside down on the baking sheet, slash it as shown here (D).

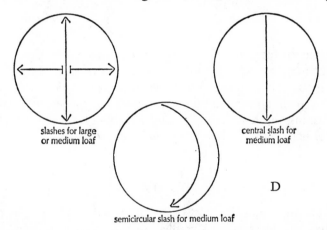

slashes for large
or medium loaf

central slash for
medium loaf

semicircular slash for medium loaf

D

Large loaves are usually slashed in a cross: make one vertical
slash and complete the horizontal cuts as illustrated. Medium
loaves may have a cross, a single central slash, or a semicircular
slash around half the circumference.

Round Rolls
[Petits Pains, Champignons]

Cut the original dough, step 5, page 95, into 10 to 12 pieces.
After they have rested 5 minutes, form them one at a time,

leaving the rest of the dough covered. The principles are the same here as for the preceding round loaves, but make the preliminary cushion shape with your fingers rather than the palms of your hands.

For the second stage, during which the ball of dough is rotated smooth side up, roll it under the palm of one hand, using your thumb and little finger to push the edges of the dough underneath and to form the pucker, where the edges join together (A).

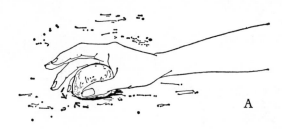

A

Place the formed ball of dough pucker side up on the flour-rubbed canvas and cover loosely while forming the rest. Space the balls 2 inches apart. When risen to almost triple its size, lift gently with lightly floured fingers and place pucker side down on baking sheet. Rolls are usually too small for a cross; make either one central slash or the semicircular cut.

THE SIMULATED BAKER'S OVEN

Baking in the ordinary way, as described in the preceding recipe, produces an acceptable loaf of bread, but does not nearly approach the glory you can achieve when you turn your home oven into a baker's oven. Merely providing yourself with the proper amount of steam, if you do nothing else, will vastly improve the crust, the colour, the slash patterns, and the volume of your bread; steam is only a matter of plopping a heated brick or stone into a pan of water in the bottom of the oven. The second provision is a hot surface upon which the naked dough can bake; this gives that added push of volume that improves both the appearance and the slash patterns.

When you have the hot baking surface, you will then also need a paddle or board upon which you can transfer dough from canvas to hot baking surface. For the complete set-up, here is what you should have, and any builders' merchant stocks these items.

For the hot baking surface

A hot baking sheet will not do because it burns the bottom of the dough. Buy a piece of asbestos cement about $\frac{1}{4}$ inch thick and cut 1 inch shorter and narrower than your oven rack. Set this on the rack in the upper third of your oven while pre-heating, and slide the dough on to it for baking.

For unmoulding the risen dough from its canvas

A piece of $\frac{3}{16}$-inch plywood about 20 inches long and 8 inches wide.

For sliding the dough on to the hot asbestos

When you are doing 3 long loaves, you must slide them together on to the hot asbestos; to do so you unmould them one at a time from the canvas with one board and arrange them side by side on the second board, which takes the place of the baker's wooden paddle, *la pelle*. Buy a piece of $\frac{3}{16}$-inch plywood slightly longer but 2 inches narrower than your oven rack.

To prevent dough from sticking to unmoulding and sliding boards

White cornmeal or small pasta pulverized in the electric blender until it is the consistency of table salt. This is called *fleurage*.

The steam contraption

Something that you can heat to sizzling hot on top of the stove and then slide into a pan of water in the oven to make a great burst of steam: a brick, a solid 10-pound rock, piece of cast iron or other metal. A 9-by-12-inch roasting pan 2 inches deep to hold an inch of water and the hot brick.

Non-essential professional equipment

Instead of letting the formed dough rise on canvas, *sur couche*, many French bakers place each piece in a canvas-lined wicker or plastic form called a *banneton*; from this you turn the risen dough upside down directly on to a board and then slide it into the oven. Various sizes and shapes are available in French bakery-supply houses.

banneton – 24 inches long

These are bakers' blades, *lames*, for slashing dough; they are about 4 inches long and $\frac{1}{4}$ inch wide, with very sharp, curved ends.

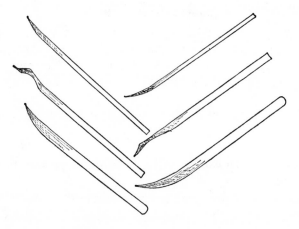

USING THE SIMULATED BAKER'S OVEN

At least 30 to 40 minutes before the end of the final rise, step 7 in master recipe, place the sheet of asbestos cement on the rack in the upper third of the oven and preheat oven to 450°F., Mark 8. At the same time set the brick or metal over very high heat on top of the stove so that it will get sizzling hot, the hotter the better. Provide yourself with 2 stiff spoons or spatulas, or with fire tongs for lifting brick (A) from stove top into pan of water in bottom of oven when the time comes, and test lifting the brick to be sure you have the instruments to do the job.

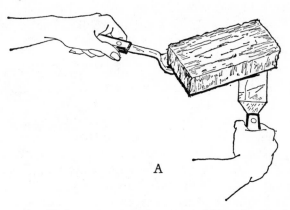

A

When the final rise is complete, sprinkle pulverised corn-meal or pasta on the long side of the unmoulding board and on the surface of the sliding board. Your object now is to un-mould the loaves one at a time from the canvas to the sliding board, then to slide the 3 of them together on to the hot asbestos in the oven. Place the long side of board at one side of the

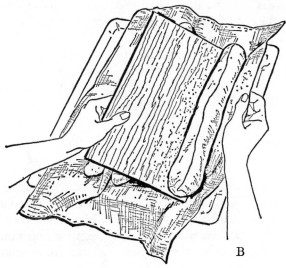

B

dough, then raise and flip the dough softly upside down on to board (B). Slip the dough, still upside down, from the unmoulding board on to the right side of the sliding board. Line up the rest of the dough side by side in the same manner.

Slash the dough as described in step 9, page 102.

Place pan of cold water on the lowest rack of an electric oven, or on the floor of a gas oven, add sizzling hot brick, and close oven door.

The 3 pieces of dough are now to be slid together off the sliding board on to the hot asbestos in the oven: the movement is one quick, smooth jerk like that old magician's trick of pulling the cloth from under a tableful of dishes. Open the oven and, holding the sliding board at the two ends nearest you, rapidly extend your arms so the far end of the board rests on the far end of the asbestos at the back of the oven. Then with one quick jerk, pull the board towards you and the three loaves will slide off on to the asbestos. This must be a fast and confident action because if you pause midway, the dough will rumple off the board and once it touches the hot asbestos you cannot move or reshape it, although it will come loose after 5 to 6 minutes of baking. You may muff this every once in a while, and produce some queerly deformed shapes, but they will all bake into bread.

Remove the brick and pan of water after 5 to 8 minutes of baking; the crust will have started to brown lightly. The oven should be dry for the rest of the baking. When the bread is done, remove the asbestos and brush it clean. Total baking time will be about 25 minutes for *bâtards*; the bread is done when it makes a hollow thump if tapped, and when the crust is crisp and, hopefully, nicely browned.

SELF-CRITICISM – OR HOW TO IMPROVE THE PRODUCT

Certainly one of the fascinating aspects of cooking is that you can almost endlessly improve upon what you have done, and when you realize that professional bakers have spent years learning their trade it would be surprising indeed if your first loaves were perfect in every respect. If they seem below standard in any of the following points, here are some possible explanations.

Crust did not brown

If you have not used the hot brick and pan of water steam-contraption, you will not get a very brown crust. Or if you have used the brick, perhaps it was not really sizzling hot; heat it 15 minutes longer the next time, or use 2 bricks. On the other hand, your oven thermostat might be inaccurate, and the oven was not really at the required 450°F. A third possibility is that your dough might have been under-salted; check your measurements carefully in step 1 the next time.

Crust was too brown or too red

If you were using the brick system, you might have had too much steam in the oven; next time use a smaller brick, or heat it a little less, or take it out several minutes sooner. Another possibility is that the dough mixture in step 1 got an overdose of salt, and salt affects colour; next time be sure your teaspoons are level.

Crust was tough

A tough crust is usually due to humidity: the day was damp and sticky, or your kitchen was steamy, and the starch has coagulated and hardened on the surface of the dough.

Slashes did not bulge open in the crust

Go over the instructions in step 9 to check on whether you cut them as directed. On the other hand, it might be that the bread had over-risen in step 7, just before baking, and the yeast had no strength left for its final push in the oven. Conversely, you might not have let it rise enough in this step and the dough was too heavy to bulge out the way it should.

Bread seems heavy; no holes inside

This is always due to insufficient rising, particularly during the pre-bake rise in step 7. Next time be sure it feels light and springy, and looks swollen, and that it has risen to almost triple its original size before it goes into the oven.

Flavour is uninteresting

Again, the only reason for this is insufficient time taken for rising: the yeast has not had an opportunity to produce the slow ageing and maturing that develops flavour. For your next batch, follow the timing and temperature requirements particularly in step 3, for the first rise.

Flavour is unpleasantly yeasty or sour

A yeasty over-fermented smell and taste are due more often to the dough having risen at too high a temperature than to its having over-risen. Next time, watch the room temperature at which it is rising, and if you are making bread in hot weather, you will have to take a longer time and let it rise in the refrigerator.

MACHINE MIXING AND KNEADING OF FRENCH BREAD DOUGH

The usual home mixer is useless for kneading dough of the French bread type, but the heavy-duty table-model with dough hook, illustrated in the equipment section at the end of the book, works perfectly. The dough-hook attachment that comes with some hand-held electric mixers and the hand-cranking bread pails are slower and less efficient, to our mind, than hand kneading. In any case, when you are using electricity, follow the steps in the recipe as outlined, including the rests; do not over-knead, and for the heavy-duty mixer, do not go over a moderate speed of number 3 or 4, or you risk breaking down the gluten in the dough. When the kneading is finished, take the dough out of the bowl and give it a minute or so of hand kneading, just to be sure it is smooth and elastic throughout. Then proceed with the recipe as usual, from step 3 on.

White Sandwich Bread · *Pain de Mie*

This kind of bread can be used for sandwiches, canapés, toast, and croûtons. It is almost impossible in present-day America and England, to find the firm, close-grained, evenly rectangular, unsliced type of white bread that is essential for professional-looking canapés, appetizers, and fancy sandwiches. In French this is *pain de mie*, meaning that the *mie*, the crumb or inside, is more important than the crust; in fact the crust exists merely as

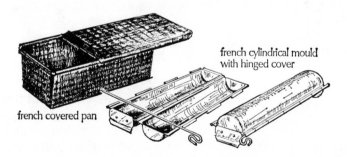

french cylindrical mould
with hinged cover

french covered pan

a thin and easily sliced covering. French *boulangeries* form and bake the bread in special covered moulds; the bread rises during baking so that it fills the mould completely and emerges absolutely symmetrical. The form can be round or cylindrical, but it is usually rectangular. You can easily achieve the round or the rectangular shapes by baking in any straight-sided bread tin or baking dish, covering the tin with foil and a baking sheet, and topping that with some kind of weight to keep the bread from pushing up out of shape while it is in the oven.

*Pain de Mie
[White Sandwich Bread]

[For about 1 pound of flour, to fill one 3-pint covered tin or two 1½-pint covered tins]

1. The preliminary dough mixture (*le fraisage*)

½ oz. fresh yeast, or ¼ oz. dry-active yeast
3 tbl. warm water (not over 100°F.) in a measure
2 tsp. salt
Good ½ pt tepid milk in a measure
About 1 lb. strong plain flour
A 6- or 7-pt mixing bowl with fairly straight rather than outward slanting sides
A rubber spatula
A pastry scraper or stiff metal spatula

Mix the yeast in the warm water and let it liquefy completely while measuring out the rest of the ingredients. Dissolve the salt in the tepid milk. Measure the flour into the mixing bowl. Then stir in the liquefied yeast and salted milk with a rubber spatula, cutting and pressing the dough firmly together into a mass, being sure all bits of flour and unblended pieces are gathered in. Turn dough out on to a flat kneading surface, scraping bowl clean. Dough will be quite soft and sticky; let it rest for 2 to 3 minutes while you wash and dry the bowl.

2. Kneading (*pétrissage*)

Start kneading by lifting the near side of the dough, using a scraper or spatula to help you, and flipping it over on to the other side (A). Scrape dough off surface and slap down again;

A

lift, flip over and slap down again, repeating the movement rapidly. In 2 to 3 minutes dough should have enough body so that you can give it a quick forward push with the heel of your

B

hand as you flip it over (B). If it remains too sticky for this, knead in a sprinkling of flour. When it begins to clean itself off the working surface and draw back into shape, it is ready for the next step – kneading in the butter.

3. Kneading in the butter

2 oz. chilled butter

When butter is incorporated into a dough in most French recipes, it is added after kneading.

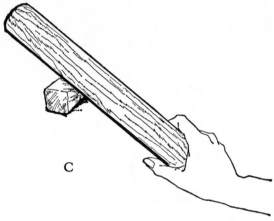

C

Soften the butter by beating it with a rolling pin (c). Smear it out with a scraper, spatula, or the heel of your hand until it is soft and malleable but still cold (D).

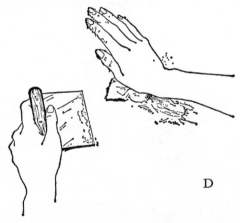

D

By small pieces, start rapidly folding and smearing the butter into the dough with the heel (not the palm) of your hand (E), then gather the dough into a mass with your scraper

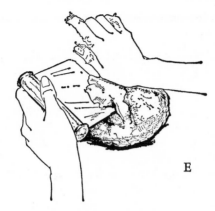

E

and smear again. Keep working in more bits of butter as each previous addition is partially absorbed. Dough will be ropy, very messy, and even stickier until it begins to absorb the butter. Work fast to prevent the butter from turning oily,

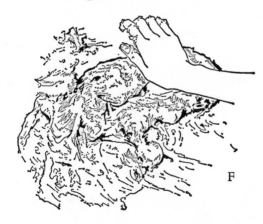

F

always using the heel of your hand (F), and also cutting the dough with scraper or spatula. In a few minutes dough will again become smooth and elastic.

Then let the dough rest 2 to 3 minutes. Knead again briefly with the heel of your hand until the dough begins to clean the butter off the kneading surface and off your hand. It is now sufficiently kneaded, although it will remain quite soft and somewhat sticky.

4. First rising (*pointage premier temps*): 3 to 4 hours at around 70°F.

The clean 6- or 7-pt. mixing bowl
A large plastic bag that bowl will fit into, or a large sheet of plastic
A bath towel

Place the dough in the bowl. Slip bowl into plastic bag or top with plastic and cover with the towel. Set on a wooden or plastic surface or on a folded towel or pillow and place at a temperature of 68–72°F.

Dough should take a minimum of 3 hours to rise for the yeast to do its best work. When dough has risen to $3\frac{1}{2}$ times its original volume, it will feel light and springy when pressed, and is ready for its second rise.

(†) *Delayed action:* See chart on page 104.

5. Deflating and second rising (*rupture*; *pointage deuxième temps*): $1\frac{1}{2}$ to 2 hours at around 70°F.

The dough is now to be thoroughly deflated and folded to expel accumulated gas, and to redistribute the yeast into an even finer network of gluten that will result in a close-grained texture when the bread is baked.

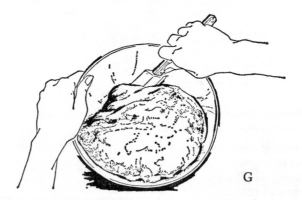

G

With a rubber spatula or the slightly cupped fingers of one hand, dislodge dough from inside of bowl (G) and turn out on to a lightly floured surface, scraping the bowl clean. If dough seems damp and sweaty, sprinkle with a tablespoon of flour.

With the lightly floured palms of your hands, pat and push the dough out into a roughly shaped rectangle 10 to 12 inches long (H). With the help of a scraper or spatula, fold the right side over towards the centre, then fold the left side over to

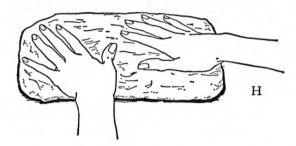

H

cover it, as though folding a business letter (I). Pat the dough out again into a rectangle, fold again in three, and put the dough back in the bowl. Cover with plastic and towel and let rise a second time, to not quite triple in volume.

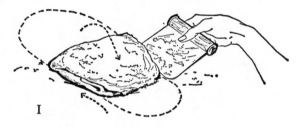

I

(†) *Delayed action:* See chart on page 104. If you want to freeze the dough, however, you can do it after the next step.

6. Moulding and final rising (*la mise en forme; l'apprêt*): 40 to 60 minutes at 75° to 80°F.

White vegetable shortening

A 3-pt rectangular bread tin with vertical or only slightly outward–slanting sides (for example, 9½ by 5½ in., 2¾ in. deep), or a round tin, or two 1½-pt tins

Remember to preheat oven to 425°F., Mark 7, in time for next step. Grease inside of bread tin (if tin is new, grease heavily then roll flour around inside and knock out excess). With a rubber spatula or the slightly cupped fingers of one hand, loosen dough from bowl and turn out on to a lightly floured surface. If you are making 2 loaves, cut dough cleanly in half with one chop of a long knife. Lift one end of dough and flip it over on to its opposite end. To relax the gluten and make dough easier to form, let it rest 7 to 8 minutes covered with plastic.

Following are illustrated directions for forming rectangular loaves. For cylindrical and circular forms, use the French bread system, pages 105–7.

With the lightly floured palms of your hands, pat and push the dough out into a roughly shaped rectangle slightly longer than your bread tin (J). Fold the dough in half lengthwise (K).

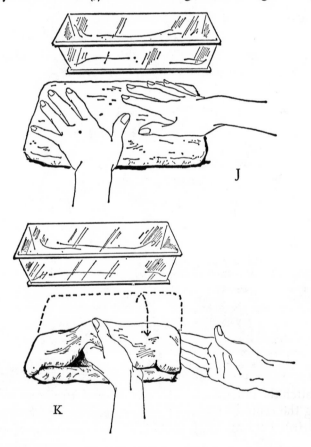

Seal edges of dough together with your thumbs as illustrated
(L), or with the heel of one hand. Roll dough a quarter turn
forwards, so seal is on top.

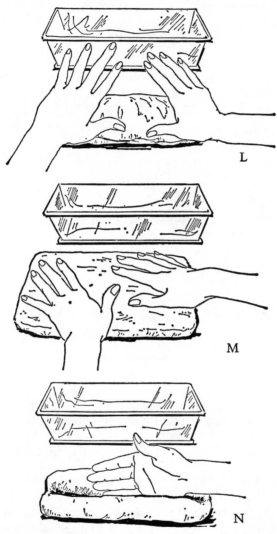

Flatten the dough again into a rectangle (M). Press a trench
along the central length of the dough with the side of your
hand (N). Fold again in two lengthwise and seal the edges

together with the heel of your hand (o). Roll dough a quarter turn towards you, so seal is underneath. Place the dough smooth side up in the prepared tin, pressing it down snugly into the corners with your knuckles (P). Tin should be no more than a third to two-fifths full.

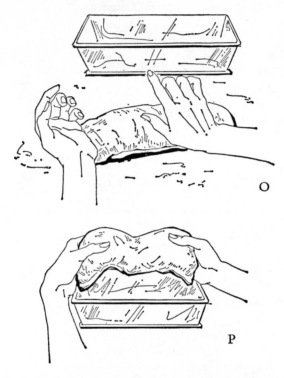

O

P

(†) You can freeze the dough at this point (see page 105), wrapping tin airtight. To continue with the recipe, let thaw for several hours in the refrigerator or at room temperature.

For the final rising, set tin uncovered at a temperature of 75° to 80°F. until dough has risen to slightly more than double, or to fill the tin by no more than $\frac{3}{4}$. It is important when you are to bake in a covered tin that you do not let the dough rise more than this, as it must have room to finish swelling and to fill the tin while it is in the oven. When dough has risen, bake at once.

(†) You can delay the rising action by setting the tin in the refrigerator, or even by weighting it down under refrigeration. In either case, the tin should be covered airtight, then set uncovered at room temperature for 20 to 30 minutes before baking. If dough has over-risen, bake it uncovered or deflate by pressing it down and letting it rise again to the correct height.

7. Baking, cooling, and storing: oven at 425°F., Mark 7; baking time 40 minutes

A perfectly smooth sheet of aluminium foil, 1½ ins. larger all around than bread tin, and greased on shiny side
A baking sheet or a tin large enough to cover entire top of bread tin
A 5-lb. weight of some sort, such as a brick
A cake rack, for cooling bread after baking

Oven has been preheated to 435°F., Mark 7. Cover bread tin with aluminium foil, greased side down. Set tin on a rack in middle level of preheated oven, cover tin with baking sheet or second tin and centre the weight on top.

Bake undisturbed for 35 to 40 minutes (30 for small loaves), then slide rack to front of oven. Standing well enough aside in case bread should burst out of tin (which could occur only if you had let it over-rise before baking), see if bread is done. The bread should have shrunk slightly from sides of tin so it will unmould easily, and the crust should be lightly browned. When thumped, the loaf should make a hollow sound. If not quite done, return to tin, cover with foil and baking sheet, and bake 5 to 10 minutes more. Unmould and cool on a rack.

When thoroughly cool, in 1½ to 2 hours, wrap airtight and refrigerate. Flavour and texture improve after 12 to 24 hours, and you should probably wait 36 hours if you want very thin slices for sandwiches or Melba toast.

This bread freezes perfectly; thaw it in its wrapper either in the refrigerator or at room temperature.

Baking in an Uncovered Tin (the conventional loaf)

If you want a loaf that swells up in the oven, bake the dough in an open tin, one that holds twice the volume of the unrisen dough, in this case a 2½-pint tin. During its final rise, step 6, let the dough come up almost to the edge of the tin. Just before baking, glaze the top of the dough by painting it with a tablespoon of milk in which you have dissolved ⅛ teaspoon of sugar. Oven temperature and timing are the same as in the preceding master recipe; if the top of the bread seems to be colouring too much, cover loosely with heavy brown paper or a sheet of aluminium foil.

Omitting the Butter

You may omit the butter in the master recipe if you wish. This will give you a lighter and whiter loaf; you may prefer it this way for Melba toast.

Melba Toast

To serve with consommé, *foie gras,* caviar.

Use 2-day-old *pain de mie.* Cut off the crusts at the two ends. With a very sharp long knife, such as a ham slicer, cut the bread into even slices less than $\frac{1}{16}$-inch thick. Arrange the slices, overlapping them by no more than a third of their length, on 1 or 2 large baking sheets and set in upper- and lower-middle levels of a 275°F., Mark 1 oven for about an hour, turning bread over once or twice and switching baking sheets from one rack to the other. Toast is done when bread is crisp, slightly curly, and a very pale brown. When cold and wrapped airtight, Melba toast freezes perfectly; thaw and re-crisp for a few minutes in a 350°F., Mark 4 oven.

Pain de Mie aux Raisins
[Raisin Bread]
This bread can be served with tea, or used for toast. See also *pain brioché aux raisins*, page 128.

[*To bake in two 2-pint covered tins or one 3-pint open tin*]

5 to 8 oz. small raisins
Ingredients for *pain de mie*, preceding master recipe

To soften the raisins, soak in 1½ pints of very hot water for 10 to 15 minutes. Drain, twist hard in the corner of a towel to squeeze out as much accumulated water as possible. Pat thoroughly dry in paper towels; spread out on a dry towel until you are ready to use them. Knead the raisins into the dough near the end of step 3, when the butter has been almost absorbed. Since the weight of the raisins will hold the dough down, the first rise, step 4, will be only to triple in the allotted time. Baking time and oven temperature are the same as for *pain de mie*.

Pain Brioché
Brioche Commune
Pain Louis XV
[Egg Bread]
This bread can be served with butter and jam, or used for fancy sandwiches, such as mousse of *foie gras*, or for toast; it is an alternative to *brioche* dough for *Koulibiac*, sausage in *brioche*, and their like. This is a lovely light-textured yellow bread. With another egg and three times the butter it would be a true *brioche*. Although you will find this dough quite a bit stickier and softer to handle than *pain de mie*, the technique for making it is the same.

[*For about 1 pound of flour, to fill two 3-pint covered tins, two 1½-pint open tins, or for 2 dozen individual rolls formed in small moulds or bun tins*]

1. Mixing and kneading the dough

½ oz. fresh yeast or ¼ oz. dry-active yeast
3 tbl. warm water in a measure
1 tbl. salt
2 tbl. sugar
3 tbl. tepid milk
About 1 lb. strong plain flour
A 6- to 7-pt mixing bowl with fairly straight rather than outward-
    slanting sides
4 large eggs (if chilled, set for 5 minutes in warm water)
Sprinklings of flour as needed
4 oz. chilled butter

Sprinkle yeast in warm water and let liquefy completely. Then stir in the salt, sugar, and milk. Measure the flour into the mixing bowl, make a well in the centre, add the eggs and the yeast mixture. Cut and mix everything together with a rubber spatula to form a dough. Turn out on to kneading surface and let dough rest for 2 to 3 minutes. Following illustrated directions for *pain de mie*, pages 117–19, knead by lifting, folding, slapping, and pushing with the heel of your hand. Dough will be stickier than that for *pain de mie*; if it remains unusually so, knead in a tablespoon or so more flour. When dough begins to clean itself off kneading surface, start working in the butter in small pieces. When butter is absorbed, let dough rest for 2 to 3 minutes. Knead again briefly until dough cleans butter off kneading surface and off your hands.

2. Completing the bread

Follow steps 4, 5, and 6 in the master recipe for the first and second risings in a covered bowl and the final rise in the bread tin. Follow step 7 for baking, except preheated oven should be at 400°F., Mark 6, and baking time will be about 35 minutes. The surrounding crust will be a little darker than for *pain de mie*. *Pain brioché* may be eaten warm or cold, although it will slice more easily after 24 hours. It freezes perfectly.

Pain Brioché aux Raisins
[Egg Bread with Raisins]

Pain brioché makes heavenly raisin bread, eaten plain with butter, or toasted. Follow directions for *pain de mie aux raisins*, page 127

Machine Mixing and Kneading for *Pain de Mie* and its Variations

Follow directions for French bread, page 114, and when you come to adding the butter, melt it, let it cool to tepid, then gradually beat it in. As soon as butter is incorporated, let dough rest for 2 to 3 minutes; finish the kneading by hand for a minute or so until dough is smooth.

Brioches

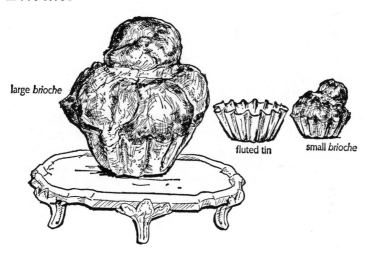

large *brioche*

fluted tin   small *brioche*

Although the wonderfully buttery, light, and thoroughly delectable texture of fresh *brioches* may persuade you they are manna from another planet, *brioche* dough differs from *pain de mie* dough only in that eggs are used rather than milk, and a very much larger proportion of butter is incorporated. Actually, you can use equal amounts of butter and flour, but we think the proportions of 3 parts butter to 4 parts flour make a much more manageable dough with a delicious texture and taste.

In France, *brioches* are served for breakfast with butter and jam, or for tea, or with the coffee break. Stale *brioche* may be sliced and toasted, or hollowed out and used as a container for sauced foods or appetizers.

*Pâte à Brioche Fine
[*Brioche* Dough]

Brioche dough is for all sizes and shapes of *brioches*, and for *Koulibiac*, sausage in *brioche*, and their like.

You must allow a minimum of 7 hours from the time you start *brioche* dough to the time it is ready for the oven. Three hours are needed for the first rise, 1½ for the second, half an hour for chilling, and 1 to 1½ hours for the final pre-bake rise. You may find it convenient to start the first rise in the late afternoon and complete the second one overnight in the refrigerator; you can then form and bake the *brioche* in the morning. However, as you will see from the delayed-action notes in the recipe, you can pretty well make it suit whatever schedule you wish.

[*For about ½ pound of flour, making enough unrisen dough to fill one 2½-pint mould or nine to ten 4-ounce moulds*]

1. The preliminary dough mixture (*le fraisage*)

3 large eggs (if chilled, place in warm water for 5 minutes)
A pt measure
A fork

Warm the eggs if chilled. Break them into the measure and blend with a fork. You should have about ¼ pint.

½ oz. fresh yeast or ¼ oz. dry-active yeast
3 tbl. warm water (not over 100°F.) in a measure
1 tsp. sugar

Mix the yeast in the warm water, add the sugar, and let yeast liquefy completely.

About 8 oz. plain flour
A 5-pt mixing bowl
A rubber spatula
2 tsp. sugar
1¼ tsp. salt
A pastry scraper or stiff spatula

Measure the flour into the mixing bowl. Make a well in the centre with the rubber spatula and pour in the eggs. Sprinkle on the additional sugar and the salt; scrape in the liquefied yeast mixture. Cut and stir liquids and flour together with a rubber spatula, then turn out on to kneading surface, scraping bowl clean. Dough will be very soft and sticky. Work it with scraper or stiff spatula for a moment to blend ingredients completely, then scrape to side of kneading surface and let dough rest while you prepare the butter, next step.

2. Preparing the butter

6 oz. chilled unsalted butter
A rolling pin

Soften the butter by beating it with a rolling pin (A). Smear it out with a scraper, spatula, or the heel of your hand until it is

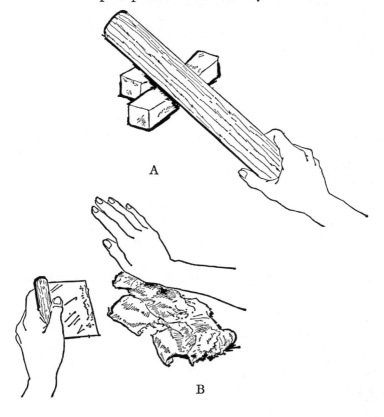

A

B

soft and malleable but still cold (B). Place at one corner of kneading surface until you are ready to use it, step 4 (refrigerate in hot weather).

3. Kneading (*pétrissage*)

This will be a very soft and sticky dough that now contains the minimum amount of flour; you will probably knead in more if dough remains too soft. Knead with one hand, keeping the other clean for emergencies.

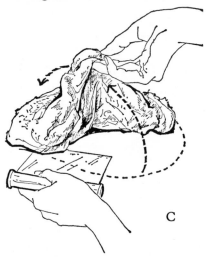

C

Using scraper or spatula, start flipping the near side of the dough over on to the far side (c), the right side on to the left, and so forth, rapidly and vigorously a dozen times or more

D

until dough begins to have body and elasticity. When dough has enough body, lift and slap it down roughly on the kneading surface repeatedly (D), using scraper to help you. Sprinkle on more flour by tablespoons (up to 3 or 4 in all if necessary) if dough remains too soft and sticky. It should be a soft dough that will stick to your fingers if you hold a pinch of it for more than 2 to 3 seconds. Knead until it has enough elasticity to draw back into shape when pushed out, probably 4 to 5 minutes, then let it rest for 2 to 3 minutes. Knead again for a moment and it is ready for the butter.

4. Kneading in the butter

By ounce pieces, start folding, kneading, and smearing the butter into the dough with the heel of your hand (E); then gather the dough into a mass, chopping it into small pieces

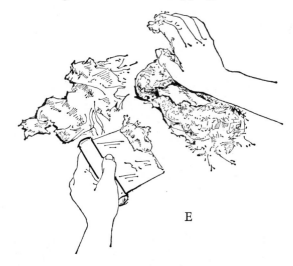

E

with your scraper and smearing again. Keep working in more pieces of butter as each previous addition is partially absorbed. Dough will be ropy, sticky, and very messy indeed until it begins to absorb the butter. Work rapidly, especially if the kitchen is warm, and be sure you are using the heel, not the palm, of your hand (F).

You may finish kneading with a scraper or spatula, which will prevent the butter from becoming too warm and turning oily. Do not hesitate to chill the dough for 20 minutes or so if this happens, and then continue.

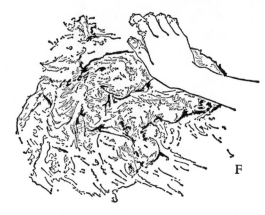

F

When all the butter is absorbed, the dough will look rather fluffy. Let it rest for 2 to 3 minutes, and knead briefly again. Kneading is finished when dough draws back into shape after being pushed out.

5. First rising (*pointage premier temps*): 5 to 6 hours at around 70°F.

A clean 5-pt mixing bowl
A large plastic bag that bowl will fit into, or a large sheet of plastic
A bath towel

The dough has to almost triple in volume. Place dough in bowl, slip into plastic bag or cover with plastic and arrange bath towel on top. Set on a wooden or plastic surface or on a towel or pillow. For best texture and flavour, dough should take 5 to 6 hours to rise sufficiently, at which point it will feel light and springy, though somewhat sticky because of the butter.

Note: In hot weather you will probably have to set bowl in refrigerator from time to time to prevent butter from melting and oozing out of dough.

(†) Set bowl in refrigerator for a short delay; for a longer one, cover with waxed paper, a plate, and a 10-pound weight to slow or even prevent its rising.

6. Deflating (*rupture*)

With a rubber spatula or the slightly cupped fingers of one hand, dislodge dough from inside of bowl (G) and turn out

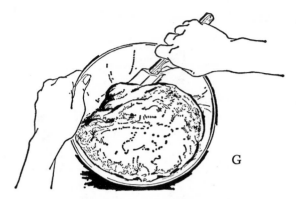

G

on to a lightly floured surface, scraping bowl clean. Sprinkle surface of dough with a teaspoon or so of flour.

With the lightly floured palms of your hands, pat and push dough out into a roughly shaped rectangle about 10 inches long (H). With the help of a scraper or spatula, flip the right

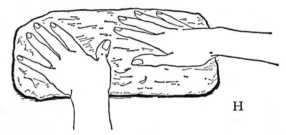

H

side of the dough over towards the centre, then flip the left side over to cover it, as though folding a business letter (I).

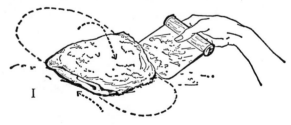

I

Pat the dough out again into a rectangle, fold again in three, and replace the dough in the bowl. Cover again with plastic and a towel.

(†) If you want to freeze *brioche* dough, this is the best time to do so, but see notes on freezing on facing page.

7. Second rising (*pointage deuxième temps*): 2 to 6 hours or more, depending on temperature

Brioche dough is usually chilled before it is formed so that it can be shaped easily; chilling may be done either during or after the second rise, whichever works out best for your cooking schedule.

(a) Room temperature method: Let dough rise to twice its original volume, at a temperature of around 70°F. This should take $1\frac{1}{2}$ to 2 hours. Then dislodge from bowl with a rubber spatula or the slightly cupped fingers of one hand, and refrigerate on a large plate or platter covered with waxed paper, another plate, and a weight. Dough should be ready to form in 30 to 40 minutes.

(b) Refrigerator method: Let dough start to rise at around 70°F. for an hour, then refrigerate. Dough will continue to rise for an hour or more until the butter congeals. If you wish to leave it overnight, cover with a plate and a weight when you refrigerate it.

Forming and baking *brioches*

Brioches are usually baked in fluted moulds with slightly outward-slanting sides. However, you can use anything you have available, from a baking dish or ovenproof bowl for large *brioches* to pyrex cups or bun tins for small ones.

Notes on final rise

The final rise before baking is to almost double in volume, until the dough feels light and softly springy when touched. The ideal rising temperature is around 75°F., and you have to watch the dough carefully on a hot day because higher temperatures melt the butter so that it oozes out of the dough. If this starts to happen, refrigerate the dough from time to time. It is difficult to predict how long the final rise will take; if the dough was thoroughly chilled before forming, it will take longer to rise. You must usually count on at least an hour, and it must really rise and soften or it will bake into a rather firm and dense *brioche*. Below are directions for forming and baking large, small, and ring *brioches*.

Freezing *brioche* dough

The best time to freeze *brioche* dough is after the second rise, but you may also do so after it has been formed and before the final rise. However, and probably because of the high butter and egg content, its life in the freezer is not long: a week to 10 days is all we would suggest.

*Grosse Brioche à Tête
[Large *Brioche* with Ball-shaped Head]

1. Forming the *brioche*

1 tsp. soft butter
A 2½-pt circular fluted mould or a cylindrical baking dish
The preceding *brioche* dough, chilled

Butter the interior of the mould or dish. With lightly floured hands on a lightly floured board, form ¾ of the dough into a smooth ball by kneading it lightly and rolling it between the palms of your hands. Place the ball in the bottom of the mould.

Make a funnel-shaped hole in the centre of the dough 2½ inches wide at the top diameter and about 2 inches deep, using your first 3 fingers. Roll the remaining dough between the lightly floured palms of your hands to make a ball, then a teardrop shape. Insert pointed end of tear drop into hole (A).

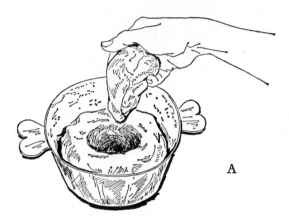

A

2. Final rising: 1 to 2 hours at 75°F.

Set uncovered and free from draughts at a temperature of
around 75°F. until dough has almost doubled in volume, and
feels light and softly springy when touched. Be sure your oven
has been preheated to 475°F., Mark 9, by the time the *brioche*
is ready to bake.

(†) *Delayed action:* You can set mould in refrigerator, covering
it with a bowl to prevent dough from crusting; you can cover
the formed dough airtight and freeze, but see notes on page
137.

3. Glazing and clipping

1 egg beaten with 1 tsp. water in a small bowl
A pastry brush
A pair of sharp-pointed scissors

Just before baking paint surface with beaten egg, being sure
not to glaze where the head joins the main body of the *brioche*
as this could glue the two together and prevent the head from
rising. In a moment, glaze with a second coat.

To help head in shaping up during baking, make 4 to 5
scissor clips in the large ball close under the head and slanting
inwards about half the width of the head (B).

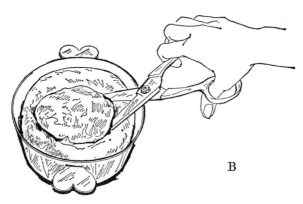

B

4. Baking, cooling, and storing: oven at 475°F., Mark 9, then 350°F., Mark 4; baking time: 40 to 50 minutes

Place the mould with the risen, glazed, and clipped *brioche* on a baking sheet in the middle or lower-middle level of the pre-heated 475°F., Mark 9 oven. In 15 to 20 minutes, when the *brioche* has risen and started to brown lightly, turn thermostat down to 350°F., Mark 4. Total baking time will be 40 to 50 minutes; *brioche* is done when it has begun to show a very faint line of shrinkage from the mould, or when a knife or straw plunged down through the centre comes out clean. If, during baking, *brioche* seems to be browning too much, cover loosely with heavy brown paper or foil.

Cool on a rack for 15 to 20 minutes before serving. *Brioches* may be eaten slightly warm or cool; cold *brioches* may be warmed for 10 to 15 minutes in a 350°F., Mark 4 oven.

(†) *Brioches* dry out and become stale almost within 12 hours of baking. To preserve their freshness, wrap airtight and freeze; large frozen *brioches* take about half an hour to thaw in a 350°F., Mark 4 oven.

Petites Brioches à Tête
[Small Individual *Brioches* with Ball-shaped Heads]
Choose either 4-ounce, slant-sided fluted moulds for small *brioches*, or baking cups or bun tins. Form in the same way as large *brioches*, filling the moulds half full and letting dough rise

to almost double. Paint twice with egg glaze and clip under the heads in several places just before baking. Bake about 15 minutes at 475°F., Mark 9 in middle level of oven.

Brioche en Couronne
[Ring-shaped *Brioche*]

The *brioche* dough, chilled
A baking sheet
Optional: an ovenproof bowl or cup

Knead the chilled dough into a ball and place on a lightly floured surface. Make a hole in the centre with your finger, twirling dough around your finger to enlarge the hole and inserting more fingers as the hole gets bigger (A). When hole

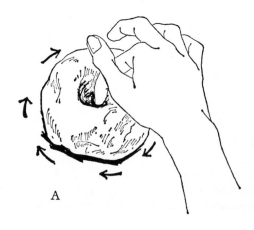

A

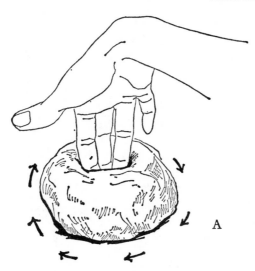

is large enough to do so, insert both hands and gently stretch dough while twirling it in floured surface (B). The object is to make a doughnut shape 10 to 12 inches in diameter. Place shaped dough on a lightly buttered baking sheet and let rest 10

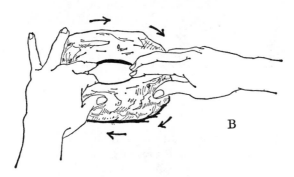

minutes to relax gluten, then widen the circle a little more. To keep centre of dough from closing in during rising and baking, insert a lightly buttered ovenproof bowl or cup in hole (C).

Let dough rise, uncovered, to almost double at a temperature of around 75°F., until dough is light and springy to the touch. Paint with a double coating of egg glaze (1 egg beaten with 1 teaspoonful of water) just before baking. Then clip top

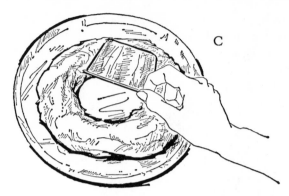

of dough at 1-inch intervals, making cuts about 1 inch deep, pointing scissors towards outside of ring at a 45-degree angle (D).

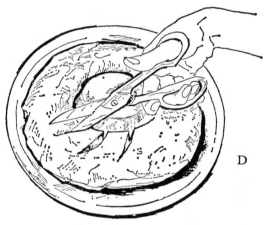

Bake 20 to 30 minutes in the middle level of a preheated 475°F., Mark 9 oven until nicely puffed and browned. A knife or straw plunged into the centre of one side should come out clean. If *brioche* browns too much during baking, cover loosely with heavy brown paper or aluminium foil.

Kougloff
[*Brioche* with Raisins]
Whether or not this moulded ring-shaped raisin *brioche* originated with Viennese bakers, it is usually considered by the

French to be an Alsatian raisin cake of uncertain orthography, as you will see it spelled also *Kugelhopf*, *Kougelhof*, *Gougelhop*, and even *Gugelhupf*. Bakers frequently make *Kougloff* out of left-over *brioche* dough, softening it with a little milk or additional butter as they knead in the raisins just before dropping the dough into its mould.

Kougloff mould

baked *Kougloff*

[*For a 2½-pint* Kougloff]

Special requirements

4 oz. small currant raisins
1 to 1½ tsp. soft butter
A 2½-pt *Kougloff* mould, or any fluted ring mould 3½ to 4 ins. deep
    and about 8½ in. at rim diameter that holds 2½ pts
3 tbl. shaved blanched almonds

To soften raisins soak 10 to 15 minutes in very hot water; drain, twist hard in the corner of kitchen towel to squeeze out accumulated water, and spread out on a paper towel until needed. Butter the mould heavily, then sprinkle a tablespoon of the almonds in the bottom, reserving the rest until later.

1. Softening the dough

Brioche dough, master recipe, page 130
If needed, 3 to 4 tbl. milk and /or butter

So that it will mould smoothly, dough for a *Kougloff* must be soft and sticky. If you are making the dough specifically for a *Kougloff*, knead in only 4 of the 6 ounces of butter called for in steps 2 and 4 of the master recipe and complete the recipe through step 7. After the second rise, knead in the remaining 2 ounces of butter and the raisins. If you are using left-over *brioche* dough, soften it by kneading in milk and/or butter half a tablespoon at a time, then knead in the raisins.

2. Filling the mould and final rise

A pastry scraper or stiff metal spatula
A rubber spatula
The remaining almonds
A tbl. or so of flour

Gather a 2-tablespoon gob of the soft dough on the end of your scraper or metal spatula and use the rubber spatula to dislodge it and place it on the bottom of the prepared mould. Continue spreading it around the mould to make a layer. Sprinkle or press more almonds against inside of mould, and add another layer of dough; continue thus until all dough is used. Sprinkle lightly with flour and press dough gently against sides and cone of mould with floured fingers. Mould will be about half filled. Let rise uncovered at around 75°F. for an hour or more, until mould is almost filled.

3. Baking: oven at 475°F., Mark 9, then at 350°F., Mark 4; 30 to 40 minutes

Bake at 475°F., Mark 9, in middle or lower-middle level of preheated oven for about 15 minutes, or until dough has risen and started to colour. Then lower thermostat to 350°F., Mark 4 for rest of baking. *Kougloff* is done when it shows a faint line of shrinkage from sides of mould and when the sides are nicely browned. Serve slightly warm or cool, with butter.

Electric Mixer *Brioche* Dough

Those who hate to work with their hands can use an ordinary home-model electric mixer for *brioche* dough, lifting it up out of the dough when necessary to unclog the mixer blades. Those who want to double or triple the recipe will find a heavy-duty mixer with dough hook a great time saver. In either case, use the ingredients called for in the master recipe, but melt the butter and set aside until tepid. Blend the liquefied yeast, and the eggs, salt, and sugar into the flour, using large bowl of mixer, then gradually beat in the tepid melted butter. Beat at moderate speed for 3 to 5 minutes, until dough has enough elasticity to retreat back into shape when a piece is lifted with a spatula. Dough will be very soft and sticky. (If it looks too soft and oily, set bowl in cold water for a few minutes in order to cool and partially congeal the butter, then turn out on to a lightly floured board and sprinkle with a tablespoon or so of flour.) Scrape dough into a lightly floured bowl, sprinkle with a teaspoon of flour, and proceed with the 2 rises as described in the master recipe, steps 5 to 7.

Croissants

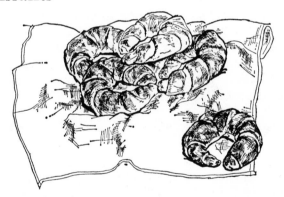

The most delicious of French croissants, to our mind, are those called *croissants de boulanger*, which are made of risen yeast-milk-and-flour dough that is flattened out, slathered with butter, folded in three, and rolled and folded again three times as though you were making French puff pastry. After rising and baking, the resulting croissant is a tenderly layered, puffy, deliciously buttery roll like nothing else. There are other croissant formulas on the market, some of which are either puff pastry or *brioche* dough rolled into crescent shapes, others have a little egg in the mixture, still others are made with butter substitutes. We do not think any of them compare with the classic formula.

Croissants

The minimum time required for making croissants is 11 to 12 hours. Included are 3 hours and 1½ hours for the rising of the initial dough, two rest periods of 1½ to 2 hours each, and a final pre-baking rise of about an hour. Therefore, if you want freshly baked croissants for breakfast you will have to stay up all night as the bakers do. However, they will taste just as fresh if you make them ahead and freeze them either fully baked or ready to bake, as indicated in the recipe.

[*For one dozen 5½-inch rolls*]

1. The basic dough

¼ oz. fresh yeast or 1¼ tsp. dry-active yeast
3 tbl. warm water (not over 100°F.) in a measure
1 tsp. sugar

Mix the yeast in the warm water with the sugar and let liquefy completely while measuring out the rest of the ingredients.

About ½ lb. strong plain flour
A 5-pt mixing bowl
2 tsp. sugar
1½ tsp. salt
¼ pt milk warmed to tepid in a small saucepan
2 tbl. tasteless salad oil
A rubber spatula
A pastry scraper or stiff metal spatula

Measure the flour into the mixing bowl. Dissolve the additional sugar and the salt in the tepid milk. When yeast has liquefied, pour it along with the milk mixture and oil into the flour. Blend the elements into a dough by cutting and pressing with the rubber spatula, being sure all bits of flour are gathered in. Turn dough out on to kneading surface, scraping bowl clean. Let rest for 2 to 3 minutes while you wash and dry the bowl.

The short rest allows flour to absorb liquid; dough will be quite soft and sticky.

Start kneading by lifting near edge, using scraper or spatula to help you, and flipping it over on to the other side (A).

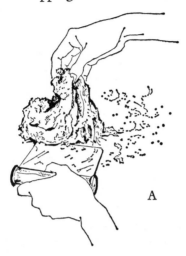

A

Rapidly repeat the movement from one side to the other and end over end 8 to 10 times until dough feels smooth and begins to draw back into shape when pushed out. This is all the kneading it should have; you want just enough body so dough will hold together when eventually rolled, but you do not want to over-activate the gluten and make dough difficult to handle.

2. The two rises – first about 3 hours; second about 1½ hours – at 70–72°F.

The clean 5-pt mixing bowl
A large plastic bag or sheet of plastic
A bath towel

The dough is to rise to 3½ times its original volume. Put it in the bowl. Cover with plastic and bath towel, and place at a temperature of between 70 and 72°F. In 3 or 4 hours dough should have risen sufficiently, and will be light and springy when touched.

Deflate by loosening dough from edges of bowl with a rubber spatula or the cupped fingers of one hand, and turn it out on to a lightly floured surface. With the lightly floured palms of your hands, pat and push the dough out into a rectangle about 8 by 12 inches. Fold in three as though folding a business letter. Return dough to bowl; cover again with plastic and bath towel.

Let rise a second time, but only to double the original volume. Then loosen dough from edges of bowl and turn out on to a lightly floured plate. Cover airtight and refrigerate for 20 minutes, which will make the next step easier.

(†) *Delayed action:* Set dough in a colder place to rise, or let it rise the second time overnight in the refrigerator. After second rise, when dough has been turned out of bowl on to plate, you may freeze it for a week, but see page 137.

3. Rolling in the butter; turns 1 and 2

¼ lb. chilled unsalted butter
A rolling pin (see page 691 for illustrated comments)
Flour as needed
A pastry scraper or stiff metal spatula
Waxed or plastic paper
A plastic bag

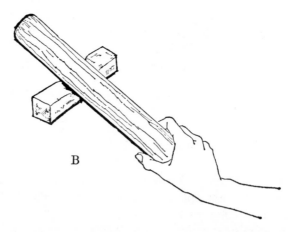

B

Butter must now be worked into a smooth but still cold paste that can be spread evenly on the dough and then rolled with it. Beat butter with rolling pin to soften it (B). Then smear it out

with the heel of your hand or a scraper or spatula (C) until it is
of very easy spreading consistency but still cold; it must not
become soft and oily – refrigerate if necessary.

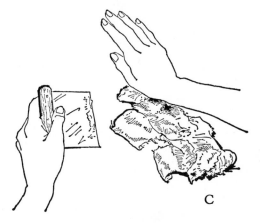

C

Place chilled dough on a lightly floured pastry marble or
board. With the lightly floured palms of your hands push and
pat it out into a rectangle about 14 by 8 inches (D). Spread

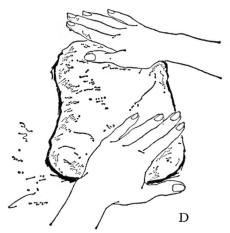

D

butter as evenly as possible over the upper two thirds of the
dough rectangle, leaving a $\frac{1}{4}$-inch unbuttered border all around
(E). Dough is now to be folded into three layers, just as though
you were folding a business letter. Fold the bottom (un-

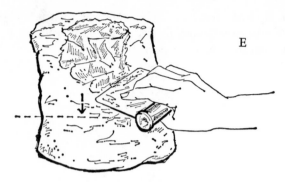

buttered) third up to the middle (F). Fold the top (buttered) third down to cover it (G), making 3 even layers of dough separated by 2 layers of butter. This is called 'turn number 1'.

For 'turn number 2', lightly flour the top of the dough and your rolling surface, turn the dough so the edge of the top flap is to your right, as though it were a book you were going

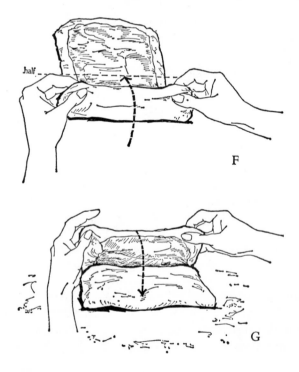

to open. Roll the dough into a rectangle about 14 inches by 6 inches. Roll rapidly, starting an inch from the near end and going to within an inch of the far end (H). Fold again in three.

H

You now have 7 layers of dough separated by 6 layers of butter; at the end of the fourth roll there will be 55 layers of dough.

Sprinkle dough lightly with flour, wrap in waxed paper or plastic, place in a plastic bag and refrigerate. Dough must now rest for 1 to 1½ hours to deactivate the gluten so that you can make the two final rolls without difficulty.

4. Turns 3 and 4 – after a rest of 1½ to 2 hours in the refrigerator

Unwrap dough, sprinkle lightly with flour, and deflate by tapping lightly several times with rolling pin. Cover and let rest for 8 to 10 minutes, again to relax gluten. Being sure that the top and bottom of dough are always lightly floured, start rolling dough into a rectangle 14 by 6 inches. If you notice that butter has congealed into hard flakes, beat dough with light firm taps for a minute or so, going from one side to the other until butter has softened: it must be able to extend the length and width of the rectangle inside the dough as you roll it out. Fold rectangle in three, roll again into a rectangle, and fold in three to complete the final turn. Wrap and chill for 2 hours before forming dough into croissants, or leave overnight covered with a board and a 5-pound weight.

5. Forming croissants – after dough has rested 2 hours in refrigerator

The dough is now ready to be rolled out into the usual rectangle and then cut into triangles that are rolled up and twisted into crescent shapes. Professionals use either the ingenious triangle-cutting roller illustrated, or do all the cutting by hand. To make everything as easy as possible for yourself, refrigerate all pieces of dough you are not actually working on.

(a) Preliminaries

A large sheet of plastic
A large, lightly buttered baking sheet (14 by 16 ins. at least)

Unwrap chilled dough, place on a lightly floured surface, and deflate by tapping several times gently with rolling pin. Cover with plastic and let rest 10 minutes, to relax gluten.

(b) Forming triangles by hand:

Roll dough into a rectangle 20 by 5 inches; cut in half, crosswise (A and B) and chill 1 half (B).

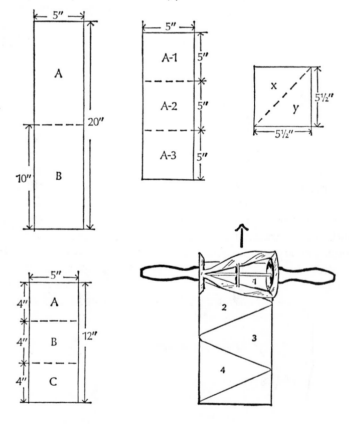

Roll piece of dough (A) into a rectangle 15 by 5 inches; cut into 3, (A-1, A-2, A-3) crosswise, and chill 2 of the 3 pieces.
Roll piece of dough (A-1) into a 5½-inch square and cut into 2 triangles (x and y).

(c) *Forming triangles with a cutter:*
Roll chilled dough into a rectangle 12 by 5 inches; cut into 3, crosswise (A, B, and C), and chill 2 pieces.
Roll piece of dough into a rectangle 15 by 5 inches, roll the cutter over it, and you will have formed 4 triangles (1, 2, 3, 4).

(d) *Turning triangles into crescents or croissants:*
Holding one of the triangles of dough by its large end, roll it out towards the point to make the triangle about 7 inches long (A). Then, to extend the large end slightly, stretch the 2 top

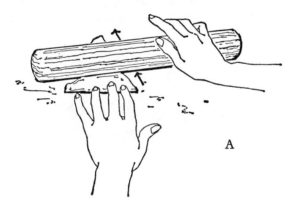

A

angles of the triangle lightly between your thumbs and forefingers, enlarging end about an inch in all (B). Start rolling up

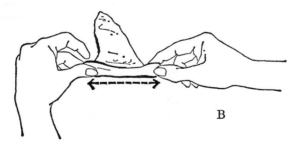

B

the croissant first by folding the large end forwards on to itself (c). Then, holding the point with the fingers of your left hand, finish the roll under the fingers and palm of your right hand.

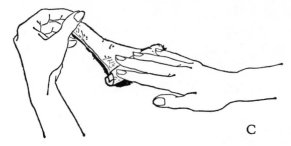

C

Bend the 2 ends down to form a crescent shape and place on a lightly buttered baking sheet, with point resting inside curve and against surface of baking sheet (D). Form the rest of the triangles into croissants in the same manner.

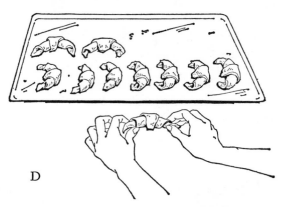

D

(†) *Delayed action:* Formed croissants may be wrapped air-tight and frozen for a week, if dough was not frozen before.

6. Final rise: about 1 hour at 75°F.

Cover croissants loosely with a large sheet of plastic and set at a temperature of around 75°F. for their final pre-baking rise. Dough should almost double in size and feel light and springy when touched; if it does not rise and feel light, the baked croissants will be heavy and hard rather than tender, puffy, and light. In hot weather you may have to set dough in refrigerator from time to time to prevent butter from softening and oozing out.

(†) *Delayed action:* For a slower rise, set dough in a colder place or refrigerate; if thoroughly chilled, leave at room temperature 20 to 30 minutes before baking. Risen croissants may be frozen for a few days and baked in their frozen state.

7. Glazing, baking, and storing: oven preheated to 475°F., Mark 9

A pastry brush
1 egg beaten with 1 tsp. water in a small bowl
A cake rack

Just before baking, paint the croissants with egg glaze, then set in middle level of preheated oven for 12 to 15 minutes, until croissants are nicely puffed and brown. Cool on a rack for 10 to 15 minutes before serving.

Croissants are at their best when freshly baked; even refrigerated in an airtight container, they are never as good the next day. Freezing is the best preservation: wrap airtight when croissants are thoroughly cool and freeze. To thaw and serve, set frozen croissants on a lightly buttered baking sheet and place in a preheated 400°F., Mark 6 oven for 5 minutes.

Pastry Doughs

Pastry dough, both tart and pie doughs and puff pastry, play an immensely important part in every phase of French cooking from little hot appetizers to *quiches*, and from *pâtés en croûte* to strawberry tarts, *mille feuilles* and *Pithiviers*. If pie dough has always been your culinary bugaboo, remember that no one is born a pastry chef, everyone has had to learn, and that the first big step is to make the decision that you are now, today, going to learn to make a decent pie crust. Then make pie dough every day or two for a week or more; serve everything you can think of in pastry. You will be surprised how quickly you develop the technique, and you will then be in the masterful position of having an endless number of delicious concoctions at your fingertips. All the recipes here are for at least 1 pound of flour. Our feeling is that if you are going to make dough at all you might as well make a lot, because it keeps beautifully in the freezer.

Tart and Pie Doughs · *Pâtes Brisées –* *Pâtes à Croustades*

French pastry dough is flour and butter worked together and then moistened with liquid. Liquid forces the gluten molecules in the flour to join into a continuous web so that the dough will keep its shape when rolled out; the dough must have its stated amount of liquid for this effect to take place. Butter gives the pastry its flavour and texture; as always, we suggest that about $\frac{1}{4}$ of the butter proportions be given over to vegetable shortening.

It is in the first step, working the butter and flour together, that many people have difficulty. Trying to do everything just right, they work too slowly and carefully, lingering over each squeeze of butter and flour until their hot fingers melt the butter; thus the liquid cannot mix in properly, and the dough is a wet, oily mess that, even after chilling, bakes into a miserable piece of cardboard.

ELECTRIC MIXER PIE DOUGH

An electric mixer will eliminate the hot-hand syndrome, see following recipe. Even a small hand-held model does an admirable job of cutting butter into flour, and the heavy-duty mixer with its flat-beater attachment is, as always, marvellous, especially when you are doubling or tripling quantities. Any pastry dough formula may be done by machine following this general method. Directions for hand mixing are in Volume I.

Pâte Brisée à l'Œuf
Pâte à Croustade
[Egg Pastry Dough]

For free-standing shells and cases, and for turnovers.

The following dough formula, for making with an electric mixer, is designed especially for pastry shells formed on up-side-down tins, an informal and wonderfully easy way to make *quiche* and pie shells that is described and illustrated on pages 159–61. Whatever your dough formula, you can use exactly the same system outlined here.

[For about 1 pound of flour, enough for three 10-inch shells]

1. Cutting the fat into the flour

1 lb plain flour
The large bowl of your electric mixer, or a 4- to 5-pt mixing bowl with
   sloping sides
8 oz. chilled unsalted butter
A 16-in. piece of waxed paper (reserve also for next step)
A table knife
3 oz. chilled white vegetable shortening
A home-style electric mixer on stand, or a hand-held mixer, or a
   heavy-duty mixer with flat beater blade

Measure the flour into the bowl. Place chilled butter on waxed paper and rapidly cut into 8 lengthwise, then cut strips into $\frac{1}{4}$-inch pieces and add to flour along with the chilled shortening. Run machine at moderate speed, pushing fat and flour into blades with a rubber spatula if you are using the home-model machine on a stand. Continue only until mixture looks like very coarse meal (5 minutes with a home mixer). The object here is to break the butter into very small pieces, less than $\frac{1}{16}$ inch in size; each little piece of butter remains cold enough to be a separate identity coated with flour. If room is hot and butter seems to be softening, stop where you are, refrigerate bowl and beater blades for 30 minutes, then continue.

2. Blending in the liquid

8 fl. oz. liquid as follows: 1 large egg plus necessary iced water in a pt
  measure
2 tsp. salt
¼ tsp. sugar
A table fork
Few more drops iced water if necessary
A plastic bag

Measure out the liquid, add the salt and sugar, and blend
together with a fork. Pour into the flour mixture and beat at
moderate speed for only a few seconds, just until dough has
absorbed liquid and clogs in the blades. Turn massed dough
out on to waxed paper; sprinkle drops of iced water on any
unmassed bits and press together with rubber spatula as you
add to rest of dough. With lightly floured hands, press pastry
rapidly into a roughly shaped cushion, wrap in waxed paper,
and place in plastic bag.

3. Chilling the dough before forming: about 2 hours

Once dough has been mixed, it must be well rested and
chilled before you roll it out. The rest relaxes the gluten in the
flour, so the dough will roll easily; chilling firms the butter,
giving the dough enough body for rolling. Also, granular
'instant-blending' flour must have at least an hour to re-
hydrate or it will be very difficult to roll and will be very
tough when baked.

(†) Dough may remain in refrigerator several days, or may be
frozen for several months.

UPSIDE-DOWN PASTRY SHELLS AND CASES

The classic free-standing French pastry shell is formed by
rolling out the dough and pressing it inside a flan ring or
mould. The dough is then braced in place with another
mould or with buttered foil and dried beans so that it will not
collapse during baking. This method is illustrated in Volume I,
pages 162–6, and produces the most professional result.

ring mould   oval baking dish

pastry shell
from ringed mould

tartlet shells from
bun tins

pastry shell from
oval mould

bun tins

A more informal and simpler method is to bake the shell on an upside-down cake tin, or on any upside-down fireproof object whose shape appeals to you, such as a pie tin, bread tin, ring mould, saucepan, baking dish, or even bun tin. For this type of shell you must have a pastry that is light and buttery but will hold its shape when moulded and baked upside down. The preceding egg pastry dough was designed especially for upside-down shells.

Upside-down Pastry Shells

[*For a 10- by 1-inch round shell, or any shell formed on any 2½- to 3-pint mould*]

1. Forming shells

1 tsp. soft butter

The mould: a round cake tin or baking dish 9 to 10 ins. bottom
   diameter

½ the preceding egg pastry dough, chilled

Butter the outside of the mould and set upside down. Rapidly roll out the dough into a circle ⅛ inch thick and at least 2½ to 3 inches wider in diameter than your mould. (Illustrated directions for rolling dough are in Volume I.)

Roll dough up on pin and unroll over upturned bottom of mould (A), then run pin lightly over dough to smooth it in place. With lightly floured fingers, press dough snugly against sides of mould, being very careful not to pull or stretch dough; it must retain its uniform thickness of ⅛ inch. Even off the edges around the sides of the mould with a ravioli wheel

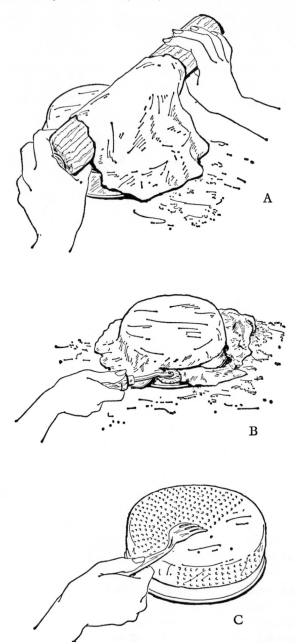

A

B

C

or knife, making shell about 1 inch deep (B). To prevent shell from puffing out of shape during baking, prick all over at $\frac{1}{8}$-inch intervals with a table fork (C). To even the sides all around press flat of fork against pastry, being careful not to reduce thickness (D). In case any section of sides seems too thin, paint lightly with cold water and patch with raw dough.

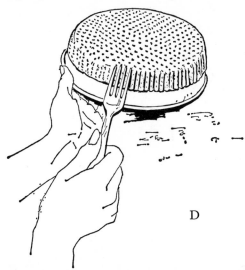

D

So that dough will bake properly and not draw up or out of shape, it should now be refrigerated for at least an hour before it goes into the oven; this relaxes the gluten in the flour. Press raw left-over dough into a ball, wrap and refrigerate; you may need a little later on, after baking.

(†) Shell may be frozen at this point. Set as it is in freezer for an hour or so until hardened, then wrap airtight. Bake shell while still frozen.

2. Baking shells – after a rest of 1 hour

Preheat oven to 425°F., Mark 7. You will need to weight down the top of the dough after it has baked for 4 to 5 minutes, otherwise the top will puff and draw the sides up: choose a saucepan or baking dish weighing about 2 pounds, or a pie plate filled with dried beans, and butter the bottom of the pan, dish, or plate.

Place chilled dough-covered mould, still upside down, on a baking sheet and set in middle level of oven. In 4 to 5 minutes, place the buttered weight on top, remove 2 to 3 minutes before shell is done.

A partially baked shell, the type used for *quiches* and over-baked tarts and pies, needs 6 to 10 minutes in all depending on the thickness of the dough. It is sufficiently baked when it has started to colour and can be raised gently from the mould. Fully baked shells usually need 10 to 15 minutes in all, until the shell is nicely browned and crisp. When done, remove from oven and let cool on mould for 8 to 10 minutes, then, being very careful not to crack shell, unmould on a rack.

REFERENCE CHART FOR PASTRY DOUGH FORMULAS

DESCRIPTION	USES	FORMULA
ENTRÉE PASTRIES		
1. *Pâte Brisée Ordinaire*		
Ordinary pastry dough with less butter than the following, therefore easier to roll and form	For general pie crusts, plain *quiches*, turnovers, meat mixtures	1 lb. flour; 9 oz. butter; 2½ oz. shortening; 2 tsp. salt; ¼ tsp. sugar; 8 fl. oz. iced water
2. *Pâte Brisée Fine*		
Finest pastry dough – delicate texture, fine flavour, fragile (Volume I, page 159)	For fancy appetizers and tartlets, rich *quiches*, and the best quality of pre-baked shells	1 lb. flour; 11 oz. butter; 3 oz. shortening; 2 tsp. salt; ¼ tsp. sugar; 8 fl. oz. iced water
3. *Pâte Brisée à l'Œuf*		
A light, crisp dough	Especially for shells and cases moulded and baked on upside-down forms, and for turnovers	1 lb. flour; 9 oz. butter; 2½ oz. shortening; 2 tsp. salt; ¼ tsp. sugar; 8 fl. oz. liquid (1 egg plus necessary iced water)

(*continued on next page*)

DESCRIPTION	USES	FORMULA

SWEET PASTRIES

Pâtes Sucrées

| Any of the previous dough formulas | For the same uses | Same formulas except for salt and sugar proportions, which should be changed to: ⅛ tsp. salt; 5 tbl. sugar |

4. *Pâte Sucrée aux Jaunes d'Œuf*

| Less rich than No. 2, finer texture than No. 1 and No. 3 | For baked tarts and tartlets, and pre-baked shells | 1 lb. flour; 9 oz. butter; 2½ oz. shortening; ⅛ tsp. salt; 5 tbl. sugar; 8 fl. oz. liquid (2 egg yolks plus necessary iced water) |

5. *Pâte Sablée – Pâte Sèche*

| Sweet biscuit dough, crisp and buttery; the more sugar you add the more difficult the dough is to handle | For biscuits, sweet tarts and tartlets, and especially for pre-baked shells | 20 oz. flour; 9 oz. butter; 2½ oz. shortening; 8 to 18 tbl. sugar; ¼ tsp. baking powder; 3 eggs; 1½ tsp. vanilla extract; ⅛ tsp. salt |

PÂTÉ DOUGHS

6. *Pâte à Croustade – Pâte à Pâté*

| An excellent *pâté* dough that is also good to eat | For *pâtés* and meat pies that are moulded in raw dough either in the spring-form *pâté* mould, or in a baking dish | 1 lb. flour; 5½ oz. butter; 3 oz. lard; 2 tsp. salt; 8 fl. oz. liquid (4 egg yolks plus necessary iced water) |

7. *Pâte à Croustade à l'Envers*

| A *pâté* dough that will hold its shape and is also good to eat | For *pâté* cases that are partially baked on upside-down forms before being filled with meat mixtures and baked; also for free-form *pâtés en croûte* | 20 oz. flour; 7 oz. butter; 3½ oz. lard; 2½ tsp. salt; ½ pt liquid (2 eggs plus necessary iced water) |

First aid for cracked shells

If a partially baked shell develops a small split or crack, paint the area with beaten egg and patch with raw dough just before filling and baking. If sides seem thin or weak, you may paint with beaten egg and patch or strengthen them with a strip of raw dough, or you may fill the shell by no more than $\frac{1}{3}$ so sides will not be under any strain during baking.

Freezing and left-overs

Baked shells may be wrapped airtight and frozen; it is wise to put them in a protective container of some sort. Left-over dough may be frozen and used again or combined with more of the same dough when you make another batch.

French Puff Pastry · *Pâte Feuilletée*

French puff pastry, *pâte feuilletée*, is literally what the French title implies: hundreds of leaves or layers of dough separated by hundreds of layers of butter. A piece half an inch thick puffs up 4 to 5 inches in the oven and is unbelievably light and tender to bite into. With almost as many uses as it has layers, puff pastry is the dough for *vol-au-vent* and Napoleons, for *coqs en pâte, gigots en croûte*, and all kinds of turnovers, tarts, pie toppings, first-course pastries, and luxurious cocktail titbits. It dresses up the simplest shop-bought cheese mixture, can add the final flourish to the grandest platter, and since it freezes perfectly for several months, puff pastry is tremendously useful to have available on those occasions when you need something fast to assemble that looks impressive.

If you enjoy working with your hands you will find it is the most fascinating of doughs to make, and if you want to acquire a facility in pastry, *pâte feuilletée* will teach you all the tricks. It most definitely takes practice to perfect, but when you have mastered puff pastry you will find it such a satisfying and splendid accomplishment you will bless yourself for every moment you spent learning its techniques.

THE TWO KINDS OF PUFF PASTRY

The classical, best-quality puff pastry, *pâte feuilletée fine*, contains equal parts of butter and flour, is made in a rigidly traditional manner, and you must count on 6 to 7 hours from the time you start it to the time you can form and bake it. This is what you use for *vol-au-vent*, patty shells, and fine desserts such as that most wonderful of almond tarts called the *Pithiviers*. However, it is not at all necessary to be so grand for cocktail appetizers, cheese-filled cases, leg of lamb baked in a crust, beef Wellington, and a host of other delicious items. For these, and in fact for most of your puff pastry needs, simple puff pastry, *demi-feuilletée*, is very good indeed and can be made in half the time. Because it is so much easier to make, we suggest that you start your career on *demi-feuilletée*, and when you get around to the classic method it will then seem like only a variation on a familiar theme.

EQUIPMENT

Although you can mix pastry on a wooden table and roll it out with a broom handle, you will find it easier to make when you have a pastry marble and a good rolling pin. This is particularly true for puff pastry. For notes on a pastry marble and rolling pins, see pages 690-91.

KEEPING COOL AND RELAXED

You will have very little trouble with puff pastry when you remember that you must keep the dough cold and that you must let it have the rest periods it needs.

Because of its high butter content, puff-pastry dough begins to soften as soon as you remove it from the refrigerator, just as butter softens. When you leave it too long at room temperature it becomes limp, sticky, and utterly impossible to work with until you refrigerate it again. Thus, if at any point your dough becomes limp and soft, stop where you are, refrigerate the dough for 30 minutes, then continue. Do the same if the dough retracts after rolling, or if it turns rubbery and refuses to extend itself; this means that the gluten in the dough is over-activated from having been rolled out, and the way to calm it down is to stop rolling and let the dough relax in the refrigerator for an hour or two. Most of the troubles most people have with puff pastry spring from unchilled dough and over-activated gluten.

*Pâte Demi-feuilletée
[Simple Puff Pastry – Flaky Pastry – Mock Puff Pastry]

For the many recipes like turnovers, toppings for meat pies, meats baked in a crust, appetizers, and so forth where you want a flaky, light dough, *demi-feuilletée* can be ready for baking in 3 to 4 hours. The pastry consists of an initial dough made of flour, water, salt, and a little oil, which acts as a tenderizer; this is pushed out into a 16-inch rectangle that is spread with softened butter. Then the rectangle is folded into three, making a sandwich that has 3 dough layers and 2 butter layers. Rolled out and folded again 3 more times, as sketched in the recipe, the layers build up in geometric progression to make 72 layers of butter after the fourth fold. When the pastry finally goes into the oven, each of the many layers of dough puffs up between the layers of butter and the pastry bakes into a light, airy delight to both eye and tongue.

[*For about 1 pound of flour, making 2¼ pounds of dough, enough for 2 of the 6- by 16-inch covered entrée pastries on page 205, or about 3 dozen of the cornets, or horns, described on pages 198–201.*]

1. The dough mixture (*la détrempe*)

1 lb. strong plain flour
A 5-pt mixing bowl
4 tbl. tasteless salad oil
A rubber spatula
2 tsp. salt
8 fl. oz. iced water, plus a tbl. or so more if needed
A 2-ft sheet of waxed paper
A plastic bag

Put all but 2 ounces of the flour into the mixing bowl. Reserve the 2 ounces for step 2. Stir the oil into the flour and mix thoroughly with rubber spatula (A) – you could use an electric mixer for this, but it hardly seems worthwhile. Then stir in the salt and the water, cutting and pressing ingredients firmly

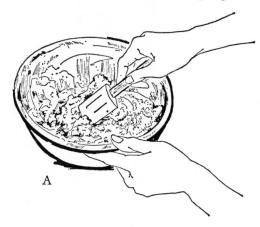

A

into a mass with spatula and then with the cupped fingers of one hand. Lift massed parts of dough out of bowl and place on pastry marble or board. Sprinkle unmassed bits of flour with drops of water in bowl; press together and add to dough.

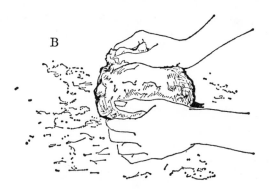

B

Press dough firmly and rapidly into a cushion shape (B). Do not try to make a smooth surface; it will smooth out later. Consistency should be pliable, though not at all damp or sticky. If you are in a terrible rush you can complete the next 2 steps now, but the dough will be easier to handle if you

sprinkle it lightly with flour, wrap in waxed paper (C), slip
it into a plastic bag, and refrigerate it for 40 minutes to an
hour.

2. Turn 1: adding the butter, and the first fold (*premier tour*)

12 oz. chilled unsalted butter
A pastry scraper or stiff broad spatula
The 2 oz. flour reserved from step 1

When you are ready to roll out the dough, beat the butter
with a rolling pin to soften it (D). Smear out with scraper or

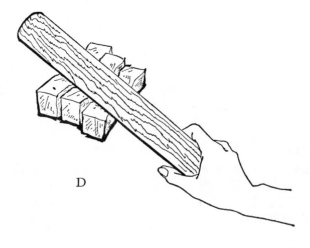

the heel, not the palm, of your hand (E). When partially softened, work in the flour and continue until butter is perfectly smooth and of easy spreading consistency but still cold. If butter is not supple enough you cannot spread it over the dough; if it is too soft it will ooze out as the dough is rolled. Chill briefly if you have softened it too much.

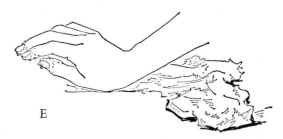

E

Lightly flour the dough and your hands. Push and pat the dough out, in front of you, into a rectangle 16 to 18 inches long and about 8 inches wide (F). Dough is being pushed rather than rolled so that you will activate the gluten as little

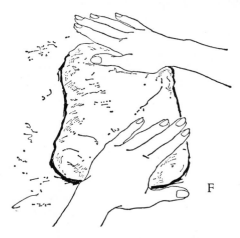

F

as possible for this first operation. (Dough will be very soft and sticky if you have not chilled it.) Using a scraper or stiff spatula, spread the softened butter over the upper two-thirds of the dough leaving a $\frac{1}{8}$-inch unbuttered border all around (G). The lower third is unbuttered.

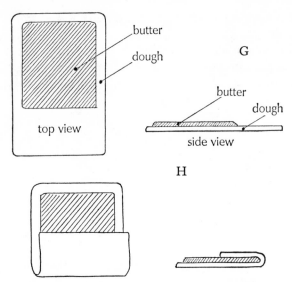

Fold the dough into three as follows: fold the bottom (unbuttered) third up to the middle (H). Fold the top (buttered) third down to cover it (I), just as though you were folding a business letter. You have made 2 layers of butter but only 3 of dough, because the middle layers, which touch, join to form a single layer.

Rotate the dough a quarter turn counter-clockwise so the top flap of dough is to your right (J), as though it were a book you were about to open. Dough will still look rather rough and the spotty damp patches are oil; all will smooth out by the final turn.

3. Turn 2: the 4-layer fold (*deuxième tour*)

In the second turn, you will roll out the dough and fold it so that it makes 4 layers. During the roll, be sure top and bottom of dough are always lightly floured and that your rolling surface is always scraped clean, to prevent dough from sticking; lift dough and slide it about between rolls to make sure.

Starting about an inch in from the near edge of the dough, roll your pin rapidly to within an inch of the far end, extending the dough as you roll (κ). The rolling movement is a firm,

K

even push away from you at a 45-degree angle. You are aiming for as even a rectangle of dough as possible, after several rolls you wish it to be 16 to 18 inches long and about 8 inches wide. Even the sides of the rectangle with the side of your pin when necessary and occasionally roll across the rectangle to widen it. Sprinkle any breaks in the dough with flour. (If you did not chill the initial dough it will look messy and soft at this point; do not worry.)

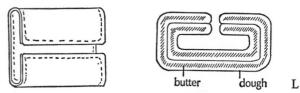

butter   dough   L

Fold the top and the bottom edges of the rectangle so that they meet at the centre of the dough (L). Fold them together again, as though you were closing a book (M). Now you have completed the second turn, and have 8 layers of butter sandwiched in between 9 layers of dough.

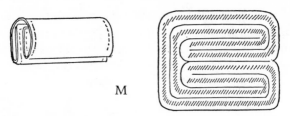

M

So that you will remember that you have now made 2 turns – you may decide to freeze the dough at this point – press 2 depressions in the top of the dough with the ball-ends, not the nails, of your fingers (N).

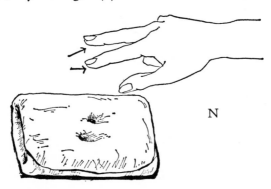

N

Wrap the dough in waxed paper, slip it into a plastic bag and refrigerate for 40 to 60 minutes (or overnight if you wish) until dough is much firmer and the gluten has relaxed; it will then be easy to roll out for the final 2 turns.

4. Finishing the dough: turns 3 and 4 – after a 40- to 60-minute rest

Unwrap the chilled dough and flour it sparingly top and bottom. If it is cold and hard, beat it evenly and firmly but not too heavily with your rolling pin to start it moving: beat crosswise and lengthwise, and keep the even rectangular shape (o).

Then roll dough rapidly out into a rectangle 16 to 18 inches long. (Again, if dough is very cold and you have not beaten it sufficiently to soften the butter, the sides may split when you roll out the dough. Do not worry if this happens;

remember to beat it a little longer the next time.) Fold rectangle of dough into three, again as though folding a business
letter and as diagrammed in turn 1. Rotate dough so top flap
is to your right, book-opening fashion; roll again into a

rectangle and fold into three. You now have completed the
fourth turn, and have 72 layers of butter. With the ball-ends
of your fingers, make 4 depression marks in the surface of the
dough. Wrap and chill for at least 2 hours to firm the butter
and to relax the gluten. It is then ready for forming and baking
in any way your recipe directs. (You may, of course, give the
dough 2 more turns after it has chilled, tripling the layer
count twice again to a total of 648; this is called for only
rarely, however.)

Storage, ahead-of-time notes, and freezing

You may wrap and store puff-pastry dough in the refrigerator
at any step during its manufacture; however, remember that
if you have not completed 4 turns the butter will be distri-
buted in rather thick layers. Thus if the pastry is very cold,
the congealed butter will break into lumps and flakes unless
you give it a careful and thorough beating with your rolling
pin before you attempt to roll it out. Puff-pastry dough may
be frozen for as much as a year, when wrapped airtight and
kept at zero degrees or less; thaw at room temperature or
overnight in the refrigerator.

Forming and baking the dough – after a rest of 2 hours
A complete listing of recipes using this dough is in the Index under 'pastry, puff'.

Use of left-over dough
See illustrated directions on page 196.

Pâte Feuilletée Fine
[Classic French Puff Pastry]
For *vol-au-vent*, patty shells, fine desserts, and *petits fours*.

Classic French puff pastry has equal amounts of butter and flour, 6 rollings out and foldings, and develops 729 layers of butter sandwiched between 730 layers of dough. You may use it for any recipe requiring puff pastry, but its particular role lies in the realm of the patty shell, the fine dessert, and the elegant tea pastry. As you will see, the dough mixture contains butter rather than oil, and is made like pie dough; rather than being spread on, the main part of the butter is enclosed in the dough. Otherwise the technique for classic puff pastry does not differ too much from simple puff pastry. You must allow, however, a minimum of 6 to 7 hours from the time you start it to the time you can form and bake it. As usual, most of this time is taken up with rest periods; the actual work involved is probably not more than 30 minutes, and this can be spread over a period of several days.

[*For about 1 pound of flour, making 2½ pounds of dough, enough for one 8-inch vol-au-vent 5 inches high or 8 to 10 patty shells, plus left-overs which will make a 6- by 16-inch covered pastry such as the one on page 205, or 2 dozen of the cheese appetizers on page 198*]

1. The dough mixture (*la détrempe*)
1 lb. strong plain flour
A 6-pt mixing bowl, or the large bowl of an electric mixer
3 oz. chilled unsalted butter
A 2-ft length of waxed paper

Measure 14 ounces of the flour into the mixing bowl. Reserve 2 ounces for step 2. Place chilled butter on waxed paper and cut into quarters lengthwise; rapidly cut quarters into ¼-inch pieces and add to the flour in the bowl. The butter is now to be cut into the flour and the liquid then added, just as though you were making pie dough. You may use an electric mixer as described in the *pâte brisée* recipe on page 157, or rub the flour and butter rapidly together between the tips of your fingers (A) until the butter is the size of small oatmeal flakes, or chop with a pastry blender until the mixture resembles coarse meal (B).

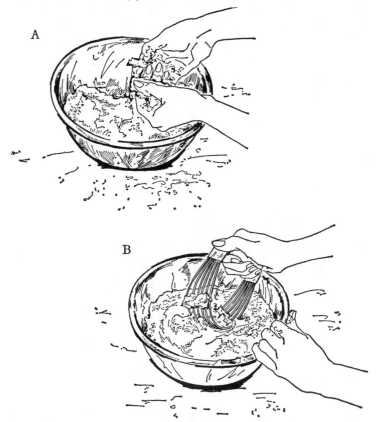

2 tsp. salt
9 fl. oz. iced water in a pt measure, plus a few droplets more if needed
A plastic bag

Blend the salt into the iced water and pour into the flour and butter mixture. If you are using an electric mixer, mix for just a few seconds, stopping the machine as soon as dough clogs in the blades. Otherwise blend with a rubber spatula, pressing dough firmly into a mass with spatula and then with cupped fingers of one hand. Lift massed dough out on to marble or board; sprinkle unmassed bits in bowl with droplets of water, press together and add to main body of dough.

Press dough firmly and rapidly into a rough cushion shape; consistency should be pliable, though not at all damp and sticky. Sprinkle lightly with flour, wrap in waxed paper, and slide into a plastic bag. Refrigerate for 40 minutes to relax gluten and firm the dough.

2. Preparing the butter – after dough has rested 40 minutes

12 oz. chilled unsalted butter
The 2 oz. flour reserved from step 1
A pastry scraper or stiff metal spatula

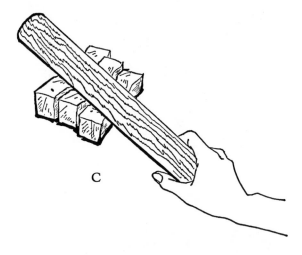

C

Beat the butter with a rolling pin to soften it (c), smear it out with the heel, not the palm, of your hand (d), or a pastry scraper or spatula. When partially softened, work in the flour. Butter must be absolutely smooth and supple, yet still cold. Form into a 5-inch square, place at the corner of your working surface, and proceed to the next step.

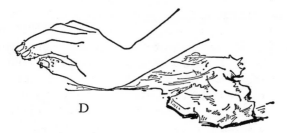

D

3. The dough package

Roll the chilled dough into a circle 12 to 13 inches in diameter; it will still look rough. Place the butter in the centre (E). Bring the edges of the dough over the butter (F) to enclose it com-

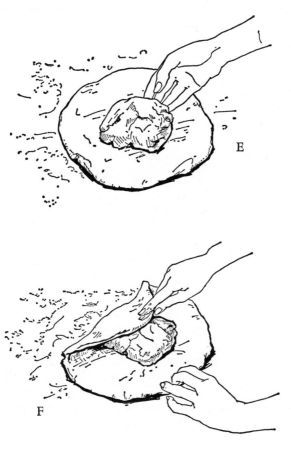

E

F

pletely, being very careful not to stretch dough because you want it to have a uniform thickness at the sides of the square. Press dough well together on top of package and seal edges with your fingers (G). Dough will still look rough and uneven, which is as it should be.

G

4. Turns 1 and 2

You now have a package with a layer of dough at the top and the bottom, and a layer of butter in between. Your object is to roll the package out into a rectangle, extending the butter the whole length and width of the rectangle between the 2 layers of dough: beat the package lightly but firmly its length and width with your rolling pin to get the butter moving, dust flour on the bottom and top of the dough, and rapidly roll it out into a rectangle 16 inches long and 8 inches wide. It is now to be folded in three, as though folding a business letter.

Fold the bottom third up over the centre of the dough (H).

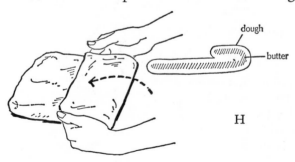

dough

butter

H

Fold the top third down to cover it, making 3 even layers (I).
By folding the dough in 3, you have made 3 layers of butter
but only 4 of dough, because the middle layers, which touch,
join to form a single layer.

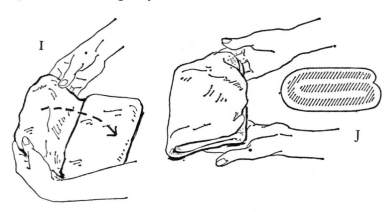

Place dough in front of you so that top flap is to your right, as
though it were a book (J). Roll again into a 16-inch rectangle
and again fold in three, making 9 layers of butter (K). Press 2
depressions in the top of the dough with the ball-ends, not
the nails, of your fingers so that you will remember you have
made 2 turns.

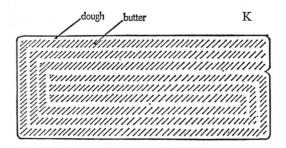

Wrap dough in waxed paper and slip it into a plastic bag.
Refrigerate for 40 to 60 minutes to relax the gluten and to firm
butter for next turns, which it is best to complete within an
hour if you can so that layers of butter do not become too
firm and congealed.

5. Turns 3 and 4 – after a rest of 40 to 60 minutes

If dough is hard and cold, beat with firm even strokes to soften butter. Complete turns 3 and 4 in the same way as the previous turns. You may find during the rolling out that the bottom layer of dough does not stretch out to meet the top and middle layers at each end: turn dough over and roll upside down to even the layers. Make 4 depression marks in the dough to indicate the 4 turns: wrap and chill again for at least an hour before starting turns 5 and 6.

(†) *Delayed action:* This is the best point to refrigerate the dough for several days, or to freeze it for several months.

6. Turns 5 and 6 – after a rest of at least 1 hour, and 2 hours before you wish to form and bake the dough

Complete turns 5 and 6 in the same manner. (It is here that if you have given the dough only its minimum rest period you may find it hard to roll out and inclined to retract rather severely when extended. If this happens, stop immediately; forcing it will only make the gluten more tenacious and the dough more bulky. Wrap and refrigerate the dough for an hour more before continuing.) Make 3 pairs of depression marks in the top of the dough to indicate the 6 turns. Wrap and refrigerate for 2 hours before forming and baking.

(†) *Delayed-action notes:* When you are making the dough for a *vol-au-vent*, you will usually get the highest rise when you form and bake the dough about 2 hours after the final turn. For all other purposes, dough may be refrigerated for several days, or frozen for several months.

Forming and baking the dough – after a rest of 2 hours

Except for the *vol-au-vent* and patty shells, which follow here, all other recipes using puff pastry will be found in their appropriate chapters, and there is a complete listing of recipes under 'pastry, puff' in the Index.

Use of left-over dough

See illustrated directions on page 196.

PATTY SHELLS

That beautifully sauced combination of sweetbreads, *quenelles*, truffles, mushrooms, and olives known as *ris de veau financière* has nowhere else to go but into a patty shell so light and airy it can fly with the wind, as the French title, *vol-au-vent*, suggests. Our litany ever seems to be 'your own are so much better', and how true it is when your own puff pastry makes shells so light, buttery, and flaky you can hardly believe they are real even while the pastry is melting in your mouth. Whether you wish to serve individual shells or one dramatic large one for the whole table, small and large shells are constructed in similar fashion.

You are aiming for a hollow cylinder of pastry. To achieve it, you make 2 layers: a ring of dough that is set on a disc of dough. The ring forms the sides of the cylinder, and the disc, its bottom. Both ring and disc puff up in the oven, and when the pastry is done, you cut an opening in the top, as you will see, fork out the small amount of uncooked pastry inside, and you have a case ready for filling with creamed lobster, shrimps, mushrooms, or whatever delectable mixture you may have concocted. We shall start with individual pastry shells.

DOUGH TALK

Both large and small shells require an extravagant amount of dough, and you will have as much left over as you have in the shells. However, the left-over dough is converted into puff pastry again as described and illustrated at the end of this section on page 196.

Bouchées
[Patty Shells for Individual Servings]

[For 9 shells 3½ inches in diameter]

1. Forming the dough

The preceding recipe for 2½ lb. chilled classic puff pastry
A pastry-cutting wheel or long knife
A 3½-in. plain, round cutter
A 2-in. plain, round cutter
A large baking sheet 12 by 16 ins. at least
1 or 2 trays or baking sheets in the refrigerator for storing pieces of dough
A sharp, thin skewer (or large darning needle)

Because puff pastry softens so quickly out of the refrigerator, you will find it best to work on only part of the dough at a time, keeping the rest chilled. Each piece will make 3 patty shells. Roll the dough into a rectangle 18 inches long and 8 inches wide, cut into thirds crosswise using pastry wheel or long knife, and refrigerate 2 of the pieces of dough. Roll the remaining piece of dough into a 10- by 14-inch rectangle ¼ inch thick. Work rapidly from now on so that dough will not soften before you are through; if it does, stop immediately, refrigerate everything for 15 to 20 minutes and then continue. Soft, limp dough is impossible to work with.

    With the 3½-inch round cutter, cut 6 discs in the pastry, spacing them half an inch from the edges of the pastry and from each other. With the 2-inch cutter, cut circles from the centre of three of the discs to make 3 rings (A). (Carefully arrange all left-over dough in one layer and refrigerate; see page 196 for instructions.)

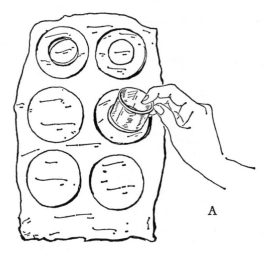

A

Rinse pastry sheet in cold water, shake off excess water, and place the 3 discs upside down on the sheet, spacing them ½ inch from edge of sheet and from each other. Paint tops of discs lightly with cold water and press a ring of dough on each disc (B). Seal each ring to each disc by making slanting

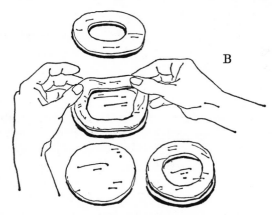

B

indentations ⅛ inch apart with the back of a knife, going all around the circumference, and pressing the 2 layers of dough together with the balls of your fingers as you go (C).

Prick all over exposed centre of bottom discs with the tines of a table fork (D). Plunge a skewer down through the pastry

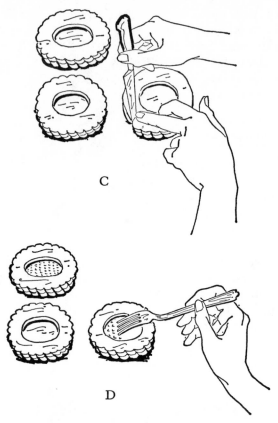

C

D

at 3 points in the centre of the pastry and 4 around the ring; this, hopefully, will ensure a vertical, even rise in the oven. With a 2-inch round cutter or a knife, press a circle outline $\frac{1}{16}$ inch deep in each disc, where the inside edge of the ring meets it (E); this will then be cut out after baking and serve as a cover.

E

Pastry will probably have softened; refrigerate baking sheet for 10 minutes, or at least while you are rolling out and cutting the next 2 pieces of dough. When all 9 *bouchées* are assembled on the sheet, cover with waxed paper and refrigerate for at least 40 minutes before baking, so that dough can relax and *bouchées* will not shrink or bake out of shape.

(†) The formed pastry may be frozen at this point, and taken right from freezer to oven.

2. Baking: 20 to 25 minutes in a preheated 425°F., Mark 7, oven

Just before baking, paint top surfaces of *bouchées*, not the sides, with a double coating of egg glaze (1 egg beaten with 1 teaspoonful water), and decorate with cross-hatch knife or fork marks. (See *vol-au-vent*, step 2, pages 189–90.) Bake in the middle level of preheated oven about 25 minutes. They are done when risen and brown, and when the sides are brown and crisp. Remove to a rack.

With a sharp small knife held vertically, cut out covers with an up-and-down sawing motion (F). Delicately scrape out any uncooked pastry from inside with the back of a teaspoon or the tines of a small table fork. Cool on a rack.

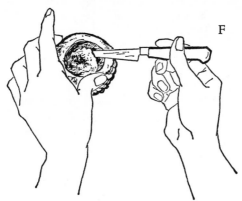

F

3. Storing and serving

The sooner you can fill and serve patty shells, the fresher, lighter, and more delicious they will be. If you are serving the same day, keep in a warm oven or the turned-off oven.

Otherwise arrange in a covered pan and freeze them. To re-heat and crisp shells, either frozen or not, preheat oven to 425°F., Mark 7, place shells on a lightly buttered baking sheet and set in middle level of oven. Turn oven off and shells will be crisp in 5 to 8 minutes.

Vol-au-vent
[Large Patty Shell]

A large patty shell is somewhat reminiscent of the old-time *haute cuisine*; it is wonderfully dramatic to serve and always greatly enjoyed by your guests just because it is an unusual treat. The decorative cover, which is formed and baked separately, is optional and depends on how your table serving works out. If you have a cover, the filled *vol-au-vent* with cover poised on top of the food is presented for all to admire, then the cover must be removed to a separate dish for cutting and serving.

[For an 8-inch shell about 5 inches deep, serving 6 people]

1. Forming the dough

The preceding recipe for 2½ lb. classic puff pastry, page 174
An 8-in. and a 5-in. round *vol-au-vent* cutter, pan cover, plate, or saucer for cutting circles of dough
A heavy rolling pin with rolling surface at least 14 ins. long
A baking sheet or round pizza tray rinsed in cold water and not dried
1 or 2 baking sheets or trays in the refrigerator for left-over dough

Place chilled puff pastry on a lightly floured marble or pastry board and roll rapidly into a rectangle ⅜ inch thick, 12 inches wide, and 20 inches long. (To ensure that stresses and strains are equalized for even baking, be sure to roll dough cross-wise as well as lengthwise.)

Work as rapidly as possible from now on so that dough will not soften and become difficult to handle; if it does soften, immediately stop whatever you are doing and re-frigerate everything for 15 to 20 minutes, then continue.

Cut two 8-inch discs out of pastry, spacing them at least ½ inch from edges of dough and from each other (A). Lift

A

surrounding dough off the discs and arrange in one layer on
baking sheet or tray and refrigerate; directions for re-forming
it into puff pastry are on page 196.

Roll one of the discs up on the pin and unroll upside down
on damp baking sheet (B). (Damp surface makes pastry stick
to sheet, giving it a grip so it can rise in the oven.) Paint a $1\frac{1}{2}$-
inch border around the top of the circle with cold water.

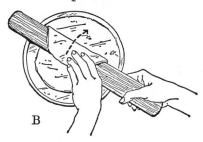

B

Using a round cutter or guide 5 inches in diameter, centre
it in the second disc of dough and cut around it to make the
8-inch ring for the second layer of the *vol-au-vent* (C). So that
you will not stretch the ring of dough as you remove it from
the circle, brush lightly with flour and fold it in half, then in
quarters. Unfold it on the dampened circumference of the
first disc (D), pressing it in place with the balls of your fingers.
(Refrigerate disc of left-over dough.) Seal the 2 layers of dough
with the back of a small knife, by pressing slanting lines $\frac{1}{8}$ inch
deep and about $\frac{3}{4}$ inch apart all around the circumference (E),
also pressing top of circle with the balls of your fingers as you
go. (It is now wise to cover and refrigerate *vol-au-vent* for an

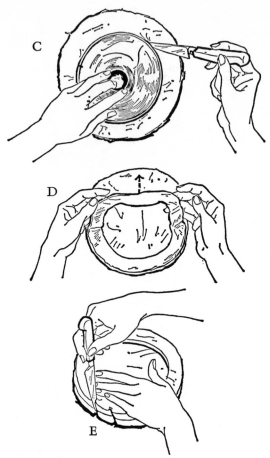

hour before baking; this will relax dough so that it will bake evenly.)

(†) Unbaked *vol-au-vent* may be refrigerated for a day or so, or frozen, but you will usually get a higher rise if you bake it within an hour of forming.

2. Final decoration and baking: about 1 hour; oven preheated to 425°F., Mark 7

Egg glaze (1 egg beaten with 1 tsp. water in a bowl or cup)
A pastry brush
A small knife
A thin, sharp skewer or large darning needle

When oven has been preheated, paint top of ring and exposed top of disc with egg glaze. (Do not paint sides, because egg could prevent them from rising.)

With a small knife, cut lines $\frac{1}{8}$ inch deep and $1\frac{1}{2}$ inches apart (at outside edge) in top of ring, pointing knife always to centre of *vol-au-vent* so the marks will be evenly spaced, like the spokes of a wheel (F).

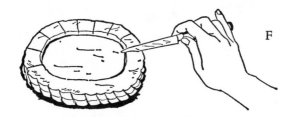

F

Cut a line $\frac{1}{4}$ inch deep in the bottom disc, where inner edge of circle meets it (G); this marks the cover, which is removed after baking so that interior of *vol-au-vent* may be cleaned out.

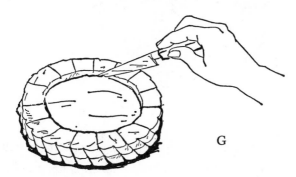

G

Make decorative, shallow cross-hatch marks in the top of the dough through the glaze with the point of a knife (H) or the tines of a table fork.

Finally, plunge skewer or needle down through the top of the pastry sheet at 4 to 5 places around the circumference and 3 places in the centre (I). The purpose of this operation is presumably to hold the puff-pastry layers in place and help the *vol-au-vent* rise evenly.

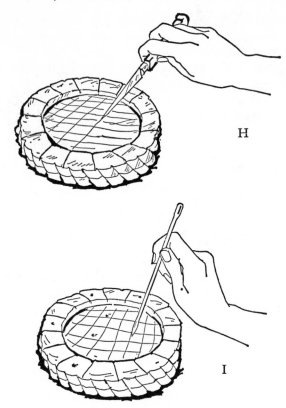

Immediately place *vol-au-vent* in lower-middle level of pre-heated oven and bake at 425°F., Mark 7 for about 20 minutes, until the pastry has tripled in height and is beginning to brown. Lower thermostat to 350°F., Mark 4 and bake 30 to 40 minutes longer, until sides are brown and crisp. If pastry is colouring too much, lay a sheet of aluminium foil or heavy brown paper loosely over the top.

3. Final touches

As soon as you remove the *vol-au-vent* from the oven and while it is still hot, cut around the inside edge of the ring to remove the cover you marked in the bottom disc; this has now risen, along with the rest of the dough. (Cover will probably break and should be eaten by the cook, who must sample the pastry anyway.) Being very careful not to pierce sides or bottom of crust, scrape uncooked pastry out of *vol-au-vent* with the tines of a table fork or the handle of a spoon (J). (You may turn this into a cheese ramekin, but you should use it while still fresh; see following recipe.)

J

Set *vol-au-vent* again on its pastry sheet and put in the oven for 5 minutes, to dry out, then let cool on a rack. If bottom of pastry burned or darkened unduly during baking, shave off the discoloured part with a sharp knife.

Storing and reheating

If you have a warming oven, set it at around 100°F. where pastry will keep for a day or two, drying and crisping to a delicious texture. Otherwise, the sooner you can eat the *vol-au-vent* the better, unless you are going to wrap it airtight and freeze, where it will keep for several weeks. To reheat cold or frozen *vol-au-vent*, set on a lightly buttered pastry sheet in a preheated 425°F., Mark 7 oven for 5 minutes, then turn oven off and leave a few minutes more, until crisp.

Ramequin du Juste Milieu
[A Hot Puffed Cheese Dish]

This dish uses the uncooked insides of the *vol-au-vent* (see above); to serve as an entrée or in place of potatoes.

[*For 4 to 6 servings*]

The fresh, preferably still warm, uncooked insides of a *vol-au-vent*
½ pt milk
2 eggs
Salt, pepper, and nutmeg
1 oz. grated Parmesan cheese
A 1½-pt baking and serving dish about 1½ ins. deep, lightly buttered

Purée the uncooked pastry and milk for a minute or so in an electric blender until perfectly smooth. Add eggs, seasonings, and cheese, and purée 5 seconds. Pour into buttered dish.

(†) May now be covered and refrigerated until the next day.

Half an hour before serving, bake in the middle level of a pre-heated 375°F., Mark 5 oven until nicely puffed and browned. Serve immediately.

Making a *Vol-au-Vent* Cover

When you want a cover for the *vol-au-vent* form it separately, and bake the 2 together on the same pastry sheet.

Use the circle of left-over dough you cut from the second disc of pastry that made the *vol-au-vent* ring. After it has rested in the refrigerator while you were making the *vol-au-vent* itself, roll it out into a disc about 9½ inches in diameter; loosen it from the rolling surface to let it shrink if it will. Roll it up on your pin and unroll upside down on a lightly buttered pastry sheet. Then trim it into a neat circle using an 8½-inch cutter or plate as a guide.

Place a slightly smaller cutter, cover, or other round object on top and draw the back of a knife from edge of pastry to edge of cutter at ¾-inch intervals all around to make a scalloped edging (A).

To discourage dough from rising more than a little in the oven, prick all over (except on scalloped edges) at ⅛-inch intervals with the tines of a table fork (B), going right down through the pastry to the pastry sheet. Cover and chill the dough for about an hour, so that gluten will relax and dough will bake evenly without shrinking.

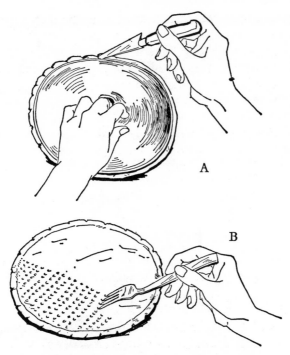

Using scraps of dough left over from the *vol-au-vent*, make
decorative cut-outs ⅛-inch thick and of any shape and design
you wish. After painting top of dough with egg glaze, affix
the designs and paint them also. Then make shallow, all-over
cross-hatch marks through the glaze and into the dough with a
small knife or the tines of a fork. The design illustrated (c) is a

very simple one of circular cut-outs, which puff up in an amusing manner; you may use ovals, leaves, strips of dough, or anything you wish, but remember that everything rises, and if you cut your shapes too thick and narrow, they may topple off in the oven.

Baking

Whether baked separately or along with the *vol-au-vent*, put the cover in a preheated 425°F., Mark 7 oven for about 20 minutes, until nicely browned, then turn oven down to 350°F., Mark 4. Pastry is done when it feels crisp and light, which should be 30 minutes or so in all. Let cool on a rack.

Fleurons
[Puff-pastry Puffs, for Decorations and Garnitures]

baked

raw

When you are not making a cover for the *vol-au-vent*, you may want some extra bits of puff pastry to decorate the edge of the platter around the shell. These are called *fleurons*, or flowered shapes, because they are small and decorative, usually fluted ovals or crescents. Classic French recipes often suggest *fleurons* as a garnish to some of the beautiful fillet of sole or scallop dishes, where pastry elegantly takes the place of a mundane starchy vegetable. You may make *fleurons* either out of the carefully preserved trimmings from your *vol-au-vent* or *bouchée* cuttings, or from the re-formed and reconstituted dough described after the next recipe.

Roll dough ¼ to ⅜ inch thick and make discs with a round, 3-inch, fluted cutter. With one stroke of the cutter through the centre, cut each disc into an oval and a crescent.

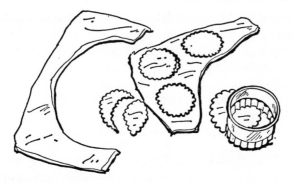

Place ½ inch apart on a dampened pastry sheet and chill for at least half an hour to relax the dough – an hour or more would be better. Glaze with beaten egg, decorate with cross-hatching, and bake in middle level of a preheated 450°F., Mark 8 oven for 12 to 15 minutes, until nicely puffed, brown, and crisp.

Petites Bouchées
[Cocktail Shells of Puff Pastry]

Cocktail-size patty shells, *petites bouchées* or little mouthfuls 2 inches in diameter, are made in 1 layer. Use the left-over circles cut from the second layer, or rings, of larger patty shells, or cut circles from the left-over and reconstituted puff-pastry dough in the following recipe.

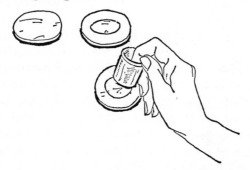

Roll the dough ¼ to ⅜ inch thick, cut with a 2-inch fluted cutter, and arrange on a dampened baking sheet. With a 1-inch cutter or a small knife, press a cover outline in the top of the dough, going ⅛ inch deep. Glaze and bake, following the preceding directions for *fleurons*. When baked and still warm, delicately cut out the cover and remove any uncooked pastry from interiors.

These small shells may then be filled and reheated for serving, or you may freeze them until needed.

Utilization des Rognures
[Reconstituting Left-over Dough into Puff Pastry Again]

You will have as much dough left over from cutting a *vol-au--vent* as you have in the *vol-au-vent* itself (A), and almost as

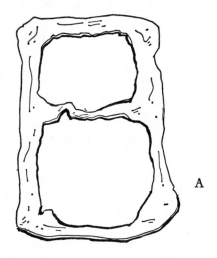

A

much from *bouchées*. You can even make another *vol-au-vent* from these scraps, or half a dozen *bouchées*, or anything else calling for puff pastry. *Demi-feuilletée*, the simpler puff pastry, is treated the same way. Puff-pastry left-overs are called *rognures*, meaning trimmings or scraps. Your object is to join the scraps into one piece of dough in such a way that the layers of butter and flour in each scrap are horizontal, as they were when the dough was first made.

Cut the scraps as necessary (B). Arrange them so that they will form a rectangle (C). Then paint an edge of each with cold

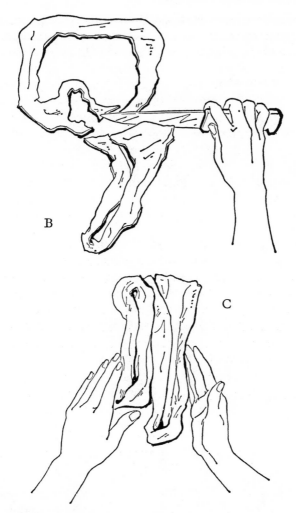

B

C

water, overlap it slightly upon its neighbour, and seal the seam with the balls of your fingers.

If you are very skilful, you can manage to make a few careful rolls with your pastry pin and join the seams of dough so perfectly that you can cut it out for patty shells or the 2 large discs needed for a *Pithiviers*. The surest system, however, is to flour dough lightly, roll into a rectangle, spread the top two thirds with a tablespoon of softened butter and fold in three.

Wrap, chill an hour or two, and finish off with 2 more turns. Refrigerate for several hours or overnight, or freeze, so that dough will relax thoroughly before you use it again.

Re-use of left-overs

You can still get puffing and flakiness out of the left-over of left-overs, using the preceding system. The pastry will not be as tender when baked as it was at first, and it may well offer a bit of resistance when you roll it out. However, it works very well for most appetizers, as well as for biscuits and for the *fleurons* and the *petites bouchées* in the 2 preceding recipes.

PUFF-PASTRY ENTRÉES

Just a few of the many delicious pastries you can make with *pâte feuilletée* are described and illustrated in the following pages; dessert pastries and biscuits are on pages 593–616, and 621–7. One could easily write a book on puff pastry alone, and we find it hard to limit ourselves to a sensible few. We hope, however, that these recipes will give you a feel for how to use it so that you can go off on your own and be confident with other recipes you find elsewhere.

Cornets
[Puff-pastry Horns – Cream Horns]

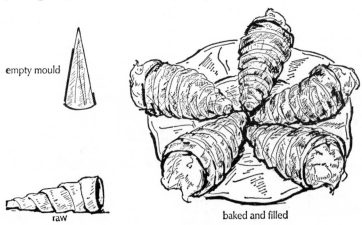

empty mould

raw   baked and filled

Strips of puff pastry are rolled around cone-shaped forms, baked until the pastry has browned and set, and baked again with a creamy cheese filling to make a most attractive first-course fantasy. (Encrusted with sugar, they come out of the oven with a caramel coating for dessert creams, as suggested on page 610.)

[For 18 to 20 horns about 5 inches long, serving 8 to 10 people]

1. Forming the dough

18 to 20 buttered cream-horn moulds (or bake the pastry in several batches)
2 large pastry sheets rinsed in cold water but not dried
½ the recipe for chilled simple puff pastry, page 166
A tray lined with wax paper for refrigerating pieces of dough you are not actually working on
A ruler or cutting guide
A ravioli wheel
A pastry brush and cup of cold water

Stand the buttered moulds within easy reach, and have the pastry sheets near you. Roll the chilled pastry out into a rectangle 14 inches long, cut in half crosswise, and refrigerate 1 piece of dough. Roll remaining piece of dough rapidly into a rectangle ⅛ inch thick and slightly more than 8 by 13 or 14 inches in size. Trim off ragged edges. (If kitchen is hot, work very rapidly, and refrigerate all pieces or strips of dough you are not actually working on in the following steps.)

Cut strips of pastry ¾ to 1 inch wide and 13 to 14 inches long, using cutting guide and pastry wheel as shown (A). Paint a

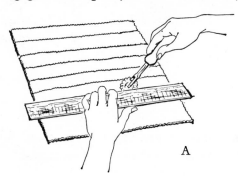

A

$\frac{1}{2}$-inch band of cold water along top length of a strip of dough.
Hold mould by its large end; slip tip of mould under right end
of dough strip (B), then pinch dough all around the tip of the

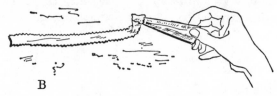

B

mould to seal it. Holding tip of mould with your left hand,
with your right hand rotate its large end clockwise – to your
right – winding the dough on to the mould in a spiral from tip
to large end (c), and letting dough overlap $\frac{1}{8}$ inch upon itself

C

as you go. Be careful not to stretch the dough which should
remain an even $\frac{1}{8}$ inch thick. When dough is cold and firm, you
will find it easy to work with. Seal end of dough at large end
of mould, pressing with your fingers (D). Place horn on baking

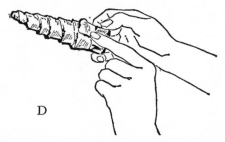

D

sheet, sealed-side of dough against sheet; press lightly to hold
the horn in place. Proceed with the rest of the horns in the
same manner.

2. Chilling, glazing, and baking

Chill at least 30 minutes, but an hour is preferable, to relax dough before baking. When ready to bake, preheat oven to 425°F., Mark 7, and set rack in middle level. Just before baking paint tops and sides of horns with egg glaze (1 egg beaten in a small bowl with 1 teaspoonful water), and make cross-hatching on surface with the point of a knife or the tines of a fork. Bake immediately; horns are done in 15 to 20 minutes, when moulds slip easily out of them. For recipes where you are to fill the horns and bake them again, remove from oven when a pale brown so they will not darken too much during their second baking; otherwise leave them in a few minutes longer, to brown nicely.

(†) Pastries are at their best when eaten within a few hours of baking; you may keep them, however, in a warming oven at around 100°F., for a day or so; otherwise wrap airtight and freeze them. To thaw, place on a lightly buttered baking sheet in a 400°F., Mark 6 oven; turn oven off, and leave about 10 minutes.

Fondue de Fromage pour Cornets, Rouleaux, Mille-feuilles, et Croquettes
[Cheese Filling for Cream Horns, *Mille-feuilles*, and Croquettes]

This is a very thick sauce that will not run or flow out of shape when heated in pastries, or when coated with beaten eggs and breadcrumbs and deep-fried. Rather than cooking it in the usual way, with a flour and butter *roux* that is moistened with hot milk, you beat the milk into the flour and then add the butter, making what is technically known as a *bouillie*.

¼ pt or more milk
2 oz. plain flour
A heavy 3-pt saucepan
A wire whisk and a rubber spatula
1 oz. butter
2 large eggs

Salt, pepper, pinch of nutmeg, and drops of Tabasco sauce or a pinch of
  Cayenne pepper
4 oz. coarsely grated Gruyère cheese
2 oz. grated Parmesan cheese
3 to 4 tbl. double cream

Gradually beat driblets of milk into the flour, in saucepan,
adding ¼ pint and beating to a smooth consistency. Add butter,
and set pan over moderate heat, stirring. When mixture comes
near the boil and begins to be lumpy, remove from heat and
beat vigorously to smooth it out. One by one, beat in the eggs,
and bring to the boil, beating constantly. Sauce must be a
thick paste; if very stiff, thin out over heat, beating in more
milk by dribbles. Remove from heat, season with salt, pepper,
a pinch of nutmeg, and rather strongly with Tabasco or
Cayenne pepper. Let cool for a few minutes, then fold in the
cheese. Fold in just enough cream to soften it slightly, but sauce
must hold its shape when mounded in a spoon; it should not
spread out later, when cooked with pastries.

(†) May be made several days in advance of using; may be
frozen. Clean off sides of pan, and press a sheet of plastic wrap
over the surface of the sauce to prevent a skin or crust from
forming.

Additions

Use half the amount of cheese called for in the preceding
filling, and fold in 1 to 2 ounces of either diced ham or mushroom *duxelles* (diced fresh mushrooms sautéed in butter,
Volume I, page 552).

Cornets à la Fondue de Fromage
[Cream Horns Baked with Cheese Filling]

The preceding cheese filling
A pastry bag with round tube opening
Puff-pastry cream horns, baked but barely browned, page 198
Rather soft cheese
A grater (small holes)
A lightly buttered baking sheet

Preheat oven to 400°F., Mark 6. Pack the cheese filling into the pastry bag and squeeze it into each pastry horn (A). Grate the soft cheese so that you have rather long whiskery wisps, and pack a large pinch into opening of each horn (B).

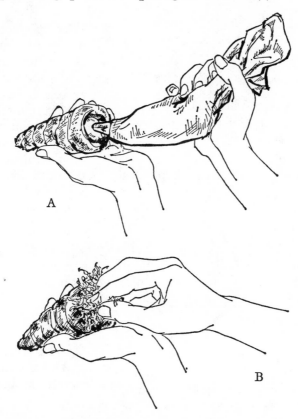

A

B

Bake in upper third of preheated oven 10 to 12 minutes, to melt cheese and heat filling to bubbling hot. Serve as soon as possible.

Rouleaux
[Puff-pastry Cream Rolls]

If you cannot find moulds for cream horns, you may find metal moulds suitable for pastry rolls; or use pieces of well-oiled unvarnished wood 5 to 6 inches long, such as a cut-up broom handle. Form, bake, and fill puff-pastry rolls in the same general manner described and illustrated for horns, starting

empty
mould

raw

baked and filled

on page 198. When baked with the preceding cheese filling, stuff whiskers of cheese into both ends to prevent filling from oozing out.

Mille-feuilles à la Fondue de Fromage
[Cheese Napoleons]

You will probably find far more use for cheese Napoleons than for pastry-cream dessert Napoleons. They make an elegant first course or luncheon dish and are practically as easy to assemble as the count of one-two-three – when you have ready-made puff pastry on hand. A thin sheet of baked puff pastry is cut into squares or rectangles that are sandwiched together with the cheese *fondue* filling and baked until the filling is bubbling hot.

[*For 6 to 8 servings*]

1 sheet of baked puff pastry 12 by 16 ins. (Napoleons,
    page 603; steps 1 and 2)
A ruler or cutting guide
A pastry wheel or very sharp knife

Cut the baked puff pastry either into three 4- by 16-inch strips, and cut each strip into squares 4 inches to a side; or cut the pastry into four 3-inch strips 16 inches long, and cut each into 4 rectangles (making 12 squares, or 16 rectangles).

The cheese *fondue* filling on page 201
3 to 4 tbl. grated Parmesan cheese
A lightly buttered baking sheet

Preheat oven to 375°F., Mark 5, about half an hour before you wish to serve. Have the filling and grated cheese ready. Place half the puff-pastry pieces on the baking sheet. Spread a 3-tablespoon lump of the filling on each, but leaving a $\frac{1}{4}$-inch free border of pastry all around. Lightly press a second piece of pastry, best side uppermost, on top. Sprinkle on a $\frac{1}{2}$ teaspoon of grated cheese.

Bake for about 15 minutes in preheated oven, upper-middle level, until cheese topping has coloured lightly and cheese filling is bubbling hot – be careful not to bake too long and burn the pastry. Serve immediately.

(†) You may form the *mille-feuilles* for baking an hour or so in advance.

Feuilletée au Fromage
Jalousie au Fromage
[Peekaboo Cheese Tart of French Puff Pastry]

Another delicious puff pastry for first courses, luncheons, or for slicing and serving with cocktails is the *feuilletée*. Quick to assemble, when you have puff-pastry dough on hand, it is done exactly like the jam tart on page 600.

[*For a 6- by 16-inch tart, serving 6 people*]

1. Forming the tart

½ the recipe for simple puff pastry, page 166, or reconstituted left-overs,
　page 196
A dampened pastry sheet
A table fork
Either: ½ to ⅔ the cheese *fondue* filling on page 201;
Or: 4 to 6 oz. Roquefort cheese or blue cheese, and 1 egg beaten with
　6 tbl. *crème fraîche* or double cream, salt, pepper, and Tabasco sauce

Roll half the pastry into an 8- by 18-inch rectangle ⅛ inch thick.
Roll up on pin, and unroll topside down on to dampened
pastry sheet. Prick all over at ¼-inch intervals with tines of
fork, going right down through to pastry sheet.

　Either spread the *fondue* filling on the pastry, leaving a ¾-
inch border all around (A); or cut cheese into thin slices and
spread over pastry, leaving border. Turn borders of pastry up
over filling at sides; wet corners, and turn ends over (B), sealing
corners with fingers. If you are using Roquefort or blue
cheese, spoon the egg and cream over it, tilting pastry in all
directions, allowing liquid to flow all over enclosed area.

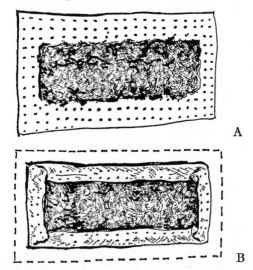

A

B

　Roll out second piece of pastry into a 7- by 17-inch rectangle ⅛ inch thick. Flour surface lightly, and fold in half lengthwise. Measure opening of filled pastry and mark folded pastry

to guide you. Cut slits in dough from folded edge as shown, making them ⅜ inch apart and half as long as width of opening in tart (c).

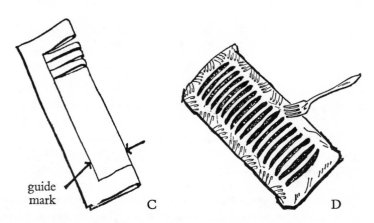

guide mark   C   D

Wet edges of filled bottom layer of pastry with cold water. Unfold top layer over it; brush off accumulated flour, and press pastry in place with fingers. Then with back tines of a fork, press a decorative vertical edging all around sides of tart (D). Cover and chill for at least 30 minutes before baking.

(†) When chilled and firm, may be wrapped airtight and frozen for several months. Remove from freezer, glaze, and bake as in step 2.

2. Baking and serving: about 1 hour at 450°F., Mark 8, and 400°F., Mark 6

Egg glaze (1 egg beaten in a small bowl with 1 tsp. water)
A pastry brush
A table fork or small knife
A rack
A serving tray or board

When oven has been preheated to 450°F., Mark 8, set rack in lower-middle level. Paint surface of chilled tart with egg glaze; wait a moment, and give it a second coat. Make cross-hatchings on top of sides and ends through glaze, and set in oven. In about 20 minutes, when pastry has risen and started to brown, turn oven down to 400°F., Mark 6. Cover loosely with foil or brown paper if surface is browning too much. Sides should be firm and crusty. Slide on to a rack when done. Serve warm or tepid cutting into crosswise slices.

(†) Tart is best when freshly made, but you can store it for several hours in a warming oven at about 100°F.

GARNITURES FOR *BOUCHÉES* AND *VOL-AU-VENT*

*Ris de Veau à la Financière
[Braised Sweetbreads Garnished with *Quenelles*, Truffles, Mushrooms, and Olives]

This is certainly one of the great classic fillings for *bouchées* and large *vol-au-vent*, and delicious when properly done. Unfortunately, like beef Wellington in the hands of the profane and cynical, gummy sauces, clumsy flavouring, and bad pastry have ruined its reputation. We urge you to give it another try, and you will understand why it has long been so popular with great chefs. You may not want to add all of the items listed, but you will have a delicious creamed sweetbread filling even if you do not do the full *financière*, which could also include cockscombs and white kidneys (*crêtes et rognons de coq*), although we have not listed them in the ingredients.

MANUFACTURING NOTE

This is the kind of filling that you can prepare the day before serving. We shall not give proportions of how much filling is to go into each pastry, because there is no way of knowing what size and how many you are to make; left-over filling will be just as good the next day, with scrambled eggs or as the filling for an omelette.

[*For 6 to 8 people*]

1. The sweetbreads and the sauce base

2 lb. soaked and peeled sweetbreads braised in wine, stock, and aromatic vegetables, Volume I, page 443
½ lb. fresh baby mushrooms, or larger mushrooms quartered

1 pt liquid as follows: the cooking stock from the sweetbreads plus half
    veal or chicken stock and half milk to complete the measure
A heavy-bottomed 5-pt saucepan, enamelled or stainless
2 oz. butter
5 tbl. flour
A wooden spoon and a wire whisk
¼ pt or more double cream

Remove sweetbreads to a plate, and strain cooking stock into a
bowl. Return stock to braising dish. Trim mushrooms, wash
rapidly in cold water, and quarter if necessary. Add mushrooms
to liquid in braising dish and simmer 5 minutes. Dip or strain
them out, and add to sweetbreads. In the heavy saucepan, melt
the butter, blend in the flour and stir over moderate heat with
wooden spoon until flour and butter foam together for 2
minutes without browning. Remove from heat, and as soon
as this *roux* stops bubbling, pour in all the hot braising liquid
at once, blending vigorously with wire whisk until perfectly
smooth.

Return over moderately high heat, and stir with wire whisk
as sauce thickens and comes to the boil. It will be quite thick.
Thin out, still simmering, with spoonfuls of cream; sauce
should coat spoon fairly heavily.

Salt and white pepper to taste
If needed: more white wine, Sercial Madeira, more stock, a pinch more
    thyme or bay leaf

Taste sauce very carefully for seasoning and strength. It may
need simmering with more wine, or strengthening with
Madeira, veal stock, a little beef stock, or herbs. If so, simmer
it, stirring, and tasting until you are satisfied. The egg yolks,
butter, and the other ingredients will give it more interest, but
it should be delicious at this point. (You will need about equal
quantities of sauce and garniture.)

2. The rest of the garniture, and final flavourings and enrichment

1 or more truffles and the juices from the tin
Veal or chicken *quenelles*, poached, and cut into ½-in. pieces, Volume I,
    page 211 (or tinned imported *quenelles* of veal or chicken), 6 to 8 oz.,
    depending on how much you have or need

3 oz. small green stoned olives simmered 5 minutes in 1½ pts of water
Salt and white pepper to taste
Drops of lemon juice
2 egg yolks blended with 3 tbl. double cream in a small bowl
1 to 2 oz. soft butter
Hot *bouchées* or *vol-au-vent*
Optional: truffle slices or a fluted cooked mushroom cap (Volume I,
 pages 547–8) for each serving

Cut the braised sweetbreads into ½-inch slices or into ½-inch
dice, and set aside. Fold the mushrooms into the sauce. If you
have several truffles, slice one and use for decoration later; dice
the rest into small pieces and add to the sauce along with their
juices. Fold in the diced *quenelles* and the olives. Bring to the
simmer for 3 to 4 minutes to blend flavours, and taste very
carefully for seasoning, adding salt, pepper, and lemon as
needed. Remove from heat, beat several spoonfuls of hot sauce
gradually into the cream and egg yolks, then fold the egg-
yolk mixture back into the saucepan along with the sweetbreads. Reheat, folding slowly, to below the simmer. Remove
from heat and fold in the butter, a spoonful at a time. Spoon
into the hot *bouchées* or *vol-au-vent*, and serve immediately,
topped, if you wish, with truffle slices or fluted mushrooms.

Garniture Dieppoise
Garniture aux Fruits de Mer
[Creamed Seafood Filling]

Adapt the *marmite dieppoise*, with its sole, halibut, shrimp,
scallops, mussels, and lobsters, to the preceding recipe. Follow
the *marmite* recipe, page 75, steps 1 and 2, then boil the cooking
liquid down to a pint or so, and proceed with the sauce in the
preceding recipe, steps 1 and 2. Use sliced truffles or fluted
mushrooms to garnish each serving.

Garniture de Volaille, Financière
[Diced Chicken in White-wine Sauce with *Quenelles*,
Truffles, Mushrooms, and Olives]

Poach chicken pieces in white wine and aromatic vegetables,

following the recipe for *poulet poché au vin blanc*, page 343, steps 1 and 2. Peel and dice the chicken, and then proceed as for the sweetbreads, simply substituting chicken and chicken stock.

3. Meats: From Country Kitchen to *Haute Cuisine*

Braised Beef · *Bœuf Braisé, Paupiettes, et Daubes*

Whether it is one large piece or a dozen small ones, whether you use red wine or white, whether or not you marinate it, lard it, flour it, thicken its juices at the beginning or at the end, all beef that is braised undergoes much the same process, and if you have done one you can do all. This is comforting to remember when you run into a new pot roast or stew: it is only the small differences in method, garnishing, or flavour that distinguish one recipe from another. For example, the fine *bœuf en daube à la provençale* on page 229 sounds as though it were quite a different dish from the *bœuf à la mode* in Volume I on page 336, but you will see they are very much related: while the beef for the *daube* is larded with ham, and is put into a thickened sauce from the beginning of its braise, the sauce for the *bœuf à la mode* is thickened at the end of the cooking. Again, in a comparison of beef stews you find the *bœuf bourguignon* in Volume I braising in a flour-thickened sauce, while the *bœuf aux oignons* here follows the simpler pattern of having its sauce thickened at the end with *beurre manié* (flour-butter paste). The methods are actually interchangeable, and you can conduct any braise exactly as you wish; the more techniques you have absorbed, the more you are master of *la cuisine*.

MARINATING THE BEEF BEFORE COOKING

An aromatic wine marinade adds its own special flavour to beef, and is always an effective tenderizer for the tougher cuts. Marinate or not, as you wish, for any of the following recipes, using the formula for the *daube* on page 230 and dry white wine rather than red, if you wish. For the marinade to be effective, stew meat or meat for *paupiettes* needs at least 6 hours, and a roast, 12 hours. Several days of marination in the refrigerator will be even more penetrating, and the marinade will also preserve the meat a little longer. In other words, rather than freezing it, if you are a once-a-week shopper, marinate it. Drain and dry the beef thoroughly before proceeding with any recipe. Substitute the marinade vegetables and wine for whatever is called for in the recipe, and if carrots are not one of the ingredients listed, for instance, add the marinade carrots anyway, since such details are of small importance.

LARDONS, PORK FAT, BACON, AND SUET

Lardons, those stick-shaped bits of fat-and-lean pork 1½ inches long and ¼ inch thick, are typical of French stews. Their rendered fat browns the beef, and their flavour adds a subtle touch to its sauce. Fresh, unsalted, and unsmoked pork belly is the cut to use if you can find it, otherwise substitute chunk bacon, cut, and blanched (simmered) 10 minutes in a quart of water to remove its salty, smoky taste. (Fat-and-lean salt pork, if very fresh and fine, is another alternative, but it must also be blanched.) Pork fat for larding and for draping over the meat is discussed in the *charcuterie* chapter on page 423. If you prefer suet, although it tends to shrink up, use fat from the outside of a rib or a loin of beef.

BEEF CUTS FOR STEWS

Cuts from the round (hind leg) (*la cuisse*)

Topside, *tende de tranche*. This is rather expensive, but furnishes solid pieces of meat with no muscle separations.

Bottom round or silverside, *gîte à la noix*. This also furnishes solid pieces, but the cooked meat will tend to be somewhat grainy; be sure not to overcook it, to avoid an accentuation of this quality. The eye of silverside, part of this cut, *rond de gîte à la noix*, is not at all recommended for stewing because of its excessive graininess.

Thick flank, *tranche grasse*. Lower parts and outside of this cut, when clear of gristle, can be used for stewing.

Shin, *nerveux gîte à la noix*. This gristly piece, when boned and trimmed, makes excellent gelatinous stew meat, but benefits from a marinade and longer cooking.

Cuts from the chuck (shoulder end)

Bladebone, *paleron*; clod, *macreuse* and *jumeau*; chuck ribs, *surlonges* or *basses côtes*. There are numerous fine stewing cuts from this section, and a good butcher will know them.

Cuts from the underside and short ribs (*caparaçon et plat de côtes*)

These include the brisket, *poitrine*, which is really too grainy for stewing but fine for braising whole; the flank, *tendron*, with its mixture of fat and lean and its cartilaginous bones, which make for good sauce consistency; and the upper flank, *flanchet*, which is not for stewing in pieces but may be stuffed and braised whole if it is not scored and grilled for steak. The short ribs, *plat de côtes couvert* (ribs 7 to 9), are excellent in a stew but take up a lot of room in your casserole because the bones are left in; however, they have excellent flavour and the meat with bones makes a delicious sauce.

*Bœuf aux Oignons
[Beef Stew with Onions and Red Wine]

This is the most elemental of beef stews, with its *lardons* of pork that render the fat that browns the beef that simmers in wine, along with onions, herbs, garlic, and a hint of tomato. Delicious just as it is, the inclusion of other elements changes its character as well as its name, making it, in fact, the perfect stew for our game of theme and variations. Buttered noodles, buttered peas, and little tomatoes go beautifully with this stew, but if you wish to branch into more exotic preparations you might choose one of the aubergine recipes, such as the *sauté en persillade*, page 459, or the grilled aubergine slices on page 457, accompanied, perhaps, with individual servings of potatoes in the form of *pommes duchesse*, page 524. A full and hearty red wine like Beaujolais or Côtes-du-Rhône is called for here.

[*For 6 people*]

1. Browning the beef and other preliminaries

5 to 6 oz. *lardons* (1½-in. sticks of blanched bacon ¼ in. thick, page 213)
Olive oil or cooking oil
A large (11-in.) frying pan (non-stick recommended)
A heavy, covered, 8- or 9-pt casserole (such as a round one, 10 by
    4 ins.)

Brown the *lardons* lightly with a tablespoon of the oil in the frying pan; transfer with a slotted spoon to the casserole, leaving fat in frying pan.

3½ to 4 lb. boned and trimmed beef stew meat cut into chunks about
    2 by 3 by 1 ins. (list of cuts is on pages 213–14)
Paper towels
1 tsp. salt
⅛ tsp. pepper

While *lardons* are browning, dry meat thoroughly in paper towels, and when *lardons* are done, raise heat under pan to moderately high. When fat in pan is very hot but not smoking, add as many pieces of beef as will fit easily in one layer. Turn every 2 to 3 minutes, browning meat nicely on all sides. (Add a tablespoon or so more oil if needed.) As some pieces are browned, transfer to casserole and brown additional ones until all are done and transferred to casserole. Toss and turn the meat with the salt and pepper.

2. Assembling braising ingredients

1 lb. onions, sliced
2 large cloves garlic, mashed
¾ pt beef stock or bouillon (more if needed)
A medium herb bouquet tied in washed cheesecloth (1 bay leaf, 4
    parsley sprigs, and ½ tsp. thyme)
1 tomato, peeled, seeded, and roughly chopped
Optional, but desirable for sauce consistency: 1 or 2 chopped or sawed
    veal knuckle bones or beef marrow bones, and/or an 8-in. square of
    blanched pork rind (Volume I, page 434)
¾ pt full-bodied, young, red wine (such as Mâcon or Beaujolais)

If fat in frying pan has burned and blackened, discard it and pour ⅛ inch of oil into pan. Add onions and cook over moderate heat, stirring occasionally, for 8 to 10 minutes or until fairly tender and beginning to brown lightly. Meanwhile add to the meat in the casserole the garlic, bouillon, herbs, tomato, and optional ingredients. When the onions are done, stir them in. To deglaze frying pan, pour in the wine, scraping around with a wooden spoon to dislodge all cooking juices. Finally, pour wine into casserole, adding a little more (or more stock), if necessary, so ingredients are just covered.

(†) Recipe may be done a day or two in advance to this point. When cold, cover and refrigerate.

3. Braising

Bring stew to simmer on top of stove, cover casserole, and either maintain at slow simmer on top of stove or place in lower-middle level of preheated 350°F., Mark 4 oven; regulate heat so that stew simmers slowly throughout cooking. Turn and baste the meat occasionally. Stew is done when you can pierce the beef quite easily with a knife; slice into it and sample several pieces if you have any doubts.

Timing: Note that aged prime beef will cook faster than other grades, regardless of cut.

Round, rump, topside: 1½ to 2½ hours.

Thick flank, silverside, shoulder blade, chuck, short ribs: 2 to 3 hours.

Shin, and other gelatinous cuts with muscle separation and gristle: 3 to 4 hours.

4. Sauce

A 4- to 5-pt saucepan
4 tbl. flour
1½ oz. soft butter in a 2-pt bowl
A rubber spatula
A wire whisk

Set cover askew and pour cooking liquid out of casserole into saucepan. Discard herb bouquet and bones from casserole. With a large spoon, skim as much surface fat as you can from liquid, then bring to the simmer, skimming, to remove more fat.

Taste carefully for strength and seasoning; if weak, boil down rapidly to concentrate flavour, adding, if you think it necessary, a little tomato paste, another clove of mashed garlic, more herbs, salt, and pepper. When you are satisfied, remove from heat; you should have about 1 pint of rich and delicious liquid that must now be thickened into a sauce with *beurre manié*. To do so, blend flour and butter to a smooth paste with rubber spatula; beat vigorously into hot liquid with wire whisk. When perfectly smooth, bring liquid to the simmer, stirring with wire whisk, and simmer 2 minutes. Sauce should be thick enough to coat a spoon, meaning it will coat the meat nicely. If too thin, add half as much again *beurre manié*; if too thick, stir in stock or bouillon. Fold the sauce into the meat in the casserole.

(†) If you are not serving immediately, set cover askew and keep warm in a very low oven, over simmering water, or on a hot-plate. For serving several hours or several days later, let cool; lay plastic wrap over surface, cover, and refrigerate (or wrap airtight and freeze for several weeks).

5. Serving

If needed: a warm lightly buttered platter
Parsley sprigs, watercress, or whatever vegetables you wish to use as a
    garnish

If stew is warm, bring to the simmer again before serving. If it has been chilled, it should simmer 5 to 10 minutes after it has either warmed through slowly on top of the stove or been about 30 minutes in a 350°F., Mark 4 oven. Taste carefully again for seasoning and if sauce has thickened too much, fold in a little stock or bouillon. Serve either from casserole or turn out on to platter; decorate with greenery or vegetables.

Bœuf au Pistou

[Beef Stew with a Herb, Cheese, and Garlic Finish]

This delicious enrichment comes at the very end, after the sauce has been thickened and just before you are ready to serve the beef. The fresh garlic, herbs, cheese, and a bit of tomato will pep up any stew, and is particularly useful for left-overs and tinned or frozen mixtures.

To be added just before serving the stew, step 5.

2 large cloves garlic; a garlic press
A small bowl or mortar
A pestle or wooden spoon
A dozen large leaves of fresh minced basil, or 1 tsp. dried basil or
    oregano
1 oz. freshly grated imported Parmesan cheese
3 tbl. tomato paste
4 dashes Tabasco sauce

Purée garlic through press into bowl. With pestle or wooden spoon, mash it to a paste, then mash with the herbs. Stir in the cheese, tomato paste, and Tabasco. Cover and set aside until you are ready to serve. Stir the *pistou* into finished stew, basting meat with sauce to blend it thoroughly with the *pistou*.

Bœuf à la Provençale
[Beef Stew with Garlic and Anchovy Finish]

The mixture of anchovies, capers, garlic, and parsley described in Volume I, pages 352–3, is an alternate enrichment. Add it as directed for the *pistou* in the preceding recipe.

Bœuf en Pipérade
[Beef Stew with a Garnish of Peppers and Tomatoes]

Another enlivening finish to a stew is the *pipérade*, a fresh sauté of green peppers, tomatoes, garlic, and herbs.

To be added just before serving the *bœuf aux oignons*, master recipe, step 5, page 217.

2 medium-sized green bell peppers, seeded and diced
2 to 3 tbl. olive oil or cooking oil in a frying pan
3 or 4 firm, fresh, ripe tomatoes, peeled, seeded, juiced, and diced
2 large cloves of garlic, mashed or minced
A cover for the pan
Salt and pepper to taste
8 large fresh basil leaves, minced, or ½ tsp. dried basil or oregano and
    3 tbl. fresh minced parsley

Sauté the diced peppers in the oil over moderately low heat for 5 to 6 minutes, or until almost tender. Fold in the diced tomato pulp and garlic; cover pan and cook slowly for several minutes until tomatoes have rendered their juice. Raise heat and toss vegetables for several minutes over high heat to evaporate almost all liquid. Fold in salt and pepper to taste, and the herbs. Set aside until stew is finished. When reheating stew for serving, fold the *pipérade* into the stew, and simmer 5 minutes to blend flavours.

Bœuf aux Olives
[Beef Stew with Olives and Potatoes]

Olives give a very Mediterranean touch and subtle flavour to anything they cook with, and potatoes make the stew practically a one-dish meal. Any of the three preceding garnishes – peppers, anchovies, or *pistou* – may be included as well, if you wish.

To be added near the end of the braising period, when beef has about ½ hour more to cook (master recipe for *bœuf aux oignons*, step 3, page 216).

1. Preparing the olives and potatoes

2 oz. each: small, stoned green olives, and black, Mediterranean-type olives, stoned
1½ pts of water in a saucepan

To remove excess salt and too strong a taste, simmer the olives for 10 minutes; drain. If black olives are still too strong for your taste, simmer them separately 10 minutes more. Leave olives whole if small (¾ inch long), quarter lengthwise if larger.

2½ to 3 lb. potatoes all of a size, about 3 ins. long
A bowl of cold water

Peel potatoes, halve lengthwise, and trim into the shape of large garlic cloves about 2½ inches long and 1½ inches at their thickest, making 3 or 4 pieces per person. Reserve in cold water.

2. Adding olives and potatoes to stew

A saucepan of salted water for the potatoes
The *bœuf aux oignons*, braised until almost tender, step 3, page 216
A round of waxed paper or of aluminium foil

A few minutes before they are to be added to the stew, drain the potatoes and place in a saucepan of cold water; bring rapidly to the boil, and boil 1 minute. Drain. Meanwhile, skim accumulated fat off top of stew, remove from casserole any bones, rind, or other extraneous matter, including herb bouquet, and carefully correct seasoning of cooking liquid. Stir in the olives. Spread the potatoes over the top of the stew, press them down into the cooking liquid, and baste with the liquid. Bring stew again to simmer on top of stove, lay paper or foil over potatoes, cover casserole again, and maintain at simmer for about 30 minutes, or until potatoes are tender, basting them once or twice with the cooking liquid.

3. Finishing the stew

Optional but attractive: one of the 3 garnishes in the preceding recipes (*pistou* especially)
Beurre manié if needed: 2 tbl. flour blended to a paste with ¾ oz. soft butter
If you wish: a hot, buttered platter
Parsley sprigs or minced fresh parsley

You may find that the cooking liquid is sufficiently degreased and sufficiently thickened so that you can serve the stew as it is. Otherwise, set cover askew and drain cooking liquid into a saucepan; skim off fat, and correct seasoning. If liquid is lightly thickened and you are using the *pistou*, which will thicken it a little more, simply blend the *pistou* into the cooking liquid and pour back into the casserole. If liquid is thin, beat in the *beurre manié*, bring to the boil, mix in the *pistou* or other garnish if you are using one, and pour back into casserole. Reheat the stew just before serving, and bring to the table either in its casserole or arranged on a platter and decorated with herbs.

Bœuf au Gingembre
[Beef Stew Flavoured with Ginger, Capers, and Herbs]
Ginger gives an especially attractive and unusual flavour to beef, and this dish has rather Chinese overtones of sweet and sour. Because of the special flavours, including vinegar, the usual red wine of the beef stew is omitted in this recipe.

Complete master recipe for *bœuf aux oignons*, through step 2, page 215, but omit the red wine; substitute ¾ pint stock or bouillon and the following ingredients.

2 oz. *pain d'épices* (page 627), gingerbread, or gingersnaps
1½ tbl. fresh ginger, grated, or 2 tsp. powdered ginger
2 tbl. capers
3 tbl. wine vinegar
2 tbl. fresh tarragon or basil, or 1 tsp. dried herbs
¾ pt of the bouillon called for in the master recipe
An electric blender

Purée the bread or gingersnaps, ginger, capers, vinegar, herbs, and half of the bouillon in the blender. Pour mixture into casserole of beef, rinse out blender jar with more bouillon, pour into casserole, and proceed with recipe.

Note: When beef is tender, at end of step 3, and you have drained out, skimmed, boiled down, and seasoned the cooking liquid as directed in the next step, you will probably find that it has thickened enough so that you need do nothing more to it.

STUFFED BEEF ROLLS

Thin slices of beef rolled around a stuffing and braised in wine (*paupiettes de bœuf* or *roulades*) is only a more elaborate way of presenting the familiar beef stew. *Paupiettes* with a pork and veal stuffing and mustard sauce appear in Volume I on page 346, an excellent recipe. The first one here is a gaint *paupiette de Gargantua*, serving 6 people, while variations are for individual rolls. Stuffings include a Provençal mixture of greens, onions, pork, and ham, an olive mixture, a pepper mixture, and a final combination of rice, garlic, and herbs.

BEEF CUTS FOR *PAUPIETTES*

Look for solid pieces of meat that will make large, thin, cross-grain slices with no muscle separations. Avoid cuts like brisket, which tend to fall into long, loose fibres after cooking. Top-side (*tende de tranche, noix*) is our first choice, and a cut from the upper-middle portion will give perfect slices 10 to 12 inches across by 5 to 7 inches. Rump (*rumsteck*) works nicely, of course, but it is a waste to spend the extra money for rump when topside is equally good. Bottom round or silverside (*gîte à la noix*) is a little grainier than topside, but a satisfactory alternative. Clod (shoulder arm) (*macreuse*) is fourth choice only because of the gristle running through part of the slice, but you can clip the gristle in several places so that it will not draw the meat out of shape.

*La Paupiette de Gargantua
[Giant Stuffed Beef Roll]

Rather than making a number of individual *paupiettes*, this recipe rolls them all into one, and, because the stuffing is green, you need no green vegetable garnish. You could accompany the *paupiette* with grilled tomatoes, sautéed mushrooms, and glazed carrots, or with braised lettuce or endives and sautéed potatoes. Another suggestion is one of the unusual purées starting on page 530, pumpkin and white beans, rice and turnips with garlic, or swedes. A full red wine is called for, as in all beef dishes; Burgundy, Moulin-à-Vent, Côtes-du-Rhône.

[*For 6 people*]

1. Preparing the meat

A 2- to 2½-lb. slice of topside of beef approximately 12 by 6 ins. and ¾ to 1 in. thick (other choices on pages 213–14)
3 tbl. strong Dijon-type prepared mustard
½ tsp. mixed herbs such as thyme and bay leaf

Trim outside fat and gristle off meat. You are now to cut the slice of beef so that you can open it up like a book, making 2 flaps of meat hinged together at one side. To do so, lay it flat on table and start at one of the long sides with a long, very sharp knife; slice through centre of meat, parallel to table, ending ½ inch from other long side. Open up the meat, spread mustard and herbs on inside surface, and set aside while preparing stuffing, next step.

2. Green stuffing with pork, ham, and onions

2 large onions, minced
2 tbl. tendered pork fat or cooking oil
An 8-in. enamelled or non-stick frying pan

Cook the onions with the fat or oil in the pan over moderately low heat until tender but not browned.

About ½ lb. greens (kale, turnip, or spinach, fresh or frozen)
A large stainless-steel knife
A 5-pt mixing bowl (or heavy-duty electric mixer)
1 egg
1 tsp. salt
½ tsp. *épices fines* (page 385), or mixture of allspice, thyme, and bay leaf
¼ tsp. pepper
1 large clove garlic, mashed
1 oz. dry crumbs from a white loaf
6 oz. diced boiled ham
4 oz. fresh sausage meat

If greens are fresh, pick them over to remove stems; drop leaves into a large pan of boiling, salted water, and boil until wilted and fairly tender (2–3 minutes for spinach, more for the others). If frozen, boil for sufficient time in a covered pan with ¼ pint salted water until defrosted and fairly tender. Drain cooked greens, refresh in cold water, squeeze out as much water as possible, and chop fine. Then add greens to onions, and stir over moderate heat for several minutes to evaporate moisture and to finish cooking. Scrape greens and onions into mixing bowl and vigorously beat in the rest of the ingredients listed. Sauté a spoonful, taste, and correct seasoning.

3. Assembling the *paupiette*

Either: a 14-in. square of caul fat, page 384;
Or: a 12- by 8-in. sheet of pork fat ¼ in. thick;
Or: 6 to 8 strips of thick bacon or salt pork, and a 12- by 6-in. piece of
  beef suet ¼ in. thick
White kitchen string

(If using salt pork or bacon, blanch 10 minutes in 3 pints of water, and pat dry.) Spread the stuffing over the meat, leaving an inch border of clear meat all around. Starting at one long side, roll the meat rather loosely around the stuffing, making a sausage shape about 4 inches in diameter. Fold over the two ends. If you have caul fat, roll the meat in a double thickness of it; tie lengthwise and in several places around the circumference. Otherwise, place strips of pork fat, bacon, or salt pork over length, particularly the seam, and the ends; tie in place, and reserve remaining pieces of fat for later.

4. Browning the *paupiette*: preheat oven to 450°F., Mark 8

Pork fat or cooking oil
A heavy casserole, preferably oval, and just large enough to hold the meat
A medium onion, roughly sliced
A medium carrot, roughly sliced

(The *paupiette* is soft and must be handled carefully to prevent stuffing from bursting out; it will stiffen after browning.) Pat meat gently with paper towels to dry it. Film casserole with ⅛ inch of fat or oil, and place meat seam-side up in casserole. Strew vegetables around meat. Brown over moderate heat, loosening bottom of meat carefully with a spatula from time to time to prevent sticking. Baste top of meat with fat in pan and set uncovered in upper-middle level of oven to brown top and sides. Baste every 3 to 4 minutes with fat or oil for the 12 to 15 minutes it will take to brown. Remove casserole from oven.

5. Braising: 1½ to 2 hours; oven at 325°F., Mark 3

Salt, pepper, and more of the same herbs
½ pt dry white wine or dry white French vermouth
½ pt or more beef stock or bouillon
Aluminium foil and the casserole cover

Turn down oven to 325°F., Mark 3. Season the meat with salt, pepper, and herbs. Pour in the wine and enough stock or bouillon to come ½ to ⅔ the way up the meat. Bring to the simmer on top of the stove. If you are using it, drape suet over meat. Place foil on top, cover the casserole, and place in middle level of oven. Baste meat several times during cooking, and regulate oven heat so that liquid is only slowly simmering in casserole. *Paupiette* is done when a knife will pierce the meat easily.

Timing: 1½ to 2 hours for top-grade beef; as much as an hour more for other cuts and qualities.

(†) Meat may be either stuffed or browned in advance of braising. Braised meat may be kept warm in a very low oven for an hour or more. It may be cooled and reheated, but will not have quite the same delicious texture.

6. Sauce and serving

A hot serving platter
A sieve set over a saucepan
If needed: 1 tbl. of cornflour blended with 2 tbl. white wine, vermouth, or stock
1 oz. soft butter
A hot sauce bowl
Watercress, parsley, or whatever vegetables you wish, to garnish platter

Remove *paupiette* to hot platter, discard strings and fat, replace foil cover over meat, and keep warm in turned-off oven. Strain cooking liquid into saucepan, pressing juice out of braising ingredients. Skim off fat. You should have ½ to ¾ pint liquid slightly thickened by the braising ingredients and the crumbs in the stuffing. (If thin, remove from heat, beat in cornflour mixture, and simmer for 2 minutes.) Correct seasoning. Just before serving stir in butter, a half spoonful at a time, spoon a little sauce over meat, and pour rest into sauce bowl. Garnish platter with greenery or vegetables, and serve immediately.

Other stuffings, other garnishings

In addition to the green-pepper stuffing and the garlic and rice stuffing in the following variations, and the veal and pork stuffing on page 346 in Volume I, other possibilities are listed on pages 664–6. Rather than the braising and sauce-making system described here, you may follow that for the *daube* on page 229, or for the beef stews and their variations beginning on page 217, which include *pistou*, *pipérade*, and ginger flavourings.

VARIATION

The following recipe describes the procedure for making individual *paupiettes*. We have suggested large and luxurious slices of meat; the stuffing is spread over them, and the slice is rolled up like a rug. When you wish to be more economical, make twice the amount of stuffing, use beef slices half as large, and rather than rolling like a rug, fold the meat around the stuffing to enclose it, almost exactly as illustrated for the stuffed cabbage leaves on pages 504–5.

Paupiettes de Bœuf à la Catalane
[Beef Rolls Stuffed with Peppers, Onions, and Mustard Bread]

[*For 4* paupiettes, *1 per person*]

1. Preparing the beef for stuffing

4 slices of topside of beef 10 to 12 by 6 to 7 ins. and ⅜ in. thick (other
    choices, pages 213–14)
Waxed paper
A mallet or rolling pin
Salt and pepper
½ tsp. thyme or oregano

(If you cannot have the beef sliced to your order and have difficulty at home, you can freeze the piece of beef and slice when not quite stiffened, or when partially thawed. This will not harm the meat at all.) Trim off all outside fat and gristle. One by one, pound each slice between sheets of waxed paper with a mallet or rolling pin, to break down the fibres somewhat and to prevent meat from cooking out of shape. Lay out flat, season tops with salt, pepper, and herbs.

2. Green-pepper, onion, and mustard-bread stuffing

3 large onions, minced
1 tsp. mixed, ground thyme, bay leaf, and oregano, or mixed herbs
Olive oil or cooking oil as needed
A medium (10-in.) frying pan (non-stick recommended)
2 medium green peppers, diced
A mixing bowl
3 slices light rye bread

4 to 5 tbl. strong, Dijon-type prepared mustard
2 or 3 large cloves of garlic, mashed or minced
1 egg, lightly beaten
Salt and pepper

Cook the onions and herbs with 3 tablespoons of the oil in the frying pan for 8 to 10 minutes over moderate heat, stirring occasionally, until tender and starting to brown. Stir in the diced peppers and cook, stirring, 4 to 5 minutes more, until peppers are almost tender. Scoop into mixing bowl. Spread both sides of the bread with mustard, film frying pan with $\frac{1}{8}$ inch more oil, and brown bread lightly on both sides. Dice the bread and add to the bowl; stir in the garlic, egg, and salt and pepper to taste.

3. Stuffing the *paupiettes*
The seasoned beef slices
The stuffing
Toothpicks
Strips of fresh pork fat, blanched bacon, or suet (page 423)

Assuming that the beef slices are roughly rectangular in shape, choose the neatest of the small sides to be the exposed end of the roll. Divide stuffing in four, spread one part over each slice, leaving an inch of clear meat for the exposed end and $\frac{1}{2}$ inch at the sides. Roll the meat up to enclose the stuffing and secure with 2 or 3 toothpicks.

4. Browning, braising, and serving the *paupiettes*
Follow the ingredients and method in the master recipe, steps 4 through 6, starting on page 224.

OTHER STUFFINGS FOR *PAUPIETTES*

Farce Niçoise
[Olive and Pimento Stuffing with Garlic and Herbs]

[*For 4* paupiettes]

2 tbl. stale, not-too-fine crumbs from a white loaf
2 to 3 tbl. wine vinegar
Two $2\frac{1}{4}$-oz. tins ripe black olives, chopped

About 3 oz. tinned red pimentos, diced
2 large cloves of garlic, mashed or minced
½ tsp. sage
1½ oz. grated Parmesan cheese
Salt and pepper to taste
Drops of Tabasco sauce
2 oz. finely minced fresh pork fat or blanched bacon
4 tbl. strong, Dijon-type prepared mustard (to spread on *paupiettes*)

Stir the breadcrumbs in a small bowl with enough vinegar barely to moisten them; let sit for a few minutes. Stir the olives, pimentos, garlic, sage, and cheese in a mixing bowl. Blend in the moistened crumbs, and season strongly with salt, pepper, and Tabasco. Blend in the minced pork fat or bacon. Just before you are ready to stuff the *paupiettes*, spread the meat with mustard, then with the stuffing.

La Farce à l'Ail de Mme Cassiot
[Rice and Garlic Stuffing with Herbs]

This fine and very simple stuffing for garlic lovers may have either rice or rather coarse stale breadcrumbs for a base. If it is breadcrumbs, however, they must come from the type of bread that has texture and body, like your own French bread from page 89. Because the typical shop-bought, white, squashy bread disintegrates into mush, we have confined our recipe to rice. If you want crumbs and have the right sort, stir ¼ pint beef stock or bouillon into 6 ounces of stale crumbs; let sit 5 minutes, then squeeze crumbs as dry as possible in the corner of a towel.

[*For 4* paupiettes]

3 oz. cooked rice
6 oz. fresh pork fat or blanched bacon
6 to 8 large cloves of garlic, very finely minced
½ tsp. thyme or oregano
3 tbl. chopped fresh parsley
½ tsp. salt
⅛ tsp. pepper
4 tbl. strong, Dijon-type prepared mustard

Either put the rice and pork fat or bacon through the coarse blade of a meat grinder, or put rice through a food mill and finely mince the fat or bacon. Stir together in a bowl with the garlic, herbs, salt and pepper. Just before you are ready to stuff *paupiettes*, spread top of each slice with mustard, then with the stuffing.

*Bœuf en Daube à la Provençale
[Braised Pot Roast of Beef with Wine, Tomatoes, and Provençal Flavourings]

This is a large, whole piece of braising beef larded with strips of ham, marinated in red wine and herbs, and slowly simmered in a lightly thickened mixture of the marinade liquid, beef stock, and tomatoes, which turns into a rich ready-made sauce at the end of the cooking. It is a splendid braising method, and one you can adapt to stews as well as pot roasts, and to duck, goose, lamb, livers, and hearts as well as to beef. Rather than the usual potatoes or pasta and buttered peas or beans, or glazed carrots and onions, and sautéed mushrooms, you could serve the little white turnips sautéed in butter on page 534, or the onions stuffed with rice on page 494, and either the broccoli braised in butter on page 450 or one of the sautéed courgettes starting on page 479. A full-bodied red wine is definitely called for here – a Burgundy, a Côtes-du-Rhône, or a Châteauneuf-du-Pape.

TIMING NOTES

Braised beef may be made ready for cooking a day ahead or may be fully cooked a day or two in advance, if need be. Allow yourself enough leeway for the actual braising, however, if you wish to serve soon after it has cooked. Unless you are sure of your meat quality, allow 5 hours from the moment you put it into the oven to the moment you wish to serve. This will give you extra time for tough meat, and leisure for the details of trimming and sauce making.

BEEF CUTS FOR BRAISING WHOLE

Topside, *tende de tranche*. This is a first-choice piece for braising whole because it is solid meat with no separations, and is not fibrous when cooked.

Undercut chuck, *basses côtes découvertes*. The continuation of the roast rib of beef section into the shoulder end, usually ribs 2 to 5, makes a choice and tender morsel. A boneless chuck pot roast can substitute for it.

Bottom round or silverside, *gîte à la noix*. This cut always looks attractive, although somewhat fibrous when cooked.

Thick flank, *tranche grasse*. This cut from the round has numerous muscle separations. It braises well, but needs firm tying to give it an attractive shape.

Middle of brisket, *milieu de poitrine*. Although coarse-grained when cooked, brisket has excellent flavour; slice it on the bias like flank steak. A good butcher will bone and de-fat it for you; if it is a long, flat piece, roll and tie it for braising.

[*For 8 to 10 people*]

1. Preparing the beef

A trimmed and boned 6-lb. piece of braising beef from preceding list (preferably one that can be tied into a cylindrical shape 10 to 12 ins. long)

For optional larding of meat: a 4- by 6-in. slice of prosciutto or ready-to-cook ham slice about $\frac{1}{4}$ in. thick

Trim meat, if necessary, to make a fairly even cylinder or rectangle with no loose fat or gristly pieces. To lard the meat, follow directions illustrated on pages 240–42, using ham rather than the pork fat called for in the larding directions. Whether or not you have larded it, tie the beef, also as illustrated there, to keep it in shape during cooking.

2. Marinating the meat: at least 12 hours or for several days

Note: You may omit this step and proceed directly to step 3.

1 bottle full, strong, young, red wine (Mâcon, Beaujolais)
6 tbl. red-wine vinegar
3 tbl. olive oil

6 cloves unpeeled garlic, halved
2 medium-sized onions and 2 carrots, sliced
1 tbl. coarse salt or table salt
The following herb bouquet, tied in washed cheesecloth: 2 bay leaves,
    4 cloves or allspice berries, 6 peppercorns, ½ tsp. each of dried fennel
    seeds, oregano, thyme, and marjoram
An enamelled, glazed, or stainless bowl or casserole just large enough
    to hold meat comfortably

Mix the marinade ingredients in the bowl or casserole, add the beef and baste it. (Liquid should come at least halfway up.) Marinate, turning and basting meat several times a day, for at least 12 hours or for several days either at a temperature of 40 to 50°F. or in the refrigerator. When you are ready for the next step, drain beef, and wipe thoroughly dry with paper towels. Strain marinade, reserving both liquid and vegetables for step 5.

3. Browning the beef and the braising ingredients

Note: If you have not marinated the beef, add all the ingredients from step 2, except the vinegar, to the ingredients here.

Either: 4 tbl. rendered fresh pork fat or goose fat;
Or: olive oil or cooking oil
6 oz. *lardons* (1½-in. sticks of blanched bacon ¼ in. thick, page 213)
A heavy, covered casserole or roaster large enough to hold meat
    comfortably (or brown meat in a large frying pan and transfer to
    roaster afterwards)
For added flavour and body: 1 or 2 sawed veal knuckle bones and/or
    beef soup bones; or a split and blanched calf's foot
The drained marinade vegetables
The marinade liquid
A strip of fresh pork fat ⅛ in. thick and long and wide enough to cover
    top and sides of beef; or beef suet
White string
The marinade bouquet of herbs
Optional but desirable for the sauce: a 6-in. square of blanched pork
    rind (Volume I, page 434)

Cook the *lardons* slowly in the fat or oil in the casserole (or frying pan) until very lightly browned. Remove with a slotted spoon and reserve. Pour 4 to 5 tablespoons of fat out of the casserole and reserve for the *roux*, next step. Raise heat to moderately high and brown the well-dried beef on all sides and ends, lifting and turning it with the help of its trussing strings. (This will take 10 minutes or more; regulate heat so meat browns nicely but fat does not burn. Add more fat or oil if needed.) Remove beef and brown the optional bones or calf's foot and the marinade vegetables for 4 to 5 minutes, stirring and tossing over high heat. Set cover askew on casserole, drain out cooking fat, and pour in marinade liquid. Stir with wooden spoon to dislodge all coagulated bits of brown flavour into liquid. Tie strip of fat about beef (illustrations are on page 246), push bones aside, and lay the beef, fat-covered side up, in casserole. Add the bouquet of herbs, the *lardons*, and the optional pork rind to the casserole, and set aside until you are ready to braise, step 5.

4. The brown *roux* to thicken the braising sauce

A heavy-bottomed saucepan, in thick, cast aluminium or a heavy
   cast-iron frying pan, about 6 in. bottom diameter
The 4 tbl. reserved fat from step 3
5 tbl. flour
A wooden spoon
½ pt beef stock (or bouillon) heated in a small saucepan
A wire whisk
A ladle

Note: You will have a better *roux* if you cook it separately rather than in the casserole after browning meat and bones.

Be sure to pick a heavy pan; melt the fat in it over moderate heat, blend in the flour, and stir continuously for about 15 minutes until flour slowly turns a dark, nutty brown. (It must not blacken, burn, and turn bitter, but it must brown properly so as to give the right flavour and colour to the sauce.) Remove from heat, and when *roux* has stopped bubbling, blend in all the hot stock at once with wire whisk. When perfectly smooth, ladle in some of the liquid from the casserole to thin the sauce, mix well, then stir all into the casserole, blending liquids thoroughly together.

5. Braising the beef: 3½ to 4 hours or longer at 350°F., Mark 4

1 lb. (4 to 5 medium) tomatoes, not peeled, but halved, seeded, juiced, and roughly chopped (or a mixture of fresh tomatoes and strained tinned tomatoes)

A 3- by 1-in. piece of dried orange peel, or 1 tsp. dried pulverized orange peel

Optional Provençal flavouring: 6 to 7 anchovies packed in olive oil, drained, and mashed to a paste

More beef stock if needed

Stir the tomatoes, orange peel, and optional anchovies into the casserole, and more stock, if needed, so that liquid comes ⅔ to ¾ the way up the beef.

(†) May be prepared in advance to this point; when cool, cover and refrigerate.

Salt to taste
Aluminium foil

Bring to simmer on top of the stove; salt lightly to taste if necessary. Lay the foil over the beef, cover the casserole, and set in lower third of preheated, 350°F., Mark 4 oven.

In about half an hour, check to see that liquid is simmering slowly, not bubbling fast: regulate oven throughout cooking so that liquid remains at a slow but definite simmer. Baste and turn the beef several times during cooking.

Beef is done when a fork pierces it easily, but it must not be cooked so long that it begins to fall apart. Aged, top-quality beef usually takes 3½ hours; other grades or qualities may take an hour or so longer.

6. Trimming the beef and finishing the sauce

Remove beef from casserole to a board or platter. Cut and discard trussing string, discard fat covering beef (or trim off suet adhering to beef and the gristle under it); trim off any loose bits of meat.

Remove bones from casserole, then pour contents of casserole through a sieve set over a large saucepan; press juices out of ingredients and into saucepan with a wooden spoon.

Discard contents of sieve. Let liquid settle a few minutes in saucepan, then skim off all surface fat with a spoon; bring liquid back to the simmer, skimming off additional fat. Taste very carefully for seasoning and strength. You should have about 2 pints of richly fragrant sauce, deep reddish brown, and the consistency of a lightly thickened soup that would coat the meat nicely, and coats the spoon. If you feel sauce should be thicker or lacks depth of flavour, boil it down rapidly to concentrate it. If it seems necessary, add and simmer a pinch of herbs, garlic, or tomato paste or a little concentrated bouillon. (If sauce has reduced too much during braising, thin out with more stock or water.)

(†) You may complete recipe to this point; return beef to casserole and pour the sauce over it. Cover and keep warm, basting occasionally, in a very low oven or upon 2 asbestos mats over low heat on top of the stove. For serving several hours or 2 days later, let cool, then cover and refrigerate; reheat for $\frac{1}{2}$ an hour or so, basting and turning meat several times, in a 325°F., Mark 3 oven.

7. Serving

(a) Carving at the table: Place the meat on a warm platter, spoon a little of the hot sauce over it to glaze its surface. Decorate platter with sprigs of parsley or watercress. Pass separately the rest of the sauce and whatever vegetables you are serving.

(b) Serving the meat sliced, on a platter: Carve the meat in the kitchen and arrange in overlapping slices on a warm, slightly buttered platter. Spoon some of the sauce around the meat, and decorate platter with parsley or watercress, or with whatever vegetable garnish you wish. Pass rest of sauce and other vegetables separately.

Left-overs

Left-overs, whether sliced or not, may be reheated in the sauce, if any is left over, or in another sauce with the same flavourings. See also the *tous nus* on page 407, and the list of stuffings on pages 664–6, both calling for minced left-over braised beef.

To serve cold

A delicious *salade de bœuf à la parisienne* is made with cold braised beef in Volume I, page 580, or an aspic, *bœuf mode en gelée*, again in Volume I, on page 594.

Bœuf en Caisse, Surprise
[Stuffed, Braised Pot Roast of Beef – Beef Case]

Like that present for the man who has everything, this is an enjoyable conceit for the cook who has cooked everything who wants to surprise guests who have eaten everything. A splendid piece of beef comes to the table looking like a typical *bœuf mode*. But no, it is not. When the host begins to serve, it is revealed that the beef was ingeniously hollowed out before braising, filled with a fragrant garniture of onions, mushrooms, olives, and herbs, and these slowly imparted their flavours to the meat while it cooked. You might accompany this with the purée of pumpkin and white beans, page 530, or the purée of rice and turnips with herbs and garlic on page 532. Either a plainly cooked green vegetable or grilled tiny tomatoes might also be included, and the red wine choices would again be Burgundy, Côtes-du-Rhône, or Châteauneuf-du-Pape.

[*For 8 to 10 people*]

1. Forming the beef case

A solid, boneless 6- to 7-lb. piece of braising beef, preferably loaf
  shaped (topside, rump, or bottom round)

Trim all fat and gristle from outside of meat and cut off any protruding pieces, to make a neat shape. (The loaf shape illustrated is easiest to stuff and to carve, but a thick wedge will do.)

White string
Rendered pork fat, goose fat, or cooking oil
A heavy, 12-in. frying pan (non-stick recommended)

Meat is now to be browned, because it is easier to do so now than later; dry thoroughly in paper towels, and make several firm ties around its length and circumference, to hold its shape. Heat fat or oil in pan to very hot but not smoking, and brown meat on all sides and the two ends. Remove meat to a cutting board and discard trussing string. (If browning fat has burned, discard it, otherwise leave in pan for step 2.)

The first step is to make the cover: starting at one end of what you have decided is the top side of the beef, cut an even slice $\frac{1}{2}$ inch thick to within $\frac{1}{2}$ inch at the other end, where slice remains attached like the cover of a book.

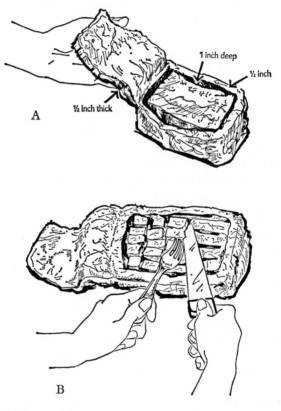

Bend the cover back. In the main body of the meat, cut a rectangular incision 1 inch deep and $\frac{1}{2}$ inch from outside edges (A). Make lengthwise and crosswise cuts 1 inch deep and about $\frac{3}{4}$ inch apart, to form cubes (B). Cut out cubes of meat with scissors (c) or with a knife. You now have a hinged case of beef with probably 2 inches of solid meat at the bottom, ½ inch at the sides, and an inch of hollow space underneath the cover.

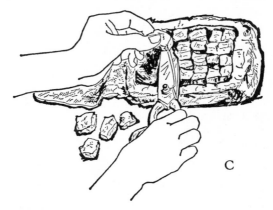

C

2. The mushroom and olive garniture or filling: for about 2 cups

The cubes of beef removed from the case
The frying pan from step 1, and more fat or oil as needed
A mixing bowl
6 oz. quartered fresh mushrooms, washed and dried
3 medium onions, sliced
1½ oz. mild-cured ham, cut into ¼-in. dice
1 to 2 large cloves garlic, mashed
4 medium-sized black, oil-cured olives, stoned and diced
½ tsp. thyme
1 egg
Pepper and salt

Cut the beef cubes so all are approximately ⅜ inch across; dry in paper towels. Heat fat or oil in pan until very hot but not smoking; rapidly brown beef cubes, tossing and turning them for several minutes, shaking and swirling the pan by its handle. When browned, scoop into bowl, leaving fat in pan. Add more fat or oil, if necessary, to film pan by 1/16 inch, and brown the mushrooms, tossing and turning for several minutes over high heat. Scoop into bowl; add the onions to the pan with a little more fat or oil if needed. Turn heat to low, stir up onions, cover pan, and cook slowly for 8 to 10 minutes until tender; raise heat, and stir for 2 to 3 minutes until onions are very lightly browned. Scoop into the mixing bowl, stirring in also the ham, garlic, diced olives, herbs, and egg. Season to taste, but be careful of salt because olives are salty.

3. Filling and tying the case

White string
Either: a sheet of pork fat ¼ in. thick and large enough to cover top and sides of beef (page 423);
Or: caul fat (page 384);
Or: well-washed cheesecloth

Sprinkle interior of beef case with salt and pepper, heap in the garniture, and turn the hinged cover down to enclose it (D). Make one or two loops of string around length of beef

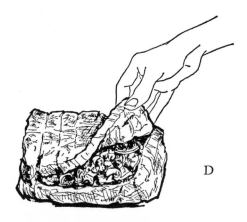

D

and enough around circumference to hold cover securely in place over garniture (E).

Either drape the fat over the beef and tie in place with string, or wrap and tie the entire case in caul fat or a double thickness of damp cheesecloth.

(†) May be completed to this point as much as a day in advance; wrap in plastic and refrigerate.

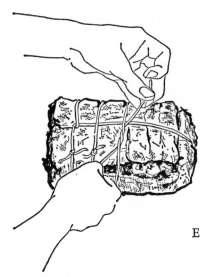

E

4. Braising the beef: 3 to 4 hours

Because the beef has already been browned, you need only follow the general method outlined for the preceding *daube* with its brown *roux*, pages 229–34, or the simpler braising method for the beef stew on page 214 with its *beurre-manié* sauce thickening.

5. Serving

Unless the beef is carved and served at the table, there will be no *surprise*. After removing strings and other extraneous matter, place beef on a hot platter, spoon a little of the sauce over it, and decorate platter with vegetables or parsley. To serve, pry cover loose and lift it, so that the garniture may be admired, then replace and cut straight through the meat as though it were a loaf of bread. Heap the garniture of mushrooms, olives, and beef cubes over each serving, and moisten with a big spoonful of sauce.

HOW TO LARD A PIECE OF MEAT

In the old days, when meat was tougher and far leaner than it is today, and when venison and game were plentiful, strips of pork fat were inserted through it to baste and moisten the interior of the meat during cooking. Now meat is larded more often because it is the stylish thing to do, and the bits of pork fat, ham, or whatever has been inserted make attractive designs when the meat is sliced.

Larding fat: pork fat and beef suet

The best fat to use is fresh pork fat back because it is hard and smooth. If you cannot find it, use blanched fat bacon or salt pork, or fat from the outside of a fresh pork loin. (If you do not wish to use pork fat, substitute suet from the outside of a rib or loin of beef.) Cut the fat into whatever length and width will fit your larding needle, making a test piece first to be sure you will have a snug fit; chill the fat for easy handling.

The larding process

In order to lard meat you must have a larding needle, or *lardoire*, a hollow tube or trough of steel shaped like a giant steel pen point with a wooden handle. Starting just back from the point, press the strip of fat down into the trough of the *lardoire* (A), being sure fat fits snugly so that it will not slip out when the *lardoire* is pushed through the meat.

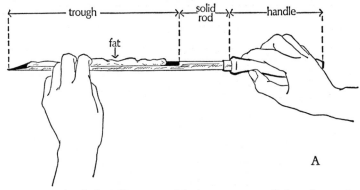

Meat is larded with strips of fat running parallel to the grain, so that when the meat is sliced you will cut across the strips of fat. Insert point of *lardoire* into one end of meat, and with a continuous, slow, clockwise rotation, push the instrument gradually through (B) until point of *lardoire* and $\frac{1}{2}$ inch of fat protrude from the other end of the meat. With the point of a small knife, gently dig end of fat-strip out of trough at

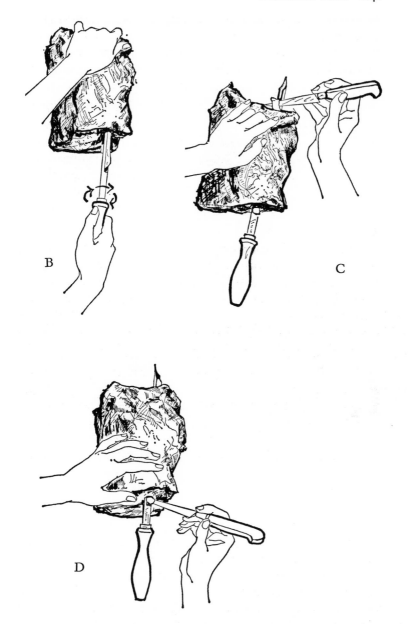

protruding end of *lardoire* (c). Then dig other end of fat-strip out of trough at the other end of the *lardoire* (D). Hold the thumb of your left hand in the trough of the *lardoire* against the fat-strip, thus preventing fat from slipping out of meat while you slowly, with a slight rocking rotation left and right, withdraw the *lardoire* from the meat leaving the fat in its place (E).

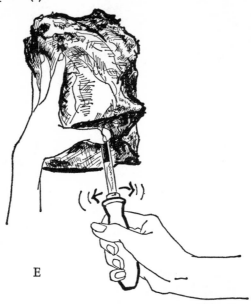

E

Insert as many other fat-strips as you wish – a piece of meat $4\frac{1}{2}$ to 5 inches in diameter will take 4 to 6. Tie the meat into shape with strong white string (F).

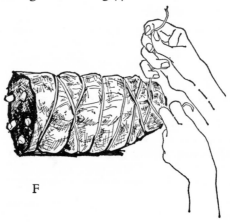

F

Whole Fillet of Beef · *Filet de Bœuf*

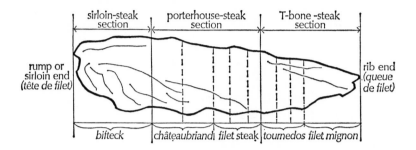

The central and the right-hand sections, in this drawing, constitute what is usually meant in British butchers' shops by a
whole fillet. To be technically correct, it should be called the
whole short-loin fillet. It weighs $4\frac{1}{2}$ to 5 pounds untrimmed,
and contains $3\frac{1}{2}$ to 4 pounds of usable meat. When you are
serving 6 to 8 people, you may wish the central section only,
le cœur du filet, which will give you a roast of $2\frac{1}{2}$ to 3 pounds
that averages 8 to 10 inches in length. For 10 to 12 people
you will need the whole piece, and may fold the last 2 inches
of the tail (right-hand side) back upon itself as illustrated
further on, to make a 12-inch roast that is $3\frac{1}{2}$ to 4 inches in
diameter when tied.

If by chance your butcher does cut whole sides of beef, you
may be able to buy the whole fillet with butt end attached.
Depending on the cutting method, the butt alone contains
only a little over $1\frac{1}{2}$ pounds of usable meat, although it weighs
slightly more than 3 pounds; to be deprived of it, therefore,
is no great loss, fillets costing what they do.

TRIMMING A FILLET

Most butchers will usually trim, tie, and lard the fillet for
you, but you should be able to do it yourself so that you will
know how the meat is constructed.

When you have an untrimmed fillet in front of you, you will note a definite difference in the two long, flat sides. On one there is a series of thick ridges and depressions more or less marbled with fat depending on the grade of the beef carcass; this side is where the fillet rested against the 6 vertebrae of the backbone in the small of the back. We shall call this the underside. The other side, which we shall call the top, will have some loose fat clinging to it, mostly at the large end and at the edges; along the central length you will see the main muscle of the fillet, covered with a shiny membrane. Starting on this side, rather gingerly pull the loose fat from the top of the membrane and along the edges, being very careful not to detach the two long straps of meat lying against each side of the main muscle. The smaller of the two straps is flattish, as though it were a flaplike continuation of the underside; underneath the larger of the straps, *la chaînette*, is a line of fat that should not be disturbed because it attaches the meat to the main muscle.

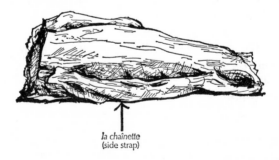

la chaînette
(side strap)

This is the whole short-loin fillet (central and right-hand portions of drawing on page 243), showing the 2 chains of meat attached to the length of the main muscle. Do not worry too much if you partially detach them; you are going to tie the meat anyway before roasting, and the ties will make the chains adhere. Although some people advise removing these chains of meat, you will diminish your roast by more than half its weight if you do so: you will end up with two thin strings of meat good only for sautéing or skewering, and your *filet* proper will weigh only 2 pounds. This is entirely a matter of your own preference, of course; we leave them on.

After pulling excess fat from the top of the meat, you must also remove the shiny membrane that covers the main muscle on this side, and as much of it on the large chain of meat as you easily can. Remove the membrane in half-inch strips the length of the meat, scraping under it with a small, sharp knife. (If you happen to have an actual whole fillet with butt included, you will notice that the main muscle with its membrane continues into the butt for several inches before it loses itself. You may wish to separate this main muscle from the rest, making it a continuation of your roast. The surrounding meat will make excellent steaks or sautés. It is rather a question of how it looks to you while you are trimming: as long as all the membranes are removed, all of the meat is good either for roasting or sautéing.)

Finally, inspect the underside of the meat and remove what you consider to be obviously excess fat; a reasonable amount left on will help to baste the meat as it roasts. Meat is now trimmed and ready for cooking. The following directions are for roasting; directions for steaks are in Volume I, pages 316 and 322–6. Do not forget the sautés of beef, Volume I, pages 353–6, which are delicious for meat from the butt, the chains, and the tail; you may also adapt sautés for any leftover cooked fillet.

TYING AND LARDING THE FILLET

Whether it is roasted or braised, and whether you are using the heart (central section, page 243) or the whole fillet, the circumference must be tied to keep the meat together and to force it into cylindrical rather than oval shape for even cooking. Use the rather thick, soft, white butcher's string, often called corned-beef twine, if you can find it. The top of the meat is the side formerly covered by a shiny membrane, as opposed to the ridged side, which rested against the backbone. When you are roasting the whole fillet, turn the last 2 inches of the tail back under its ridged side (A) to make the roast even in diameter throughout its length.

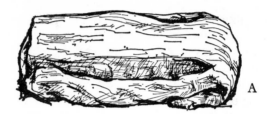

A

When you wish to tie the meat without larding it, tie or wind firm loops of string around the circumference at 1¼-inch intervals (B). To lard and tie the meat, drape pork fat or suet

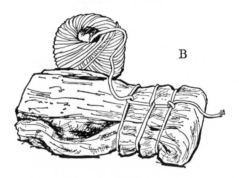

B

over the top of the meat and down under the folded tail to hold it in place. Tie a loop of string around the length of the meat (c). (If you do not have long strips of fat, overlap short ones as shown in the illustrations.) Then arrange strips of fat over the sides of the meat; tie loops of string around the circumference (D).

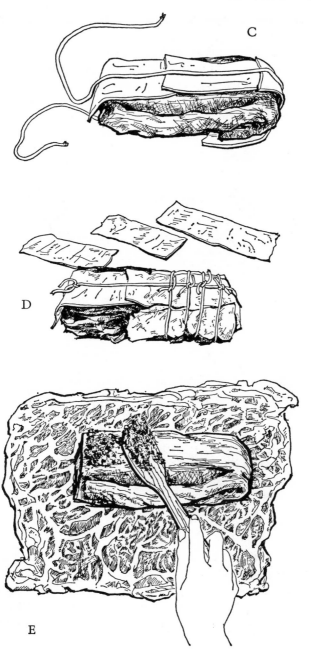

C

D

E

If you can find or order caul fat, that marvellous membrane webbed with fat that comes from inside the pig, it is perfect for wrapping a fillet that is roasted with a covering of mushroom *duxelles* or *mirepoix*, or for the sliced, stuffed fillet on page 253. Here (E) the fillet is laid on the caul fat and the flavouring is being spread over it. Fold a double thickness of caul fat around the meat to enclose it completely, and tie in place (F). The caul fat browns and tends to merge with the meat and stuffing.

F

*Filet de Bœuf Poêlé
[Fillet of Beef, Casserole-roasted with Aromatic Vegetables]

A favourite roasting method that comes to us from the old classic cuisine is *poêlage*, meaning to brown the meat and then roast it in a covered casserole with *les aromates*. This is particularly successful with beef fillet because the aromatic ingredients, even though their contact with the meat is brief, subtly enhance its flavour and aroma. In addition, you have a deliciously flavoured base for the sauce. Because internal meat temperature rises very quickly when beef is done in a covered roaster, watch it carefully after your meat thermometer reaches 110°F. (Make a guess if your thermometer starts at 130°F.)

Suggested accompaniments: a garnish of watercress and sautéed mushrooms around the meat, and *endives à la dauphinoise* (*gratin* of chicory and sliced potatoes, page 510); a Mèdoc or other claret.

[*For 10 to 12 people*]

1. Preliminaries to roasting

A fillet of beef, 3½ to 4 lb., trimmed and tied (pages 243–8)
Olive oil or cooking oil
A heavy 12-in. frying pan (an oval 'fish fryer' is ideal for this)
Salt and pepper
A heavy, oval, flameproof casserole just large enough to hold beef
  (such as 12 by 9 ins.)
1 medium onion, sliced
1 medium carrot, sliced
1 bay leaf, broken
½ tsp. thyme
A piece of fresh pork fat or suet 12 by 9 ins. and ¼ in. thick
1 pt veal stock or beef bouillon
A cover for the casserole

Dry the beef thoroughly on paper towels. Film the pan with
⅛ inch of oil and set over moderately high heat. When very
hot but not smoking, brown beef lightly on all sides, season
with salt and pepper, and place in casserole. Brown the
vegetables lightly in the same fat, season, stir in the herbs, and
strew the vegetables over, under, and around the beef. Drape
the fat over the meat. Spoon oil out of frying pan, pour in
bouillon and boil for a moment, scraping up any coagulated
cooking juices. Pour liquid into a cup and reserve for step 3.

2. Roasting the beef: 35 to 45 minutes in a preheated 375°F., Mark 5 oven

At least an hour before serving, cover casserole and set over
moderately high heat until beef is sizzling, then place in
middle level of a preheated oven. Turn and baste beef once in
15 minutes, and rearrange fat on top. Meat is done to very
rare at 125°F. on a meat thermometer and to medium rare
at 130°F.; juices will run rosy red when meat is pricked, and
roast will feel slightly springy rather than squashy (like raw
beef) when pressed. Set beef on a warm platter and leave at
room temperature for 10 to 15 minutes while finishing sauce.

3. Sauce

Optional: 1 medium tomato
The bouillon from step 1

½ tbl. cornflour blended in a cup with 3 tbl. dry port wine or vermouth
Salt and pepper to taste
1 to 1½ oz. soft butter
A hot sauce boat

Tip casserole and skim most of fat off cooking juices; bring to the boil. Chop optional tomato and add to casserole along with the bouillon. Boil slowly for 4 to 5 minutes to concentrate flavour. Remove from heat, stir in cornflour and wine mixture, and bring to the simmer. Simmer 2 to 3 minutes until sauce turns from cloudy to clear. Carefully correct seasoning. Just before serving, remove from heat and beat in the butter, a tablespoon at a time. Strain into sauce boat, pressing juices out of vegetables.

4. Serving

Cut and discard trussing strings, and arrange beef on hot platter with whatever vegetables or garnish you have chosen. Pour several spoonfuls of sauce over the beef to glaze it, and serve at once. (If beef is to be carved in the kitchen, place on a carving board that will collect juices; rapidly cut meat into slices ½ inch thick and rearrange on warm platter with garnish around them. Pour carving juices over meat, and pass sauce separately.)

(†) If you cannot serve immediately, remove strings but do not carve meat; after it has rested 10 to 15 minutes and the sauce is made except for the final butter enrichment, return meat to casserole and baste with the sauce. Set cover askew and place either over barely simmering water or in an oven no hotter than 120°F. Meat can stay thus for a good hour before serving.

Fillet Baked in a Cloak of Mushrooms or of *Matignon*

To give the meat more flavour, you may either slice it and re-form with a stuffing between each slice as in the beef *en feuilletons*, page 253, or you may use that same mushroom stuffing but spread it over the whole fillet as suggested in the drawing on page 247. In this second case, however, you must have caul fat to hold the mushrooms in place. Rather than mushrooms, you may wish to use the *matignon* of diced cooked carrots, onions, celery, ham, and wine in Volume I, page 330. In any case, when the meat is wrapped, brown it as described in the preceding recipe, and casserole-roast it in exactly the same way.

Filet de Bœuf à la Bourgeoise
[Fillet of Beef with Onions, Mushrooms, and Olives]

Whether casserole-roasted, plain roasted, or braised, a fillet of beef surrounded with onions, mushrooms, and green olives is as attractive to look at as it is to eat. The garniture is cooked in advance, and simmers in the sauce to blend flavours before being arranged around the beef; you may wish to add sautéed potatoes to the platter, or the courgette *timbale* on page 488. Cook the fillet and prepare the sauce as in the preceding master recipe, or braise it with or without a stuffing as described in Volume I, page 329. Prepare the garniture as follows:

1. Preparing the garniture
(a) The small onions:

1 lb. small white onions about 1 in. in diameter
A saucepan of boiling water
A 6- to 7-in. frying pan or saucepan (non-stick recommended)
1 oz. butter and 2 tsp. olive oil
Salt and pepper to taste
Pinch thyme
¼ pt bouillon
A cover for the pan

Drop onions in boiling water, bring rapidly back to boil ,and boil 1 minute. Drain, and refresh in cold water. Shave off two ends and peel onions; pierce a cross ⅓ inch deep in root ends. Heat butter and oil in pan; when foam is subsiding add onions and sauté over moderately high heat to brown lightly. Reduce heat, add rest of ingredients, cover, and simmer very slowly for 20 to 30 minutes, or until onions are tender when pierced with a knife. Set aside with cooking juices.

(b) *The mushrooms:*

½ lb. fresh mushrooms
1 oz. butter and 2 tsp. olive oil
An 8-in. frying pan (non-stick recommended)
2 tbl. minced shallots or spring onions
Salt and pepper to taste

Trim and wash the mushrooms; dry in a towel and cut into quarters. Heat butter and oil in pan until foam is subsiding, add mushrooms and sauté over high heat, tossing frequently, until mushrooms begin to brown. Reduce heat, add shallots, and toss a moment more. Season lightly, tossing, and add mushrooms to onions.

(c) *The olives:*

4 to 5 oz. stoned green olives, medium size, about ¾ in. long
3 pts simmering water in a saucepan

Drain and wash the olives; drop into simmering water. Simmer 10 minutes, to remove excess saltiness. Drain, rinse in cold water, and add to onions and mushrooms.

(†) Garniture may be prepared in advance.

2. Serving

The cooked fillet of beef and its pt or so of sauce
The onions, mushrooms, and olives
1 to 1½ oz. soft butter

When the beef is done and the sauce is made, add the onions, mushrooms, and olives to the sauce and simmer 3 to 4 minutes to blend flavours. (If meat is being held in casserole, return sauce and garniture to it.) To serve, place meat on platter, and dip out the onions, mushrooms, and olives with a slotted spoon, arranging them around the beef. Beat the enrichment butter into the sauce a tablespoon at a time, spoon a little over the beef to glaze it and pour the rest of the sauce into a warm gravy boat. Serve, along with whatever other vegetables you may have chosen.

Filet de Bœuf en Feuilletons, Duxelles
[Fillet of Beef, Sliced, Stuffed with Mushrooms and Roasted]

By slicing the raw fillet, seasoning each slice, and spreading it with wine-flavoured mushroom *duxelles* and then re-forming the roast, you will have a deliciously flavoured fillet that practically serves itself. For this you should have as long a piece of the main fillet muscle as possible with no under-turning tail, so that you will have large slices. (Drawings and discussion of fillet are at the beginning of this section, pages 243-4.)

[For 16 slices ⅜ inch thick, serving 8 to 10]

1. The *duxelles* stuffing

1 lb. fresh mushrooms
A heavy-bottomed 8-in. frying pan (non-stick recommended)
1½ oz. butter
2 tbl. minced shallots or spring onions
2 tbl. finely minced mild-cured ready-cooked ham
1½ tbl. flour
4 tbl. dry Madeira (Sercial)
1½ oz. *foie gras en bloc*, liver paste, or very finely minced cooked ham fat
1 egg yolk
½ tsp. dried tarragon
Salt and pepper to taste

Trim and wash mushrooms. Cut into $\frac{1}{16}$-inch dice, using either a big knife or the vegetable mincing attachment of an electric mixer or a food mill if you wish. Twist a handful at a time in the corner of a towel to extract as much juice as possible. Heat butter to foaming in frying pan, stir in mushrooms, shallots, and ham. Sauté over moderately high heat, stirring frequently, until mushroom pieces begin to separate and start to brown lightly (5 minutes or so). Sprinkle in the flour and stir over moderate heat for 2 minutes. Remove from heat, blend in the wine, and stir again over heat for 1 minute. Remove from heat, beat in *foie gras*, liver paste, or fat, the egg yolk, tarragon, and salt and pepper to taste. Set aside.

2. Stuffing and tying the fillet

The heart of the fillet, 8 to 10 ins. long and as even in diameter as possible (2½ lb. or more)

A double thickness of well-washed damp cheesecloth large enough to envelop beef (see also notes on caul fat, page 384)

A tray and a pastry brush

Rendered goose fat, pork fat, or cooking oil

Salt and pepper

The *duxelles* stuffing

White string

With a very sharp knife, cut the meat into 16 even slices, each about ½ inch thick, setting them aside in the order in which you cut them. Lay the cheesecloth on the tray and paint with fat or cooking oil. Salt and pepper each slice, spread with a tablespoon and a half of stuffing, and re-form the roast, arranging the slices against each other on the cheesecloth. Tie one loop of string around the length of the re-formed roast to hold the slices against each other, then stretch the cheesecloth tightly over the meat to enclose it. Twist each end of the cheesecloth closely against each end of the meat; tie securely with string. Then twist a tight spiral of string around the circumference from one end to the other and back again, so that meat will keep its shape. It will look like a fat sausage about 12 inches long and 4 inches in diameter.

(†) When stuffed, tied, wrapped in plastic, and refrigerated a day before roasting, it will pick up added flavour.

3. Browning and cover-roasting the beef: at least 1 hour before serving

Brown the beef and the aromatic vegetables that accompany it as described in the master recipe, step 1, page 249. (It will brown perfectly well in its cheesecloth covering.) Roast, as directed in step 2, counting 30 to 40 minutes and leaving the meat red-rare (125°F. on a meat thermometer). Remove from casserole as soon as it is done, and leave at room temperature for 15 minutes while finishing the sauce described in step 3.

4. Serving

Set beef on hot serving platter and cut string and cheesecloth, carefully pulling them out from around and under the meat (15 minutes' rest will have drawn slices of meat together). Spoon enough sauce over meat to glaze it nicely, arrange around it whatever garnish you have chosen, and serve, passing rest of sauce separately. Server need only spread top of meat apart with large fork and spoon to show location of each slice, which is then served with its share of *duxelles* stuffing.

(†) Use the same system as in the master recipe, but do not untie meat until just before serving.

Filet de Bœuf en Croûte
[Fillet of Beef Baked in Pastry – Beef Wellington *Brioché*]

Whether the English, the Irish, or the French baked the first fillet of beef in a crust we shall probably never know, but it is certain that the French would not have named it after Wellington. It is a remarkably handsome, sumptuous dish when properly made. Most good recipes specify a whole piece of fillet that is pre-roasted 25 minutes, cooled, surrounded with a mushroom and *foie gras* stuffing, then wrapped in French puff pastry and baked. We think it a great improvement to substitute *brioche* dough for puff pastry: fully risen *brioche* dough is deflated, thoroughly chilled, then rolled thin, draped over the meat and baked immediately before the dough has a chance to rise again. The resulting crust is beautiful to look at as well as being light, thin, cooked all the way through and delicious to eat; this is never the case with puff pastry, which cannot bake properly under such circumstances and is always damply dumpling under its handsome exterior. Another improvement is to bake the fillet in slices with stuffing in between as in the preceding recipe: the serving is easy and the taste is vastly improved.

VEGETABLE AND WINE SUGGESTIONS

An important dish like this should be surrounded with few distractions; we would suggest only something green and fresh like buttered new peas or green beans, broccoli flowerets, or, in season, sliced, fresh, green asparagus spears tossed in butter. Again, a fine Médoc or other claret would be an excellent choice of wine.

THE SAUCE

Anything as extravagant as this *filet de bœuf* demands an unusually good sauce. We suggest $\frac{3}{4}$ to 1 pint of the brown sauce or the *sauce ragoût* in Volume I, pages 87 and 88, simmered several hours for maximum flavour; it will then be further enriched with the cooking juices and deglazing wine from the beef, step 1 in the following recipe.

[For 16 slices of beef $\frac{1}{2}$ inch thick, serving 8 to 10]

1. Preliminaries: to do in the morning or the day before serving

$\frac{1}{2}$ the recipe for *pain brioché* dough, page 127 ($\frac{1}{2}$ lb. flour)
One of the brown sauces described in preceding paragraph
$2\frac{1}{2}$ to 3 lb. of the heart of the fillet, sliced, stuffed, wrapped, and tied
  (*filet de bœuf en feuilletons*, page 253, steps 1 and 2)
Rendered goose or pork fat, or cooking oil
A shallow roasting pan
$\frac{1}{4}$ pt dry port wine or Sercial Madeira

Prepare the dough as described, letting it finish its second rise in the refrigerator. Then deflate it, cover with plastic wrap, a plate, and a 5-pound weight so that it will not rise again; refrigerate. Make the brown-sauce base and refrigerate. Prepare the stuffed fillet as described, baste well with fat or oil, and place in roasting pan. Preheat oven to 425°F., Mark 7, and set rack in upper-third level. Roast the beef for 25 minutes, basting and turning it several times. Transfer beef to a platter or tray (reserve roasting pan) and let meat cool to room temperature. (If you are pre-roasting a day ahead, cover and refrigerate the meat after it has cooled, but set at room temperature for 2 hours before final baking in step 3, for accurate timing.) Spoon fat out of roasting pan, pour in wine and boil down by half, scraping up any roasting juices with a wooden spoon; scrape liquid into the sauce base.

2. Enclosing beef in *brioche*: 1 to 1½ hours before serving, and just before roasting

The cool, room-temperature, pre-roasted beef
Heavy shears
The chilled *brioche* dough
Flour, a rolling surface, a rolling pin, a ravioli wheel, a small knife
An oiled Swiss-roll tin or pizza tray (raised edges needed to catch roasting juices)
Egg glaze (1 egg beaten with 1 tsp. water in a small bowl)
A pastry brush
Optional: a meat thermometer

Preheat oven to 425°F., Mark 7, and slide rack on to lower-middle level. Set out all the equipment and ingredients listed. Cut wrapping and string from beef. Working rapidly from now on so that *brioche* dough softens as little as possible, roll ¼ of the dough into a rectangle ¼ inch thick and the length and width of the beef. Roll it up on your pin and unroll it on to the oiled pan. Its most attractive side up, place the beef on the rectangle of dough (A). Trim off excess dough from around the beef. Roll the remaining dough into a rectangle ¼ inch

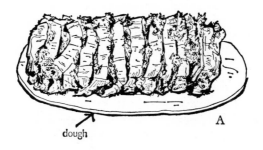

dough   A

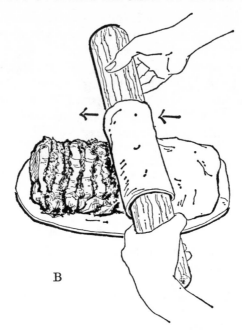

B

thick and large enough to enclose beef (probably 18 by 8 inches), roll it up on your pin and unroll over the beef (b).

Trim off any excess dough and reserve for decorations. Tuck the covering dough against the bottom rectangle of dough and under bottom of meat, sealing edges with your fingers. Paint dough covering with egg glaze; in a moment paint with a second coat.

So that any decorations on the crust will show after baking they must be either deep cuts with raised edges, or dough paste-ons. For instance, you may wish to lay on strips of left-over dough in a design, and paint with egg glaze. Decorate blank spaces by cutting into surface of dough with scissors, a knife, or the metal end of a pastry tube, making definite edges that stick up (c). (Cuts are made after glazing, so that the cut portion of the dough will remain pale, accenting the design when dough is baked.)

Immediately the decorations are complete, set beef in oven. The object here is to make sure the dough remains a crust, a thin and crisp covering; if it rises, it will be thick and bready.

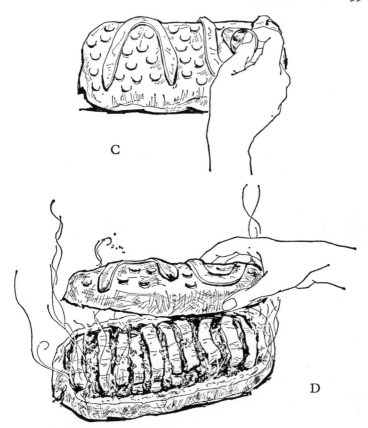

C

D

3. Baking: 30 to 40 minutes

Bake in lower-middle level of preheated 425°F., Mark 7 oven
for 20 to 25 minutes, or until pastry has browned nicely.
Lower thermostat to 350°F., Mark 4, for rest of baking, and
cover crust loosely with a sheet of foil or brown paper if it
seems to be browning too much. Indications that the meat is
done are that you can begin to smell the beef and the stuffing,
and that juices begin to escape into the pan; meat thermometer
reading for rare beef is 125°F.

4. Serving and ahead-of-time notes

A hot platter or a board wide enough to hold beef and removed top
crust

A flexible-blade spatula
A hot sauce in a warmed bowl
The hot accompanying vegetable
Serving implements: a sharp knife for cutting the crust, and a serving
  spoon and fork

When beef is done, remove from oven and slide on to platter
or board. Beef will stay warm for 20 minutes; if you still cannot serve it, set in a warming oven no hotter than 120°F. To
serve, cut all around the crust and half an inch up from its
bottom. Lift the top crust off on to the platter (D), and cut into
serving portions. Separate the slices of meat with spoon and
fork and cut down through the bottom crust so that each slice
is served with a portion of stuffing and crust. Spoon a little
sauce around the meat, and add a piece of the top crust.

Lamb · *Agneau et Mouton*

The French take great pride in their lamb and the marvellous
quality of their mutton. Although we thought we had covered
a great deal in Volume I, with lamb stew, roasts in mustard
coatings, garlic sauces, and even a boiled leg of lamb, there is
more to tell. We now add full instructions on boning the leg,
step-by-step illustrated directions on how to carve the saddle
like a major-domo, a recipe for stuffed and braised shoulder,
and complete drawings on how to make a *gigot farci en croûte*.

HOW TO BONE A LEG OF LAMB

A fully or partially boned leg of lamb is easy to carve, and you
can stuff the cavities where the bones used to be. If only the tail
and hip assembly has been removed from the raw meat, that
alone is a great help to the carver, and when the main leg bone
is also gone, carving is no problem at all. To show that it really
is a leg of lamb you are serving, leave the shank bone in unless
you want a rolled leg for spit roasting. Although most butchers
will cut out the tail and hip for you, they may not want to take
the time for a careful boning of the main leg portion. If you

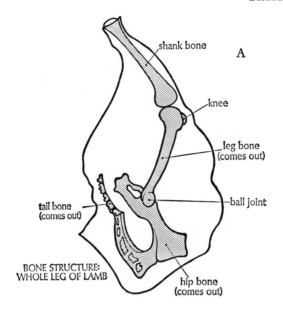

A

shank bone

knee

leg bone
(comes out)

tail bone
(comes out)

ball joint

BONE STRUCTURE:
WHOLE LEG OF LAMB

hip bone
(comes out)

enjoy working with your hands, do all the boning yourself and you will learn more about meat and carving, because you will become familiar with the bones, their shapes, and their positions.

Furnish yourself with two stout-bladed, very sharp knives, one small and one larger. Always keeping the knife blade against the bone, scrape all around against the complicated structure of the tail-hip assembly, disfiguring the meat as little as possible, until you are able to cut the tendons that join the hip to the ball joint of the main leg bone, thus releasing the hip (B).

To remove the main leg bone, cut around its exposed ball joint buried in the thick end of the meat. Loosen flesh all around and down the bone inside the meat until you come to its opposite ball joint at the knee. You now have two choices, one easier and the other longer but cleverer. The easiest way to remove the bone is to slit the underside of the meat at the knee to expose the bones; making as small a hole outside as possible, cut around knee joint, sever tendons, and draw the bone out from the large end of the meat. Close the meat neatly

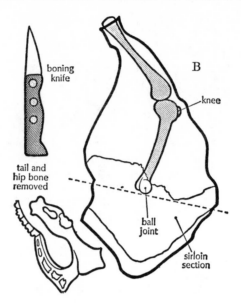

at the knee by sewing or skewering. The longer manœuvre is to get the bone without piercing the skin at the knee. By persistent poking and cutting around the bone inside the meat at the joint, by twisting the bone, by turning the meat inside out around the bone as far down as you can for better visibility, you will finally be able to free it from the tendons attaching it to the knee and pull the bone out.

The flap of meat that contained the hip and tail, at the large end of the leg, is called the sirloin (B). You may slice it off and use at another meal for roasting, steaks, or shishkebab, or you may grind part of it for stuffing back into the leg as suggested in the following recipe. (If you wish to leave the flap on, skewer it against the main body of the leg after stuffing.) With the sirloin off, you have what is known as a short (or Frenched) leg of lamb (c). (For *gigot farci en croûte*, this is what you need.)

Either fill the pocket with stuffing, pushing it well down into all spaces left by the bones, or sprinkle in a flavouring of salt, pepper, minced parsley, a clove of minced garlic, and a big pinch of rosemary or thyme. Whether filled or not, close the pocket with skewers and string (D).

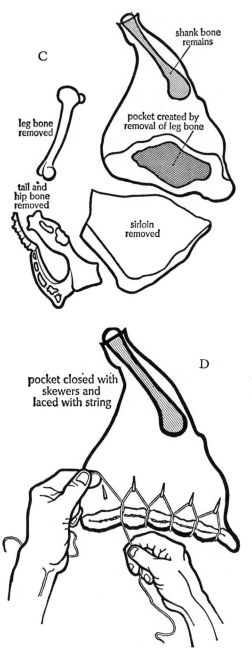

C

leg bone
removed

shank bone
remains

pocket created by
removal of leg bone

tail and
hip bone
removed

sirloin
removed

D

pocket closed with
skewers and
laced with string

RECIPES FOR BONED LEG OF LAMB

You may proceed with the recipe for *gigot farci en croûte*, or you may roast the boned, stuffed, and skewered leg of lamb just as it is, following the master recipe in Volume I, page 361; it is also delicious roasted with the herbal mustard coating also in Volume I, on page 363. After the roast has rested 15 to 20 minutes out of the oven, the meat will have settled into place and you can remove the string and skewers. To carve, cut down in bias (diagonal) slices across the grain, first from one side of the large end, then from the other; if the first few slices contain no stuffing, set aside for second helpings. When you come to the thinner portion of the meat nearer the shank, you can cut straight across.

Gigot Farci, en Croûte
[Boned, Stuffed Lamb Baked in Pastry]

At least one great French provincial restaurant has made its reputation on *gigot farci en croûte*, and any home cook who has mastered French puff pastry or *brioche* dough can make this splendidly dramatic presentation every bit as well. The recipe consists of the boned and stuffed leg of lamb, illustrated in the preceding pages, which is first roasted in a very hot oven until partially cooked, then draped in pastry, decorated with pastry cut-outs, glazed, and set back in the oven again to cook and brown the crust. Although you have to watch your timing on this so as not to overcook the lamb, it is reasonably amenable to delays as indicated by the daggers (†) at the end of most of the steps in the recipe. Do go over it well before starting, so that you will have a good idea of timing and of stopping points. We suggest that you make the pastry dough the day before serving. You might also bone the lamb, prepare the stuffing, and simmer the sauce called for in step 7; the actual cooking will then be much simplified.

Even though you have the crust, there is not much of it per serving and you may also wish a potato dish such as the scalloped potatoes, *gratin dauphinois*, in Volume I on page 560, the *gratin* with cheese and cream following it, or the unusual potato and chicory *gratin* here, on page 510. Brussels sprouts, broccoli, buttered spinach, or fresh green peas might also be included. This *gigot* naturally calls for the best in wines, giving you an opportunity to bring out your finest château-bottled claret.

THE CRUST, AND PUFF PASTRY VERSUS *BRIOCHE* DOUGH

Although puff pastry is traditional, it never quite cooks through when it covers rare-roasted meat, while *brioche* dough, if it is not allowed its final rise before baking, will form a crisp, brown crust. This question is discussed in the preamble to beef Wellington on page 255, where you have the same choice.

[*For 8 to 10 people*]

1. Boning the lamb

A 6- to 7-lb. leg of lamb (about 4 lb. boned and minus sirloin)

Following illustrated directions preceding this recipe, remove tail and hip bones, main leg bone, and sirloin meat from leg of lamb. (If you are going to make the brown sauce suggested for step 7, start it now, using the bones and scraps from the lamb.)

2. Mushroom and kidney stuffing (*farce duxelles aux rognons*)

½ lb. fresh mushrooms
1 oz. butter and 1 tbl. olive oil or cooking oil (more of each if needed)
A medium (10-in.) frying pan (non-stick recommended)
4 fine, fresh lamb kidneys, peeled and minced
3 tbl. finely minced shallots or spring onions
3 tbl. port, Madeira, or cognac
⅛ tsp. each of ground thyme and rosemary
4 oz. minced raw lamb (from the removed piece of sirloin)
2 oz. *foie gras* or *mousse de foie* (tinned goose liver or liver mousse)
Optional but recommended: 1 or 2 minced truffles and their juice
Salt and pepper to taste
If needed: 2 or more tbl. stale, not-too-fine breadcrumbs

Trim, wash, and dry the mushrooms. Chop into a fine mince with a big knife; a handful at a time twist into a tight ball in the corner of a towel to extract as much juice as possible. Heat butter and oil in pan, and when butter foam has begun to subside, add the mushrooms. Sauté over moderately high heat, stirring, for several minutes, until mushroom pieces begin to separate from each other. Stir in the kidneys and shallots, adding a little more butter if you feel it necessary. Sauté, stirring, for 2 minutes, just to stiffen the kidneys. Pour in the wine or cognac and herbs; boil down rapidly for 1 minute. Remove from heat. Stir in the minced lamb. Mash *foie gras* or *mousse* with a fork and stir in also, along with optional truffles and their juice. Season carefully to taste. (If by any chance mixture seems too damp or loose stir in a tablespoon or so of breadcrumbs to hold it together more.)

3. Stuffing, tying, and skewering the lamb

Skewers and white string

Following illustrated directions on page 263, pack the stuffing into the pockets left in the meat by the bones, skewer the large end of the meat, and lace closed with string.

(†) Recipe may be prepared to this point a day in advance. Note also that you may prepare the sauce, step 7, in advance.

4. Preliminary roasting: 30 minutes 425°F., Mark 7, and a 30-minute rest

The stuffed and skewered lamb
Cooking oil
A shallow roasting pan with rack
Optional but recommended: an accurate meat thermometer

Preheat oven to 425°F., Mark 7. Wipe lamb thoroughly dry with paper towels and brush with cooking oil, especially on exposed lean-meat surfaces. Place on rack in roasting pan and set in upper-middle level of preheated oven. Basting once or twice with oil and turning meat once, roast 25 to 30 minutes, until lamb has swelled slightly and feels a little springy in contrast to its softer raw state. Meat thermometer reading: 120°F. Remove lamb from oven but leave string and skewers in place.

(†) *Resting and ahead-of-time notes:* Lamb must rest for 30 minutes at least before final cooking, so that meat will draw together and hold stuffing in place. It must also cool off a little bit so that it will not overcook under its pastry, but it must not cool so much that it loses its juicy, freshly cooked character. If you are not ready to continue for some time, you may keep it perfectly for an hour or more anywhere that you can maintain a temperature of around 100° to 110°F., such as a warming oven, or the turned-off oven, reheating it for a moment every now and then.

5. Enclosing the lamb in pastry; preheat oven to 450°F., Mark 8, for next step

The still warm leg of lamb
A lightly greased Swiss-roll tin, or edged baking sheet
Either: the recipe for simple puff pastry, page 166;
Or: the recipe for *pain brioché* dough, fully risen and ready to bake, but chilled, page 127.
Egg glaze (1 egg beaten with 1 tsp. water in a small bowl)
A pastry brush
Optional but recommended: the meat thermometer

Remove string and skewers, and set lamb on tin or baking sheet. It is now to be enclosed in pastry; do so rapidly to prevent dough from softening and, in the case of *brioche* dough, from rising.

Rapidly roll pastry out into a flattened pear shape $\frac{1}{4}$ inch thick, 6 inches longer at the large end, and 6 inches wider than the leg of lamb. Starting at large end, unroll or unfold the pastry over the lamb (A). Leaving an inch of the shank bone

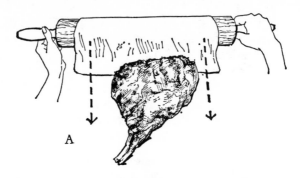

A

exposed, allow enough pastry to tuck in all around and enclose lamb completely; trim off excess. Push the pastry against the undersides of the meat with your fingers (B); the bottom of the lamb rests on the pan, and the pastry simply encloses all visible meat.

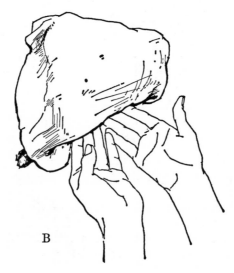

B

Make pastry cut-outs with left-over dough, such as long strips ⅜ inch wide cut with a pastry wheel, and 2-inch ovals formed with a fluted biscuit cutter. Paint top of covering dough with egg glaze, and press the decorations into place (c).

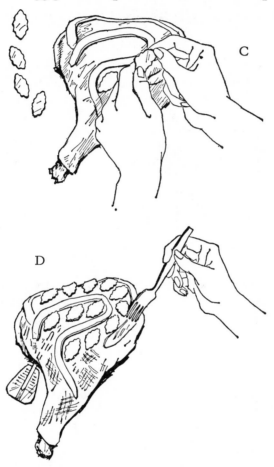

When all decorations are in place, brush surface of dough and decorations with egg glaze. Draw the tines of a table fork over glaze and lightly into dough, to make cross-hatch marks on entire surface (D). Insert optional meat thermometer where indicated (D), at a downward-slanting angle from shank so that point of thermometer lodges in the thickest portion of solid meat near large end. Immediately proceed to next step. (Note that if you are using *brioche* dough, you are not to let it rise; it is to be baked immediately.)

6. Final baking: 25 to 30 minutes at 450°F., Mark 8, and 400°F., Mark 6

Place in middle level of preheated oven and bake for 15 to 20 minutes, until pastry has started to brown nicely; reduce heat to 400°F., Mark 6, for the final 5 to 10 minutes of baking. Lamb is done to rosy rare at a thermometer reading of 130°F., or at the first sign of juices exuding from underside of lamb on to baking sheet. (*Note:* Some prefer lamb rarer, 125°F. on the thermometer, while others like it medium rare, or around 140° to 145°F. Roast the lamb to the thermometer reading you prefer.)

Remove lamb from oven as soon as it is done; carefully lift it, and slide a rack under it so that the juices will not moisten the crust. Lamb should rest 15 to 20 minutes before carving. (When ready to serve, place lamb on platter, and pour any accumulated juices into whatever sauce you have prepared.)

(†) Lamb will stay warm enough in its crust for 30 minutes; after that return to warming oven or anywhere that you can maintain a temperature of 110° to 120°F., where it may remain another half hour at least.

7. Serving

A hot, lightly buttered serving platter or a carving board
Optional but desirable: 1 pt excellent brown sauce made from the lamb bones and meat scraps (Volume I, pages 87–90), in a hot sauce bowl

Transfer lamb to platter or carving board, and pour any roasting juices into sauce. Make a presentation of the *gigot*, for all to admire. To carve, cut down in bias (diagonal) slices across the grain, first from one side of the large end, then from the other; if the first few slices contain no stuffing, set aside for second helpings. When you come to the thinner portion of the meat nearer the shank, you can cut straight across. Pass sauce separately, along with whatever vegetables you have chosen.

Épaule d'Agneau Farcie, Viroflay
[Braised, Stuffed Shoulder of Lamb]

Shoulder of lamb is far less expensive than leg of lamb, usually by at least a third, and is an elegant roast when stuffed and braised. The spinach and mushroom mixture suggested here makes attractive slices, and if you serve the potatoes in basil on page 509 and whole baked tomatoes, you will have a colourful and fragrant main course. A Saint-Émilion would be an excellent choice of wine.

A NOTE ON BONED SHOULDER OF LAMB

Most butchers will bone a lamb shoulder for you, or you will find them ready-boned, rolled, and tied; you untie and unroll them for stuffing. Ask also for a pound or so of sawed lamb bones, or for veal or beef bones, to give character to your braising liquid. (Full information on lamb shoulders is in Volume I, page 358.)

[*For 8 people*]

1. The mushroom *duxelles* and spinach stuffing (*farce Viroflay*)

½ lb. fresh mushrooms
½ oz. butter
½ tbl. cooking oil
A medium (10-in.) frying pan (non-stick recommended)
Salt and pepper
A 5-pt mixing bowl

Make a *duxelles* as follows: Trim, wash, and dry the mushrooms, and cut into $\frac{1}{16}$-inch dice with a large knife. A handful at a time, twist hard in the corner of a towel, to extract as much of their juice as possible. Heat oil and butter to bubbling in pan, add mushrooms, and cook over moderately high heat, stirring frequently, until pieces begin to separate from each other, and start to brown very lightly. Stir in salt and pepper to taste, and scrape into mixing bowl.

10 oz. cooked spinach (or a 10-oz. package frozen spinach, thawed in a
  pan of cold water and drained)
1 oz. butter
3 tbl. minced shallots or spring onions
A large clove garlic, mashed
Salt and pepper

A handful at a time, squeeze as much water as possible out of
the spinach; chop fine with a large stainless-steel knife. Melt
the additional butter in the frying pan over moderately high
heat, stir in the shallots or spring onions, and cook for 1 minute.
Then stir in the spinach and garlic, and cook, stirring, for
several minutes to evaporate remaining liquid from spinach.
When it begins sticking lightly to bottom of pan, remove from
heat; season to taste with salt and pepper, and scrape into bowl
with mushrooms.

1½ oz. not-too-fine stale crumbs from a white loaf, in a small bowl
2 to 3 tbl. stock, bouillon, or milk
4 oz. finely diced ham fat, fresh pork fat, or blanched bacon
1 egg
8 to 10 large fresh basil leaves, minced, or ½ tsp. fragrant dried basil,
  thyme, or rosemary
Salt and pepper

Soften the crumbs with the stock, bouillon, or milk and let
stand for a few minutes. Beat the ham fat, egg, and herbs into
the mushrooms and spinach. Squeeze excess liquid out of
crumbs and beat them in too. Taste stuffing very carefully for
seasoning.

(†) May be done a day in advance; cover and refrigerate.

2. Stuffing the lamb

A 5- to 6-lb. shoulder of lamb, fell intact, all excess fat cut out; bones
  removed, chopped, and reserved (ready-to-stuff weight about 3½ lb.)
A trussing needle or skewers
White string

Spread boned shoulder on a board, fell (skin) side down. Tuck
stuffing into pockets left by bones, and pile rest of stuffing in a
loaf shape down centre of meat. Sew or skewer edges of meat

together to enclose stuffing completely. (Do not overfill lamb.)
Tie into a sausage shape with loops of string at 1-inch intervals
around circumference. Dry thoroughly with paper towels
before browning, next step.

(†) When both lamb and stuffing are chilled, the meat may be
stuffed a day in advance; wrap and refrigerate.

3. Browning the lamb

2 to 3 tbl. rendered pork or goose fat, or cooking oil; more if needed
A heavy, flameproof casserole just large enough to hold lamb
    comfortably
The chopped lamb bones
A large onion, sliced
A large carrot, sliced
For sauce consistency: a 6-in. square of blanched pork rind, Volume I,
    page 434, and/or 1 or 2 chopped veal knuckle bones

Preheat oven to 325°F., Mark 3 in time for step 4. Heat fat or
oil in casserole to very hot but not smoking, add bones (including optional knuckle bones at end of list) and sliced
vegetables; sauté over moderately high heat for 5 to 6 minutes,
until lightly browned. Remove with a slotted spoon to a side
dish. Film pan with more fat or oil if necessary, set lamb in it,
seam-side down, and brown for several minutes, lifting
occasionally with spoon to prevent lamb from sticking. Turn
and brown on another side, and continue turning and browning until lamb is nicely coloured on all sides and the two ends.
Strew the browned bones and vegetables around the meat, and
add the optional pork rind.

4. Braising the lamb: 2½ hours at 325°F., Mark 3

Salt
½ pt dry white wine or dry white French vermouth
¾ pt or more brown stock or bouillon
The following tied in washed cheesecloth: 6 parsley sprigs, 1 bay leaf,
    ½ tsp. thyme, 2 cloves garlic
A piece of waxed paper or foil
Casserole cover

Salt the lamb, add the wine and enough stock for bouillon to come $\frac{2}{3}$ the way up the lamb. Bury herb packet in the liquid, and bring casserole to simmer on top of stove. Lay paper or foil over meat, cover casserole, and set in middle level of oven; regulate oven heat so that lamb simmers quietly for $2\frac{1}{2}$ hours. Turn several times during cooking, and baste with liquid in the casserole. Lamb is done when a fork will pierce it fairly easily.

5. Sauce and serving

A hot serving platter
A sieve set over a saucepan
1 tbl. cornflour blended to a paste with 2 tbl. wine or stock in a small
    bowl
A warm sauce bowl
Parsley, watercress, or whatever vegetable garnish you wish

Remove lamb to hot platter. Do not untie yet; cover with waxed paper or foil and set in turned-off oven with door ajar while finishing sauce as follows: Strain braising liquid into saucepan, pressing juices out of ingredients. Skim surface fat off liquid, bring to simmer, skimming off additional fat, and taste carefully for seasoning and strength. Boil down rapidly, if necessary; you should have about a pint. Remove from heat, and beat in cornflour mixture; return over heat and simmer, stirring, for 2 minutes. Remove string and trussings from lamb, pour a spoonful of sauce over the meat to glaze it, and pour rest of sauce into warm bowl. Decorate platter with greenery or vegetables, and serve.

    To carve, cut down in bias (diagonal) slices across the grain, first from one side of the short end, then from the other, and spoon a little sauce around the edge of each serving. (If the stuffing does not hold in place, carver should arrange meat attractively around it on plate, for each slice.)

(†) If you are not to serve the lamb at once, replace it in the casserole, pour the sauce around, cover loosely, and set in a 120°F. warming oven, or over barely simmering water, where it will keep nicely for at least 30 minutes.

Other stuffings

Other stuffing possibilities are listed on pages 664–6, and 6 stuffings specifically for lamb are in Volume I, pages 364–7.

BREAST OF LAMB

Breast of lamb, *poitrine d'agneau* (the bottom of the rib cage, similar to that of veal illustrated on page 296) is the most reasonably priced of any cut of meat, and is delicious when boned, stuffed, and braised. However, it must be very carefully peeled, and all the fat from the flank must be cut out, as well as other extraneous fat. If you do find a well-trimmed breast, follow the general system outlined for stuffed breast of veal on page 298, using either that stuffing or any of the preceding suggestions for shoulder of lamb.

SADDLE OF LAMB

A saddle of lamb, *selle d'agneau*, is one of the most luxurious and attractive roasts you could pick to serve at a small, elegant dinner party for 4 to 6 people. When you have prepared it for the oven, which is not difficult as you will see from the illustrated directions, you will find it far easier to roast and to carve than a leg of lamb, and absolutely delicious to eat.

HOW TO ORDER A SADDLE OF LAMB

The saddle of lamb is the loin. On a beef carcass it would be the whole porterhouse and T-bone steak section on both sides, and on lamb it is the whole loin-chop area. It is, in fact, a giant butterfly loin chop 8 to 10 inches thick, consisting of the two meaty loin strips that run along either side of the backbone on top, and the two smaller fillet strips that run its length underneath. What would constitute the tail of the chop is the flank, or flap of meat attached to each side.

If your butcher is not sure just what cut you want, show him this picture, or point the saddle out to him on yourself. It is equivalent to the small of your back on both sides of the backbone, and includes the front part of you; in other words, it is

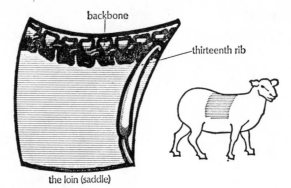

the loin (saddle)

the whole area from the top of your hip bone to where your ribs begin. Tell him to leave it whole; he is not to saw it in two at the backbone. The choicest saddle will come from a carcass of spring lamb that weighs not more than 45 pounds; the saddle will weigh around 6½ pounds untrimmed, 3½ pounds ready to roast.

FRENCH TERMINOLOGY

You may also have communication problems in France, because the saddle can be called *selle d'agneau*, *selle anglaise*, or *les deux filets réunis*. Again, point it out on yourself if there is any confusion. Their saddle of lamb will be a little smaller than an English one, while a *selle de mouton* from their excellent mutton will be a little larger and should be well aged (*bien rassie*).

HOW TO PREPARE A SADDLE OF LAMB FOR ROASTING

The drawing (A) shows the way the topside of the saddle will look before the flanks have been trimmed off. Ask that the fell (skin) be removed, which will leave a covering of fat over the top of the meat. Have the thirteenth rib removed also, if attached.

Remove all excess fat from the underside (B); this may include the kidneys. The fillet strips run parallel to the backbone

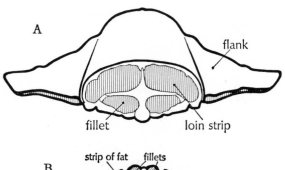

A

flank

fillet   loin strip

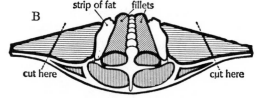

strip of fat   fillets

B

cut here   cut here

on either side, and parallel to their outside edge is a partially hidden strip of fat. Cut and pull fat out, being careful not to pierce the flanks and make holes in outside covering of meat. Cut off all but about 3 inches of flank, leaving enough on each side for flanks to cover the underside of the backbone.

Shave off all but $\frac{1}{8}$-inch layer of covering fat on the topside and make a criss-cross of bias cuts $\frac{1}{2}$ inch apart in the surface, going just down to the flesh (c). These will help the meat to cook evenly, and make attractive decorations on the crisp, roasted surface later on.

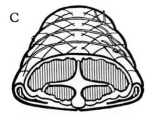

C

Sprinkle underside with salt, pepper, and a big pinch of thyme or rosemary, fold flanks against backbone to cover fillets, and tie circumference of saddle in 3 or more places with white string. If you are not to cook the saddle now, wrap and refrigerate it.

(†) Saddle may be prepared to this point a day before roasting.

*Selle d'Agneau Rôtie
[Roast Saddle of Lamb]

A plain roast saddle of lamb is so good in itself that you need go into no elaborations, although one or two are suggested at the end of this recipe. A classic accompaniment is that crusty, buttery mound of sliced potatoes, *pommes Anna*, on page 517, or one of the two variations following it, and either braised lettuce or braised chicory. Another suggestion would be aubergine, such as the *gratin provençal* with its tomatoes and cheese on page 467; you would then need only an excellent loaf of home-made French bread. A Médoc would be your best choice of wine.

[*For 4 to 6 people*]

1. Preparations for roasting

A saddle of lamb trimmed, seasoned, and tied according to the preceding
   directions (about 3½ lb. trimmed weight)
A heavy, shallow baking dish just large enough to hold the saddle
   comfortably
2 oz. melted butter in a pan and a basting brush
Optional but recommended: a meat thermometer
A carrot and an onion, sliced
2 large cloves garlic, unpeeled

Preheat oven to 475°F., Mark 9, for step 2. Set saddle right side up in the roasting pan and paint exposed ends of meat with melted butter, reserving rest for later. If you are using a meat thermometer, insert it at a long, slanting angle into the thickest part of one of the loin strips. Be sure point of thermometer reaches middle of meat and does not touch bone. Prepare the vegetables and garlic, and reserve in a bowl for step 2.

2. Roasting: 40 to 45 minutes; oven preheated to 450°F., Mark 8

Roasting start: Set lamb in upper-middle level of preheated oven for 15 minutes.

15-minute mark: Turn thermostat down to 425°F., Mark 7. Working quickly, baste 2 ends of saddle with melted butter, and strew the vegetables and garlic around the meat. Baste vegetables with fat in baking dish, or with butter.

22-minute mark: Rapidly baste meat and vegetables again with fat in dish.

30-minute mark: Baste again rapidly. If vegetables are blackening, turn thermostat down to 400°F., Mark 6.

37-minute mark: Baste again. If you are using a meat thermometer, it should be nearly at 130°F. for rosy rare meat. Meat should feel springy rather than squashy and raw, and the first juices should be exuding from the meat into the pan. Roast a few minutes longer if necessary; if you wish your meat medium rare and pink rather than red, roast to 140°F. (Note that if meat was chilled when it went into the oven, it may take a few minutes longer to roast. A heavier saddle, 4½ pounds, will take 50 to 55 minutes in all. Baste every 4 to 5 minutes when roasting longer.)

When done: Turn off oven and set lamb on a platter near outside end of open oven door; a rest of 10 to 15 minutes before carving will permit juices to retreat back into meat tissues. Discard trussing strings after the rest period. Meanwhile, make the sauce, next step.

3. The sauce

4 tbl. dry white wine or dry white French vermouth
½ pt beef stock or bouillon
Optional: 1 medium tomato, chopped (not peeled)
Salt and pepper
A sieve
A small saucepan

Spoon all but a tablespoon of fat out of roasting dish, pour in wine and stock, and add optional tomato. Set over high heat and boil, scraping up coagulated roasting juices with a wooden spoon; mash cooking vegetables into liquid as it boils. Reduce liquid by about half, correct seasoning, strain into saucepan, and keep warm. You will have only enough sauce to moisten each serving of meat.

(†) If you can control the heat, you may leave the finished lamb in a warming oven of no more than 120°F. for at least half an hour. With your sauce all made, you can then serve immediately.

4. Carving and serving

(a) Carving, at the table: If you wish to carve at the table you may follow the system of many *maîtres d'hôtel*, which is to make long, thin slices on each side, parallel to the backbone. (The first slice, which shaves off the fat, is not served.) Then turn the saddle upside down, cut off the flanks, and reserve for second helpings; cut out the fillets, and slice into crosswise pieces.

(b) Carving in the kitchen and reassembling: This works out nicely, and the carved pieces are replaced on the saddle bone. Although you may cut the long thin slices described in the preceding paragraph, we suggest cutting across the grain for better eating texture. Provide yourself with a long, very sharp knife, a fork, and a carving board; heat oven to 475°F., Mark 9, for a brief warm-up after the reassembly, and carve rapidly, as follows.

Turn saddle upside down and slice off the flanks. Cutting down parallel against the backbone and then following its outward curve, slice out first one whole fillet, then the other (A).

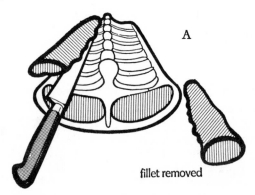

A

fillet removed

Turn the saddle right side up, shave off outside fat on each side if you wish, then cut down parallel against backbone and follow its outward curve to slice off the whole loin strip on each side. Slanting knife at a 45-degree angle parallel to board, rapidly slice each strip into cross-grain pieces ¾ inch thick; season lightly with salt and pepper but keep slices in order, so that you may replace them again on the bone. Slice and season the fillets.

Arrange the flanks lengthwise on a hot ovenproof serving platter and settle the saddle bone on top (B). Pile the fillet pieces at each end of the saddle, and rearrange the loin slices back in place on each side of the backbone (C).

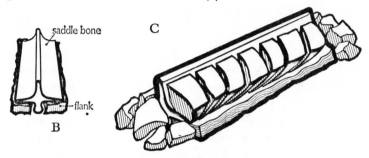

Pour the carving juices over the meat; set platter for 2 minutes in oven to give a sizzling impression. Pour a spoonful or two of sauce over the meat, rapidly decorate platter with parsley, watercress, or a vegetable garnish, and serve immediately.

Selle d'Agneau, Persillade
[Saddle of Lamb Garnished with Parsley and Buttered Breadcrumbs]

A garnish of breadcrumbs sautéed in butter with shallots and seasonings, tossed with parsley, and spread over the finished saddle of lamb is fragrant, attractive, and especially called for when you are carving in the kitchen and serving the reassembled lamb on the saddle bone. Make the *persillade* at any convenient time as long as it is ready to serve with the roast, as follows:

2 oz. clarified butter (melted butter, skimmed; clear liquid butter poured off milky residue)
A medium (10-in.) frying pan
2 tbl. finely minced shallots or spring onions

2 oz. moderately fine, fresh white breadcrumbs
Salt and pepper
3 to 4 tbl. minced fresh parsley

Melt butter to bubbling in pan, add shallots and stir for 1 minute, then add breadcrumbs and stir over moderately high heat for several minutes until a nice, golden brown. Remove from heat, stir in salt and pepper to taste, and set aside. When the meat is on its platter, mix the parsley into the crumbs and spread the *persillade* over the lamb; reheat for a moment in hot oven, and serve.

Selle d'Agneau, Milanaise
[Saddle of Lamb Garnished with Parmesan Cheese and Breadcrumbs]

Another attractive finish to a roast saddle of lamb is to spread on a coating of cheese and breadcrumbs, then set it into the oven for a moment to brown. Make the mixture as follows:

2 oz. melted butter
4 tbl. fairly fine, stale breadcrumbs
1½ oz. grated Parmesan cheese
A small bowl
Pepper to taste

Preheat oven to 475°F., Mark 9, in time for serving. Blend the butter, crumbs, and cheese together in the bowl; season to taste with pepper and set aside. When saddle is roasted, has rested, and is ready to serve, spread on the crumbs and cheese. Set in upper third of preheated oven for 2 to 3 minutes to brown lightly; serve immediately.

Veal · *Veau*

Some 25 pages are devoted to veal, its quality, and its cuts, in Volume I, starting on page 380. Recipes include casserole roasts with herbs and aromatic vegetables, the sumptuous *veau Orloff*, veal stuffed with ham and cheese, two fine stews, a detailed section on how to prepare your own scallops, another on chops, and some useful suggestions for minced veal patties, an excellent solution for the quite reasonably priced little pieces of neck meat you sometimes find packaged at the meat counter. Here we have three groups of recipes for braising veal: shoulder chops, stews, and illustrated directions on how to bone and stuff a breast of veal in the French manner. We end with two dishes from the *haute cuisine* – *veau en feuilletons* and *noisettes de veau*, *périgourdine* – both requiring the ultimate in fine wines, truffles, *foie gras*, and well-filled *porte-feuilles*.

BRAISED VEAL CHOPS AND STEAKS

Both steaks cut from the leg of veal and shoulder chops benefit deliciously from the slow, moist cooking of a braise, as do rib and loin chops from veal that is not of the pale and tender quality one had hoped to find. Because weights of veal carcasses and cutting methods for veal vary so tremendously, we shall simply specify the weight and the thickness of the meat. For shoulder chops, count on ¾ pound per person, and each chop should be ¾ to 1 inch thick. Cross-grain slices from the leg (round) should also be ¾ to 1 inch thick, and 1½ to 2 pounds will serve 4 people.

*Côtes de Veau dans leur Jus
[Veal Chops or Steaks Braised in Wine]

This is a lovely, simple, basic method for braising veal chops or steaks. Serve just as it is, enriching the braising juices with a little butter, or elaborating with cream and mushrooms or other trimmings, as described in the variations following this recipe. You might arrange the chops on a bed of creamed spinach or on the potatoes simmered in cream and tarragon, page 510. Or you could accompany them with the *gratin* of chard or of spinach and onions, pages 472 or 474. The delicious courgette *timbale* on page 488 would make the dinner much dressier, of course, and if you did not wish a rice or potato dish, a fresh loaf of your own French bread would very nicely take the place of a starchy vegetable. For wine, we suggest a Médoc.

[For 4 people]

1. Browning the chops

4 veal shoulder chops ¾ to 1 in. thick and ¾ lb. each; or 1½ to 2 lb. veal
   steak ¾ to 1 in. thick
1½ to 2 oz. butter
1 to 2 tbl. olive oil or cooking oil
An electric frying pan large enough to hold all the meat in 1 layer; or a
   medium pan and a baking dish or casserole

If using chops, cut off extra backbone pieces and remove any loose ribs, gristle, and excess fat; if tail is loose, wind it around the body of the meat and skewer in place. (Leave steaks whole or cut into serving pieces, whichever you prefer.) Dry meat thoroughly on paper towels. Heat 1 ounce butter and 1 tablespoon of oil in pan, and when butter foam begins to subside, arrange as much meat in pan as will easily fit in 1 layer. Brown 3 to 4 minutes on each side, regulating heat so butter is very hot but not browning. Remove meat to a side dish if you have not browned all at once, and brown the rest of the veal with more butter or oil if needed.

2. Braising the chops

Salt and pepper
3 tbl. minced shallots or spring onions
¼ pt dry white wine or dry white French vermouth
About ½ pt veal stock, chicken stock, or a combination of tinned
   chicken and beef bouillon
½ tsp. tarragon, thyme, or mixed Provençal herbs

(You may braise the chops either on top of the stove or in a preheated 325°F., Mark 3 oven; if they will not fit flat in one layer, overlap slightly and plan to baste more frequently.) Season meat on both sides with salt and pepper, and arrange in the pan. Set over moderate heat, stir in the shallots or spring onions, and cook 2 minutes, then pour in the wine or vermouth, and enough stock or bouillon to come half way up the meat. Add the herbs. Bring to the simmer on top of the stove, cover pan, and maintain at a slow, steady simmer throughout cooking, basting meat several times with liquid in pan. Whether chops or steak, meat should be done in 50 to 60 minutes, and should be tender when pierced with a knife: if not tender, cook 5 to 10 minutes longer.

3. Sauce and serving

A hot platter
Salt and pepper
Drops of fresh lemon juice
1 to 1½ oz. soft butter
Minced fresh parsley and whatever vegetables you wish

Arrange the veal on the platter; cover and keep warm in turned-off oven, door ajar, for the few minutes it will take to finish the sauce. Skim surface fat off cooking juices, bring to the boil, skimming, and boil down rapidly until liquid is almost syrupy. Carefully correct seasoning, adding lemon juice to taste. Remove from heat and swish in the enrichment butter, half a tablespoon at a time. Spoon the sauce over the chops, sprinkle with parsley, and serve immediately.

(†) If you are not serving immediately, prepare the sauce by boiling down the cooking juices to concentrate them, but do not reduce the quantity quite so much. Return veal to pan, baste with sauce, lay waxed paper over it and cover pan loosely. The meat will keep nicely for at least half an hour on a hot-plate or warming oven at 110° to 120°F.; finish sauce just before serving.

Côtes de Veau Gratinées au Fromage
[Braised Veal Chops or Steaks Gratinéed with Cheese]

This is a delicious variation with cheese.

Brown and braise the veal, steps 1 and 2 in the preceding master recipe, and make the sauce, step 3. Shortly before serving them, gratiné as follows.

3 oz. coarsely grated Gruyère cheese
3 tbl. dry white wine, or dry white French vermouth

Preheat grill to moderately hot. Arrange the braised veal in a shallow baking dish, if not already in one, and spread the cheese over the meat. Sprinkle the wine or vermouth on top, and set under grill for several minutes, until cheese has melted and browned nicely. Arrange the chops on their platter, pour the sauce around them, and serve.

Côtes de Veau Braisées aux Champignons
[Veal Chops or Steaks Braised with Mushrooms and Cream]

Mushrooms and veal, like mushrooms and chicken, always go well together and one reason undoubtedly is that the natural monosodium glutamate in the mushrooms points up the delicate flavour of the meat.

Brown and braise the veal, steps 1 and 2 in the master recipe, pages 284–5, but about 10 minutes before veal is done add the mushrooms as follows.

¼ lb. fresh mushrooms
1 oz. butter in a medium (10-in.) frying pan
Salt and pepper

Trim, wash, and dry the mushrooms; slice or quarter them. Heat butter to foaming, add mushrooms, and sauté, tossing and turning for 2 to 3 minutes; season lightly and set aside. (A short sauté in butter gives them added flavour.) When you estimate the veal has around 10 minutes more in the oven, add the mushrooms, basting them with the juices in the casserole.

Sauce and serving

¼ pt or more *crème fraîche* or double cream
Salt and pepper
Drops of lemon juice
1 to 1½ oz. soft butter
2 to 3 tbl. minced, fresh parley, parsley sprigs, or whatever vegetable
    you may have chosen

When done, remove veal to hot platter; cover and keep warm. Set mushrooms aside on a plate. Skim surface fat off cooking juices and boil liquid down, if necessary, until almost syrupy. Add the cream and boil down again rapidly until sauce is lightly thickened. Return mushrooms to sauce and simmer a moment. Correct seasoning, adding drops of lemon juice as needed. Remove from heat, swish in enrichment butter, then pour sauce and mushrooms over veal, decorate with parsley or vegetables, and serve.

(†) If you are not to serve immediately, complete sauce, except for enrichment butter; return veal to pan and baste with sauce and mushrooms. Cover and keep warm (110° to 120°F.). Thin out sauce before serving, if necessary, with more cream or stock; swish in enrichment butter, basting meat with sauce until butter is absorbed.

Côtes de Veau Champvallon, Gratinées
[Veal Chops or Steaks Braised with Potatoes]

This is almost a meal in a dish, and needs only a fresh green accompaniment like broccoli, peas, beans, or spinach; or you may prefer a combination salad in a separate course. Here the potatoes, cooking with the veal and their juices, absorb marvellous flavour, and the cheese and breadcrumb topping at the end not only thickens the cooking juices but also makes attractive serving. Although the general method is almost the same as the master recipe, we give a shortened full account because of slight differences.

Note: Here you must trim the meat in some way so that it will all fit in one layer in a casserole or baking dish; see step 2.

[For 4 people]

1. Browning the veal

4 oz. lardons (blanched bacon sticks, 1½ ins. long and ¼ in. thick, page 213)
3 tbl. olive oil or cooking oil
4 veal shoulder chops or steaks ¾ to 1 in. thick, dried in paper towels
1 large onion, minced
2 large cloves garlic, mashed or minced

Cut the blanched lardons of bacon into ¼-inch dice, and brown slowly with the oil in a frying pan. Remove with a slotted spoon and set aside, leaving fat in pan. Add the chops or steaks; brown for 3 to 4 minutes on each side, being sure fat is very hot but not burning. Remove veal. Stir in the onions and garlic, cover, and cook slowly, stirring occasionally, for 8 to 10 minutes, until tender. Scoop onions and garlic into a dish, leaving fat in pan. Remove pan from heat.

2. Braising the veal

Salt and pepper
½ tsp. tarragon, thyme, or mixed Provençal herbs
A covered flameproof casserole or baking dish that will just hold all the meat in one layer (or use two dishes)
1½ lb. potatoes, peeled and cut into ⅛-in. slices
4 tbl. fresh, rather roughly minced parsley
¼ pt dry white wine or dry white French vermouth
About ½ pt veal stock, chicken stock, or a combination of tinned chicken and beef bouillon
Buttered aluminium foil
A bulb baster

Preheat oven to 350°F., Mark 4. Season veal with salt, pepper, and herbs, and arrange in one close layer in casserole with the onions and garlic, and half the browned, diced *lardons*. Strew the potatoes over the veal, seasoning each layer with salt, pepper, and a sprinkling of parsley. (You should have no more than ¾ inch of potatoes in all.) Pour in the wine, and enough stock or bouillon to come ⅓ the way up the potatoes. Spoon a tablespoon or 2 of the cooking fat over the potatoes (unless it has browned, in which case use melted butter). Sprinkle the remaining *lardon* bits over the potatoes, and bring contents of casserole to simmer on top of stove. Drape buttered foil over potatoes, cover casserole, and set in middle level of preheated oven. Bake for about an hour, basting several times with liquid in pan.

3. Gratinéeing and serving

4 tbl. not-too-fine white breadcrumbs
1½ oz. finely grated Gruyère or Parmesan cheese

Turn oven thermostat to 425°F., Mark 7. When veal and potatoes are tender, taste cooking liquid and correct seasoning if necessary. Mix the crumbs and cheese together, and spread over the potatoes. Baste with juices in casserole and set in upper-third level of oven. Baste several times while juices boil down and thicken with the crumbs, and topping browns nicely; this will take 10 to 15 minutes. Either serve from casserole or baking dish, or remove each piece of veal with its topping, and transfer to a hot platter; pour juices around.

(†) If you are not to serve immediately, let juices reduce and thicken a little less; keep warm, loosely covered with foil, on a hot-plate or 120°F. warming oven. Baste with more stock or with melted butter, if necessary, before serving.

Other ideas for veal chops and steaks

Starting out with the simple braise in the master recipe on page 283, you might stir the reduced cooking juices, step 3, into a *pistou* flavouring, page 217, or into the Provençal mixture of anchovies, capers, garlic, and parsley described in Volume I, page 353. Another idea would be to spread a *pipérade* of sautéed green peppers, tomatoes, garlic, and herbs over the braised veal; cover and let them warm together for a few minutes, then spoon on the sauce and serve. You could use the *pistouille* mixture, page 463, of sautéed aubergine, tomatoes, and peppers in the same way. Finally, there is the always attractive garniture *bonne femme*, a combination of bacon *lardons*, partially cooked small onions, and blanched small potatoes, which you add to the veal the last half hour of braising so all finish their cooking together; for this, adapt the *poulet en cocotte bonne femme* recipe in Volume I, page 275.

VEAL STEWS

Veal makes lovely stew, and it cooks in a little more than an hour. Volume I contains the well-known *blanquette de veau*, with its onions, mushrooms, and creamy sauce, as well as a hearty brown stew with tomatoes. Here are several more stews, including *ossobuco*.

VEAL CUTS FOR STEWING

The part of the veal breast called 'flank', illustrated on page 296, is a favourite French stewing cut, but one that is not

290 MEATS: COUNTRY KITCHEN TO HAUTE CUISINE

popular with everyone because of the crunchy cartilage of the breast bone and rib ends. The scrag end, shin, and middle neck all give good stew meat. The hind shin is the *ossobuco*, with the marrow bone, and the choicest; the front shin has more bone and the meat more separations; it requires half an hour longer cooking, but makes a good stew because of its gelatinous quality. (If the veal you buy is not of the palest and tenderest quality, the best way to cook it is by stewing or braising; the leg can be used for boneless stewing meat in this case.)

A pound of boneless meat will serve 2 to 3 people, but you will need ¾ to 1 pound per person for meat with bone. You may use a combination of both in any of the recipes except for *ossobuco*, but we shall usually specify boneless meat simply to eliminate cumbersome either-or choices. Bones, however, will add texture and flavour to the stew; if your meat is boneless it is a good idea to tie a cupful or so of chopped veal marrow and knuckle bones in washed cheesecloth, and simmer them with the meat.

*Ragoût de Veau aux Champignons
[Veal Stew with Tomatoes, Mushrooms, and Cream]

There are endless ways of flavouring and finishing off a veal stew, because veal, like chicken, is amenable to infinite variety. Here is a master recipe for starting out the veal, and a number of ways to vary its presentation. Serve this with rice or pasta, and a fresh green vegetable or a salad. For wine, choose a light, young red like Beaujolais or Cabernet Sauvignon, or a rather strong, dry white of the Côtes-du-Rhône type.

[*For 4 to 6 people*]

1. Browning the veal and the onions

2½ to 3 lb. trimmed and boneless lean stewing veal cut into 1½-in.
  chunks (see notes preceding recipe)
Salt and pepper
2 oz. flour on a plate
2 or more tbl. olive oil or cooking oil
A heavy frying pan, non-stick recommended

Dry veal on paper towels, season with salt and pepper, and just before browning, roll in flour and shake off excess. (Shaking in a sieve works nicely.) Film pan with ⅛ inch of oil, set over moderately high heat, and when very hot but not smoking, add as many pieces of veal as will fit easily in 1 layer. Brown nicely on all sides, which will take 4 to 5 minutes or more; remove veal, as it is browned, to a side dish, and continue with the rest.

1 lb. onions, sliced
2 tbl. oil
A heavy 10- by 2-in. chicken fryer, electric frying pan, or 5-pt flameproof casserole

While veal is browning, cook onions in oil over moderate heat, stirring occasionally, for 8 to 10 minutes. When tender, raise heat and brown very lightly. When the veal is done, add it to the onions.

2. Braising the veal

¼ pt dry white wine or dry white French vermouth
½ pt brown veal stock, or chicken stock, or a combination of tinned chicken broth and beef bouillon
1 tsp. tarragon, basil, or oregano
1 bay leaf
1 or 2 large cloves garlic, mashed or minced
1 or 2 tomatoes, peeled, seeded, juiced, and roughly chopped

Discard oil from veal sauté pan and deglaze pan with the wine, scraping up coagulated browning juices. Pour the wine into the veal and onions; stir in the stock, herbs, garlic, and tomatoes. Bring to the simmer, cover and simmer slowly, basting meat occasionally with liquids in pan, for 1 to 1¼ hours, or until veal is tender when pierced with a knife. Do not overcook; meat should not fall apart.

3. The mushrooms

6 to 8 oz. fresh mushrooms
More oil
The frying pan that browned the veal
Salt and pepper

While veal is simmering, trim, wash, dry, and quarter the mushrooms. Film pan with ⅛ inch of oil, and set over moderately high heat; when oil is hot but not smoking, sauté the mushrooms, tossing and turning, for 3 to 4 minutes, just until they are starting to brown lightly. Season to taste, and set aside.

4. Sauce and serving

If needed: *beurre manié* (1 tbl. flour blended to a paste with ½ oz. soft
  butter), and a wire whisk
¼ pt *crème fraîche* or double cream
The mushrooms
Minced fresh parsley, or mixed fresh green herbs (parsley, chives, and
  tarragon, basil, or oregano)

When veal is tender, scoop it out into a side dish with a slotted spoon. Skim off surface fat, and boil down cooking liquid, if necessary, to concentrate its flavour. If it seems too thin (it must be thick enough to cover the meat nicely), remove from heat, beat in *beurre manié* with wire whisk, and bring to the simmer. Stir in the cream and the mushrooms, bring to the boil, and boil slowly 2 to 3 minutes to thicken the sauce again, and to blend flavours. Carefully correct seasoning. Return veal to casserole and simmer again for 2 to 3 minutes, basting the veal with the sauce; correct seasoning again. Either serve from pan or casserole, or arrange on a hot platter surrounded with whatever vegetables you have chosen. Decorate with herbs, and bring immediately to the table.

(†) May be kept warm for a good ½ hour on a hot-plate or over simmering water. May be cooked a day before serving; when cold, spread plastic wrap over surface, cover, and refrigerate. When ready to serve, bring to simmer slowly, and simmer about 10 minutes, basting frequently, until thoroughly reheated but not overcooked. If sauce seems too thick, thin out with stock or cream.

Ragoût de Veau, Printanier
[Veal Stew Garnished with Carrots, Onions,
New Potatoes, and Green Peas]

When all the vegetables are fresh, this is delicious indeed and very attractive to serve because of the various colours. If you are cooking and serving with no delay, the vegetables may do all of their simmering in the stew, and you add them at different times, according to how long they take to cook. Otherwise do as suggested here, giving them a separate start, and letting them finish off in the stew just before serving; in this method, you may prepare everything ahead except for the potatoes.

Follow method and ingredients for preceding master recipe, steps 1 and 2, using only ½ pound of onions in step 1, and omitting the garlic in step 2. Meanwhile, prepare vegetables.

The carrots and onions

4 to 6 fine, fresh carrots
24 to 30 small, white, fresh onions ¾ to 1 in. in diameter
A heavy covered saucepan
½ pt water
¾ oz. butter
½ tsp. salt

Peel the carrots, halve or quarter them depending on size, and cut into 1½-inch lengths; trim edges to round them, if you wish. Drop onions into boiling water, boil 1 minute, drain, and slip off peel; pierce a cross ¼ inch deep in root ends for even cooking. Place carrots and onions in pan with the water, butter, and salt; cover and simmer slowly about 25 minutes, until just tender. Set aside.

The peas

1 to 1½ lb. fresh peas (1 to 1½ cups, shelled)
A saucepan containing 5-pts of rapidly boiling, salted water

Drop the peas into the rapidly boiling water, bring quickly back to the boil again, and boil uncovered 4 to 8 minutes or more, depending on tenderness. Test frequently by tasting; they should be almost, but not quite, done. Drain immediately, run cold water over them to stop the cooking and retain their fresh colour; drain again and set aside.

The potatoes

About 2 lb. new potatoes all of a size for easy cutting (2¾ to 3 ins. long, for instance)

A bowl of cold water

When needed: a saucepan of boiling, salted water

Peel the potatoes and trim into ovals about $2\frac{1}{4}$ inches long and $1\frac{1}{2}$ inches thick; drop into bowl of cold water and set aside. (About $\frac{1}{2}$ hour before you plan to serve the stew, drain the potatoes and drop into boiling water to cover. Boil slowly, uncovered, until almost tender, drain and add to stew as indicated in last paragraph.)

Finishing the stew

If needed: more stock or bouillon

When veal is tender, tip pan and skim off surface fat. If sauce has reduced too much, add a little more stock or bouillon so that you will have enough liquid to cook and baste the vegetables.

About 10 minutes before serving, arrange the carrots, onions, potatoes, and peas in the casserole, pushing them gently down into the meat and cooking juices. Pour any cooking juices from carrots and onions over meat, and baste both meat and vegetables with juices in casserole. Bring to the simmer, cover closely, and simmer about 10 minutes, basting several times, until vegetables are tender. Correct seasoning. Either serve from casserole, or turn the stew out on to a hot platter.

Ossobuco
Jarret de Veau à la Provençale
[Braised Shin of Veal with Wine, Tomatoes, Lemon, and Orange]

Osso is bone and *buco* is round, meaning the shin with the round bone, which is the hind leg with the marrow bone. This favourite Italian veal stew is also done in France, and here is the Provençal version. Although you may use the foreleg, pieces from the hind leg are so much more attractive to serve because the bone is small and the meat holds around it nicely, that we counsel you to order hind shin, and do the recipe when you have the right meat. Veal shin, sawed into

1½-inch pieces and ready to cook, will freeze perfectly for several weeks; therefore pick up whatever you can whenever you can.

[*For 4 people – 2 pounds shin of veal, sawed into crosswise pieces 1½ inches thick*]

Season, flour, and brown the shin; arrange in the braising liquid with the onions, garlic, tomatoes, and herbs as described in the master recipe, steps 1 and 2, pages 290–91. Then proceed as follows.

1 orange
1 lemon
A vegetable peeler
A saucepan containing a quart or so of boiling water

Cut the zests (coloured parts of the peel) from the orange and lemon, then cut zests into julienne strips $\frac{1}{16}$ inch wide. To remove bitterness (but none of the flavour), simmer 10 minutes; drain, refresh in cold water, drain again, and stir into the casserole with the veal stew.

Bring stew to simmer, cover casserole, and simmer either in a preheated 325°F., Mark 3 oven or on top of the stove for 1¼ hours, or until meat is tender when pierced with a fork. Do not overcook: meat must not come loose from bone. When tender, tip casserole and skim surface fat from cooking liquid. Set casserole over high heat, if necessary, and boil down sauce to concentrate flavour. Correct seasoning. Serve either from casserole, or on a hot platter. Decorate with parsley sprigs.

Other ideas

Use other veal stew meat, such as cuts from the shoulder or the leg, and give it the *ossobuco* flavouring. Vary the *ossobuco* recipe with olives: blanch a handful each of stoned green olives and stoned black olives for 10 minutes in a quart of boiling water; drain, and add to the stew the last 15 to 20 minutes of cooking. See also the variations at the end of beef stews, pages 217–21, which include a herb cheese, and garlic finish, another with anchovies and garlic, a *pipérade* with peppers and tomatoes, and a final one with olives and pota-toes; any of these may be added to the cooked veal at the end of step 2, master recipe, page 291, instead of the mushrooms and cream. You thus have a wide choice, and need never serve the same stew twice.

STUFFED BREAST OF VEAL

Breast of veal boned, stuffed with a well-seasoned filling, braised, and sauced makes a handsome as well as tasty main-course party dish, and one that is far more reasonable in price than most. French and English meat cutting methods differ, and as we find the French version much the more attractive to serve, here is how to buy and prepare it. If you cannot have the butchering done properly for you, and if you enjoy working with meat yourself, you will find the whole breast not at all difficult to handle, and you may even be able to buy it at a far more interesting price than if it were boned and trimmed in the shop.

HOW TO BUY A BREAST OF VEAL

In England and America, a breast of veal (or of lamb) comprises the whole brisket–flank section. From a large, pale, prime carcass of veal, such as you can find in France and at some butchers here, this will weigh 7 to 7½ pounds before boning and trimming. The boned brisket weighs 2½ pounds; the breastbone, 1 pound; the flank and skirt (flap of meat

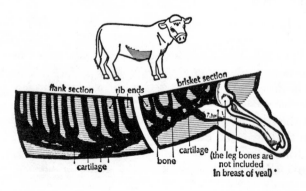

flank section   rib ends   brisket section

cartilage   bone   cartilage   (the leg bones are not included in breast of veal) *

falling over ribs), with the ribs and cartilage, 3½ pounds. It is the boned brisket that is stuffed for French recipes; a 2½-pound brisket, stuffed, will be 12 inches long, 7 to 8 inches across, and can easily serve 8 people.

Adapt whatever you find to the general idea of the recipe even if your butcher does not stock breasts of the desired weight, or follows different cutting methods. You might, for instance, sew or skewer 2 flanks together for stuffing, or 2 briskets, if they are smaller than you think they should be. If you have trouble making your wishes known, show your butcher this picture; he might be willing to order one for you, and to prepare it according to your specifications.

Actually, the whole brisket–flank combination is a good buy because not only will you have the brisket to stuff, but you can also save the thick part of the flank for stew, you can mince the rest of the flank along with the skirt for your stuffing, and when you boil up the breastbone and ribs, you will have a fine veal stock for braising the *poitrine farcie*.

FRENCH TERMINOLOGY

Brisket is *poitrine*, and the *poitrine* also includes the skirt, *hampe*; ask for a *poitrine de veau désossée, avec poche*. The flank is called *tendron*, and is a favourite French cut for *blanquette de veau*, particularly the thick part containing the breastbone cartilage.

DIRECTIONS FOR THE HOME BUTCHER

Note: In the drawing, the breast has been separated in two – the right-hand piece, minus leg bones, is the brisket; the left-hand piece the flank.

To bone the whole breast, start with the breastbone (right side in drawing), which is attached to the ribs by cartilages: first, place the meat rib-side up, with the breastbone hanging over the edge of the table. Lean hard on the bone to break it from the cartilages at the rib ends, then cut around its ridges and follow its cartilaginous prolongation into the flank, to remove the entire bone from the meat. The next step is to separate the brisket from the flank: slice through the meat between ribs 5 and 6 to make two pieces, as in the drawing. Slice off the skirt, a flap of meat on the rib side, attached to the thick part of the flank. Remove the rib bones from both brisket and flank by cutting around them, then underneath each bone to loosen it from the meat. The thick part of the flank that contained the prolongation of the breastbone (bottom left in drawing) can make an excellent stew for 2 people; cut it off from the rest of the flank, and freeze it for another meal. Trim excess fat off brisket with a long, sharp knife. Then carefully slice a pocket in the brisket (right-hand piece), going in from the large or flank end; the brisket will now be like a pouch, and you will close it by sewing or skewering after you stuff it. Scrape usable meat from membranes covering flank and skirt, and mince it. Chop up the breastbone, and brown bones and scraps half an hour in a 450°F., Mark 8 oven with a sliced carrot and onion; then simmer for 3 to 4 hours in water, herbs, and seasonings to make a simple but delicious veal stock (detailed directions are in Volume I, pages 125–8).

Poitrine de Veau, Farcie
[Breast of Veal Stuffed and Braised – hot or cold]

Green stuffings provide attractive serving slices and should be made of chard leaves, if you can find them; spinach, if you cannot. The rest of the stuffing consists of boiled rice, minced veal, a little ham, and a bit of onion. There is no pork here, no garlic, and the delicate taste of the veal does seem to come through beautifully. Accompany the dish with braised onions and carrots or baked tomatoes. A not-too-heavy red wine would be the one to choose, like a Bordeaux, a young Beaujolais, or a Cabernet Sauvignon; a rosé would also go well. Serve cold breast of veal with sliced tomatoes, the French potato salad, *pommes à l'huile*, Volume I, page 578, and either a rosé or a dry white from the Rhône like Chante Alouette.

[*For 8 people*]

1. Chard or spinach stuffing with rice, veal, and ham

2 oz. rendered fresh pork fat, ham fat, or chicken or goose fat
6 tbl. finely minced onions
A medium (10-in.) frying pan, enamelled or non-stick
4 or 5 large, green chard leaves minus white part of stalks (or 8 oz.
   cooked, chopped spinach or 8-oz. frozen spinach, thawed and
   squeezed dry)
Salt
The bowl of a heavy-duty mixer, or a large mixing bowl and wooden
   spoon
2 oz. boiled rice
$\frac{3}{4}$ lb. lean raw veal finely minced with 2 oz. lean mild-cured boiled ham
2 to 3 oz. grated Parmesan cheese
1 large egg
Large pinch grated nutmeg
$\frac{1}{4}$ tsp. pepper

Melt the fat in the frying pan, stir in the onions, cover, and
cook slowly, stirring occasionally for 10 minutes, until tender
and just beginning to brown lightly. Set aside. Meanwhile
blanch the chard leaves in a large pan of boiling salted water
for 3 to 4 minutes, until wilted; drain, refresh in cold water,
squeeze hard to rid leaves of water, and chop moderately fine
($\frac{1}{4}$-inch pieces). Blend chard (or spinach) into onions; stir
over moderately high heat for a few moments to evaporate
remaining liquid; cover and cook slowly several minutes
more, until fairly tender. Season to taste and scrape into bowl.
Vigorously beat in the boiled rice, minced meat, cheese, egg,
nutmeg, and pepper. Sauté a small spoonful in frying pan
until cooked through, taste carefully, and add more seasonings
if you feel them necessary.

2. Stuffing the veal

A boned breast of veal, weighing, if possible, around $2\frac{1}{2}$ lb. (see
   directions, description, and alternatives, pages 296–8)
Salt and pepper
A trussing needle or small poultry-lacing skewers
White string

Open the pocket in the meat and sprinkle lightly with salt
and pepper. Insert the stuffing, pushing it well down into the
meat, but do not overfill. Close opening of meat by sewing

with string, or with skewers and string. If by chance you have pierced a hole in the surface of the meat, close it by sewing or skewering.

The ridged side, where the ribs were, is the underside; turn small end of the meat under and sew or skewer it in place, thus giving the veal a rectangular cushion shape about 12 inches long and 8 inches across. If meat seems solid and stuffing securely in place, tying is not necessary; otherwise, with string, make 2 loops around length and several around circumference, but do not tie too tightly. Dry the meat thoroughly before proceeding to next step.

(†) If you wish to prepare and refrigerate the veal the day before cooking, chill stuffing before inserting it into the meat, just to be sure and safe.

3. Browning and braising the veal: 2½ hours

Rendered pork fat, goose fat, or cooking oil
A heavy casserole or roaster just large enough to hold veal comfortably
   (a 10- by 12-in. oval, for example)
1 or 2 carrots and onions, roughly sliced
Optional but desirable, if you have no home-made veal stock: 1 or 2
   veal bones, chopped
Salt
A bulb baster
¼ pt dry white wine, or dry white French vermouth
1 pt or more home-made veal stock, or rich chicken stock, or a
   combination of tinned beef bouillon and chicken broth
½ tsp. thyme
1 bay leaf
A sheet of fresh pork fat or suet, or aluminium foil

Preheat oven to 450°F., Mark 8. Film casserole with ⅛ inch of fat or oil; when very hot but not smoking, brown the vegetables and optional bones. Remove to a side dish, add more fat or oil if needed, and brown bottom (former rib side) of veal, lifting carefully from time to time with wooden spoon to be sure meat is not sticking. When browned, in 5 to 6 minutes, baste top with fat and set uncovered in upper-middle level of preheated oven for about 15 minutes, basting with fat in casserole several times, until top and sides of meat have browned nicely. Remove from oven; turn thermostat down to 350°F., Mark 4. Salt the meat lightly, strew the browned bones and vegetables around, pour in the wine and enough stock or bouillon to come ⅔ the way up meat. Add the thyme and bay leaf, and drape the fat or foil over the meat.

Bring to the simmer on top of stove, cover the casserole, and braise in lower-middle level of oven, regulating heat so that liquid in casserole remains at a slow, even simmer. If meat is easy to turn, do so several times during cooking, replacing fat or foil on top; otherwise, baste every 20 minutes or so with the liquids in the casserole. Meat should be done in about 2 hours, when it feels tender if pierced with a fork. It should retain its shape perfectly; in other words, do not let it overcook.

4. Sauce and serving

A hot platter
A sieve set over a saucepan
If needed: 1 tbl. cornflour mixed to a paste with 2 tbl. wine or vermouth
Salt and pepper
1 to 1½ oz. soft butter
Parsley, watercress, or whatever vegetable garnish you have chosen
A warm sauce bowl

Remove veal to hot platter. Do not untie or unskewer it yet, but cover with its fat or foil, and set in turned-off oven, door ajar. Strain braising liquid into saucepan, pressing juices out of vegetables. Skim off surface fat, bring liquid to the simmer, skimming, and boil down rapidly, if necessary, to around ¾ pint.

If sauce needs thickening, remove from heat, beat in the cornflour mixture, and simmer 2 minutes. Carefully correct seasoning. Just before serving, remove from heat and beat in the enrichment butter half a tablespoon at a time. Remove trussings from veal, spoon a little sauce over to glaze it, and decorate the platter as you wish. Pour remaining sauce into bowl. Serve immediately.

To carve, cut crosswise slices ⅜ to ½ inch thick, as though meat were a loaf of bread. Ring each slice with a spoonful or two of sauce.

(†) If you are not serving for half an hour or so, finish the sauce except for butter enrichment; return meat and sauce to casserole. Set cover askew and keep anywhere that you can maintain a temperature of 120°F. An occasional basting of the meat will keep it moist; if sauce thickens during wait, thin with stock before serving.

Other stuffings

Breast of veal takes kindly to many stuffings. Another combination with chard includes the sausage meat, ham, and breadcrumbs used for *paupiette* of beef on page 222, and there is the mushroom *duxelles* and spinach stuffing for shoulder of lamb Viroflay on page 271. Either the mushroom and kidney stuffing for boned leg of lamb, page 266, or the kidney and rice stuffing in Volume I, page 365, would be delicious and unusual, as would be the *boudin blanc* and mushrooms mixture in the chicken section, page 371. A complete run-down of stuffing possibilities is on pages 664–6.

*Veau en Feuilletons
[Sliced and Stuffed Roast of Veal]

Veal wants stuffing, as the British would say, and here is a typically French *grande cuisine farce fine* of pork, veal, truffles, *foie gras*, and cognac. This is sliced veal marinated in wine and truffles, then tied together in the form of a roast with the stuffing between each slice. Braised with stock and aromatic vegetables, it produces a most heavenly sauce combining all of the luxurious flavours. Very definitely a dish for a select group of friends, it calls for your finest château-bottled claret, and the best vegetables. You might surround the meat platter with a fluted border of *pommes duchesse* (page 524) and pass separately something like braised spinach, chopped broccoli simmered in cream (page 452), braised chicory or lettuce, or fresh, buttered peas.

THE VEAL

If you can get it, the top round from a large, pale, prime leg would give you solid scallops with no muscle separations.

Otherwise settle either for cuts from the full round that you can separate and regroup, or thin scallopini. These latter you could regroup or spread separately with stuffing. Play it by look and feel, aiming for a re-formed roast about 10 inches long and 5 inches in diameter.

[*For 10 to 12 people*]

1. Marinating the veal in cognac and truffles

2 to 2½ lb. veal scallops preferably from the top round, making 10 to 12 slices 6 by 4 ins. in diameter and $\frac{3}{16}$ in. thick (or scallopini, 2 or 3 per person)
Waxed paper and a mallet or rolling pin
A dish large enough to hold scallops in several layers
¼ pt cognac
1 or 2 tinned truffles, minced, and their juice
Plastic wrap

Trim all filaments, fat, and extraneous matter from scallops. Place them one by one between sheets of waxed paper and pound not too heavily, to break down filaments slightly, and to spread the meat out a little. (This will not be necessary with scallopini.) Arrange the scallops in layers interspersed with sprinklings of cognac and minced truffles. Pour remaining cognac and the truffle juices over meat, cover with plastic wrap, and set aside while preparing stuffing.

2. Minced pork stuffing with ham, truffles, and *foie gras*

2 tbl. finely minced shallots or spring onions
¾ oz. butter
A small frying pan
Bowl of heavy-duty mixer, or a large mixing bowl

Sauté the shallots or spring onions slowly in the butter for 2 to 3 minutes until tender but not browned. Scrape into bowl.

The following, finely minced together:
12 oz. lean pork
4 oz. fresh pork fat (page 423)
4 oz. lean veal
4 oz. mild-cured ham
1 tsp. salt

⅛ tsp. white pepper
Big pinch ground allspice
½ tsp. tarragon leaves, finely chopped or powdered
1 egg
The juices from the marinated scallops, and the truffles

Add all of the rest of the ingredients listed, except the final item, and beat vigorously by machine or with a wooden spoon to blend thoroughly. Just before starting step 3, drain marinade liquid into stuffing, scrape truffles off veal, and beat vigorously into stuffing. To check seasoning, sauté a spoonful until cooked through, taste, and add more salt, pepper, or herbs if needed. (The *foie gras* comes in step 3.)

3. Assembling the veal

Either: a piece of caul fat 16 to 18 ins. square (page 384);
Or: well-washed cheesecloth, melted butter, and a pastry brush
Salt and pepper
4 to 6 oz. tinned *foie gras en bloc*
White string

(If your veal slices are smaller or thinner than the ideal, group them together, adapting meat to the method outlined here.) Spread the caul fat or cheesecloth on a board or tray. Season each scallop of veal lightly with salt and pepper, and build the slices into a closely packed loaf shape, with stuffing and a slice of *foie gras* between each scallop.

If you are using caul fat, fold it securely around the meat; if using cheesecloth, first paint it with melted butter, roll it tightly around circumference, then twist each end tight and tie close against meat with string. Tie a loop of string around length of meat, and wind string back and forth around circumference to keep all in place. You should have a fat sausage shape about 10 inches long.

(†) Recipe may be prepared a day in advance to this point; wrap airtight and refrigerate.

4. Browning and braising the veal: about 2 hours

A heavy, covered, flameproof casserole just large enough to hold
    meat comfortably, such as a 10- by 12-in. oval 5 in. deep
Rendered goose fat, pork fat, or cooking oil

1 or 2 veal knuckle and marrow bones, chopped
1 medium carrot, roughly chopped
1 medium onion, roughly chopped
¾ pt. excellent veal stock, beef stock, or a mixture of chicken broth and
    beef bouillon
½ tsp. thyme
1 bay leaf
Useful: a meat thermometer

Preheat oven to 350°F., Mark 4. Dry the meat in paper
towels. Set casserole over moderately high heat with the fat
or oil, and when very hot but not smoking, brown the meat
on all sides. (It will brown through cheesecloth perfectly
well.) Remove to a side dish and brown the bones and
vegetables. Push them to sides and return meat to casserole;
pour in enough stock or bouillon to come half way up. Strew
the herbs around the meat. Bring liquid to the simmer, cover
casserole, and set in lower-middle level of preheated oven.

   Check casserole in about 20 minutes, and when contents
are quietly simmering, reduce oven heat to 325°F., Mark 3.
Turn the meat twice during cooking and braise about 2 hours
in all, or to a meat thermometer reading of 165° to 170°F.
When done, remove veal to a side dish and let rest 20 minutes
in turned-off oven, door ajar; meat must settle before serving
so pieces will hold in place.

5. Sauce and serving

A sieve set over a saucepan
Salt and pepper to taste
2 tsp. cornflour blended with 3 tbl. dry Madeira (Sercial), dry port, or
    cognac
A wire whisk
A hot platter
Watercress, parsley sprigs, or whatever vegetable garnish you may
    have chosen
1 to 1½ oz. soft butter
A warm serving bowl

Strain braising liquid into saucepan. Skim off as much surface
fat as you can, and bring liquid to the simmer, skimming off
additional fat. Boil down rapidly, if necessary, to about ¾
pint; carefully correct seasoning. Remove from heat, blend

in the cornflour mixture, and simmer 2 minutes. Sauce should be lightly thickened.

Disturbing meat as little as possible, untie it. If you have used caul fat, it will have mostly disintegrated during cooking; remove any bits that have not. If you have used cheesecloth, carefully cut it off with shears. Using two spatulas, lift meat on to hot platter. (If by chance the slices come apart, push them together.) Spoon a little sauce over meat to glaze it, and decorate platter with whatever you have chosen. Reheat sauce, remove from heat, and beat in the enrichment butter a half tablespoon at a time, and pour into hot sauce bowl. Serve immediately. For serving, spread scallops slightly apart with spoon and fork, to display the meat. Be sure each slice comes off with its share of stuffing, and surround with a spoonful of sauce.

(†) You may complete the sauce except for the final butter enrichment, and arrange the meat on its platter, cover it, and keep warm for a good half hour at 120°F.

Feuilletons de Veau en Croûte
[Stuffed Roast of Veal Baked in a Pastry Crust]
The presentation of a roast baked in brown, decorated pastry is always dramatic. For the stuffed veal, follow the preceding master recipe exactly through steps 1, 2, and 3, and braise the meat in step 4 for about 1½ hours, or to a thermometer reading of 150°F. Remove the meat, and let it rest 30 minutes. Then untie it, remove covering, and drape the roast either in puff pastry as described for the *gigot en croûte* on page 264, or in chilled *brioche* dough as for the fillet of beef on page 255. Decorate the dough, glaze it with egg, and return to a 425°F., Mark 7 oven for 25 to 30 minutes, to cook and brown the crust, and to finish cooking the meat. Serve with the same sauce described in step 5 of the preceding recipe.

Noisettes de Veau, Périgourdine
[Individual Stuffed Loin Scallops with *Foie Gras* and Truffles]
Less dramatic but exquisite in taste are *noisettes* of veal, meaning the boneless loin section of a veal chop, surrounded with

the stuffing, braised in wine, and served with a brown, truffled sauce. You can do this dish, however, only if you have caul fat to hold the stuffing in place; it disintegrates during cooking. You might serve the *noisettes* on a platter garnished with very carefully sautéed potatoes, glazed onions, glazed carrots, sautéed mushrooms, and a decoration of fresh parsley sprigs. Another suggestion would be *pommes Anna*, page 517, or the *gratin Crécy* of scalloped potatoes and carrots in cream, Volume I, page 562, and the chopped, sautéed broccoli on page 451. A good Médoc would again be indicated.

[*For 6 people*]

1. Preparing the *noisettes* for cooking

12 *noisettes* of veal (boneless large eye of meat in loin or rib chops, ½ in. thick and 2½ ins. in diameter if possible; 3 per person if smaller)
½ the marinade ingredients in step 1, master recipe, page 303
2 tbl. finely minced shallots
About 3 oz. clarified butter (melted butter, skimmed; clear liquid butter spooned off milky residue)
A medium (10-in.) frying pan, non-stick recommended

Trim all fat, filaments and gristle from *noisettes*. Salt and pepper lightly, and marinate in a covered bowl with the cognac, truffles, and shallots for at least half an hour, or overnight. Scrape marinade off meat, and beat it into the stuffing (next step) along with the marinade liquid. Dry *noisettes* thoroughly on paper towels. Film pan with ⅛ inch of the clarified butter, heat to bubbling hot, and sauté a few scallops at a time for a minute or so on each side, just to stiffen the meat slightly. Remove to a side dish, reserving butter in pan.

½ the stuffing ingredients in step 2, master recipe, pages 303–4
3 oz. tinned *foie gras en bloc*
A piece of caul fat about 24 ins. square (page 384)

Divide stuffing and *foie gras* into 12 (or 18) portions. Spread a piece of caul fat (about 8 inches square) on a board or tray. Centre a half portion of stuffing upon it, and a half portion of *foie gras* upon that. Place a *noisette* of veal over the stuffing, top with its remaining share of *foie gras*, and spread with its

308 MEATS: COUNTRY KITCHEN TO HAUTE CUISINE

final share of stuffing. Fold caul fat around it, to enclose meat and stuffing. Continue with the rest of the *noisettes* in the same way.

(†) May be done a day in advance to this point; cover and refrigerate.

2. Cooking and serving

The frying pan and the clarified butter
The *noisettes* of veal wrapped in caul fat
A covered flameproof baking dish large enough to hold scallops in one slightly overlapping layer
A *brunoise* (3 tbl. each very finely diced – $\frac{1}{16}$ in. – carrots, onions, and celery)
3 tbl. dry Madeira (Sercial) wine
$\frac{1}{4}$ pt veal stock, beef stock, or bouillon
A hot platter, and whatever decorative garnish you have chosen
A small tinned truffle, minced, and its juices
1 to $1\frac{1}{2}$ oz. soft butter

Preheat oven to 375°F., Mark 5. Add more butter to pan, if necessary, to film it by $\frac{1}{8}$ inch. Heat to bubbling hot, and brown the meat again lightly on each side for a minute or so. Arrange in baking dish. Stir *brunoise* vegetables into pan, lower heat, and cook rather slowly for 5 to 6 minutes, until tender and barely browned. Pour in the Madeira, scraping up coagulated sauté juices with a wooden spoon. With a rubber spatula, scrape wine and vegetables over *noisettes*. Add the stock or bouillon, bring to the simmer, cover, and braise in middle level of preheated oven for 25 minutes.

Remove any bits of caul fat that have not disintegrated, and arrange *noisettes* on hot platter, cover and keep warm. Skim surface fat off cooking juices, and boil down rapidly until almost syrupy and reduced to around $\frac{1}{4}$ pint. Add minced truffle and its juices; simmer 2 minutes. Remove from heat, and swirl in the enrichment butter by half tablespoonfuls. Spoon sauce and *brunoise* vegetables over *noisettes*. Serve immediately.

(†) If you cannot serve immediately, finish sauce except for butter enrichment. Return meat to baking dish, baste with sauce, cover partially, and keep warm on a hot-plate or in a 120°F. warming oven.

Suckling Pig · *Cochon de Lait*

Roast suckling pig is wonderfully dramatic to serve, delicious to eat, and is hardly more difficult to cook than a turkey. Your only absolute requirement is an oven large enough to hold the roasting pan that will be large enough for the pig; the pig will be around 20 inches long from end of rump to tip of snout, but it can be arranged either in the traditional straight crouch, illustrated farther on, or in a comfortable curl; a pan 12 by 18 inches and 2 inches deep would be the minimum size. You must also have something upon which to serve the pig, like a platter, a large tray, a carving board, or a piece of plywood covered with foil. You will want leaves, flowers, fruits, and vegetables for decoration; suggestions are in step 7 of the recipe, page 315. Your final decision will be whether or not to stuff the pig. If you choose not to stuff, you should spread a flavouring of cooked chopped celery and onions, herbs (thyme, bay, sage), salt, and pepper in the cavity. Stuffing, however, not only flavours the meat, but also allows you to serve more people; use anything suitable for turkey or goose, such as sausages and apples, breadcrumbs and onions, one of the appropriate suggestions listed on pages 664–6, or the unusual *farce Trébizonde* suggested in the recipe here.

HOW TO ORDER A SUCKLING PIG

Be sure to order suckling pig well in advance, because this is not an everyday item. Specify the genuine milk-fed suckling pig, weighing 10 to 12 pounds and no more; heavier animals are too fatty and the skin is tough. After 14 pounds a pig is no longer suckling and would probably not fit into your oven anyway. It may be that when the pig is available, you are not, but you can have it wrapped airtight and frozen, where it will keep perfectly for several weeks at zero degrees or less. (Fresh pork is perishable; plan to roast the pig within a day or two of purchasing or defrosting it.) Ask that it be thoroughly cleaned inside and out, and that the eyeballs be removed because they burst during cooking. If the heart, liver, and kidneys come along with the pig, save them for your stuffing or use in the Provencal sausages, *caillettes*, page 405.

PREPARING THE PIG FOR ROASTING

To prepare the pig for roasting, soak for several hours in cold water with 3 tablespoons of vinegar and 2 tablespoons of salt for each 6 pints of water. If your pig is frozen, it will defrost at the same time. Scrub inside the ears, nostrils, and mouth with a vegetable brush to be sure all is clean; scrub the feet also. Go over the pig to remove any hairs that might have been missed. Dry the pig thoroughly inside and out, and it is ready to stuff and roast.

Cochon de Lait, Farci à la Trébizonde
[Roast Suckling Pig Stuffed with Rice,
Sausages, Apricots, and Raisins]

With this exotic mixture stuffed into your suckling pig you need just a green vegetable accompaniment, like buttered brussels sprouts or broccoli. A smooth and not-too-heavy red wine would be your best choice, such as a Graves or Médoc.

[*For 12 to 14 people*]

1. Preparing the pig for stuffing: 3 to 4 hours
A 10- to 12-lb. suckling pig

Prepare the pig for roasting, soak it and dry it as described above.

2. The rice, sausage, and apricot stuffing (*farce Trébizonde*)
Note: Many of the steps in this stuffing may be carried on at once; we have separated each process, and leave the time sequences up to you.

1 lb. pure pork sausages (preferably home-made, page 386)
A medium (10-in.) frying pan with cover
3 tbl. water
A 9- or 10-pt mixing bowl
A slotted spoon

Prick skin of sausages with a pin, arrange in pan with water, cover, and simmer 5 minutes. Uncover, drain off water, and sauté sausages slowly for several minutes, until lightly browned. Remove, leaving fat in pan. Cut sausages into ½-inch lengths, and place in mixing bowl.

Either: the pig's liver, heart, and kidneys cut into ⅜-in. dice;
Or: ¾ lb. liver, calf or chicken, diced
2 tbl. minced shallots or spring onions
¼ tsp. thyme
Salt and pepper

Heat fat in pan to very hot but not smoking, and stir in the liver mixture, shallots or spring onions, and thyme. Toss and turn for 2 minutes, just to stiffen liver. Season, and scoop out into mixing bowl, leaving fat in pan.

1 lb. onions, minced

Stir the onions into the pan, cover and cook slowly 8 to 10 minutes, stirring occasionally, until tender and translucent. Season lightly, scoop half into mixing bowl, and leave the rest in the pan.

1 whole head of garlic
A pan of boiling water
Butter if needed
3 oz. plain, raw, white untreated rice
4 tbl. dry, white wine or dry, white French vermouth
½ pt chicken broth, hot
½ pt hot water
½ tsp. salt
½ bay leaf
¼ tsp. thyme
Big pinch saffron threads

Separate garlic cloves, drop them unpeeled into boiling water, and boil 2 minutes. Drain, refresh in cold water, slip off peel, quarter garlic lengthwise, and reserve. If fat in frying pan has darkened, drain onions and return them to pan with 1½ ounces butter. Blend in rice, and stir over moderate heat for several minutes until rice becomes translucent, then milky in colour. Stir in the wine or vermouth, chicken broth, hot water, salt, herbs, and saffron. Bring to the slow boil, add the garlic, and stir once; cover, and boil slowly for about 15 minutes, or until all liquid has been absorbed and rice is almost but not quite tender. Set aside, uncovered.

3 to 4 oz. seedless black raisins or currants
A bowl of very hot water

Drop raisins into hot water and let soften 10 to 15 minutes. Drain, squeeze dry in the corner of a towel, and add to mixing bowl.

½ lb. best-quality dried apricots
A bowl of very hot water
½ pt beef stock or bouillon
A heavy covered saucepan
Big pinch allspice

Soak apricots for 10 to 15 minutes until somewhat softened. Drain, and simmer slowly in bouillon with allspice until just tender enough to eat (not mushy). Drain, reserving any liquid for your final sauce. Cut apricots into ¾-inch pieces and add to mixing bowl.

A rubber spatula
¼ tsp. each: ground fennel seeds, thyme, and oregano
⅛ tsp. ground bay leaf
⅛ tsp. white pepper
Salt

Gradually blend the cooked rice into the mixing bowl, turning gently with the rest of the ingredients and the herbs and seasonings listed here. Taste very critically for seasoning, adding more salt, pepper, and herbs if you think them necessary.

(†) Stuffing may be made a day in advance; cover and refrigerate.

3. Stuffing the pig

2 tsp. salt
⅛ tsp. white pepper

6 to 8 skewers or finishing nails about 3 ins. long
White string
Aluminium foil

Turn the pig on its back, and season cavity with salt and
pepper. Spread in the stuffing, filling the cavity completely
but not forcing it. (Reserve any extra stuffing; cook separately,
in a covered dish.) Close cavity with skewers and lace them
in place with string. If there is a slit under the skin, season with
salt and pepper, but it need not be closed. Crumple foil into a
ball 2 to 2½ inches in diameter, force pig's jaws open, and
insert ball to keep them open.

4. Into the roasting pan

¼ pt or more olive oil or cooking oil in a small pan
A basting brush
A shallow roasting pan at least 20 ins. long, with rack
More skewers and string, if needed
Aluminium foil
Optional but recommended: a meat thermometer

Dry surface of pig again with paper towels, and paint pig all
over with oil. If pig will fit in a straight crouch in pan (A),

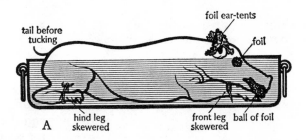

foil ear-tents
tail before
tucking
foil
hind leg   front leg   ball of foil
A   skewered   skewered

skewer and tie hindlegs and forelegs in place to brace pig in
position; let head rest between forelegs. Or arrange pig in a
less formal position (B), hind legs extended forward, and
forelegs curled under.
  If chin sticks out over lip of pan in either position, put a
double thickness of foil under it so that roasting juices will
drain back into pan. Insert balls of foil into the eye sockets;
make tents of foil to cover the ears and protect them during

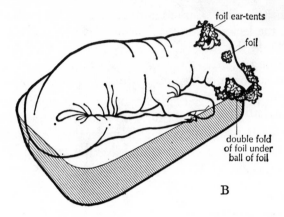

foil ear-tents

foil

double fold
of foil under
ball of foil

B

roasting. To protect tail, tuck into rear opening. Insert meat thermometer into thickest portion of thigh, being sure its point is not touching any bone.

(†) Although pig may be stuffed the day before roasting if both stuffing and pig have been chilled separately beforehand, you will have to leave the pig out at room temperature for 2 to 3 hours before roasting or timing will be difficult and roasting may be uneven.

5. Roasting: oven preheated to 450°F., Mark 8; 3 to 3½ hours (2½ to 3 hours roasting plus a 30-minute rest)

The oil and the basting brush
½ lb. onions, roughly sliced
½ lb. carrots, roughly sliced
4 cloves of garlic, whole and unpeeled

Set pan with pig in lower-middle level of preheated 450°F., Mark 8 oven. In 15 minutes, rapidly brush entire surface of pig with oil. Roast 15 minutes more, baste again with oil, and turn thermostat down to 350°F., Mark 4.

Baste in 20 minutes. Twenty minutes later, after pig has roasted a little more than an hour in all, baste again, and strew the onions, carrots, and garlic cloves in the pan. Continue basting every 20 minutes or so, using fat in pan when oil is used up; basting helps the skin to crisp and brown nicely. In a total of 2½ to 3 hours, meat thermometer should have reached 180° to 185°F., the thigh meat should be tender when pressed, the legs should move in their sockets, and the pig is done. (Note that a chilled, stuffed pig may take up to 30 minutes longer to roast, as may a 14-pound pig.)

Pig must now rest 30 minutes before carving, so that meat juices will retreat back into tissues. Turn oven off and leave door ajar, letting pig remain warm.

(†) Pig can wait a good hour before carving; when oven has cooled for 20 minutes, reset thermostat to 140°F. and close the door (or reheat oven briefly every 10 minutes).

6. The sauce

The serving platter, tray, or board
¾ pt veal stock or beef stock, or beef bouillon
½ pt dry port, Sercial Madeira, dry white wine, or dry white French vermouth
1 tbl. dry mustard blended with 2 tbl. of the stock or wine
A strainer set over a bowl or a saucepan
Salt and pepper
A warm sauce bowl

Lift pig, and drain its juices back into the roasting pan; set it on platter, remove foil, skewers, string, etc., and pluck end of tail from its hiding place. Remove rack, tilt pan, and spoon fat off roasting juices. Pour the stock or bouillon into the pan, and the wine; beat in the mustard mixture, and bring to the simmer, scraping coagulated roasting juices into liquid. Simmer slowly for 10 to 15 minutes while pig is being carved. (You may wish to scrape all of this liquid into a saucepan rather than simmering in the roasting pan.) When you are ready to serve, pour accumulated carving juices into sauce, and strain sauce into bowl or pan, pressing juices out of vegetables. Skim off any surface fat, carefully correct seasoning, and pour sauce into warm bowl for serving.

7. Decorations and presentation

Decorate the platter with leaves, and flowers or fruit, placing a garland of flowers around the pig's neck, if you wish. Stick flowers in the eyes, and replace the ball of foil in its mouth with a shining red apple or a tangerine. (Orange blossoms, shiny green leaves, and yellow zinnias, for instance, are very attractive; at Christmas-time, holly, cranberries, and white daisies would be appropriate.) Bring the pig to the table or parade it around the room, so that everyone may enjoy its splendour. Although you may carve at the table, we suggest the seclusion of the kitchen unless an expert in suckling pigs is among the party.

8. Carving and serving

Provide yourself with 1 or 2 very sharp carving knives, a carving or kitchen fork, a big spoon, and a large pair of kitchen shears or poultry shears; an electric carving knife can be helpful in making the first cuts in the skin. We suggest you carve and serve one side, and return to the kitchen to carve the second side of the pig. Arrange it attractively again for the second serving at the table.

First (c), slit the skin the length of the backbone, using an electric carving knife if you have one. Then cut around skin

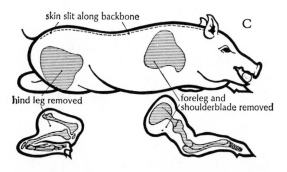

skin slit along backbone

C

hind leg removed

foreleg and shoulderblade removed

where you feel the outline of the shoulder; lift off shoulder and foreleg portion. Do the same for the hind leg. Divide both into serving pieces, and set aside.

Drawing (D) illustrates what you will find when you take your knife and cut down along the backbone and ribs to remove flesh and skin. Most of the meat is against the upper part of the ribs, and at the loin (from rump to ribs). Between meat and skin will be a layer of fat, more or less of it according to the age and size of the pig. Remove meat from fat, and

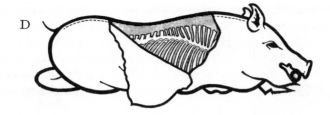

carve meat into serving portions. Scrape fat from skin, and cut skin into serving strips about 1 inch wide and 3 to 4 inches long. (Shears would be useful here.)

Pull out the exposed rib bones, which will come loose easily. Spread part of stuffing out from cavity of pig, arrange meat over the stuffing, and cover with strips of skin. If you have chosen brussels sprouts, broccoli, or other decorative vegetables, arrange them attractively around the meat. Re-decorate platter with leaves and flowers as necessary, and serve the pig with its sauce. (The other side of the pig will stay warm for second servings because the skin holds in the heat.)

Ox Tongue · *Langue de Bœuf*

A beautiful ox tongue braising in aromatic sauce smells so good while it is cooking, looks so splendid when you bring it to the table, and makes such a welcome change from the usual fare in main-course dishes that you need have no hesitation at all in serving it for company. Half the price of beef, tongue is all solid meat and therefore something well worth adding to your culinary repertoire. Because ox tongue has the best flavour and texture, we shall concentrate on that; pork, veal, and lamb tongues, which are treated in the same general way, are taken up in the next section, on page 330.

NOTES ON FRESH TONGUE

Fresh ox tongue is perishable: it has a total refrigerated life of only about eight days. Because it is already several days old when it reaches your butcher, you should plan to soak and salt it, or boil it, within a day of bringing it home. Because it is perishable, tongue is often smoked, brined, or pickled (corned) to preserve it longer, or it may be frozen. Although smoked and pickled tongue may be cooked like fresh tongue, we prefer the taste of fresh tongue, and have so geared our recipes.

HOW TO PREPARE AN OX TONGUE FOR COOKING – FRESH OR FROZEN

To freshen the tongue, first scrub it with a vegetable brush under warm running water, then let it soak for 2 to 3 hours in a sinkful of cold water. Drain and dry it. (If tongue has been frozen, let it thaw in the cold water, then scrub it, and soak it an hour more.)

Optional salting

To improve flavour and tenderness, as well as to preserve the tongue for several days before cooking, you may salt it. To do so, find an enamelled bowl or casserole that will just hold the tongue comfortably, spread a $\frac{1}{4}$-inch layer of coarse salt in the bottom, and lay the soaked and dried tongue on top. Cover tongue with a $\frac{1}{4}$-inch layer of salt, and place waxed paper on top. Weight down with a plate and 5 pounds of tinned food, for instance, or parts of a meat mincer. Refrigerate at least overnight, but 2 days will have more effect. When you are ready to cook the tongue, wash off the salt. (If you salt the tongue longer than 2 days, soak for 2 to 3 hours in cold water to remove excess salt.)

A NOTE ON COOKING METHODS

Tongue may be either boiled – meaning, of course, simmered slowly – or braised. When it is braised it receives a preliminary boiling until it is $\frac{2}{3}$ cooked (2 hours for a 4-pound tongue); it is then peeled, and either braised whole or braised in slices. Whether the tongue is boiled until tender or boiled until ready to peel, the boiling method is the same and so is the peeling. We therefore give directions for each, and follow with recipes, sauces, and serving suggestions for both boiled and braised tongue.

Boiling the Tongue – a Preliminary to Braising or a Complete Cooking

When you are boiling the tongue until tender, you will need aromatic vegetables and herbs to flavour it. Even better would be your decision to make the simple meat stock in Volume I, page 126, or the *pot-au-feu* in Volume I, page 333, and let the tongue simmer along in the same pot, where it will pick up even finer flavour. Tongue that will finish its cooking in a braising stock needs only salted water for this preliminary boiling.

A fully trimmed fresh ox tongue weighing 3½ to 4 lb.
A pan of cold water just large enough to hold tongue easily
If tongue was not salted: 1½ tsp. salt per 1½ pts of water
If tongue is to be boiled until tender: 1 lb. each of carrots and onions,
   sliced; 4 stalks celery, sliced; a large herb bouquet (8 parsley sprigs,
   1 tsp. thyme, 2 bay leaves, 4 allspice berries, and 2 unpeeled cloves
   of garlic, all tied in washed cheesecloth)
A cover for the pan

Prepare the tongue for cooking as described in the preceding pages. Place in pan, being sure that water covers tongue by 5 inches. (If tongue was not salted, measure water, adding salt accordingly.) Bring to the simmer; skim off greyish scum for 5 minutes or more, until it ceases to rise. Add vegetables and herb bouquet if you are using them. Set cover askew over pan, for slight air circulation, and maintain liquid at a slow simmer. If tongue is to be braised, simmer it for 2 hours only. If tongue is to be cooked completely, simmer 3 to 3½ hours or until meat is tender when pierced with a knife. Remove tongue from pan and proceed immediately to the peeling, next paragraph.

Peeling the tongue

Remove tongue from pan and plunge it into a basin or sinkful of cold water. As soon as it is cool enough to handle (it should still be warm), slit the nubbly skin-covering all around the top circumference of the tongue. Using your fingers, and a knife if you need one, peel the top surface of the tongue; skin should come off quite easily. The skin on the underside will usually adhere to the meat; make lengthwise slits and remove strips of skin with a knife. Trim any fatty parts and loose bits off the thick underside of the tongue, and pull out any bones that may be buried in the butt end. The tongue is now ready either for braising, if it simmered only 2 hours, or for saucing and serving if it is fully cooked.

(†) If you are now ready to serve a fully cooked tongue, return it to the pan and remove pan from heat; tongue will stay warm and retain its juiciness. For tongue that is to be braised, let it cool, then wrap airtight and refrigerate it; you may finish the cooking a day or two later.

Langue de Bœuf, à l'Aigre-douce
[Boiled Ox Tongue with Sweet-and-Sour Sauce, Pearl Onions, and Currants]

Because plain boiled tongue is so supremely easy to do, you owe something rather special in the way of a sauce both to the tongue and to those who are about to eat it. Brown sweet-and-sour sauce with pearl onions and currants is a delicious solution, and more than a dozen other possibilities are listed at the end of the recipe. Accompany the dish with buttered peas or asparagus tips, a purée of chestnuts or mashed potatoes, or French bread, and a red Bordeaux wine.

[*For 6 to 8 people*]

1. Boiling the tongue: 2 hours of soaking; 3 to 3½ hours of boiling

A fully trimmed fresh ox tongue weighing about 4 lb.

Scrub, soak, and, if you wish, salt the tongue; simmer 3 to 3½ hours until tender, and peel it, as described in the preceding pages. While tongue is cooking, or at any other convenient time beforehand, prepare the following sauce and garniture.

(†) If you are not ready to serve the tongue, keep it warm, re-heating it if necessary, in its cooking liquid.

2. Brown mustard sauce with pearl onions and currants

For *mirepoix*: 3 tbl. finely minced onions, 3 tbl. finely minced carrots,
   2 tbl. finely minced celery, 1 tbl. finely minced boiled ham, 1 oz.
   butter
A heavy-bottomed 3-pt saucepan with cover
10 oz. (40 to 50) small white pearl onions about ¾ in. in diameter
A pan of boiling water

Cook the diced vegetables and ham slowly in the butter for 10 to 12 minutes, stirring frequently, until tender and just starting to brown. While *mirepoix* is cooking, drop onions into boiling water, and boil 1 minute to loosen skins; drain, shave off 2 ends, slip off peel, and pierce a cross in the root end of each; set aside.

½ pt dry white wine or dry white French vermouth
½ pt tongue cooking stock; more if needed
¼ pt rich beef stock or bouillon; more if needed
2 oz. currants
1 bay leaf
A cover for the pan

Pour the wine or vermouth into the *mirepoix* and boil down rapidly until reduced by ⅓ of its volume. Then add the tongue stock, the beef stock or bouillon, currants, bay leaf, and peeled onions. Bring to simmer, cover pan, and simmer very slowly for 40 to 60 minutes, or until onions are tender. (Add more liquid if needed; you should end up with about ¾ pint.)

3 tbl. strong Dijon-type prepared mustard blended to a paste with
   1 tbl. cornflour in a small bowl
Salt and pepper
1 to 1½ oz. soft butter

When onions are tender, remove from heat; gradually beat about ¼ pint of their cooking liquid into the mustard and cornflour mixture. Fold mixture into onions, and when smoothly blended, return over heat; simmer 2 minutes. Sauce should be lightly thickened. Carefully correct seasoning, and set aside. Reheat just before serving; remove from heat, and fold in the butter, a small piece at a time.

3. Slicing the tongue and serving

When slicing the tongue, try for even pieces ⅜ inch thick and as uniform in diameter as possible: place the hot tongue on a carving board and cut several vertical slices off the thick end; then, continuing at the thick end, start gradually slicing on the bias, angling the back of your knife progressively down towards the board as you come off the hump; your blade will be almost horizontal as you reach the tip of the tongue.

Either arrange the slices of tongue down the centre of a hot, lightly buttered, oval platter, spoon a little sauce with raisins and onions over the tongue, decorate sides with green vegetables, and pass rest of sauce separately, *or* arrange the slices of tongue against a mound of puréed chestnuts, or mashed potatoes, spoon a little sauce over each slice, surround with onions, currants, and the rest of the sauce, and pass the vegetables separately.

OTHER SAUCES TO SERVE WITH BOILED TONGUE

Tomato sauces, brown sauces, white sauces, and oil and vinegar sauces all go well with boiled tongue. With one exception, these come from Volume I. Use tongue cooking broth boiled down or fortified, if necessary, with chicken stock or beef bouillon for the liquids called for in the various recipes.

Tomato Sauces

The classic tomato sauce in Volume I on page 95, the excellent Provençal sauce with fresh tomatoes following it, or an alternative using tinned tomatoes here in Volume II, page 468.

Brown Sauces

Pick any of the brown sauces in Volume I, pages 85 to 95. Particularly recommended are the *sauce piquante* with pickles and capers, the *sauce brune au cari*, brown curry sauce, the *sauce chasseur* with mushrooms, tomatoes, and herbs, and the *sauce à l'italienne* with ham and mushrooms.

White Sauces

Sauce au cari, a light curry sauce with onions, cream, and lemon (Volume I, page 82); or *sauce soubise*, an excellent onion sauce, to which you may add 2 to 3 tablespoons of chopped capers and minced parsley, if you wish (Volume I, page 83); or *sauce aux câpres, sauce à la moutarde, sauce aux anchois*, caper, mustard, or anchovy sauces, easy to make, and all variations of the mock hollandaise, *sauce au beurre* (Volume I, page 84).

Oil and Vinegar Sauces

Sauce de Sorges, delicious and unusual herbal mayonnaise made with shallots, capers, and soft-boiled eggs (Volume I, page 112), for tongue served either hot or cold; or *sauce ravigote, vinaigrette* with onions and capers, or the two variations following it, one with sour cream and dill, the other with mustard – all three good for tongue served hot or cold (Volume I, page 114).

Langue de Bœuf Braisée, au Madère
[Ox Tongue Braised Whole, Madeira Sauce]

When you want a splendid presentation and have an able carver at the table, braise the tongue whole and present it glazed in its sauce and surrounded by a handsome display of vegetables. We suggest a garniture of glazed carrots, onions, and turnips, whole baby mushrooms – all fresh vegetables, because of their fine taste and texture. A Médoc would be your best choice of wine.

[*For 6 to 8 people*]

1. Preliminaries to braising: 2 hours of soaking; 2 hours of boiling

A fully trimmed fresh ox tongue weighing about 4 lb.

Following directions starting on page 318, scrub, soak, salt if you wish, and simmer the tongue for 2 hours; peel it.

(†) This may be done the day before braising.

2. Braising the tongue: 2 hours at 350° to 325°F., Marks 4–3

½ lb. each of carrots and onions, sliced
4 oz. mild-cured boiled ham, diced
1½ oz. butter
A heavy, covered, flameproof casserole just large enough to hold
   tongue comfortably

Preheat oven to 350°F., Mark 4. Cook vegetables and ham with butter for about 10 minutes in covered casserole over moderately low heat, stirring frequently, until vegetables are tender and beginning to brown lightly.

Salt and pepper
The skinned ox tongue

Salt and pepper the tongue and place in the casserole, turning and basting it with the vegetables and butter. Cover casserole and let tongue sweat (*suer*) over moderately low heat for 10 minutes; turn the tongue, baste again, cover casserole, and sweat it 10 minutes more. (If tongue was refrigerated, double the number of minutes.)

4 tbl. dry Madeira (Sercial)
¼ pt dry white wine or dry white French vermouth
Optional, to improve flavour and texture of sauce: 1 or 2 chopped or
   sawed veal knuckle bones and/or beef marrow bones; a piece of
   blanched pork rind, 6 ins. square
1 whole washed tomato, unpeeled, roughly chopped
1 large clove of garlic, unpeeled, halved
1 bay leaf
½ tsp. thyme
½ pt or more rich beef stock or beef bouillon
A sheet of pork rind or beef suet ¼ in. thick and large enough to cover
   tongue; or washed cheesecloth

Pour the Madeira and the wine or vermouth into the casserole; boil down rapidly until liquid has almost evaporated. Strew optional bones and the pork rind around the tongue, along with the tomato, garlic, and herbs. Pour in enough stock or bouillon to come ⅔ the way up the tongue. Cover tongue with fat or cheesecloth, bring liquid in casserole to the simmer, cover casserole, and set in lower-middle level of preheated oven. In 20 minutes, check to see that liquid in casserole is simmering slowly and steadily; lift fat or cloth and baste tongue rapidly with liquid in casserole. Turn thermostat down to 325°F., Mark 3. Baste tongue several times again during cooking, and when it has braised 1 hour, turn on its other side, covering again with fat or cheesecloth. Tongue should be done in 2 to 2½ hours, when a knife will pierce the meat easily; do not overcook. (While tongue is braising, prepare vegetable garnish; although the vegetables may braise with the tongue, we find it easier to cook them separately.)

3. The vegetable garnish

24 to 32 small fresh white onions 1 to 1¼ ins. in diameter
A saucepan of boiling water
A wide (9- to 10-in.) saucepan, chicken fryer, or electric frying pan, and a cover for the pan
½ to ¾ pt water
Salt
1½ oz. butter
10 to 12 fine, fresh, medium-sized carrots, all of a size
10 to 12 firm, fresh, white turnips all of a size, 2 to 2½ ins. in diameter

Drop onions into boiling water, bring rapidly back to the boil for exactly 1 minute; drain. Shave off tops and bottoms, and peel the onions; pierce a cross ⅓ inch deep in the root ends for even cooking. Place in pan with the water, salt, and butter; bring to the simmer, cover, and simmer slowly while preparing the carrots. Rapidly peel the carrots, quarter them lengthwise, cut into 1½-inch lengths, trim off sharp edges, and add to the simmering onions. Then rapidly peel the turnips, quarter them, trim off sharp edges, and add to the pan after onions have cooked 20 minutes. Continue to simmer slowly until vegetables are tender (about 20 minutes longer), adding a little more water if all has evaporated. Correct seasoning, and set aside.

¾ lb. fresh button mushrooms (or larger fresh mushrooms, quartered)
A large (11-in.) frying pan
1 oz. butter and ½ tbl. cooking oil
2 tbl. minced shallots or spring onions
Salt and pepper

Trim the mushrooms, wash rapidly, and dry in a towel. Set frying pan over moderately high heat with the butter and oil. When butter foam is beginning to subside, add the mushrooms; sauté 3 to 4 minutes, tossing frequently, shaking and swirling the pan by its handle until mushrooms are just beginning to brown lightly. Toss for a moment with the shallots or spring onions, season to taste, scrape into a side dish, and reserve.

4. Sauce and serving

A hot, lightly buttered platter
A sieve set over a saucepan
3 tbl. dry Madeira (Sercial)
1 tbl. arrowroot or cornflour, in a small bowl
A wire whisk and rubber spatula
Salt and pepper
1½ to 2 oz. soft butter
Parsley sprigs

When tongue is tender, remove to platter, cover, and keep warm in turned-off oven (or warming oven at 120°F.) while finishing the sauce. Pour contents of casserole through sieve, pressing juices out of braising ingredients. Skim surface fat off liquid in saucepan, and bring liquid to the simmer, skimming. You should have about ¾ pint.

Blend the Madeira into the arrowroot or cornflour; remove cooking liquid from heat and blend the wine mixture into it. When smooth, return saucepan to heat and fold in the cooked onions, carrots, turnips, and mushrooms along with any of their cooking juices. Simmer, swirling pan by its handle and gently turning vegetables in sauce for 4 to 5 minutes. Sauce should be thick enough to coat the tongue nicely; carefully correct seasoning. Just before serving, fold in the enrichment butter, a small piece at a time, gently basting vegetables with sauce until butter is absorbed.

Arrange the tongue humped side up on the platter, glaze with spoonfuls of the sauce, and arrange the vegetables around it, basting both tongue and vegetables with remaining sauce. Decorate with parsley sprigs, and serve immediately.

(†) If you are not ready to serve when tongue is tender, complete the sauce but omit the final butter enrichment. Return tongue, sauce, and vegetable garnish to casserole; cover tongue again with its fat or cheesecloth, put on casserole cover slightly askew, and set in a very low oven, or over simmering water. Tongue will stay warm safely for a good hour. If sauce has thickened too much when you are ready to serve, thin it out with a little stock or bouillon.

Other sauces, flavourings, garnitures

You may braise tongue with any of the flavourings and garnishings you would use for beef; you might even slice it after its preliminary 2-hour boiling and peeling, re-form it with a mushroom stuffing between each slice, and then braise it, as for the sliced and stuffed fillet of beef *en feuilletons*, page 253. The garniture *à la bourgeoise*, of onions, mushrooms, and olives, page 251, would be attractive, as would some of the variations following beef stew, pages 217–21. Particularly recommended among these are the *pistou* and the Provençal flavourings, the *pipérade* with its peppers and tomatoes, and the final suggestion on page 220, for ginger, capers, and herbs. For any of these suggestions, the general cooking procedure for the tongue follows the same pattern and timing as the master recipe; you are simply substituting other flavourings.

Langue de Bœuf Braisée, Calcutta
[Sliced Fresh Ox Tongue Braised with Curry]

Tongue is much easier to prepare and serve when you braise it in slices after its preliminary 2-hour boil and its peeling. Sliced tongue cooks in 30 to 40 minutes, the flavour of the sauce penetrates the meat beautifully, and sliced tongue lends itself to prearrangements, pre-cooking, and numerous ahead-of-time manoeuvres that are not possible with whole tongue. Using the general method of the following recipe, you can add sliced tongue to cook with the brown mustard sauce, pearl onions, and raisins in the boiled tongue recipe on page 320, or use one of the ideas either in the preceding paragraph or in those suggested for boiled tongue on pages 322–3.

French curry sauce does not have the strong, mouth-searing quality of Indian curry; the French version is more a flavour than an experience, because if the curry were strong it would ruin the accompanying wine. You might serve this tongue on a bed of mashed potatoes, rice, or braised spinach, on a purée of peas or lentils, or on the purée of pumpkin and white beans on page 530. Your own fresh French bread could take the place of a second vegetable. For wines, claret would go nicely, or a rather strong dry white like a Hermitage, from the Rhône valley.

[*For 6 to 8 people*]

1. Preliminaries to braising: 2 hours of soaking; 2 hours of boiling

A fully trimmed fresh ox tongue weighing about 4 lb.

Following directions starting on page 318, scrub, soak, salt if you wish, and simmer the tongue for 2 hours; peel it.

(†) This may be done the day before braising.

2. The braising sauce

1 lb. onions, sliced
1 oz. butter and ½ tbl. cooking oil (more if needed)
A 10- to 12-in. casserole, chicken fryer, or electric frying pan
About 2 tbl. fragrant curry powder (depending on its strength and your inclinations)
2 tbl. flour

Cook the onions slowly in the butter and oil over low heat, stirring occasionally, for 8 to 10 minutes until tender and translucent but not browned. Blend in the curry powder and cook, stirring, for 2 minutes. Blend in the flour, and a little more butter or oil if flour makes too stiff a paste; cook, stirring, for 2 minutes more. Remove from heat.

About 1 pt heated meat stock (a combination of beef stock or bouillon and tongue cooking stock or chicken broth)
A wire whisk
½ pt dry white wine or dry white French vermouth
2 large cloves garlic, mashed
1 oz. currants

1 sour cooking apple, peeled and diced (or an eating apple and 1 tbl.
    lemon juice)
½ tsp. thyme
1 bay leaf
Salt and pepper to taste

When casserole contents have stopped bubbling, pour in ¾ pint of the hot stock and blend vigorously into the onions, curry, and flour with wire whisk. Pour in the wine or vermouth; add the garlic, currants, diced apple, thyme, and bay leaf. Bring to the simmer, stirring, and simmer 2 minutes. Sauce should be lightly thickened. Taste carefully, and correct seasoning.

3. Braising the tongue: 30 to 40 minutes

Cut the peeled tongue into even slices ⅜ inch thick. (Directions for slicing are in step 3, page 322, in the master recipe for boiled tongue.) Arrange the slices in the casserole, overlapping as necessary, and baste the tongue with the sauce.

(†) Recipe may be prepared in advance to this point; when cool, cover surface with plastic wrap, a cover, and refrigerate.

Bring to the simmer, cover, and simmer 30 to 40 minutes, tilting casserole and basting tongue several times with the sauce. When tender if pierced with a fork, meat is done, but do not overcook; eat a piece if you have any doubts about its being done.

4. Serving

A hot, lightly buttered serving platter
Optional: 4 to 6 tbl. *crème fraîche* or double cream
Salt, pepper, and drops of lemon juice
½ to 1½ oz. soft butter
A hot gravy bowl
If needed: fresh minced parsley

When tongue is done, arrange the hot slices on the platter (or over a bed of vegetables if you wish); cover and keep warm while you finish the sauce. You should have ½ to ¾ pint of sauce thick enough to coat a spoon nicely. Stir in optional cream; boil down if sauce is too thin or, conversely, add a little more stock if it seems too thick. Taste carefully, stirring in more salt, pepper, and drops of lemon juice if you feel them necessary. Just before serving, remove sauce from heat, and swish in the enrichment butter a small piece at a time. Spoon hot sauce over the slices of tongue, and pour rest of sauce into hot serving bowl. (You may strain the sauce; the onions and currants, however, give it an attractive informal look and texture.) Decorate tongue with parsley, if you wish, and serve immediately.

(†) *Ahead-of-time note:* You may complete the sauce except for the final butter enrichment; return tongue slices to sauce, and baste them with it. Reheat to bubbling hot before serving, but be careful not to overcook the tongue.

Veal, Pork, and Lamb Tongues · *Langues de Veau, de Porc, et de Mouton*

Veal, pork, and lamb tongues have the same consistency as ox tongue, and although they do not have quite the same fine flavour you may substitute them for ox tongue in any of the preceding recipes. Braising is particularly recommended, because the braising stock adds the flavour that these tongues lack. Here are notes on each.

VEAL TONGUES

Weights and measures: These will weigh 6 to 8 ounces on the average, and will be 5 to 6 inches long, although tongues from large carcasses can weigh up to $1\frac{1}{4}$ pounds. Count on one 6- to 8-ounce tongue per person, or 2 tongues for 3 people.

　　Preparation for cooking: Scrub, soak, and, if you wish, salt the tongues exactly as directed for ox tongue, page 318.

　　Preliminary boiling, and peeling: Simmer the tongues for 45 minutes (1 hour for large tongues) in salted water, refresh briefly in cold water, and peel as described for ox tongue, page 319.

Cooking methods: Braise the tongues whole, or cut in half lengthwise, following the ox-tongue recipes and variations starting on page 323. Braising time will be about 1½ hours.

PORK TONGUES

Weights and measures: Pork tongues weigh ¾ to 1 pound, and are 8 to 9 inches long. Count on 1 tongue for 2 people, or 2 large tongues for 5 people.

Preparation, boiling, peeling, and cooking methods: Follow preceding directions for veal tongues.

LAMB TONGUES

Weights and measures: 3 to 4 ounces each, and 3 to 4 inches long. Count on 2 tongues per person, or 1½ to 2 if the tongues are cut in two lengthwise.

Preparation, boiling, peeling, and cooking methods: Follow directions for veal tongues, but the final braising will probably be 45 minutes to 1 hour only.

Tripe · *Tripes*

Those who love tripe speak of it with passionate enjoyment and will travel miles to dine upon it. Like brawn, it is a rather old-fashioned taste – a fragrant, earthy reminder of the past when every edible morsel of the beast was used. Many people today who have heard of tripe have neither seen nor eaten it, but our forefathers consumed it with relish. The Parker House in Boston became famous throughout the nation for its fried tripe, and the fine Parisian restaurant, Pharamond, in the heart of the old markets, Les Halles, made its reputation serving steaming bowls of *tripes à la mode de Caen*, a recipe you will find in so many cookbooks that we shall not repeat it again here. Instead, we present a much simpler dish from Provence, and one that we like immensely: the tripe first cooks to a golden yellow with onions, then finishes off in an aromatic mixture of tomatoes, wine, and herbs. If you are one of those who has never tried tripe before, yet enjoys new foods and new tastes, we think you will find this a happy introduction.

HOW TO BUY TRIPE

There are four kinds of tripe, and any or all may be used in any recipe, but the only one usually available today is honey-comb tripe (*bonnet*, in French). Although you can buy it tinned, frozen, and fully cooked, or pickled, we are interested here only in ready-to-cook tripe. This means that it has been scraped, washed, blanched, often bleached, and is, in fact, ready for cooking. Fresh tripe is perishable; plan to cook it within a day or two of buying it.

A NOTE ON FRENCH TRIPE

In France, tripe is bought *chez le tripier*, who sells cleaned and blanched tripe of all four varieties. *Gras double*, a term you will run into in French recipes and at *la triperie* itself, can mean either the heaviest and meatiest of the four, *la panse*, or it can mean the four varieties rolled together fully cooked, and needing only to be reheated in whatever sauce you plan to use.

Ready-to-cook tripe, on the other hand, should be soaked several hours or overnight in several changes of cold water, then blanched. Although some cooks do not blanch fresh ready-to-cook tripe, we find that blanching freshens the flavour and we suggest the following preliminaries to cooking. Wash the tripe thoroughly under cold, running water. Then place it in a large saucepan, and cover by 3 inches with cold water; bring to the boil, and boil slowly 5 minutes. Drain, run cold water into the pan, soak the tripe for several minutes, drain, and blanch again for 5 minutes. Repeat the process a third time, and the tripe is ready to cook.

Because you will occasionally run into them in French recipes, the technical names for beef tripe are as follows:

first stomach, rumen, or paunch – *panse* or *gras double*; second stomach, reticulum, or honeycomb tripe – *bonnet*; third stomach, omasum, psalterium, or manyplies – *feuillet* or *franche mule*; fourth stomach, abomasum, or reed – *caillette* or *millet*.

Tripes à la Niçoise

[Tripe Baked with Onions, Tomatoes, Wine, and Provençal Seasonings]

As an alternative to *tripes à la mode de Caen*, we find this a wonderfully satisfying recipe. The tripe is cooked several hours just with onions; then tomatoes, other flavourings, and wine go in for another session of slow, penetrating simmer. You could, if you wished, finish off the recipe in another way after the onion-cooking session, or pick the tripe out of its tomato sauce at the end of the recipe here, grill or deep-fry it, and serve the tomato sauce separately. We shall leave these possibilities to you, and present the recipe in its own straightforward way. Serve boiled rice or boiled potatoes with the tripe. No green vegetable is needed, but a salad could follow. For wines, we suggest a strong, dry white like a Mâcon or Hermitage, or a young red like Beaujolais, or a strong, dry rosé like Tavel.

[*For 6 people*]

1. Preliminary cooking of tripe and onions: 2 to 2½ hours

Optional, for additional flavour: 4 or 5 slices, ¼ in. thick, of fat-and-lean
    fresh pork belly or blanched bacon (page 213)
¼ pt olive oil
A heavy, 7- to 8-pt covered casserole (earthenware preferred for looks,
    and for heat-holding properties)
2 lb. onions, sliced

Preheat oven to 325°F., Mark 3. Cut optional pork or bacon into 2-inch lengths. Cook slowly without browning in the oil for 5 minutes to render some of the fat. Then stir in the onions, cover the casserole, and cook onions slowly 10 minutes or more, stirring frequently, until tender but not at all browned.

2½ to 3 lb. ready-to-cook tripe (see notes preceding recipe)
Heavy shears
1 tsp. salt
A round of waxed paper
A piece of aluminium foil

While onions are cooking, cut tripe into strips 2 inches wide; cut the strips into triangles about 3 inches on the long side. When onions are ready, fold the tripe into them, along with the salt. Lay a round of waxed paper over tripe to keep it from browning, drape foil over top of casserole to keep in the steam, and place casserole cover on top of foil. Set in middle level of preheated oven, and bake slowly for 2½ hours, regulating thermostat so that tripe cooks very slowly and steadily but does not brown. When time is up, tripe will be a golden yellow.

2. Finishing the cooking, and serving: 2 to 2½ hours

6 medium tomatoes, peeled, seeded, juiced, and chopped, or a
    combination of fresh pulp and tinned, drained, sieved Italian plum
    tomatoes
4 large cloves garlic, mashed or minced
½ pt dry white wine, or dry white French vermouth
To thicken cooking liquid: an 8-in. square of blanched pork rind
    (Volume I, page 434) and/or 2 or 3 veal knuckle bones, chopped and
    tied in washed cheesecloth
The following tied in washed cheesecloth: 6 peppercorns, 6 allspice
    berries, 1 tsp. fennel seeds, a 3-in. piece of dried orange peel or 1 tsp.
    bottled peel, 1 tsp. thyme, 1 bay leaf
½ to ¾ pt veal stock, or beef stock or bouillon
Salt as needed
Optional, to be added last ½ hour of cooking: 2 oz. black, Mediterranean-
    type olives, stoned, and blanched 10 minutes (page 219)

Fold the tomatoes and garlic into the tripe; pour in the wine. Bury the pork rind and bones in the tripe, and the packet of seasonings. (Remove these later, when tripe is done.) Pour in enough stock just to cover ingredients. Bring to simmer on top of stove, and salt lightly to taste. Cover tripe again with the waxed paper, foil, and casserole cover, and return to oven for another 2 hours of slow simmering. Test tripe by eating a piece; it should be tender enough to chew easily, but should still have some texture. Skim off surface fat; carefully correct seasoning. Bake $\frac{1}{2}$ an hour, an hour, or longer, until tripe is of the desired consistency. (Add a little more white wine or stock if liquid has evaporated too much. Stir in optional olives about $\frac{1}{2}$ an hour before estimated end of cooking.)

Serve bubbling hot from casserole on to very hot plates.

(†) Tripe may be cooked several days in advance of serving, and reheats perfectly.

Rabbit · *Lapin*

Rabbit, if you have never tried it, is very much like chicken in taste and texture, but the meat is firmer and therefore does very well in a stew. Most rabbit stews are called sautés in French, and the recipe you usually encounter is *sauté de lapin au vin blanc*, in which the pieces of rabbit are browned in the pan, seasoned, floured, and simmered in white wine with onions, mushrooms, and *lardons* of bacon. Rather than repeat this too-familiar version, we give a red wine stew.

BUYING A RABBIT AND PREPARING IT FOR COOKING

In many parts of the country you can now buy an excellent quality of frozen young rabbit pieces, cut up and ready for cooking as soon as you have defrosted them. If fresh whole rabbit is available, have it cut so that the forelegs are disjointed from the body at the shoulder, the hind legs at the hip, and the rib section separated from the loin. Then separate the hind legs at the knee, to make 2 pieces; cut the loin (*rable*) and the rib sections in two crosswise and, if you wish, trim off with scissors the lower part of the ribs, which is mostly bone.

Cut up this way, you will have 10 pieces, the choicest of which are the second joints and the 2 pieces of loin; the 2 front legs are second best, and the rib sections have the least meat. Use the liver and heart like chicken liver, or you may wish to add it to the stew.

Two and a half pounds of cut-up ready-to-cook rabbit will serve 4 to 5 people.

TO THAW FROZEN RABBIT

Let it defrost for 24 hours in the refrigerator, or defrost it in a wine marinade as suggested in the following recipe.

Lapin au Saupiquet
[Rabbit Marinated in Vinegar and Herbs,
and Stewed in Red Wine]

This French recipe is very much like the German *Hasenpfeffer*, in that both use a wine-vinegar marinade before the stew begins; this tenderizes the rabbit as well as giving it an excellent flavour. Serve the rabbit with parslied potatoes, buttered noodles, or steamed and buttered rice, and a simple green vegetable such as the sautéed courgettes on page 479, buttered broccoli, or green beans. A full red wine is definitely the type to choose – a Hermitage, Côtes-du-Rhône, or Châteauneuf-du-Pape.

[*For 4 to 5 people*]

1. Marinating the rabbit: at least 24 hours

¼ pt red wine vinegar
½ tsp. cracked peppercorns
3 tbl. olive oil or cooking oil
2 onions, sliced
2 large cloves of garlic, unpeeled, halved
4 juniper berries
½ tsp. oregano
1 bay leaf
½ tsp. thyme
An enamelled or stainless bowl or casserole large enough to hold rabbit comfortably
2½ lb. cut-up ready-to-cook frying rabbit, fresh or frozen
A bulb baster

Mix all the ingredients in the bowl, add the rabbit, and baste with the marinade. (If rabbit is frozen, let it defrost in the bowl at room temperature, basting frequently, and pulling pieces apart from each other when possible, until completely defrosted.) Cover bowl and refrigerate it, basting and turning the rabbit occasionally. Marinate at least 24 hours, although you can leave the rabbit safely for 2 or 3 days because the marinade also preserves the meat.

2. The braising sauce (*sauce au saupiquet*)

4 oz. *lardons* (1½-in. sticks ¼ in. thick of bacon blanched 10 minutes in
   1½ pts water)
2 tbl. olive oil or cooking oil, more if needed
A large (11-in.) frying pan (non-stick recommended)
1 lb. onions, sliced
A heavy, covered, flameproof casserole large enough to hold rabbit
   pieces easily

Preheat oven to 450°F., Mark 8. Brown the *lardons* lightly with oil in the pan over moderate heat. Then stir in the onions, and cook for about 10 minutes, stirring frequently, until onions are tender and lightly browned. Transfer onions and *lardons* to the casserole with a slotted spoon, leaving fat in pan.

The rabbit and its marinade
Paper towels
Salt and pepper
Optional: the rabbit's liver, quartered, seasoned, and floured
3 tbl. flour

While onions are cooking, remove rabbit from marinade, and dry thoroughly with paper towels; reserve the marinade. When onions are out of pan add more oil if necessary, so that pan is filmed by ⅛ inch, raise heat to moderately high, and brown the rabbit pieces nicely on all sides. Season with salt and pepper, and add the rabbit to the casserole. (Brown optional liver at the same time, and set aside for later.) Sprinkle on half the flour, toss rabbit in casserole, sprinkle on rest of flour, and toss again.

   Heat casserole to sizzling on top of stove, then set uncovered in upper third of preheated 450°F., Mark 8 oven for 5 minutes;

toss again, and return casserole to oven for 5 minutes more. (The oven is an easier way to brown and cook the flour than sautéing on top of the stove; but if you do not wish to use your oven, you may sauté.)

The marinade
1 bottle of full-bodied, young, red wine (Mâcon, Côtes-du-Rhône)
¾ pt beef or veal stock, or beef bouillon

While casserole is in oven, pour the browning fat out of the frying pan, pour in the marinade, and boil down until liquid has almost evaporated. Pour in the wine, boil down to half its volume, then add the bouillon, bring to the boil, and set aside.

Remove casserole from oven and add the hot wine and bouillon mixture, stirring rabbit pieces, onions, and *lardons* so that all is well blended.

3. Stewing the rabbit: about 1 hour

Bring contents of casserole to the simmer on top of the stove, cover and simmer slowly either on the stove or in a preheated 350°F., Mark 4 oven; regulate heat in either case so that stew bubbles slowly and regularly throughout the cooking, and baste rabbit pieces several times with the sauce. Rabbit should be done in about 1 hour, when the meat is tender if pierced with a knife. (While rabbit is stewing, prepare prunes in step 4.)

4. Sauce and serving

A hot, lightly buttered, serving platter
Stock or bouillon if needed
20 to 25 large prunes, simmered 10 to 15 minutes in 3 tbl. cognac,
    ¼ pt bouillon, and 1 oz. butter
The optional sautéed liver pieces from step 2
Optional: 8 to 10 croûtons or *fleurons* (triangles of white bread sautéed
    in clarified butter; puff pastry crescents, page 194)
Fresh parsley sprigs

When rabbit pieces are tender, arrange them on the serving platter, cover, and keep warm while finishing the sauce. Remove bay leaf, and skim surface fat off braising sauce.

Bring to the simmer, skimming. You should have $\frac{1}{2}$ to $\frac{3}{4}$ pint of sauce thick enough to coat a spoon nicely; thin out with stock or bouillon if too thick, or boil down rapidly if too thin. Then add the prunes with their liquid, and the optional liver; simmer 2 to 3 minutes, and carefully correct seasoning. Spoon the sauce and prunes over the rabbit, decorate with croûtons or *fleurons* and parsley sprigs, and serve.

(†) If you are not ready to serve, return rabbit to casserole, baste with sauce, and reheat later.

4. Chickens, Poached and Sauced – and a *Coq en Pâte*

When grilling and frying chickens are among our most reasonably priced meats today, it is hard to realize that great-great-grandmother's, or even great-grandmother's, Sunday chicken was a luxurious treat, since chicken was expensive in those days. To have it so accessible now is a great boon to the cook, because you can prepare it in such a vast number of ways. Volume I takes up roasting, casserole roasting, sautés, fricassees, *coq au vin*, and chicken breasts, as well as details on chicken types and qualities, trussing directions, and timing charts. There is not a word, however, about one of the easiest and most delicious ways to cook chicken – poaching in white wine. The chicken practically cooks itself, produces its own sauce base, and can be served in numerous ways from very plain to extremely elegant.

We start with chicken in pieces, taking it from the simple wine stew through a cheese casserole, an aspic, a *chaud-froid*, and finally a *bouillabaisse* and a *bourride*. For more formal chickens, there is a roaster or capon poached whole in white wine and aromatic vegetables, plus various stuffings and white-wine sauces; an illustrated guide to boning follows; and we conclude with a glamorous *coq en pâte* with the whimsical title *poularde en soutien-gorge*.

Chicken in Pieces

How fortunate we are to have chicken in pieces – those who like dark meat may feast upon thighs, white-meat-only people are welcome to breasts, while wings at half price make lovely finger food when the budget is low.

PREPARING READY-CUT CHICKEN FOR COOKING

Rather than being disjointed, meaning that thighs are removed from backbones at the connecting ball joints and wings from shoulders in the same fashion, most supermarket ready-cut chicken is done with a meat saw which neatly halves or quarters the chicken in a matter of seconds. This saving of man-hours is passed on to us, of course, in reasonable prices for chicken but does leave us with some unwanted bones and bits. If these do not bother you, simply wash the chicken under cold running water, dry in paper towels, and proceed to the cooking. If you have time for surgery, however, you can make the chicken easier to cook, especially for sautés and fricassees but also for poaching, because the pieces will lie flatter and take up less room; in addition, they will be far easier to eat. You will also have some useful scraps for chicken stock. The illustrated goose on page 415 will help you locate bones and joints because goose and chicken have the same bone structure; see also the illustrated semi-boned chicken on page 363. Here, then, is how to trim the various pieces of chicken.

Drumsticks and second joints (legs and thighs)

When drumsticks and second joints come joined together, the thigh bone is usually attached to the hip, making a clumsy piece of chicken – the hip should be off. On the hip, however, at either side of its attachment to the ball joint of the thigh, are two nuggets of meat, the oysters, which should remain part of the second joint: scrape this meat from the hip bone up to and around the joint, leaving meat attached to joint. Then bend and cut joint free from the piece of hip: this is picky work because the hip bone is small, but it is really worth the trouble. Then, to make the second joint even more attractive, scrape meat away from this same ball joint, and whack off its bulbous end with your chopping knife. In French cooking, the drumstick is separated from the second joint: flex the two pieces to locate ball joint at knee, and cut through it to separate drumstick from second joint.

Breast–wing sections

The breast–wing sections (or wingless breasts) usually come already split so that you have one whole side in one piece, and another whole side as the other piece. On the bone-and-flesh side you may see the long ridge of the breastbone, if it was left in that half, running the length of the thick portion of the meat. Below it is the rest of the breastbone and below that the cross-hatch of ribs; attached to the ribs you may find a piece of the backbone. Again, this is a clumsy piece to cook as it is, but easy to trim.

If the wing has been left on, you will be able to make 2 full servings out of the breast by cutting it in the French manner, meaning that the lower third of the breast meat remains attached to the wing as follows: Set the breast in front of you, skin-side up and top of breast (long side with thickest meat) away from you. We shall suppose that you have a left breast with the wing on the right. By wiggling the wing, locate with your finger where the ball joint of its upper arm attaches to the shoulder. Then make a semicircular cut through the skin and breast meat, starting at the lower left side of the long end facing you and ending at the shoulder joint. Scrape meat from rib bones the length of the cut (scrap·ng towards you, not towards the thick side of the meat), separate wing at shoulder by cutting through ball joint, and free the wing with its strip of breast meat. With shears, cut the bony nubbin off the elbow of the wing; trim rib bones from main part of breast along with backbone if it is attached. For a right-sided breast use the same system, but you may find it is easier to set the breast in front of you lengthwise, the wing end facing you and the thick part of the meat to your left.

Wingless breasts will be improved when you scrape the lower third of the flesh from the ribs at the long thin side, and cut off ribs at this point; the breast will then lie flatter.

Save all scraps for chicken stock

Even a small handful of scraps and bones are worth boiling up with a bit of onion, celery, carrot, a bay leaf, pinch of salt, and water to cover. Full directions for chicken stock are in Volume I, pages 257–8.

HOW MUCH TO BUY

We shall arbitrarily call for 2½ pounds of ready-cut frying chicken to serve 4 people in the following recipes, but you would normally buy by eye – the equivalent of 1 whole breast-half with a wing or 1 drumstick–second joint per serving is usually sufficient. The total weight will probably be between 2 and 2½ pounds, depending on the weight of the frying chicken and on what pieces you buy.

*Poulet Poché au Vin Blanc
[Chicken Pieces Poached in White Wine, Herbs, and Aromatic Vegetables]

This very simple, basic poaching recipe can be even simpler if you are on a fat-free diet: rather than cooking the vegetables in butter, simmer them 15 minutes in chicken stock before you add the chicken and the wine. Butter does seem to bring out more of their flavour, however. Because the vegetables cook along with the chicken and are served with it you could precede or follow the chicken with fresh artichokes or asparagus. You then need nothing more for the chicken course than steamed rice, a parsley garnish, and either more of the same white wine that cooked with the chicken, or a claret, or a rosé.

[For 4 people]

1. Sautéing the vegetables

2 medium-sized carrots
1 medium-sized onion and the white part of 1 leek (or 2 onions)
3 medium-sized celery stalks
1½ oz. butter
A heavy 5-pt flameproof casserole with cover (such as a round terracotta one, 9 by 3 ins. set on an asbestos mat)

(This step is optional: see preceding paragraph.) Peel the carrots and onion; quarter leek lengthwise and wash; trim and wash celery. Depending on what effect you want, cut the vegetables either into thin slices or into julienne matchsticks 1½ inches long. Cook slowly with the butter in the covered casserole over moderately low heat, stirring frequently, until vegetables are tender but not browned – about 10 minutes. Meanwhile, prepare the chicken, step 2.

2. Poaching the chicken

2½ lb. ready-cut frying chicken, washed, dried, and trimmed, if you
    wish, according to directions preceding this recipe
Salt
½ pt dry white wine or dry white French vermouth
About ¾ chicken stock or tinned chicken broth
The following herbs tied in washed cheesecloth: either ½ tsp. tarragon;
    or ½ bay leaf, ¼ tsp. thyme, and 4 parsley sprigs
Salt to taste

Preheat oven to 325°F., Mark 3, if you wish to use it. Prepare the chicken for cooking, salt lightly, and arrange in the
casserole, spreading the cooked vegetables around and over it.
Cover casserole and let chicken sweat for 10 minutes over
moderate heat, turning it once. (Omit this step if you are not
sautéing vegetables in butter.) Then pour in the wine or
vermouth and enough chicken stock or broth barely to cover
the chicken. Bury the herb packet in the chicken, and bring
casserole to the simmer. Taste, and salt lightly if necessary.

Cover the casserole and regulate heat to maintain liquid at a
slow, quiet simmer either on top of the stove or in a preheated
325°F., Mark 3 oven. (*Note:* Poaching means slow cooking,
so that chicken pieces will retain their shape, and will be
tender; boiling not only toughens the meat, but also warps its
contour.) Dark meat of chicken will take 20 to 25 minutes;
light meat, probably 5 minutes less and should be removed
when done, if you have mixed dark and light together. Juices,
when either dark or light meat is pricked deeply, should run
clear yellow, with no trace of rose, and meat should feel
tender when pierced. Do not overcook, however.

3. Serving

Tilt casserole and skim off surface fat; taste liquid and correct
seasoning. Discard herb bouquet. Either serve directly from
casserole, or arrange the chicken and vegetables on a bed of
steamed rice, decorate with parsley, and pass the cooking
liquid separately.

(†) If you aren't ready to serve, chicken will keep perfectly
for a good hour. Skim off surface fat, and correct seasoning,

then set casserole cover slightly askew for air circulation; keep warm in a very low oven, on a hot-plate, or over barely simmering water.

Stewing Chicken - Fowl

A fine stewing chicken 10 to 12 months old, as it is supposed to be when you buy from a reputable shop, does beautifully when poached in white wine. Use the same general system as in the preceding master recipe with the following slight changes.

If the chicken has not been cut up for you and you wish to cut it up yourself, follow the directions for goose, page 415. Reserve neck, back, gizzard, and heart as well as all scraps; place them in the bottom of the casserole to cook along with the chicken and give additional flavour to the broth. Mature chickens have much more flavour than young fryers, and you need only wine and water for the cooking stock. Stewing time will be about 2½ hours, or until the meat is tender when pierced with a knife. Because the vegetables will have cooked this length of time, they will not be of further use; if you want vegetables to cook and serve with the chicken, add a fresh batch before end of cooking time.

Serve the chicken on a bed of steamed rice or *risotto*, and you may turn its cooking stock into a cream sauce as suggested for whole poached chicken on page 357 or one of its variations on pages 368, 369-75. You may gratiné the chicken in cheese sauce, as in the recipe on page 347, or change the seasonings altogether by simmering the chicken in *bouillabaisse* flavourings, as suggested on page 352.

Poulet en Gelée
[Chicken in Aspic]

Chicken poached in white wine makes delicious chicken in aspic, and you may be as elegant as the formal recipe in Volume I, page 587, where the chicken is arranged on an aspic-lined platter; each piece is coated with aspic and tarragon leaves, chopped aspic fills in the empty spaces, and aspic cut-outs abound. On the other hand, you may be much less formal and just as attractive, but in a different way, with either of the two following arrangements. (*Note:* In neither of these is the cooking stock clarified – rendered clear and sparkling with egg whites; if you wish to clarify it, however, directions are in Volume I, page 130.)

A sieve set over a saucepan
A quart measure
Chicken broth if needed
1½ packages (1½ tbl.) plain, unflavoured, powdered gelatine
Salt and pepper

Set cover askew over casserole and drain out cooking liquid into the saucepan. Skim off surface fat and pour liquid into quart measure; skim again, and pour in additional stock, if necessary, to make 1¼ pints. Return liquid to saucepan, sprinkle on the gelatine, and let it soften for several minutes. Then stir over moderate heat until gelatine has completely dissolved and liquid is free of gelatine granules. Taste, and correct seasoning.

Rearrange chicken attractively with vegetables, either in the same casserole or in a serving bowl or dish that will just hold the pieces. Pour on the cooking stock and chill several hours, or until gelatine has set; scrape any congealed fat from surface, and chicken is ready to serve.

Moulded Aspic

You may wish to unmould the chicken on to a platter rather than serve it from a bowl or casserole. Use the same method as in the preceding recipe, but you may need more jellied stock – proportions are 1 envelope (1 tablespoon) gelatine for each ¾ pint of stock. Use a decorative metal mould, a metal cake tin, or even a bread tin; pour in a ⅛-inch layer of jellied stock and chill until set. Then arrange the chicken and vegetables attractively in the mould or pan, and chill 20 minutes, or until remaining stock is cold, almost syrupy, and on the point of setting; immediately pour it over the chicken. Chill several hours or overnight to set the gelatine completely. To un-mould, first scrape off any surface fat, then dip mould or pan for 4 to 5 seconds in very hot water, rapidly run a knife around edge of aspic, turn a chilled platter upside down over mould, and reverse the two. If aspic does not dislodge itself in a minute or two, repeat the process. Keep chilled until serving time, then decorate platter with lettuce, watercress, parsley, or appropriate vegetables.

Note: A more formal method for lining a mould with aspic is in Volume I, page 596, but would only be necessary if you were using clarified jellied stock.

Poulet Mornay, Gratiné
[Poached Chicken Pieces Gratinéed with Cheese Sauce]

When you want a casserole of chicken that you may prepare ahead for a party, this is a useful dish. After the chicken has poached, the cooking liquid is turned into a cheese sauce, which then enrobes the chicken in a baking dish; reheat and brown in the oven when the time comes. Serve this with steamed rice or buttered pasta, and either a simply done green vegetable such as buttered broccoli, peas, or asparagus tips, or a salad. A white Burgundy would be good here, or a claret.

Follow method and ingredients for chicken poached in white wine, master recipe, steps 1 and 2, pages 343–4. When chicken is done proceed as follows.

The cheese sauce (*sauce mornay*)

A sieve set over a saucepan
1¾ oz. butter
A heavy-bottomed 3-pt enamelled, non-stick, or stainless saucepan
1 oz. flour
A wooden spoon and a wire whisk

Set cover askew and drain cooking liquid out of casserole. Skim off surface fat, and bring liquid to simmer, skimming. You should have about 1 pint; boil down rapidly, if necessary. Meanwhile, make a white *roux* and a *velouté* sauce as follows: melt butter in saucepan, blend in flour, and stir over moderate heat with a wooden spoon until flour and butter foam together for 2 minutes without browning. Remove from heat, and as soon as *roux* stops bubbling, pour in all of the hot chicken cooking liquid at once, blending vigorously with a wire whisk.

Return sauce over moderately high heat, and stir with wire whisk as sauce thickens and comes to the boil. Boil, stirring, for 2 minutes, and remove from heat. Sauce should be thick enough to coat a spoon nicely; if too thin, boil down rapidly and if too thick, thin with milk, stock, or cream. Let cool for several minutes, stirring occasionally to prevent top from crusting while you prepare for the next step.

Final assembly

A buttered *gratin* dish that will hold the chicken comfortably (such as a 9- by 12-in. oval, 2 in. deep)
About 3 oz. coarsely grated Gruyère cheese
Salt and pepper
Speck of nutmeg
1 oz. melted butter

When you have buttered the dish, and grated and measured the cheese, fold all but 3 to 4 tablespoons of the cheese into the sauce. Taste, and correct seasoning as necessary with salt, pepper, and a speck of nutmeg. Smooth a thin layer of sauce in the bottom of the dish, and arrange the chicken over it, including the vegetables, if you wish.

Spoon the rest of the sauce over the chicken, masking each piece completely. Spread on the cheese, and sprinkle melted butter over the cheese.

(†) May be prepared a day in advance to this point; when cold, cover and refrigerate.

Reheating and serving

When both chicken and sauce are hot, and you are serving almost immediately, set dish 3 or 4 inches from a moderately hot grill and let topping brown slowly while contents of dish come to the bubble; you may then keep chicken warm for half an hour or so at 120°F., but be very careful not to let it overcook and lose the delicious quality of freshly cooked chicken.

When chicken has been refrigerated, set dish in upper third of a preheated 375°F., Mark 5 oven for 25 to 30 minutes, or until top has browned nicely and contents are bubbling hot. Again, be careful not to overcook.

Chaud-froid de Poulet, Morvandelle
[Chicken in *Chaud-froid* – a cold dish]

A simple chicken poached in white wine with aromatic vegetables can very easily be transformed into a dressy *chaud-froid* when you enrich the poaching broth with cream and egg yolks, which will thicken the broth just enough as it cools to enrobe the chicken pieces with a yellow-ivory cloak. Light, creamy, with a lovely texture and flavour, yet no trace of flour or gelatine, this is by far the most attractive *chaud-froid* we know. Serve it with cold vegetables or a tossed salad, French bread, and a chilled Chablis, Riesling, or Gewürztraminer.

Poach the chicken in wine and aromatic vegetables using the method and ingredients in the master recipe, steps 1 and 2, pages 343–4. When chicken is done, continue as follows.

The *chaud-froid* sauce

A sieve set over a heavy-bottomed 3-pt enamelled or stainless saucepan
6 egg yolks in a mixing bowl
½ pt *crème fraîche* or double cream
A wire whisk, a ladle, and a wooden spoon
Salt, white pepper, and drops of lemon juice

Set cover askew, and drain chicken cooking stock out of casserole into saucepan. Skim off surface fat, bring liquid to the simmer, skimming, then boil down rapidly until reduced to a generous ½ pint. Beat the egg yolks and cream to blend. Still beating, gradually ladle in driblets of the hot chicken cooking liquid. When half has gone in, gradually beat the creamy mixture into the remaining chicken cooking liquid in the saucepan.

Set pan over moderate heat and stir slowly and continuously with wooden spoon, reaching all over bottom of pan, for 5 to 6 minutes, or until sauce thickens enough to film spoon with a creamy layer. (Be careful sauce does not come near the simmer and curdle the egg yolks; however, you must heat it to the point where it thickens.)

Immediately remove from heat, and stir vigorously for 1 minute to cool slightly and stop the cooking. Taste very carefully, adding salt, white pepper, and drops of lemon juice; sauce should be quite highly seasoned because flavour becomes somewhat subdued in a cold dish. Shortly before coating chicken, set saucepan in a large bowl of cold water and ice cubes; stir frequently until sauce is cool and has begun to thicken. Meanwhile, prepare the chicken for the next step.

Final assembly and serving

A chilled shallow serving dish, just large enough to hold chicken easily
For decoration: either minced fresh tarragon, parsley sprigs, or
watercress; or 1 or 2 truffles to mince and stir into the sauce with the
juices from the tin; or a fluted mushroom cap to top each piece of
chicken (Volume I, pages 547–9, for fluting and cooking)

Peel the skin off each piece of chicken, removing as much as you easily can without tearing the meat. Arrange chicken in dish. (If you are stirring truffles into sauce, do so now.) Spoon a thin layer of sauce over each piece, using about ⅓ of the sauce at this point. Cover chicken and chill for 15 to 20 minutes (or longer). When sauce has set on chicken and you are ready to continue, re-warm the remaining sauce briefly, only enough to liquefy it. Beat with wire whisk until perfectly smooth, and spoon it over the chicken to mask each piece completely. Cover chicken with a bowl and chill.

Remove chicken from refrigerator about half an hour before serving (unless weather is too hot), to take off the chill; decorate as you wish with any of the elements suggested.

Waterzooi de Poulet
[Chicken Poached in White Wine and a Julienne
of Vegetables, Cream, and Egg-yolk Sauce]
The preceding *chaud-froid* turns out to be an almost exact replica of the famous Belgian *bouillabaisse* of chicken, *waterzooi*. The Belgian dish is served hot, however, and the sauce is

more like a soup – a *waterzooi* is ladled into deep plates, and you eat it with a knife, fork, and soup spoon. Although its general method is almost identical to that of the *chaud-froid*, as well as the *poulet en bourride* on page 355, the recipe will be easier for you to follow when you have the full details for its sauce and serving even if it means repeating familiar instructions. Accompany the *waterzooi* with boiled potatoes, French bread, and a white Graves or Burgundy. It is a separate course, and a rich one – precede with a cold vegetable or something like the *salade niçoise* in Volume I, page 579, and follow with fresh fruit, a fruit tart, or a sorbet.

SHOWMANSHIP

In the fine Brussels restaurants where this dish is served, the chicken is poached whole; the *maître d'hôtel* carves it in front of you, and warms the pieces of chicken in the sauce while you savour its delicious perfume. If you can carve like a master and enjoy the drama of table-top cooking, by all means poach the chicken whole, page 357; carve it at the table, and make the sauce as described here, but in a chafing dish.

[*For 4 people*]

Follow the master recipe for chicken pieces poached in white wine, steps 1 and 2, pages 343–4, but cut the aromatic vegetables into julienne matchsticks for step 1. When chicken is done, continue as follows.

Sauce and serving

If needed: more chicken broth
6 egg yolks in a mixing bowl
½ pt *crème fraîche* or double cream
A wire whisk and a ladle
Salt and white pepper
2 tbl. rather roughly chopped fresh parsley
If you wish, a serving casserole or a soup tureen
Wide soup plates

(You should have 1 to 1¼ pints of cooking stock for the sauce; add extra broth if necessary.) When you are ready to serve, beat the egg yolks and cream to blend; continue beating, and ladle in driblets of the hot chicken cooking liquid until about ½ pint has gone in. Remove casserole from heat; swirling it with one hand, gradually pour creamy mixture back over chicken. Taste carefully, and correct seasoning.

Set casserole over moderate heat and continue to swirl it slowly for 4 to 5 minutes, until sauce thickens into a light cream as the egg yolks gradually poach in the mixture; you must be very careful here not to heat the sauce too much or it will turn granular as the egg yolks scramble, but you must heat it to the point where it thickens. Serve immediately, either from casserole or turned into a tureen; decorate with parsley.

The chicken and sauce, which is more like a cream soup, are ladled into soup plates, along with a serving of potatoes, and eaten with knife, fork, and soup spoon.

(†) Although you may make the egg yolk and cream liaison, pour it over the chicken, and reheat later, it is safer to keep the poached chicken warm, and finish the dish just before serving. Finished *waterzooi* risks curdling if you try to keep it warm; in other words, this is not a dish adaptable to complete ahead-of-time cookery.

Bouillabaisse de Poulet
[Chicken Poached in White Wine with Provençal Vegetables, Herbs, and Flavourings]

Famous and successful recipes have a way of turning up in other guises, chicken has a habit of wearing other costumes, and there should be nothing surprising about chicken swimming in the robust flavours of a *bouillabaisse*. Although the method here is almost the same as that for the previous poachings, the ingredients differ; we therefore outline all the steps. Serve this with steamed rice or boiled potatoes, French bread, and a strong young white wine like a Riesling or Pinot Blanc, a rather light red like a Beaujolais, or a rosé.

[*For 4 people*]

1. Preliminary cooking of vegetables

½ lb. onions, sliced
½ lb. white of leek, sliced (or more onion)
3 tbl. olive oil
A heavy 5-pt flameproof casserole with cover

Cook the onions and leeks slowly with the oil in the covered cassserole for about 10 minutes, stirring fairly frequently, until tender but not browned.

4 or 5 tomatoes, peeled, seeded, and juiced, or a combination of fresh
   tomatoes and tinned Italian-type plum tomatoes, drained and sieved
2 cloves garlic, minced or mashed

While vegetables are cooking, prepare the tomatoes; when vegetables are tender, stir tomatoes in along with the garlic. Cover, and cook 5 minutes so that tomatoes will render their juices; then uncover, raise heat, and let juices almost entirely evaporate.

2. Poaching the chicken

2½ lb. ready-cut chicken, prepared as described on pages 340–42
Salt

When tomatoes are done, salt chicken lightly, and arrange in casserole, spreading vegetables around and on top. Cover and cook 10 minutes over moderate heat, turning once.

½ pt dry white wine or dry white French vermouth
About ¾ pt chicken stock or tinned chicken broth
1 bay leaf
½ tsp. thyme
¼ tsp. fennel seeds, crushed
2 pinches saffron threads
A 2-in. piece of dried orange peel, or ½ tsp. bottled dried orange peel
Big pinch pepper
Pinch Cayenne pepper or drops Tabasco sauce
Salt as needed

Pour the wine or vermouth over the chicken, and enough stock or broth barely to cover the meat. Add the herbs and seasonings, bring to the simmer, and salt lightly as necessary.

Cover casserole and simmer slowly either on top of the stove or in a preheated 325°F., Mark 3 oven for 20 to 25 minutes, or until chicken is tender.

3. Serving

Tip casserole and skim off surface fat; remove bay leaf and orange peel, and carefully correct seasoning. Serve as it is, from casserole, or arrange chicken and vegetables on a bed of steamed rice, decorate with parsley sprigs, and pass rest of cooking liquid separately.

(†) May be kept warm for at least half an hour; set cover askew for air circulation and place in a very low oven, on a hot-plate, or over barely simmering water. Do not overheat and let chicken overcook.

To Serve Cold or in Aspic

This is delicious as a cold dish. When chicken is done, skim off surface fat, remove bay leaf and orange peel, and correct seasoning. When cool, cover and refrigerate for several hours. Scrape off congealed fat and serve the chicken as it is; cooking stock will set lightly, like jellied consommé. (If you want a firmer jellied effect, strain cooking stock out of casserole when chicken is done, degrease completely, and dissolve in it 1 package (1 tablespoon) of gelatine for each ¾ pint of liquid; pour back over the chicken and vegetables, and chill.)

Final Touches – *Rouille* and *Pistou*

You might pass a *rouille* with the chicken – the garlic, pimento, and chilli-pepper sauce given at the end of the fish soup recipe in Volume I, page 70. Another excellent sauce would be the *pistou* on page 217, a fragrant combination of basil, tomato, garlic, and cheese that may either be incorporated into the cooking liquid just before serving, or be passed separately. Finally there is the marvellous garlic mayonnaise, *aïoli*, in the next variation.

Poulet en Bourride

[*Bouillabaisse* of Chicken with *Aïoli* Sauce]

What the Belgians do to chicken in their *waterzooi*, their rivals on the Mediterranean accomplish in a most Provençal manner. In fact, the two recipes are almost exact parallels – egg yolks and cream thicken the broth of the *waterzooi* on page 350, while it is egg yolks and olive oil for the *bourride*. This is a very rich and splendid dish; we would suggest only oiled potatoes to go with it, a very simple beginning to the meal, such as asparagus vinaigrette, and a sorbet or fruits for dessert. A strong, dry wine like Burgundy or Côtes-du-Rhône would be our suggestion for wine.

Poach the chicken exactly as described for the *bouillabaisse* of chicken, page 353, steps 1 and 2; skim off surface fat, and keep chicken warm. While it simmers, prepare the *aïoli* as follows.

The *aïoli* sauce

3 tbl. fresh breadcrumbs
Wine vinegar
A heavy bowl or mortar, a pestle or wooden masher, and wire whisk
6 to 8 large cloves garlic, mashed
$\frac{1}{4}$ tsp. salt
6 egg yolks
$\frac{1}{4}$ to $\frac{1}{2}$ pt olive oil

Following the procedure for *aïoli* sauce in Volume I, page 111, moisten the crumbs with drops of vinegar and pound to a paste in the bowl or mortar. Add garlic and salt, and continue pounding until smooth. Then add egg yolks and pound until thick and sticky. Finally begin beating in drops of olive oil; when sauce is thick and heavy, thin with vinegar, and continue beating in oil with wire whisk. Season to taste, and cover airtight until ready to use.

Combining chicken and *aïoli*

A ladle
Optional: a warm soup tureen
Rather roughly chopped fresh parsley
Wide soup plates

When chicken is done and just before you are ready to serve, remove from heat. Gradually ladle driblets of the hot chicken cooking liquid into the *aïoli* sauce, beating sauce with wire whisk; when a cup of liquid has gone in, pour mixture back into chicken and vegetables, swirling casserole with one hand as you do so, to blend.

Set casserole over moderate heat and continue to swirl it slowly for 4 to 5 minutes, until sauce thickens into a light cream; be careful not to heat sauce to the simmer or it will turn granular as the egg yolks scramble, but you must heat it to the point where it thickens. Serve immediately, either from casserole or turned into a tureen; decorate with parsley.

Like *waterzooi*, the chicken and the soup-like sauce are ladled into soup plates, along with a serving of potatoes, and eaten with knife, fork, and soup spoon.

(†) *Ahead-of-time note:* See remarks for *waterzooi*, pages 350–52.

Casserole-Poached Chicken · *Poularde Pochée à Court Mouillement*

Roasting and stewing are not the only ways to cook a whole chicken; there are also casserole roasting, which produces the savoury brown *poulet poêlé à l'estragon* and its variations in Volume I, pages 272–7, and casserole poaching, for those times when you wish to serve a whole chicken with one of the many white-wine sauces. This is called *pocher à mouillement* because the chicken is set in a casserole that will just hold it, and the poaching liquid comes only part way up – the dark meat of the legs and thighs simmers and the white meat of the breast steams. This gives you not only a beautifully tender and juicy chicken, but also a perfectly flavoured white-wine chicken broth for a sauce, or, if you are serving the chicken cold, for your aspic or *chaud-froid*. You may cook the chicken with or without stuffing, and serve it any number of ways. We begin with chicken in a white-wine and tarragon sauce.

THE CHICKEN TO BUY – PREPARING IT FOR
POACHING

Roasting chickens and capons are best for casserole poaching
because their flesh is mature enough to hold up under the
steam and moisture. To prepare the chicken for cooking,
first remove the package of giblets from inside the cavity.
The giblets should include the liver, heart, gizzard, and neck.
If you are not stuffing the chicken, you may season the liver
and return it to the cavity to cook and serve with the chicken,
or save it for another purpose. Reserve the rest of the giblets
for the casserole; they will give added flavour to the broth.

Pull loose fat from around inside of vent opening; you may
render it (page 419), and use for general cooking or for rubbing
over the chicken instead of butter. Cut off nubbins attached to
wing elbows and, to make carving easier, remove the wishbone by cutting round its forked outline from inside the neck
end of the chicken, then break its two ends loose from bottom
of breast and pull it free. Run cold water all around inside and
outside of chicken, and dry thoroughly with paper towels.
(We were not enthusiastic about washing chickens in Volume
I; we now think it is a wise precaution.) After you have
inserted whatever flavouring or stuffing is called for, truss the
chicken as illustrated in Volume I, pages 258–60 (or in less
detail here on page 365).

*Poularde Pochée à l'Estragon

[Casserole-poached Chicken with White-wine and Tarragon
Sauce]

A fine roasting chicken is a *poularde* in French, and capon is
chapon; either one is recommended for this delicious recipe.
Rather than a stuffing, we have suggested a herbal flavouring
inside the chicken, which is typical of many French recipes;
if you do wish a stuffing, see the variations at the end of the
recipe as well as the list of stuffings on page 664.

Nothing that accompanies the chicken should mask the
lovely flavour of the tarragon, and with this in mind, we
would suggest steamed rice and the garniture of mushrooms
and onions used for chicken fricassee (Volume I, page 284);

or either the unusual rice and onion *soubise* in Volume I on page 519 or the stuffed onions here on page 494, with buttered peas or asparagus tips. This is definitely an occasion for one of the great white Burgundy wines.

[*For 5 to 6 people*]

1. Preparations for poaching

2 carrots, sliced
2 onions, sliced
1 oz. butter
A heavy enamelled casserole or roaster just large enough to hold the chicken comfortably, breast up

Preheat oven to 325°F., Mark 3 in time for step 2. Cook the onions and carrots in the covered casserole, stirring occasionally, until vegetables are tender but not brown. Meanwhile, prepare the chicken as follows.

A 4½-lb. ready-to-cook roasting chicken or capon
1½ oz. soft butter (half for inside and half for outside of chicken)
½ tsp. salt (for inside and outside of chicken)
A medium-sized branch of fresh tarragon, or 1 tsp. dried tarragon

Prepare chicken for roasting as described in paragraph preceding recipe, but before trussing it, put half the butter inside the chicken, sprinkle with half the salt, and add the tarragon; then truss the chicken. When vegetables are tender, massage the rest of the butter into the chicken skin, sprinkle with remaining salt, and arrange the chicken breast up in the casserole.

½ pt dry white wine or dry white French vermouth
¾ pt or more chicken stock or tinned chicken broth
1 bay leaf
6 parsley sprigs
A medium-sized branch of fresh tarragon, or ½ tbl. dried tarragon
The washed chicken giblets (neck, gizzard, heart, wing nubbins, wishbone)
Salt as needed
A double thickness of well-washed and rinsed damp cheesecloth to cover chicken breast and thighs
1 oz. soft butter
Waxed paper

Pour the wine into the casserole, and enough chicken stock or broth to reach about ⅓ the way up the chicken. Add the herbs, and giblets. Bring to simmer on top of the stove, taste liquid, and salt lightly, as needed. Drape the damp, washed cheesecloth over the breast and thighs; it should be long enough to fall into the liquid all around so that it will draw the broth over the chicken and baste it during the cooking. Smear the butter over the cheesecloth, top with waxed paper, cover the casserole, and set in middle level of preheated oven.

(†) You may arrange the chicken in the casserole with wine, broth, cloth, and trimmings, then refrigerate, and poach it the next day.

2. Poaching the chicken: 1 hour and 30 to 40 minutes at 325°F., Mark 3

After chicken has been in the oven about 20 minutes, check casserole to be sure liquid is at the very slow simmer – if liquid bubbles actively, flesh can break apart. Regulate thermostat accordingly; except for making sure cooking is slow and gentle, you have nothing more to do until chicken is done.

When chicken flesh is tender if pressed and drumsticks move in their sockets, chicken should be ready. Test by lifting it carefully (use trussing strings between thighs and elbows) and drain juices on to a white plate; if last drops to come out are clear yellow with no trace of rose, chicken is definitely done.

3. The sauce (sauce à l'estragon)

A sieve set over a 4- to 5-pt stainless saucepan
2 oz. butter
A second 4- to 5-pt saucepan, heavy-bottomed and enamelled or
    stainless
5 tbl. flour
A wooden spoon and a wire whisk

When chicken is done and juices have been drained from vent, set it on a platter or side dish. Strain cooking stock into saucepan, pressing juices out of ingredients in sieve; skim surface fat off stock. Return chicken to casserole with a cup of the cooking stock, replace cheesecloth, set casserole cover askew, and keep chicken warm, either in turned-off oven, on a hot-plate, or over barely simmering water while you prepare a *sauce velouté*.

Bring cooking stock to the simmer, skimming off additional fat, and maintain at slow simmer while making the *roux*: melt butter in saucepan, blend in flour with wooden spoon, and stir over moderate heat until butter and flour foam together for 2 minutes without browning. Remove from heat, and as soon as *roux* stops bubbling, pour in ¾ pint of the hot chicken stock, blending vigorously with wire whisk. When smooth, return over moderate heat and stir rather slowly with wire whisk as sauce thickens and comes to the boil. Boil, stirring, for 2 minutes – sauce will be quite thick.

¼ pt or so double cream
Salt, white pepper, and drops of lemon juice
1 to 2 oz. soft butter

Simmering the sauce, pour in 4 tablespoons of the cream, and add successive spoonfuls until sauce thins out but is still thick enough to coat a spoon nicely. Taste very carefully for seasoning, adding salt, white pepper, and lemon juice to taste. Just before serving, remove from heat and beat in the enrichment butter a small piece at a time.

4. Serving

A hot, lightly buttered serving platter
Either: 10 to 12 large fresh tarragon leaves dropped 30 seconds in boiling water and laid on a plate:
Or: slices of truffle or fluted and cooked mushrooms, and parsley or watercress if needed
A warmed sauce bowl

Remove trussing strings from chicken, and set it on platter; wipe up any juices. Spoon enough sauce over chicken to mask it attractively, and decorate with tarragon leaves or whatever you have chosen. Pour rest of sauce into bowl. Make a presentation of the chicken to your guests, who will want to admire it. Then, if it is not to be carved at the table, carve in the kitchen; arrange the pieces over a bed of rice, and spoon a little of the sauce over each. Decorate again with tarragon leaves or whatever you have chosen, and serve.

(†) You may keep the chicken warm for half an hour at least as suggested at the end of the first part in step 3. Complete the sauce except for the final butter enrichment, clean sauce off sides of pan with a rubber spatula, and dot a tablespoon of soft butter on surface of sauce, spreading it lightly and evenly with the back of a spoon; keep sauce warm, uncovered, over simmering water.

To serve cold, see recipe below.

Poularde en Chaud-froid
Poularde en Gelée
[Chicken in *Chaud-froid* – Chicken in Aspic]
The tender fragrant quality of chicken poached in white wine and the excellence of its cooking broth make it ideal for *chaud-froid* or simply chicken in aspic. For *chaud-froid*, you might use half the broth for an initial creamy coating on the chicken pieces following either the cream and egg-yolk sauce on page 349, or the recipe in Volume I, page 589, with cream and gelatine. You could then decorate the chicken with tarragon leaves, and glaze with clear aspic made from the rest of the broth. Full directions for *chaud-froids* are in this volume and in Volume I as indicated; for aspics see page 345 in this volume, and page 582 in Volume I.

Stuffed Chicken – Boned Chicken

When you want to serve stuffed chicken, either roasted or poached, it is easier to carve it if you bone the breast of the raw chicken, meaning that you slit the skin and peel it back from the breast, remove the meat, and cut out the breastbone and upper half of the ribs. This gives you a boat-shaped trough; its bottom is formed by the backbone, and its sides by the lower ribs, the wings, and the legs. Pile the stuffing into the trough, top with breast meat cut into strips, fold the skin back into place, and the chicken is reconstituted again for cooking. To serve, cut right down the length of the breast to reveal white meat and stuffing, while the legs and wings come off in the usual way. Because white meat picks up flavour when in direct contact with the stuffing, most of the dark-meat-only people will shift over to 'a little of both, please'. You will also find this semi-boning a successful way to treat the enormous breasts of modern turkeys, and a turkey is boned exactly like the chicken illustrated here.

Volaille Demi-désossée
[Half-boned Chicken]
Also for turkey, other poultry, and game birds.

Set chicken breast up, and with a sharp knife, slit the skin from neck to tail, following ridge of breastbone. With your fingers, peel the skin back from the breast first on one side, then on the other (A), going down to the shoulders and the second joints to expose the whole expanse of breast.

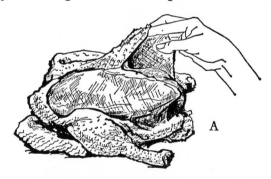

A

Starting on one side of ridge of breastbone, cut through flesh to bone all along its length from neck end to tail. Always angling the cutting edge of knife against bone and not against flesh, continue cutting down against outward curve of breast-bone and then against ribs, pulling flesh from bone with your fingers as you cut (B). Be careful not to slit skin at sides of breast as you release meat from lower rib cage; cut off the meat where it joins the ball joint of the wing at the shoulder,

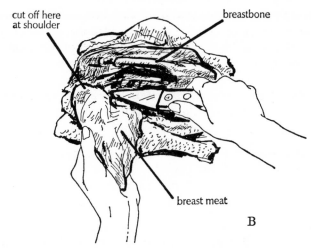

cut off here at shoulder

breastbone

breast meat

B

and you have removed one side of the breast meat. Remove the other side in the same manner.

With heavy shears and starting at the tail end, cut through the upper half of the breastbone–rib structure midway on each side, where the backward-slanting top ribs join the forward-slanting bottom ribs. Continue the cut through the V-shaped bone at the neck end, and the breastbone is freed.

With the breastbone removed, you now have a boat-shaped open cavity to fill with stuffing (c). The 2 boneless

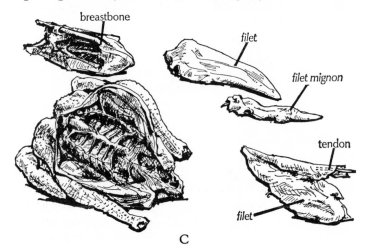

breastbone

filet

filet mignon

tendon

filet

C

pieces of meat, one removed from each side of the breast, are called *suprêmes*, and each is composed of 2 layers. The larger layer is the *filet*; the smaller layer is the *filet mignon*. On the underside of each *filet mignon* is a clearly visible white tendon. Grasp the end of it in a towel held in one hand; slit flesh on either side with a small knife and, scraping it against your knife as you gently pull, draw it out; repeat for the second tendon.

(†) If you are not ready to stuff the chicken at this point, place the *suprêmes* in the cavity, draw the chicken skin over them, wrap the chicken, and refrigerate it. Chop up the breastbone and add it to your chicken stock.

When you are ready to stuff the chicken, cut the breast meat into strips $\frac{3}{8}$ inch wide. (You may wish to marinate them in oil, herbs, and wine or drops of lemon juice, or in cognac as suggested in the following recipe.) Raise the legs upright, then flex them, pushing knees against armpits (where wings join shoulders). Run a skewer or knitting needle through the carcass at knees as shown; this will hold legs in place for the rest of the operation. Mound whatever stuffing you have chosen in the cavity, building it into a dome at the front to simulate a full breast. Lay the strips of breast meat over the stuffing (D).

Fold the breast skin over the stuffing and breast meat, covering it completely (E). One edge of skin should overlap

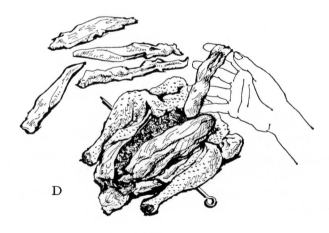

D

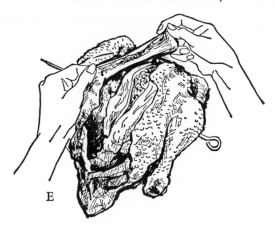

E

the other by $\frac{3}{8}$ to $\frac{1}{2}$ inch; remove a little stuffing if necessary. With white string and either an 8-inch trussing needle, a long mattress needle, or a plastic knitting needle with a hole drilled in the end, truss the chicken (F).

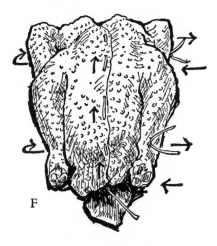

F

(1) Sew the 2 flaps of breast skin together as follows: start at the tail end, and leaving a 3-inch piece of string free at that end, stitch a straight line up to the neck. Turn the chicken over and sew the neck skin to the back, completely enclosing the stuffing at the neck end.

(2) The second tie is to secure the lower part of the drumsticks and to close the vent opening. Push needle through the lower part of the carcass and the tail piece; come back through skin on top of one drumstick, through lower end of breast, and top of second drumstick. Pull string tight, and tie.

(3) For the final tie, remove skewer, and go through carcass at the knees; fold wings akimbo and come back through the underside of one wing, through a bit of the backbone, then through the underside of the second wing. Pull string tight and tie.

Chicken is now ready for roasting, casserole roasting, or for the *poularde poché, à la d'Albuféra*, in the following recipe.

*Poularde à la d'Albuféra

[Half-boned Chicken Stuffed with *Foie Gras*,
Truffles, Chicken Livers, and Rice, Poached in
White Wine; *Sauce Suprême Pimentée*]

One of the most famous chickens boned, stuffed, and poached in white wine is this one, created to honour Maréchal Suchet, who was made Duc d'Albuféra by a grateful Napoleon after the General's victories in Spain. The dukedom, a large lagoon surrounded by rice fields with an outlet to the bay of Valencia, was lost in another battle the next year, 1813, but both duke and recipe retained their titles. Curiously enough, as a gastronomical aside to history, the grateful Spanish, in recognition of his role in returning the lost territories to them, awarded the revenues from the Albufera to the Duke of Wellington – perhaps at the very moment a famous *filet* of beef was being named after him. Numerous versions, as is always the way, exist for *poularde à la d'Albuféra*, and we have picked the one we prefer. Not all of them include a small pinch of saffron in the rice, but all do have a Spanish echo of pimento in the sauce.

The vegetable accompaniment should be fresh and simple, we think. Something like the parslied baked cucumbers in Volume I, page 536, or fresh new peas or asparagus tips, or the tender, peeled, fresh broccoli in Chapter 6 here, page 446. We prefer one of the great white Burgundies with this dish,

or one of the lovely white Graves – Haut-Brion or La
Mission-Haut-Brion.

[*For 6 people*]

1. Preparing the chicken

A 4½-lb. roasting chicken or capon
A dish to hold the strips of breast meat
1½ tbl. each of dry port or dry (Sercial) Madeira, and cognac
1 tbl. very finely minced shallots or spring onions
Freshly ground white pepper
Pinches of tarragon or thyme
1 or more 1-oz. tins of truffles
2 or more oz. tinned *foie gras en bloc*, chilled for easy cutting

Following preceding directions, bone out the breast of the
chicken. Cut breast meat into strips ⅜ inch wide and turn about
in the dish with the wine, shallots, pepper, herbs, and the
uncut truffles and their juice. Dipping your knife in hot water
for each slice, cut the *foie gras* into ¼-inch dice; place at side of
dish, and baste with the marinade. Cover marinade dish
with plastic wrap, and refrigerate while making the stuffing;
wrap and refrigerate the chicken.

2. The stuffing (*farce à la d'Albuféra*)

The chicken liver and heart (if you have the minimum of *foie gras*, add
    an extra chicken liver)
1½ oz. butter
A heavy-bottomed, 3- to 4-pt enamelled or stainless saucepan with cover
A large mixing bowl
2 tbl. very finely minced onion
2 oz. plain, raw, white, untreated rice
3 tbl. dry white wine or dry white French vermouth
¾ pt chicken stock or tinned chicken broth
A small pinch of saffron threads
A bay leaf
Salt and pepper to taste
1 egg, lightly beaten

Cut the chicken liver or livers and heart into ¼-inch dice, and
sauté over moderate heat in ½ ounce of the butter, just to
stiffen them slightly; scrape into mixing bowl. Melt the rest
of the butter in the pan, add the onions, and cook slowly,

stirring frequently, for 4 to 5 minutes until fairly tender but not browned. Stir in the rice, and cook, stirring, for several minutes over moderate heat until rice turns translucent, then milky, indicating that the covering starch has coagulated. Pour in the wine and let cook for a moment to evaporate the alcohol.

Then pour in the chicken stock or broth, add the small pinch of saffron, the bay leaf, and bring to the simmer. Add salt and pepper as needed, stir up once, cover pan, and let cook at a moderately fast simmer, without touching it again, for 15 minutes. Rice should be almost but not quite done, needing only 2 to 3 minutes more cooking; liquid should have been entirely absorbed. Uncover pan, discard bay leaf, turn rice into mixing bowl, and let it cool to tepid. Stir in the egg.

Remove the truffles from their marinade, and cut into dice (or mince if you have only a small amount). Fold with a rubber spatula into the rice and chicken livers, and carefully correct seasoning. (Reserve the *foie gras* until next step.)

3. Stuffing and trussing the chicken

Salt cavity of chicken lightly, spread a layer of rice stuffing in it, and then a few pieces of the diced *foie gras*. Continue in layers, moulding rice into a dome at the breast end. Cover with the breast strips, as illustrated on page 364, fold skin over breast, sew, and truss the chicken also as illustrated. (Reserve marinade juices.)

(†) If both stuffing and chicken are cold, you may stuff and truss the chicken a day in advance of cooking.

4. Poaching the chicken: 1½ to 1¾ hours

Poach the chicken as directed in steps 1 and 2, master recipe, pages 357–9, but use a big pinch of thyme and a bay leaf rather than tarragon in the casserole.

5. The sauce

Make the sauce as described in step 3 of the master recipe, page 359, but omit the tarragon, and stir the marinade liquid into it. Rather than enriching it with plain butter, use pimento butter as follows.

3 tbl. canned red pimento
1½ oz. soft butter
A fine-meshed sieve set over a bowl
A wooden spoon and a rubber spatula
Pinch of Cayenne pepper, or drops of Tabasco sauce

Drain the pimento and gently press out liquid. Rub it with the butter through the sieve, scraping all residue off bottom of sieve as well as banging sieve on bowl to dislodge as much as possible. Beat in Cayenne or Tabasco. Just before serving, remove sauce from heat and beat in the pimento butter, a small piece at a time.

6. Serving

When ready to serve, remove trussing strings and place chicken on platter. Spoon a little of the sauce over the chicken, and decorate as you wish, with truffle slices or fluted mushrooms. To carve, cut straight down through top of breast from neck end to tail end, and spread apart. Remove wings and legs. Remove breast meat with stuffing, using a serving spoon and fork, and give each guest both dark meat, light meat, and stuffing; spoon some of the sauce around or over each serving.

(†) See directions at end of master recipe, page 361.

OTHER STUFFINGS, OTHER SAUCES

Farce Évocation d'Albuféra
[Rice, Mushroom, and Chicken-liver Stuffing with
Purée of Garlic]

More Mediterranean in feeling than the original is the following stuffing for those occasions when you do not wish to indulge in truffles and *foie gras*.

[*Stuffing to fill a 4¼-pound half-boned chicken*]

1 head of garlic
3 tbl. dry white wine or dry white French vermouth
½ pt chicken stock or tinned chicken broth
A small covered saucepan

Separate the garlic cloves and drop into a pan of boiling water, boil 1 minute, drain, and slip off the peel. Then simmer the garlic cloves very slowly for 30 minutes with the wine and stock. Meanwhile, continue with the rest of the stuffing.

¼ lb. fresh mushrooms, trimmed, washed, dried, and quartered
2 tbl. minced shallots or spring onions
½ oz. butter and 1 tsp. oil
A heavy-bottomed 4- to 5-pt enamelled or stainless saucepan
3 chicken livers, cut into ⅜-in. pieces
3 tbl. dry (Sercial) Madeira or dry port
A mixing bowl

Sauté the mushrooms and spring onions in butter and oil over moderately high heat, tossing and turning, until fat reappears on surface of mushrooms; then add diced livers and sauté a minute more, tossing. Pour in the Madeira or port and boil rapidly until liquid is almost entirely evaporated. Scrape into mixing bowl.

5 to 6 oz. plain boiled white rice
¼ tsp. thyme or oregano
1 egg, lightly beaten
The cooked garlic in its broth
A fine-meshed sieve
Salt and pepper to taste

Blend the rice, herbs, and egg into the mixing bowl. Drain cooked garlic, and mash through sieve into mixing bowl; blend in, along with 2 tablespoons of the cooking liquid. (Reserve rest of liquid for sauce, including it as part of the chicken cooking stock.) Taste stuffing, and carefully correct seasoning.

Stuff, truss, and poach the chicken as directed in the preceding recipe; either make the same sauce with pimento-butter enrichment, or make a light curry sauce by stirring 2 teaspoons of fragrant curry powder into the butter as you make the *roux*, beginning of step 3, master recipe, page 359.

Farce Normande, aux Boudins Blancs
[White Forcemeat Stuffing with Mushroom *Duxelles*]

Boudin blanc, with its minced chicken, veal, or pork and onions, is so good one is always happy to find other uses for it. Use half the recipe on page 387, but there is no need to encase the mixture in sausage skins: roll it, instead, into one big sausage shape in cheesecloth, as illustrated on page 383; poach it in the wine and chicken stock you will use for poaching the chicken, making the stock even better than usual for your final sauce. Then proceed as follows.

The poached *boudin* described in preceding paragraph
About 5 tbl. cooked mushroom *duxelles* (finely diced mushrooms
    sautéed in butter, page 271), still in their sauté pan
2 tbl. minced shallots or spring onions
3 tbl. dry (Sercial) Madeira or dry port wine
Salt and pepper to taste

Cut the *boudin* into ½-inch dice and set aside. Heat the *duxelles* with the shallots or spring onions, tossing and turning over moderately high heat for 2 minutes to cook the shallots, then pour in the wine. Boil rapidly for a minute or two, to evaporate liquid almost completely. Taste, and carefully correct seasoning.

Stuff the chicken with layers of diced *boudin* interspersed with sprinklings of *duxelles*, and top with the slices of breast meat. Truss the chicken as illustrated on page 365, and poach as directed in the master recipe for chicken poached in white wine, starting on page 357. Rather than flavouring the sauce with tarragon, you might make an additional 2 or 3 tablespoons of wine-flavoured *duxelles* initially, and reserve it to simmer a moment in your finished sauce before adding the final butter enrichment. A sprinkling of minced fresh green herbs, such as parsley, tarragon, or chives could go in too at the last minute.

Poularde en Soutien-gorge
Coq en Pâte
Poularde en Croûte
[Half-boned and Stuffed Chicken in a Pastry Crust]

Once you have boned, stuffed, and enrobed a *coq en pâte,* you may put it away in the refrigerator and bake it the next day. Amusing to prepare and always a success when served, it is a great dish for a party. Not only are the chicken's breastworks removed, but its skin is also peeled off; thus the French title, *soutien-gorge,* is as primly nondescriptive as would be our brassière; the German *Büstenhalter* would give a more exact explanation of what the pastry must do to hold the breast and stuffing in place during baking. The dough, *pâte à croustade,* is designed for something like a *pâté* or a chicken that must bake for an hour or more: the pastry is crisp, tender, and delicious to eat as well as being easy to handle; if you make it in the electric mixer you will find it very easy to do.

CHICKEN NOTES

Rather than the $4\frac{1}{4}$-pound roaster or capon for 6, suggested in the recipe, you may use 3- to $3\frac{1}{2}$-pound frying chickens, and 3 of them would serve 12 to 16 people. You will need only $\frac{1}{2}$ the pastry recipe per frying chicken, and less stuffing. Roasting time for 1 frying chicken would be 1 hour and 20 to 30 minutes; for 3 chickens in one oven, probably 1¾ to 2 hours.

[*For 6 people*]

1. The pastry: made at least 2 hours before baking

Pastry formula 6, page 163, *pâte à croustade*

Make the pastry either by hand in the usual way, or by machine as described on page 157. Wrap and chill the dough for at least 2 hours, or overnight. (Actually you will need only ⅔ of the dough for this recipe; freeze any left-overs and use for turnovers or appetizer pastries.)

2. Preparing and stuffing the chicken

A 4½-lb. roasting chicken or capon

Slit the skin of the chicken along the breastbone from neck end to tail; turn chicken over and slit skin from neck to tail ¼ inch from edge of backbone on each side.

Cut off wings at elbows. Then, except for strip of skin at backbone, peel the rest of the skin off the chicken. Being careful not to detach the following pieces from the chicken, cut through ball joints attaching wings to shoulders, second joints to hips, and drumsticks to second joints; this is to prevent these appendages from kicking through the pastry during cooking. Remove breast meat, and cut out upper half of breastbone–rib structure as illustrated on pages 362–3. Cut the breast meat in strips and marinate, if you wish, in wine and herbs as described in the master recipe, page 367, step 1. Make a brown chicken stock with the giblets, skin, and scraps (Volume I, page 257).

¾ lb. of any stuffing for chicken, pages 664–6, the *évocation d'Albuféra* being particularly recommended
A skewer or knitting needle just long enough to go through carcass at knees and to protrude ¼ to ½ in. on each side

Following illustrated directions on pages 364–5, stuff the chicken and lay the breast strips on top. Insert skewer as in the illustration (D), to keep legs in place during baking; it will be drawn out from the crust before serving.

3. Enclosing chicken in pastry

The chilled pastry from step 1
White wine, or vermouth, or chicken stock; or the garlic cooking
  liquid if you are using *farce évocation d'Albuféra*
A pastry brush
A shallow buttered roasting pan or edged baking sheet large enough to
  hold chicken easily
Egg glaze (1 egg beaten in a small bowl with 1 tsp. water)

Preheat oven to 400°F., Mark 6, in time for step 4. Roll ⅔ of the pastry out on a lightly floured board, making an oval ³⁄₁₆ inch thick and large enough to cover top and sides of chicken. Paint chicken with wine or stock, and press the pastry in place over the flesh. (Leave a small opening at one side or both for removal of skewer after baking.) Trim off any extra pastry, leaving only enough to cover sides of chicken completely. (Bare bottom of chicken rests on baking surface.)

Roll out pastry scraps, cut into whatever designs you wish, paint undersides with egg glaze, and affix to the pastry.

(†) If both stuffing and chicken were cold before being combined, chicken may be covered, refrigerated, and baked the next day. Note, however, that roasting time may be 15 to 20 minutes longer than time indicated in step 4.

4. Baking: 1½ to 1¾ hours

The egg glaze and the pastry brush
Aluminium foil or brown paper

When oven has been preheated to 400°F., Mark 6, paint surface of pastry and decorations with egg glaze. Draw the point of a knife over glaze into pastry to make decorative cross-hatch marks.

Immediately set chicken in middle level of preheated oven. In 20 to 25 minutes, when pastry has begun to brown nicely, turn thermostat down to 350°F., Mark 4. Look again in another 30 minutes, and if pastry is browning too much, cover loosely with foil or brown paper. Chicken is close to being done when juices begin to exude in pan, and is definitely done when pan is removed, tipped, and last juices running from under crust are clear yellow with no trace of rose. As soon as chicken is done, remove from oven.

5. Sauce and serving

A lightly buttered serving platter
2 tbl. minced shallots or spring onions
3 tbl. dry (Sercial) Madeira, dry port wine, or dry white French vermouth
A saucepan containing ½ pt of brown chicken stock (or a combination of chicken broth and beef bouillon)
4 tbl. *crème fraîche* or double cream
If needed: 1 tsp. cornflour blended with 1 tbl. stock or wine
1 to 1½ oz. soft butter
A warm sauce boat

Remove chicken to serving platter, and carefully extract skewer that has held legs in place. Stir the shallots or spring onions and wine into the juices in the roasting pan, set over moderate heat, and scrape up all coagulated bits of flavour into juices and wine with a wooden spoon. Scrape liquid into saucepan with the stock, and boil down rapidly to concentrate flavour. Add cream, and boil a few minutes to thicken lightly. (If it seems necessary, remove from heat, beat in cornflour mixture, and simmer 2 minutes more to thicken.) Carefully correct seasoning. Just before serving, remove from heat and swirl in butter a small piece at a time. (You will have only ½ pint, just enough to moisten each serving.)

To serve, cut straight down through top of crust from neck to tail, and spread crust to sides of chicken. Remove legs and wings, and cut into serving pieces. Give each guest both white and dark meat, stuffing, and a piece of the crust; spoon a bit of the sauce over or around the meat.

(†) You may keep chicken warm for an hour, if necessary; let it sit out at room temperature for 20 minutes, then keep in a very low oven (or in the turned-off oven, reheating briefly from time to time if necessary).

5. *Charcuterie*: Sausages, Salted Pork and Goose, *Pâtés* and *Terrines*

The foundation and mainstay of French *charcuterie* is pork in all its forms, from sausages and stuffings to hams, *pâtés*, and *terrines*. *Chair cuite*, meaning meat that is cooked, was obviously the derivation of this marvellous keystone of French civilization, but modern *charcuterie* shops, like American delicatessens, have branched out and sell all manner of edibles, such as aspics and ready-to-heat *escargots*, heat-and-serve lobster dishes, ready-made salads, mayonnaise, relishes, tinned goods, fine wines, and liqueurs. In the best establishments, all the cooking is done on the premises; they cure their own hams, make their own salt pork and fresh and smoked sausages, and have their own formulas for their beautiful display of *pâtés*. Let us all pray that this delicious way of life will long remain, because there are few things more satisfying to the soul than the look and smell of a French *charcuterie*.

Sausages · *Saucisses et Saucissons*

With the virtual disappearance of local butchers making their own sausages, it behoves every serious cook to have a few sausage formulas on hand for such delicious concoctions as *saucisson en croûte, saucisson en brioche, saucisson chaud et pommes à l'huile* – that wonderfully simple dish of hot, sliced sausages and potato salad, little pork sausages for breakfast and garnitures, and those lovely white-meat sausages with truffles, *boudins blancs*. A sausage is only ground meat and seasonings, a mixture no more complicated than a meat loaf, and for fresh unsmoked sausages you need no special equipment at all. An electric mincer and a heavy-duty mixer will make things easier, but a sausage-stuffing mechanism and sausage casings are not necessary because you can use other means to arrive at the sausage shape. In French terminology a *saucisse* is primarily a small and thin sausage, usually fresh, and a *saucisson* is a large sausage usually smoked or otherwise cured; the one may be called the other, however, if it is a question of size. Here are directions for forming them in casings and a practical substitute for casings, as well as a short discussion on caul fat.

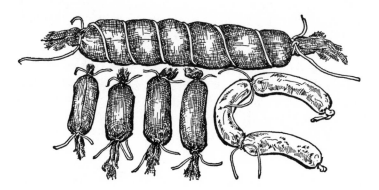

SAUSAGE CASINGS

Natural sausage casings, the flexible, tubular membrane that holds the sausage together and forms its skin, are made from the thoroughly scraped and cleaned intestines of pigs, cattle, and sheep, from the stomachs of pigs, and from the bladders of all three. Sheep casings are the most valuable and expensive of all, and also the most fragile; varying in diameter from $\frac{5}{8}$ to 1 inch, they are used mostly for fresh pork breakfast sausages and the small cocktail or garnishing sausages called chipolatas. Beef casings are for large sausages like bolognas, salamis, and blood sausages, and middle sizes like cervelats and *Mettwürste*. Pig casings come in various lengths and widths: bungs (*gros boyaux*), or the large intestine; pig middles (*fuseaux*), or the middle intestines; small casings (*les menus*), which are the small intestine.

The most practical and easily obtainable for the home sausage stuffer are small pig casings, the kind a butcher would use to make fresh pork sausages or fresh Italian sausages. If he cannot supply you with a few pieces, he can order them for you; or look up in the classified telephone directory under Butcher's Supplies. Ask for a set of small pig casings, medium width. You will get a bundle of 16 to 18 casings, each 20 feet long, which are twisted into a complicated swirl resembling wet spaghetti. To disentangle the pieces, unwind the set on a very large table. Then start with one piece from the middle and gently pull it through the maze, first on one side, then on the other. Disentangle all the pieces, winding each up on your fingers as you do so, like string. Pack the pieces between layers of coarse salt in a large screw-top jar and store in the refrigerator. They will keep safely for years as long as they are well covered with salt.

Before using a piece of casing, wash it off in cold water, then soak for 1 but not more than 2 hours in cold water. Any casing you do not use may be thoroughly rinsed inside and out, wound up again, and repacked with salt in your casing container.

How to use sausage casing

Casing is ideal for sausages because it holds the meat in perfect symmetry; the problem is finding a way to get the meat into these marvellous containers. Professionals use a stuffing machine, *poussoir*, which is a large cylinder with a pushing plate at one end and a nozzle at the other: the meat goes into the cylinder, the casing is slid up the outside of the nozzle, and a crank operates the plate, pushing the meat from the cylinder through the nozzle and into the casing, which slowly and evenly fills with meat as it slides off the nozzle. There are home models available from some butcher supply houses and mail-order sources; anyone going into serious sausage making should certainly have one, since alternatives can only be makeshift and more or less successful depending on your sausage mixture. Here are the alternatives, including hand stuffer, meat mincer, and pastry bag. You will work out your own system.

Whichever of the three methods you choose, you will need a nozzle of some sort on to the outside of which you slide the sausage casing. This can be a funnel, the metal tube that fits a professional-size pastry bag, or an ordinary sausage stuffing nozzle; whatever it is, we shall call it by its official name, stuffing horn. After the sausage casing has soaked for an hour in cold water, cut it into 2- to 3-foot lengths so it will be easy to deal with.

Wet horn in cold water; fit one end of a piece of casing on to the small end (A). Hold the large end of the horn under

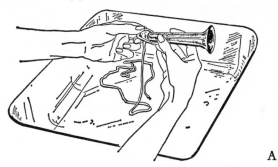

A

a slowly running cold water tap, and push casing up outside with your fingers, being careful not to tear casing with your fingernails (B). If you have cut casing into lengths, string them all on to the horn, one after the other. To permit freedom of

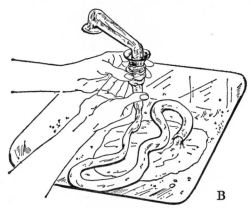

B

action, always leave 3 to 4 inches of empty casing dangling from end of horn and, unless your sausage mixture is very soft and liable to dribble out, do not knot end of casing until the whole length is filled.

With the casing in place, you are now ready to stuff it. Have in mind how long you want your sausages to be, how many, if any, you want linked together, and, if they are to be linked, whether the meat mixture is soft enough so that you can safely twist the filled casing into lengths without bursting it. This is mostly a matter of trial and error; if you want no errors and have plenty of casing, fill and either link or cut and tie one sausage at a time. To minimize air spaces and bubbles, watch casing carefully as you are filling it; when air spaces develop, push filled casing against end of horn to force air back into stuffer. In severe instances, when you are making linked sausages, you will have to cut the casing, tie it, and start a new series of links.

A pastry bag works surprisingly well for either stiff or soft sausage mixtures. You will need 2 metal tubes 2 inches long with $\frac{1}{2}$-inch openings at the small end. One is holding the casing around its outside; the other is fitted inside a 12- to 14-inch bag (c).

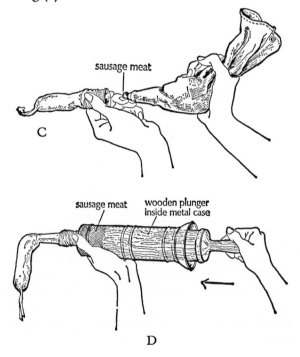

sausage meat

C

sausage meat   wooden plunger
inside metal case

D

The oversize hypodermic (D) consists of wooden plunger, cylinder, and detachable horn. It works well for soft mixtures like the *boudin blanc*. For stiffer blends, you have to brace the end of the tube against the edge of a table. A pastry bag is easier in this case.

A stuffing horn of plastic or metal 4 inches long, $\frac{3}{4}$ inch in diameter at the small end, and $2\frac{1}{4}$ at the large end fits most mincers of the type illustrated here (E). They often come as

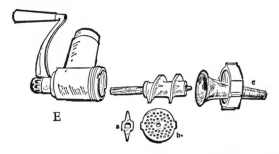

extra equipment, or can be ordered from butcher equipment suppliers or mail-order houses. Sometimes the mincer is operated with cutting knife (a) and disc (b) as well as horn (c), and sometimes not; if you have no instructions, you will have to try both ways. Some mincers work fairly well as sausage

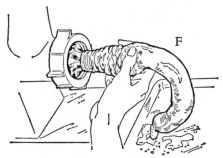

stuffers; others are maddeningly unsatisfactory. Operate mincer at slow speed if it is electric, and hold casing horizontal with horn as meat goes in (F); this is to avoid air bubbles.

When sausage meat has gone into casing, slip a free 3 or 4 inches of empty casing from horn and cut off with scissors.

Tie a knot in the casing close against the meat at each end.
For linked sausages, twist slowly and carefully to make the
separations (G). Tie a piece of white string at each separation.

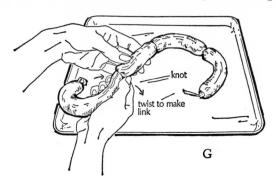

knot

twist to make
link

G

HOW TO FORM SAUSAGES IN CHEESECLOTH CASINGS

Cheesecloth works very well indeed as an alternative to professional casing when it is of no aesthetic importance that the
sausage be perfectly symmetrical, such as those to be baked in
pastry, served in slices, or crumbled and grilled. The illustrations are for small sausages; large ones are formed in the same
way.

As an example, for 5-inch sausages, provide yourself with
sufficient pieces of well-washed, damp, double-thickness
cheesecloth about 8 inches square, and sufficient 4-inch
pieces of white string to secure the 2 ends of each. Form
sausages one at a time. Start by spreading cheesecloth on a
tray and painting it with melted lard or shortening (A). Form

A

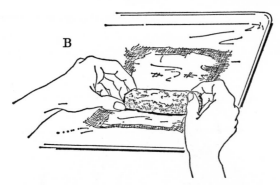

a neat rectangular loaf of sausage meat 5 inches long on lower end of cheesecloth (B). Smooth meat into a cylindrical shape; roll up tightly and neatly in cheesecloth (C). Tie one end

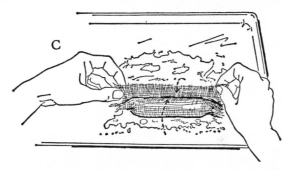

securely with white string. Twist other end of cheesecloth to pack meat into place, tie it with string, and the casing is finished (D). These sausages are often refrigerated for 2 hours or so to firm them up before anything else is done to them.

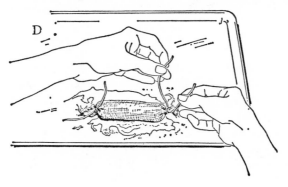

CAUL FAT

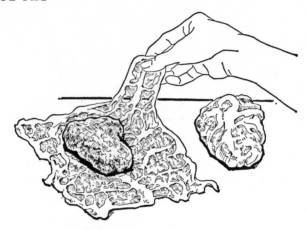

A marvellously useful product of the pig is its caul fat (*crêpine, toilette*), the spider-web-like membrane laced with fat that lines the visceral cavity. Caul fat makes a perfect and perfectly edible container for the fresh sausage patties called *saucisses plates* or *crêpinettes*. You can use caul fat instead of casing for *boudins*, for the large sausages you bake in *brioche* dough, and it is marvellous for wrapping up the stuffed fillet on pages 247–8, meats roasted in a cloak of mushroom *duxelles*, or the *noisettes de veau* on page 306. Caul fat is little known to the general public in this country but you should be able to order it from a good butcher. As it will keep 2 months or more in the freezer, get several pieces while you are at it; each will average 30 inches square.

SALT AND SPICES

Seasoning is always an important part of sausage making and of *charcuterie* in general, since this is what gives the meat character, making your own brand different from any other. Furthermore, the salt and spices that enter into the preparation retard oxidation in the meat and are thus preservatives. French recipes often specify simply *épices, sel épicé* or *quatre épices*, meaning use your own spice formula. The old standby, *quatre épices*, is a bottled mixture available everywhere in France; the four spices are usually pepper, clove, ginger or cinnamon, and nutmeg. *Sel épicé* is spiced salt that is usually 2 parts white pepper and 2 parts mixed spices for every 10 parts of salt.

You will find it useful to have your own spice mixture that you can keep at hand in a screw-top jar. Use it not only for sausages but for *pâtés*, meat loaf, as a marinade before cooking pork chops, and so forth. Here is a suggested formula: be sure all items are fresh-tasting and fragrant.

[*For 1 cup* épices fines]

1 tbl. each: bay, clove, mace, nutmeg, paprika, thyme
1½ tsp. each: basil, cinnamon, marjoram or oregano, sage, savory
½ cup white peppercorns

If ingredients are not finely ground, pulverize either in an electric blender or a coffee grinder (finest grind), then pass through a fine-meshed sieve, and re-pulverize any residue.

[*For each 3 pounds of meat mixture: suggested proportions of spice and salt*]

1 level tsp. (2 grammes) *épices fines*
Plus other flavours such as more pepper, garlic, more of a specific herb, and so forth, depending on your taste and recipe
For fresh sausages, *pâté* mixtures, and stuffings: 1 level tbl. (½ oz.) table salt
For sausages that are to be air-dried 2 or more days: 1½ tbl. table salt

Note: These proportions are what seem correct to us. Salts and spices vary in strength, and you may find you prefer a little more or a little less per pound.

PORK CUTS AND PORK FAT FOR SAUSAGES

Sausages, and *charcuterie* in general, are a by-product of butchering. If you raise your own pigs and do your own butchering, you will have all the lean meat you need out of the trimmings from hams, loins, necks, and other large pieces. You will have, as well, the various types of fat, such as the hard fat from the back of the pig between the meat of the loin and the skin; this is the fat back, which is used not only for sausages and *pâtés* but also for larding roasts. You will have the leaf lard, almost impossible to find nowadays, which comes from inside the pig around the kidneys. You will have fat from the jowl, the neck, the belly, the hams, and the shoulders. Those of us not so fortunate have to buy retail cuts from the butcher or the supermarkets; our sausages will be a little more expensive to make, but they will be far better than anything we can buy because we will be using fresh meat of the best quality.

Rather than the difficult-to-find fat back, you may use fat trimmed from the outside of a loin roast; it works well because it is neither too soft nor too hard. Fat trimmed from the outside of fresh hams and hands is less desirable because a little soft, but it is quite usable when you have no alternatives. If you have a fat-and-lean cut like boneless bladebone, make a guess at the proportion of fat to lean and add whichever is lacking according to your recipe requirements.

Chair à Saucisse
[Plain Pork Sausage Meat]

For sausage cakes, breakfast sausages, chipolatas, and as a stuffing ingredient for *pâtés*, poultry, and so forth.

It is so easy to make your own sausage meat and it is so good that you will wonder, once you have made it, why you ever were so foolish as to buy it. Usual French proportions of fat to lean are one to one; you may cut it down to 1 part fat and 2 parts lean, particularly when you are using the retail pork cuts suggested here rather than trimmings; less fat than this will give you less tender sausages.

[*For 3 pounds sausage-meat mixture*]

1. The sausage mixture

2 lb. lean fresh pork meat such as fresh ham, hand, or loin
1 lb. fresh pork fat, such as fat back, fat trimmed from loin roast, or fresh leaf fat
A meat mincer
A heavy-duty mixer with flat beater blade, or large bowl and wooden spoon

1 tbl. salt

1 tsp. *épices fines* (page 385) or ½ tsp. white pepper and ½ tsp. pulverized
mixed herbs and spices to your taste

Put meat and fat through finest blade of meat mincer; for a
very smooth mixture, you may put it through the mincer
again. If you have a heavy-duty mixer, beat thoroughly with
the seasonings until very well blended. Otherwise, blend
thoroughly with a wooden spoon and/or your hands, first
dipping them in cold water. To test for flavour, sauté a small
spoonful for several minutes until cooked through; taste,
and add more seasoning if you feel it necessary, but remember
that the spice flavour will not develop to its full in the meat
for 12 hours or more.

2. Forming and cooking

(a) Sausage cakes or sausage roll: Either form into sausage
cakes with a wet spatula on waxed paper, or with your hands,
dipping them in cold water frequently; then, if you wish,
wrap cakes in caul fat (page 384). Or form into a cylinder 2
inches in diameter in cheesecloth as illustrated at the beginning
of this section and chill; then unwrap and cut into cakes.
Sauté slowly in a frying pan until nicely browned and thoroughly cooked through.

(b) Sausage links and chipolatas: For these you should have
narrow sheep casings ⅝ inch in diameter, if you can get them.
Breakfast links are usually 3 inches long; chipolatas, the tiny
sausages used for cocktails and garnitures, 1½ to 2 inches.
Form as illustrated at the beginning of this section. To cook,
prick in several places with a pin and place in a frying pan
with ½ inch of water, cover and cook at just below the simmer
for 5 minutes or until sausages have stiffened slightly. Pour
off water and sauté, turning frequently, until nicely browned.

Boudin Blanc
[White-meat Sausages – Chicken and Veal
or Chicken and Pork Forcemeat Stuffing]

White-meat sausages are found everywhere in Europe, from
the German and Swiss *Bratwürste* and *Weisswürste* to England's

quaintly titled white puddings. It has even been suggested that the French *boudin* and the English pudding sprang from a single etymological root. The *boudin* is more like a *quenelle* than a sausage, delicate in flavour and texture. In France, where a truffled *boudin* is traditional at the midnight *réveillon* of Christmas and New Year, mashed potatoes is the accompaniment. However, you may treat them like roast chicken or roast veal, adding green vegetables to the platter, such as creamed spinach, broccoli, peas, braised chicory, or whatever else you feel appropriate.

[*To make 10 to 12* boudins, *5 by 1¼ inches*]

1. The sausage mixture

(a) *The pork fat:*

4 oz. fresh pork leaf fat, outside loin fat, or fat back
A meat mincer with finest blade
An 8-in. frying pan with cover

Put the pork fat through the mincer. Return half to top of mincer. Cook the rest in the frying pan over low heat for 4 to 5 minutes until it has rendered 2 to 3 tablespoons of fat but has not browned at all.

(b) *Cooking the onions:*

¾ lb. onions, sliced

(If you want a mild onion flavour, drop them into 3 pints of boiling water and boil 4 minutes; drain, rinse in cold water, and thoroughly shake off excess water.) Add onions to pork fat and fat pieces in frying pan, cover and cook very slowly, stirring frequently, for 15 minutes or more; they should be perfectly tender and translucent, but no more than a pale cream in colour.

(c) *The* panade:

1½ oz. stale white breadcrumbs
½ pt milk
A heavy-bottomed 3-pt saucepan
A wooden spoon
The large bowl of your electric mixer, or a 5-pt bowl

Meanwhile, bring the breadcrumbs and milk to the boil and boil, stirring constantly with wooden spoon to prevent scorching, for several minutes until mixture is thick enough almost to hold its shape on the spoon. (This is now a *panade*, in the true and original sense of the word.) Scrape into bowl.

(d) The final mixture:

½ lb. skinless and boneless raw breast of chicken
½ lb. lean fresh veal or pork from hand or loin
2 tsp. salt
⅛ tsp. each: nutmeg, allspice, and white pepper
1 egg
2 to 3 egg whites
¼ pt double cream
Optional: a 1-oz. truffle and juices from the tin

When onions are tender, pass them with the remaining pork fat, the chicken, and the veal or pork through mincer twice. Place meat in bowl with *panade*; add seasonings, and beat with the electric mixer or by hand until well blended. Beat in the egg and continue beating for 1 minute, then beat in half the egg whites, and in another minute the remainder of the egg whites. Finally beat in the cream 2 tablespoons at a time, beating a minute between additions. If you are using a truffle, chop it into ⅛-inch pieces and beat it in along with juices from the tin.

To check seasoning, sauté a small spoonful until cooked through, taste, and add more if you feel it is necessary, but remember that the *boudin* is supposed to be rather delicate and mild in flavour.

2. Forming the *boudins*

Form either in small pig casings or in cheesecloth, as shown on pages 378–83. Sausages will improve in flavour if refrigerated at least 12 hours before cooking.

(†) *Storage notes:* May be refrigerated for 2 to 3 days, or may be frozen for a month or so.

3. Preliminary cooking

(If you have formed the *boudins* in sausage casing, prick them in several places with a pin.) Arrange *boudins* in a baking pan, roaster, or large frying pan at least 3 inches deep, and on a rack or grill if you have one that fits. Measure in enough pints of boiling water or half-and-half boiling water and milk to cover *boudins* by 1½ inches. Add 1½ teaspoons salt for each pint and a half of liquid, and lay 2 bay leaves on top. Bring liquid barely to the simmer and poach uncovered at just below the simmer for 25 minutes. Remove from liquid and cool on several thicknesses of paper towels. If you have used cheesecloth casings, cut off the two ends with scissors and peel the sausages while still warm. (Sausage-casing *boudins* are peeled just before final cooking.)

(†) If the *boudins* are not to have their final cooking promptly, wrap and refrigerate when cool. They will keep 3 to 4 days in the refrigerator, a month or so in the freezer.

4. Final cooking and serving

Of the several cooking methods available, oven baking is not recommended because it toughens the outside of the *boudins* before they have had time to brown. Dredging in flour and browning slowly in a frying pan in clarified butter or rendered pork fat is preferable, but the best method, we think, is under the grill as follows: roll the peeled *boudins* in fresh white breadcrumbs, pressing the crumbs in place with your fingers. Arrange in a buttered baking dish and dribble on droplets of melted butter. Grill slowly, turning and basting with fat in pan several times, for 10 to 12 minutes, until *boudins* are nicely browned. Arrange on a hot platter, over a bed of hot mashed potatoes if you wish, and decorate with sprigs of parsley or watercress. Serve as soon as possible.

*Saucissons à Cuire
[Large Fresh Sausages for Cooking]

These sausages are for cooking and serving with potatoes, sauerkraut, or *cassoulet*, or for baking in *brioche* or pastry dough.

The following formula produces a fine substitute for those marvellous creations you read about but cannot find except in a French *charcuterie*. This recipe is for the home sausage-maker, and requires no special equipment; for that reason you cannot call your product a *saucisson de Lyon*, which is hung for 8 days in a drying shed, or a *saucisson de Morteau*, which finishes in a smokehouse. But *saucisson de ménage, saucisson de Toulouse, saucisson à l'ail, saucisson truffé, cervelas de Paris* – any of these names will do, and any Frenchman you invite for a meal will think you brought the sausage back from France.

The sausages will develop their best flavour when you are able to hang them in a dry, airy part of the room at a temperature of 70° to 80°F. for 2 to 3 days before cooking. If the weather is very damp, or much over 80°F., however, omit the hanging; several days in the refrigerator instead will help develop flavour. The saltpetre (potassium nitrate), which you should be able to buy at any prescription counter, is omitted if you are not hanging the sausages; its role is to give the meat an appetizing, rosy colour that only develops after several days of hanging. Use the coarse or the fine blade of your mincer, whichever you prefer, but the coarse texture is more typical of a sausage that is to be hung.

French sausages of this type are not heavily spiced, and peppered, like some of the Spanish and Italian varieties. We have suggested 3 special flavourings, and you will eventually develop the proportions or other additions that will make your own sausage *le saucisson de chez nous.*

[*For 3 pounds sausage-meat mixture, making 10 to 12 sausages 5 by 1¼ inches, or 2 sausages 12 by 2 inches*]

1. The sausage mixture

2 lb. lean fresh pork such as fresh ham, hand, or loin
1 lb. fresh pork fat such as fat back, fat trimmed from a loin roast, fresh leaf fat
Either: 1 tsp. *épices fines* (page 385) plus ¼ tsp. white pepper;
Or: ¾ tsp. white pepper and ½ tsp. pulverized herbs and spices of your choice
1 tbl. salt
3 tbl. cognac

(*a*) *If you are to hang the sausage:*
¼ tsp. saltpetre, ¾ tsp. sugar, and 1½ tsp. more salt

(b) Special flavourings:

Either: a 1- to 2-oz. tin of truffles and the juice from the tin;
Or: 3 tbl. chopped pistachios and 1 small clove garlic, mashed;
Or: 2 or 3 medium cloves garlic, mashed, and ½ tsp. cracked peppercorns

Put meat and fat through mincer. With either a heavy-duty mixer and flat beater, or your hands and/or a wooden spoon, mix in the rest of the ingredients to blend vigorously and completely. Sauté a small spoonful to cook through thoroughly, taste, and correct seasoning, if necessary.

Note: Nitrites and nitrates are added to cured meats to give them colour and to act as a preservative, but excessive amounts are considered dangerous to human health. Saltpetre is potassium nitrate, which slowly converts into nitrite salt as a result of bacterial activity, but it is a slow process resulting in low levels of nitrite, considered perfectly safe. Leave out the saltpetre, however, if you wish.

2. Forming and curing the sausages

Form the sausages either in casings or in cheesecloth as illustrated at the beginning of this chapter. If you are forming a 12- by 2-inch sausage in cheesecloth, wind a spiral of string around the length to keep it in shape; if you are hanging cheesecloth-wrapped sausages, paint again with melted lard after forming and tying. Hang sausages up on a nail or hook, in the dry airy part of your kitchen where the temperature is generally around 70°F. and rarely over 80°F. After 2 to 3 days, they are ready for cooking.

(†) *Storage note:* After curing, sausages may be wrapped securely and refrigerated for a week, or frozen for a month.

3. Cooking and serving suggestions

Saucissons à cuire need 30 to 40 minutes of slow cooking in liquid, and if you have formed them in casings, prick them in several places with a pin so that the fat will run out. When you are braising sauerkraut or cabbage, doing a bean or lentil dish or a *pot au feu*, add the sausages to the dish 30 to 40 minutes before the end of the cooking period. When you wish to serve them separately, as with French potato salad, or baked in *brioche* or pastry dough, poach them at just below the simmer for 30 to 40 minutes in a wine-flavoured beef bouillon, selecting a container, such as a bread tin or casserole, that will just hold them easily. There is no need to brown them afterwards, but if you want a more elegant presentation for sausages formed in cheesecloth, roll them in fresh breadcrumbs, dribble on melted butter, and brown them under the grill.

Other suggestions

You can make delicious fresh sausages out of the all-purpose pork and veal *pâté* mixture in Volume I on page 605, plus, if you wish, diced ham, diced marinated bits of veal or game, or diced and briefly sautéed liver, as suggested in the *pâté* mixtures following it. You may also adapt any of the *pâté* mixtures in the next section of this chapter. Form and cook the sausages as described in the preceding recipe; this type of sausage, and the chicken-liver sausage in the next recipe, are particularly good when baked in *brioche* or pastry dough.

Saucisson Truffé au Foie Gras ou aux Foies de Volaille
[Pork and Veal Sausages with Truffles and
Foie Gras or with Chicken Livers]

These sausages are intended especially for baking in *brioche* or pastry dough, or as a stuffing for *pâtés*, poultry, or *chaussons*.

[*To make two 12- by 1½-inch sausages*]

1 oz. pork fat, chicken fat, or butter
2 tbl. minced shallots or spring onions
Either: ¾ lb. chicken livers;
Or: a mixture of chicken livers and tinned *foie gras en bloc*, half-and-half
    if you wish to pay the price(*foie gras* is used in next step)

Heat the fat or butter in an 8-inch frying pan, add the shallots or spring onions and the chicken livers (not the *foie gras*); toss over moderately high heat for several minutes until liver has just stiffened to the touch; it should feel springy, but remain rosy inside. If you are using chicken liver only, cut half into ¼-inch dice and place in a bowl.

The diced liver or the *foie gras*
2 tbl. cognac
Pinch *épices fines*, page 385, or allspice
Salt and pepper

If you are using *foie gras*, cut into ¼-inch dice and place in a bowl. Fold *foie gras* or liver gently with the cognac and flavourings and let marinate until needed.

1 oz. stale white breadcrumbs
¼ pt milk

Simmer breadcrumbs in milk, stirring constantly, for several minutes until thick enough to mass on a spoon. Scrape into large bowl of mixer, or a large mixing bowl. (This is a *panade*.)

½ lb. lean veal
Either: 1 lb. *chair à saucisse*, page 386;
Or: ½ lb. lean pork loin, hand, or fresh ham, and ½ lb. fresh pork fat back or outside loin fat
The sautéed undiced chicken livers

Put meats, fat, and chicken livers through finest blade of mincer and add to mixing bowl.

The marinade from the diced *foie gras* or chicken livers
2 tsp. salt
Either: ¾ tsp. *épices fines* and ¼ tsp. white pepper;
Or: ½ tsp. white pepper and big pinches each allspice and nutmeg
¼ tsp. thyme
Either: 3 tbl. peeled pistachio nuts, quartered lengthwise;
Or: 1 or 2 diced truffles and their tinned juices
1 egg
3 tbl. dry port wine or Sercial Madeira
The marinated *foie gras* or diced chicken livers

Beat in the marinade, salt, flavourings, pistachios or truffles and juice, and egg. When well blended, gradually beat in the wine. Finally, fold in the diced *foie gras* or chicken livers, being careful not to break the diced shapes. Mixture will be fairly soft. Sauté a spoonful and taste; correct seasoning as necessary. Form into sausages using either casings or cheese-cloth as described on pages 377–83. (If you are using the mixture for a filling or stuffing that is to be baked later, pack into a covered bowl.) Flavour will improve when refrigerated a day or two before cooking.

Cook and serve sausages as suggested in preceding master recipe, or bake in *brioche* dough as in the following recipe.

(†) *Storage note:* Sausages may be frozen for a month or so.

Saucisson de Foies de Volaille
Pâté de Foies de Volaille
Farce à Gratin

[Chicken-liver Sausage for Baking in *Brioche* Dough – Chicken-liver *Pâté* – Chicken-liver Spread or Filling]

This all-purpose liver mixture is so versatile it can serve as a sausage, a *pâté*, a spread for sandwiches and hors d'œuvre, a filling for poultry or meat, and can generally be used any-where you need the depth and strength of a liver accent. Liver alone is such a concentrated flavour that you must have something else with it to temper the taste: the sausage uses cream cheese and breadcrumbs, while the *pâté* includes cheese and butter, and the filling, *farce à gratin*, calls for the traditional pork fat. Two other liver *pâtés* or spreads are the pork-liver *pâté* on page 423 and the mousse of chicken livers in Volume I, page 598.

The basic chicken-liver mixture

3 tbl. very finely minced onions
1½ oz. chicken fat or butter
¾ lb. chicken livers
Either: ¼ tsp. *épices fines*, page 385;
Or: a big pinch each of allspice, mace, and white pepper
A big pinch thyme
¼ tsp. salt
4 tbl. cognac
Optional: 5 tbl. diced fresh mushrooms, squeezed dry and sautéed in
   ½ oz. butter

Cook the onions slowly in the fat or butter for 12 to 15 minutes, until very tender but not brown. Add livers and seasonings, and toss over moderately high heat just until stiffened slightly, 2 to 3 minutes; livers should remain rosy inside. Pour in the cognac, heat to bubbling, and flame with a lighted match; in 1 minute, extinguish flames with a cover and remove pan from heat. Stir in optional mushrooms. The liver mixture is now ready to be used either in *brioche* dough or in another form as follows.

For sausage in *brioche*, page 399

1 oz. dry white breadcrumbs
4 oz. cream cheese
The basic chicken-liver mixture

Stir the breadcrumbs and cheese into the liver mixture, and purée through a food mill, mincer, or blender. Correct seasoning. Roll into a cylindrical shape in aluminium foil and chill until firm; however, bring to room temperature before encasing it in the dough so that dough will rise easily.

For liver spread or *pâté*

The basic chicken-liver mixture
4 oz. softened butter
4 oz. cream cheese

Purée liver mixture through a food mill, mincer, or blender, then beat in softened butter and cream cheese. Correct seasoning. If you plan to use this as a *pâté*, pack into a covered jar or mould and chill.

For *farce à gratin*: to use as a spread, filling, or *pâté*

The basic chicken-liver mixture but substitute 6 oz. fresh pork fat back
    or outside loin fat for the butter

Rather than using butter for cooking the onions and chicken livers, use the 6 ounces pork fat as follows: mince it, and cook slowly for 8 to 10 minutes in the sauté pan until pieces of fat are translucent but not browned, and 4 tablespoons or so of fat has rendered. Then proceed with the recipe. Purée in a blender, food mill, or mincer, pack into a jar or decorative bowl, and chill.

(†) *Storage note:* Any of these will keep for 4 to 5 days in the refrigerator, and they freeze successfully for several months.

Sausages and Other Meat Mixtures Baked in *Brioche* Dough · *Saucissons et Pâtés en Brioche*

When you want to be dramatic and dressy with sausage, bake it in a *brioche* case. For cocktails, slice it warm and thin and serve on little plates. When it is a hot first course or the mainstay for luncheon or supper, include a succulent brown sauce to pour over each serving. Although reminiscent of *pâté en croûte*, sausage in *brioche* is usually served warm, and is lighter in general impression. Unlike the real *pâté*, which goes raw into its covering of dough for baking, the sausage or meat mixture that is enclosed in *brioche* dough has already been cooked, and remains in the oven only long enough to heat through as the *brioche* bakes.

FORMING NOTE

The rectangular loaf shape that encloses a large cylindrical sausage is the most typical form, and the one we shall illustrate. With your own sausage or cooked meat mixture, however, you may make it round, square, heart-shaped, or whatever you wish.

CLOSING THE GAP

Because you are working with live dough, that is, yeast dough, you may run into one problem that does not occur with pastry dough: this is a sometimes ugly space between the meat and the *brioche* that only reveals itself when you are slicing through the structure to serve.

It is particularly true of home-cured or shop-bought sausages, less true of soft mixtures like chicken livers, and more liable to be troublesome with sausages baked in a tin (as on page 402) than with those formed on a pastry sheet (page 400). One way to minimize the gap or eliminate it completely is to be sure that the sausage is very hot at the moment you enclose it in the dough. Heat kills the yeast in a thin layer of dough, about $\frac{1}{8}$ inch, all around the sausage, and this layer should cling to the sausage while the rest of the dough rises around it. Another way to close the gap is to bake the sausage in a closed tin, as suggested in a variation at the end of the master recipe. We are only giving prominence to this problem so that you will be aware of it and pleased with yourself when you have avoided it but not unduly disturbed when you have not. In such instances, however, when you want to serve a cold liver *pâté en brioche*, you will welcome the gap because you can siphon a deliciously flavoured aspic into that space between meat and *brioche*, which will add immensely to the taste and appearance of the *pâté* slices when you serve them.

TIMING NOTE

With your *brioche* dough made the day before, and your sausage or meat mixture ready for pre-cooking, you should count on $2\frac{1}{4}$ to $3\frac{1}{2}$ hours from the time you start the process until the time you can serve. You will need 40 minutes for poaching, if you are using a sausage, an hour for the dough-with-sausage to rise before baking, an hour for baking, and 20 to 30 minutes for meat and *brioche* to settle before slicing. Remember that you can control the rising of dough (page 104), and you can keep the baked result warm; thus you may arrange your schedule as you wish.

*Saucisson en Brioche
[Sausage Baked in *Brioche* Dough]
This is for a large sausage about 12 inches long and 1½ to 2 inches in diameter, such as the *saucisson à cuire* on page 390 and the liver or *foie gras* sausage following it, or for a shop-bought sausage that is to be cooked and served hot, like a Polish sausage (*kielbasa*) or Italian *cotechino*. You may also use the cooked chicken-liver sausage mixture on page 395; in this case, omit step 2 in the following recipe.

[*For a 12-inch case, serving 6 as a hot first course, or 4 as a main course, or giving 18 slices for a cocktail appetizer*]

1. The *brioche* dough: started the day before you plan to serve

Either: the *pain brioché* dough on page 127;
Or: the richer *pâte à brioche fine* on page 130 (proportions for ½ lb. flour in either case)

Make the *brioche* dough, giving it one rise at room temperature and a second rise that finishes in the refrigerator. Dough must be well chilled before you form it in step 3.

2. Poaching the sausage: about 40 minutes; omit this step if you are using the already cooked chicken-liver sausage mixture

The sausage (see introductory paragraph)
A loaf tin just large enough to hold the sausage (loaf shape recommended)
¼ pt dry white wine or dry white French vermouth
1¼ pts or more beef bouillon simmering in a saucepan
1 bay leaf

Salt and pepper
Useful: a meat thermometer

Prick the sausage in several places with a pin and place in tin.
Pour in the wine and enough simmering bouillon to cover
sausage by 1 inch. Add seasonings and bring liquid to just
below the simmer (water is shivering and almost bubbling).
Cover loosely and maintain liquid at this state for 40 minutes.
Remove sausage, peel off casing, and return to liquid until you
are ready to proceed to step 3. Sausage should be hot (around
165°F.) for next step; reheat if necessary.

3. Achieving the free-form *brioche* shape

The chilled dough
A large pastry sheet or tray 16 by 24 ins., covered with lightly floured
  waxed paper
The hot, cooked, and peeled sausage (or room-temperature chicken-liver
  sausage)
A lightly buttered pastry sheet at least 12 by 16 ins. in diameter

Rapidly roll the chilled *brioche* dough into a rectangle approximately 24 by 10 inches. With a pastry wheel or knife,
cut off a 4- by 10-inch strip and refrigerate it. Roll remaining
dough up on your pin and unroll it on to the waxed-paper-
covered sheet or tray.

Centre sausage on dough and quickly fold the two sides up
over it (A); they should overlap by about 2 inches. Working

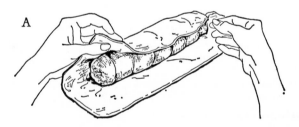

A

rapidly, fold over the 2 ends of the dough to enclose the
sausage completely (B). Then to prevent sausage from breaking through dough, turn the buttered pastry sheet upside down
on top of it, and reverse the two so that sausage will unmould
itself seam-side down on the buttered sheet. Brush off any

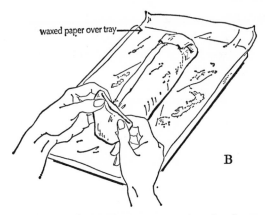

waxed paper over tray

B

flour on top of dough. Roll out reserved and refrigerated strip to about 15 by 4 inches in diameter; roll up on pin and then unroll over sausage (c).

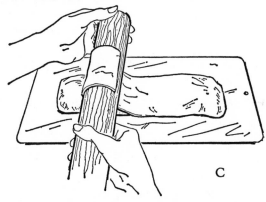

C

Trim off excess dough from 2 ends, and press dough cover in place lightly with fingers. Set uncovered at a temperature of no more than 75° to 80°F. Let dough rise until it feels light and spongy-springy when touched – 40 to 60 minutes. (Preheat oven in time for next step.)

4. Baking: about 1 hour; oven preheated to 425°F., Mark 7

1 egg beaten with 1 tsp. water in a small bowl
A pastry brush
Scissors
A cooling rack

Just before baking, paint top of dough with egg glaze; let set a moment, and paint again. Clip top of dough with scissors, going in at a slant about $\frac{3}{8}$ inch deep and 2 inches across (D).

D

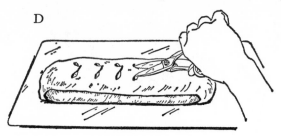

Set in middle level of preheated 425°F., Mark 7 oven and bake for 20 minutes, or until *brioche* has risen about double its height and begun to brown. Turn oven down to 350°F., Mark 4, for 30 to 40 minutes more. It is done when you can begin to smell the sausage cooking, and when the *brioche* itself feels solid and makes a rather dry thumping noise when tapped. (Cover lightly with foil or brown paper if it is colouring too much before it is done.) Slide off pastry sheet on to rack, and let cool 20 to 30 minutes before serving.

5. Serving suggestions

Serve the sausage hot, warm, tepid, or cold (although a sausage is usually better warm or tepid than cold). When serving it hot as a first or main course, you can make a delicious brown sauce with the sausage-poaching liquid, using any of the suggestions in Volume I, pages 90–94.

(†) You may keep the sausage warm for an hour or more in a very low oven. If for some reason you cannot serve it when baked, let cool, then wrap airtight; reheat uncovered on a lightly buttered pastry sheet in a 400°F., Mark 6 oven for 20 minutes or so.

Forming the Sausage in a Loaf Tin

For a 12- by 2-inch sausage you will need a long, rectangular 3-pint loaf tin, about 12 by $3\frac{1}{4}$ inches bottom diameter and $2\frac{1}{2}$ inches deep. Follow steps 1 and 2 in the master recipe, butter the inside of the loaf tin, then wrap the hot sausage in the dough on a paper-covered pastry sheet or tray as illustrated (A and B). Turn a buttered 12-inch loaf tin upside down over the sausage (E). Reverse tray with sausage on to tin, unmoulding

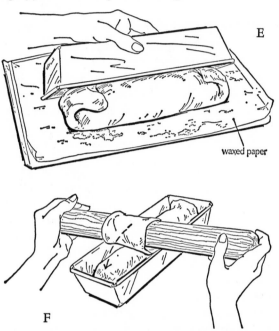

E

waxed paper

F

sausage seam-side down into tin. Brush off any flour from top of dough, and unroll reserved dough strip over sausage (F). Press dough cover into place with fingers, pushing it lightly down against top, sides, and ends of sausage (G).

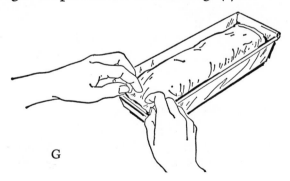

G

Let rise at a temperature of no more than 75° to 80°F. for 40 to 60 minutes, until dough is light and springy; it will fill the tin by about three quarters. Glaze, clip top with scissors, and bake as described in preceding master recipe.

Baking in a Covered Tin

When you want to be sure there is no gap between meat and *brioche*, follow the preceding recipe, but rather than glazing and clipping the top of the dough when it has risen, cover the tin as described and illustrated for *pain de mie*, pages 115–16. This works because the risen dough fills the tin only by three quarters; then, while it bakes, the dough will not only fill the covered tin completely, but will also press itself against the sausage meat. You may use any shape of tin you wish, including a fluted *brioche* tin. The imported hinged cylindrical mould shown in the illustration, page 115, can easily be adapted for sausage in *brioche*.

Cold *Pâté en Brioche* with Aspic

Sausages, to our mind, are at their best when served hot or warm in *brioche* dough, while liver mixtures are delicious cold. We suggest the chicken-liver mixture on page 395, or the cooked pork and liver *pâté* with onions on page 426. Follow any of the preceding methods you wish; when the meat is fully encased and ready to rise, make a hole in the top of the dough and insert a well-oiled cone of foil or the tube from a pastry bag, letting its end touch the meat. After rising and baking, and when completely cold, pour in through the cone as much almost-set wine-flavoured meat-jelly aspic as the case will hold. (See illustrated directions in the *pâté en croûte* section, page 439.) Then remove cone, wrap *pâté* airtight, and chill several hours or overnight. *Pâté* should be eaten within 4 to 5 days.

Saucisson en Croûte
[Sausage Baked in Plain Pastry or in Puff Pastry]
Equally delicious, though naturally different in texture, is any one of the suggested sausages poached in bouillon, peeled,

and baked in plain pie crust dough or in that wonderfully high-rising flaky dough known as French puff pastry. Use the *pâte brisée à l'œuf*, page 157, or the *demi-feuilletée* on page 166. Form the dough around the sausage as described in the free-form system, master recipe, page 400. Paint top with beaten egg, press on decorative pastry cut-outs, and bake exactly as described in the master recipe. (Illustrated directions for decorating this type of pastry are in Volume I, page 614.)

*Caillettes
Gayettes
[Pork and Liver Sausages with Greens]

These hearty green and brown sausages are made in the countryside where pigs are slaughtered, and the farmer uses every edible morsel for some speciality. His recipe usually includes lungs and spleen as well as the heart and liver we have specified, and, if he lives in Provence, he puts in plenty of garlic. Swiss chard (*blettes*) is the preferred green, but because it is not always to be had in this country, we have suggested kale or spinach as substitutes. Traditionally the sausages are formed into cushion or dumpling shapes 2 to 3 inches in diameter, wrapped in caul fat, and baked in a big pottery dish. You may also form them like ordinary sausages, like sausage cakes, or turn the whole mixture into a meat loaf. (*Note:* Flavour will improve if you can make the mixture a day before cooking.)

Serve with mashed or scalloped potatoes and grilled tomatoes, or an aubergine and tomato casserole such as that on page 470, or the *ratatouille* in Volume I, page 539, or simply a green salad and French bread. A rosé wine or light red would go nicely.

[*To make a dozen sausages*]

1. The greens

6 tbl. minced onions
1 oz. pork fat or 2 tbl. olive oil
A heavy-bottomed saucepan with cover
Either: 1½ to 2 lb. fresh Swiss chard, kale, or spinach;

Or: 1½ lb. frozen spinach defrosted in a basin of cold water
A large pan of boiling salted water
The large bowl of an electric mixer, or 5-pt mixing bowl

Cook onions and oil in covered pan over moderate heat, stirring occasionally, for 10 minutes or so, until tender and translucent. Meanwhile, pick over fresh greens, wash thoroughly, and if you have chard use both the green leaves and the white stems; drop into boiling water and boil uncovered until wilted and just edibly tender – 1 minute for spinach, 5 or more for other greens. Drain immediately, refresh in cold water, and drain again. (Fresh and defrosted greens may now be treated alike.) A smallish handful at a time, squeeze to extract as much water as possible; chop roughly with a big knife. Stir into the onions, raise heat, and stir for several minutes to evaporate excess moisture. Scrape into mixing bowl.

2. The sausage mixture

Either: 1½ lb. fat-and-lean fresh pork blade-bone;
Or: ¾ lb. lean pork from fresh ham or loin, and ¾ lb. fresh pork fat back or fat trimmed from outside loin
Either: ½ lb. fresh liver (pork, lamb, or beef) and ¼ lb. heart (pork, lamb, or calf);
Or: liver only
1 tbl. salt
Either: ¾ tsp. *épices fines*, page 385, ¼ tsp. pepper, and ¼ tsp. savory;
Or: ⅛ tsp. allspice, ⅛ tsp. mace, ⅛ tsp. bay leaf, ¼ tsp. savory, and ½ tsp. pepper
Optional: 1 or more cloves of garlic, finely minced or mashed

Put meat, fat, and liver once through the coarsest blade of the mincer, or chop by hand into ¼-inch pieces. Add to bowl along with the seasonings, and mix thoroughly by electricity or by hand. Sauté a small spoonful until thoroughly cooked, taste, and correct seasoning if necessary. (Whether you form the sausages now or later, their flavour will improve if you wait 24 hours before cooking.)

(†) *Storage note:* May be refrigerated for 2 to 3 days; may be frozen for a month or two.

3. Forming and cooking

(a) Caul fat: Form sausage mixture into a dozen balls or cylindrical shapes, wrap in caul fat (page 384), arrange in one layer in a greased baking dish, and baste with melted lard or butter. Bake for 40 to 45 minutes in the upper third of a preheated 375°F., Mark 5 oven until nicely browned.

(b) Sausage casings: Form in sausage casings (page 377), prick in several places with a pin, and either bake as described in preceding paragraph or poach in almost simmering water for 5 minutes, then brown in a frying pan.

(c) Sausage cakes: Form into sausage cakes with dampened hands. Just before cooking, dredge lightly in flour; sauté slowly in lard or cooking oil for 6 to 8 minutes on each side until nicely browned.

(d) Meat loaf (this is particularly recommended when you want something to serve cold): Either grease a 2½-pint loaf tin or baking dish and pack the sausage mixing into it; or form the mixture into a loaf shape, wrap in caul fat, and place on a greased baking dish. Bake in upper third of a preheated 375°F., Mark 5 oven, basting several times with melted fat for an hour or more, or until juices, when meat is pricked deeply, run clear yellow with no trace of rosy colour (180° to 185°F. on a meat thermometer).

Les Tous Nus
Quenelles de Bœuf Provençales
[Provençal Sausages of Left-over Braised Beef and Greens]

The naked ones, *les tous nus*, are sausages without casings, and a Provençal speciality. These are formed by hand, rolled in flour, and dropped for a moment in boiling water before they are baked in a shallow dish with a spicy tomato sauce. They are so fragrant and appetizing that you will find yourself braising beef just as an excuse for making *les tous nus* with the left-overs.

[*For 4 to 6 people*]

1. The sausage mixture

1 to 1½ lb. blanched and squeezed greens
2 tbl. minced onions cooked with 2 tbl. olive oil
¾ pt minced cooked beef, preferably braised
Optional, to flavour boiled or roast beef: 2 oz. raw sausage meat and
    1 tbl. cognac
1 tsp. salt
Either: ¼ tsp. *épices fines*;
Or: allspice and mace
¼ tsp. savory or oregano
¼ tsp. pepper
Big pinch of cayenne or drops of Tabasco sauce
2 large cloves of garlic, minced or puréed
1½ oz. grated Parmesan cheese
1 to 2 beaten eggs

(If you have chard, use green leaves only.) Blanch, squeeze, and chop the greens as described in step 1 of the preceding recipe, and cook with the onions 2 to 3 minutes until all liquid has evaporated; greens must be as dry as possible. Blend them in a large mixing bowl with the beef, seasonings, and cheese. Beat in 3 tablespoons of egg; beat in driblets more egg, moistening only enough so that mixture will hold its shape for forming. Sauté a spoonful and taste; correct seasoning as necessary.

2. Forming the sausages

4 oz. flour on a large tray
A large frying pan full of boiling water
A skimmer
A rack, or paper towels on a tray
1 or 2 shallow, greased baking dishes
1 pt or so good tomato sauce, page 468, or Volume I, pages 95 or 96
1 oz. grated Parmesan cheese
1 to 2 tbl. olive oil

Take up a 3-tablespoon gob of the mixture and roll into a sausage shape ¾ inch in diameter; roll in flour and set aside. When all the sausages are formed, drop half into the boiling water, bring back to the simmer for ½ minute. Dip out on to rack and continue with the rest. Arrange closely together in baking dish or dishes. Pour over the tomato sauce, which should barely cover them. Sprinkle on the cheese and dribble the oil over it.

(†) May be completed a day in advance to this point.

3. Cooking the sausages: oven preheated to 425°F., Mark 7

About 30 minutes before serving, bring to simmer on top of stove, then set in upper third of oven until sauce has browned and crusted lightly on upper part of sausages, and is bubbling underneath.

Variations

Like the *caillette* mixture in the master recipe, step 3, the *tous nus* mixture may also be formed in caul fat or sausage casings, or may become sausage cakes or meat loaf.

Jambon Persillé and Home-cured Pork

Jambon persillé is the traditional Easter ham of Burgundy. Simmered in wine, then cut up or shredded and packed into a big bowl between layers of chopped parsley, aspic, and seasonings, each slice when served is beautifully patterned with wavy lines of bright green. It is a marvellous dish for cold lunches, supper parties, and receptions. The real Burgundian recipe is made with salt-cured ham, known in France as *jambon demi-sel*. Although you may certainly use ordinary ham for the dish, the salt cure is so easy – all you need is 2 weeks of refrigerator space for the large bowl that holds the meat – we highly recommend that you try it. It is not only that you will have the authentic meat for *jambon persillé*, but also that you can cure a loin of pork for chops or roasting, since salted pork makes a delicious change from ordinary pork and is grilled or roasted in exactly the same way. At the same time, if you can find any pork jowls or bellies, you can also make your own salt pork.

Salaison à Sec
(Home Dry-curing of Pork)

The object of curing pork is not only to preserve it but to give it that special maturity of taste that only comes through salting. For our purposes here, we are more concerned with taste than with preservation. There is no need for brines, vats, and smokehouses, only for saltpetre, sugar, spices, and salt. Saltpetre imparts an attractive rosy colour to the meat, sugar develops its flavour and counteracts the drying effects of saltpetre, spices play their habitual role, and salt preserves the meat while it matures. The following 15-day cure is for the boned fresh ham or shoulder that may be used for *jambon persillé*, and for loin roasts and salt-pork cuts; these are all pieces, in other words, that are no thicker than 4 to 5 inches.

TEMPERATURE FOR CURING

Curing should take place at around 38°F., which is the range of most refrigerators. At temperatures over 40°F, the meat may spoil before the salt can penetrate, and at below 36°F. the salt penetration is too much slowed down.

THE MEAT AND ITS PREPARATION FOR THE CURE

For *jambon persillé* you may use either fresh ham (leg of pork) or fresh hand; hand is usually cheaper and weighs around 6½ pounds, or half as much as a ham. Before curing, remove the rind, which is to be cured and cooked along with the meat, and slice off as much fat from rind and outside of meat as you easily can; bone the meat as neatly as possible so that you do not end up with any more small pieces of meat than necessary. Render the fat, if you wish (page 418), and use it for general cooking. Simmer the bones with vegetables and herbs as for an ordinary meat stock, and store in the freezer until it is finally time to cook the meat. If you want to add a loin roast of pork to the cure, bone it or not, as you choose, and slice off all but a ⅛-inch layer of covering fat. Pork jowls, belly, and fat back are cut into whatever sizes you find convenient, and are cured as they are, with the rind left on.

Note on meat-to-bone ratios

The amount of usable meat you will get from a fresh ham on the bone or hand is roughly 60 per cent. In other words, a 6½-pound hand will yield approximately 4½ pounds of meat.

[*Dry-salt cure for 10 pounds of pork*]

10 lb. fresh pork prepared as described in preceding paragraph (include rind if making *jambon persillé*)

A glazed or enamelled bowl or casserole large enough to hold meat closely packed

6 oz. salt (sea salt, coarse salt, or table salt)

2 oz. sugar

1 tsp. saltpetre (potassium nitrate from a pharmacy)

1½ tsp. crushed juniper berries

Either: 1½ tsp. *épices fines*, page 385; or: ¾ tsp. white pepper, and ¼ tsp. each of allspice, pulverized thyme, and bay leaf

A bowl to mix salt and spices in

A large tray to salt meat on

Plastic wrap, a large plate, and a 7- to 10-lb. weight, mincer, brick, stone, or other heavy object

Prepare the pork as described and be sure curing bowl is the right size. Stir the salt and other ingredients thoroughly in the small bowl and divide in 2, reserving ½ for later salting. Starting with the largest pieces of meat, rub salt thoroughly into all sides, corners, and crevices. Pat a $\frac{1}{16}$-inch layer over meat and pack into bowl. Continue with the smaller pieces and end with the rind, if you are using it, placing it fat side down over the meat. Cover meat with plastic wrap, plate, and weights. Refrigerate (or place in cold-room) at 36° to 40°F. for 5 days. Then remove meat, leaving accumulated brine in bowl, re-salt with reserved mixture, and return to bowl with plastic, plate, and weight on top. Refrigerate for 10 days more, turning meat once or twice to be sure everything is well salted; meat is then ready to use.

(†) *Storage note:* Meat may remain in cure for 6 to 8 weeks in all, but be sure all pieces are well covered with salt.

Cooking note: Salted meat must be de-salted before cooking – soak in several changes of cold water overnight if cured 15 days, 24 hours if cured several weeks.

*Jambon Persillé
[Mould of Parslied Ham in Aspic]

As described in the introduction to this section, *jambon persillé* is a Burgundian creation. Inevitably when dealing with well-known regional specialities, there are dozens of variations and minor versions, and always hundreds of very definite opinions on how to conduct each step. Among the considerable number of serious and trustworthy formulas we have studied, this is the one we prefer.

A NOTE ON SHOP-BOUGHT HAM

If you are not using home-cured ham, buy 6½ to 8 pounds of ready-to-bake, mild-cured smoked ham on the bone or hand. Omit step 1, proceeding directly to the simmering in step 2; skin and bone the ham after cooking.

[*For 4 to 5 pints of ham, serving 12 to 16 people*]

1. Soaking the ham: 12 to 24 hours

4 to 6 lb. of boned, home-salted fresh ham or hand, and the salted ham rind (preceding recipe; or see preceding note)

Soak the ham and the rind in a large basin of cold water, changing water 2 to 3 times. Overnight is enough for ham cured about 15 days; soak for 18 to 24 hours if ham has cured longer. (Soaking removes the preserving salt, not the flavour.)

2. Simmering the ham

A pan just large enough to hold ham comfortably
Either: 1 bottle best quality, young, strong, dry white wine (Côtes-du-Rhône or Pinot Blanc);
Or: 1¼ pts dry white French vermouth
1¼ pts bouillon (made from fresh ham bones, or a mixture of beef and chicken bouillon)
Necessary water
1 tsp. thyme, 2 tbl. tarragon, 4 allspice berries, 2 bay leaves, and 2 large cloves of garlic tied in washed cheesecloth

1 large onion, roughly chopped
1 medium carrot, roughly chopped
1 celery stalk

Place soaked ham (and rind) in pan, add wine, bouillon, and enough water to cover by an inch. Add rest of ingredients listed, bring to the simmer, and skim for several minutes until scum ceases to rise. Cover partially and maintain at the simmer until ham is tender when pierced with a sharp knife (about 2 hours for boned, home-cured ham). Let ham cool in liquid an hour or two.

While still warm, remove rind from pan (or from the bought ham), scrape off and discard as much fat as possible, and purée rind through coarse disc of food mill or fine blade of mincer; reserve in a 2-pint bowl. Tear ham apart with your fingers, discarding fat and gristle. Cut ham into pieces about ½ inch thick and 1½ to 2 inches square, and place in a 4-pint bowl along with any meat scraps. Moisten with a tablespoon or so of cooking stock, and set aside. Thoroughly degrease cooking stock, boil down rapidly to concentrate flavour if necessary, and correct seasoning.

3. The aspic: for about 1½ pints

2 pts. thoroughly degreased ham cooking stock in a saucepan
2 to 3 egg whites
Optional for added flavour: 4 to 6 tbl. minced green tops from leeks or spring onions
2 packages (2 tbl.) powdered unflavoured gelatine

Following directions in Volume I, pages 130–32, clarify the cooking stock with the egg whites, add optional greenery, strain, and then dissolve the gelatine in it.

4. The parsley and aspic flavouring

The bowl of puréed rind
2 oz. chopped fresh parsley
1 clove of garlic, mashed
1 tbl. dried tarragon or 3 tbl. fresh minced tarragon leaves
1 tbl. wine vinegar
Salt and pepper to taste
½ pt of the aspic, cool but not set

Mix all ingredients except the aspic in the bowl, and just before assembling the ham in step 5, stir in the cup of aspic.

5. Assembling and serving

The following assembly method is informal: the meat is packed into a bowl, and slices are cut and served directly from it. If you want a dressier presentation, line the bowl with aspic before filling it, and unmould on to a platter for serving.

A 4- to 5-pt serving bowl, casserole, or crock (this can be of clear glass through which you can see the design of the ham and parsley)
The parsley and aspic mixture
The cooked and cut ham
A rack and/or plate that will fit into the bowl
A weight of some sort
The remaining aspic, cool but not set

Chill the bowl and spread a layer of parsley-aspic in the bottom. Then pack with layers of ham and of parsley-aspic. When filled, cover with rack and/or plate and weight, and chill for an hour or so, until set. (If you do not weight down the ham, it will be difficult to cut into slices later.) Remove the rack and so forth, scumble the top a bit with a fork (to disguise plate or rack marks), and pour on the cool aspic. Cover and chill until serving time.

To serve, cut into slices, like a large pie.

(†) *Storage note: Jambon persillé* will keep nicely for a week under refrigeration. It may be frozen, but will lose character after 2 to 3 weeks.

Preserved Goose · *Confit d'Oie*

Like the salting of pork, the preserving of goose is an age-old method for keeping meats during the winter months, and is typical of the *foie gras* regions in France, where geese are raised to produce those magnificent livers. The goose for *confit* is given a brief preliminary salting, then is slowly simmered in

its own fat, a process that not only cooks it but also renders
out most of the heavy layer of fat under the skin, just as most
of the fat is rendered out of bacon when you cook it. Traditionally, the cooked pieces of goose are then packed in crocks
and sealed in the fat for storage. The taste of preserved goose,
like the taste of salted pork, has a very special quality quite unlike fresh goose or pork, and it is an easy process as well as an
interesting one to do. Besides having goose to eat in the
numerous ways described at the end of the recipe, you will
have its big carcass for soup and, during the weeks to come, a
goodly supply of the best cooking fat imaginable, which is
marvellous for browning meats and sautéing potatoes, for
basting roasts, frying eggs, and grilling chickens, as well as
for flavouring vegetable dishes like cabbage and sauerkraut.

HOW TO DISJOINT POULTRY, AS ILLUSTRATED WITH A GOOSE

In the following directions, the goose is cut so that each wing
makes a serving portion, the breast is halved lengthwise, and
the drumstick–second-joint pieces are left intact for separation
before serving.

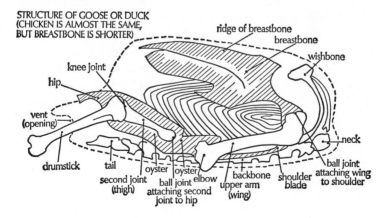

STRUCTURE OF GOOSE OR DUCK (CHICKEN IS ALMOST THE SAME, BUT BREASTBONE IS SHORTER) — ridge of breastbone — breastbone — wishbone — knee joint — hip — vent (opening) — neck — drumstick — tail — oyster — oyster — elbow — backbone — shoulder blade — ball joint attaching wing to shoulder — second joint (thigh) — ball joint attaching second joint to hip — upper arm (wing)

Preliminaries

Pull all fat out of cavity; you will have about a pound from a
ready-to-cook shop-bought goose, twice as much or more

from a farm goose. Cut off wings at elbows and save for the stock pot, along with the neck and gizzard; save the heart and liver for the sausage suggestion at the end of the *confit* recipe. As a preliminary to disjointing the goose, slit skin the length of the back, going down to the bone from neck opening to beginning of tail piece. Then place goose in front of you, its legs to your left.

Removing the wing section

So that the wing will make an adequate serving, you want to include the lower third of the breast with it as follows. Starting an inch to the right of where second joint is attached to hip, in the drawing, cut through breast meat to bone in a shallow semicircle reaching up to the joint where wing is attached to shoulder. Bend wing at a right angle away from breast and then down towards back, to break open the joint; cut through joint to free wing, and scrape breast meat off carcass from initial cut down towards backbone to free the entire section.

Removing drumstick–second-joint section

Follow end of drumstick with your finger to find knee. Holding knee in your left hand, slit around it from vent to ribs (where wing section was removed). Again with your finger, follow second joint (thigh) from knee to hip, to locate ball joint attaching it to the hip bone. At either side of this joint along the hip are two nuggets of meat, the oysters, which should come off as part of the drumstick–second-joint section: scrape this meat from hip bone up to and around joint. Then bend knee away from carcass at a right angle and down towards backbone to break open ball joint at hip. Cut through joint to detach it, then cut drumstick–second-joint from carcass. Remove wing–breast piece and drumstick–second-joint from other side of goose.

The breast

You now have only the upper two thirds of the breast meat left on the carcass. Cut through ribs just below breast meat on either side. Then, grasping tail end (at left in drawing), lift breast structure up at right angles and bend it towards neck end, to break it free at shoulder. Chop off the 2 tusk-shaped shoulder-blade bones at neck end and trim off excess skin.

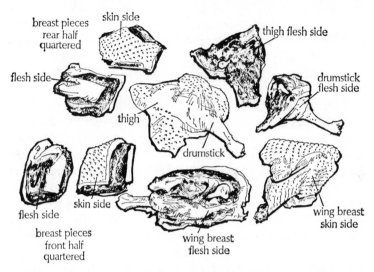

Locate ridge of breastbone with your finger, then slit down through skin to bone close along one side of ridge. With cleaver and mallet, chop the breastbone in half along this slit. (You may then wish to chop each piece in half, crosswise, if you are serving the goose in a *ragoût* rather than a *confit*.)

Trim fatty edges of skin from each piece of goose; feel with your fingers for any knobs of fat buried under the flesh at edges of breast, wings, second joints, and remove them. Cut into ½-inch pieces with shears, and reserve all of this for rendering, step 2 in the recipe.

A NOTE ON COOKING-FAT

Ideally the goose is cooked in goose fat and fresh pork leaf fat (also called fresh leaf lard), which comes from around the pork kidneys. This is very difficult to find unless there is a pork-slaughtering business in your area: substitute fresh pork fat back or the fat from a loin roast. If you have no success in finding this, render only the fresh fat and skin from the goose, and after you have strained it, add shop-bought leaf lard, which you can usually buy in 1-pound packages. Failing this, use white vegetable shortening.

Confit d'Oie
[Preserved Goose]

Preserved goose is a disjointed and salted goose cooked in its own fat.

Modern refrigerators and freezers have made changes in the *confit* traditions. In the old days you had to simmer the goose for at least 2½ hours, until every bit of moisture had evaporated and a straw would pierce the meat with ease; you then were sure it would keep through the winter, packed in its jars of fat in your cold-room or cellar. For our purposes, since we are more interested in taste than tradition, the goose is cooked only until done, and is stored in its fat in the refrigerator, or is wrapped and frozen.

Note: Pork, small game, duck, and turkey are done exactly the same way after being cut into serving pieces. Use only pork fat for the rendering and cooking.

[*For a 10- to 12-pound ready-to-cook roasting goose. Thaw if frozen, and disjoint as described and illustrated in preceding directions; you will have 5 to 6 pounds of goose*]

1. Salting the goose: 24 hours

Half the ingredients for the dry-salt cure on page 411, or add goose
　　to the cure along with the pork you are doing

Follow directions for salt curing but leave goose in the cure for 24 hours only. (If you have to leave it longer, you may de-salt the meat by soaking the goose pieces several hours in cold water before cooking.)

2. Rendering fat: 45 minutes

6 lb. fresh fat (goose fat and fatty skin pieces, plus fresh pork leaf fat,
　　other fresh pork fat, or see notes preceding recipe)
A heavy 10-pt pan or casserole (which may also serve to cook the goose)
½ pt water
A deep-fat-frying thermometer

Pull papery filaments from pork leaf fat if you are using it, and chop all fat into ¼-inch pieces. Place in pan with water, cover loosely, and set over low heat so that fat liquefies slowly. When it reaches 212°F. it will crackle and spit as water content evaporates. When it stops spitting, in about 25 minutes, remove cover and raise heat slightly to 250°F. (Do not ever allow fat to go over 325°F. or it will lose its clear, pale-yellow colour.) In 20 to 30 minutes more, the fat pieces will be lightly golden brown, and the fat may be considered rendered. Strain through a fine sieve, pressing liquid fat out of browned residue. (Save residue for *frittons*, at end of recipe.) Return fat to pan. Cover when cool, and set in a cool place or refrigerate.

3. Cooking the goose: 1½ to 1¾ hours for a roaster goose

The pan of rendered fat
The salted goose
More fat if needed
The thermometer

Set pan over low heat to liquefy fat. Meanwhile, wipe off salt and dry the goose with paper towels; place goose in pan. (Fat should cover goose pieces by at least an inch.) Start timing when fat begins to bubble quietly and temperature is between 200° and 205°F., where it should remain throughout cooking.

Goose is done when meat is tender if pierced with a knife and when juices run clear yellow; meat and skin should colour no more than a deep golden yellow and fat should remain pale yellow. Remove goose. Raise heat slightly and cook fat for 5 to 6 minutes (but not over 325°F.) until it stops crackling, which indicates all liquid has evaporated and fat has clarified. Strain through a fine sieve, pressing fat out of residue. Save residue for *frittons*, page 420.

4. Storing of goose and of fat

You may serve the goose as it is, hot or cold, and it is delicious when freshly cooked. It will keep 4 to 5 days in a covered dish in the refrigerator, or you may wrap it airtight and freeze for 6 to 8 weeks. However, it seems to retain its best flavour, if you wish to preserve the meat for some time, when you pack it into a bowl and cover completely with the liquid fat in which it cooked; when fat has cooled and congealed, cover airtight with plastic wrap, and refrigerate. It will keep 2 to 3 months at least. To remove pieces of goose, set bowl at room temperature for several hours so that fat will soften enough for you to remove as many pieces of goose as you wish with a wooden spoon. Be sure the remaining pieces are completely covered with fat when you cover and refrigerate them again.

Any fat not being used to preserve the goose will keep for a month or more in covered jars in the refrigerator.

Serving suggestions

Besides the cabbage soup of Béarn, *garbure*, and the baked beans of Toulouse and Castelnaudary, *cassoulet*, you may add the goose to warm up in a casserole of lentils or beans, or in the braised sauerkraut or red cabbage in Volume 1, pages 532–3. Another idea is to warm the goose in a covered dish in a medium hot oven for 10 to 15 minutes, until it is hot and tender, then roll it in breadcrumbs, sprinkle with goose fat and brown under a hot grill; serve with the purée of beans and pumpkin on page 530, the turnip and rice purée, page 532, the garlic mashed potatoes or rice and onion *soubise* in Volume I, pages 557 and 519, or with sliced potatoes sautéed in goose fat. Accompany with Brussels sprouts or broccoli and a light red wine or a rosé.

Arrange cold goose on a platter garnished with lettuce, watercress, or parsley, and accompany with French potato salad, cold mixed vegetables, or a tossed green salad, and beer or chilled dry white wine.

Frittons – Grattons
[Cracklings]

All the residue from rendering the fat and cooking the goose goes into this spread for toast or crackers, which you can serve with cocktails or accompanying a green salad and cold meats.

The fat-rendering and goose-cooking residue
Salt, pepper, and *épices fines* or allspice to taste
An attractive jar or pot
Melted goose fat

Pound the cracklings in a mortar or put through a mincer, then warm briefly in a frying pan. Season to taste and pack tightly into jar or pot. Chill, and when cold, pour on a $\frac{1}{4}$-inch layer of melted goose fat. Cover and refrigerate. Will keep for a month or so.

Cou d'Oie Farci
[Goose-Neck Sausage]

If you have a farm goose, you can ask that the whole neck from head to backbone be saved for you intact and as it is. Pluck and singe skin thoroughly, then peel it off the neck in one piece, turning skin inside out as you go. Sprinkle with salt and pepper, turn it skin side out, and it is ready to be a sausage casing. Use the truffled pork, veal, and liver formula on page 393, substituting goose liver and heart for chicken liver. Tie or sew the two ends, and poach the sausage in fat along with the goose.

Pâtés and *Terrines*

The French are famous for the splendour of their *pâtés* and *terrines*, those glorious looking, intoxicating smelling, rich, and unforgettable mixtures of pork, veal, chicken, duck, truffles, liver, *foie gras*, wines, and spices that are packed into long earthen dishes in the *charcuterie*, or in great round bowls, or are formed in cunningly decorated brown crusts. No other cuisine has developed the art quite like the French, and no other formulas are quite as delicious and subtle. However, if you have done some of the recipes in Volume I beginning on page 603, you will know how easy it is to make a *terrine*: it is only a matter of grinding up meat, seasoning it, slicing or dicing a garniture, and packing everything into a fat-lined dish before setting it in the oven. You know also that your own is almost invariably better than anything you can buy because you are using the best ingredients rather than scraps, and that most *pâtés* and *terrines* are expensive to buy and just as expensive to make. They come in the category of necessary luxuries.

An excellent pork-liver *pâté* starts off this new series in a fairly economical manner. This is followed by a *pâté de campagne*, then a *pâté* baked in bread dough, and an unusual porkless *terrine*. The next section has fully illustrated directions on how to form and bake *pâtés en croûte*.

A NOTE ON LIAISONS AND BINDERS

Almost all *pâté* mixtures have something in addition to meat to bind them together, preventing the meat from crumbling when the *pâté* is sliced. Eggs are usually present, sometimes breadcrumbs, and rice can also serve. The following *panade* is an alternative to the breadcrumb type of *panade* used for the *boudin* sausages on page 388.

Panade au Riz

[*For about 1 cup*]

2½ oz. plain raw white rice
½ pt or more of meat stock or bouillon
1½ oz. butter
A heavy-bottomed 2½-pt saucepan (non-stick recommended)

Simmer the rice in the liquid and butter for 25 to 30 minutes, or until it is very tender. Add a little more bouillon if necessary, to keep rice from sticking, but liquid should be entirely absorbed when rice is done.

To use the *panade*

Purée in an electric blender, food mill, or mincer along with any liquids or egg you are using. (Your recipe will direct you.) Any left-over *panade* may be frozen.

A NOTE ON PORK FAT, BAKING DISHES, AND OTHER MATTERS

Full notes on what to bake a *pâté* in, and so forth, can be found in Volume I, pages 603–4, and in the master recipe for *terrine de porc, veau, et jambon*, also in Volume I, starting on page 605. Our only additional comment here is on pork fat. Except in the case of the porkless *pâté*, which uses suet or chicken fat, all of the following recipes call for fresh pork as part of the meat mixture and also as a liner for the baking dish. We realize how difficult it is to find fresh pork fat back (*lard gras*). For the fat in the meat mixture itself, you can use fat-and-lean pork from a fresh hand or bladebone, or fat from the outside of a loin roast; outside fresh ham- and hand-fat are less satisfactory because softer, but perfectly possible. Although you can line the mould with blanched salt pork or bacon, fresh pork fat is very much better both in taste and appearance. Lacking fresh fat back, you can pound strips of fresh outside loin fat between 2 sheets of waxed paper, to reduce them to $\frac{1}{8}$ inch thickness and to weld them together.

THREE LIVER *PÂTÉS*

Down on the farm, you naturally use every bit of the pig for something, and some of the very best *pâtés* contain pork liver, either as the main ingredient or combined with other meat. These have far more character than chicken-liver *pâtés*, and your own home-made mixture is always surprisingly better than anything you seem to be able to buy, even in the best French *charcuterie*.

Liver note

You may substitute ox liver for pork liver; we have not found any significant difference in effect. Calf's liver is lovely but insanely expensive for this type of dish.

*Terrine de Foie de Porc
[Pork-liver *Pâté*]

To translate a *terrine de foie de porc* into familiar language: it is like the very best liver sausage; you could easily mistake it for *pâté de foie gras*. Simple to make, it consists only of liver, pork fat, flavourings, plus an egg and either rice or breadcrumbs to bind everything together. Of all the mixtures, this necessarily contains the most fat; if you used any less you would not achieve perfection. Serve slices of *pâté* and French bread or toast as a first course; it is also delicious as a spread for sandwiches or cocktail appetizers.

[*For a 2½-pint baking dish: 18 to 20 slices*]

The *pâté* dish: a 2½-pt *terrine* or baking dish (rectangular, round, oval)
or bread tin
A pan of water
Sheets of pork fat to line *pâté* dish

Preheat oven to 350°F., Mark 4, and place rack in middle level. Set *pâté* dish in pan to check water level: it should come ⅔ up outside of dish. Remove dish and place pan of water in oven. Line bottom and sides of *pâté* dish with strips of pork fat ⅛ inch thick. (See notes preceding this recipe as well as illustrations on page 436.)

1 lb. fresh pork fat back or fat from outside a loin roast
12 oz. liver (pork, beef, or calf)
1 cup rice *panade*, page 422
A meat mincer
An electric mixer with large bowl
2 eggs
2 tbl. cognac
2½ tsp. salt
Either: 1 tsp. *épices fines*, page 385;
Or: ½ tsp. pepper and big pinches of allspice, nutmeg, and cayenne
Optional: a 1-oz. truffle, minced, and its juice

Put the pork fat, liver, and rice *panade* through the finest blade of mincer and into the bowl. Beat in the rest of the ingredients. Sauté a spoonful and taste; correct seasoning as necessary. Turn mixture into *pâté* dish.

A piece of fresh pork fat to cover the meat
1 bay leaf
A branch of thyme, or ¼ tsp. dried thyme
Sufficient aluminium foil to cover *pâté* with 1 in. extra all around

Cover with the fat, lay the bay leaf and thyme on top, and then the foil. Cover, and set in pan of water in oven. Bake for $1\frac{1}{4}$ to $1\frac{1}{2}$ hours or longer; *pâté* is done at a temperature of 160°F., or when juices and fat surrounding *pâté* are clear yellow with no trace of rosy colour (press *pâté* with a spatula to check on this).

A cover for the dish, or a pastry sheet and weight
Useful: a meat thermometer

When done, remove *pâté* dish from pan, discard water, and return dish to pan. Cover with board, or pan and weight (to press meat together and prevent air pockets) and let cool to room temperature. Remove board and weights and refrigerate.

Serving

Pâté will improve in flavour after 2 to 3 days. Cut slices $\frac{3}{8}$ to $\frac{1}{2}$ inch thick directly from dish; or heat bottom of dish gently, run a knife around between *pâté* and dish, and unmould on a serving plate or board.

Storage

Pâté will keep nicely for 8 to 10 days under refrigeration. It may be frozen, and results are more successful for liver *pâtés* than for meat *pâtés*.

Pâté de Campagne
[Pork and Liver *Pâté* with Veal or Chicken]

These *pâtés* vary in content and flavour throughout France, but always contain pork liver, pork, and sometimes other meats, as well as pork fat, a binder, and the usual seasoning. The following formula is one we like; whether you serve it in its baking dish or unmould it, the name is always *pâté de campagne* and never *terrine*.

[*For a 2½-pint baking dish*]

8 oz. fat-and-lean fresh pork (such as bladebone or loin, or the *chair à saucisse*, page 386)
8 oz. fresh pork fat back or fat from outside a loin roast
8 oz. raw lean veal, or raw chicken meat
8 oz. liver (pork, beef, or calf)

½ cup rice *panade*, page 422
3 tbl. minced onions, cooked until soft in 1 oz. pork fat or butter
1 egg
2 tbl. cognac
1 medium clove of garlic, mashed
Either: 1 tsp. *épices fines*, page 385;
Or: ½ tsp. pepper and big pinches of ground allspice, thyme, bay leaf
½ tsp. additional pepper
1 tbl. salt

Be sure all gristle, bones, skin, or other extraneous matter have been trimmed from meat before weighing. Pass meats, fat, and liver through finest blade of mincer along with the *panade*. Beat in rest of ingredients. Sauté a spoonful and taste. Correct seasoning as necessary. Pack into a fat-lined dish, and bake as in the master recipe.

Pâté de Foie et de Porc en Brioche
[Pork and Pork-liver *Pâté* Baked in *Brioche* Dough]

This is a *pâté* baked in *brioche* dough in a round tin. It is always dramatic because the dough rises luxuriously and the whole effect is one of effulgent *gourmandise*. The *pâté* is served cold, and it must be baked at least a day ahead of serving so that the meat will settle, which means that you will probably need to make the dough a day before baking.

[*For a 9- by 1¼- to 2-inch round mould, serving 12 to 16 people*]

1. The *pâté* ingredients

The *pain brioché* dough mixture on page 127, chilled and ready to form
8 oz. fresh pork fat back or fat from outside a loin roast
A 12-in. frying pan
¾ lb. onions, minced
8 oz. fresh pork hand or loin
1 lb. liver (pork, beef, or calf)
1 medium clove of garlic, mashed
Either: 1 tsp. *épices fines*, page 385;
Or: ½ tsp. pepper and big pinches of ground allspice, thyme and bay leaf
¼ tsp. additional pepper
2 tsp. salt
2 tbl. dry white breadcrumbs, moistened in a small bowl with 3 tbl.
    double cream and 1 tbl. cognac

Prepare the dough the day before baking. Put the pork fat through the medium blade of the mincer. Place half in bowl of electric mixer and heat other half slowly in frying pan until fat has rendered. Add onions to pan and cook slowly about 15 minutes until tender and translucent. Meanwhile, mince the pork and set aside, then the liver, and set aside separately. When onions are done, add the pork and cook 4 to 5 minutes, stirring until meat is grey rather than rosy. Add the liver and cook for several minutes until somewhat stiffened and puffed, and beginning to look greyish-ruddy-brown. Scrape into mixing bowl and beat in all the rest of the ingredients. Sauté a spoonful and taste; correct seasoning as necessary.

2. Forming the *pâté en brioche*

A buttered 9- by 1½-in. (2½-pt) false-bottomed cake tin or fluted mould; or a flan ring set on a baking sheet
The chilled dough
A piece of floured waxed paper on a small baking sheet
The hot meat mixture
A pastry brush
Cold water
A 2-in. chimney, such as a small, buttered metal funnel or the metal tube from a pastry bag

On a lightly floured board, roll ¼ of the dough into a circle the diameter of your tin or mould, set on floured paper, and chill until needed. Rapidly roll out the rest of the dough into a circle about ¼ inch thick and 12 inches in diameter. Lightly press it into the tin or mould, letting edges overhang all around. Turn the hot meat mixture into the dough-lined tin; fold the edges of the dough over on to the meat. Paint dough lightly with cold water, and unroll reserved circle of dough on top, pressing edges lightly with your fingers to seal. Make a hole in the centre top of the dough and insert chimney. (You will probably have enough dough left over for a small loaf of bread.)

3. Rising: about 1 hour

Set the *pâté* in a draught-free place at a temperature of no more than 75° to 80°F. until top of dough feels spongy-springy when touched and the whole structure has risen ½ inch or more up from the rim of the mould. Preheat oven in time for next step.

4. Baking: about 1 hour in a preheated 425°F., Mark 7 oven

Egg glaze (1 egg beaten in a small bowl with 1 tsp. water)
Sharp-pointed scissors
Useful: a meat thermometer

Just before baking, paint top (not sides) of dough with egg glaze; in a moment paint it again. Make scissor clips 1½ inches apart all around top circumference of dough, going in at a slant ¾ inch deep and 2 inches wide. Set *pâté* in middle level of preheated 425°F., Mark 7 oven and bake for 18 to 20 minutes, until *brioche* has risen and begun to brown nicely. Reduce heat to 350°F., Mark 4, baking about 40 minutes more. *Pâté* is done when fat is bubbling up in funnel; temperature on meat thermometer should be 160° to 165°F.

5. Cooling

Remove from oven and let cool in mould for ½ hour, then unmould on to a rack. When thoroughly cold, cover airtight and refrigerate for at least 12 hours before serving.

6. Serving suggestions

Serve as it is, cutting it into wedges like a pie. When you want an even more attractive dish, pour almost-set aspic into chilled *pâté* through chimney hole, and chill an hour or more before serving. (This is described in the *pâté en croûte* section, page 440.)

A PORKLESS VARIATION

La Terrine Verte
Pâté Sans Porc
[A Porkless *Pâté*]

Slice into this unusual *pâté*, and it is a beautiful green with decorations of white and brown. It has a meaty, hearty taste, yet is made without a trace of pork meat or pork fat: it is veal, chicken, and calf's brains spiced with onions, garlic, herbs, and cognac, garnished with chicken breasts and livers, and turned green with spinach. The fat is either veal- or beef-kidney fat, or goose or chicken fat. Bake the *pâté* at least 2 and preferably

3 days before serving, so that all the flavours may blend into perfect harmony.

[*For a 3½-pint* terrine *serving 12 to 16*]

1. The *pâté* mixture

The boned and skinned breast from 1 frying chicken
3 chicken livers
3 tbl. cognac
Salt and pepper

Cut the breast meat and the chicken livers into strips ⅜ inch wide; place in a bowl with the cognac and a sprinkling of salt and pepper. Let marinate while preparing rest of *pâté* mixture.

The *terrine:* a 3½-pt mould, baking dish, or bread tin of any shape,
   although a rectangular one is easy for serving
1 lb. fresh veal-kidney fat, beef suet, or goose fat or chicken fat
A mincer
An electric mixer with large bowl

Chill *terrine* in freezer. Trim off any filaments or extraneous matter and put fat through fine blade of mincer. Place ½ in large bowl of mixer and render the rest of the fat. (Directions are on page 418.) When strained, cooled, and almost congealed, spread ¾ of it inside the chilled *terrine*. Refrigerate *terrine* until you are ready to fill it.

½ lb. boneless raw light or dark meat from a frying chicken
½ lb. raw, lean veal
1 lb. brains (calf, beef, or lamb), blanched and peeled (they need not be
   trimmed of tubes and extraneous matter)
½ lb. onions, minced
Either: 1 lb. blanched, chopped fresh spinach;
Or: 1 lb. frozen spinach, thawed (squeezed dry)
1 medium clove garlic, mashed
2 eggs
1 tbl. salt
Either: 1 tsp. *épices fines*, page 385;
Or: ½ tsp. thyme, ¼ tsp. allspice, and ¼ tsp. nutmeg
6 tbl. dry white breadcrumbs, moistened with 3 tbl. chicken broth or
   milk

Mince the chicken, veal, and brains into the mixing bowl along with the minced raw fat. In 1 oz. of the rendered fat, cook the onions for 8 to 10 minutes over low heat until tender and translucent, then blend in the spinach and stir several minutes to evaporate excess moisture. Add spinach and onions to mixing bowl, along with the garlic, eggs, salt, seasonings, and bread-crumbs. Beat vigorously to blend all ingredients. Sauté a spoonful until cooked through, taste, and correct seasoning.

2. Filling the *terrine* and baking: preheat oven to 350°F., Mark 4

The marinating strips of chicken breast and chicken livers
The *pâté* mixture
The chilled, fat-lined *terrine*
The remaining rendered fat
1 bay leaf
1 branch thyme, or ¼ tsp. dried thyme
2 sheets of aluminium foil
A cover for the *terrine* (or pastry sheet and weight, such as a brick)
A pan of boiling water in middle level of pre-heated oven

Beat the cognac marinade into the *pâté* mixture. Spread ⅓ of the *pâté* mixture in the *terrine*, cover with ½ of the chicken meat and livers in alternating strips. Spread with ½ the remaining *pâté* mixture, then with the remaining strips of chicken and liver, ending with the last of the *pâté*. Spread reserved and rendered fat over the *pâté*, and top with the bay leaf and thyme. Fold the foil closely over top of *terrine* to enclose it completely; set on the cover, and place in pan of boiling water in oven. Bake for about 1½ hours, or until *pâté* starts to shrink from sides of mould, and when pressed with the back of a spoon no rose-coloured juices exude. (Temperature on a meat thermometer should be 160° to 165°F.)

3. Cooling and serving

Cool under a board or pan and weight, then refrigerate, covered, for 2 to 3 days before serving as described in the master recipe, page 425.

Pâtés Baked in Pastry Crust · *Pâtés en Croûte*

When it appears in pastry dough, any *pâté* mixture becomes a *pâté en croûte*, certainly one of the great visual delights of French *charcuterie*. A hinged metal *pâté* mould provides the most professional as well as the easiest system for *pâté en croûte*, and you can buy a variety of shapes in most kitchen stores. The mould, which sits on a baking sheet when filled, has neither top nor bottom, only 2 sides hinged at 1 end and closed by a removable pin at the other. It is a kind of corset, which actually moulds the *pâté* dough in its decorative embrace, and holds it tight while it bakes and cools. If you have no mould, a workable alternative described on page 442-3 produces an equally attractive result; it is a baked bottom case of dough, which you fill as though it were a *pâté* mould and top with a decorated cover of dough. A third alternative is the free-form shape, *pâté pantin*, baked on a pastry sheet like the sausage in *brioche* on pages 400-402. The first 2 methods are outlined in the following directions.

TIMING

A *pâté* always develops more taste 2 to 3 days after baking. Allowing 2 days for the maturing process, you will need at least 1½ days for baking, cooling, chilling: start the *pâté*, then,

4 to 5 days in advance of any date you wish to serve it. The finished *pâté* will keep 7 to 10 days under refrigeration.

THE *PÂTÉ* MIXTURE

Although you may use any of the preceding *pâtés* for *pâté en croûte*, the more traditional mixture is the all-purpose pork and veal stuffing in Volume I, page 604, and a garniture of strips of veal and ham, or of game such as rabbit, hare, partridge, or pheasant, or of duck, turkey, or chicken. Follow one of the recipes in Volume I, starting on page 605, and including the duck *pâté* on page 610. For a 3½-pint mould you will need approximately 2 pounds of stuffing and 1 pound of garnishing strips. You will also need sheets of fresh pork fat for lining the dough.

THE DOUGH FORMULA

For *pâtés* moulded in a hinged form, use the *pâté à croustade*, formula 6, page 163, which contains flour, butter, lard, and egg yolks. When you are forming the dough on an upside-down case, use formula 7, with whole eggs. These are both excellent doughs for *pâtés*; they hold their shape through the long baking, and are also good to eat. Either one is easy to make in an electric mixer as described on page 157; it is best to prepare the dough several hours ahead or the day before forming and baking, so that it will be well chilled, rested, and easy to roll.

Forming and Baking *Pâté en Croûte* in a Hinged *Pâté* Mould

1. Lining the mould with dough

Your first step is to line the bottom and sides of the mould with an even ⅜ inch layer of dough. An ingenious professional method is to form ¾ of the dough into a pouch, the bottom and sides of which fit neatly against the mould with a minimum of wrinkles while the open top falls around the outside leaving the mould open for filling. In French this is a *calotte*, a skull cap. (The following illustrations are for an oval mould; adapt the same system for rectangular and round moulds.)

A hinged 2½- to 3½-pt *pâté* mould
A piece of heavy paper to serve as a pattern
Sheets of fresh pork fat ⅛ in. thick, enough to line bottom, sides, and top of mould (page 423)

Using *pâté* mould as a guide, cut a pattern out of the paper to fit the opening of the mould (A). Cut 2 pieces of pork fat, using pattern, and set aside; these will line bottom and top of *pâté* later. Reserve pattern for dough cover, later.

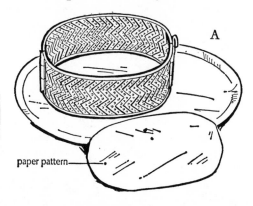

A

paper pattern

Chilled *pâté à croustade* dough made with 1 lb. of flour (page 157)
A pastry brush and cup of cold water

Roll ¾ of the chilled dough into a circle about 1 inch thick and 2 inches larger in diameter than the long side of the mould – dough must be very thick at this point so that when you are through rolling and forming it you will still have a ⅜-inch layer lining the mould.

Paint a 1-inch strip down each side, right and left, with water (B). As the first step in making the pouch shape, dough is to be folded in half and corners are to be bent down as follows. Except at the 2 sides, sprinkle circle of dough liberally with flour to prevent sticking when folded in half. Bring top down to bottom, making a semicircle with its curved side facing you. Gently press 2 sides, right and left, together to seal them, then pull the 2 corners (right and left at

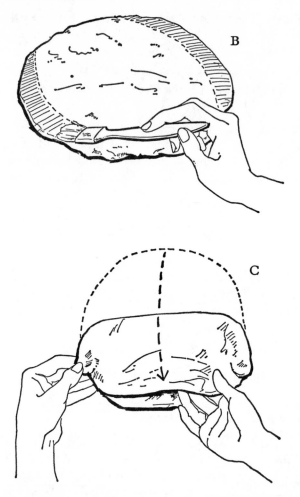

top of fold) down towards you as illustrated (c). Now, rather than a semicircle, you have a pocket or the beginning of a pouch.

Starting with open side facing you, and making several passes with your pin, roll dough away from you to deepen pouch, so that when it is spread into the mould you will have an overhang of 2 inches: for a mould 4 inches high and 5 inches across, the pouch should be $8\frac{1}{2}$ to 9 inches deep (D). Be very careful here that you roll the dough evenly and that the final com-

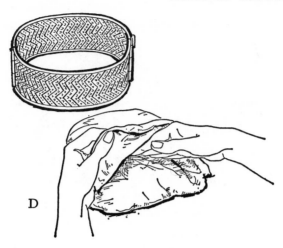

D

bined thickness of top and bottom layers is no less than ¾ inch; when the dough is thinner you risk breakage and leakage problems later on. (If by any chance you muff this on your first try, briefly knead dough into a ball, chill an hour or more to relax it, and start over again.)

1 to 1½ oz. lard or shortening
A baking sheet with raised edges (to catch cooking juices)
Scissors

Grease inside the mould and baking sheet, and set mould on sheet. Fold dough lightly in half lengthwise and centre in mould. Unfold and ease it gently into place by lifting sides of dough, being careful always that you do not stretch the dough and make it thinner at any point. Clip off a gob of extra dough and use it as a tampon, rather than your fingers, to press dough against pastry sheet and sides of mould. Leaving a 1½- to 2-inch overhang, trim off excess dough with scissors (E).

The sheets of fresh pork fat

Place an oval of pork fat on the bottom of the mould, and line the sides (F). This fat is your insurance against crust-cracking.

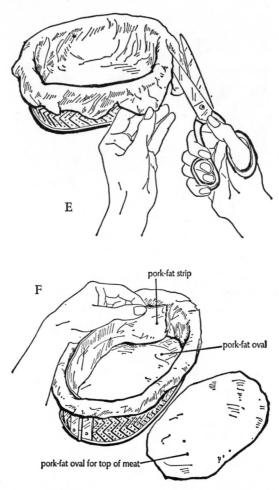

E

F

pork-fat strip

pork-fat oval

pork-fat oval for top of meat

2. Filling the mould

The *pâté* mixture and the strips of garniture (see notes preceding **recipe**)
The lined pâté mould
A bowl of cold water

With your *pâté* mixture made, your garniture in strips, and
your mould ready, you can now assemble the *pâté*. Have **a**
bowl of cold water handy to dip your hands into when you
spread in the meat mixture (G). Preheat oven to 375°F., Mark 5.

Fill the mould, starting with a layer of *pâté*, then a layer of garniture strips, a layer of *pâté*, another of garniture, and a final layer of *pâté* mixture (H). Fill mould just to rim, making only a slightly domed shape in centre: if mould is too full, juices will bubble out over crust during baking.

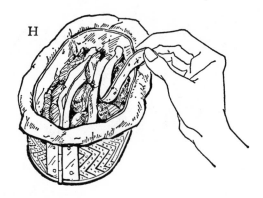

1 bay leaf
A sprig or 2 of thyme (or ¼ tsp. dried thyme)
The second oval of fresh pork fat

Place bay leaf and thyme on top of *pâté*; cover with the second oval of pork fat (I).

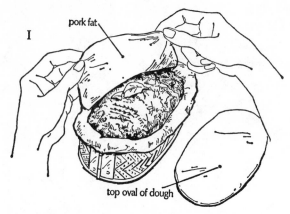

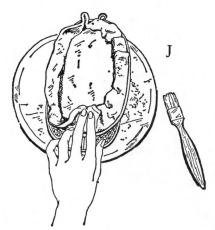

The reserved dough (or chilled left-over dough)
The paper pattern (size of mould opening)
A pastry brush and cold water
A table fork

Roll the reserved dough out ½ inch thick, cut into an oval
following pattern, and place on top of pork-fat oval. Paint
circumference with cold water and fold edges over, pressing

first with fingers to seal (J), and then with the back tines of a
table fork. (*Note*: Cover must be thick so that it will rise only
a little, otherwise you will have too large a gap between meat
and top of crust after baking. Another reason for making it

thick is that it will barely cook through and thus will not crumble when you eventually slice the *pâté*.)

Pastry cut-outs made from left-over dough
Egg glaze (1 egg beaten with 1 tsp. water)

Make pastry cut-outs of any shape you wish. (Illustrations are in Volume I, page 614.) One by one, paint bottoms of cut-outs with egg glaze and press in place on top of *pâté*, completely covering seam where edges of pastry overlap (K).

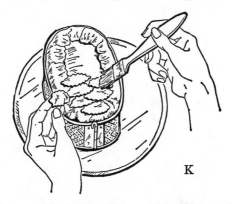

K

2 greased chimneys 1½ in. high, such as metal funnels, metal tubes from a pastry bag, or aluminium foil

With a sharp-pointed knife, make 2 holes ¼ inch in diameter in top of *pâté*, going down through to touch the meat; insert chimneys (L). They allow cooking steam to escape rather than

L

to gather in the crust, possibly bursting it. Just before baking, paint top of *pâté* with egg glaze, being careful none drips down into mould.

(†) *Pâté* mixture, garniture, and dough may be made a day or two in advance of baking, or *pâté* may be assembled (but not glazed), covered, and refrigerated for a day or two if meat is fresh. Add 20 to 30 minutes more to baking time if *pâté* has been chilled before going into oven.

3. Baking: 1½ to 2 hours; oven preheated to 375°F., Mark 5

Useful: a meat thermometer
A pan, spoon, and bulb baster for removing fat from pan

Place in lower-middle or middle-level of oven and bake for 20 to 25 minutes until crust begins to colour, then lower thermostat to 350°F., Mark 4, for rest of baking. Inspect *pâté* every 20 to 30 minutes: suck up fat from baking sheet with bulb baster and wipe off sheet with paper towels. An accumulation of fat can burn bottom of *pâté*, and it also smokes up the kitchen.

Pâté is done when juices begin bubbling up into funnel; they should be clear yellow. Check temperature by removing funnel and inserting meat thermometer, which should read between 160° and 165°F.

4. Cooling the *pâté*; the aspic

Remove *pâté* from oven, but do not attempt to slide *pâté* off baking sheet or to remove mould from *pâté* at this point, since you might tear or crack the crust, which must remain intact. Let cool completely for several hours or overnight, then chill in refrigerator for at least 4 hours.

A funnel
1½ pts wine-flavoured aspic (2 tbl. gelatine dissolved in 4 tbl.
    port or cognac combined with rather over 1¼ pts beef bouillon)
A bowl of cracked ice

During baking, the meat shrinks slightly from the top and sides of the crust, and you want to fill this space with aspic, which is delicious both visually and gastronomically. When *pâté* is thoroughly chilled, and with the mould still in place, insert funnel in a chimney hole in top of *pâté*. Being sure aspic has been well tested for consistency so that it will hold its shape when cold, stir over cracked ice until almost syrupy and on the point of setting; pour through funnel into *pâté*, tilting *pâté* in all directions, allowing aspic to run all over and around it. Chill again for several hours.

Finally, when aspic has chilled, remove pin from mould and carefully nudge sides of mould from sides of *pâté* (M). Once mould is off, *pâté* will hold its shape perfectly.

M

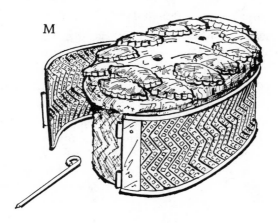

5. Serving

To serve, cut pie-shaped wedges going around circumference of *pâté*. For a rectangular *pâté*, cut straight across, as though it were a loaf of bread.

6. Storing

Pâté en croûte will keep a week to 10 days at 37°F. It is the aspic that might go off first, and then the crust with the meat juices in it. If you wish to keep left-overs a little longer, remove the crust, scrape off the aspic and the fat-covering, and wrap the meat in plastic or foil. A cooked *pâté* can be frozen, but will never have the same fresh texture again.

Forming and Baking the *Pâté* without a Mould

Although the hinged mould is easier to manage, baking a bottom case of dough to act as a mould works very nicely and is not difficult to do. The dough is formed on an upside-down casserole or bread tin, upon which it is baked, just as upside-down pastry shells are formed and baked on pages 158–62. The baked case is then lined with fat, filled with the *pâté*, draped with a close-fitting sheet of dough, decorated, and baked as usual.

1. The bottom case of dough

The *pâté à croustade à l'envers*, formula 7, page 163, for 20 oz. of flour
A 2½-pt mould, such as an oval casserole or bread tin greased on the
  outside with lard or shortening

Roll ⅔ of the dough into a circle, 2 inches more in diameter than the length of your mould, and 1½ inches thick. Form a pouch exactly as thick and exactly as illustrated for the spring-form mould, pages 433–5. Press lightly on to mould and trim off excess dough with a knife or pastry wheel. Cover and chill 2 hours or overnight (to relax dough and prevent shrinkage during baking). Set as it is, mould still upside down, on a baking sheet in a preheated 425°F., Mark 7 oven for 12 to 15 minutes, until pastry is starting to colour. Turn thermostat down to 350°F., Mark 4, and bake 10 minutes more, or until pastry just loosens from mould but is not cooked through: it holds its shape but is not browned. Cool 15 minutes on mould, then unmould carefully on to a rack and cool 30 minutes until pastry is firm and set.

2. Filling the case

Lard or shortening
A baking sheet
Pâté ingredients listed in preceding recipe, including sheets of pork
  fat and paper pattern

Grease just the area where pastry case will sit on baking sheet, and set case on sheet. Following directions in preceding recipe, pages 432–8, cut pork fat to fit bottom, sides, and top of *pâté*, line the case with the pork fat, and fill with *pâté* mixture topping with a sheet of pork fat.

3. The cover, and finishing the *pâté*

Chilled left-over dough and remaining dough
Egg glaze, pastry brush, pastry cut-outs, chimneys, as described in
preceding recipe

To discourage a gap from developing between top of meat and crust after baking, roll out a preliminary cover of dough $\frac{1}{4}$ inch thick, to fit top of pork fat. Set in place on *pâté*. Then roll remaining dough into a sheet $\frac{1}{4}$ to $\frac{3}{8}$ inch thick and large enough to cover top of pastry case and to fall $\frac{2}{3}$ the way down the case all around. Paint sides of case with egg glaze and arrange covering sheet of dough over *pâté*. Trim edges all around with scissors, then press dough in place against sides of case. Decorate with cut-outs, insert chimneys, glaze, bake, cool, chill, and fill with aspic as described and illustrated in preceding recipe.

6. A Choice of Vegetables

When you buy vegetables fresh and cook them lovingly, you may find yourself more renowned for your remarkable courgettes stuffed with almonds than for your spectacular *crêpes Suzette*. And why not, when flaming desserts are becoming status symbols and hand-whittled fresh vegetables more and more of a rarity? Recipes for vegetables consume over 100 pages in Volume I, and describe some of the ways to prepare rice and potatoes as well as almost everything to do with artichokes, asparagus, green beans, and spinach, plus how to braise chicory, how to turn a mushroom, and where to peel the chestnut. There are gaps, however, and while the present chapter will fill some of them we are more interested in giving you fresh ideas for old favourites than in completing the vegetable roster. Although we have included a number of classics, like *pommes Anna*, most of the recipes here are new ones that you will not have seen before – the sautéed broccoli, for instance, on page 449, the unusual purées starting on page 530, the spinach with onions on page 474. While some dishes are as elaborate as the stuffed artichoke hearts on page 541, others are as fast and simple as the grated courgettes on page 484. Seldom-honoured notables like swedes, chard, and pumpkin receive attention, and stuffed whole cabbage gets a revolutionary, new, and fully illustrated treatment. Here, then, are 100 more pages of recipes for fresh vegetables, beginning with broccoli and ending with a splendid dish of cold artichokes.

Broccoli · *Choux Brocoli, Choux Asperges*

Although green sprouting broccoli, asparagus broccoli, Italian broccoli, *Brassica oleracea var. italica*, or whatever you wish to call just plain green broccoli has been around for centuries, it was not widely known until the early 1920s. Despite its re-known in England and, especially, in America, it continues to remain almost unknown in France (where it is spelled with only one 'c'); that is their loss, because fresh broccoli, properly prepared, is certainly one of our most attractive vegetables, both visually and gastronomically. With its delicate cabbage flavour, it is more tender in taste and texture than cauliflower as well as being far more colourful. It goes beautifully with such subtleties as fish in fine white sauces, chicken breasts, brains, and sweetbreads; in fact, anything that spinach does to dress up a dish, broccoli does equally well, sometimes better. Thus, whether or not it ever becomes a French vegetable, we shall give broccoli the full treatment à la française.

BUYING BROCCOLI

When buying broccoli, choose clean, firm, smooth, fresh-smelling dark green or purplish-green bunches with fresh-looking, closely bunched, all-green bud clusters. Over-mature broccoli will have thick, woody stems that are often hollow; the buds will be partially open, yellowish, and have a rather strong odour. Broccoli is perishable, and will become limp and bruised-looking and develop an unpleasant stale-cabbage smell if not properly handled. Bring it home from the shop as soon as possible, refrigerate in a plastic bag immediately, and plan to cook it within 2 to 3 days.

The usual bunch of broccoli, containing several stalks tied together, weighs between 1½ and 2 pounds and will serve 4 to 6 people.

PREPARING BROCCOLI FOR COOKING

When we speak of the delights of fresh broccoli properly pre-pared, we are talking about peeling the stems and stalks before cooking the broccoli. If you have subsisted on unpeeled broccoli, you will find that peeled broccoli is an entirely different vegetable which cooks in 5 to 6 minutes, remains fresh and green, and is tender from stalk to tip. In fact we have the same feeling about unpeeled broccoli that we do about unpeeled asparagus – neither is a gastronomical object.

To prepare broccoli for cooking, you may quarter the whole stalks lengthwise from butt to head, and peel each stem of each piece. We, however, prefer smaller pieces for easier handling and more even cooking. We suggest that you begin by discarding the tough leaves, retaining only the small ones that seem as tender as the buds. Then cut off the top 2½ to 3 inches of each head, usually at the point where the branches separate themselves from the central stalk. Halve or quarter the branches lengthwise, depending on their size, to make them all no more than ½ inch in diameter at the base. Using a small knife and starting at the bottom of each branch peel off the skin in strips, coming almost up to the flower buds. Cut off and discard the tough ½ inch at the butt of each central stalk and strip off the skin, cutting deeply enough when necessary to expose the tender whitish flesh. (Slightly off-season broccoli that has fresh, tight bud clusters may have very thick central stalks with hollow cores; quartering lengthwise and deep peeling, however, will make the stalks tender and edible.) Cut stalks lengthwise into pieces ½ inch in diameter, and then into bias (diagonal) pieces about 1½ inches long.

Place the prepared broccoli in a covered bowl or plastic bag and refrigerate until you are ready to cook it. Wash rapidly under cold, running water just before cooking.

COOKING METHODS

Peeled broccoli cooks so fast, 5 to 6 minutes, that if you are serving it simply, with melted butter or a sauce, you should cook it only just before serving. If this works in with your schedule, it is easily accomplished between courses, otherwise pick one of the alternative methods, where the broccoli is sautéed or finishes in the oven.

*Choux Brocoli Blanchis

[Blanched Broccoli – Plain Boiled Broccoli]

When you have not peeled your broccoli, you must resort to all sorts of subterfuges such as boiling the stalks while steaming the heads, steaming the whole vegetable, or pressure cooking; by the time the stalks are done the heads usually droop, the colour has darkened, and the broccoli has lost much of its fresh taste and texture as well as those nutrients considered so important by the very people who feel the peel is the best part. When you have peeled your broccoli, you may use the French method of green-vegetable cookery – blanching. Because peeled broccoli is so tender, we recommend the wire salad basket for plunging it into its boiling bath and snatching it out again.

[*For 4 to 6 servings*]

1½ to 2 lb. fresh broccoli
A wire salad basket (or a vegetable rack, or a large skimmer)
A pan containing at least 6 pts of rapidly boiling water and 2 tbl. salt
(1 tsp. per pt)

Cut, peel, and wash the broccoli as described in preceding directions, and place in salad basket. Plunge into the rapidly boiling water over highest heat. As soon as water returns to the boil again, boil slowly uncovered, for 4 to 6 minutes (depending on freshness of broccoli). It is done when a knife pierces the stalks easily. Taste a piece as a test; it should be just tender, with a slight crunch of texture. Remove immediately from the boiling water and serve as directed in one of the following suggestions.

(†) If by some chance you plan to serve the hot broccoli with a sauce, and cannot do so immediately when it is done, let it cool, spreading out on a tray if necessary so it will cool quickly. Keep the water boiling. Return broccoli to salad basket just before you wish to serve and re-plunge it for a moment in the rapidly boiling water so that it will just heat through.

Serving Suggestions for Plain Boiled Broccoli

Brocoli au citron (broccoli for dieters): broccoli, like asparagus, is great for dieters because it has its own natural flavour, which a little lemon juice will enhance. Arrange the hot broccoli on a hot serving dish, sprinkle with salt and pepper, and decorate with wedges of lemon.

Brocoli au beurre noir (broccoli with brown butter sauce): before cooking the broccoli, melt about 3 ounces of butter, skim off foam and pour the clear yellow butter off the milky residue and into another saucepan. When broccoli is done, arrange it on a hot serving dish; sprinkle with salt, pepper, and drops of lemon juice. Heat butter until it turns a light, nutty brown and pour it bubbling hot over the broccoli. Serve immediately.

Beurre au citron (a lemon-butter sauce), Volume I, page 117.

Sauce hollandaise, its variations with cream (*sauce mousseline*), or the orange-flavoured variation (*sauce maltaise*), all of which are in Volume I, pages 97–103.

*Brocoli à la Polonaise

[Broccoli with Sautéed Breadcrumbs and Chopped Egg]

This more elaborate presentation of the brown butter sauce includes breadcrumbs and sieved egg. You might serve it as a first course or in place of a salad. It would also go with plain grilled or roast chicken, chops, steak, hamburger, or grilled fish.

[*For 1½ to 2 pounds broccoli, serving 4 to 6*]

¼ lb. butter
A saucepan
An 8-in. frying pan
4 tbl. white breadcrumbs
Salt and pepper
1 hard-boiled egg
A sieve set over a bowl

Before cooking the broccoli (master recipe, page 446) melt the butter in the saucepan, skim off foam, and pour clear butter off milky residue and into frying pan. Stir in the breadcrumbs and sauté over moderately high heat, stirring for several minutes until crumbs are lightly browned. Season to taste with salt and pepper, and set aside. Peel the hard-boiled egg, rub through sieve into bowl, and season with salt and pepper.

When broccoli is done, arrange on a hot serving dish and sprinkle lightly with salt and pepper. Reheat the breadcrumbs, mix in the sieved egg, strew over the broccoli, and serve immediately.

Broccoli with Poached Eggs

Omit the hard-boiled egg in the preceding recipe, and substitute 1 hot poached egg per person. When broccoli is cooked, arrange on hot serving dish and place hot poached eggs on top. Sprinkle the hot, browned breadcrumbs over all and serve immediately.

Cold Boiled Broccoli

Broccoli, peeled and blanched in the French manner, is delicious in cold vegetable combinations, accompanied by a vinaigrette or mayonnaise. So that it will retain all its fresh colour and texture after cooking, spread it out on a clean towel as soon as you have removed it from the boiling water. When cold, refrigerate in a covered bowl.

BROCCOLI RECIPES THAT MAY BE
PREPARED AHEAD

Brocoli Sautés à la Niçoise

[Broccoli Sautéed with Onions, Bacon, and Breadcrumbs]

Like the *brocoli à la polonaise*, this could well be a first course or served in place of the salad, or it could accompany poached or scrambled eggs, plain grilled chicken or fish, or pork or veal chops. In this recipe you may blanch the broccoli in advance, and sauté it just before serving.

[*For 1½ to 2 pounds broccoli, serving 4 to 6*]

3 rashers bacon
An 8-in. frying pan, non-stick recommended
3 tbl. white breadcrumbs
3 tbl. finely minced onions
3 tbl. olive oil

1 large clove garlic, mashed
The blanched broccoli
Salt and pepper

Before blanching the broccoli (master recipe, page 446) prepare the following garniture. Cook the bacon until lightly
browned, and drain on paper towels; crumble when crisped
and cool. Sauté the breadcrumbs in the bacon fat, stirring, and
when light brown scrape into a side dish. In the same pan,
cook the onions in the olive oil for 8 to 10 minutes or more,
until tender and translucent; stir in the garlic, and set pan aside.

Just before serving, reheat onions, add the cooked broccoli
pieces, season lightly with salt and pepper, and toss and turn
gently over moderately high heat, shaking and swirling the
pan by its handle. When heated through, add browned
crumbs and crumbled bacon, swirling and tossing for a moment more. Turn out on to a hot dish and serve immediately.

*Brocoli Étuvés au Beurre
[Broccoli Braised in Butter]

When you cannot give broccoli last-minute attention you may
blanch it *al dente*, meaning until it is not quite completely
cooked, pack it into a casserole, and bake it with butter. It
finishes cooking while you are having the first course, but do
not leave it in the oven too long or it will lose its lovely fresh
quality.

[*For 1½ to 2 pounds broccoli, serving 4 to 6*]

½ oz. soft butter
A 2½-pt flameproof casserole or baking dish
The broccoli, blanched for 4 minutes only, page 446
Salt and pepper
2 to 3 oz. melted butter
A round of waxed paper
A cover for the casserole

Smear inside of dish with butter. Arrange cooked broccoli
stalks in bottom of dish, season lightly and dribble on ⅓ of the
butter. Arrange broccoli heads attractively on top, season, and
dribble on the rest of the butter. Lay waxed paper on top and

set aside until about 20 minutes before you are ready to serve. Preheat oven to 350°F., Mark 4, in plenty of time. If casserole is heavy, heat on top of the stove. Cover, and set in middle level of oven until broccoli is bubbling hot. Serve as soon as possible, to preserve fresh taste and green colour.

Brocoli Gratinés au Fromage ou à la Milanaise
[Buttered Broccoli Gratinéed with Cheese]

Follow the preceding recipe but add 2 ounces finely grated Parmesan cheese to the ingredients. Sprinkle 2 tablespoons of cheese inside the buttered dish before arranging the broccoli on it, and sprinkle cheese over each layer of broccoli along with the butter. Cover and heat until bubbling in the oven, then set under a low grill for a moment or two to brown cheese lightly.

CHOPPED BROCCOLI
Another solution for the chef-host-butler is to blanch the broccoli, cool it quickly, then chop it and reheat at leisure in one of the following ways.

*Sauté de Brocoli
[Chopped Broccoli Sautéed in Butter]

This very simple way with broccoli is also one of the most delicious, because the hot butter penetrates every surface. As well as being an almost all-purpose vegetable accompaniment, chopped sautéed broccoli may serve as a bed for poached fish fillets, poached eggs, chicken breasts, veal scallops, brains, or sweetbreads; these may then be sauced and, if called for, browned under the grill.

[*For 1½ to 2 pounds fresh broccoli, serving 4 to 6*]

The broccoli, peeled, washed, and blanched as directed in the master recipe, page 446, but for 4 minutes only

Spread the blanched broccoli on a towel to cool. Then chop on a board with a big knife to make pieces between ⅛ and ¼ inch in size. If not to be cooked immediately, refrigerate in a covered bowl.

2 oz. butter (1 to 1½ oz. more if you wish)
A 10- to 12-in. frying pan, non-stick recommended
Salt and pepper to taste

Several minutes before serving, melt the butter in the frying pan over moderately high heat. When bubbling hot, pour in the chopped broccoli and immediately begin shaking and swirling the pan by the handle to toss the broccoli pieces in the butter until well heated through. Sprinkle with salt and pepper, toss a moment more, and turn into a hot dish. Serve immediately.

Brocoli Étuvés à la Crème
[Chopped Broccoli, Simmered in Cream]
Serve this tender, creamy broccoli dish with grilled or roast chicken, sautéed chicken breasts, veal scallops, brains or sweetbreads, or grilled or sautéed fish.

[*For 1½ to 2 pounds fresh broccoli, serving 4 to 6*]

The preceding recipe for blanched chopped broccoli sautéed in 1½ oz.
   butter
½ pt double cream
2 tsp. cornflour in a 2-pt bowl
A wire whisk
A rubber spatula

After the broccoli has been warmed in butter and seasoned, blend 2 tablespoons cream into the cornflour. When smooth, blend in the rest and fold into the broccoli. Simmer, folding gently for 2 to 3 minutes, to cook starch and thicken cream. Taste for seasoning. Turn into a hot vegetable dish and serve immediately.

(†) May be set aside and just heated through before serving.

Gratin de Brocoli, Mornay
[Chopped Broccoli Gratinéed with Cheese Sauce]
This is an especially good recipe to accompany roast turkey or chicken, and a boon for Christmas because you may assemble the whole dish the day before and set it in the oven ½ hour before serving. It also goes well with roast red meats, steaks, chops, and grilled fish or could be the hot entrée at an informal luncheon where you were serving cold ham or poultry, or poached or scrambled eggs.

[*For 1½ to 2 pounds fresh broccoli, serving 4 to 6*]

1. The broccoli and the cheese sauce
The peeled, blanched, and chopped broccoli, sautéed in butter, page 451
2 oz. butter
A heavy-bottomed 4-pt saucepan
3 tbl. flour
½ pt hot milk in a small saucepan (more if needed)
A wooden spoon, wire whisk, and rubber spatula
2 oz. grated cheese, Parmesan and Gruyère mixed (save 3 tbl. for later)
½ tsp. salt or to taste
Big pinch white pepper

Prepare the broccoli and set aside. Make a white sauce as follows, starting with a butter and flour *roux*: melt the butter in the saucepan, blend in the flour, and stir over moderate heat until flour and butter foam together for 2 minutes without browning at all. Remove from heat, and when *roux* stops foaming, vigorously blend in all of the hot milk at once with wire whisk, beating until mixture is perfectly smooth. Return over moderately high heat, stirring with whisk as sauce thickens and comes to the boil. Boil, stirring, for 2 minutes, and remove from heat. Let cool for a moment. Fold in all but 3 tablespoons of the cheese, and salt and pepper to taste.

2. Assembling the dish
A 2½-pt baking dish about 2 ins. deep
1 oz. soft butter

Smear a small piece of butter inside the baking dish and spread 2 to 3 tablespoons of sauce in the bottom. Spread half the

454 A CHOICE OF VEGETABLES

broccoli in the dish, and cover with half the sauce. (If sauce seems too thick for spreading, beat in a little more milk, a spoonful at a time.) Cover with the remaining broccoli and sauce; sprinkle the 3 tablespoons reserved cheese over the sauce. Dot with remaining butter.

(†) Recipe may be completed to this point a day in advance. When cool, cover and refrigerate.

3. Baking: about 30 minutes 375°F., Mark 5

About 30 minutes before serving, place broccoli in upper-third level of preheated oven and bake until bubbling hot and cheese has browned nicely on top. Do not overcook, or broccoli will lose its attractive flavour and texture. You may keep the dish warm for 15 minutes or so in turned-off oven or warming oven, but the sooner you serve it the better the flavour.

Timbales de Brocoli
[Broccoli Moulds]

These are dish custards that are unmoulded for serving as first-course or luncheon dishes, or as an accompaniment to roast chicken or veal, grilled chicken, veal chops, or grilled fish. Use about 1½ pounds peeled, blanched, and chopped broccoli in place of the courgettes on page 488, or in place of the asparagus in Volume 1, page 474.

Aubergines

Aubergines, like broccoli, are in season all year round, and are marvellously versatile vegetables. You may bake, grill, boil, sauté, stuff, soufflé, and gratiné aubergines, as well as serve them hot, cold, alone, or together with meat, fish, fowl, or other vegetables. Volume I contains a splendid aubergine stuffed with mushrooms, and *moussaka* and *ratatouille*, the first a marvellous mould of aubergine and lamb, and the second a

Provençal casserole of aubergines, courgettes, tomatoes, and onions. Here you will find it grilled, cold *à la grecque* with tomatoes and herbs, sautéed in various unusual forms, baked with meat, with cheese, and souffléed. Aubergines will also turn up in other parts of this book, as a filling, stuffing, or accompaniment to many a main dish.

HOW TO BUY AUBERGINES

Although you will occasionally see baby aubergines and small sizes, either round or egg-shaped, almost the entire large-scale commercially raised crop consists of the big, dark-purple varieties weighing 1 to 2 pounds. They are roundish, egg-shaped or bell-shaped.

Size is no signal of quality, because all aubergines are harvested when the fruit is still immature – the seeds sparse and soft, the flesh firm. When aubergines mature, the flesh softens, the seeds grow larger and tougher, and both seeds and flesh turn bitter.

When you are buying aubergines, therefore, look at each one carefully all over, which means that if they are packed in a plastic-covered carton you must open it up. Make sure that the skin is sleek and shiny, that it is taut over the flesh, that there are no pockmarks, brown spots, or wrinkles anywhere. Press each fruit gently all over to be sure the flesh is firm and resistant. Avoid any aubergine that is dull, wrinkled, blemished, or even slightly soft, because the flesh will have an off-flavour you can do nothing to correct.

STORING AUBERGINES

Unlike most other vegetables, aubergines store best at 45° to 50°F., but even under these conditions the storage limit is only about 10 days. Unless you have a cold-room, therefore, buy aubergines only a day or two before you plan to cook them. In a cool kitchen, keep them in a plastic bag with a damp paper towel for humidity; in summer, you will have to refrigerate them. Under refrigeration, however, they will develop surface pitting and brown spots within 4 to 5 days, and begin to soften.

You may have wondered why a particular aubergine recipe sometimes comes off perfectly and at other times does not have the tender delicious quality you remembered before. The answer is probably either that the aubergine was not really firm, fresh, and immature when you bought it, or that it had been kept too long under refrigerated storage.

PRELIMINARIES TO COOKING: PEELING, SALTING, BLANCHING

Aubergine skin is edible when cooked long enough, as in a *moussaka*, gratinéed dish, or other recipe involving an hour in the oven. For the rapidly done sautés and for aubergine simmered *à la grecque*, cooking is so short that the skin remains rather tough and stringy.

Most aubergine recipes direct that it be either macerated in salt or blanched in boiling salted water before the main cooking begins. There are three reasons for this. The first is to eliminate the slight bitterness usually present in even the youngest and freshest specimens, the second is to remove excess vegetable water that otherwise exudes during cooking, and the final one is to prevent the aubergine from absorbing too much oil or fat. You will find, in a comparison of sautés, that plain cubed aubergine will blot up 3 times more sautéing oil than blanched aubergine, that salted aubergine will use half as much as plain aubergine, and that blanched aubergine, which requires the least oil, will be the most tender of the three but have slightly less flavour. We therefore recommend salting in most recipes, and blanching only when we have found it is the best solution.

Salting, however, requires a wait of 30 minutes while the excess vegetable water slowly works its way out of the flesh, and if you are in a tearing hurry do not hesitate to blanch. To do so, drop the aubergine into salted boiling water after you have peeled and cubed or sliced it; boil slowly, uncovered, for 3 to 5 minutes or until it is almost tender but still holds its shape, then proceed with the recipe.

Aubergines en Tranches, Gratinées
[Grilled Aubergine Slices]

Grilling and sautéing are by far the easiest ways of cooking aubergine, and thick slices of grilled aubergine are attractive to serve. Actually, the following recipe is a combination of baking, to soften the aubergine, then grilling, with a topping of tomatoes and breadcrumbs. Serve with steaks, chops, roast lamb, grilled fish or chicken, or as a garnish with poached, scrambled, or fried eggs.

[*For 4 people*]

1. Salting the aubergines

2 to 2½ lb. fresh, shiny, firm, unblemished aubergines
A large tray
1½ tsp. salt
Paper towels

Cut off cap, shave nubbin off bottom, and wash the aubergines, but do not peel. You are now to cut them into slices all somewhat the same dimension, 3 to 4 inches long, 2 inches wide, and ½ to ¾ inch thick. If you have large ones, for instance, cut the centre slices into 4, other sizes into 3 or 2. Arrange on tray. Sprinkle salt on both sides and let sit for 20 to 30 minutes. Drain and press dry with paper towels.

2. Preliminary baking of the aubergines: oven preheated to 400°F., Mark 6

¼ pt olive oil
Either: 1 or 2 cloves garlic, mashed;
Or: 3 tbl. minced shallots or spring onions
¼ to ½ tsp. mixed herbs (*herbes de Provence* or thyme, oregano, and rosemary)
Big pinch pepper
A 4-in. bowl
A 14-in. pizza tray or Swiss-roll tin
A cover, or aluminium foil

Blend the oil, the garlic or shallots or spring onions, and the herbs and pepper in the bowl, dip each slice into the mixture, drain, and arrange slices slightly overlapping on pizza tray or tin. Reserve remaining oil mixture for later. Cover aubergine and bake in middle level of preheated 400°F., Mark 6 oven for 10 to 15 minutes, until aubergine is almost but not quite tender; do not let it overcook and turn limp, but it must cook long enough to soften.

3. Tomato and breadcrumb topping

5 to 6 medium tomatoes, peeled, seeded, juiced, and chopped
⅛ tsp. salt
Big pinch pepper
4 tbl. dry white breadcrumbs
More oil if needed

When you have prepared the tomatoes, toss gently in a bowl with salt and pepper; drain in a few minutes and spread over the aubergine slices. Sprinkle lightly with breadcrumbs and drizzle on oil.

(†) Recipe may be prepared an hour in advance to this point. Cover loosely and set aside.

4. Grilling and serving

A hot serving platter, or the meat platter
A flexible-blade spatula

About 5 minutes before serving, set aubergine 4 to 5 inches under a moderately hot grill and let brown slowly to finish cooking. Arrange on platter, again overlapping slices slightly in an attractive design. Serve as soon as possible because aubergine will soften if kept warm.

Other suggestions for toppings

Sprinkle aubergine with a mixture of breadcrumbs, cheese, and parsley, and finish with drops of oil, or mask the slices with the thick cheese sauce described for *brocoli mornay* on page 453, and top with a sprinkling of cheese and melted butter. In either case, reheat and brown under a moderate grill as described in the preceding step.

*Aubergines en Persillade, Sautées

[Sautéed Aubergines Garnished with Garlic, Breadcrumbs, and Herbs]

Sautéed aubergine is easier to serve than the preceding grilled aubergine, and certainly easier to finish off at the last moment. It also lends itself to several variations, as you will see. Serve sautéed aubergine with steaks, chops, roast lamb, grilled fish, or grilled chicken. Whole, small baked tomatoes are probably the most attractive additional accompaniment.

[For 4 to 6 people]

1. Preparing the aubergines

2 lb. shiny, firm, unblemished aubergines
A 5-pt mixing bowl
1½ tsp. salt
A colander
Paper towels

Peel the aubergines. Cut into lengthwise slices ¾ inch thick, cut slices into ¾-inch strips, and the strips into ¾-inch cubes. Toss in the bowl with the salt and let stand 20 to 30 minutes. Just before sautéing, drain in colander and pat dry in paper towels.

2. Sautéing the aubergines

Olive oil or cooking oil
A 12-in. frying pan, preferably non-stick (or an 8-in. pan for sautéing in 2 batches)
The colander set over the drained mixing bowl

Pour a ⅛-inch layer of oil into the pan and heat until very hot but not smoking. Add enough aubergine to make 1 layer. Toss and turn the aubergine frequently, shaking and swirling the pan by its handle; sauté for 5 to 8 minutes until aubergine is tender and very lightly browned. (Aubergine burns easily, and you must keep your eye on it. If it has browned but is not tender, lower heat and cover the pan for 2 to 3 minutes until it is tender.) Drain in colander and return any accumulated oil from bowl to frying pan. Continue with the rest of the aubergine if you are sautéing in several batches.

3. The *persillade*

The oil
3 tbl. coarse, dry white breadcrumbs
2 tbl. minced shallots or spring onions
1 to 2 large cloves of garlic, mashed or finely minced
3 tbl. fresh chopped parsley
Optional other herbs, such as thyme, basil, or oregano
A hot serving dish

Add more oil to pan to make about 2 tablespoons. Heat to very hot, add the breadcrumbs, and toss for a minute or two to brown lightly. Then add the shallots or spring onions and garlic, and toss a moment more.

(†) Recipe may be completed in advance to this point.

Just before serving, reheat pan with breadcrumb mixture, add aubergine, and toss over moderately high heat until aubergine is sizzling. Toss with parsley and optional herbs, turn into hot dish, and serve immediately.

Aubergines en Persillade, Gratinées
[Aubergines Baked with Parsley, Garlic, and *Béchamel*]
Sautéed aubergines tossed with garlic and parsley then folded into a *béchamel* sauce and browned in the oven make a fine accompaniment to steaks, chops, hamburgers, grilled chicken, or fish.

[*For 4 to 6 people*]

Ingredients for 2 lb. aubergines in the preceding master recipe, steps
    1, 2, and 3

Peel, cube, salt, and drain the aubergines; then sauté in oil until lightly browned. Reserve the breadcrumbs, tossing the aubergine with only the shallots or spring onions, garlic, and herbs. Set aside.

For ¾ pint *béchamel*

2 oz. butter
A heavy 3-pt saucepan
5 tbl. flour

A wooden spoon and a wire whisk
¾ pt milk heated in a small saucepan
Salt and pepper to taste
A rubber spatula
A lightly buttered 2½-pt baking dish about 1½ ins. deep
2 to 3 tbl. of the reserved breadcrumbs
½ oz. melted butter

For the *béchamel* sauce (which you can make while the aubergine macerates), melt the butter in the saucepan, blend in the flour, and stir over moderate heat until flour and butter foam together for 2 minutes without browning at all. Remove this *roux* from heat, and when it stops bubbling, vigorously blend in all of the hot milk at once with wire whisk, beating until mixture is perfectly smooth. Return over moderately high heat, stirring with whisk as sauce thickens and comes to the boil. Boil, stirring, for 2 minutes, season lightly to taste, and remove from heat. Sauce should be quite thick; if too thick for easy spreading, beat in more milk by droplets. (If done ahead, clean off sides of pan and press a sheet of plastic wrap on surface of sauce to prevent a skin from forming.)

Spread a ⅛-inch layer of sauce in the bottom of the baking dish with spatula, spread half the aubergine on top, and cover with half the sauce. Spread rest of aubergine over this and cover with the last of the sauce. Sprinkle the crumbs on top and dribble melted butter over the crumbs.

(†) Recipe may be completed to this point and set aside.

To gratiné, if sauce and aubergine are still warm, set 4 to 5 inches under a moderately hot grill for several minutes, until aubergine is bubbling and crumbs have browned lightly. Otherwise bake in upper third of a 425°F., Mark 7 oven for 15 to 20 minutes, but do not overcook.

Soufflé d'Aubergines en Persillade
[Aubergine Soufflé]
Fold beaten egg whites into the preceding sautéed and sauced aubergine, and you turn it into a soufflé – not the airy cheese type, of course, but something that puffs dramatically in a wide

baking dish with removable collar. Serve it, along with a fine tomato sauce, to accompany boiled beef, roast lamb, grilled or roast chicken, or let it be the main course for an informal luncheon.

[*For 8 servings*]

The soufflé base

Ingredients for the preceding 2 lb. of sautéed aubergines baked in *béchamel*

Following the preceding recipe, peel, cube, salt, drain, and dry the aubergines; sauté in oil until thoroughly tender and very lightly browned. Toss with the shallots or spring onions and garlic.

Chop rather roughly with a big knife on a board. Fold into the pan of *béchamel* sauce, along with the chopped parsley. Carefully correct seasoning.

(†) May be completed in advance to this point; clean off sides of pan and lay a sheet of plastic wrap on top of the sauce. You may also fill the mould (next step), cover with a bowl, and bake an hour later.

Assembling and baking: 25 to 30 minutes at 400°F., Mark 6

½ oz. soft butter
2½- to 3-pt baking dish about 2 ins. deep (such as a round one 10 to
   11 ins. in diameter, or a casserole)
3 tbl. grated Parmesan cheese
Waxed paper
Heavy aluminium foil and 2 straight pins
3 egg yolks
5 egg whites
½ to ¾ pt tomato sauce, page 468, or the fresh tomato *coulis*, Volume I,
   page 96

Preheat oven in time for baking. Smear butter inside baking dish, sprinkle cheese inside to coat bottom and sides. Shake or knock out excess cheese on to waxed paper and reserve. Encircle circumference of dish with a double thickness of well-buttered aluminium foil secured by pins; foil should rise 1½ inches above rim of dish. Reheat soufflé base, folding over moderate heat. Stir in the egg yolks. Beat the egg whites to stiff peaks (directions are on page 685); stir ¼ of them into the soufflé base along with all but 1 tablespoon of the reserved Parmesan cheese. Scoop rest of egg whites on top of soufflé base and delicately fold in with a rubber spatula.

Turn the mixture into the prepared dish. Sprinkle on the remaining cheese and set soufflé immediately in lower third of preheated oven. Bake for 25 to 30 minutes until soufflé has risen about double and is nicely browned. (If served as soon as it has risen, the inside will be soft and the soufflé will sink rapidly; if baked 5 minutes more, the soufflé will be drier but will hold up longer. Follow your own preference, but these additional minutes give you some leeway.)

As soon as the soufflé is done, remove from oven, undo aluminium collar, and serve immediately, accompanied by the tomato sauce in a warm bowl.

Pistouille
[Sautéed Aubergines with Tomatoes, Peppers, Garlic and Basil]

Pistou, a Provençal purée of fresh garlic and basil, is stirred into sautéed aubergines that have simmered with tomatoes, peppers, and onions, making a dish reminiscent of that famous Mediterranean medley, *ratatouille*, but much easier to produce. Good hot or cold, *pistouille* can be served with grilled fish, grilled chicken, roasts, steaks, chops, cold roast pork, veal, or lamb, and any left-overs can stuff eggs, tomatoes, or other vegetables.

Note: This dish is naturally at its best when fresh basil and local tomatoes are in season. Out of season, use fresh tomatoes plus a tablespoon or so of tinned tomato sauce or purée, and if you cannot find fragrant-smelling dried basil, use oregano.

[*For 4 to 6 people*]

Ingredients for salting and sautéing 2 lb. aubergines, as in the master recipe, steps 1 and 2, page 459

Peel, salt, drain, dry, and then sauté the aubergines in oil until lightly browned as described in the master recipe.

The onion, pepper, and tomato garnish

1 medium onion, minced
1 medium green bell pepper, diced
2 tbl. olive oil
A 4-pt saucepan or another frying pan
2 lb. tomatoes, peeled, seeded, juiced, and chopped

While the aubergine is macerating in salt, cook the onion and pepper in oil in the pan for 10 to 15 minutes, until tender and translucent but not brown. Add the tomato pulp, cover pan, and simmer 5 minutes to render its juice; uncover pan and simmer over moderate heat for 5 minutes or more until juices have almost entirely evaporated. Set aside.

When aubergine has been sautéed and drained, return it to the frying pan with the tomato mixture and simmer uncovered for about 10 minutes to blend flavours and evaporate more liquid. Mixture should form a thick mass.

The *pistou*

2 large cloves of garlic
A garlic press
12 to 14 large, fresh basil leaves, minced (or about ½ tbl. dried basil or oregano)
A small bowl and a pestle, or small wooden spoon
3 tbl. fresh minced parsley

Purée garlic through press, then mash with the basil or oregano in the bowl to make a smooth paste; fold into the hot aubergine.

(†) May be completed to this point. Set aside.

Reheat just before serving, correct seasoning, and fold in the parsley.

To Serve Cold

2 to 3 tomatoes
Salt and pepper
3 tbl. fresh minced parsley
½ tbl. olive oil

Whether the aubergine is cooked and cooled or left over, a little ripe tomato will freshen the taste. Peel, seed, and juice the tomatoes; dice the pulp. Place in a bowl and fold with the seasonings, parsley, and oil. Let stand 10 minutes, drain, and fold into the aubergine.

Aubergines en Pistouille, Froides
[Cold Aubergines *à la Grecque* with Tomatoes and Basil]

Much the same as cold *pistouille*, but with a more piquant flavour, is aubergine simmered in a *court bouillon*, turned briefly in oil to enhance its flavour, then folded into tomatoes that have also cooked in the *court bouillon*. A final touch is the *pistou* of garlic and basil, which makes this an especially good cold hors d'œuvre with sardines, tuna, hard-boiled eggs, anchovies, olives, or other Provençal trimmings.

For the *court bouillon*

1¼ pts water in a 5-pt stainless saucepan
1½ tbl. lemon juice
3 tbl. olive oil
1½ tsp. salt
6 coriander seeds
¼ tsp. thyme
1 bay leaf
2 large cloves garlic, mashed
2 lb. firm, fresh, shiny aubergines
A colander set over a bowl
Olive oil
A heavy non-stick frying pan (10 to 12 ins. in diameter if possible)
A serving dish

Combine the *court bouillon* ingredients in the saucepan and simmer at least 5 minutes, or while you are preparing the aubergines. Peel aubergines and cut into ¾-inch cubes. Place half in the simmering *court bouillon*, bring to the boil, and simmer 5 minutes. Drain into bowl, return *court bouillon* to pan, and simmer the rest of the aubergine. Drain, return *court bouillon* again to pan, boil down rapidly to ½ pint, and reserve. Meanwhile, pour a $\frac{1}{16}$-inch layer of oil into frying pan and sauté drained aubergine (adding only half if pan is small), using moderately high heat. Shake and swirl the pan frequently by its handle to toss the aubergine, and sauté for several minutes, until it is tender but not browned. Turn into serving dish, leaving oil in pan.

3 to 4 tbl. minced shallots or spring onions
1½ lb. (6 medium) tomatoes, peeled, seeded, juiced, and cut into ½-in. dice
1 or 2 cloves garlic
A garlic press
2 tbl. fresh basil, minced (or about ½ tbl. dried basil or oregano)
3 tbl. fresh minced parsley

Stir the shallots or spring onions into the frying pan and cook for a moment, then add the tomatoes and the reduced *court bouillon*. Boil slowly for 5 minutes, then raise heat and boil rapidly until liquid has almost evaporated and tomatoes are quite thick. Correct seasoning. Purée garlic through press into a small bowl; using a wooden spoon, mash with herbs to make a smooth paste; fold this *pistou* into the hot tomatoes. Then fold the tomatoes into the aubergines. When cold, cover and chill. Sprinkle on the parsley before serving.

La Tentation de Bramafam

[Aubergine Caviare with Walnuts – A Cold Spread or Filling]
Recipes for aubergine caviare have been around for years, but this is the only one we know that combines aubergine and walnuts. Tremendously easy to do in the electric mixer, this is something you can keep on hand in the refrigerator for a week or more, and use on toast or crackers, or as a dip for cocktail titbits, as a filling for hard-boiled eggs or tomato shells, or to pass with cold meats or chicken.

About 2 lb. firm, shiny, unblemished aubergines
An electic mixer
7 to 8 oz. ground walnuts (grind them in an electric blender)
¾ tsp. salt, and more as needed
⅛ tsp. pepper
1 to 4 large cloves garlic, puréed in a press

4 to 6 squirts Tabasco sauce
¼ tsp. ground allspice
1 tsp. freshly grated ginger root or ¼ tsp. powdered ginger
5 to 8 tbl. olive oil
Optional, to bring out flavour: ½ tsp. monosodium glutamate

Preheat oven to 425°F., Mark 7. Cut off green caps and place aubergines in a shallow roasting dish or pie plate. Bake 30 to 35 minutes or until thoroughly soft to the touch. Cut in half lengthwise and scoop flesh into bowl of mixer. Beat several minutes at high speed to purée the aubergine flesh, then beat in the ground walnuts, salt, pepper, garlic to taste, Tabasco, allspice, and ginger. By driblets, as though making mayonnaise, beat in enough oil to make a creamy mass, but not so much as to thin the mixture; it should hold its shape softly when lifted with a spoon. Taste carefully; correct seasoning, adding the monosodium glutamate if you wish, and the *tentation* is ready to use.

(†) Will keep several days under refrigeration; may be frozen.

*Gratin d'Aubergines, Provençal
[Sliced Aubergines Baked with Cheese and Tomatoes]
When you have the time for it, this is a most attractive way to serve aubergines: they are sliced but the peel is left on, and the slices are arranged upright in the baking dish with tomatoes and cheese in between. When baked, the purple-skinned slices form dark ripples separated by hints of red and brown, and the same effect is carried over on to the plates when you serve. This is a particularly good dish to go with roast lamb or veal.

Note: Fresh tomato sauce, *coulis de tomates*, in Volume I, page 96, is the most desirable one here, but the following sauce with tinned Italian tomatoes is an excellent alternative. We prefer tinned tomatoes to tomato purée because they are less concentrated and the resulting sauce, we think, tastes more like the fresh.

[*For 4 to 6 servings*]

1. The tomato sauce (using tinned tomatoes): for about ½ pint

2 large onions, minced
2 tbl. olive oil or cooking oil
A heavy bottomed 3-pt saucepan with cover
A 1-lb. tin of peeled Italian-style plum (pear-shaped) tomatoes
A sieve set over a bowl
1 bay leaf
¼ tsp. thyme or oregano
A 1-in. piece of dried orange peel or ¼ tsp. bottled dried peel
A pinch of saffron threads
1 large clove garlic, mashed
¼ tsp. salt

Stir the onions into the oil, cover pan, and cook over low heat, stirring occasionally, for 8 to 10 minutes or until onions are tender and translucent but not browned. Meanwhile drain the tomatoes, collecting their juice in the bowl; pour juice back into the tin and reserve. Rub the tomatoes through the sieve to eliminate seeds. When onions are tender, stir in the sieved tomato pulp and the herbs, orange peel, saffron, garlic, and salt. Cover pan loosely and simmer, stirring occasionally, and adding a little of the tomato juice if sauce becomes too thick. Let sauce simmer at least 30 minutes, although a total of 45 to 60 minutes will make it even better. Taste carefully and correct seasoning. Sauce should be thick enough to hold its shape softly in a spoon.

(†) May be made several days in advance and refrigerated; may be frozen.

2. Blanching and sautéing the aubergines

2 lb. firm, fresh, shiny aubergines

A

Cut off green caps, and wash the aubergines but do not peel them. Halve or quarter them (A), depending on size, and cut into slices $\frac{3}{8}$ inch thick and about 2 inches from skin side to bottom of slice.

A large saucepan of boiling salted water (1 tsp. salt per pt)
A skimmer or slotted spoon
A tray covered with several thicknesses of paper towelling, and additional paper towels
Olive oil or cooking oil
A large (11-in.) frying pan, preferably non-stick
A flexible-blade spatula
A second tray or a platter to hold sautéed aubergine

A dozen slices or so at a time, blanch in the boiling water for 2 minutes – barely to soften, not to cook through; dip out with skimmer or spoon, and drain on paper towels.

Pat tops of slices dry with towels. Pour a $\frac{1}{8}$-inch layer of oil into frying pan; heat to very hot but not smoking. Sauté for a minute as many slices in pan as will fit in 1 layer, on each side, barely browning them, and transfer to second tray. Continue with rest of slices, adding more oil to pan as necessary. (Although all of this is somewhat of a nuisance, it is this step that gives the final dish its distinction.)

3. Assembling

An oiled 2- to $2\frac{1}{2}$-pt flameproof *gratin* dish, such as an oval one 10 to 11 ins. long and 2 ins. deep
About 4 oz. Gruyère cheese sliced $\frac{1}{16}$ in. thick
The reserved tomato juice
Aluminium foil

Arrange the aubergine slices purple side uppermost in overlapping rows, each row spread with tomato sauce and covered with slices of cheese as shown (B).

If you need more room, push the rows more closely together as you go; if you need less, let them lie flatter. Pour in about $\frac{1}{4}$ pint of the tomato juice, enough to come $\frac{1}{2}$ to $\frac{2}{3}$ the way up the aubergine. Cover closely with the foil.

(†) May be prepared in advance to this point; refrigerate if you are not going to bake within an hour or so.

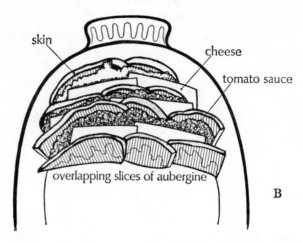

skin
cheese
tomato sauce
overlapping slices of aubergine
B

4. Baking and serving: preheat oven to 375°F., Mark 5

Heat briefly on top of stove just until contents start to bubble, then bake for 45 minutes to an hour in the middle level of the preheated oven. Aubergine is done when the slices are tender and juices have thickened but are not quite absorbed. Uncover for last 10 minutes of baking so that cheese will brown and liquid will thicken more. (Add more tomato juice if there is danger of aubergine drying out before it is done.) Serve bubbling hot.

(†) This may be baked well in advance of serving, and then reheated. If so, take it out of the oven before liquid is quite absorbed, so there will be enough to moisten the aubergine during its reheating. Any left-overs may be transferred to a smaller dish and reheated under a low grill.

Gratin d'Aubergines Farcies
[Main-course Aubergine and Tomato Casserole for Left-over Meat]

Sautéed sliced aubergines, an excellent tomato sauce, and grated cheese are just the elements for turning yesterday's roast into a splendid new main course. Turkey, veal, or pork respond especially well to this treatment. The meat is minced and flavoured, while the other elements are the same as in the preceding recipe. You may arrange the aubergine in upright slices if you wish to take the time, or lay them flat as suggested here and build the casserole in layers. Serve this hot with French bread and a chilled rosé wine, and follow with a tossed green salad. It is also delicious served cold.

Note: As in most recipes of this type, exact proportions are not of vital importance. If you have less or more meat, add fewer or more onions and the other ingredients that flavour it.

[For 6 to 8 people]

The meat mixture

2 large onions, minced
2 tbl. olive oil or cooking oil
An 8-in. frying pan with cover

Stir the onions into the oil, cover the pan, and cook over low heat, stirring occasionally, for 8 to 10 minutes or until onions are tender. Raise heat and stir to brown onions lightly for 2 to 3 minutes.

About 1 lb minced cooked veal, pork, or turkey (previously trimmed of all fat, skin, and gristle)
About ¼ lb. minced baked or boiled ham, or ready-to-cook packaged ham slice (you may include some of the fat)
About ¼ tsp. of whatever herb you prefer and are using in the tomato sauce (thyme, oregano, fresh basil, rosemary)
¼ pt thickened gravy from the roast, or ¼ pt stock or bouillon blended with 1½ tsp. cornflour
1 clove garlic, mashed
Salt and pepper to taste
1 egg
3 to 4 tbl. chopped fresh parsley

Stir the minced meat into the onions, along with the herbs, the gravy or bouillon, and garlic. Simmer 2 to 3 minutes to blend flavours. Season carefully with salt and pepper to taste, and a little more of the herb if you think it necessary. Let cool while you are completing other parts of the recipe. When tepid or cold, blend in the egg and the parsley.

Assembling the casserole

Ingredients for the 2 lb. sliced, blanched, and sautéed aubergines in
  preceding recipe, but ¾ pt tomato sauce, and the tomato juice and
  4 oz. coarsely grated Gruyère cheese (or 3 oz. Parmesan if you prefer)
An oiled 5-pt baking dish or casserole such as a round earthenware one
  10 ins. in diameter at the top and 3 ins. deep
2 tbl. coarse white breadcrumbs, fresh or stale
2 tbl. olive oil or melted butter
A rubber spatula
½ pt tomato juice
A cover for the casserole, or aluminium foil

For a round casserole 10 by 3 inches, you will have 4 layers
each of aubergine, meat, tomato sauce, and cheese. Arrange
them, then, in the casserole in that order, ending with a mixture of cheese and breadcrumbs tossed together. Dribble olive
oil or melted butter over the top. Drawing edges of ingredients ¼ inch towards centre of casserole in several places, pour
in the ½ pint of tomato juice.

(†) May be assembled a day in advance of baking.

Baking and serving: about 1¼ hours at 375°F., Mark 5

Cover, heat to simmer on top of stove, and bake as directed
in step 4 of preceding master recipe.

(†) May be baked in advance and reheated.

Two Recipes for Greens

Blettes Gratinées
[Swiss Chard Gratinéed with Cheese Sauce]

This way of serving chard brings out its special flavour, and
makes it a most attractive accompaniment to roast beef or
chicken. Here both the long white stems and the large green
leaves are used, but they are cooked separately before being
combined.

[*For 6 to 8 servings*]

1. Preparing the chard

About 10 stalks (2 bunches) fresh chard

Cut the green part of the leaves off the white of the stalk that runs up the centre of the leaves. Wash leaves and set aside. Trim off any discoloured bits and ends, wash the long white stalks thoroughly, and cut into ¼-inch slices.

2. Cooking the white stalks

1 oz. flour
A heavy-bottomed 4-pt saucepan (non-stick is useful)
A wire whisk
¼ pt cold water and 1 pt hot water
1 tsp. salt
1 tbl. lemon juice
The sliced stalks
A wooden spoon
A sieve set over a bowl

Place flour in saucepan. Beating with wire whisk, gradually blend in the cold water to make a smooth mixture. Beat in the hot water, salt, and lemon juice, and bring to the simmer, stirring. Add chard stalks and simmer about 30 minutes or until they are tender, stirring occasionally, and adding a little more water, if necessary, to prevent scorching. Drain, reserving cooking liquid. (You will note that the chard stalks acquire a subtle flavour when finally tender, and that they leave a sticky film on the bottom of the pan.)

3. Cooking the green leaves

The green leaves
A large pan of boiling salted water
A colander

While the stalks are simmering, drop the leaves into the boiling water, bring rapidly back to the boil, and boil uncovered for 5 to 6 minutes or until leaves are fairly tender. Drain, refresh in cold water, squeeze dry a handful at a time, and chop. Mix them into the cooked stalks.

4. Sauce and assembly

1 egg yolk
3 tbl. double cream
A clean saucepan
The stalk cooking liquid (plus milk if necessary to make ¾ pt)
Salt and pepper to taste
A buttered 2- to 2½-pt baking dish about 2 ins. deep
1 oz. grated Parmesan cheese
½ oz. butter

Blend the egg yolk and cream in the saucepan with a wire whisk, then gradually blend in the stalk cooking liquid. Bring to the simmer, stirring, and simmer 1 minute. Correct seasoning. Spoon a layer on to the bottom of the baking dish. Taste the cooked stalks and leaves, and season if necessary. Spread half in the dish, spread on half the sauce and half the cheese. Repeat with the remaining chard, sauce, and cheese and top with the butter, cut into dots.

(†) May be completed a day before serving; cover with plastic and refrigerate.

5. Serving

If chard is still warm, set under a low grill until just beginning to bubble and top is nicely browned. If cold, set in upper third of preheated 375°F., Mark 5 oven for about 30 minutes just until bubbling hot and top has browned.

Gratin d'Épinards aux Oignons
[Spinach Braised with Onions]

This is creamed spinach with character, which will stand up to steaks, chops, roasts, and grilled fish; you can also serve it with poached eggs and *croûtons*. Although fresh is best, frozen spinach is very successful done this way, as are other greens such as sorrel, chard, and kale.

[*For 4 people*]

2 large onions, minced
3 tbl. olive oil
An 8-in. heavy-bottomed non-stick or enamelled frying pan
Optional: 1 to 2 large cloves garlic, mashed
2 lb. fresh spinach boiled 3 minutes, drained, squeezed dry, and chopped
2 tbl. flour
½ pt hot milk
Salt and pepper to taste
2 to 4 tbl. double cream

Cook the onions in the oil for 8 to 10 minutes or more until tender and just beginning to brown lightly. Add optional garlic and cook for a few seconds, then stir in the spinach and cook over moderate heat, stirring, for 2 minutes. Blend in the flour and stir over moderate heat for 2 minutes more. Remove pan from heat; gradually blend in the milk. Set again over heat, bring to the simmer, stirring, and add seasonings to taste. Simmer slowly over low heat for 10 to 15 minutes, stirring occasionally to be sure spinach is not sticking to pan. Spinach is done when it is tender and has absorbed the milk. (If you are doing other greens you may have to cook them longer, and add a little more milk.) Just before serving, taste carefully for seasoning and stir in the cream, a tablespoon at a time.

(†) *Ahead-of-time note:* Set spinach aside after it has simmered in the milk; smooth it with a rubber spatula and spread 2 tablespoons of cream over it. Reheat and finish seasoning just before serving.

Pumpkins

Before Columbus sailed back from his famous voyage of 1492 the squash family was unknown in Europe. The only written accounts date from after his return, and this seems as good a reason as any to trace the origin of squash from the Americas. The American word, 'squash', is of Algonquin origin; the Latin generic is *Cucurbita*, and the French, *courge*.

Le Potiron tout Rond
[Stuffed Pumpkin or Pumpkin Soup served in a Pumpkin]

[*As a vegetable serving 6 to 8*]

3 oz. fresh white breadcrumbs
A roasting pan
A fine, hard, unblemished 4-lb. pumpkin (about 6 ins. in diameter) with
    2 in. stem
½ oz. soft butter
Salt

Spread the breadcrumbs in the roasting pan and let them dry out in a 300°F., Mark 2 oven, stirring occasionally; this will take about 15 minutes. Meanwhile, with a short, stout knife, cut a cover 4 inches in diameter out of the top of the pumpkin. Scrape all the stringy material and seeds from cover and inside of pumpkin (an ice-cream spoon and grapefruit knife are useful for this). Rub inside of pumpkin and the cover with the soft butter and sprinkle lightly with salt.

2 onions, finely minced
3 oz. butter
An 8-in. frying pan
½ tsp. salt
Pinch of pepper and nutmeg
½ tsp. ground sage
2 oz. finely diced or coarsely grated Gruyère cheese
¾ to 1 pt single cream
1 bay leaf
A shallow lightly buttered baking/serving dish to hold the pumpkin

While breadcrumbs are drying, cook the onions in the butter for 8 to 10 minutes over low heat until tender and translucent. Then stir in the crumbs and let them cook slowly for 2 minutes to absorb the butter. Stir in seasonings and sage. Remove from heat and stir in the cheese, then spoon the mixture into the pumpkin. Pour in the cream, adding enough so mixture comes to within ½ inch of pumpkin rim. Lay bay leaf on top and replace cover.

(†) May be prepared in advance to this point.

Baking and serving: baking time about 2 hours

Bake in a preheated 400°F., Mark 6 oven for about 1½ hours, until pumpkin is beginning to soften on the outside and the inside is beginning to bubble. Reduce oven thermostat to 350°F., Mark 4, and bake another ½ hour until pumpkin is tender but still holds its shape solidly. (If pumpkin is browning too much, cover loosely with foil or brown paper.)

(†) May be kept warm in a very low oven for ½ hour at least.

To serve, remove cover and dip into pumpkin with a long-handled spoon, scraping flesh off bottom and sides of pumpkin with each serving of the filling.

Pumpkin Soup

Use a 6- to 7-pound pumpkin and the same ingredients, except replace the cream with enough chicken stock to come within ½ inch of rim. Stir ¼ pint or so of double cream and a handful of chopped parsley into soup just before serving.

Courgettes

HOW TO BUY AND STORE COURGETTES

When you are buying courgettes, look for obviously fresh, clean specimens that feel heavy, are firm to the touch all over, and have skin so tender you can pierce it easily with a fingernail. Fully edible courgettes are immature: when you cut them open the seeds are soft and the tissue surrounding the seeds is moist and crisp. Size indicates quality; beware of foot-long courgettes. However, if you do find yourself with slightly over-age ones you can peel them if the skin seems tough, quarter them lengthwise, and cut out the pulpy core and tough seeds; use only the moist, crisp flesh between skin and core. Store courgettes in a plastic bag in the refrigerator, where they will keep for a week to 10 days if very fresh.

PRELIMINARIES TO COOKING: PEELING, SALTING, BLANCHING

Courgettes need no peeling; their flavour is delicate anyway, and to remove the peel makes them taste even milder. They contain a large amount of vegetable water, and if you do not deal with it in some way before the serious cooking begins, you will have watery casseroles and overcooked sautés. There are two methods for eliminating the water, both equally good because neither removes essential flavour. The easiest method, when you are to sauté chunks of courgettes, for instance, or hollow them out for a stuffing, is to drop the whole vegetables into boiling salted water and boil about 10 minutes, just until the flesh begins to yield to pressure. This is called blanching. The second method, for cut or grated courgettes, is to salt them, let them stand for 20 minutes until the water oozes out of the tissues, then squeeze or pat them dry. We shall use both systems here, starting out with a number of unusual recipes for blanched, sautéed courgettes.

You will notice that only twice is any herb but parsley used in the following recipes, in order that the delicate flavour of the courgettes may be pointed up rather than masked. Preliminary sautéing of the courgettes before saucing or simmering does much to bring out their flavour, and shallots, onions, garlic, and cheese seem to be their natural complements.

WEIGHTS AND MEASURES

One courgette 8 inches long and $1\frac{3}{4}$ inches at its widest diameter weighs 5 to 6 ounces; 3 of this size weigh about 1 pound.

One pound of courgettes will provide 2 to 3 servings as a vegetable garnish.

TO BLANCH WHOLE COURGETTES

The object in blanching courgettes is to boil them just long enough to minimize the oozing out of their vegetable water, but not long enough to cook them quite through. In other words, they are not tender; they hold their shape.

Shave the stem and the tip off each courgette, and scrub thoroughly but not harshly with a vegetable brush under cold, running water to remove any clinging sand or dirt. Plunge them into a large saucepan of boiling, salted water; when water returns again to the boil, boil them slowly, uncovered, for 10 to 12 minutes usually, until the flesh will just yield slightly to pressure. Test each courgette, and remove one by one as they are done, plunging them into cold water. Drain, and the courgettes are ready for sautéing, stuffing, creaming or whatever the following recipes direct. If you are not continuing the recipe until the next day, cover and refrigerate them.

*Courgettes Sautées, Maître d'Hôtel

[Courgettes Sautéed in Butter with Lemon and Parsley]

One of the very easiest and most delicious ways to serve courgettes is to blanch them whole, cut them into large dice, then toss in butter and seasonings, finishing off with lemon juice and parsley. Cooked this way, courgettes go with anything, and they are particularly recommended when you want a simply done green vegetable to go with something rather elaborate, such as *escalopes de veau à la crème* or a chicken fricassee.

[*For 6 people*]

1. Sautéing the courgettes

2 to 2½ lb. blanched courgettes (6 to 7 courgettes 8 by 1¾ ins., for
  example)
Paper towels
About 2 oz. butter
1 to 2 tbl. olive oil or cooking oil
A large (11-in.) non-stick or enamelled frying pan
A cover for the pan
Salt and pepper

After the courgettes have been scrubbed, blanched, and drained as in the directions above, cut them in quarters or sixths lengthwise, depending on their diameter. Cut the lengths crosswise into 1-inch pieces, and pat dry with paper towels. Melt 1 ounce butter with 1 tablespoon oil over high heat.

When butter foam has begun to subside, toss in the courgettes. Toss and turn frequently, shaking and swirling the pan by its handle, for 5 minutes or more, until they are beginning to brown very lightly. By this time, they should be just tender; if not, cover pan and cook over low heat for several minutes. (If you are using a smaller pan, sauté in several batches and turn each batch out on to a dish until all is done, then return them all to the pan.) Toss with salt and pepper to taste.

(†) May be done in advance to this point. Set aside. Reheat to sizzling before continuing.

2. The *maître d'hôtel* seasoning

Drops of fresh lemon juice
Remaining butter from step 1
2 to 3 tbl. fresh minced parsley
A hot serving dish or the meat platter

Just before serving, toss with drops of lemon juice; correct seasoning, and add a little more lemon juice if you feel it is necessary. Then toss with another ounce of butter and the parsley. Turn out on to hot dish and serve immediately.

Courgettes Sautées à la Provençale
[Courgettes Sautéed in Olive Oil with Garlic and Parsley]
Garlic and olive oil are especially good with courgettes and this dish goes well with steaks, chops, grilled chicken, and fish.

2 to 2½ lb. blanched courgettes (page 478), quartered lengthwise and
    cut into 1-in. pieces
3 to 4 tbl. olive oil
Salt and pepper to taste
2 to 3 cloves garlic, mashed or finely minced
Optional: 2 tbl. dry, fairly coarse white breadcrumbs
3 to 4 tbl. fresh minced parsley

Dry the courgette pieces with paper towelling and sauté, tossing frequently, in hot olive oil until just tender and very lightly browned. The moment before serving, toss over moderately high heat with the seasonings, garlic, and optional breadcrumbs, then with the parsley.

Courgettes Gratinées à la Milanaise
[Courgette Pieces Sautéed, then Baked with Cheese]

This is a convenient ahead-of-time preparation that goes nicely with grilled chicken or fish and with steaks or chops.

2 to 2½ lb. courgettes prepared as in either of the 2 preceding recipes
A heavily buttered 2½- to 3-pt baking and serving dish about 2½ ins.
    deep
2 oz. grated Parmesan or Gruyère and Parmesan cheese
2 tbl. melted butter or olive oil

Prepare the courgettes as directed, but leave them slightly undercooked. Sprinkle baking dish with cheese, and fill with layers of courgettes and cheese, dribbling butter or oil over all. If courgettes are still warm, reheat and brown lightly for several minutes under the grill; otherwise, reheat to sizzling for about 15 minutes in upper third of a 425°F., Mark 7 oven.

Courgettes Étuvées à la Crème
[Courgettes Simmered in Cream and Tarragon]

The French word *moelleux* can probably best describe the tender, melting, softly fragrant quality of courgettes warmed in butter and shallots and then simmered in cream and tarragon. This lovely dish goes particularly well with roast chicken and veal.

Preliminary note: Cut the courgettes into any shape you wish. Although the 1-inch pieces used in the preceding recipes are easiest to cook, round slices ½ inch thick or lengthwise strips ⅜ inch thick and 2½ to 3 inches long are attractive to serve. Choose for the cooking an 11- to 12-inch non-stick or enamelled frying pan, straight-sided chicken fryer, electric frying-pan, or casserole. If you decide to cut the courgettes into strips, you will have to do the preliminary sauté in several batches.

[*For 6 people*]

2 to 2½ lb. courgettes blanched whole as directed on page 478
About 2 oz. butter
One of the pans discussed in preceding paragraph
Salt and white pepper
2 tbl. minced shallots or spring onions
1 tsp. fresh minced tarragon or ¼ tsp. dried tarragon (more if needed)
About ½ pt *crème fraîche* or double cream

Cut the blanched courgettes as discussed in preceding paragraph; dry well on paper towels. Over moderate heat, melt enough butter in pan to film it by $\frac{1}{16}$ inch. When butter foam begins to subside, sauté the courgettes for 2 to 3 minutes, tossing or turning, until they are well warmed through but not browning. Season to taste with salt and pepper, sprinkle on the shallots or spring onions and tarragon, and pour in the cream. Simmer for about 10 minutes, basting frequently with the cream, until courgettes are tender and cream has reduced enough to enrobe the pieces.

(†) May be done in advance to this point; set aside uncovered. Reheat to simmer before proceeding.

More cream if needed, and the remaining butter
A hot serving dish
2 tbl. fresh minced parsley plus 1 tsp. fresh minced tarragon if available

Just before serving, taste carefully for seasoning, adding a little more tarragon as well as salt and pepper if needed. If sauce has reduced too much or if it looks slightly curdled, add 2 to 3 tablespoons more cream; bring to simmer, remove from heat, and baste the courgettes to smooth out the sauce. Add also another ½ ounce of butter, basting until it has been absorbed. Arrange on hot dish, sprinkle on the herbs, and serve immediately.

A Slightly Less Fattening Variation

Rather than simmering the courgettes in pure cream, you may use a thin cream sauce, such as that in which the sliced potatoes and basil simmer on page 509.

Courgettes Gratinées, Mornay
[Courgettes Gratinéed with Cheese Sauce]

When you want a creamy vegetable dish to go with grilled meats or roast chicken, and one that you can get ready for the oven well ahead of time, prepare sautéed courgettes with lemon and parsley as in the master recipe on page 479. Then turn to the *brocoli mornay* recipe on page 453; fold the courgettes into the cheese sauce, arrange in a baking dish, and finish it off with cheese and butter in the oven as described for the broccoli.

Courgettes en Persillade, Gratinées
[Courgettes Baked with Garlic, Parsley, and *Béchamel*]

An alternative to the preceding cheese sauce is courgettes sautéed in olive oil with garlic and parsley, as on page 480, then baked in a *béchamel* sauce topped with breadcrumbs and butter, following the aubergine recipe on page 460. The little hint of garlic here is delicious, and the dish goes nicely with steaks, chops, and roast lamb.

Courgettes en Pistouille
[Courgettes with Tomatoes, Peppers, Garlic, and Basil]

Here sautéed courgettes are simmered in a mixture of cooked onions, peppers, and tomatoes, and given a final *pistou* flavouring of garlic and basil. This goes hot with grilled fish, chicken, roasts, steaks, and chops, and cold on picnics. Follow the recipe in the aubergine section on page 463, substituting blanched, sautéed courgette pieces for aubergine.

TO GRATE AND SALT COURGETTES

An interesting and easy way to serve courgettes is to grate them, salt them so the vegetable water runs out, squeeze gently dry, and sauté in butter or olive oil for a few minutes until tender. You can then serve the vegetable as it is, simmer it with cream, bake it in a sauce, or turn it into a moulded custard.

The preliminary sauté gives added flavour, as well as removing extra vegetable water. Anyone eating grated courgettes for the first time is almost certain to think it is a remarkable new vegetable.

Shave the stem and the tip off each courgette, scrub the vegetable thoroughly but not harshly with a brush under cold running water to remove any clinging sand or dirt. If vegetables are large, halve or quarter them. If seeds are large and at all tough, and surrounding flesh is coarse rather than moist and crisp, cut out and discard the cores. Rub the courgette against the coarse side of a grater, and place grated flesh in a colander set over a bowl. For each 1 pound of grated courgette, toss with 1 teaspoon of salt, mixing thoroughly. Let drain 3 or 4 minutes, or until you are ready to proceed. Just before cooking, squeeze a handful dry and taste. If by any chance the courgette is too salty, rinse in a large bowl of cold water, taste again; rinse and drain again if necessary. Then squeeze gently by handfuls, letting juices run back into bowl. Dry on paper towels. The courgettes will not be fluffy; they are still dampish, but the excess liquid is out.

The pale-green, slightly saline juice drained and squeezed out of the courgettes has a certain faint flavour that can find its uses in vegetable soups, canned soups, or vegetable sauces.

*Courgettes Rapées, Sautées
[Grated Courgettes Sautéed in Butter and Shallots]

This is the base recipe for sautéed grated courgettes. Serve it as it is, with the addition of a little more butter, or turn it into one of the variations that follow. Like the blanched and sautéed courgette pieces, this recipe goes with anything and is particularly useful when you want a rather neutral but attractive green accompaniment to creamed dishes like sweetbreads and elaborate soles in white wine sauces. You may also use it rather than spinach as a bed for poached eggs in hollandaise sauce, creamed chicken, and their like.

[*For 4 to 6 servings*]

1. Preliminary sautéing

2 to $2\frac{1}{2}$ lb. courgettes (6 to 7 courgettes 8 by $1\frac{3}{4}$ ins., for example)
1 oz. butter
1 tbl. olive oil or cooking oil
A large (11-in.) non-stick or enamelled frying pan
2 to 3 tbl. minced shallots or spring onions
A cover for the pan if needed

Trim, wash, grate, salt, squeeze, and dry the courgettes as directed in notes preceding this recipe. Melt the butter with the olive oil over moderate heat, stir in the shallots or spring onions, and cook for a moment, then raise heat to moderately high. When butter foam has begun to subside, add courgettes. Toss and turn frequently for 4 to 5 minutes, shaking and swirling the pan by its handle. Courgettes are ready to serve as soon as they are tender; taste to check. (If you wish, you may cover the pan and finish cooking for a few more minutes over low heat.)

(†) Courgettes may be completed to this point several hours in advance of serving. Set aside uncovered; cover when cool, and reheat before proceeding.

2. Final flavouring and serving

More salt if needed, and white pepper
1 to $1\frac{1}{2}$ oz. soft butter, more if you wish
A rubber spatula
A hot serving dish

Shortly before serving, reheat the courgettes, tossing and turning them. Taste carefully for seasoning. Remove from heat and fold in the butter, a small piece at a time, with rubber spatula. Turn into hot dish and serve immediately.

Courgettes Rapées à la Crème
[Grated Courgettes Simmered in Cream]

After sautéing the courgettes, step 1 in the preceding master recipe, pour in about 1 pint of *crème fraîche* or double cream; simmer the courgettes for several minutes until cream has been absorbed and has thickened. Reheat just before serving, and fold in $\frac{1}{2}$ ounce or so of soft butter.

Courgettes Rapées, Sautées à la Provençale
[Grated Courgettes Sautéed in Olive Oil with Garlic]
Rather than sautéing the grated courgettes in butter, use olive oil for step 1 in the master recipe. Retain the shallots or spring onions if you wish, and add to them 1 or 2 cloves of garlic mashed, or finely minced.

Courgettes aux Épinards
[Sauté of Grated Courgettes and Chopped Spinach]
The addition of spinach gives more character to a courgette dish or courgettes give more tenderness to a spinach dish, whichever way you want to look at it. Substitute this attractive combination for plain courgettes in any of the preceding or following variations. We have suggested olive oil and garlic here, but you may prefer the butter and shallots of the master recipe on page 484. We have also directed that the spinach receive a brief preliminary blanching in boiling water; however, this may be dispensed with if your spinach is young, tender, and fresh from the garden.

[*For 6 to 8 servings*]

2 to 2½ lb. courgettes
About 2 lb. fresh spinach
A large pan of boiling salted water
A colander

Following the directions on page 483, trim, wash, grate, salt, squeeze, and dry the courgettes. While they are draining with salt, trim and wash the spinach; drop it into the rapidly boiling water and boil for a minute or two, just until limp. Drain, refresh in cold water, squeeze dry, and chop.

2 to 3 tbl. olive oil
1 or 2 large cloves of garlic, mashed
Salt and pepper
1 to 1½ oz. soft butter

When courgettes have been squeezed and dried, sauté, tossing and turning frequently, in the hot oil with the garlic. When almost tender, stir in the chopped spinach. About 10 minutes before serving, reheat, tossing and stirring, then cover pan and let cook several minutes over low heat, until spinach is as tender as you wish it to be. Season carefully to taste. Remove from heat and fold in the butter, a small piece at a time. Turn into a hot dish and serve immediately.

Tian de Courgettes au Riz
[*Gratin* of Courgettes, Rice, and Onions with Cheese]

The *tian* is, or was in the old days, a shallow, rectangular, earthenware Provençal baking dish. Anything cooked in it becomes a *tian*, just as something like chicken cooked in a casserole becomes a casserole of chicken. The *tian*, as a name, has been in vogue lately, but its shape and contents can vary considerably. Courgettes and rice are typical, as are additions of Swiss chard and spinach; thus you could use the preceding combination of courgettes and spinach, if you wish, rather than courgettes alone as suggested here. Serve with roasts, steaks, chops, calf's liver, grilled fish or chicken, or as a first course.

[*For 6 people*]

2 to 2½ lb. courgettes
4 oz. plain, raw, untreated white rice
2 large onions, minced
3 to 4 tbl. olive oil
2 large cloves garlic, mashed or finely minced
2 tbl. flour
About 1 pt hot liquid: courgette juices plus milk, heated in a pan
About 3 oz. grated Parmesan cheese (save 2 tbl. for later)
Salt and pepper
A heavily buttered 2½- to 3-pt flameproof baking and serving dish about 1½ ins. deep
2 tbl. olive oil

Following directions on page 483, trim, wash, grate, salt, squeeze, and dry the courgettes. While they are draining (reserve the juices), drop the rice into boiling salted water, bring rapidly back to the boil, and boil exactly 5 minutes; drain and set aside. In a large (11-inch) frying pan, cook the onions

slowly in the oil for 8 to 10 minutes until tender and translucent. Raise heat slightly and stir several minutes until very
lightly browned. Then stir in the grated and dried courgettes
and the garlic. Toss and turn for 5 to 6 minutes until courgettes
are almost tender. Sprinkle in the flour, stir over moderate
heat for 2 minutes, and remove from heat. Gradually stir in the
hot liquid, being sure the flour is well blended and smooth.
Return over moderately high heat and bring to the simmer,
stirring. Remove from heat again, stir in the blanched rice
and all but 2 tablespoons of the cheese. Taste very carefully for
seasoning. Turn into buttered baking dish, strew remaining
cheese on top, and dribble the olive oil over the cheese. (Preheat oven in time for baking.)

(†) May be prepared several hours or a day in advance of final
cooking.

About ½ hour before serving, bring to simmer on top of stove
then set in upper third of a preheated 425°F., Mark 7 oven until
tian is bubbling and top has browned nicely. The rice should
absorb all the liquid.

Timbale de Courgettes
[Moulded Custard of Courgettes, Onions, and Cheese]
Here is a delightful concoction that is elegant to serve either
as a first course, a luncheon dish, or to accompany roast or
grilled chicken, a saddle of lamb, or veal or lamb chops. It is a
mixture of grated and sautéed courgettes, cooked onions,
cheese, cream, and eggs that is unmoulded after baking, and
then sprinkled with buttered breadcrumbs and parsley. One
of its most attractive qualities, besides its flavour, is the rather
moist texture given it by the cheese, reminiscent of the soft
centre in a fine soufflé.

[*For 6 people*]

1. The courgette mixture
About 2 lb. courgettes
1 lb. onions, minced
1½ oz. butter

1 tbl. olive oil or cooking oil
A large frying pan
Salt and pepper
A 2-pt measure
A rubber spatula

Following directions on page 483, trim, wash, grate, salt, squeeze, and dry the courgettes. While they are draining, cook the onions slowly for 12 to 15 minutes or longer, with the butter and oil, in a large (11-inch) frying pan until onions are very tender, translucent, and just beginning to brown. Raise heat, stir in the courgettes; toss and turn for 5 to 6 minutes. Cover pan and cook courgettes several minutes longer over low heat, until tender. Season to taste and scrape into the measure.

2. The custard mixture

4 oz. mixed grated Parmesan and Gruyère cheese
About $\frac{1}{2}$ pt cream
A 4- to 5-pt mixing bowl and a wire whisk
8 large eggs
Salt and pepper to taste
A heavily buttered 2$\frac{1}{2}$-pt cylindrically shaped baking dish about 3$\frac{1}{2}$ ins.
  deep (such as a *charlotte*), bottom lined with buttered waxed paper

Add the cheese to the vegetables in the measure, and pour in enough cream, stirring, to reach the 1$\frac{1}{2}$-pint mark. Turn the mixture into the bowl, scraping measure clean. Break eggs into measure; beat to blend yolks and whites, and fold into the courgette mixture. Taste carefully for seasoning, and turn into baking dish.

(†) May be completed in advance to this point; cover and refrigerate. Stir up gently before proceeding. Chilled custard will probably take 10 to 15 minutes longer to bake than unchilled custard.

3. Baking: allow 1 hour; preheat oven to 375°F., Mark 5

A pan about 3 ins. deep and large enough to hold baking dish easily
Boiling water

When you are ready to bake the custard, set baking dish in pan; pour in enough boiling water to come about $\frac{2}{3}$ the way up outside of dish. Place in lower-middle level of preheated oven. To assure yourself of a smooth, bubble-free custard, regulate oven heat so that water in pan never quite simmers throughout the cooking; lower thermostat to 350°F., Mark 4, in 15 minutes, and you will probably lower it to 325° or 300°F., Mark 3 or 2, near end of baking. Custard should be done in 35 to 40 minutes: the top centre will look set rather than loosely liquid when you gently shake the pan. A knife or skewer plunged down through middle of custard will emerge almost clean, looking slightly oily with perhaps a tiny curd of custard clinging here and there. Remove baking dish from pan and let custard settle for 20 minutes before unmoulding it.

4. Serving

1½ to 2 oz. clarified butter (melted butter, skimmed; clear liquid butter
    spooned off milky residue)
A small (7- to 8-in.) frying pan
4 tbl. dry, not-too-fine white breadcrumbs
3 to 4 tbl. minced fresh parsley
Salt and pepper to taste
A hot, lightly buttered serving plate

While custard is baking or cooling, or at any other convenient time, prepare breadcrumb and parsley garnish as follows: heat clarified butter in pan, and when bubbling stir in bread-crumbs. Sauté for several minutes over moderately high heat, stirring continuously until crumbs are lightly browned. Remove from heat, and when cool, stir in the parsley and season-ings.

After custard has settled 20 minutes, run a thin knife around edge of custard. Turn serving plate upside down over baking dish, reverse the two and unmould custard on to plate. Sprinkle with the parsley and crumbs, and serve as soon as possible.

(†) If you are not ready to serve, do not unmould custard, but leave it in its dish in the pan of hot water and in the turned-off oven. It will stay warm for a good ½ hour or longer, and may then be unmoulded immediately.

STUFFED COURGETTES

Stuffed courgettes can well be a first course, especially when the stuffing is rice or vegetables. The best sizes for stuffing are 6 to 8 inches, and 1 courgette half is usually sufficient for a first course or as a vegetable garnish to go with the meat course. Serve 2 or even 3 halves per person when the courgettes are the main course.

*Courgettes Farcies aux Amandes
[Courgettes Stuffed with Almonds and Cheese]

This is a particularly attractive stuffing, not only because almonds are unusual, but also because the flavour of the courgettes survives the stuffing. Serve as a separate course, or with veal chops or scallops, or roast, grilled or sautéed chicken.

[*For 6 servings*]

1. Preparing the courgettes for stuffing

3 courgettes all of a size, about 8 by 2 ins.
A large pan of boiling, salted water
A grapefruit knife
Salt
Paper towels

Trim and scrub the courgettes; blanch about 10 minutes in boiling salted water, just until flesh yields to pressure, as directed on page 478. Cut in half lengthwise. Using grapefruit knife, hollow out the cores of each half, to make boat-shaped cases with the sides and bottoms about ⅜ inch thick. Salt lightly and drain hollow side down on towels. Chop the removed flesh, squeeze out vegetable water in paper towels, and reserve flesh for stuffing.

2. The almond, cheese, and breadcrumb stuffing

2 tbl. finely minced onions
1½ tbl. olive oil or cooking oil
A 6- to 8-in. pan
The chopped courgette flesh
A 3-pt mixing bowl

2½ oz. ground blanched almonds (grind them in an electric blender)
¼ pt double cream
2 to 3 tbl. dry, fairly fine white breadcrumbs
2 oz. grated Gruyère cheese
1 large egg
Salt and pepper to taste
2 to 3 big pinches powdered clove

Stir the onions into the oil, cover pan, and cook over low heat, stirring occasionally, for 8 to 10 minutes, or until onions are tender and translucent. Uncover, raise heat and let them just begin to brown, then stir in the chopped courgette flesh and sauté for several minutes, until tender. Scrape into bowl, and stir in the almonds and cream. Stir in 2 tablespoons of the breadcrumbs, blending thoroughly, then all but 1 tablespoon of the cheese, and finally the egg. Mixture should hold its shape softly when lifted in a spoon; if too soft, beat in more crumbs by small spoonfuls, mixing thoroughly. Blend in salt and pepper to taste, and the powdered clove.

3. Stuffing and baking the courgettes: 25 to 30 minutes at 400°F., Mark 6

A heavily buttered rectangular or oval baking and serving dish just
    large enough to hold the 6 courgette halves in 1 layer
1 tbl. each of the remaining breadcrumbs and cheese, mixed in a small
    bowl
1½ oz. melted butter

Arrange the courgette halves skin side down in the baking dish and fill with the stuffing, heaping it into a dome on each half. Sprinkle each with the cheese and breadcrumbs, and dribble on the melted butter.

(†) May be prepared to this point a day in advance of baking; cover and refrigerate.

Bake in upper third of preheated oven for 25 to 30 minutes, until bubbling hot and browned on top. (Do not overcook, letting courgette shells become too soft for serving.) Serve from baking dish, or arrange around meat platter.

(†) May be kept warm, but again, do not let courgette shells soften.

Courgettes Farcies au Riz et aux Poivrons
[Courgettes Stuffed with Rice and Peppers]
Another stuffing for courgettes: this one is equally good cold
or hot. Prepare, stuff, and bake the courgettes exactly as
described in the preceding recipe, but make the stuffing as
follows.

Rice and pepper stuffing with tomato topping; for six 8- by 2-inch courgette halves

1 medium onion, diced
4 tbl. olive oil (save 2 tbl. for later)
A medium-sized frying pan
1 medium green pepper, diced
A large clove garlic, mashed
The chopped courgette cores
2½ oz. plain, raw, white, untreated, long-grain rice
1 egg
1½ oz. grated Parmesan cheese (save 2 tbl. for later)
3 tbl. fresh minced parsley
Salt and pepper
3 medium-sized tomatoes, peeled, seeded, juiced, and chopped

Stir the onions into the oil in a medium-sized (10-inch) frying
pan, cover and cook over low heat, stirring occasionally, for
8 to 10 minutes until tender. Uncover, raise heat and brown
very lightly, stirring, then add the green peppers, garlic, and
courgette cores. Cover and cook slowly for several minutes
more until peppers are tender. Turn into mixing bowl. Meanwhile, in a pan of boiling salted water, boil the rice for exactly
10 minutes, drain, and add to mixing bowl. Beat in the egg,
then the cheese and parsley. Season carefully with salt and
pepper. Mound the stuffing in the blanched and hollowed-out
courgette halves. Season tomato pulp with salt and pepper,
spread over the stuffing, cover with the remaining cheese, and
sprinkle on the remaining olive oil. Bake for 25 to 30 minutes
in upper third of preheated 425°F., Mark 7 oven until bubbling
hot and cheese topping has browned lightly.

Other stuffings
You may stuff courgettes, following the general method outlined in the master recipe, with all kinds of mixtures, including

other vegetables, left-over meat combinations, sausage mixtures, and so forth. A complete list of possibilities is on pages 664–6.

Stuffed Onions – Stuffed Cabbage
Oignons Farcis – Choux Farcis

Oignons Farcis au Riz
[Onions Stuffed with Rice, Cheese, and Herbs]

Onions hollowed out and stuffed with rice and chopped, cooked onion cores need only a little cheese, cream, and a pinch of herbs to point up their flavour. Served hot, they add great distinction to a platter of grilled chicken or fish, and are always attractive with roasts, steaks, and chops. Serve them cold with cold meats or fish, or as part of an hors d'œuvre display. The following recipe is for giant onions, but smaller ones are done the same way: whatever their size, you hollow them out raw, blanch them until barely tender, then stuff and bake them. If you do not blanch them first, they will take hours to cook and might well burst out of shape in the process. (A list of other stuffing possibilities is on pages 664–6.)

[For 6 large onions]

1. Coring and blanching the onions

6 very large, firm, fresh, perfect onions at least $3\frac{1}{2}$ ins. in diameter if possible, yellow or white
A small, sharp knife and a grapefruit knife
A large pan of boiling salted water
A slotted spoon and a colander

One at a time, shave off pointed end and root end of onions (A), and peel off skin along with one outside layer of flesh. Whole onions are now to be hollowed out to form onion cups. With sharp knife, cut cone-shaped core out of the top side of the onion (B). (Reserve all onion flesh for step 2.) Being careful not to make sides and bottom too thin (they should be almost $\frac{1}{2}$

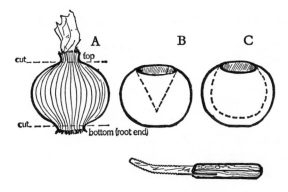

inch thick, or about 4 layers for onions this size), use grapefruit knife to dig circular sections out of body of onion to make
a cup shape (c).

Drop the onion cups into boiling water. When it comes
back to the boil, boil slowly, uncovered, for 10 to 15 minutes
until onions are just tender when pierced but still very
definitely hold their shape. Remove carefully and drain upside
down in a colander. (Reserve boiling water for next step.)

2. The rice, onion, and cheese stuffing

The onion cores
1½ to 2 oz. butter
A large frying pan with cover
A 5-pt mixing bowl

While onion cups are blanching, mince all usable onion left-
overs. Cook slowly in butter in covered pan 8 to 10 minutes,
stirring occasionally, until tender and translucent; uncover pan,
raise heat, and brown very lightly, stirring. Turn into mixing
bowl.

2½ oz. plain, raw, white untreated rice
The boiling water from the onion cups

After onion cups have been blanched and removed, stir rice
into boiling water and boil slowly for 10 to 12 minutes, until
rice is almost but not quite tender. Drain thoroughly, and add
to mixing bowl.

1½ oz. grated Parmesan cheese
3 tbl. *crème fraîche* or double cream
4 tbl. dry, not-too-fine white breadcrumbs (for now and for step 3)
3 tbl. minced parsley
2 tbl. fresh minced basil or 1 tsp. fresh minced tarragon (or ¼ to ½ tbl.
  dried basil, oregano, sage, or tarragon)
Salt and pepper to taste

Stir the cheese and cream into the rice and onions, then 2 tablespoons of the breadcrumbs. If mixture does not hold its shape softly, blend in a spoonful or so more crumbs to thicken and bind it. Stir in the herbs and seasonings.

3. Stuffing and baking the onions: 1 to 1¼ hours at 375°F., Mark 5

1½ to 2 oz. melted butter
A heavily buttered flameproof baking dish just large enough to hold
  onions easily, such as a 12-in. casserole 3 ins. deep
The breadcrumbs remaining from step 2
6 tbl. dry white wine or dry white French vermouth
¼ pt or more beef stock of bouillon
A bulb baster

Preheat oven to 375°F., Mark 5. Butter or oil the outside of the onion cups and arrange in the baking dish. Sprinkle interiors lightly with salt and pepper, and fill with the stuffing, heaping it into a ½-inch dome. Sprinkle with a teaspoon of breadcrumbs and of melted butter. Pour the wine around the onions, and enough stock or bouillon to come a third of the way up the onions. Bring to simmer on top of stove, then set in lower middle of preheated oven.

Bake uncovered for 1 to 1¼ hours, regulating oven so that liquid remains at the slow simmer, and basting outside of onions several times with liquid in dish. Onions are done when a knife pierces them easily, but they should not overcook and lose their shape. Outside layer will toughen slightly, but insides will be tender. Top of stuffing should brown attractively, but if it is browning too much, cover loosely with foil or brown paper. Serve from baking dish, or arrange around the meat or vegetable platter. Add any onion juices to whatever sauce you are making.

(†) May be baked in advance and kept warm or reheated.

*Chou Farci
[Stuffed Whole Cabbage]

Stuffed cabbage is the kind of dish that guests and family always seem to love because it has the hearty, earthy look and the rich, satisfying aroma that promise good eating. To stuff a whole cabbage you first make a delicious mixture using something like the fresh sausage and ham suggested here, or leftover meat as in the variation following it. You then pull off the cabbage leaves, boiling them until pliable, and re-form the cabbage into approximately its original shape with your delicious mixture spread between layers of leaves. Finally you braise, sauce, and serve it up, and it looks just like a beautiful, decorated, whole cabbage sitting on the serving platter. You must, of course, have some method for holding the cabbage leaves in the shape of the whole while braising. If you have struggled to mould cabbage with string, towels, cheesecloth, or even the net shopping bag that is occasionally used in Provence, we think you will welcome the ease of the following bowl-moulding method. Parslied boiled potatoes, French bread, and rosé wine would go well with the cabbage.

Note: Braised stuffed cabbage is equally good cold, and could well be baked specially for a cold lunch or a picnic. If so, drain and unmould it as soon as it is done, so there will be no bits of congealed fat on the leaves.

[*For 8 to 10 people*]

1. Fresh sausage, rice, and ham stuffing

1 lb. fresh sausage meat, preferably home-made, page 386
A medium sized (10-in.) frying pan
An 8- to 9-pt mixing bowl and large wooden spoon
½ lb. diced mild-cured ham
1 lb. onions, minced
6 oz. boiled rice
½ tsp. sage
½ tsp. caraway seeds
3 tbl. minced fresh parsley
2 cloves garlic, mashed
1 egg
Salt and pepper

(Start the water boiling for step 2.) Break up the sausage meat and sauté over moderate heat for 5 to 6 minutes, just until it is beginning to brown lightly. Remove to mixing bowl, leaving fat in pan. Brown the ham lightly in the fat; remove it to the bowl, again leaving fat in pan. Finally stir in the onions and cook slowly for 8 to 10 minutes, until tender and beginning to brown very lightly. Scrape them into the bowl and beat in all the rest of the ingredients. Taste carefully for seasoning, adding more salt and herbs if you feel them necessary. (Chopped, blanched leaves from the heart of the cabbage will be stirred in later.)

2. Preparing the cabbage for stuffing

A firm, fresh, crisp 2¼- to 2½-lb. cabbage (about 8 ins. in diameter),
    either the crinkle-leafed Savoy or the smooth-leafed winter cabbage
A large pan of boiling salted water
A large tray covered with a towel

With a small, stout knife, make a bias cut all around the stem of the cabbage, going 2 to 2½ inches deep, and removing the tough core. Discard any outside leaves that seem tough or wilted.

If you have the crinkle-leafed Savoy cabbage, you usually need not blanch it to remove the leaves. Peel them off carefully so as not to tear them, until you come to the heart, where leaves are small and bend inward. Drop as many cabbage leaves as will easily fit into the boiling water and boil, uncovered, for 3 to 4 minutes, until leaves are pliable enough to bend without breaking. (This is called blanching.) Drain on towel and continue with the rest of the leaves and the heart, boiling it 5 minutes.

If you have a smooth-leafed cabbage (or an unpeelable Savoy), drop the whole cabbage core side down into the boiling water. In 5 minutes, start loosening leaves carefully, nudging them off the cabbage with 2 long spoons as they free themselves from the core. Remove these leaves to the tray. Continue loosening and removing leaves to tray until you come to the heart, where leaves bend inward. Leave heart to boil for 5 minutes, and add as many of the removed leaves as will easily fit, boiling them 3 to 4 minutes or until they are just pliable. Continue with the rest of the leaves. (Do not discard boiling water yet.) Chop the heart of the cabbage, salt and pepper lightly, and stir into the already prepared stuffing from step 1.

3. Other miscellaneous preliminaries

10 to 12 slices of lean salt pork or bacon approximately 4 by 1½ ins. and
   ⅜ in. thick
The boiling cabbage water
1 medium onion, sliced
1 medium carrot, sliced
2 tbl. rendered goose or pork fat, or cooking oil
The frying pan

Drop the slices of salt pork or bacon into the boiling water and boil slowly for 10 minutes. Drain, rinse in cold water, and set aside on paper towelling. Meanwhile, cook the vegetables in the fat or oil until tender and just beginning to brown, then remove to a side dish. (Note that there is also a sauce base in step 6, which you may prepare now if you wish.)

4. Stuffing the cabbage

A lightly buttered 4- to 5-pt stainless-steel bowl, flameproof mould,
   baking dish, or *charlotte* mould 3½ to 4 ins. deep (with a cover)
Salt and pepper
1 to 1½ pts excellent brown stock or bouillon

Lay several strips of the blanched pork or bacon in the bottom of the stainless steel bowl or flameproof mould and cover with the lightly browned carrot and onion slices.

Starting with the largest and greenest of the blanched cabbage leaves, lay them curved side down and stem end up in the mould (A), to cover bottom and sides. Sprinkle lightly with

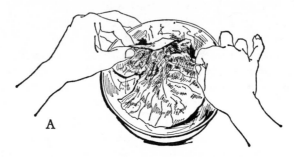

A

salt and pepper. Spread a layer of stuffing over the lower third of the leaves (B). Cover the stuffing with cabbage leaves. Salt

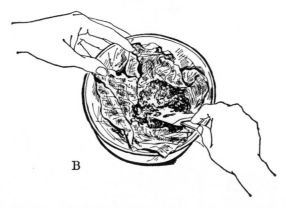

B

and pepper them lightly, and spread on more stuffing. As you build up layers, slip leaves down side of mould to be sure sides are well covered (c).

When you have used all the stuffing, and mould is filled to within ½ inch of top, cover filling with a final layer of leaves and arrange the rest of the blanched salt pork or bacon on top (D). Pour enough stock or bouillon between outside leaves and side of mould to come about an inch from the top (E).

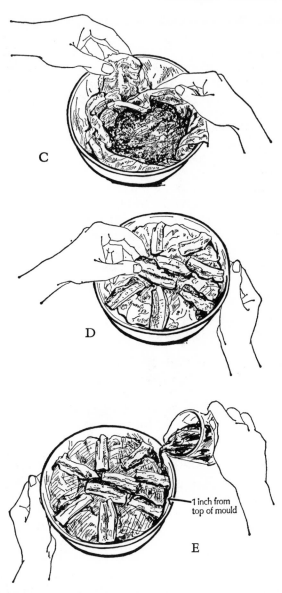

C

D

E

1 inch from
top of mould

(†) May be prepared in advance to this point and cooked the
next day. Cover with plastic wrap and refrigerate. Add 20 to
30 minutes more to cooking time if cabbage has been chilled.

5. Braising: 2½ to 3 hours at 400°F., Mark 6, and 350°F., Mark 4

Waxed paper
The cover for the mould
A pan to hold the mould and to catch drips
A bulb baster
Additional stock or bouillon if needed
Optional: a meat thermometer

Preheat oven to 400°F., Mark 6. Bring filled mould slowly to the full simmer on top of the stove. Lay the waxed paper over the cabbage and cover the mould. Set in pan and place in lower middle of preheated oven. In 20 to 30 minutes, when liquid in mould is slowly and steadily simmering, turn thermostat down to 350°F., Mark 4, and regulate oven heat so that liquid is always very slowly simmering throughout the 2½ to 3 hours of cooking. Baste occasionally with the cooking liquid and add a little more stock if liquid evaporates below the half-way mark. (Two and a half to 3 hours are needed for heat to penetrate into centre of cabbage, where a meat thermometer should read 165° to 170°F.)

(†) Ahead-of-time notes are at end of step 6.

6. Sauce and serving

3 tbl. finely minced onions
1 tbl. rendered goose or pork fat, or cooking oil
A heavy-bottomed, 3-pt enamelled or stainless saucepan with cover
1 clove garlic, mashed
1 lb. tomatoes peeled, seeded, juiced, and chopped; or part fresh
   tomatoes and part sieved, tinned Italian-type plum tomatoes
½ tsp. sage
Salt and pepper to taste

While cabbage is braising, or at any other convenient time, make the sauce base as follows: stir the onions into the fat, cover pan, and cook over low heat, stirring occasionally, for 8 to 10 minutes or until onions are tender and translucent but not browned. Add the garlic, tomatoes, and sage; cover and simmer 10 minutes. Uncover, season to taste, and set aside.

If needed: ½ tbl. cornflour blended with 1 tbl. tomato juice or bouillon
A hot serving dish
A frying pan
3 tbl. minced fresh parsley

When cabbage is done, keep cover on mould and drain cooking liquid into the tomato-sauce base; let simmer while you are finishing the cabbage. Sauce should thicken lightly. If it does not, remove from heat, blend in cornflour, and simmer 2 minutes more. Carefully correct seasoning.

Remove pork or bacon pieces from top of cabbage and set aside. Drain cabbage again, then turn serving dish upside down over mould and reverse the two, unmoulding cabbage on to the dish. Remove vegetables and pork from top of cabbage. Pat pork or bacon strips dry on paper towels, and brown very lightly in frying pan; arrange them decoratively over the cabbage. Spoon the sauce around the cabbage, decorate with the parsley, and serve as soon as possible.

(†) Sauce may be finished and pork or bacon sautéed well in advance of serving, then reheated. Keep cabbage warm, loosely covered, and unmould at last minute. (Omit sautéing the pork strips at bottom of mould.) However, if you leave the cabbage too long, or cool and reheat it, you risk losing its freshly cooked quality.

Feuilles de Chou Farcies
[Stuffed Cabbage Leaves for Individual Servings]

When you want a less elaborate presentation, a little quicker cooking, have fewer people to serve, or want an attractive way to use a bit of left-over meat, you may make as many or as few servings as you wish by wrapping a stuffing in individual cabbage leaves. Usually served hot, these are also delicious cold on a bed of lettuce or watercress, and garnished with sliced tomatoes and cucumbers in a vinaigrette sauce.

[For 12 stuffed cabbages leaves, serving 4 to 6]

12 large blanched cabbage leaves 7 to 8 ins. long (step 2 in preceding master recipe)

One at a time, lay blanched cabbage leaves curved side down on cutting board and cut a wedge about 2 inches long out of the tough bottom stem (A).

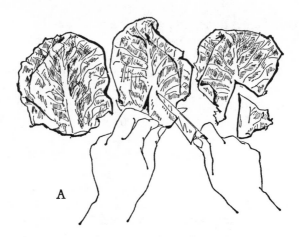

A

Stuffing: use that in the preceding recipe, page 498 (about $\frac{1}{3}$ to $\frac{1}{2}$ the amount listed), or $\frac{1}{3}$ to $\frac{1}{2}$ of the stuffing at the end of this section, page 506; or use one of the stuffings from the list on pages 664–6

Place a loaf-shaped mound of stuffing in lower third of leaf just above wedge cut (B). Start rolling leaf towards tip. At the

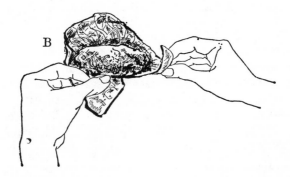

B

halfway mark, fold each side over stuffing to enclose it (C). Finish rolling up the leaf (D), and complete the rest of the leaves in the same manner.

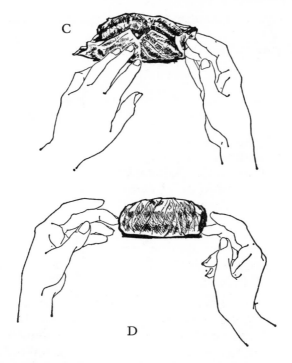

1 each: medium sized carrot and onion, sliced and lightly browned
    (step 3 in preceding recipe)
A lightly buttered 3-pt flameproof baking and serving dish 2 ins. deep
    (such as a 9- by 12-in. oval)
Optional: the rest of the cabbage leaves, blanched and roughly chopped
Salt, pepper, and ¼ tsp. ground sage, rosemary, or thyme
12 slices of lean salt pork or bacon, 4 by 1½ ins. and ⅜ in. thick,
    blanched (step 3 in preceding recipe)
About ¾ pt of excellent brown stock or bouillon
Aluminium foil
A bulb baster
The tomato-sauce base, step 6 in preceding master recipe
2 tbl. minced fresh parsley

Strew the sliced cooked carrots and onions in the bottom of
the baking dish and spread the optional blanched and chopped
cabbage over it. Season with salt, pepper, and sage, rosemary,
or thyme. Lay the stuffed cabbage leaves on top, seam-side
down and close together. Salt and pepper them lightly, cover

each with a strip of blanched salt pork or bacon, and pour around them enough stock or bouillon almost to cover. Enclose top of dish tightly with aluminium foil.

(†) May be completed in advance to this point. Refrigerate, and bake the next day if you wish.

Bake for 1 to 1¼ hours in a preheated 350°F., Mark 4 oven, basting occasionally with the liquid in the dish. Drain cooking liquid into the tomato-sauce base and boil down rapidly to thicken. Carefully correct seasoning and pour back over the cabbage rolls. Brown the pork or bacon strips lightly in a frying pan and arrange over the cabbage, sprinkle with parsley, and serve.

Petits Choux Farcis
[Ball-shaped Stuffed Cabbage Leaves]
Rather than sausage shapes, you may form the leaves into round shapes resembling individual cabbages. To do so, blanch the leaves as directed and cut a wedge out of bottom of stem. Place leaf curved side down on the corner of a towel. Heap 2 to 3 tablespoons of stuffing in the centre, fold rest of leaf over stuffing, then twist into a ball in the towel to force a round shape. Arrange balls smooth side up and close together in a dish, and bake as in preceding recipe, but 1 hour of cooking should be sufficient.

Braised Beef and Ham Stuffing
This is another stuffing suitable for whole cabbage or cabbage leaves.

¾ lb. onions, minced
3 tbl. rendered goose or pork fat, or cooking oil
4 tbl. dry white breadcrumbs
¼ pt single cream
1½ lb. minced cooked lean beef, preferably braised, but any type of cooked beef will do
¾ lb. minced cooked lean ham
2 oz. grated Parmesan cheese

2 to 3 cloves garlic, mashed
¾ tsp. ground rosemary or thyme
2 eggs
4 tbl. minced fresh parsley
Salt and pepper to taste

Cook the onions in fat or oil in a covered saucepan over low heat for 8 to 10 minutes until tender; raise heat and cook a few minutes more until lightly browned. Meanwhile blend the breadcrumbs and cream in a small bowl and let stand while assembling rest of ingredients. Finally beat the cooked onions, crumbs, meats, cheese, garlic, herbs, eggs, and parsley vigorously together to blend. Carefully season to taste, adding more herbs if you feel them necessary.

Potato Dishes · *Pommes de Terre*

Ounce for ounce, potatoes have fewer calories than fresh peas, lima beans, or sweet corn, yet potatoes come so near to being the complete food that one can survive healthily on a diet of potatoes only, plus a very small amount of fat, for as much as 5 months. Nutrition aside, the potato is an endlessly fascinating gastronomical object which, since its introduction by Parmentier into France during the reign of Louis XVI, has received tremendous French culinary attention. We shall not, in this short section, go into the fundamental cooking methods because they are available in any good basic cook-book. We offer instead a number of out-of-the-ordinary simmers and sautés, a deliciously fattening potato pie, two of the classics illustrated, *pommes Anna* and *pommes duchesse*, and we begin with a group of useful potato facts.

NOTES ON BUYING AND STORING POTATOES

When you are buying potatoes, choose those that look clean and healthy, that are firm to the touch, smooth, dry, free from cracks, and with no suggestion of sprouting (greenish-white nubbins of growth appearing at the small depressions called the eyes). Be sure, also that the potatoes are potato-coloured, that is, uniformly brownish or reddish with no hint of green. Green means that they have been exposed to sun or light, either in the field or in storage, and green potatoes develop a bitter taste. Potatoes are sometimes waxed and sometimes coloured reddish, a harmless cosmetic treatment designed to enhance their customer appeal; if so, this fact should be indicated clearly on the bin or package.

Unless you happen to have a proper root cellar where you can store potatoes in the dark at a temperature of 55°F. and at a humidity of 85 to 90 per cent, buy only what you will use within a week or so. Potatoes kept at 60° to 70°F. have the best cooking flavour, but they begin to sprout after a few weeks. Potatoes stored at below 40°F., the temperature of your refrigerator, resist sprouting and withering but gradually develop a sweet taste because the potato starches transform themselves into sugar. Thus, keep your small store of potatoes at normal room temperature in heavy brown paper sacks so they will be protected from light. Separate different types or you will run into cooking irregularities.

POTATO TYPES

Potatoes are a far more complicated vegetable to grow, harvest, store, and classify than any of us who are not in the business would ever dream. New varieties are constantly being tested out that will survive in specific climates, that will resist the myriad viruses and diseases which attack potato plants, and that will more perfectly meet public tastes and the specific demands of dehydrators, chip manufacturers, and other industrial users. Potatoes of one variety can vary from one year to the next in a certain growing locality because of weather, or the same variety will be mealy in one area and not in another because of soil and climatic differences. The tradition of choosing old potatoes for baking and mashing, and new potatoes for boiling still holds true in part, but so much has happened to the potato since grandmother's day that a list of varieties classified according to buying areas and uses would be out of date almost as soon as it appeared in print. Thus we shall go no further than specifying boiling potatoes when we mean the type that holds its shape in cooking, and baking potatoes when we want a mealy, floury potato for baking or mashing. If your greengrocery does not have its potatoes clearly labelled as to baking and mashing, frying, boiling, or all-purpose, ask the shopkeeper to help you.

Pommes de Terre au Basilic
[Sliced Potatoes Simmered in Cream and Basil]

This is a top-of-the-stove recipe in which sliced potatoes are boiled briefly in water to neutralize any milk-curdling properties they may possess, then simmered until tender in a cream sauce with garlic and basil. You may set them aside and reheat again just before turning them into a vegetable dish with more basil, parsley, and butter. Serve with roast red meats, steaks, chops, or grilled chicken.

[*For 4 to 6 people*]

2 lb. boiling potatoes
A large saucepan of boiling salted water
A colander

Peel the potatoes. Cut into slices about $\frac{1}{4}$ inch thick and $1\frac{1}{4}$ inches in diameter. Drop them into the boiling water, bring rapidly back to the boil again, and boil for 3 minutes. Drain immediately.

$1\frac{1}{2}$ oz. butter
A heavy-bottomed 5-pt saucepan (non-stick recommended)
$1\frac{1}{2}$ tbl. flour
A wooden spoon and a wire whisk
$\frac{1}{2}$ pt milk heated in a small saucepan
$\frac{1}{4}$ pt double cream; more cream (or milk) if needed
About 1 tbl. fresh minced basil; or $\frac{1}{2}$ tsp. dried basil (or oregano)
1 to 2 large cloves of garlic, mashed
$\frac{1}{2}$ tsp. salt
Big pinch of white pepper
A cover for the pan

Make a white *roux* as follows: melt the butter in the saucepan, blend in the flour, and stir over moderate heat for 2 minutes to cook the flour without browning. Remove from heat, and when *roux* has stopped bubbling, vigorously blend in all of the hot milk at once with your wire whisk, beating until mixture is perfectly smooth. Blend in the $\frac{1}{4}$ pint of cream, the herb, garlic, salt, and pepper. Return over moderately high heat, stirring with whisk as sauce thickens very lightly and comes to the boil. Simmer 2 minutes, then fold in the potatoes. Sauce should just cover potatoes; add a little more cream or milk if necessary. Bring to simmer, correct seasoning, cover pan, and simmer very slowly for 10 to 15 minutes, until potatoes are tender. Stir up gently from bottom once or twice to be sure potatoes are not sticking; they will have absorbed half of the liquid before they are done and if sauce seems too thick you may always add a little more milk.

(†) May be completed in advance to this point. Spoon a little milk or cream over top of potatoes and either set aside uncovered or keep warm, partially covered, in a pan of simmering water.

1 to 2 oz. soft butter
2 to 3 tbl. fresh minced basil and parsley, or parsley only
A warm, lightly buttered vegetable dish

Reheat potatoes just before serving. Carefully correct seasoning. Gently fold in the butter and $\frac{2}{3}$ of the herbs with a rubber spatula. Turn into vegetable dish, decorate with the remaining herbs, and serve at once.

A Different Herb – Tarragon

The preceding potatoes are delicious with tarragon rather than basil, a good solution for wintertime, since dried tarragon is usually far more fragrant than dried basil.

Gratin Dauphinois aux Endives
[*Gratin* of Sliced Potatoes and Chicory]

Both chicory and potatoes go beautifully with chicken or veal, and here they are combined into one dish. The natural moisture in the chicory provides enough liquid for the potatoes, while the butter, lemon juice, shallots, and cheese that bake along with them contribute delicious additional flavours.

[*For 8 people; baking time about 1¼ hours*]

2½ lb. very fresh, white, firm Belgian chicory with leaves tightly closed at the tips
1¼ lb. boiling potatoes
1 oz. soft butter
A 5- to 6-pt baking dish about 2½ ins. deep (such as a 12-in. round one, or an 11- by 16-in. oval)
1 tbl. lemon juice
4 oz. melted butter
Salt and white pepper
3 oz. coarsely grated Gruyère cheese
2 tbl. finely minced shallots or spring onions
Buttered waxed paper
A cover for the dish

Preheat oven to 400°F., Mark 6. Trim root ends, and wash chicory rapidly under cold running water. Slice crosswise into pieces ¾ inch thick and set aside. Wash and peel potatoes, cut into slices ¼ inch thick and about 1¼ inches in diameter. Smear the butter in the baking dish and arrange in it half the sliced chicory. Sprinkle with half the lemon juice, and 1 ounce of melted butter. Season lightly with salt and pepper, and spread on half the cheese. Over this arrange the potatoes in layers, sprinkling each with salt and pepper, a little of the butter, and the minced shallots or spring onions. Spread the rest of the chicory over the potatoes, seasoning them with lemon juice, salt and pepper, and all but ½ ounce of the remaining butter. Omit the cheese, reserving for later.

Lay the buttered waxed paper over the chicory, cover the dish, and bake in middle level of 400°F., Mark 6 oven for 15 to 20 minutes, or until you can hear the contents bubbling. Turn oven down to 350° or even 325°F., Mark 4 or 3, for the rest of the baking, regulating heat so that vegetables simmer slowly throughout the rest of the cooking, which will be 1 to 1¼ hours. When potatoes are tender if pierced with a fork, remove dish from oven, and reset thermostat to 425°F., Mark

7. Spread remaining cheese over the vegetables and dribble on the remaining butter.

(†) Dish may be completed an hour or so in advance up to this point. Set partially uncovered in a warming oven, or over a pan of almost simmering water. As long as potatoes are warm and have a little ventilation, they will not lose their fresh-tasting quality.

About 15 minutes before serving, set dish uncovered in upper third of preheated 425°F., Mark 7 oven until contents are bubbling hot and cheese topping has browned lightly.

Pommes de Terre Sautées, Calabraise
[Sliced Potatoes Sautéed with Lemon and Garlic]

This excellent, crusty sauté of potatoes needs to be done in a large non-sticking pan where the potatoes have room to toss, turn, and crust. Serve them with eggs, sausages, pork chops, grilled chicken, steaks, or fish.

[*For 6 servings*]

2 lb. boiling potatoes all of a size for even slices
A large saucepan with just enough boiling salted water to cover potatoes
Olive oil (or 1½ oz. butter and 2 or more tbl. olive oil or cooking oil)
A large (11-in.) frying pan (non-stick recommended especially for this recipe)
The grated peel of ½ lemon
2 large cloves of garlic, mashed
Big pinch of nutmeg
Salt and pepper

Peel the potatoes, cut into slices ¼ inch thick and 1¼ inches in diameter (or cut into ½-inch dice, if you prefer. Drop into boiling, salted water, and boil about 5 minutes, or until barely tender. (Eat a piece to check; do not overcook.) Drain thoroughly. Film frying pan with a ⅛-inch layer of oil (or butter and oil), set over moderately high heat, and when very hot but not smoking add enough potatoes to make 1 full layer. Toss and turn frequently for several minutes, shaking and swirling the pan by its handle, until potatoes are beginning to brown lightly. Add some more potatoes, and continue to toss them in the pan until the new addition is beginning to brown. If necessary, add a little more oil and continue with more potatoes; however, about ¾ inch of potatoes will be the maximum you can handle in the pan.

When all potatoes are lightly brown toss with the lemon peel, garlic, nutmeg, salt and pepper. Continue sautéing and tossing several minutes more until potatoes are as brown as you wish them to be.

(†) May be kept warm at this point, pan set partially covered over 2 asbestos mats over low heat. As long as they are warm and ventilated, potatoes will retain their fresh taste for at least ½ hour.

If available: 1 tbl. minced fresh basil
2 to 3 tbl. minced fresh parsley
1 oz. or more butter
About 1 tbl. lemon juice
A hot serving plate or the meat platter

Just before you are ready to serve, reheat to sizzling and toss with the herbs and butter. Check seasoning again, and toss with lemon juice to taste. Turn out on to plate and serve immediately.

Galette de Pommes de Terre aux Tomates
[Hashed Brown Potatoes with Tomatoes and Herbs]
Another recipe for sautéed potatoes, this time with pork bits, onions, and tomatoes, calls for the potatoes to be mashed down with a fork when soft so that they look like an omelette when turned out on to their serving plate. Arrange sausages, sautéed chicken, chops, hamburgers, or poached or fried eggs around the potatoes, and you need only a green vegetable or salad for the perfect informal meal.

[For 6 servings]

1. The pork and onions
4 to 5 oz. bacon chunk or lean salt pork cut into ¼ in. dice
A pan with 3 pts water

1 tbl. olive oil or cooking oil
A large (11-in.) frying pan (non-stick recommended especially for this
   recipe)
1 medium onion, minced
A cover for the pan
A sieve set over a small bowl

Simmer the diced bacon or pork in the water for 10 minutes, drain and dry in paper towels. Cook for several minutes with the olive oil in the frying pan until it begins to brown lightly. Stir in the onion, cover the pan, and cook over low heat, stirring occasionally, for 8 to 10 minutes until onions are tender. Raise heat and cook, stirring, to brown the onions very lightly. Scrape into sieve, pressing fat out of ingredients into bowl. Return fat to frying pan; reserve pork and onions for step 3.

2. Sautéing the potatoes

About 2 lb. boiling potatoes
Paper towels
More oil as needed
A mixing fork or a wooden spoon
Salt and pepper

While onions are cooking, peel the potatoes, cut into slices about $\frac{1}{8}$ inch thick and $1\frac{1}{4}$ inches in diameter. Dry thoroughly in paper towels. Add more oil to pan if needed, to film it by $\frac{1}{16}$ inch. Raise heat to moderately high, and when fat is very hot but not smoking, add the potatoes. Toss and turn frequently for several minutes, shaking and swirling the pan by its handle, until potatoes begin to brown. Lower heat slightly, cover pan, and cook for 5 to 10 minutes, tossing frequently, until potatoes are tender. Uncover, mash roughly with mixing fork or wooden spoon, and season to taste.

3. Finishing the recipe

1 lb. tomatoes, peeled, seeded, juiced, and chopped
1 to 2 large cloves garlic, mashed
$\frac{1}{4}$ tsp. mixed herbs such as *herbes de Provence*
The cooked pork bits and minced onion
A hot serving dish

Raise heat to high. Fold in the tomatoes, garlic, and herbs along with the cooked pork bits and onions. Season again to taste, and sauté uncovered for several minutes to brown. Potatoes should slide around in a mass, and you may be able to flip them over, to brown both sides.

(†) If you are not ready to serve, set partially uncovered over low heat and 2 asbestos mats, where potatoes will keep warm without harm for $\frac{1}{2}$ hour at least. Reheat to sizzling just before serving.

If you have browned top and bottom of the potato mass, you may serve it like a flat cake, sliding potatoes from pan on to plate. Otherwise they will be most attractive in the form of an oval omelette: flip the two sides over the middle, and reverse the pan on to the serving plate so the potatoes land browned side up.

POMMES ANNA

Pommes Anna looks like a brown cake 6 to 8 inches in diameter and 2 inches high, and it smells marvellously of potatoes and butter. That, in effect, is all it is: thinly sliced potatoes packed in layers in a heavy pan, bathed in clarified butter, and baked in a very hot oven so that the outside crusts enough for the potatoes to be unmoulded without collapsing. The contrast of crusty exterior and tender, buttery interior is quite unlike anything else in potato cookery, and to many *pommes Anna* is the supreme potato recipe of all time. It was created during the era of Napoleon III and named, as were many culinary triumphs in those days, after one of the *grandes cocottes* of the period. Whether is was an Anna Deslions, an Anna Judic, or simply Anna Untel, she has also immortalized the special double baking dish itself, *la cocotte à pommes Anna*, which is still being made and which you can still buy at a fancy price. It is of heavy copper.

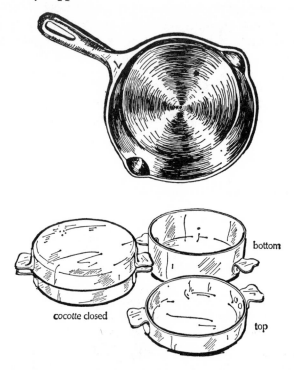

cocotte closed

bottom

top

A thick, flameproof baking dish of some sort is actually one of the keys to *pommes Anna*, because it must be an excellent heat conductor. Although the copper *cocotte Anna* is a beautiful object, its absolutely vertical sides, 3-inch depth, and frequent tendency to sticky-bottom troubles make it less easy to use than other possibilities.

The familiar cast-iron frying pan with its fairly vertical sides and short, straight handle is actually the best of all for *pommes Anna*. The potatoes are easier to unmould from this than from the French type of iron frying pan with its sloping sides and long handle. However either will do as will a thick, flameproof, ceramic baking dish or a thick cast-aluminium one with nonstick interior. The essential is to have a material that will get thoroughly hot all over, to brown and crust the outside of the potatoes.

Having furnished yourself with the right pan, you then want to make sure the potato slices will not stick to it, because you must be able to unmould them at the end of the cooking. Therefore, use clarified butter, dry the potatoes thoroughly before the cooking begins, and finish the cooking once you have begun it, or else the potatoes will exude moisture and stick to the pan. As you will note in the recipe, cooking begins at once, on the top of the stove as you are arranging the potatoes in the pan; this is to dry the bottom layers and start the brown crust forming. In the classic recipe you then finish the cooking in a hot oven, which usually gives a more professional result, but you may complete the cooking on top of the stove, as suggested in the cheese variation following the master recipe.

Pommes Anna and its variations go especially well with roast saddle of lamb, leg of lamb, roast beef, chops, sautéed chicken, plain or fancy steaks, and roast game.

*Pommes Anna
[Mould of Sliced Potatoes Baked in Butter]

Your object, in arranging the sliced potatoes in their dish for this very special recipe, is not only to fill the dish but to make a reasonably neat design in the bottom and around the sides so that when the potatoes are unmoulded they will present a handsome exterior. For the sides you may either arrange an edging of overlapping upright slices braced by horizontal interior layers, or build up a wall of evenly spaced horizontal slices as you fill the pan. We have suggested the latter, simpler, system here.

[For 6 people]

1. Preliminaries

½ lb. butter
3 lb. boiling potatoes (more if needed)
Paper towels

Preheat oven to 450°F., Mark 8. Set one rack in very bottom level, and another just above it. Clarify the butter: melt it, skim off scum, and spoon the clear liquid butter off the milky residue. Peel the potatoes, trim into cylinders about 1¼ inches in diameter so that you will have uniform slices, then slice cylinders into even rounds ⅛ inch thick. Dry thoroughly in paper towels. (Do not wash potatoes after peeling, because you want the starch to remain in, so potatoes will mass more easily into a cake.)

2. Arranging the potatoes in the dish

A heavy cast-iron frying pan about 8 ins. top diameter and 2 to 2½ ins.
    deep, or one of the other possibilities in paragraphs preceding recipe
Salt and pepper

Pour ¼ inch of the clarified butter into the pan and set over moderate heat. When hot, start rapidly arranging the first layer of potatoes in the bottom of the pan as follows. Arrange one potato slice in the centre of the pan. Overlap a circle of potato slices around it (A). Overlapping in the opposite

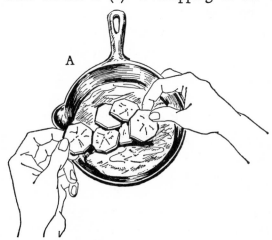

A

(counter-clockwise) direction rapidly arrange a second circle around the first and continue with another (clockwise) overlapping circle if necessary, to rim the edge of the pan. Pour on a spoonful of the clarified butter. Reversing direction again, rapidly arrange an evenly overlapping layer of potatoes around circumference of pan, fill in the centre with more potatoes (B), and baste with another spoonful of butter. Shake pan not too roughly by handle to be sure potatoes are not sticking, and sprinkle on salt and pepper.

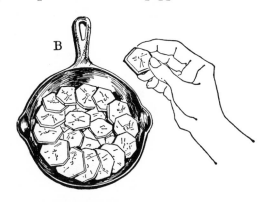

Continue filling the pan with layers of potatoes basted with butter and seasoned with salt and pepper, always being sure that the layer around the circumference of the pan is evenly spaced. Remember, also, to shake the pan by its handle from time to time, to be sure potatoes are not sticking. Fill the pan completely, allowing potatoes to form a $\frac{1}{4}$- to $\frac{1}{2}$-inch dome in the centre; they will sink during cooking. You should have added enough butter so that you can see it bubbling up the sides of the pan; excess will be poured out after cooking.

3. Baking

A heavy saucepan, 7 ins. bottom diameter, or whatever will fit into the potato pan

A heavy, close-fitting cover for the potato pan

A pizza tray or roasting pan to catch drips

Butter bottom of saucepan and press it down hard on the potatoes (C), forcing the layers together. Butter underside of

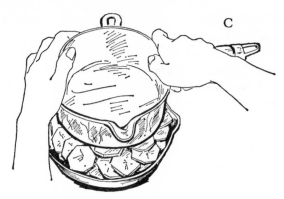

C

cover, place it on the potato pan set on upper of the two oven racks. Set drip pan under the potatoes, on rack below, to catch bubblings-up of butter (which could otherwise set fire to your oven).

Bake for 20 minutes. Uncover, press potatoes down hard again with bottom of saucepan, and continue baking 20 to 25 minutes more, uncovered. (If baked all the time with cover on, potatoes tend to pick up an off taste.) Press down potatoes again before end of baking, Gently draw an edge of the potatoes away from side of dish: potatoes are done if brown and crusty. Bake 5 minutes or so more if necessary.

4. Unmoulding and serving

A bowl for excess butter
A flexible-blade spatula
If needed: a buttered baking sheet
A lightly buttered, hot serving dish

When potatoes are done, place cover slightly askew on pan and drain out excess butter, which may be used again in other cooking. Run spatula around edge of pan. Shake pan, and if potatoes have stuck to bottom, run spatula carefully under potatoes to loosen them, but disturb them as little as possible. If you feel it will be easier to unmould them first on to a baking sheet and slide them on to the serving dish, do so; otherwise invert the dish over the potato pan, reverse the two, and potatoes will drop on to dish. They should look like a brown cake.

Unmoulding troubles

You should have no trouble, but if some potatoes do stick to pan, scrape them off and put them in place on the potato cake. If you have had trouble and potatoes look messy or pale, simply push or mound them into a reasonable shape, sprinkle with cheese or breadcrumbs, drizzle on a little butter, and brown briefly under the grill.

(†) After unmoulding the potatoes, cover loosely with foil and set in a warming oven, or on an electric hot-plate, or over simmering water. They will keep nicely for ½ hour at least as long as they are warm and have a little circulation of air.

Pommes de Terre Sarladaise
[Truffled Sliced Potatoes Baked in Butter]

All you need for this variation is the wherewithal for a number of sliced truffles, as many as you wish. Proceed as in the master recipe, but intersperse truffles with the potato slices after the first layer of potatoes has been arranged in the pan, and end with a layer of potatoes.

Galette de Pommes de Terre au Fromage
[Mould of Sliced Potatoes and Cheese Cooked in Butter]

This is a more informal method of forming *pommes Anna*, and you may omit the cheese if you wish. Here all the cooking is done on top of the stove, which is a convenience when your oven is in use.

[For 6 people]

2 to 2½ oz. clarified butter
A heavy, medium-sized (10-in.) frying pan, either cast-iron or non-stick
About 2½ lb. boiling potatoes in round, 1¼-in. slices ⅛ in. thick, well dried
About 4 oz. Gruyère cheese cut into 1-in. slices less than ⅛ in. thick (use slicing slot of a grater)
Salt and pepper
Small pinches of nutmeg

A cover for the frying pan
A flexible-blade spatula
A hot serving dish

Following illustrated directions in preceding master recipe, pour ¼ inch of butter into frying pan. Set over moderate heat and rapidly arrange an over-lapping layer of potato slices in the pan, shaking pan gently from time to time to prevent sticking. Baste with a sprinkling of butter, arrange a second layer over the first, and over this second layer of potatoes arrange a layer of cheese slices. Season the third layer of potatoes with salt, pepper, and a speck of nutmeg. Continue filling the pan with potatoes, cheese, seasonings and end with a layer of potatoes. When filled, shake pan gently again and let cook 3 to 5 minutes over moderately high heat to be sure the bottom of potatoes is crusting. Then cover pan and set over low heat for about 45 minutes, or until potatoes are tender when pierced with a small knife. (Be sure heat is not too high, or bottom of potatoes will brown too much.) Run spatula all around edge of pan and underneath to loosen potatoes, and unmould upside down on serving dish.

Tourte Limousine
[Potato Pie with Herbs and Cream]

Another attractive way to serve potatoes is to mould them in pastry, and bake in a flan ring or false-bottomed cake tin, which comes off when the potatoes are done; the pie then stands free on a serving dish. In this excellent recipe, the sliced potatoes are seasoned with melted butter and herbs, and when they are tender inside their crust, a mixture of cream and beaten egg is poured into them through the chimney hole. The *tourte* can well be the main course for a lunch or supper, along with a mixed vegetable salad, possibly some cold meat, and a Riesling, Sylvaner, or rosé wine. Or serve it with steaks, hamburgers, grilled chicken, or fish. Any left-overs may be reheated, but are also good cold.

[*For a 9-inch pie, 8 to 12 servings*]

1 tsp. soft butter
The mould: a 9-in. flan ring set on a baking sheet, or a round, 9-in.
   false-bottomed cake tin
Either: ½ the recipe for *pâte brisée ordinaire*, formula 1, page 162;
Or: a ready-mix pastry dough
3 tbl. chopped fresh parsley
Either: 2 tbl. minced fresh green herbs (basil and chives);
Or: 1½ tbl. minced shallots or spring onions and ¼ tsp. dried oregano
   or sage
2 oz. butter melted in a saucepan
2 lb. all-purpose potatoes, thinly sliced, in a bowl of cold water
Salt and pepper
A pastry brush and cup of cold water
A chimney: the metal tube end of a pastry bag or a small metal funnel,
   buttered
1 egg beaten with 1 tsp. water in a measure
4 tbl. double cream

Preheat oven to 425°F., Mark 7. Butter inside of flan ring and surface of baking sheet, or inside of cake tin. Roll ⅔ of the pastry into a circle 14 inches in diameter (so that you will have a 1½-inch overhang), and line the mould, letting overhang fall around outside rim. Stir the parsley and herbs into the butter. Drain and dry the potatoes and spread ⅓ on the bottom of the lined mould. Stirring butter and herb mixture, pour ⅓ of it over the potatoes and sprinkle potatoes with salt and pepper. Complete filling mould in same manner. Fold overhanging pastry over potatoes, and moisten top of pastry with water. Roll out remaining pastry into a circle 9½ inches in diameter, roll up on pin, and unroll over mould. Roll pin over pastry to trim it the size of the mould, then press it down with the balls of your fingers over the moistened bottom layer to seal. Make a chimney hole in top of pastry and insert funnel. Paint top of pastry with beaten egg, and make cross-hatch marks over pastry with the back of a knife or the tines of a table fork. Blend cream into remainder of beaten egg, and refrigerate for later.

Baking: about 1 hour

Immediately set *tourte* in lower-middle level of preheated 425°F., Mark 7 oven and bake for about 30 minutes, until pastry is nicely but not too deeply browned. Then turn thermostat down to 350°F., Mark 4 for rest of baking; cover *tourte* loosely with foil or brown paper if it is browning too much. As soon as potatoes are tender when you poke them through the chimney hole, *tourte* is done. A spoonful at a time, pour the egg and cream mixture into the pie through the chimney, tilting pie in all directions so that cream will flow all over. Bake another 5 minutes or so to set the mixture, and *tourte* is ready to serve; unmould and slide on to a hot serving dish.

(†) If *tourte* is done before you are ready to serve, keep it warm, uncovered, in a turned off oven or warming oven. If wait is to be more than 15 minutes, do not add egg and cream until a few minutes before serving, then reheat in a 350°F., Mark 4 oven.

*Pommes Duchesse

[Mashed Potato Mixture for Borders and Other Decorations]

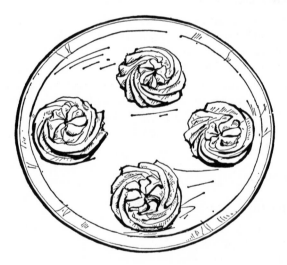

Even hamburgers look dressy in a fluted border of *pommes duchesse*, and fluted mounds of potatoes placed around a meat platter are elegant indeed. Consisting only of mashed potatoes, egg yolks, butter, and cream, *pommes duchesse* is a very simple

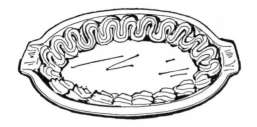

mixture and perfectly delicious when you use the best ingredients, meaning live potatoes rather than dehydrated ones.
Serve *pommes duchesse* anywhere that mashed potatoes would
naturally go, such as around a platter that is to hold *bœuf
bourguignon* or *coq au vin*, or piped around the creamed eggs or
fish that are to be gratinéed, or with steaks, chops, or grilled
fish.

TECHNICAL NOTES

You may prepare and form the potatoes in advance, and bake
them just before serving; once baked and browned, however,
they must be served fairly soon or they will lose their light,
freshly cooked quality. We prefer egg yolks to whole eggs in
the mixture because we think that egg whites have a drying-
out effect, although they do give the potatoes a slight puff.
If you like a puff anyway, use 1 egg and 1 yolk for each pound
of potatoes rather than the 3 yolks for a pound (6 for 2 pounds)
suggested here.

[*For 2 pounds of mashed potatoes, serving 6 to 8*]

1. The potato mixture

2½ lb. baking potatoes all of a size for even cooking (6 or 7 potatoes
    4½ by 2 ins., for instance)
A heavy-bottomed saucepan
Cold water
1 tsp. salt per 1 pt of water
A cover for the pan
A colander or sieve
A potato ricer, or a food mill with medium disc, or an electric mixer

A rubber spatula and a wooden spoon
6 egg yolks in a small bowl
3 oz. soft butter
4 to 6 tbl. *crème fraîche* or double cream
¾ to 1 tsp. salt
⅛ tsp. white pepper
Pinch of nutmeg
A pan of hot but not simmering water large enough to hold potato pan

Scrub the potatoes under warm water, drop into saucepan of cold water to cover, add salt, and set over high heat. When water comes to the boil, boil slowly, partially covered, for about 25 minutes usually. Test for doneness by cutting a potato in half, taking a slice from inside the half and eating it: potato should hold its shape, but should be cooked through, tender, mealy, and ready to eat. Drain, and peel at once, holding potato on a fork. Immediately put potatoes through a ricer or food mill, or beat with electric mixer, to make a smooth, lump-free purée. Put into saucepan and stir over moderate heat for 2 to 3 minutes until potatoes film bottom of pan, indicating that most of excess moisture has evaporated. Remove from heat, beat in the egg yolks, then the butter and 4 tablespoons of the cream. Beat in a little more cream by dribbles if you think the potatoes will take it, but mixture must be fairly firm so that it will hold its shape when formed. Beat in the salt, pepper, and nutmeg; taste carefully and correct seasoning as necessary. Set potato pan in pan of hot water.

(†) Potatoes must be warm if you are to form them smoothly and easily. If you are not quite ready, cover pan partially and beat rather frequently with a wooden spoon. Note that warm potatoes are never covered airtight; a slight circulation of air prevents them from developing an off taste.

2. Forming a fluted border of *pommes duchesse*

A wooden spoon
The warm *pommes duchesse* mixture
A rubber spatula
A 12- to 14-in. canvas pastry bag with ¾-in. cannelated nozzle
A lightly buttered, flameproof serving platter, such as a 12- by 14-in. oval

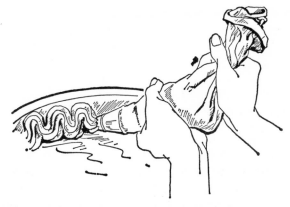

Vigorously beat the warm potato mixture to be sure it is smooth and pliable, then scoop into pastry bag. Squeeze out into a decorative design around the edge of the platter. Use a winding ribbon design, for instance, and add rosettes if you wish. When you have a small pastry bag and run out of potatoes rather quickly, rosettes hide breaks in the pattern.

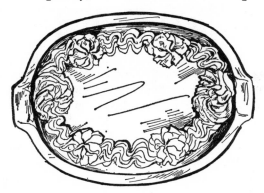

2 to 3 tbl. finely grated Gruyère or Parmesan cheese
$1\frac{1}{2}$ to 2 oz. melted butter

Sprinkle the potatoes with a dusting of cheese and dribble on melted butter. (Although egg glaze may be used and gives better over-all colour, we do not like the taste and texture of egg film when it has hardened over the browned potatoes.)

(†) Set aside; cover loosely when cool and refrigerate.

3. Browning and serving

Either bake in upper third of a preheated 400°F., Mark 6 oven for 25 to 30 minutes until lightly browned, or brown slowly for 5 minutes or so under a low grill. Browning under the grill leaves a moister texture but you must watch carefully that the potatoes do not burn. Once browned, serve as soon as possible because the potatoes will taste dry and stale if cooled and re-heated.

Individual Nests or Mounds of *Pommes Duchesse*

Using the same general method as described in the master recipe, flute individual nests of the potato mixture on buttered heatproof serving dishes, shells, or plates; sprinkle the potatoes with cheese and melted butter, and brown as described in step 3. For individual mounds, squeeze the potatoes out on a buttered baking sheet and proceed in the same manner, lifting them off with a spatula for serving.

Pommes Duchesse au Fromage
[Cheese-flavoured *Pommes Duchesse*]

For cheese-flavoured *pommes duchesse*, which you may use in any of the preceding or following suggestions, beat 2 table-spoons finely grated Parmesan cheese into the finished potato mixture in step 1 of the master recipe. In this case, because the cheese is strong, you may use instant mashed potatoes, adding the minimum amount of liquid suggested on the package, so that you may beat in enough cream to give the potatoes flavour and interest without making them too soft to form.

Galettes de Pommes Duchesse
[Mashed Potato Pancakes from the Left-overs]

Left-over *pommes duchesse* is delicious when formed into cakes and sautéed in butter. This works for browned *pommes duchesse* but is more successful with the uncooked mixture, and although you may bake rather than sauté the potatoes, which is easier to do, much the best flavour and texture comes from sautéing.

[*For a dozen 3-inch cakes, serving 4 to 6 people*]

About 1 lb. of the *pommes duchesse* mixture, step 1 in preceding master recipe
4 oz. dry, not-too-fine white breadcrumbs
A sheet of waxed paper on a tray
2½ to 3 oz. clarified butter (melted butter, skimmed; clear liquid butter spooned off milky residue)
A large (11-in.) frying pan, preferably non-stick
A buttered baking sheet

If the potato mixture is freshly made, let it cool. Either rolling and patting them in the lightly floured palms of your hands, or forming them on waxed paper with a wet rubber spatula, make smooth cakes of the potato mixture 3 inches in diameter and ¾ inch thick. As each is formed, place it on the bread-crumbs, heap crumbs on top, pat a thin layer in place, and arrange the cakes in 1 layer on waxed paper.

(†) If you are not going to sauté them immediately, cover and refrigerate; they will keep perfectly well until the next day.

Preheat oven to 200°F., Mark ¼. Shortly before serving, film frying pan with ⅛ inch of the clarified butter, heat to very hot but not browning, and arrange as many potato cakes in pan as will easily fit in 1 layer. Sauté for 3 to 4 minutes on one side, until nicely browned and crusted, turn and sauté on the other side. Arrange on baking sheet and keep warm in oven while sautéing the rest, adding more butter to pan as necessary. The potato cakes may be kept warm for 15 minutes or more, but are at their best and freshest the sooner you serve them.

Galettes de Pommes de Terre Farcies
[Filled Potato Cakes]

With a stuffing of ham, mushrooms, and cheese, potato cakes become a main course. Serve them with a green vegetable or a salad. Rather than sautéing them, you may find baking easier.

[*For 8 cakes 3½ inches in diameter, serving 4 or more people*]

Ingredients for the preceding potato cakes plus:
¼ lb. fresh mushrooms, finely diced
1 tbl. minced shallots or spring onions
Salt and pepper
2 oz. ham, finely minced
2 oz. Gruyère cheese, grated

Sauté the mushrooms and shallots or spring onions in ½ ounce of the butter in a small pan until mushroom pieces begin to separate from each other and to brown very lightly. Season with salt and pepper, add the minced ham, and sauté a minute more. Set aside. Form half of the potato mixture into 8 discs 3½ inches in diameter and about ¼ inch thick. Spread the ham and mushrooms in the centre of each, and top with grated cheese. Cover with discs made from the remaining potatoes.

To cook, either dredge in breadcrumbs and sauté in clarified butter as in preceding recipe, or arrange on a buttered baking sheet, sprinkle with breadcrumbs and melted butter, and bake in upper third of a preheated 400°F., Mark 6 oven for 25 to 30 minutes until lightly browned.

A Bean Purée, Three Turnip Recipes, and a *Crêpe*

Any change from routine is a happy event, particularly when it is a substitute for the usual starchy vegetable choices. Here is a clever purée of beans and pumpkin, two purées involving turnips, plus a turnip sauté, and a new kind of *crêpe* made of green peppers and tomatoes.

Gratin de Potiron d'Arpajon
[Purée of Pumpkin and White Beans]
A combination of pumpkin and beans goes especially well with goose, duck, turkey, pork, or sausages. This is also one of the few vegetable recipes where you may successfully substitute

tinned or frozen ingredients for fresh, as noted near the end of the directions in step 1, and in the ingredients for step 2.

[*For 4 to 6 people*]

1. The pumpkin

10 tbl. *mirepoix* vegetables (4 tbl. each of finely diced onions and celery; 2 tbl. diced carrots)
1½ oz. butter
A covered 4- to 5-pt flameproof baking and serving dish 2½ to 3 ins. deep
2 lb. pumpkin, peeled and roughly sliced
Optional: 1 to 2 cloves garlic, mashed
1 bay leaf
⅛ tsp. thyme
½ tsp. salt
¼ pt water
Waxed paper cut to fit top of dish

Preheat oven to 350°F., Mark 4. Cook the *mirepoix* vegetables in butter in the covered dish over low heat, stirring occasionally, for 8 to 10 minutes, until vegetables are tender but not browned. Stir in the pumpkin, optional garlic, herbs, salt, and water. Bring to a simmer on top of stove, lay waxed paper over vegetables, cover, and bake in middle level of preheated oven for 30 to 40 minutes, stirring up once or twice to be sure vegetables are not browning. Add 2 to 3 tablespoons more liquid if all has evaporated before pumpkin is tender. (If using tinned or frozen pumpkin, cook *mirepoix* vegetables until tender, then add garlic, herbs, and 3 tablespoons water; cover and boil slowly for about 10 minutes until liquid has evaporated.) Remove bay leaf.

2. The beans; baking and serving

About 10 oz. cooked or tinned white beans (for quick soaking and pressure cooking of dried beans, see Volume I, page 433)
A food mill with medium disc
A large mixing bowl
A rubber spatula and wooden spoon
2 large eggs
¼ pt double cream

2 oz. grated Gruyère cheese
Salt and white pepper
1½ oz. butter

Preheat oven to 425°F., Mark 7, in time for baking. Purée the
pumpkin mixture along with the beans through food mill
into bowl. Beat in the eggs, cream, all but 2 tablespoons of the
cheese, and salt and pepper to taste. Smear ½ ounce of the
butter in the baking dish, spoon in the purée, sprinkle reserved cheese on top and dot with the remaining butter.

(†) May be completed a day ahead to this point. When cold,
cover and refrigerate. Allow 10 to 15 minutes longer in oven
if mixture is chilled.

About ½ hour before serving, bake uncovered in upper third
of preheated 425°F., Mark 7 oven until bubbling hot and top
has browned nicely.

Purée Freneuse
[Purée of Rice and Turnips with Herbs and Garlic]

Unless your guests know that Freneuse is Turnipville, on one
of the serpentine twists of the Seine north-west of Paris, they
will have no other clue to identify this marvellous mixture.
Serve it with red meats, pork, sausages, chops, goose, and
ducklings.

[*For 4 to 6 people*]

¾ pt milk, more if needed
A heavy-bottomed 3-pt saucepan (non-stick would be useful)
½ lb. rice
½ tsp. salt
1 oz. butter
2 to 3 large cloves of garlic, mashed
¼ tsp. thyme and bay leaf
3 to 4 white turnips, about 3 in. in diameter, peeled and roughly
    chopped
A food mill

Bring the milk to the simmer, add the rice, salt, butter, garlic,
and seasonings. Simmer, stirring occasionally, for 10 minutes,
until rice is partially tender. Stir in the turnips, adding more

milk, if necessary, to submerge the vegetables. Cover and simmer 10 to 15 minutes more, stirring occasionally, until turnips are tender. Liquid should be almost entirely absorbed; if not, uncover and boil, stirring, to evaporate it. Purée through food mill and return to pan.

(†) May be completed ahead of time to this point.

Salt and white pepper to taste
1 to 1½ oz. butter or 2 to 3 tbl. double cream
A hot serving dish
Minced parsley

Shortly before serving, reheat, stirring. Carefully correct seasoning. Stir in the butter or cream by spoonfuls. Turn into a hot serving dish and decorate with the parsley.

La Purée, Châteaux en Suède
[Purée of Swedes]
Firm, fresh swedes with their crisp, moist flesh and fine, sweet flavour are every bit as good as the best white turnips, especially when they are simmered with butter and turned into a fragrant, yellow purée. Serve with a roast goose or duck, a loin of pork, a dinner of home-made sausages, or a lamb or beef stew.

[*For 4 to 6 people*]

1½ to 2 lb. firm, crisp swedes, peeled and cut into 1 in. pieces
A heavy-bottomed 3-pt saucepan
About ¾ pt water
1½ tsp. salt
1½ oz. butter
A cover for the pan
A food mill set over a mixing bowl

Place swede chunks in saucepan with enough water to come two thirds of the way up the vegetables. Add salt and butter, bring to the boil, cover and boil slowly, tossing occasionally, for about 30 minutes or until tender. Drain, reserving cooking liquid, and purée swedes through food mill into bowl.

2 oz. rendered goose fat, pork fat, or butter
1½ oz. plain flour
A wooden spoon and wire whisk
The hot cooking juices from the swedes
3 tbl. double cream
Salt and pepper
A lightly buttered warm vegetable dish
Fresh parsley

Melt the fat or butter in the saucepan, blend in the flour, and stir over moderate heat until flour and fat foam together for 2 minutes without browning at all. Remove from heat, and when it has stopped bubbling blend in ½ pint of the cooking juices, beating vigorously with wire whisk until mixture is perfectly smooth. Return over moderately high heat, stirring with whisk as mixture thickens and comes to the boil. Boil, stirring, for 2 minutes. Sauce should be very thick, but not so thick that it will not combine with the puréed swedes: beat in more cooking liquid (or milk) by spoonfuls if you think it necessary. Finally beat the swede purée and the cream into the sauce, and season carefully to taste.

(†) May be prepared even a day in advance; cover and refrigerate when cool.

About 30 minutes before serving, cover and reheat over simmering water, stirring occasionally. To serve, turn into a hot vegetable dish and decorate with parsley.

Petits Navets Sautés, en Garniture
[Fresh, Young White Turnips Sautéed in Butter]

Winter and early spring are the time for early crop turnips, which are tender enough to need no blanching and are at their best cooked simply in butter. Whether round, oval, or top-shaped and with or without their green leaves, buy them smooth, firm, small, clean, unblemished, and all of a size for even cutting and shaping. Their flesh, when you cut into them raw, must be moist, crisp, and sweetly turnipy. Serve sautéed turnips with duck, goose, turkey, pork, roast beef or lamb, steaks or chops. They are also attractive as part of a vegetable garnish in combination with such others as glazed carrots and sautéed mushrooms, or buttered fresh peas. The following recipe is for a small amount, but if you wish to cook more, do the preliminary sauté in batches, and finish them off all together in a covered casserole in a 325°F., Mark 3 oven.

[*For 4 to 6 servings*]

About 12 fresh, young white turnips 2 to 2½ ins. in diameter (2½ lb. without tops)
1 oz. or more butter
1 or more tbl. olive oil or cooking oil
A large (11-in.) frying pan (non-stick recommended)
¼ tsp. salt, more as necessary
Big pinch pepper
A cover for the pan

With a small, sharp knife, peel the turnips, removing outer skin and the white underskin that covers the moist flesh. You now want to cut them in the form of large garlic cloves, all pieces approximately the same size: if you have round turnips, for example, quarter them lengthwise, and round off the sharp edges, saving trimmings for turnip soup or adding them to one of the preceding purées.

Melt 1 ounce of butter with 1 tablespoon of oil in frying pan over moderately high heat. When butter foam is beginning to subside, indicating fat is hot enough, add as many turnips as will fit in 1 crowded layer. Toss and turn frequently, shaking and swirling the pan by its handle, for 4 to 5 minutes, until turnips are beginning to brown very lightly. (If you are sautéing in 2 batches, turn browned turnips into a side dish, add more butter and oil if needed, brown the second batch, then return all to the pan.) Toss turnips with the salt and pepper, cover pan, and cook over very low heat, tossing occasionally, for about 10 minutes more or until turnips are tender. Be careful turnips do not brown too much. Be sure also not to overcook them; they should be just tender but still hold their shape.

Salt and pepper as needed
1 to 1½ oz. more butter
3 to 4 tbl. fresh minced parsley
A hot vegetable dish or the meat platter

Just before serving, reheat to sizzling, toss with more salt and pepper as needed, then with the additional butter, and finally with the parsley. Turn into hot vegetable dish or on to platter and serve.

Crêpes à la Pipérade
[Pepper, Onion, Tomato, and Cheese Pancakes]

Cooked bell peppers, onions, tomatoes, cheese, and herbs plus a light batter to bind them all together are the basic ingredients for this attactive vegetable combination, which is cooked like pancakes. Serve them with roasts, chops, or grilled chicken, and any left-overs are delicious with cold hors d'œuvre or on a picnic. They are, in addition, a splendid background for diced poultry, veal, or pork left-overs, which you may include in the mixture; topped with a poached or fried egg and a tomato or cheese sauce, they are an ample main course for informal meals.

[*For twelve 4-inch pancakes*]

1. The *crêpe* batter

1½ oz. flour
1 large egg
¼ tsp. salt
1½ tsp. cooking oil
4 tbl. milk, plus a little more if needed
An electric blender, or a bowl, whisk, and sieve

Either whirl all ingredients in a blender; or place flour in bowl, beat in rest of ingredients, and strain through sieve. Batter should be like double cream; if too thick, thin out with drops of milk. You may use it immediately if you have instant-blending flour; otherwise let it rest for an hour at least.

2. The *pipérade* mixture

4 medium onions, sliced
3 tbl. olive oil or cooking oil
An 8-in. frying pan with cover
3 or 4 medium green bell peppers, sliced
3 to 4 ripe, red tomatoes, peeled, seeded, juiced, and sliced

2 to 3 large cloves of garlic, mashed
Salt and pepper to taste
2 tbl. fresh minced parsley, plus 1 tbl. fresh minced basil or ½ tsp. of
   dried oregano

Cook the onions in the oil for 8 to 10 minutes, or until tender
and translucent. Add the peppers and cook another 3 to 4
minutes to soften slightly. Then add the sliced tomato pulp
and garlic; cover pan for several minutes until tomatoes have
rendered their juice. Uncover, raise heat, and boil for several
minutes, tossing pan by handle to blend ingredients, until
liquid has almost completely evaporated. Season carefully to
taste, and toss with the herbs.

3. Cooking the *crêpes*

(You may prefer several 8-inch *crêpes* cut into wedges; the
following is for 4-inch *crêpes* cooked 3 at a time in a 10-inch
pan.)

5 oz. Gruyère cheese cut into ⅜-in. dice
The *pipérade* turned into a 3-pt bowl
A rubber spatula
6 tbl. or more of the *crêpe* batter
Cooking oil
A heavy-10-in. frying pan (non-stick recommended)
1 or 2 oiled baking sheets
A pancake turner

Blend the cheese into the *pipérade* along with 6 tablespoons of
the batter. Brush frying pan with oil and set over moderately
high heat. When hot but not quite smoking, ladle in 3 tablespoons of the *crêpe* mixture as a test. Cook about 2 minutes on
one side, until little holes appear through the surface, at which
time bottom should be nicely browned. Turn and cook about
1 minute on other side, then remove to a baking sheet. *Crêpe*
should just hold together, with only enough batter in the
mixture to enrobe the ingredients. Add a little more batter to
bowl if you feel it necessary, but too much makes for doughy
crêpes. Cook the rest of the *crêpes* and arrange on baking sheets.
   Just before serving, reheat for 5 minutes or so in a preheated
425°F., Mark 7 oven.

Including Left-overs

For the same amount of batter, use: 5 ounces each sliced onions, peppers, and tomatoes for the *pipérade*; 2 ounces diced cheese; 5 ounces diced cooked poultry, veal, pork, ham, sausages, or fish.

Three Cold Vegetables

Petits Oignons Aigre-doux
[Sweet and Sour Onions Braised with Currants – hot or cold]

Serve these hot with roast pork, duck, goose, game, or cold along with hors d'œuvre, and cold meat and poultry. They should be considered more as a garnish, relish, or condiment than a vegetable, and if you are using tiny pearl onions, 6 per serving should be sufficient.

[*For 6 to 8 people*]

10 oz. (40 to 50) small, white pearl onions
A saucepan of boiling water
A heavy-bottomed 3-pt saucepan with cover
¼ pt beef or chicken bouillon
6 tbl. water
1 tsp. dry mustard blended with 1½ tbl. wine vinegar
2 tbl. olive oil
1½ tbl. sugar
¼ tsp. salt
1 medium tomato, peeled, seeded, juiced, and chopped

3 tbl. currants
1 large clove garlic, mashed
¼ tsp. thyme
1 bay leaf
⅛ tsp. pepper
A serving dish

Drop the onions into the boiling water and boil 1 minute to loosen skins. Drain. Shave off 2 ends, peel, and pierce a cross in the root end of each to help onions retain their shape while cooking. Place onions in a saucepan with all the ingredients listed except for the herbs and pepper. Bring to the simmer, skim for several minutes, then add the thyme, bay leaf, and pepper; cover and simmer slowly about 1 hour, or until the onions are tender but still hold their shape. Add a little more water if necessary during cooking; however, liquid should be reduced to a syrup when onions are done; if not, boil down at end of cooking. Transfer to dish and serve hot or cold, decorated, if you wish, with parsley.

Salade de Poivrons, Provençale
[Peeled and Sliced Sweet Peppers in Garlic and Oil]

A typical informal first course in Provence might include the local black olives, sliced hard-boiled eggs, anchovies, capers, and slices of green or red sweet peppers turned in olive oil, salt and garlic. The only trick to this recipe is that you will have to peel the peppers, which is quite a different matter from peeling eggs. A number of pepper-peeling systems are on the books, including spearing them on a long fork and turning them one by one over a gas flame, baking in a hot oven, baking in a slow oven, boiling them, steaming them in a covered dish, dropping in hot oil, grilling them until the skin puffs and blackens. We like grilling because it is the quickest, the surest, and it cooks the flesh just enough so that the pepper is ready to cut and serve as soon as you have peeled it.

A NOTE ON SWEET PEPPERS

All sweet peppers both here and in France belong to the same species, *Capsicum annuum*, native to the tropics and including a large number of shapes and sizes. Pick peppers that are brightly coloured, glossy, firm, and thick-fleshed, with no pockmarks, brown patches, or soft spots anywhere on their surface. Like their distant cousin, the aubergine, raw peppers prefer a temperature of 45° to 50°F. and a humidity of 90 per cent. Unless you can reproduce these conditions, buy only what you will use within a day or two because they will deteriorate rapidly when stored where they are either too hot or too cold.

[For 4 medium-sized peppers]

1. Peeling the peppers

4 medium-sized peppers, green, red, yellow, or mixed
A shallow baking dish big enough to hold peppers easily, such as a pie plate
A cutting board
A sharp knife and a table fork

Preheat grill to very hot. Arrange peppers in dish and place so surface of peppers is an inch from grill element. As soon as skin facing grill has puffed and blackened, in 2 to 3 minutes, turn peppers on another face, and finally on each end, so that all of skin has puffed. Remove peppers to cutting board. One by one, rapidly cut in half lengthwise, remove stem and seeds, and scrape off skin. (This should be done as soon as possible and before peppers cool; if blackened skin remains too long on pepper, it can darken the flesh under it.)

2. Dressing the peppers

1 medium clove of garlic, mashed
¼ tsp. salt
A small bowl and a pestle or wooden spoon
4 tbl. excellent olive oil
A serving dish
Plastic wrap

Mash garlic and salt until salt has dissolved completely, then beat in olive oil. Cut peppers into lengthwise strips ⅜ inch wide and arrange layers in dish, spooning dressing over each layer. Cover and let steep, tilting dish and basting with the dressing occasionally, for 20 minutes before serving.

(†) May be made several days in advance; cover airtight and refrigerate. Remove ½ hour before serving to de-congeal oil.

Fonds d'Artichauts Farcis, Froids
Fonds d'Artichauts en Surprise
[Artichoke Hearts Stuffed with Mushroom Purée;
Poached Eggs Optional – a cold entrée]

Here is one of those perfect first-course dishes for special guests and formal dinners. Whole artichokes are boiled and the leaves carefully removed to preserve the hearts; the hearts are then filled with a mixture of puréed and marinated raw mushrooms, the scraped-off flesh from the leaves, mayonnaise, and herbs. A helping hand is welcome here, because leaf scraping is rather slow work. However, if you are alone and unhurried, you may boil the artichokes one day, scrape them the next, and fill them on the morning of the third day. When you want to serve this as a main-course luncheon dish, add *la surprise*, poached eggs, which blend perfectly with mushrooms, artichokes, and mayonnaise.

[*For 6 large artichokes*]

1. Preparing the artichokes

6 large, fresh, fine artichokes 4 to 4½ ins. in diameter
A large pan containing 10 pts boiling salted water
A food mill with middle-size disc, or a sieve

Following illustrated directions in Volume I, pages 457–8, trim the artichokes, being sure all the tough green part is cut off bottoms and small leaves are broken from circumference. Boil slowly, uncovered, for 35 to 45 minutes until bottoms are tender when pierced with a knife. (Prepare mushrooms and mayonnaise, steps 2 and 3, while the artichokes boil.)

Drain upside down in a colander. When cool, carefully remove the leaves, keeping hearts intact. Scrape out and discard hairy choke from centre of each artichoke heart. With a teaspoon, scrape flesh from the inside of leaves and the soft cone of leaves covering choke. Purée the scraped flesh through food mill or sieve, then twist hard in the corner of a towel to extract as much water as possible. Place puréed flesh in a bowl.

2. The purée of raw mushrooms

½ lb. very fresh, firm, unblemished mushrooms
¼ tsp. salt
Big pinch of pepper
2 tbl. very finely minced shallots or spring onions
1 tbl. lemon juice
A 3-pt bowl

With a large, sharp knife, chop the mushrooms into a very fine mince, almost a purée. Blend them in the bowl with the salt, pepper, shallots or spring onions, and lemon juice. Marinate for 15 to 20 minutes. Then, a handful at a time, twist mushrooms in the corner of a towel to squeeze out as much vegetable liquid as possible. Add the mushrooms to the bowl containing the puréed artichoke flesh.

3. Final assembly

About ½ pt thick home-made mayonnaise (the hard-yolk *tartare* minus the trimmings but plus the sieved egg white, Volume I, page 110, is particularly recommended)
1 tbl. fresh minced tarragon or ¼ tsp. dried tarragon
4 tbl. fresh minced parsley (reserve half for decorations)
Salt and pepper to taste
The cooked artichoke hearts
Optional: 6 cold poached eggs or 6-minute peeled eggs (*œufs mollets*)
A serving dish or individual plates lined with lettuce leaves or watercress
3 to 4 tbl. double cream, *crème fraîche*, or sour cream

The artichoke and mushroom purées are now to be seasoned and piled into the artichoke hearts: a spoonful at a time, stir mayonnaise into the vegetables, adding probably 3 to 4 tablespoons in all but not enough to thin out purée, which must remain thick and hold its shape. Stir in the herbs and taste carefully for seasoning. Sprinkle artichoke hearts lightly with salt and pepper, and mound the purée in them, smoothing it into a dome. (If you are using eggs, lay them in the artichokes between 2 layers of the purée.) Arrange the artichokes in the dish or plates. Just before serving, stir the cream into the mayonnaise, then spoon a dollop over the top of each artichoke, and decorate with parsley.

(†) It is usually perfectly safe to complete the recipe the day before serving, except for the final bit of mayonnaise, and to cover and refrigerate the artichokes. To avoid all risks of turned mayonnaise, however, we suggest that you complete the final assembly only an hour or so before serving.

7. Desserts: Extending the Repertoire

Frozen Desserts – Sorbets, Ice Creams, and Mousses · *Entremets Glacés*

As long as your freezer maintains a steady temperature of zero degrees or less, you need no other ice cream contraption to produce a marvellous parade of frozen fantasies. We start this delicious group with a simple sorbet made from sieved tinned apricots, proceed to a mousse of fresh strawberries (pausing to make some sugar-biscuit cups to serve them in), and continue with chocolate–burnt-almond ice cream, a walnut and caramel mousse, *bombe glacée*, and directions for parfaits and frozen soufflés. *Le Saint-Cyr*, a handsome mould of chocolate mousse and meringues, leads into a digression on meringue whipped cream either as a filling for cream horns or as a vanilla ice cream with chocolate sauce. *La Surprise du Vésuve* ends the section in a dramatic burst of flames.

*Mousse à l'Abricot, Glacée
[Apricot Sorbet]
Easy, delicious, and available all year round is apricot sorbet made from tinned apricots. Timing is 4 to 5 hours, but it is easier to be leisurely and start the mousse the day before serving.

[*For about 1½ pints, serving 4 to 6 people*]

1. The sorbet mixture

A tin (1 lb. 14 oz., or two 1-lb. tins) of apricot halves
A food mill with fine disc
A 2-pt measure
A 4-pt mixing bowl
2 egg whites in a small clean beating bowl

An electric mixer, with clean, dry blades
About 4 oz. caster sugar
2 tbl. lemon juice
2 or 3 drops of almond extract

Drain apricots, purée them, and put into measure. Add enough of their juice to make ¾ pint, and turn purée into mixing bowl. Beat egg whites with mixer until they form soft peaks, and set aside. Then, with mixer, beat the sugar and lemon juice into the apricot purée; continue beating for several minutes to dissolve sugar completely – until you can feel no granules on your tongue. If not sweet enough, beat in a little more sugar; be careful, however, because sugar proportions should be no more than a quarter part of the mixture or sorbet will not freeze properly. Whip in the beaten egg whites with mixer; their purpose is to discourage large ice crystals from forming. Add the drops of almond extract, which will bring out the apricot flavour.

2. Freezing the mousse: 4 to 5 hours minimum at zero degrees or less

A flat pan about 9 by 12 ins. in diameter, if you are in a hurry; or a
    mixing bowl; or ice trays if you have little room
Plastic wrap
An electric mixer or a large wire whisk
Optional: a serving bowl or ice cream mould
The apricot sauce on page 660

The mixture is now to be frozen, and beaten up once or twice during the process to break up ice crystals and give a smooth, light texture. Turn it into a flat pan or ice trays if you are rushed; leave in mixing bowl if you are not. Cover with plastic wrap and freeze for 2 to 3 hours, or until sorbet has begun to set.

When partially set, scrape into mixing bowl if sorbet is in a pan or trays. Beat vigorously with electric mixer or wire whisk; sorbet will increase in volume and begin to whiten. Cover and freeze again for an hour or so, and again beat it up; then turn it into a serving bowl or ice cream mould if you wish. Cover, and freeze for several hours more before serving. (Note: If you are in no hurry and sorbet has frozen hard before you have beaten it, leave at room temperature until softened, and beat with an electric mixer; then return to freezer and continue as usual.)

Let mousse soften for $\frac{1}{2}$ hour in the refrigerator before serving, and accompany, if you wish, with the apricot sauce. (See also the biscuit cups on page 548, which you can use instead of sorbet dishes.)

Mousse à l'Abricot, Chantilly

To make a richer and softer sorbet, really an ice cream, you may incorporate whipped cream as follows.

[*For 2¼ pints, serving 6 to 8 people*]

The preceding apricot sorbet mixture
½ pt chilled whipping cream in a beating bowl
A large bowl with a tray of ice cubes and water to cover them
A large wire whisk or hand-held electric mixer
A rubber spatula
Optional: a chilled serving bowl or ice cream mould

At the end of the first freezing, after you have beaten the apricot mixture and it has increased in volume and whitened, fold in the lightly whipped cream, *crème Chantilly*. (Cream should always be beaten separately; if beaten with the sorbet you will not get as much volume.) Set bowl of cream over ice cubes and water. Circulating whisk or beater about bowl to incorporate as much air as possible, beat until cream has doubled in volume and beater leaves light traces on surface.

Fold the cream into the sorbet, and it will need no further beating, only freezing. If you are serving in a decorative bowl or mould, turn the mixture into it now, cover, and freeze 3 to 4 hours at least before serving.

Bombe Glacée à l'Abricot

[Apricot Mousse Moulded with another Sorbet or an Ice Cream]

When you want to be more elaborate, you may pack the apricot sorbet into a bowl or mould lined with another sorbet or with ice cream, as follows.

[*For 3 pints, serving 8 to 10 people*]

1½ pts of pineapple sorbet, lemon sorbet, or vanilla ice cream
(home-made or best quality shop-bought)
A chilled 3-pt ice cream mould, or metal bowl or *charlotte*
Plastic wrap
The apricot sorbet, page 544

Let the sorbet or ice cream soften just enough so that you can spread it around the inside of the mould or bowl. Cover with plastic wrap and set in freezer to harden. When the apricot has been frozen and beaten several times, and is ready for its final freezing, pack it into the lined bowl. Cover again with plastic wrap and freeze several hours more.

To unmould, run a knife around inside rim of mould, hold for several seconds in a basin of cold water, and unmould on to a chilled serving dish. If not to be served immediately, cover with an inverted bowl and return to freezer.

Mousse aux Fraises ou aux Framboises, Glacée
[Fresh Strawberry or Raspberry Sorbet]

Your own fresh strawberry or raspberry sorbet is a delight, and just as easy to make as the preceding apricot one.

[For about 1⅓ pints, serving 4 to 6 people]

1½ lb. fresh strawberries or raspberries
A food mill with fine disc, set over a 4- to 5-pt mixing bowl
2 egg whites in a small, clean beating bowl
An electric mixer or a large wire whisk
4 oz. caster sugar
3 tbl. lemon juice

Hull the strawberries, and wash rapidly; if using raspberries, pick them over and discard any spoiled ones. Purée berries into mixing bowl. Beat the egg whites until they form soft peaks, and set aside. Beat the sugar and lemon juice into the berry purée and continue beating for several minutes to dissolve sugar completely – until you can feel no granules on your tongue. Whip in the beaten egg whites. Cover and freeze, beating several times as directed in master recipe, step 2, page 545.

Strawberry or Raspberry Ice Cream

For a softer and richer mixture, fold in ½ pint of double cream, beaten over ice, after the mousse has begun to set, as directed for the apricot ice cream, page 546.

Other Fruits

You may substitute frozen raspberries or strawberries for fresh ones in the preceding recipe; thaw, drain, and purée four 10-ounce packages, add enough of the juices to make ¾ pint, and you will need no additional sugar. Fresh, ripe, raw peaches are delicious either as a sorbet or with cream added, and you can decorate each serving with sliced peaches macerated in sugar, lemon juice, and kirsch. Use the same proportions and method for other fruit purées.

Coupelles, Langues de Chats

[Biscuit Serving Cups for Ices, Fruits, and Dessert Creams]

Simple to make and charming as containers are crisp little biscuit cups made from the French egg-white batter known as *langues de chats*, because it is usually baked in flat cat's tongue shapes. Here the batter is spread in thin discs on baking sheets; as soon as the edges have browned in a hot oven, they are removed one by one and pressed into a teacup, where they immediately crisp into shape.

[*For 8 cups 3½ inches in diameter*]

1. The biscuit batter (*pâte à langues de chats*)

2 baking sheets approximately 14 by 18 ins., buttered and floured
A *vol-au-vent* cutter, pot lid, or saucer about 5½ ins. in diameter
A rubber spatula
Tasteless salad oil
2 large tea cups or small bowls about 5 ins. in diameter at the top, 2 at
  the bottom, and 2½ ins. deep

Preheat oven to 425°F., Mark 7, and set rack in middle level.
Prepare baking sheets; then, with cutter and point of rubber
spatula, mark 4 circles on each. Lightly oil cups or bowls, and
set them at a convenient place near the oven.

An electric mixer or a wooden spoon
2 oz. soft butter
2½ oz. caster sugar
The grated rind of 1 lemon or orange
A 3-pt mixing bowl
2 egg whites
1½ oz. plain flour
A sieve or sifter
A rubber spatula

Beat the butter, sugar, and lemon or orange rind in the bowl
with electric mixer or wooden spoon until pale and fluffy.
Pour in the egg whites and mix a few seconds, only just enough
to blend. Place flour in sieve or sifter and shake it over the
batter, rapidly folding it in with rubber spatula.

2. Forming, baking, and shaping; oven preheated to 425°F., Mark 7

A rubber spatula and a dessert spoon
A kitchen timer
A flexible-blade spatula (blade should be at least 8 ins. long) for
  unmoulding biscuits
The oiled cups or bowls for unmoulding the biscuits
A cake rack or racks

Note: If this is the first time you have done this type of biscuit,
experiment with one or two first so that you will understand
the system of baking, removing, and moulding; they are easy
to do as soon as you know what to expect.

Using rubber spatula to dislodge the batter, place a 1½-tablespoon gob in the centre of each of the 4 circles on one of the baking sheets. Using back of spoon, smear the batter out to fill the circles; it will be less than ⅛ inch thick, Place in middle level of preheated oven, set timer for 5 minutes, and bake until biscuits have browned lightly, either to within an inch of the centre, or in large splotches. (Form biscuits on second sheet while these are baking.)

As soon as they are done, set baking sheet on open oven door so that biscuits will stay warm and piable – they crisp immediately they cool, and then cannot be moulded. Working rapidly, slide long side of spatula blade under one biscuit to scrape and lift it off the baking sheet; turn it upside down over one of the oiled cups or bowls, and press into the cup with your fingers. Rapidly remove a second biscuit from the sheet and press into second cup. Immediately take first biscuit out of first cup – they crisp in seconds – and place on rack. Rapidly mould the third biscuit, and finally the fourth. (They will be fragile, so handle with care.)

Close oven door and wait for a few minutes for temperature to return to 425°F., Mark 7; bake and mould second sheet of biscuits.

3. Storing and serving

Biscuits will stay crisp for several days in dry weather if stored airtight; for longer storage, freeze them. Spoon sorbet, ice cream, or fruits into the biscuit cups just before serving. For fruit sorbets or ice cream, such as strawberry, save some of the fruit to decorate top of each serving.

Le Kilimanjaro
Glace au Chocolat, Pralinée

[Chocolate–Burnt-almond Ice Cream]

For lovers of chocolate and ice cream, we think this is the best combination we know.

[For 2½ pints serving 6 to 8 people]

1. Ground caramelized almonds (*pralin aux amandes*)

4 oz. blanched almonds
A pizza tray or roasting pan

Preheat oven to 350°F., Mark 4. Spread almonds in tray or pan, set in middle level, and roast 10 to 15 minutes, stirring up several times, until they are a walnut brown. Remove from oven.

4 oz. sugar
3 tbl. water
A small, heavy saucepan with cover
The almonds in a bowl
The roasting pan, lightly oiled
An electric blender

Combine sugar and water in saucepan and set over moderately high heat. Swirl pan slowly by its handle, but do not stir sugar with a spoon while liquid is coming to the boil. Continue swirling for a moment while liquid boils and changes from cloudy to perfectly clear.

Cover pan, raise heat to high, and boil for several minutes until bubbles are thick and heavy. Uncover and continue boiling, swirling gently, until syrup turns a nice caramel brown. Remove from heat and stir in the almonds; immediately turn out into oiled pan. When cold and hard in 20 minutes or so, break up; grind 4 or 5 tablespoons at a time in electric blender.

(†) *Pralin* freezes perfectly for several months in an airtight jar.

2. The chocolate ice cream

4 oz. sugar
4 tbl. water
2½-pt saucepan with cover

2 tbl. instant coffee
8 oz. good plain chocolate
A larger saucepan of simmering water removed from heat
A wooden spoon

Combine sugar and water in saucepan; swirl over heat until sugar has dissolved completely, and liquid is perfectly clear. Remove from heat; stir in the coffee. Break up the chocolate, stir it in, cover, and set in the pan of hot water. While chocolate is melting, beat the cream into *Chantilly* as follows.

Crème Chantilly:
¾ pt chilled double cream in a 4-pt bowl
A large bowl containing a trayful of ice cubes and water to cover them
A hand-held electric beater
A rubber spatula

Set bowl of cream over ice cubes and water. Circulating beater about bowl to incorporate as much air as possible, beat until cream has doubled in volume and beater leaves light traces on surface.

The *pralin* from step 1 (save 2 to 3 tbl. for final decoration, step 3)

With the electric beater, whip the chocolate until perfectly smooth and shiny. Beat the chocolate for a moment over ice to cool it, then beat in about ½ cup of the *crème Chantilly*. Finally, fold the chocolate mixture into the *Chantilly* along with the *pralin*.

3. Moulding, freezing, and serving; freezing time 2 hours minimum

If you are in a hurry: a 2½- to 3-pt pan, or ice trays 2 ins. deep
Otherwise: a 2½-pt conical mould, or a narrow bowl or dish with rounded bottom, to give the effect of a mountain peak

Immediately turn the ice-cream mixture into pan, pans, or mould. Cover with plastic wrap, and freeze. If you have used a shallow pan, the cream should be ready to unmould in about 2 hours; you will probably need 4 hours for a mould or a bowl.

A chilled serving dish
½ pt double cream beaten into *Chantilly* (as in step 2), sweetened to
  taste with icing sugar and flavoured with ½ tsp. vanilla extract
The reserved 2 to 3 tbl. *pralin*

Just before serving, dip pan or mould in tepid water to loosen
the ice cream. Turn serving dish upside down over mould, and
reverse the two to unmould ice cream into dish. Top with the
crème Chantilly, sprinkle with the *pralin*, and announce the
name of your snow-capped mountain as you bring it to the
table.

Mousse Glacée, Pralinée aux Noix
Appareil à Bombe

[Walnut-caramel Ice Cream – or Filling for *Bombes Glacées*]

French frozen mousses are of two types, one with sugar syrup
and cream, and the other like this, with custard and cream.
Using this base, you may incorporate any flavouring you
wish, from melted chocolate to crushed pineapple, and from
crumbled peppermint sticks to ground caramelized walnuts.
It makes a tender, smooth ice cream, suitable for freezing in a
serving bowl, in a soufflé dish, in parfait glasses, or to be packed
into a decorative mould lined with ordinary ice cream.

[*For 2½ pints, serving 8 to 10 people*]

1. Ground caramclized, and caramelized, walnuts (*pralin aux noix*)

11 oz. sugar
¼ pt water
A heavy 3-pt saucepan with cover
8 oz. shelled walnuts (some may be walnut pieces; 8 perfect halves
  needed)
A lightly oiled baking sheet
A fork, for taking walnuts out of caramel
An electric blender

Combine sugar and water in saucepan, and set over moderately
high heat. Swirl pan slowly by its handle, but do not stir sugar
with a spoon while liquid is coming to the boil. Continue
swirling for a moment as liquid boils and changes from cloudy

to perfectly clear. Cover pan, raise heat to high, and boil for several minutes until bubbles are thick and heavy. Uncover, and continue boiling, swirling gently, until syrup turns a nice caramel brown.

Immediately remove from heat and add the 8 perfect walnut halves; quickly take them out one by one with fork, drain off excess caramel, and place right-side up at one end of baking sheet. If caramel has thickened or begun to harden, set over heat again to liquefy. Remove from heat and pour in the rest of the walnuts; stir about with fork, and turn out on to baking sheet. (Do not wash out the pan; reserve for next step.) When caramel-walnut mixture has hardened, in about 20 minutes, break it up into 1-inch pieces. Grind in electric blender, flicking switch on and off rapidly so that some pieces will remain $\frac{1}{8}$ inch in size, to give texture and interest to the mousse.

(†) Both *pralin* and caramelized walnuts freeze perfectly for several months in an airtight container.

2. The ice cream mixture (*appareil à bombe*)

$\frac{1}{4}$ pint milk heated in the caramel pan
4 egg yolks in a 4- to 5-pt stainless steel bowl (metal is preferable because easy to heat and cool)
A hand-held electric mixer
The ground *pralin*: some for now, some for later
A pan of almost simmering water, large enough to hold bowl for egg yolks
A wooden spoon
A second bowl with 2 trays of ice cubes and water to cover them, to hold the first bowl
3 tbl. kirsch or dark rum

Set milk over low heat, stirring occasionally, to melt the caramel. Meanwhile, beating the egg yolks, gradually incorporate a third of the *pralin* and continue beating until mixture is thick and sticky. By driblets, beat in the hot milk, then set bowl in the pan of almost simmering water. Stir rather slowly with spoon, reaching all over bottom of bowl, until custard gradually warms through and thickens enough to coat spoon with a creamy layer. (Be careful custard does not overheat and curdle the egg yolks; however, you must warm it to the point where it thickens.)

Immediately remove from heat and beat in another third of the *pralin* to stop the cooking. Then, with electric mixer, beat over ice 5 minutes or so, until thoroughly chilled and mixture forms a thick ribbon when a bit is dropped from beater back on to the surface. Beat in the kirsch or rum, and all the rest of the *pralin* (unless you wish to reserve 2 to 3 tablespoons for decorations); final addition of *pralin* does not melt, because mousse is now cold.

½ pt chilled double cream in a 3- to 4-pt bowl
The electric beater (blades need not be washed)
A rubber spatula

Remove custard mixture from ice, and replace with the cream bowl. Beat cream into *Chantilly* by circulating electric beater about bowl to incorporate as much air as possible; continue beating until cream has doubled in volume and beater leaves light traces on surface of cream. Fold the cream into the chilled custard, and mousse is ready for freezing.

3. Freezing and serving suggestions

Freezing times at zero degrees or less: 3 hours for individual servings or parfaits; 6 hours for bowls, moulds, and *bombe glacée*.

(a) *Mousse glacée* or parfait: Pile the chilled mousse into a decorative serving bowl or into individual serving dishes or parfait glasses. Cover with plastic wrap and freeze. At serving time, decorate with caramelized walnuts and/or *pralin*; parfaits are usually topped with a swirl of whipped cream before the walnuts or *pralin* go on. (See 'frozen swirls' below.)

(b) *Soufflé glacé*: Surround a 2-pint soufflé dish with a strip of lightly oiled (tasteless salad oil) foil or waxed paper tied or pinned in place, to make a collar that sticks 1½ inches above rim of dish. Pile the chilled mousse into the dish, letting it rise ½ to ¾ inch up the collar; lay plastic wrap over top of collar and freeze the mousse at least 6 hours. Remove collar just before serving, and decorate top of soufflé with caramelized walnuts and/or *pralin*.

(c) *Bombe glacée*: Follow directions for *bombe glacée à l'abricot*, page 546.

Frozen Whipped Cream Swirls

You may form whipped cream swirls, rosettes, or other designs on a plate or baking sheet lined with waxed paper; cover the swirls and freeze them. At serving time, peel them off the paper, and place upon the dessert. For this, the cream must be a little stiffer than the usual *Chantilly* so that it will hold its shape enough to be formed; when stiff enough, fold in confectioner's sugar and vanilla to taste, pack the cream into a pastry bag or paper decorating cone, and make the designs. (Directions for making paper decorating cones are on page 662.)

Le Saint-Cyr, Glacé
[Frozen Chocolate Mousse Moulded in Meringues]

Here is a handsome dessert for those happy times when you can indulge in whipped cream and chocolate. It is a mould of frozen chocolate mousse in the form of a cylinder with ribbons of white meringue marching around the circumference. It will remind you of the tall *képis*, the decorative caps, worn by the officers of Saint-Cyr, the famous French military academy. You can add a visor, edible or not, if you want to complete the picture.

A NOTE ON MERINGUES AND MANUFACTURING METHODS

This dessert is easy to make when you have an electric beater on a stand; if you don't mind holding on for a while, however, a portable beater is perfectly satisfactory. Rather than being the usual meringue of egg whites beaten to stiff peaks and sugar then folded in, this is the Italian meringue, where boiling sugar syrup is beaten into the stiff egg whites, and the beating continues for 8 to 10 minutes, or until the meringue is cool and forms stiff peaks. It has a double advantage: the meringue shapes bake in half the time of ordinary meringues and the rest of the meringue mixture can be used for the chocolate mousse. Thus you need not bother making a custard base with its attendant beating of sugar and egg yolks over heat; instead, you beat melted chocolate right into the meringue mixture, fold in the whipped cream, and the mousse is made. A further recommendation is that the mousse does not become hard and stiff when frozen; it retains a tender, creamy quality.

[For 3½-pint mould, serving 8 to 10 people]

1. The meringue mixture (*meringue italienne*): 2½ pints

Measure out all the ingredients for this step so that while the sugar is boiling you can finish beating the egg whites.

1 lb sugar
8 tbl. water
A heavy 3-pt saucepan with cover

Combine sugar and water in saucepan and set over moderately high heat. Swirl pan slowly by its handle, but do not stir sugar with a spoon while liquid is coming to the boil. Continue swirling for a moment as liquid boils and turns from cloudy to perfectly clear. Cover pan, reduce heat to low, and let simmer slowly while you beat the egg whites.

6 egg whites at room temperature
An electric mixer with large 5-pt clean, dry bowl and blades
Big pinch salt
¼ tsp. cream of tartar
Drops of vanilla essence to taste

Turn egg whites into mixer bowl, and start at slow speed for a minute or so, until egg whites begin to foam up. Beat in the salt and cream of tartar, and gradually increase speed to fast, until egg whites form stiff peaks. (Notes on beating egg whites are on page 685.) Beat in the vanilla.

Optional but useful: a sugar thermometer
A 2-pt glass measure with ¾ pt cold water and 2 ice cubes
A metal spoon

Remove cover from sugar syrup, and insert sugar thermometer if you are using one. Boil rapidly, and when bubbles begin to thicken, watch temperature or start dropping driblets into iced water. Boil to 238°F., the soft-ball stage – sugar makes a sticky but definite shape when worked in cold water with your fingers.

Immediately start beating egg whites at moderate speed, dribbling boiling syrup into them until all is used. Continue beating egg whites at moderate speed until cool, and until mixture forms stiff peaks when lifted – when you draw a spatula through it, the walls of meringue on either side of the path remain erect and unmoving. (If you are using a portable beater, you may set the meringue bowl in a basin of cold water to speed the cooling.) Beating time: 8 to 10 minutes using a beater on a stand.

2. Baking the meringue decorations: about 1 hour at 200°F., Mark ¼

2 pastry sheets about 12 by 16 ins., non-stick if possible, buttered and floured
A rubber spatula
The dessert mould: a 3½-pt cylindrical *charlotte* mould, baking dish, or even a flower pot, at least 4 ins. deep
½ the meringue mixture
A canvas pastry bag 12 to 14 ins. long with ¾-in. cannelated ribbon-tube opening
A small knife (to cut off meringue from tube when necessary)

Preheat oven to 200°F., Mark ¼. Draw guidelines on pastry sheets with point of rubber spatula to mark depth of mould, so that you will know how long to make the meringues: they are to stand upright around the sides of the mould. (Left-over

meringues are to be layered into mould with the chocolate
mousse; you may wish to decorate top of dessert, after unmoulding, with meringues either whole or crumbled.) A suggested decoration, to resemble the braid on a military cap,
would be a series of straight ribbons alternating with serpentine shapes.

Whatever you decide upon, scoop the meringue mixture
into the pastry bag, and squeeze out shapes between the guide-
lines on the pastry sheets, making the decorations $\frac{1}{8}$ to $\frac{3}{16}$ inch
thick, and no more than $1\frac{1}{2}$ inches wide. You will need 12 to
16 perfect specimens, therefore use up all the meringue in the
bag; muffed shapes can be layered with the mousse, and you
will have some breakage after baking because the meringues
will be brittle.

Set baking sheets in upper- and lower-middle levels of oven
for about an hour, or until you can gently nudge a few loose
from baking surface. They will not puff up, they will not
change shape, and they should remain pure white; they simply
dry out. While still warm, they bend slightly; as soon as they
are cool, they become crisp and fragile. Remove baking sheets
from oven, push all meringues gently loose, but leave them on
the baking sheets.

3. The chocolate mousse (*mousse au chocolat meringuée*)

1 lb. good plain chocolate
A saucepan for the chocolate, and cover for the pan
4 tbl. dark rum
A saucepan of simmering water removed from heat, large enough to
   hold chocolate pan
Waxed paper
The dessert mould from step 2
$\frac{1}{2}$ oz. soft butter

Break up the chocolate, and place in the saucepan with the
rum; cover, and set it in the pan of hot but not simmering
water. While chocolate is melting, fold an 18-inch piece of
waxed paper in half lengthwise, cut in two along fold, and
with the 2 pieces held together, cut into blunt-ended wedges
5 to 6 inches at the wide end, $2\frac{1}{2}$ inches at the blunt end, and $\frac{1}{2}$

inch longer than depth of mould. Cut a circle of waxed paper to fit in bottom of mould exactly, and place it in the mould. One at a time, dot soft butter on one side of waxed paper wedge and insert against inside edge of mould, small end of wedge at bottom; butter holds paper in place. Continue around inside of mould, overlapping paper so that mould is completely covered. Refrigerate in order to set butter and keep paper glued to mould.

The meringue mixture remaining from step 2
¾ pt chilled double cream in a beating bowl
A larger bowl with a tray of ice cubes and water to cover them
A large (balloon) wire whisk, or a hand-held electric beater with clean, dry blades

As soon as chocolate is melted, and you have beaten it to a soft, smooth texture, whip it into the meringue mixture. In its separate bowl, set cream over ice and beat, circulating beater all around bowl to incorporate air into cream, until doubled in volume; continue beating a few minutes more, until beater leaves light traces on surface, and a bit of cream lifted and dropped back softly retains its shape. This is now *crème Chantilly*.

Remove the cream from the ice, and set the chocolate-meringue mixture over it, beating for a few minutes until cool but not stiff – if chocolate is warm it will deflate the whipped cream. Then, with a rubber spatula, turn the *crème Chantilly* out on top of the chocolate, and fold the two together, cutting down from surface of cream to bottom of bowl with rubber spatula, and turning spatula against side of bowl as you draw it out; continue rapidly, rotating bowl as you fold. If the meringues are not yet ready, refrigerate the mousse.

4. Filling the mould

Not allowing it to touch sides of mould if you can help it, turn a 1-inch layer of mousse into the bottom of the mould; this will give support to the meringues you are to place against the sides. Remembering they are fragile and break easily, arrange the meringues best side out against mould and upright around its edges, spacing them about ¼ inch apart. Turn in another layer of mousse about ¾ inch thick, cover with extra meringues, and continue filling the mould with mousse and meringue layers, ending with a layer of meringues. (Do not trim off protruding ends of upright meringues at this point.) Cover mould with plastic wrap, and freeze for 6 hours at least.

5. Unmoulding and serving

Optional: either more *crème Chantilly* sweetened with icing sugar and flavoured with rum or vanilla, or *crème anglaise* (custard sauce, 652)

To unmould the dessert, bend waxed paper back from edges of mould, bend protruding meringue ends down over dessert, and turn a chilled serving dish upside down over mould. Reverse the two and dessert should unmould immediately – if not, reverse mould, run a knife between waxed paper and edge of mould, and reverse again. Carefully peel off waxed paper from top and sides. You need no decoration on top, unless you have baked meringue decorations for it or you wish to crumble left-over baked meringues over it.

Serve the *Saint-Cyr* immediately, accompanied by the optional whipped cream or custard sauce.

(†) Dessert may be unmoulded on to serving dish, covered with a bowl, and returned to freezer for an hour or so before serving; in its mould, it may remain frozen for several weeks. Left-over baked meringues should be kept either in a warming oven at about 120°F. to prevent them from softening, or wrapped airtight and frozen; if frozen, you may need to re-crisp them in a 200°F. oven for 20 to 30 minutes.

Other flavourings and serving ideas for the Chocolate Mousse

Rather than moulding the chocolate mousse in a meringue-lined mould, you may wish to mould it as it is, and decorate with *crème Chantilly* for serving; or you may turn the mousse into individual serving pots, chill rather than freeze them, and serve like the usual chocolate mousse with sweetened whipped cream on the side. Instead of using meringues, you may fold into the mousse a cup or two of *pralin* (caramelized almonds, page 551, or walnuts, page 553), which always gives an in-

teresting texture and taste to chocolate mousse. There is also
the richer chocolate mousse in Volume I, on page 644, with
its egg yolks and butter rather than meringue and whipped
cream; when you use this formula, you need not freeze the
mousse, because the butter, which congeals when refrigerated,
holds the mousse in form when it is unmoulded.

*Chantilly Meringuée
[Whipped Cream with Italian Meringue]
For cream fillings and ice cream; see following recipes.

The Italian meringue of hot sugar syrup whipped into egg
whites, so successful with the preceding *Saint-Cyr*, step 1, page
557, also serves other purposes. You may use it as a base for
butter-cream icing and fillings as described on page 636; you
may also fold it into whipped cream to give the cream more
body and stability as a filling for cream puffs, cream horns, and
Napoleons, or *mille-feuilles*. Or this same *Chantilly meringuée*
may be packed into a mould or bowl and frozen, thus becoming what can truly be called an iced cream. (Although you
can fold plain beaten egg white into whipped cream and freeze
it, the meringue does a better job because it completely dis-
courages the formation of ice crystals, giving you a wonderfully soft and smooth ice cream.)

[*For about 1½ pints of meringue whipped cream*]

½ the *meringue italienne* called for in step 1, page 557
½ pt chilled double cream in a 4-pt bowl
A large bowl with a tray of ice cubes and water to cover them
A hand-held electric mixer or a large wire whisk
Drops of vanilla essence to taste
A rubber spatula

Prepare the meringue mixture, and beat slowly until it is cold.
Meanwhile, prepare a *crème Chantilly* as follows. Set bowl of
cream over ice cubes and water. Circulate beater or whisk
about in cream to incorporate as much air as possible as you
beat; continue beating until cream has doubled in volume and
beater leaves light traces on surface. Stir the vanilla into the
meringue mixture, then fold in a quarter of the whipped cream

to lighten the meringue. Scoop rest of whipped cream on top and fold it in by rapidly cutting down through centre to bottom of bowl and then out to side with rubber spatula, rotating bowl as you do so; repeat the movement rapidly until cream and meringue are blended and deflated as little as possible.

To Use *Chantilly Meringuée* as a Filling

Use as it is, or fold in *pralin* (caramelized almonds, page 551, walnuts, page 553), or shaved chocolate, or fresh strawberries, raspberries, or sliced peaches, or bits of glacéed chestnuts or glacéed fruits macerated in rum or kirsch.

Chantilly Glacée, au Chocolat
[Vanilla Ice Cream with Chocolate Sauce; *Chantilly Meringuée* used as Ice Cream]

It is hard to improve on this universal favourite, and wonderful to have your own private brand.

[*For about 1¼ pints, serving 4 to 6 people*]

1. The vanilla ice cream (*Chantilly glacée*)

The preceding meringue whipped cream, page 562
A 1½-pt mould or metal bowl with rounded bottom
Plastic wrap

Prepare the meringue whipped cream, turn into bowl, cover with plastic wrap, and freeze 3 to 4 hours at least before unmoulding and serving. (This will be a rather soft and tender ice cream.)

2. The chocolate sauce

4 oz. good plain chocolate
¼ pt water
1 tbl. instant coffee
A 2½-pt saucepan
A larger saucepan of simmering water to hold chocolate pan
A wire whisk
1½ tbl. double cream
¾ oz. butter

1½ tbl. dark rum
Pinch of salt if needed

Break up the chocolate and combine with water and coffee in saucepan. Stir slowly over moderate heat until chocolate is melted and smooth, then set in simmering water and cook for 15 minutes, stirring occasionally. Beat in the cream, butter, rum, and, if needed, a pinch of salt. Set aside. Sauce should be tepid when it goes over the ice cream; reheat to tepid, beating it, if necessary, later.

3. Unmoulding the ice cream, and serving

A chilled serving dish
A basin of cold or tepid water

At serving time, set frozen mould in basin of water for several seconds to loosen the ice cream. Run a knife around edge of dessert; turn serving dish upside down over bowl, and reverse the two to unmould the ice cream.

Spoon the tepid chocolate sauce over the ice cream, letting it drip down the sides so that some of the white shows through. Serve immediately.

Other sauces and flavourings

Instead of chocolate sauce, serve the fresh raspberry or strawberry purée in Volume I, page 632, and surround the dish with fresh berries, as well, if you wish. Or spoon over the ice cream two or three chilled, fresh, sliced peaches macerated in sugar, lemon juice, and light rum or kirsch; the apricot sauce on page 660 in this volume is another possibility. Still another would be to fold 3 or 4 ounces of ground caramelized walnuts into the cream after it has begun to set; after pouring chocolate sauce over the ice cream, decorate it either with a sprinkling of *pralin* or with the caramelized half walnuts on page 553. Bits of glacéed chestnuts or glacéed fruits macerated in rum or kirsch would also be attractive.

Bombe Glacée

Frozen *Chantilly* is a perfect filling for *bombe glacée*, just as it is, or with any of the preceding flavour suggestions. Mould in a bowl or *bombe* lined with chocolate, coffee, or strawberry or raspberry ice cream following the directions for the *bombe glacée à l'abricot* on page 546.

La Surprise du Vésuve
[French Baked Alaska Flambée]

Vesuvius erupting is the French version of our baked Alaska ice cream dessert that is spread with meringue and browned quickly in a hot oven. Here the meringue is sprinkled with powdered sugar; the volcano is contained in half an eggshell thrust crater-like into the centre of the Vesuvius, and filled with flaming liqueur that courses down the mountain slopes like molten lava. Use any ice-cream formula you wish, either from the preceding recipes or shop-bought; the cake, which forms the base, may be your own *génoise* from page 635, the sponge cake or almond and orange cake from Volume I, pages 714 or 722, or a shop-bought sponge cake.

[*For a 14- by 8-inch dessert, serving 8 people*]

1. **Preliminaries: to be prepared before dinner**

A *génoise* or sponge cake, such as a round one 8 by 1½ ins.
A flameproof serving platter or tray 16 to 18 ins. long
¼ pt cognac, kirsch, or rum (whatever flavour will go with your sorbet or ice cream) in a small saucepan
10 egg whites at room temperature, and in an egg-beating bowl in time for step 2
An electric mixer
2 pinches salt
½ tsp. cream of tartar
¾ lb. caster sugar
Drops of vanilla essence to taste
2½ pts sorbet or ice cream frozen in a melon-shaped mould about 12 ins. long
An uncracked eggshell half with saw-tooth edge (cut with scissors)
6 oz. icing sugar in a fine-meshed sieve
Matches

(All the ingredients listed must be measured out, laid in easy reach, and ready for use when you are ready, at the last minute, to beat the meringue, unmould the ice cream, assemble the structure, and brown it rapidly in the oven. Although you can beat the meringue an hour before serving, and re-beat it at the last minute, the beating takes but a few minutes in an efficient mixer and your guests should not mind a short wait.)

Slice the cake into $\frac{1}{2}$-inch layers; cut the cake layers in such a way that you can form a large oval $\frac{1}{2}$ inch thick and 1 inch larger all around than your ice-cream mould. Arrange the oval on the platter, sprinkle with 2 to 3 tablespoons of liqueur, cover airtight with plastic wrap, and set aside. Be sure oven is preheated to 450°F., Mark 8, in time for step 2.

2. Assembling, browning, flambéeing, and serving: about 10 minutes; oven has been preheated to 450°F., Mark 8

(a) *Beating the meringue:*

Start beating the egg whites at moderate speed until they are foaming, beat in the salt and cream of tartar, then gradually increase speed to fast until egg whites form soft peaks. Gradually beat in the sugar, sprinkling in 3 tablespoons at a time, beating $\frac{1}{2}$ minute between additions. After all has gone in, add vanilla, and continue beating for several minutes at high speed until egg whites form stiff shiny peaks.

(b) *Assembling Vesuvius:*

Set ice cream mould in a basin of tepid water, run a knife around edge, and unmould the sorbet or ice cream upon the cake in the platter. Immediately spread the meringue over it with a spatula, starting at bottom of cake and bringing it up to a peak at the top of the dessert – meringue should be about 1 inch thick over the sorbet or ice cream, in order to insulate it from the heat of the oven. With spatula make vertical striations from bottom to top, which will allow flaming liqueur to flow down the sides. Insert eggshell half in peak of mountain. Sieve icing sugar all over surface of meringue, making a layer about $\frac{1}{16}$ inch thick.

(c) *Browning:*

Set in upper-middle level of preheated 450°F., Mark 8 oven for 3 to 4 minutes, to brown meringue lightly. Meanwhile, heat the liqueur.

(*d*) *Flambéeing and serving:*

As soon as meringue has browned remove from oven; ignite the hot liqueur with a lighted match, pour into the eggshell, letting excess drip down sides of meringue, and bring flaming to the table.

Fruits, Flans, and Custards, a French Shortcake, and a Flaming *Charlotte*

Gratin de Pommes, Normande
Clafouti aux Pommes

[Sliced Apples Baked with Rum, Currants, Eggs, and Cream]

This is every bit as good as the finest apple tart, but not quite as filling because the apples are baked in a dish rather than in a tart shell.

[For a 10-inch dish, serving 8 to 10 people]

1. The rum and currants

3 oz. currants, in a small bowl
3 tbl. dark rum

Preheat oven to 375°F., Mark 5. Soak the currants in the rum until you are ready to use them.

2. Baking the apple slices

¼ lb. melted butter
A baking tin with raised edges, such as a 10- by 16-in. Swiss-roll tin or a 14-in. pizza tray
4 oz. sugar
6 to 7 medium-sized eating apples (about 2 lb.) (such as Golden Delicious or Cox's Orange Pippin, or other apples that will keep their shape during cooking)
A flexible-blade spatula and a rubber spatula
A lightly buttered 2½-pt baking-and-serving dish, such as a round one 10 by 1½ ins.
More sugar if necessary

Spread $\frac{1}{2}$ the butter in the tin and sprinkle over it $\frac{1}{2}$ the sugar. Wash apples thoroughly but do not peel. Quarter them, core them, and cut into lengthwise slices about $\frac{3}{8}$ inch thick. Arrange in one over-lapping layer in the pan, sprinkle on the remaining sugar, and dribble the remaining butter over all. Bake about 25 minutes in upper-third level of preheated oven until apples are tender but still hold their shape. Transfer apple slices to baking dish in one crowded, overlapping layer. Scrape cooking juices over apples. Taste, and sprinkle on a little more sugar if you think it is needed.

(†) May be prepared to this point a day in advance. Cover when cool, and refrigerate. Preheat oven in time for step 4.

3. The rum and egg topping

The currants in their rum
A sieve over a bowl
3 large eggs
4 oz. sugar
An electric mixer
1 oz. plain flour
$\frac{1}{4}$ pt liquid (2 to 3 tbl. rum maceration plus single cream)
$\frac{1}{4}$ tsp. cinnamon

Drain the currants, pressing rum out of them lightly. Sprinkle $\frac{1}{2}$ the rum over the apples slices. Beat the eggs and sugar for 3 to 4 minutes at high speed with mixer until they are thick and pale yellow. Beat in the flour, liquids, and cinnamon. Fold in the currants, then spread the topping over the apples.

4. Baking and serving: about 25 minutes at 375°F., Mark 5

Bake in middle level of preheated 375°F., Mark 5 oven for about 25 minutes, or until topping has browned nicely and a skewer, plunged through topping, comes out clean. Serve hot, warm, or cold. You may wish to pass lightly whipped cream sweetened with powdered sugar and flavoured with rum, or home-made *crème fraîche*, although no cream or sauce is really necessary.

Flan aux Prunes
Clafouti aux Prunes
[Fresh Plums Baked in Custard]

Fresh plums are halved, baked with sugar and flavourings until just tender, and then baked again under a blanket of eggs and cream. Simple to do and delicious to eat, the same recipe can be applied to other fruits, tinned or fresh, as described at the end of the recipe.

[*For 4 people*]

1. Preliminary baking of the fruit

1 lb. fresh plums, washed, halved, and stoned
A lightly buttered baking dish, large enough to hold them in 1 layer
⅛ tsp. cinnamon
4 oz. sugar
The grated rind of 1 lemon
1 tbl. lemon juice

Preheat oven to 350°F., Mark 4. Arrange fruit skin-side down in dish, and sprinkle with the flavourings. Bake in middle level of oven about 20 minutes, or until fruit is just tender but still holds shape. Raise oven heat to 375°F., Mark 5, for next step.

2. Final baking with custard: 20 to 25 minutes at 375°F., Mark 5

A lightly buttered 10- to 11-in. baking dish 1½ to 2 ins. deep
2 large eggs
3 tbl. sugar
A mixing bowl and wire whisk
2 tbl. flour
1 tsp. vanilla extract
4 tbl. single cream

Transfer fruit, still skin-side down, to second baking dish; reserve juices. Beat eggs and sugar in bowl to blend them, then beat in the flour, vanilla, and cream. Pour over the fruit.

(†) Refrigerate if you are not baking immediately.

Bake in upper third of preheated oven for 20 to 25 minutes, until custard has puffed and browned lightly.

3. Sauce and serving

The cooking juices from step 1, in a small pan
Optional: 2 to 3 tbl. cognac, rum, or kirsch
A serving bowl
Optional: *crème Chantilly* (lightly whipped cream, page 552) sweetened with icing sugar and flavoured with cognac, rum, kirsch, or vanilla

While the dessert is baking, warm the fruit juices and flavour them with the liqueur if you wish; warm them again just before serving. Serve the flan hot, warm, or tepid, accompanied by the fruit juices and optional *crème Chantilly*.

Other ideas

Use the same system for tinned and frozen fruits, like plums, peaches, or apricots. Thaw, if frozen; drain thoroughly, and halve and stone them if necessary. Give them a preliminary baking of 10 minutes or so with 2 or 3 tablespoons of melted butter, a pinch of cinnamon, drops of lemon juice, and a sprinkling of sugar to enhance their flavour. Then pour on the custard mixture and proceed with the recipe.

Pommes Soufflées, Calvados

[Individual Apple Soufflés in Apples]

This is the attractive kind of recipe that looks much dressier than it is – apples baked in wine, then filled with an apple soufflé mixture and baked again on butter-drenched *canapés*. For an essentially simple process, the recipe is purposely detailed because you will want to use this way of baking apples with other fillings and toppings, some of which are suggested at the end of the recipe. Ahead-of-time notes follow each step in the process, so that you can do parts of the dessert whenever you have time, and be ready for the final baking several hours in advance of serving.

[*For 6 people*]

1. Preliminary cooking of the apples

6 large, firm, unblemished eating apples (such as Golden Delicious,
    or Cox's Orange Pippin, or other apples that will keep their shape
    during cooking)
1 lemon, quartered
A 10- to 12-in. flameproof baking dish 3½ ins. deep and smeared with
    ¾ oz. softened butter
6 tbl. dry white wine or vermouth
3 to 4 oz. sugar (more if apples seem sour)
½ stick cinnamon
A 10- to 12-in. round of heavily buttered waxed paper

Preheat oven to 325°F., Mark 3. Wash the apples, then prepare
one at a time: shave off bottom of apple so it will stand solidly
upright. Slanting your knife down towards the core, cut a
cap off top of apple about 2 inches in diameter. Peel, reserving
peel and all edible apple bits for step 2. With grapefruit knife
hollow out apple centres and remove seeds, leaving a ½-inch
shell of apple all around sides and bottom. Rub inside and out
with cut lemon and place in baking dish. When all apples are
done, squeeze remaining lemon juice over them and add
lemon pieces to the dish.

Pour the wine around the apples, sprinkle on the sugar, add
cinnamon, and bring to simmer on top of stove. Cover with
the waxed paper, and set in middle level of preheated oven for
about 30 minutes, regulating heat so that liquid never quite
simmers. Apples should be tender when pierced with a knife,
and ready to eat, but they must keep their shape so that they
will stand up to their final cooking. Remove from oven and
let cool for at least 10 minutes, waxed paper in place over them.

(†) May be baked even a day in advance. Remove from refrigerator at least ½ hour before final baking, step 4.

2. The apple purée (soufflé base)

The peel and all edible bits from apple centres
3 tbl. water
A heavy-bottomed 3-pt saucepan with cover
½ lb. apricot jam pushed through a sieve (3 tbl. for now, the rest for later)
A food mill or sieve
3 or more tbl. sugar

Drops of vanilla essence to taste
3 tbl. calvados, rum, or cognac
1 egg yolk blended with 3 tbl. double cream in a small mixing bowl
Optional: drops of red food colouring

While shells are cooking, simmer apple peel and trimmings with water in the covered pan over moderately low heat for about 15 minutes. When tender, purée with 3 tablespoons of the apricot jam through food mill or sieve. Add sugar, vanilla, and spirits; boil down rapidly, stirring constantly until mixture is almost thick enough to hold its shape on a spoon. Gradually stir it into bowl with cream and egg yolk. Return to saucepan and stir over moderately high heat until mixture comes almost to the boil and thickens again. Taste, adding more sugar if necessary and drops of red colouring if you think they are needed.

(†) May be completed a day in advance; film surface with plastic wrap, and refrigerate.

3. Preliminaries to baking
(a) *The canapés:*

About 4 oz. clarified butter (melted butter, skimmed; clear liquid
   spooned off milky residue)
A frying pan
6 rounds of bread 3 ins. in diameter and ⅜ in. thick (use home-made-type
   white bread)
The remaining sieved apricot jam from step 2
An unbuttered ovenproof serving platter large enough to hold apples
   easily
The cooked apples
A pastry brush

Film frying pan with ⅛ inch of clarified butter, and set over moderately high heat. When bubbling, add as many bread rounds as will fit easily in one layer, and sauté for a minute or so on each side to brown very lightly, adding a little more butter if needed to keep bread from burning. These are now called canapés; paint one side of each with a coating of apricot jam and set them jam-side up on a platter. One by one, drain the apples, pouring accumulated juices back into baking dish.

Paint inside and out with more of the strained apricot jam, and place one apple on each canapé. Dribble over them any remaining butter.

(b) The sauce:

A sieve (or the food mill)
A small saucepan
1 tsp. arrowroot blended with 3 tbl. calvados, rum, or cognac
The remaining apricot jam (plus sugar if needed, and ½ oz. or so of butter)

Discard lemon rind and cinnamon stick; strain contents of apple-baking dish into saucepan. Beat in arrowroot mixture and apricot jam; bring to the simmer. Simmer 2 to 3 minutes, until sauce has turned from cloudy to clear, and has thickened lightly. Taste for flavour, adding more sugar and butter if you feel the need.

(†) Canapés and sauce may be made a day in advance, but do not arrange apples on canapés more than an hour or two before baking.

4. Baking and serving: about 20 minutes at 375°F., Mark 5

2 egg whites at room temperature
An egg-white beating bowl and hand-held electric beater or balloon whisk
Pinches of salt and cream of tartar
The apple purée from step 2
A rubber spatula
The platter of apples
Icing sugar in a small fine-meshed sieve
The sauce, warmed
A warm sauce bowl

About 20 minutes before serving (or as much as an hour in advance) beat egg whites at moderate speed for a minute or two, until foamy; beat in the salt and cream of tartar, and gradually increase beating speed to fast until egg whites form stiff peaks. Stir a spoonful of them into the apple purée to lighten it; delicately fold the rest of the egg whites into the purée with the rubber spatula. Spoon the soufflé mixture into the apple shells, heaping it into a dome. (Invert a large bowl over the platter of apples if you are not baking immediately.)

Bake in middle level of preheated oven for 12 to 15 minutes, until soufflé filling has puffed slightly – it will not puff very much – and begun to brown. Rapidly sprinkle icing sugar over the apples and bake 2 to 3 minutes more. Serve immediately, accompanied by the sauce, a spoonful of which may be poured over part of each apple as it is served.

Other ideas

Rather than filling the apples with a soufflé mixture, you may boil down and season the apple purée as directed in step 2, and stir in 3 tablespoons dry breadcrumbs sautéed in 2 ounces of butter; fill the apples and proceed with the recipe. You may add a handful of raisins soaked first in the rum or cognac called for. Rather than breadcrumbs, you might stir in crumbled stale macaroons, which would give an attractive almond flavouring. Finally, having filled the apples with any of these stuffings, you could then cover them spectacularly with a meringue (beaten egg whites and sugar), sprinkle with shaved almonds, and brown in a hot oven, following the method for the *poires meringuées*, step 4, page 576, in the following recipe.

Poires Meringuées, au Sabayon
[Wine-poached Pears Baked in Meringue, Wine-custard Sauce]

This is a simple fruit dessert that looks satisfyingly elegant and complicated. Pears are poached in an aromatic red-wine syrup, the syrup is turned into a sauce, and at serving time the pears are baked in a cloak of meringue sprinkled with almond flakes. Pear-poaching, sauce-making, and even the little toasts the pears sit upon while baking may be done the day before serving.

[*For 8 pear halves, serving 4 to 8 people*]

1. Poaching the pears

½ lb. sugar
½ pt young red wine, such as Côtes-du-Rhône
¾ pt water

An enamelled frying pan or saucepan 2½ or more ins. deep and just large
enough to hold pear halves
4 whole cloves
The zests (coloured part of peel) of ½ orange and ½ lemon
Drops of vanilla essence to taste
4 firm, ripe, unblemished pears
A grapefruit knife

Stir the sugar into the wine and water, bring to the simmer, and
when dissolved add the cloves, zests, and vanilla. Simmer for
20 minutes, then remove from heat. One at a time, peel the
pears, halve lengthwise, retaining stems, and neatly remove
stem lines and cores. Drop each, as done, into the wine syrup.
Syrup should barely cover pears: add more liquid and sugar if
necessary (4 oz. sugar per ½ pint of liquid). Bring almost to the
simmer, and poach uncovered at just below the simmer for 10
to 15 minutes, until pears are just tender when pierced with a
knife. (Maintaining liquid at below the simmer prevents fruit
from disintegrating.) Let pears cool in syrup for at least 20
minutes so that they will firm up as well as absorb the sugar
and flavourings. (They may remain for several days in the
syrup.)

2. The _sauce sabayon_

¾ pt of the pear poaching syrup
A small saucepan
A 2½-pt enamelled or stainless saucepan and a wire whisk
3 egg yolks
2 tsp. cornflour
2 tbl. cool cooking syrup
A wooden spoon
1 oz. butter
3 to 4 tbl. orange liqueur

Rapidly boil down the cooking syrup in a small saucepan until
reduced by half. In the second saucepan beat egg yolks and
cornflour to blend smoothly, then beat in the 2 tablespoons of
cool syrup. In a thin stream of driblets, beat in the hot, reduced syrup. Set over moderate heat; stir slowly and constantly
with wooden spoon until mixture thickens enough to coat
spoon – do not let it come to the simmer and scramble the egg

yolks; however, sauce must thicken. Remove from heat. Beat in the butter, then the orange liqueur. Set aside, or cover and refrigerate when cool.

3. Preparations before cooking: an hour in advance

8 canapés (rectangles of white bread sautéed in butter, step 3, page 572)
A lightly buttered baking and serving dish, large enough to hold
  canapés easily in 1 layer

Sauté the canapés (if done a day in advance, pack airtight and freeze); arrange in 1 layer in baking dish.

3 egg whites
A clean beating bowl and electric beater
Big pinch each of salt and cream of tartar
4 oz. caster sugar
¼ tsp. vanilla extract

Beat egg whites until foaming, then beat in the salt and cream of tartar, and continue beating until soft peaks are formed. Beat in the sugar, sprinkling it on 2 spoonfuls at a time, beating ½ minute between additions. Beat in the vanilla and continue beating for several minutes at high speed until egg whites form stiff, shiny peaks. This is the meringue mixture.

A rack set over a tray

Drain pears hollow-side down on rack.

4. Baking and serving: 5 to 7 minutes: oven preheated to 425°F., Mark 7

3 tbl. sugar
The canapés in their baking dish
The drained poached pear halves
The *sauce sabayon*
The meringue mixture
4 tbl. sliced almonds
2½ oz. icing sugar in a fine-meshed sieve
A warm bowl for the sauce

(Although pears may be masked with meringue or baked ahead, they are best when assembled and baked at the last moment.) Sprinkle a teaspoon of sugar over each canapé, and place a pear half, hollow-side up, on top. Fill hollow with a teaspoon of *sauce sabayon*. If necessary, beat the meringue mixture at high speed for a moment until it again forms stiff peaks. Mask each pear half with a large spoonful of meringue. Strew sliced almonds over each and sift on a light sprinkling of icing sugar. Place in upper third of preheated oven for about 5 minutes, until meringue and almonds have lightly browned. Meanwhile, gently warm the sauce to tepid and turn into warm bowl. Serve pears as soon as possible, passing the sauce separately.

Mousse d'Oranges à l'Ananas
[Moulded Orange Mousse Garnished with Pineapple and Candied Orange Peel]

When you want a beautiful dessert that is also light and as delicious as it is refreshing, this orange Bavarian cream without cream is a perfect answer.

[For 6 to 8 people]

1. Preliminaries
(a) *Glazed pineapple*

A small (8½-oz.) tin of pineapple slices, or 4 slices and 6 tbl. juice
2½ oz. sugar
A small saucepan
A small bowl
3 tbl. kirsch

Lay pineapple slices flat on cutting board, and slice in half parallel with board to make 2 rings rather than 1; divide each into 16 wedges. Bring sugar to boil in pineapple juice, and when dissolved add the pineapple and boil 5 minutes, or until pineapple is beginning to turn a golden, light-caramel colour. Drain. Place pineapple in bowl with kirsch, and return juice to pan.

(b) *Glazed orange peel*

6 or more large, bright, juicy oranges
6 large, rectangular sugar lumps
Waxed paper

A wooden spoon
A 4-pt stainless or enamelled saucepan

Wash and dry oranges. Break sugar lumps in half. Over waxed paper, rub sugar lumps one at a time vigorously against the skin of 2 oranges, until all sides of lumps have absorbed as much oil as possible from the orange skins. Mash the sugar with the spoon and scrape into saucepan.

A vegetable peeler and a sharp chopping knife
A small saucepan with ¾ pt water
A small bowl
5 oz. sugar
¼ pt water
The pan of pineapple juice

Remove zests (orange part of peel) from 2 of the other oranges, and cut into julienne strips 1½ inches long and $\frac{1}{16}$ inch wide. Drop into the pan of water and simmer 15 minutes; drain, rinse in cold water, and squeeze dry in paper towels. Place in small bowl. Stir sugar and water into pineapple juice, swirl over heat until sugar dissolves, then boil rapidly to the thread stage (230°F.). Stir 2 tablespoons into the orange peel, reserve rest of syrup for the custard.

A 2-pt measure
1 lemon
2 packages (2 tbl.) unflavoured powdered gelatine in a small bowl

Squeeze juice out of oranges and lemon and strain into measure to make ¾ pint. Pour ¼ pint of juice into the gelatine, and stir a tablespoon of juice into the pineapple-sugar syrup to liquefy it.

2. Making and moulding the mousse

4 egg yolks
1 tbl. cornflour
The 4-pt pan with the crushed sugar lumps
A wire whisk or electric beater
The pineapple-sugar syrup
The orange and lemon juice
A wooden spoon

Beat the egg yolks and cornflour with the crushed sugar for a minute or two until yolks are thick and sticky. Gradually beat in the pineapple-sugar syrup, and continue beating vigorously for 2 minutes. Beat in the orange juice. Set over moderate heat and stir slowly (2 strokes per second), reaching all over bottom of pan. As custard warms, it will become foamy, and when a faint breath of steam rises it is beginning to thicken. Continue stirring over heat until it thickens enough to coat spoon lightly; custard must not come to the simmer and scramble the yolks, but it must thicken.

The gelatine and orange juice mixture

Remove custard from heat and immediately scrape the gelatine mixture into the hot custard, beating vigorously to be sure gelatine dissolves completely.

4 egg whites (at room temperature)
Pinch of salt
¼ tsp. cream of tartar
A clean, dry bowl and electric mixer or balloon whisk

Beat the egg whites until foaming, beat in the salt and cream of tartar, and continue until egg whites form stiff peaks. Then beat the egg whites into the hot custard with your whisk, making a foamy mass – the mousse.

The pineapple wedges
A 2½-pt metal mould, fluted or decorated if you wish
Half the orange peel
A large bowl with 2 trayfuls of ice cubes and water to cover them
A rubber spatula
Plastic wrap

Arrange a handful of pineapple wedges in the bottom of the mould for decoration. Drain the pineapple maceration liqueur into the mousse, then fold it in along with the orange peel. Set bowl with mousse in bowl of ice cubes of water; stir every few minutes with rubber spatula until mousse thickens and is about to set. (Beat with wire whisk if necessary to smooth it again.) Rapidly turn a third of the mousse into the mould, spread half the pineapple wedges over it, cover with half the remaining mousse, then the rest of the pineapple and finally the last of the mousse. Cover with plastic and refrigerate until serving time.

(†) May be made a day or two ahead; may be frozen and served either frozen or thawed.

3. Serving

A large bowl of hot water
A chilled serving dish
The rest of the orange peel
Either: *crème Chantilly* (lightly whipped cream, page 552), with icing sugar and flavouring;
Or: *crème anglaise* (custard sauce, page 652), with a little double cream stirred in

Shortly before serving dip mould for 5 seconds in hot water, turn serving dish upside down on top of mould and reverse the two, unmoulding dessert on to dish. Fold remaining orange peel into whatever sauce you have chosen, and pass separately.

Riz des Hespérides

[Mould of Orange-flavoured Rice and Cherries]

In the long-ago days before frozen strawberries and tinned apricots, the only fruits to be had during the winter were dried or glacéed; when once in a while fresh oranges came in from Italy or Spain, they would be combined into something very special, like this unusual rice dessert. You will find it a delicious illustration of what wonders can be wrought with simple and inexpensive ingredients – the rice is simmered in milk and puréed orange peel, then moulded with glacéed orange and lemon peel, cherries, and almonds; it is served with custard sauce or whipped cream.

[*For 8 to 10 people*]

Make this the morning, or the day, or several days before you wish to serve.

1. The orange rice

6 oz. plain, raw, white rice
5 pts rapidly boiling water in a saucepan

2 large, bright-skinned oranges
A vegetable peeler
An electric blender
¾ pt milk
A heavy 3-pt flameproof baking dish with cover
1 oz. butter
⅛ tsp. salt
Pinch nutmeg
Waxed paper

Preheat oven to 300°F., Mark 2. Sprinkle rice into boiling water and boil rapidly for exactly 5 minutes; drain immediately. Wash oranges. Remove the zests (orange part of peel) with vegetable peeler, and place in blender with 6 tablespoons of the milk. Purée zests and milk, and pour into baking dish; add rest of milk, blanched rice, butter, salt, and nutmeg. Bring just to the simmer on top of the stove, then lay waxed paper over surface of milk, cover dish, and place in middle level of preheated oven. Bake for 30 to 40 minutes, until rice is tender and all liquid has absorbed. While rice is cooking, prepare ingredients in next step.

2. The fruit garniture

2 oz. glacéed cherries
A pan of boiling water and a sieve
A small bowl
2 tbl. cognac
4 oz. mixed, diced glacéed orange peel, lemon peel, and citron
A small saucepan
1 package (1 tbl.) plain, unflavoured gelatine
2 tbl. strained lemon juice
3 tbl. strained orange juice
3 tbl. orange liqueur
A pan of hot water to hold the pan of glacéed fruits and gelatine

Slice cherries in half lengthwise (through stem end) and drop into boiling water to wash off preservatives. Drain, and place half in the small bowl with the cognac. Then drop rest of glacéed fruit into boiling water and leave for several minutes – to soften as well as wash them. Drain, and put into small saucepan with the remaining cherries. Sprinkle on the gelatine, and stir in the lemon juice, orange juice, and orange liqueur. Let gelatine soften for several minutes, then set the pan in hot water, stirring occasionally, so gelatine will dissolve completely by the time you are ready to use it. (Reheat water, as necessary.)

3. Assembling the mould

½ lb. sugar
½ pt water
A small, heavy saucepan and cover
A cup of iced water or a sugar thermometer
1 tsp. vanilla
4 tbl. sliced almonds with or without skins
A 2½-pt *charlotte* mould or cylindrical dish 3 to 3½ ins. deep, bottom lined with waxed paper

As soon as you remove the rice from the oven, make the sugar syrup: blend sugar and water in saucepan and bring to boil over moderately high heat, swishing pan by handle until sugar has dissolved completely and liquid is perfectly clear. Cover pan and boil rapidly for 1 to 2 minutes, until syrup is forming large, thick bubbles. Uncover and in a few seconds test; syrup should form a soft ball in the iced water, or be at a temperature of 283°F. A spoonful at a time, rapidly but gently fold the syrup into the rice. Fold in the diced fruits and gelatine mixture, and the vanilla; drain in the cognac from the cherries, and fold in along with the sliced almonds. Mixture should cool somewhat before being moulded; set in a pan of cold water or over cracked ice and water, folding occasionally until liquids and rice form a homogeneous blend.

Arrange the reserved cherry halves in the bottom of the mould, cut-side up. Spoon the rice into the mould, which will be almost filled. Cover with waxed paper or plastic, and chill for several hours, or until set.

4. Serving

A chilled serving plate
Either: 1¼ pts *crème anglaise* (custard sauce, page 652) flavoured with orange liqueur;
Or: *crème Chantilly* (lightly whipped cream, page 552) flavoured with orange liqueur and sweetened with icing sugar

Run a thin knife around edge of dessert, turn serving platter upside down over it, and reverse the two to unmould dessert on to plate. Surround with a little of the custard sauce or *crème Chantilly*, and pass the rest separately.

Le Pélerin en Timbale
[Moulded Almond Cream]

This is a cross between the rich *charlotte Malakoff* and the classic Bavarian cream: a custard sauce bound with gelatine and butter, flavoured with toasted almonds, kirsch, and apricot, and moulded in a cake-lined dish. It gets its name from the pilgrims who, in the days before modern processing, stuffed their pockets with non-perishables like dried fruits and nuts. We assume that this particular *pélerin* paid his host for the night in almonds, which his hostess put to use in the following manner. (Note that this dessert improves in flavour if made a day or two in advance of serving.)

[*For 8 to 10 people*]

1. Preliminaries

7 oz. blanched whole almonds
A roasting pan or pizza tray
A kitchen timer
An electric blender

Preheat oven to 350°F., Mark 4. Spread almonds in pan and toast for 5 minutes in middle level of oven; stir them up and toast another 5 to 6 minutes, stirring every 2 to 3 minutes to be sure they do not burn. They should be deep golden brown. When cool, pulverize 3 or 4 tablespoons at a time in electric blender; set aside.

A 2½-pt cylindrical *charlotte* mould or baking dish about 3½ ins. deep
A round of waxed paper
A long thin knife
A butter sponge cake, *génoise*, shortcake, or other cake of that type (can be shop-bought), such as a round one at least 8 by 1½ ins.
2 heavily buttered pastry sheets
1½ oz. melted butter
2 to 3 tbl. sugar
1 tbl. kirsch

Meanwhile, line bottom of mould with the waxed paper. Then slice cake into horizontal layers each no more than ⅓ inch thick. Cut a round out of the top-of-cake layer to fit bottom of mould and place round inside-side up on a baking sheet. Cut rest of cake layers into strips 1¼ inches wide and arrange on the baking sheets. Paint with melted butter and sprinkle with sugar. When almonds are done, raise thermostat to 400°F., Mark 6. Set baking sheets in middle and upper-third levels of oven and bake the cake strips for about 10 minutes, until they are lightly golden brown. Remove from oven, sprinkle with drops of kirsch, and set aside.

·2. The custard sauce (*crème anglaise*) and almond cream

1½ tbl. (1½ packages) unflavoured powdered gelatine
4 tbl. kirsch in a measure
6 oz. sugar
6 egg yolks in a heavy-bottomed 3-pt stainless or enamelled saucepan
A hand-held electric beater or a wire whisk
1 pt hot milk in a small saucepan
A wooden spoon
8 oz. butter cut into ¼-in. slices
The toasted almonds
Drops of vanilla essence to taste
If needed: a pinch of salt; a few drops of almond extract

Sprinkle the gelatine over the kirsch and set aside. Beat the sugar gradually into the egg yolks and continue beating for several minutes until mixture is thick, pale yellow, and forms a ribbon for a few seconds when a bit falls back on the surface. Gradually beat in the hot milk, adding it in a thin stream. Set mixture over moderate heat and stir slowly with wooden spoon, reaching all over bottom of pan, for 4 to 5 minutes until sauce thickens enough to film spoon with a creamy layer. (Be careful sauce does not come to the simmer and curdle the egg yolks, but you must heat it to the point where it thickens.) Immediately remove from heat and stir vigorously for 1 minute to cool slightly, then scrape the gelatine and kirsch mixture into the hot sauce, beating thoroughly for 2 minutes, to be sure gelatine dissolves completely. (A hand-held electric beater is useful here, and from now on.) Beat in the butter, 4 pieces at a time, then the almonds and vanilla. Taste carefully: add a little salt and drops of almond extract if you feel them necessary. Set aside; you will have about 2 pints of sauce, which should still be slightly warm or at least tepid when used in next step.

3. Filling the mould

Line the mould with the toasted cake, sugared sides against mould, as follows. Place circle in the bottom; cut strips to fit upright and close together side by side, trimming one or two into wedges if necessary to fill in gaps.

A ladle
The tepid almond cream
Left-over cake strips
2 to 3 oz. apricot jam
Plastic wrap

Ladle a third of the almond cream into the mould. Paint several cake strips with apricot jam and arrange in a layer over the cream. Ladle more cream into mould to fill to two thirds and cover with additional apricot-painted cake strips. Finally fill the mould with the remaining almond cream, pouring some down between cake strips and side of mould if necessary. Top with additional cake strips if any remain; cover with plastic wrap and chill several hours until set.

(†) Finished dessert will keep 4 to 5 days under refrigeration or may be frozen.

4. Serving

A chilled serving dish
1 pt apricot sauce (page 660)
Optional: 1 pt *crème Chantilly* (lightly whipped cream, page 552), sweetened, and flavoured with kirsch

Carefully run a thin knife around edge of mould several times to detach sides of dessert. Then turn dish upside down over mould, reverse the two and give a sharp downward jerk to unmould dessert on to dish. Spoon a little of the apricot sauce over top of dessert, and the rest around it on the dish.

Refrigerate if not to be served immediately. Pass optional *crème Chantilly* separately.

Le Marly
La Riposte
[French Strawberry Shortcake Made with Rum-soaked *Brioche*]

Le Marly is the French retort – *la riposte* – to the English shortcake. Rather than being biscuit dough, or a *savarin* – which it closely resembles except in shape – the cake is *brioche* dough baked in a cake tin, then split in two, hollowed out, and steeped in rum- or kirsch-flavoured syrup. The strawberry and whipped cream filling is topped with pie-shaped wedges of *brioche* that rise to a peak in the centre, giving the impression of a Chinese coolie hat. Glazed with apricot and decorated with strawberries, it is a pretty dessert, and so easy to assemble that you might well make the whole dough recipe rather than the half portion needed. You will thereby have two *brioche* cakes; freeze the second one to have on hand for those times when you need something special in a hurry. Other fruits besides strawberries are delicious too, and are suggested at the end of the recipe.

[*For a round* brioche *8 by 2¼ inches, serving 6 to 8*]

1. Making and baking the *brioche*: about 5 hours (may be baked in advance and frozen)

Note: Because it will be soaked in rum or kirsch, the flavour of the *brioche* itself is not of great importance, and there is no need to make the buttery *brioche fine*; *brioche commune*, the *pain brioché* recipe, is the dough to use here and it needs only the first rise – or 2 rises to double if you are working in a hot kitchen.

½ the *pain brioché* dough on page 127
A round cake tin 8 by 1½ ins. smeared with 1 tsp. soft butter
A cake rack

Follow the *pain brioché* recipe, but you may make the dough in an electric mixer as described on page 129.

As soon as the first rise is complete, deflate the dough, form into a ball (directions for forming a round shape are on page 105), and place seam-side down in tin; pat dough out to edges all round. Tin will be filled by about two thirds. Set uncovered at 75° to 80°F. until dough has risen to fill the tin – about 1 hour. (Preheat oven to 400°F., Mark 6, before dough has completed its rise.)

Bake in middle level of preheated 400°F., Mark 6 oven for 20 minutes, or until dough has risen about an inch above rim of tin and has begun to brown nicely, then turn thermostat down to 350°F., Mark 4, and bake another 10 to 15 minutes. *Brioche* is done when it comes easily out of the tin, is nicely browned, and makes a hollow sound when thumped. Cool on a rack.

(†) If you want to keep the *brioche* for several days or several weeks before using, wrap airtight when cool, and refrigerate or freeze it. To defrost frozen *brioche*, let it sit several hours at room temperature, or place on a lightly buttered baking sheet for about 45 minutes in a 300°F., Mark 2 oven.

2. Preliminaries to assembling the dessert
(a) *The fruit filling:*

1½ lb. fresh strawberries
A bowl
Sugar if needed

Wash the strawberries if necessary; hull them. Reserve 4 to 6 of the finest to decorate top of dessert; halve or quarter the rest, depending on size. Place in bowl, and toss lightly with sugar to taste.

(b) *The sugar syrup:*

Scant ½ pt water in a small saucepan
6 oz. sugar
6 tbl. kirsch or dark rum

Stir the water and sugar over heat until sugar is completely dissolved; remove from heat. When syrup has cooled to lukewarm, stir in the kirsch or rum. (Syrup should be tepid when it goes over the *brioche*; reheat if necessary.)

(c) *Apricot to glaze the* brioche:

About 5 oz. apricot jam forced through a sieve into a small saucepan
2 tbl. sugar
A wooden spoon

Bring the strained apricot jam and sugar to the boil, stirring, for several minutes until last drops to fall from spoon are sticky. Set aside; reheat before using.

(d) *For ¾ pint* crème Chantilly:

½ pt double cream in a mixing bowl
A large bowl with a tray of ice cubes and water to cover them
A large wire whisk or hand-held electric mixer
A rubber spatula
Drops of vanilla essence to taste
3 to 4 oz. icing sugar in a sieve

Set bowl with cream over the ice cubes and water. Circulating whisk or beater about bowl to incorporate as much air as possible, beat cream until doubled in volume. Beater should leave light traces on surface of cream. (If you wish to squeeze out whipped cream decorations later, reserve 6 tablespoons in a bowl, and refrigerate.) Fold in the vanilla, and sugar to taste. Keep over ice until needed.

3. Assembling and serving

A long knife for splitting the *brioche*, a small knife and a grapefruit
   knife for hollowing it out
A tray to hold syrup drips
A serving dish
Optional: a canvas pastry bag with round, cannelated tube opening,
   for making decorative lines of whipped cream on top of cake

Slice off the top quarter of the *brioche*, making a cover about ¾ inch thick; cut into 6 to 8 pie-shaped wedges, and place upside down on rack over tray. Hollow out remaining part of *brioche*, first outlining a circle in its top surface ¾ inch from edge all around the inside, and to within ¾ inch of bottom. Then remove interior by bits, with grapefruit knife, to make the *brioche* into a container ¾ inch thick at sides and bottom.

   Set *brioche* container hollowed-side up on serving dish. Drain the strawberries, adding their juices to the syrup. Pour successive spoonfuls of tepid syrup gradually over *brioche*, letting it absorb as much liquid as it will. At the same time, pour spoonfuls of syrup over the upside-down cover wedges. Fold the berries into the *crème Chantilly*. Paint outer sides of *brioche* container with warm apricot glaze; turn the strawberries and cream into it, heaping the filling into a dome.

Handling them carefully, set the *brioche* wedges in place on top of the filling, letting their pointed ends rise to a peak at the centre. Paint tops of wedges with warm apricot glaze. If you have decided to make whipped cream decorations, whip the reserved *Chantilly* over ice until it is a little stiffer, so that it will hold its shape when squeezed out; fold in 2 tablespoons of sifted icing sugar and a few drops of vanilla. Fill in gaps between wedges with ribbons of whipped cream. Just before serving, decorate top of *Le Marly* with the reserved strawberries. To serve, cut right down between wedges, from top to bottom of cake.

(†) May be assembled an hour or two before serving; cover with a bowl, and refrigerate.

Other fruits

Instead of fresh strawberries, use raspberries, sliced fresh peaches, frozen strawberries (thawed), a mixture of pineapple and bananas, or the apricot filling on page 660, which you could combine with diced bananas and toasted, slivered almonds. You may macerate the fruit in sugar, rum, or kirsch, if you wish, then stir the maceration into the sugar syrup.

Charlotte Jamaïque en Flammes
[Rum-cake Caramel Custard, Flambée]

This is another *riposte* to the Anglo-Saxons, a French plum pudding of rum-soaked *brioche* or sponge cake, currants, fruits, and custard baked in a caramelized mould and brought flaming to the table. A fine holiday dessert, it may be made ready for the oven hours before baking, and that takes about an hour.

[*For 6 to 8 people*]

1. Preparing the fruits

4 oz. currants
Either: 4 oz. each of glacéed cherries and apricots;
Or: 8 oz. mixed diced glacéed fruits
½ pt dark Jamaica rum in a covered bowl

Drop the currants into a pan of boiling water, and set aside to swell and soften while preparing rest of fruit. If using cherries and apricots, cut cherries in half, and drop in boiling water to wash off preservatives; drain, and set on a plate. Dice the apricots, drop in boiling water, drain, and set on another plate. (If using mixed fruits, drop in boiling water, and drain.) Then drain currants, squeeze out accumulated moisture, and steep in the rum until you are ready to use them.

2. Caramelizing the mould

4 oz. sugar and 3 tbl. water in a small, heavy saucepan
A cover for the pan
A 2½-pt cylindrical mould, such as a *charlotte* or ceramic baking dish at least 3½ ins. deep
A plate upon which mould may be reversed

Set sugar and water over moderately high heat, and swirl pan slowly by its handle (but do not stir sugar with a spoon) while liquid is coming to the boil. Continue swirling for a moment as liquid boils and turns from cloudy to perfectly clear. Cover pan, raise heat to high, and boil several minutes, until bubbles are thick and heavy. Uncover and continue boiling, swirling gently, until sugar turns a nice caramel brown.

Immediately pour the caramel into the mould (reserve caramel pan); turn mould in all directions to film bottom and sides, and continue turning slowly for a minute or so, until caramel ceases to run. Turn mould upside down over plate.

3. The custard sauce

½ pt milk
3 eggs
5 oz. sugar
A 5-pt mixing bowl and electric beater or large wire whisk
Drops of vanilla essence to taste

A clean 4- to 5-pt enamelled or stainless saucepan
A wooden spoon
A fine-meshed sieve

Pour the milk into the caramel-cooking pan, and stir over heat to dissolve caramel. Then beat eggs and sugar in mixing bowl for several minutes until pale and foamy; beat in the vanilla. Finally, in a thin stream of droplets, beat in the hot milk. Pour mixture into clean saucepan, and set over moderate heat; stir slowly with wooden spoon, reaching all over bottom of pan, for 4 to 5 minutes, or until custard thickens enough to film spoon with a creamy layer. (Be careful sauce does not come to the simmer and curdle the eggs, but you must heat it to the point where it thickens.)

Remove from heat, and stir vigorously a moment or two to cool the sauce and stop the cooking. Rinse out mixing bowl, and strain the sauce into it.

4. Filling the mould

A pan of boiling water large enough to hold dessert mould easily
About 1 lb. of *brioche*, sponge cake, or shop-bought sponge-type cake

(Preheat oven to 350°F., Mark 4, for next step.) Check water level of pan with mould set into it, and place pan (without mould) in lower-middle level of oven. Slice *brioche* or cake into 3 layers, each about ⅛ inch thick, and trim so they will fit into the mould exactly. (Each layer may consist of several pieces neatly fitted together.)

Fit a layer of cake in the bottom of the caramelized mould. Drain the currants and sprinkle 3 tablespoons of their rum maceration over the cake. Arrange a row of cherry halves (or mixed diced fruit) around the edge of the cake, and spread a third of the currants and apricots (or more diced mixed fruit) over the rest of the cake. Pour in a third of the custard. Put down a second layer of cake, sprinkle with 3 tablespoons more rum, and continue filling the mould in layers. Leave about ¼ inch of unfilled space at top of mould because dessert will swell slightly during cooking. Cover remaining rum and reserve for flambéeing.

(†) Mould may be filled a day in advance of baking; cover airtight and refrigerate. Chilled custard will probably take at least 20 minutes more to bake than the 45 to 60 minutes specified in step 5.

5. Baking the dessert: 45 to 60 minutes at 350°F., Mark 4, plus a 10-minute rest (longer if custard has been chilled)

Place the filled mould in the pan of hot water in the oven (water should come three quarters of the way up outside of mould). Bake for 45 minutes to 1 hour, regulating heat so that water in pan almost but never quite bubbles – to ensure a smooth and velvety texture to the custard. Add more boiling water, as necessary, if liquid drops below the halfway mark. Dessert is done when it begins to show a faint line of shrinkage from sides of mould.

If you wish to serve within 10 to 15 minutes, remove mould from water and allow custard to settle for 10 minutes before unmoulding, step 6; otherwise leave custard in its pan of water in turned-off oven. Dessert must be hot for successful flambée-ing.

6. Unmoulding, flambéeing, and serving

A thin-bladed flexible knife for help in unmoulding
A very hot, lightly buttered serving platter
3 or 4 broken sugar lumps and 1 tbl. sugar
The remaining rum (at least 6 tbl.) in a small saucepan
Matches
A pair of long-handled serving utensils

The moment before serving, run knife around edge of mould, turn hot platter upside down over it, and reverse the two to unmould dessert on to platter. Stick the broken sugar lumps into the dessert at various places, and sprinkle on the plain sugar. Heat the rum and pour it over the dessert. Averting your face, ignite the rum with a lighted match, and bring the *charlotte* flaming to the table. Spoon flaming rum over the dessert as you begin to serve.

Desserts Using French Puff Pastry

French puff pastry, that unbelievably tender and buttery dough, with its hundreds of thinner-than-paper layers, is ideal for desserts. Because the pastry itself is so marvellous, the rest of the ingredients are usually rather simple and easy to assemble. We give only a sampling of the many, many recipes that use puff pastry, going into enough illustrated detail, we hope, so that when you run into other puff pastry recipes elsewhere, they will seem feasible and even familiar.

Your sole problem – which need be no problem at all – is to keep the dough cold while you are working on it. At the slightest suggestion of limpness, stop where you are, refrigerate everything for 15 to 20 minutes, then continue. If you are not yet used to working with puff pastry, do not attempt anything complicated in a hot kitchen; wait for cool weather or an air-conditioned atmosphere. Chilled dough in a cool room is easy to manipulate; soft, limp dough in a warm room is impossible.

Abaisses en Feuilletage pour Tartes aux Fruits

[Forming Puff Pastry Shells for Fruit Tarts]

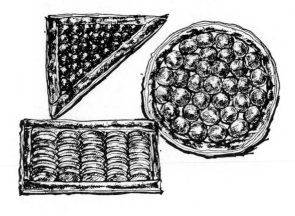

With French puff pastry you can make free-standing shells of any size and shape you wish: the sides of the pastry rise automatically in the oven while the bottom stays put, held down by the fruit or, if you want a precooked shell, by a tin. Use either the simple puff pastry on page 166, or the reconstituted left-over puff pastry described on page 196. We shall not give proportions, except to say that one fourth of the recipe, or a piece of dough $5\frac{1}{4}$ by 2 by $1\frac{3}{4}$ inches, will make a rectangular pastry 6 inches wide and 13 inches long, with a bottom layer $\frac{1}{8}$ inch thick; thus half the recipe would make a 12- to 13-inch square.

To make a square or rectangular shell

Sufficient chilled puff pastry dough
A ruler or light-weight baking sheet to use as a cutting guide
A ravioli wheel or sharp knife
A baking sheet rinsed in cold water but not dried
A cup of cold water and a pastry brush

Roll out the chilled pastry $1\frac{1}{2}$ inches larger than the size you want your tart to be. With cutting guide and ravioli wheel or knife, trim off rough edges all around. Again using your guide and ravioli wheel or knife, cut a strip $\frac{3}{4}$ inch wide from each side of the pastry (A); these will form the raised edges of

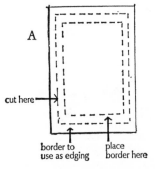

A

cut here→

border to use as edging   place border here

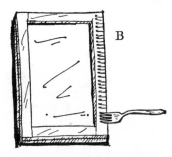

B

the tart; set them aside. Roll up the rectangle or square of pastry on your pin, and unroll it upside down on the dampened baking sheet. Paint around top edges of tart with a $\frac{3}{4}$-inch stripe of cold water. Lay a strip of pastry on top of each side, as shown. Paint corners with cold water, and lay two final strips of pastry over each end. Trim off excess. Seal the two layers together by pressing outside rim all around pastry with the back tines of a table fork (B), and pressing top strips of pastry lightly with thumb of other hand as you go. Prick interior of pastry with fork at $\frac{1}{8}$-inch intervals, going down to pastry sheet. Cover with plastic wrap and chill for an hour before proceeding; dough must be relaxed or it will not bake evenly.

(†) When chilled and firm, dough may be wrapped airtight and frozen for several months; continue with whatever your recipe, using dough in its frozen state.

Forming a round tart shell

Using *vol-au-vent* cutters, pot lids, or any convenient circular objects, pick one for the size of your eventual tart and another $\frac{3}{4}$ inch larger all around for the raised rim of the tart. Roll out pastry $\frac{1}{8}$ inch thick and $\frac{1}{4}$ inch larger all around than the larger of your two cutting guides; lift pastry and let it shrink if it will, and extend again if necessary. Centre guide on pastry and cut off excess dough.

Centre the smaller guide in the pastry and cut all around it cleanly, so that this centre disc can easily separate itself from the outside circle (C). Divide outside circle into quarters or sixths and slide out of the way; these strips will form the raised rim of the tart. Roll disc up on pin and unroll upside

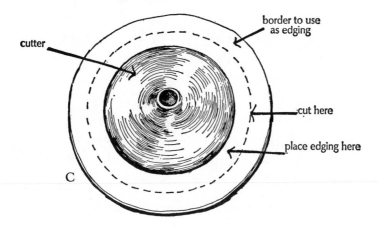

cutter

border to use as edging

cut here

place edging here

C

down on a dampened baking sheet, pressing it out gently with fingers if necessary. Paint a ¾-inch strip around the circumference of disc with cold water. Lay one of the strips of dough in place on the dampened circumference of disc, and paint one end of strip with cold water. Overlap ⅜ inch of second strip on the dampened end of the first, and press lightly with fingers to seal (D); continue around circumference with

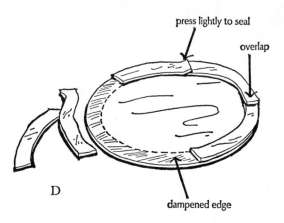

press lightly to seal

overlap

D

dampened edge

the rest of the strips, trimming final one to fit. Seal edges all around with back of a fork, prick the interior, and refrigerate as described in preceding directions.

Baked shells for fresh fruit tarts, like strawberries
A shell that is to be fully baked and then filled with fresh fruits must have something to weight down the centre during bak-

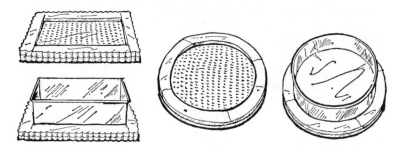

ing. The traditional solution is oiled paper and dried beans, but we think an oiled tin of some sort is far easier. Provide yourself with 3 guides, one for the outside circumference, one for cutting the inch-wide strips, and one for the area of the pan. After cutting edges and pressing them on to the dampened circumference of the pastry, prick interior of pastry, oil outside of tin, and set it in place. Chill at least an hour before baking.

To bake, preheat oven to 425°F., Mark 7. Then paint top of raised edging with egg glaze (1 egg beaten in a small bowl with 1 teaspoonful of water), and make cross-hatch markings in glaze with back of a small knife. Set the pastry, with tin in place, in middle level of oven. Bake 10 to 15 minutes, until edges of pastry have risen and begun to brown nicely. Lift off tin, prick interior, and bake 5 minutes more; look at tart, and if centre is rising, prick again, and press down. If centre is browning too much, cover loosely with foil. Baking will be 20 to 25 minutes in all. Slide shell on to a rack.

(†) Shell is at its best if eaten within a few hours; cover airtight when cold, or keep in warming oven, or freeze.

Tarte aux Pommes
Tarte aux Poires
[Apple or Pear Tart Baked in French Puff Pastry]
This is a case where the most elementary method is by far the best: the raw tart dough is painted with apricot, slices of raw apple or pear are arranged closely on top, sprinkled with sugar, and the tart is baked. It is glazed with apricot after baking, and that is all there is to it. The combination of flaky, buttery pastry, fruit, sugar, and apricot is quite heavenly.

A NOTE ON JUICY FRUITS

When you are baking raw fruits in a raw puff pastry shell you must be sure that you are using the kind of fruit that will not burst into juices before the edges of the pastry have puffed up enough to hold them in. Thus if you find yourself with soft or juicy varieties, slice them, sprinkle with sugar, and let stand in a bowl for 20 minutes so that excess juices will exude. Then drain the fruit, arrange in the tart, and add the juices to boil down with the apricot glaze.

[*For an 8- by 16-inch rectangular tart, serving 4 to 6 people*]

1. Filling the tart shell

Either: 3 to 4 large, crisp, eating apples (Golden Delicious, Cox's Orange Pippin, or other apples that will keep their shape during cooking);
Or: 5 to 6 firm, ripe pears (such as Bartlett)
A chilled 8- by 16-in. uncooked tart shell of French puff pastry (pages 594–5)
About ½ lb. strained apricot preserves in a small saucepan (apricot preserves pushed through a sieve)
A pastry brush
2 oz. sugar
Egg glaze (1 egg beaten in a small bowl with 1 tsp. water)
A small knife, or table fork

Preheat oven to 450°F., Mark 8, and set rack in lower-middle level. Peel, quarter, and core the fruit; cut into lengthwise slices ¼ inch thick. Paint interior of chilled uncooked pastry shell with strained apricot. Arrange the slices of fruit closely together and almost upright in the shell, making lengthwise or crosswise rows, whichever you find more attractive. Sprinkle the sugar over the fruit. Paint top of pastry (not sides) with egg glaze, and make cross-hatching in its surface with point of knife or tines of fork.

2. Baking: 40 to 50 minutes at 450°F., Mark 8, and 400°F., Mark 6

Set tart immediately in lower middle of preheated 450° F., Mark 8 oven, and bake for 20 minutes, or until sides of pastry have risen and begun to brown. Lower heat to 400°F., Mark 6, and continue baking another 20 minutes, or until sides of tart feel crisp and rather firm. High heat is needed to cook the layers of pastry through; cover tart loosely with foil or brown paper if edges are browning too much.

3. Glazing and serving

A rack
The remaining strained apricot
1 tbl. sugar (or juices from macerated fruits)
A wooden spoon
A kitchen spoon or pastry brush
A serving tray or board
Optional: *crème fraîche* (page 24), sweetened *crème Chantilly* (lightly
    whipped cream, page 552), or *crème anglaise* (custard sauce, page 652)

Slide tart on a rack. Boil the apricot and sugar, stirring, for several minutes until last drops to fall from spoon are sticky. Spoon or brush the apricot over the fruit to glaze it. Serve tart warm, tepid, or cold, sliding it first on to tray or board. Cut into crosswise pieces for each serving. Pass optional cream or sauce separately.

(†) The tart is at its best eaten a few hours after baking; leftovers will be delicious, but never as wonderful as the freshly baked tart.

Baking the Fruit in a Round Pastry Shell

Use the same general system, but arrange the slices of fruit in a spiral, or in rows of diminishing width from circumference to centre, like the spokes of a wheel.

Other Fruits to be Baked in Puff Pastry Shells

Fresh stoned cherries, fresh apricot or plum halves placed skin-side down, fresh sliced peaches, or well-drained tinned apricots or peach slices may be done this same way.

Fresh Fruits in Pre-baked Puff Pastry Shells

Use pre-baked puff pastry shells, page 594, just as you would pre-baked shells made from pie-crust dough, as suggested in Volume I, pages 683–4, for strawberry tart and its variations. This has a pastry-cream filling, but you may use simply a waterproofing of the red-currant glaze, arrange the straw-

berries or other fresh fruits on top, and paint with more glaze;
pass whipped cream or custard sauce separately.

Jalousie
[Peekaboo Jam or Fruit Tart of French Pastry]

Very quick to assemble and delicious, because puff pastry
turns anything into a treat, is this attractive tart with its jam or
fruit filling. Translated literally from the French, it would be
called the Venetian Blind Tart, since that is what *jalousie*
means; peekaboo seems more appealing.

[For a 6- by 16-inch tart, serving 6 people]

1. Forming the tart

½ the recipe for simple puff pastry, page 166; or reconstituted left-overs,
   page 196
A dampened pastry sheet
A table fork
½ lb. or so of excellent raspberry, strawberry, or blackberry jam, or
   other suggestions listed at end of recipe

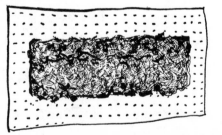

A

Roll half the pastry into an 8- by 18-inch rectangle ⅛ inch
thick. Roll up on pin, and unroll topside down on to dampened
pastry sheet. Prick all over at ⅛-inch intervals with tines of
fork, going right down through to pastry sheet.

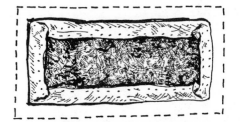

B

Spread a $\frac{1}{4}$-inch layer of jam over pastry, leaving a $\frac{3}{4}$-inch border of pastry all around (A). Turn borders of pastry up over filling at sides; wet corners, and turn ends over, sealing corners with fingers (B).

Roll out second piece of pastry into a 7- by 17-inch rectangle (slightly larger than shape of filled pastry), $\frac{1}{8}$ inch thick. Flour surface lightly; fold in half lengthwise. Measure opening of filled pastry and mark folded pastry to guide you. Cut slits in the dough from folded edge (C), as shown, making

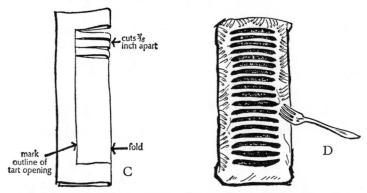

cuts $\frac{3}{8}$ inch apart

mark outline of tart opening

fold

C

D

them $\frac{3}{8}$ inch apart and half as long as width of opening in tart. Wet edges of filled bottom layer of pastry with cold water. Unfold top layer of pastry over it; brush off accumulated flour, and press pastry in place with fingers. Then, with back tines of a fork, press a decorative vertical border all around sides (D). Cover and chill for at least 30 minutes, or until baking time.

(†) When chilled and firm, may be wrapped airtight and frozen for several months. Remove from freezer, glaze, and bake as in step 2.

2. Baking and serving: about 1 hour at 450°F., Mark 8, and 400°F., Mark 6

Egg glaze (1 egg beaten in a small bowl with 1 tsp. water)
A pastry brush
A table fork or small knife
A rack
A serving tray or board
Optional: *crème fraîche, crème Chantilly,* or *crème anglaise* as suggested
for preceding recipe, step 3 (page 599)

When oven has been preheated to 450°F., Mark 8, set rack in lower-middle level. Paint surface of chilled *jalousie* with egg glaze; wait a moment, and give it a second coat. Make cross-hatchings on top of sides and ends through glaze with fork or knife, and set *jalousie* in the oven. In about 20 minutes, when pastry has risen and is browning nicely, turn heat down to 400°F., Mark 6. Bake 30 to 40 minutes more, covering loosely with foil or brown paper if surface is browning too much.

Jalousie may seem done before it actually is; sides should be firm and crusty, and object of long cooking is to dry out and crisp all inner layers of the pastry. Slide on to a rack when done. Serve warm, tepid, or cold, with optional cream or sauce passed separately. Cut into crosswise slices for each serving.

(†) As with all puff pastries, this is best when freshly baked.

Other fillings

Cooked fruits rather than jams are also desirable fillings for the *jalousie*. Among them we suggest the apricot filling on page 660. Another idea is a filling of baked apple slices, such as those for the *gratin de pommes*, step 2, page 567; spread some apricot jam over the pastry before piling on the baked apple slices, and more over the apples before you cover them with the pastry. Stoned prunes stewed in wine, butter, and sugar, and mixed with toasted almonds or chopped walnuts would be delicious. Glazed tinned pineapple and diced bananas is another idea; glaze the pineapple following the directions for the orange mousse, page 577. These are only a few possibilities, and you will think of many others yourself.

Mille-feuilles

[Napoleons – Layers of Puff Pastry Interspersed
with Pastry Cream or Whipped Cream; Iced with
Fondant and Chocolate or with Icing Sugar]

The *mille-feuilles* dessert, according to some authorities, was
not developed in France until the latter part of the nineteenth
century. The name 'Napoleon', at any event, is not associated
with it at all in any French recipes; the French icing, furthermore, is simply a layer of icing sugar. The rest of the world
has long wondered, then, how the pastry came to be named
'Napoleon' outside of France, and who changed the icing
from sugar to white fondant and lines of chocolate. The Danes
have been told for generations that a Danish royal pastry chef
invented the dessert way back in the early 1800s on the
occasion of a state visit between the Emperor Napoleon and
the King of Denmark, in Copenhagen. The Italians are sure
it is a corruption of Napolitain, because of the layered pastries
made in Naples. Some sources believe that the chocolate lines
appear to form the letter N, for Napoleon – which is far
easier for foreigners to pronounce anyway than *mille-feuilles*.
A final story, with a certain air of mischievous *fumisterie*
about it, is that the dessert was really a French invention after
all, and Napoleon's favourite pastry; he ate so many of them,
however, on the eve of Waterloo that he lost the battle. The
pastry then disappeared from view for half a century; when
it finally reappeared from banishment, it wore another icing
and a new name.

MANUFACTURING NOTES

Mille-feuilles and Napoleons are thin rectangles of crisply
baked puff pastry that are mounted in 3 layers with whipped

cream or pastry cream in between, and a topping of icing sugar for *mille-feuilles* or of white icing and lines of chocolate for Napoleons.

The traditional method of forming and cutting them, illustrated in the following recipe, is to bake the pastry in large sheets, and to cut each sheet into 3 long strips 4 inches wide, as in step 4, page 607. After the 3 strips are glazed with apricot, the first is spread with filling, the second is laid over the first and filled, then the third strip is laid on top, and covered with sugar or fondant. This giant *mille-feuilles* is finally cut crosswise into rectangular serving pieces 4 inches long and 2 inches wide, as shown in the final drawing.

This is certainly the easiest and most practical method, although you may find that it will flake or crumble a bit too much for that final cutting into serving pieces, depending on the flour you have used. You will be able to judge this when you cut the sheet of pastry into three strips; if it seems brittle, glaze the strips with apricot, then cut each into its final rectangles, and build the individual servings separately. It will take you a little longer, but you will avoid trouble. As with many recipes of this sort, be ready to adapt yourself to circumstances because the exact state of a baked pastry is impossible to predict.

[*For 16 pieces*]

1. Forming the puff pastry

4 baking sheets all of a size, 12 by 18 ins. approximately (or form and
    bake 1 pastry at a time, and use 2 baking sheets)
About ½ oz. soft butter
Chilled fresh puff pastry, either the simple dough on page 166 but with
    6 turns rather than 4, or the classic puff pastry, page 174
A large knife or a pastry wheel
A rotary pastry pricker, page 694, or 2 forks

(Please read the manufacturing notes preceding this step.) Lightly butter topsides of 2 baking sheets, and bottom sides of the 2 others. Roll chilled pastry into a 14-inch rectangle, cut in half crosswise, and chill one half. Roll remaining piece rapidly into a 13- by 19-inch rectangle ⅛ inch thick; roll up on pastry pin, and unroll over one of the buttered baking sheets.

Trim off $\frac{1}{3}$ inch of pastry all around, so that the horizontal layers of dough within the puff pastry will be even at the edges.

Prick pastry all over at $\frac{1}{8}$-inch intervals with pastry pricker or forks. Chill for at least 30 minutes to relax dough before baking. Roll and form second piece of dough in the same manner.

2. Baking the pastry: about 20 minutes at 450°F., Mark 8

Preheat oven to 450°F., Mark 8, and set racks on upper- and lower-middle levels. Cover each chilled sheet of pastry dough with a buttered baking sheet, and set in the 2 levels of the oven. The pastry is to rise as little as possible during baking; you are to prick it again, and push down the covering sheets several times, as follows. In 5 minutes, lift covering sheets and rapidly prick pastry all over to deflate it; press covering sheets down on the pastry, and bake 5 minutes more. Rapidly prick the pastry again, and switch from one level to the other, so both will bake evenly. Prick and press pastry again in 5 minutes; it should be starting to brown. Remove covering sheets if pastry has set, and let it brown and crisp 2 to 3 minutes more, but cover again with the baking sheets if it starts to puff up – watch carefully during these last few minutes that pastry does not brown too much. At end of baking, pastry should be crisp and golden, and between $\frac{1}{4}$ and $\frac{3}{8}$ inch thick. Remove from oven and cool 5 minutes, with the covering sheets in place to prevent pastry from curling. The pastry is now ready for cutting, next step.

(†) Pastry is at its best when freshly baked. Use within a few hours, but you may keep it fresh in a warming oven (100° to 150°F.) for a day or so; otherwise, wrap airtight and freeze.

3. Preliminaries to assembling *mille-feuilles* or Napoleons

(a) *Apricot glaze*:

$\frac{1}{2}$ lb. apricot jam (preserves) forced through a sieve into a small saucepan
2 tbl. sugar
A wooden spoon
A pastry brush

Bring strained apricot jam and sugar to the boil, stirring, for several minutes until last drops of jam to fall from spoon are sticky. Reheat to liquefy again before using.

(b) *The filling* – 1¼ *to* 1½ *pints needed:*

Either: one of the custard fillings in Volume I, pages 629–31, including *crème pâtissière*, *crème Saint-Honoré*, or the almond custard, *frangipane*;

Or: *crème Chantilly meringuée*, the whipped cream stiffened and sweetened with an Italian meringue mixture, page 562

If needed: 1½ packages (1½ tbl.) plain unflavoured powdered gelatine softened in 3 tbl. liquid (diluted kirsch or plain water)

Prepare one of the fillings suggested, and chill. It must hold its shape enough when spread over the pastry so that you can make layers almost ½ inch thick; if it seems too soft, strengthen it with gelatine just before using the filling as follows: sprinkle gelatine over liquid in a small saucepan; when softened, heat until completely dissolved. Let cool (or stir over ice) until almost syrupy; then fold into the filling.

(c) *Icing for* mille-feuilles:

About 6 oz. icing sugar in a fine-meshed sieve

This is all you will need for icing *mille-feuilles*.

(d) *Icing for Napoleons:*

1 cup white fondant icing, page 657, in a small saucepan with 2 tbl. kirsch
A larger saucepan of simmering water
A wooden spoon
A rubber spatula or flexible-blade metal spatula

Just before you are to ice the assembled Napoleons, step 4, stir fondant and kirsch over simmering water until perfectly smooth and just enough liquefied to coat spoon fairly heavily. Use at once.

1 tbl. instant coffee
3 tbl. water in a small saucepan with cover
8 oz. good plain chocolate
A larger saucepan of simmering water to hold chocolate pan

A wooden spoon
A paper decorating cone, page 662

Dissolve coffee in water over heat; remove from heat, break up the chocolate, and stir it in. Remove pan of simmering water from heat, set chocolate pan in it, stir up, and cover pan. Set aside to melt for several minutes, then stir vigorously until perfectly smooth and creamy. Keep over warm (not hot or simmering) water until ready to use. Prepare paper cone as described and illustrated, and cut opening about $\frac{1}{8}$ inch in diameter.

4. Assembling

Note: If pastry seems flaky or crumbly, cut it with a serrated knife rather than pastry wheel, using the knife like a saw. See also manufacturing notes, page 603, on forming individual portions rather than long strips.

Even sides and ends of pastry by trimming with pastry wheel or serrated knife. With a guide of some sort, such as a pastry sheet or a ruler, mark pastry with the point of a knife, dividing it into 3 even strips; cut through with pastry wheel (A) or with serrated knife. Cut second pastry sheet in the same manner.

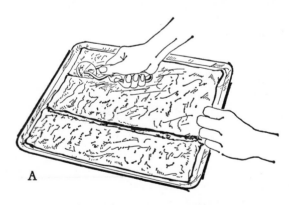

A

Paint top of each of the 6 strips with warm apricot glaze (B). Divide filling into 4 parts; spread 1 part on 1 of the glazed strips. Mount a second glazed strip upon the filled strip, and spread with its share of filling; mount a third glazed strip upon

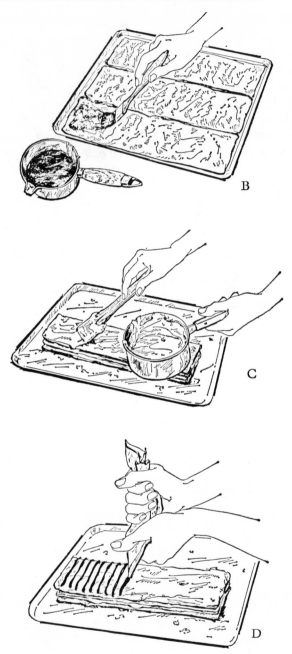

it, and set aside. Repeat with the second group of 3 strips.
You now have two 3-layered strips ready for icing. For *mille-
feuilles*, simply shake a heavy layer of icing sugar over each
of them. For Napoleons, rapidly spread as even a layer as
possible of white fondant over each (c).

Stir up melted chocolate to be sure it is smooth and velvety,
then pour it into your paper cone. Squeeze out lines of
chocolate about 1 inch apart down the length of the fondant
on each strip (D). Proceed immediately to next step, while
chocolate is still soft. Draw the back of a knife down across
the middle of the chocolate lines, then draw another line in
the opposite direction on each side, thus pulling the chocolate

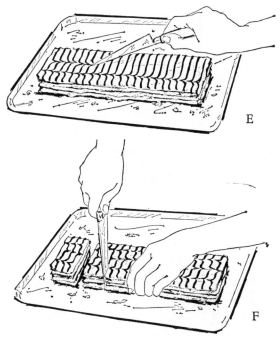

into a decorative pattern (E). As soon as chocolate has set, in
4 to 5 minutes, but before fondant has hardened, cut the strips
into crosswise pieces about 2 inches wide, using a very sharp
(or saw-edged) knife (F), and cutting very carefully with an
up-and-down sawing motion. Cut *mille-feuilles* in the same
manner.

5. Serving

Arrange the *mille-feuilles* or Napoleons on a serving tray and chill an hour. Remove Napoleons from refrigerator 20 minutes before serving, so that both chocolate and fondant will regain their glossy bloom.

(†) These pastries are at their best when freshly made, although you may keep them for 2 to 3 days under refrigeration, and you may freeze them.

Cornets et Rouleaux
[Cream Horns – Cream Rolls]

The cream horns and rolls of puff pastry described and illustrated on pages 198–204 are also useful for desserts. Rather than glazing them before baking, press the top and sides (not the bottom where pastry is sealed) in plain granulated or in coarse crystallized sugar.

Bake in the middle level of a preheated 425°F., Mark 7 oven for 15 to 20 minutes until nicely caramelized – but watch them; they burn easily. Fill with *crème Chantilly*, lightly beaten cream, sweetened and flavoured with vanilla or liqueur, or with the meringue whipped cream, *Chantilly meringuée*, page 562, or with the custard and egg-white filling,

no sugar on seam side (bottom)

crème Saint-Honoré, Volume I, page 630. A sprinkling of *pralin*, caramelized almonds or walnuts, pages 551 and 553, could nicely be folded into any of these fillings.

Pithiviers
[Almond Cream Baked in French Puff Pastry]

The small town of Pithiviers, south of Paris halfway to Bourges, may have other distinctions, but its world renown is certainly due to the famous almond pastry that every local *pâtissier* prominently and proudly displays. This is an exact illustration, drawn from our own photograph of *le veritable Pithiviers de Pithiviers*, taken only moments before we consumed it down to the last crumb in a warm and flowering meadow just outside the town itself. This buttery, flaky, tender, marvellous dessert is probably one of the most glorious uses to which you can put puff pastry; it is also a persuasive reason for you to learn how to make your own *pâte feuilletée*, because a *Pithiviers* is so easy and fast to assemble. It is two discs of dough enclosing a lump of rum-flavoured almonds, sugar, and butter; the top disc is glazed with egg just before baking, and the characteristic design is cut into it with the point of a knife. Serve the *Pithiviers* as a dessert, at a tea party, or on any occasion that calls for something special in the way of a sweet. One of the great white Sauternes would be lovely with it, or a sweet champagne, or a sparkling Vouvray.

[*For an 8-inch* Pithiviers, *serving 6 to 8 people*]

Timing note: Make the puff pastry the day before serving, as well as the almond cream, since it must be cold and hard. The assembled *Pithiviers* may be refrigerated or frozen, but once baked, it is at its best when served within 2 to 3 hours (unless you have a warming oven where it can remain safely at around 100°F. for a number of hours).

1. The almond cream: chilling time 30 to 40 minutes in freezer

$2\frac{1}{2}$ oz. sugar
2 oz. soft butter
An electric mixer, or a bowl and wooden spoon
1 large egg
$2\frac{1}{2}$ oz. ground blanched almonds – may be ground in an electric blender
$\frac{1}{4}$ tsp. almond extract
Drops of vanilla essence to taste
$1\frac{1}{2}$ tbl. dark rum

Beat sugar and butter together until light and fluffy, then beat in the egg, almonds, extracts, and rum. Cover bowl and set in freezer for 30 to 40 minutes, or in refrigerator for an hour or two; it is essential that the cream be chilled and hard before you assemble the *Pithiviers*.

2. Assembling the *Pithiviers*: about 1 hour, including 2 half-hour rests

The recipe for chilled classic French puff pastry, page 174
A round pastry cutter or upside-down cake tin 8 ins. in diameter
A small, sharp-pointed knife for cutting dough
A piece of lightly floured waxed paper on a tray
More flour and more waxed paper
A dampened baking sheet (a pizza tray is good for baking this pastry)

Preheat oven to 425°F., Mark 7, in time for step 3. Place chilled puff pastry on a lightly floured marble or board, and roll it rapidly into a rectangle $\frac{3}{8}$ inch thick, 12 inches wide, and 20 inches long. (To equalize stresses and strains within the dough for even baking, be sure to roll it crosswise as well as lengthwise.) Be sure dough is at least $\frac{1}{4}$ inch thick or it will not puff into the glorious height it should achieve, as it bakes.) Centring cutter or cake tin well on pastry for each of the discs you are to cut, and making them at least $\frac{1}{2}$ inch from edges of pastry and from each other, cut two 8-inch discs (rounds) in the dough. Lift off surrounding dough, and arrange it in 1 layer on tray; directions for its re-use as puff pastry are on page 196.

Cover this left-over dough with waxed paper, and dust paper lightly with flour; roll one of the discs up on your pin, unroll on the waxed paper, cover with another sheet of waxed paper, and refrigerate. Unroll second disc topside down on baking sheet, cover, and refrigerate for 20 to 30 minutes, or until cold and firm. (Make frequent use of the refrigerator, and you will have no troubles with puff pastry.)

Remove disc formed on the baking sheet from the refrigerator. Push dough out gently with your fingers to make it slightly more than 8 inches in diameter all around. Soften almond cream, if necessary, by kneading it; form it into a cake 4 inches in diameter and centre it on the disc of dough. It is important here that the almond cream be cold and hard, and that there be a free circumference of dough $1\frac{1}{2}$ to 2 inches wide all around; this will prevent it from leaking out of the pastry during baking.

A

Paint free circumference of dough with cold water (A). Remove remaining disc of dough from refrigerator and roll it out rapidly, rotating disc as you go, expanding it all around to about $8\frac{1}{2}$ inches. Unroll it over the almond cream on the bottom disc of dough (B). With lightly floured fingers as well as the side of your hand, firmly press top disc to bottom disc all around the lump of almond cream (C); if air pockets prevent a perfect seal, make a little hole for air to escape in centre top of dough, where chimney will be inserted later. Chill dough again for 30 minutes.

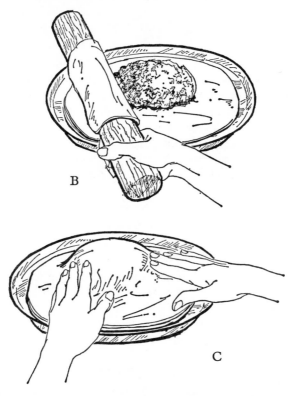

Turn a cake tin or bowl upside down over *Pithiviers*; about $\frac{3}{8}$ to $\frac{1}{2}$ inch of dough should protrude all around from its edge. With the back or the front of a small knife, whichever works best for you, cut a scalloped border all around circumference of dough, spacing indentations evenly and about $1\frac{1}{4}$ inches apart (D). Press tin or bowl rather firmly into dough as a final seal, and remove it. Chill before proceeding, if dough has softened.

(†) *Pithiviers* may be refrigerated or frozen at this point; chill to harden dough, then cover airtight. (Frozen pastry may be taken directly from freezer, and glazed and decorated as soon as top of dough is soft enough for a knife to penetrate it.)

When oven is preheated to 425°F., Mark 7, and just before baking, paint entire top surface of *Pithiviers* with egg glaze (E) (1 egg beaten in a small bowl with 1 teaspoon water). In 2

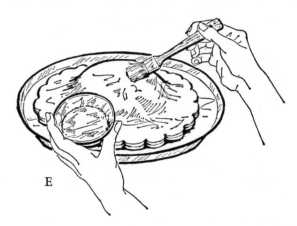

minutes, after you have made and inserted the buttered aluminium foil or brown paper chimney in illustration (F), paint with a second coat. With the point of a sharp small knife, cut decorative design into pastry as shown, going ⅛ inch deep (F). (Cutting through glaze and down into dough will make the design stand out after baking.) Proceed immediately to the baking, next step.

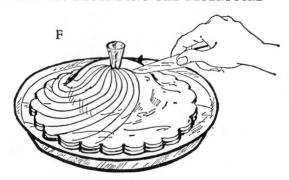

F

3. Baking: about 50 minutes at 450°F., Mark 8, and 400°F., Mark 6

As soon as *Pithiviers* has been glazed and decorated, set in middle level of preheated 450°F., Mark 8 oven. In 20 minutes, or when pastry has risen and browned nicely, reduce oven heat to 400°F., Mark 6, and continue baking 25 to 30 minutes more, until sides of pastry are brown and crisp. If *Pithiviers* seems to be browning too much during baking, lay a sheet of brown paper or foil loosely over the top.

4. Sugar glaze

About 2 oz. icing sugar in a fine-meshed sieve
A cake rack

Remove *Pithiviers* from oven, set thermostat at 475°F., Mark 9, and slide oven rack on to upper-third level.
    Remove funnel. Sieve a $\frac{1}{16}$-inch layer of the sugar over the top of the *Pithiviers*. When oven is at 475°F., Mark 9, set pastry in upper third for 4 to 5 minutes, peeking quickly every 30 seconds, until sugar has melted to a glossy sheen. Remove the *Pithiviers* and slide it on to the rack.

5. Serving and storing

A *Pithiviers* may be eaten tepid or cold, but is always at its best when freshly made and served within 2 to 3 hours of baking. It will keep successfully for a day in a warming oven at 100°F., or you may freeze it when cold and wrapped airtight. If frozen, thaw for about 30 minutes on a lightly buttered pastry sheet in a 350°F., Mark 4 oven.
    To serve, cut into wedges, like a pie.

A Little Selection of *Petits Fours*

Les Truffes aux Chocolat
[Chocolate Sweets in the Form of Truffles]

Rough balls of melted chocolate, butter, and orange liqueur rolled in cocoa look like freshly dug truffles. These home-made sweets are easy to make and, unfortunately for those who are trying not to resemble Babar the elephant, they are quite irresistible.

[For 1½ dozen]

3 tbl. strong coffee (1 tbl. instant coffee in 3 tbl. boiling water)
A covered saucepan for melting the chocolate
9 oz. good plain chocolate
A larger pan of simmering water removed from heat, to hold chocolate pan
A hand-held electric mixer
5 oz. chilled unsalted butter
3 tbl. orange liqueur

Dissolve the coffee in the saucepan with the hot water; break up the chocolate, and stir it into the liquid. Cover, and set in the pan of hot but not simmering water. When chocolate has softened, beat with electric mixer until perfectly smooth and creamy. Remove from hot water and beat a moment to cool. Cut chilled butter into ⅓-inch slices and gradually beat into the chocolate with mixer, adding a new piece as soon as a previous one is almost absorbed. When smooth, beat in the orange liqueur by dribbles. Chill for an hour or two, until firm.

A sturdy teaspoon
About 3 oz. unsweetened cocoa on a plate
Frilled paper bonbon cups

When chocolate mixture has chilled and set, remove by tea-spoon gobs, roll into rough circular shapes, then roll in the cocoa to enrobe them completely. Place in paper cups.

(†) When packed in an airtight container, *truffes* will keep perfectly for several weeks in the refrigerator, or for several months in the freezer.

Les Croquets Denison
[Walnut and Almond Puffs]

These easy-to-make mouthfuls can take the place of after-dinner mints, or go with tea, coffee, sweet liqueurs, and sweet wines. Ideally they are baked directly in fluted paper sweet cups, if you can find any that are the non-stick kind. Otherwise bake them in tiny buttered moulds, preferably not fluted ones because the batter may stick to them. Lacking proper containers, you may form the mixture on a baking sheet, like biscuits; they will not be as elegant to look at but will be just as good to eat.

Note: A heavy-duty mixer with flat beater works beautifully here; if you do not have one, beat everything together in a bowl with a wooden spoon.

[*For 3½ to 4 dozen 1¼-inch puffs*]

1. The batter

2 oz. walnuts
2 oz. blanched almonds
4 oz. icing sugar
1½ tsp. kirsch
The grated peel of ½ lemon
2 to 3 tbl. egg white

Pulverize the nuts in an electric blender and turn into a bowl. Add the sugar, kirsch, grated lemon peel, and 2 tablespoons of egg white. Mixture is now to be beaten until it forms a mass stiff enough to hold its shape when bits are rolled into balls: beat for 2 to 3 minutes, and if ingredients remain sandy and unmassed, add ½ tablespoon more egg white; continue beating, and if mixture still separates, beat in a little more egg white. (If too soft, on the other hand, beat in a tablespoon or so more pulverized nuts or icing sugar, or refrigerate for ½ hour until it becomes firmer.)

2. Forming the *petits fours*

Waxed paper on a tray
A table fork
2 egg whites in a small bowl
2 oz. icing sugar on a plate; more sugar as needed
Fluted non-stick paper sweet cups (or buttered moulds, 1 tbl. capacity)
A baking sheet, clean and dry if you are using paper cups

Preheat oven to 300°F., Mark 2. Puffs will double in size when baked, therefore cups or moulds should be filled only by half. Form mixture into balls by rolling between the palms of your hands; place each ball, as formed, on the waxed paper. Beat egg whites with fork to break up thoroughly. One by one, dip each ball in egg white, then roll in sugar, place in sweet paper or mould and arrange on baking sheet. (Or flatten the balls into disc shapes, dip in egg white, then coat with sugar and arrange on a buttered baking sheet.)

3. Baking and serving

Optional: paper sweet cups

Bake in middle level of preheated 300°F., Mark 2 oven for 15 to 20 minutes, until puffs have about doubled in size and are pale gold in colour. Let cool and crisp for 10 to 15 minutes. If you have baked them in moulds, dislodge delicately with the point of a knife and, if you wish, place each in a sweet cup.

(†) Will keep several days when covered airtight; for longer storage, freeze them.

Tuiles aux Amandes
[Lacy Curved Almond Wafers]

These delicate mouthfuls go nicely with fresh fruit desserts, ices, and afternoon tea. Rapidly mixed and baked, the wafers crisp almost immediately into the shape of old-fashioned roof tiles when they are lifted from the baking sheet to a rolling pin or bottle to cool. The only *tour de main* involved here is that you work out your own system for removing the wafers as quickly as possible from baking sheet to rolling pin; as they cool, they become too crisp to mould. Bake one sheet at a time even though you may prepare several sheets in advance, or be baking one while you are preparing another.

[*For about 45 wafers 3 inches in diameter*]

1. The batter

3 or 4 baking sheets about 12 by 16 ins.
½ to 1 oz. soft butter for the baking sheets
2 oz. soft butter in a 5-pt mixing bowl
4 oz. sugar
An electric mixer
2 egg whites

Preheat oven to 425°F., Mark 7, and set rack in middle level. Prepare baking sheets by smearing each with about 1 teaspoonful of soft butter. Beat the rest of the butter and the sugar together until soft and fluffy; add the egg whites, and beat a few seconds, only just enough to blend.

5 tbl. plain cake flour in a sieve or sifter
A rubber spatula
3 tbl. ground blanched almonds (grind them in an electric blender)
¼ tsp. almond extract
½ tsp. vanilla extract

Sieve or sift the flour over the batter, folding it in with a rubber spatula. Fold in the ground almonds, almond extract, and vanilla.

4 tbl. sliced, shaved, or slivered almonds (either blanched or with skin left on)

Using rubber spatula to dislodge batter, drop ½-teaspoon gobs on to one of the buttered baking sheets, spacing them 3 inches apart. With back of spoon, smear out each blob into a circle 2½ inches in diameter; batter will be so thin you can see baking sheet through it. Top each circle with a pinch of sliced, shaved, or slivered almonds.

2. Baking and shaping: oven has been preheated to 425°F., Mark 7

A kitchen timer
A flexible-blade spatula (blade should be at least 8 ins. long)
2 bottles or rolling pins braced to lie still
A cake rack

Place in middle level of preheated oven, and set timer for 4 minutes. (Meanwhile, make sure rolling pins are ready; then start forming batter on another baking sheet.) Wafers are done when a $\frac{1}{8}$-inch border around circumference has browned lightly. Set baking sheet on open oven door so that biscuits will keep warm and pliable.

Working rapidly, slide long side of spatula blade under one biscuit to scrape and lift it off the baking sheet, and place right side up on rolling pin or bottle. Quickly continue with the rest; the wafers crisp to shape so quickly that the first several may be removed to rack to make room for remaining wafers. (If last wafers have cooled too much for moulding, return sheet to oven for several seconds to soften them.)

Close oven door and wait a few minutes for temperature to return to 425°F., Mark 7; bake and mould the rest of the wafers in the same manner.

(†) Wafers will stay crisp for several days in dry weather when stored airtight; otherwise, freeze them.

Two Recipes for Left-over Pastry Dough

Two more good reasons for you to master French puff pastry are *couques* and *palmiers* – crisp, buttery, lightly caramelized biscuits that you can make with the left-overs. Like some of the wonderful things you concoct with left-over braised beef, *les tous nus* and *choux farcis*, to give examples from another part of the menu, it is well worth making the original just to have the residue to play with.

THE DOUGH – PUFF PASTRY VERSUS PIE-CRUST DOUGH

Most biscuits as well as many of the appetizer and entrée pastries are made with scraps of raw puff pastry left over from *bouchées, vol-au-vent, mille-feuilles,* or other recipes calling for fresh *pâte feuilletée.* These scraps need not be fully reconstituted into puff pastry again, as described on page 196: those for the *couques* should only be smooth enough to roll out and be cut fairly evenly, and those for the *palmiers* will reconstitute into smoothness as they are rolled in sugar, folded, and rolled and folded again before their final forming. You can convert butter pie-crust dough, *pâte brisée,* formulas 1 or 2, page 162 (or even packaged mixes), into a reasonable substitute for puff pastry by rolling and folding with softened butter, as described in the same recipe for reconstituting puff pastry.

Couques

[Tongue-shaped Caramelized Biscuits Made from Puff Pastry Dough]

These were made famous in the 1920s by Le Café de Paris, on the Avenue de l'Opéra. Whenever you ordered ice cream, long *couques* on embroidered napery accompanied each serving, and they soon became the most fashionable biscuits in Paris. *Couque* comes from the Flemish *koek,* whose diminutive, *koekje,* produced the American 'cookie'. We shall not give proportions because they are not necessary, but a circle of dough 3 inches in diameter and ½ inch thick will produce 6 to 8 *couques* 6 to 7 inches long.

1. Forming the biscuits

Chilled left-over French puff pastry, *pâte feuilletée* (pages 196–8)
An oval fluted cutter 3 to 3½ ins. long (or a 2-in. round cutter,
    preferably fluted)

Preheat oven to 450°F., Mark 8, in time for step 2, and set rack in upper-middle level. Roll pastry out about ⅛ inch thick and cut into ovals (or rounds). Reform left-overs, roll out again, and cut.

Sugar (ordinary granulated)
A flexible-blade spatula
A clean dry baking sheet
A rack or racks

Spread an oval-shaped layer of sugar ⅛ inch thick on your rolling surface. Lay a pastry cut-out on the sugar and roll it out into a tongue shape 6 to 7 inches long and about 1/16 inch thick; you will be encrusting sugar into the bottom of the pastry as you roll. Turn it upside down (sugared-side up) on baking sheet, and roll the rest of the cut-outs in the same manner. (Although you can bake the biscuits now, they usually cook more evenly if you cover with plastic wrap and chill them for ½ hour at least; this relaxes the dough and prevents it from shrinking or pulling out of shape during baking.)

2. Baking: oven has been preheated to 450°F., Mark 8

Bake in upper-middle level of preheated oven for 7 to 8 minutes, until sugar coating has caramelized lightly; if some biscuits are done before others, remove them to rack because they burn easily. Biscuits crisp as they cool.

(†) *Couques* will stay crisp for several days in dry weather when stored airtight; otherwise keep them in a warming oven or freeze them.

Palmiers

[Palm-leaf Caramelized Sugar Biscuits Made from Puff Pastry Dough]

This most popular of all puff-pastry biscuits is often a disappointment when shop-bought, even in France, but always delicious when you make it yourself from your own homemade buttery puff pastry. Thus if you have not been impressed with them before, try making your own; you will find them handsome to look at, wonderfully crisp, and you may make them very large as well as rather small. Size depends on the thickness of the pastry and the width of the rectangle you roll it into. You will work out your own system if you become an addicted *pâtissier* of *palmiers*, with your own palm-leaf patterns and special *tours de main*; we suggest only the basic techniques here. Again, we shall not give proportions, but a piece of pastry dough 5½ by 2 by 1½ inches will produce 2 dozen 3-inch *palmiers*.

1. Forming the biscuits

Sugar (ordinary granulated)
Chilled left-over French puff pastry, *pâte feuilletée* (pages 196–8)
A flexible-blade spatula
A clean dry baking sheet (you will probably need 2 sheets at least)
A rack or racks

Spread a layer of sugar ⅛ inch thick on your rolling surface. Sprinkling dough with more sugar as you roll, extend it into a rectangle about ³⁄₁₆ inch thick. Fold bottom up to middle, and top down to cover it, as though folding a business letter. (Illustrations are in the section on puff pastry, page 170.)

Turn pastry so top flap of dough is to your right, roll again in sugar to make a rectangle ⅜ inch thick, and fold again in three. (If pastry has softened and become difficult to handle, or if it has stiffened and become balky, refrigerate for 30 minutes to an hour, then continue.) Roll the dough out 8 inches long (for 3-inch *palmiers*), then give it a quarter turn so the 8-inch length is facing you. Extend it out in front of you now with your rolling pin, keeping the dough 8 inches wide, and rolling it to whatever length it will go to make a square or rectangle ¼ inch thick. Trim off rough edges.

Fold sides so they almost touch at the centre, as shown (A). Sprinkle top of dough with sugar and encrust it into the pastry

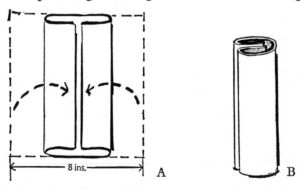

A   B

with your rolling pin, at the same time pressing the top and bottom layers of dough together with pin. Fold pastry in two, as though closing a book (B). Press with your rolling pin, to hold the 4 layers more closely together.

With a sharp knife, cut dough into crosswise pieces $\frac{3}{8}$ inch thick (c). Depending on what effect you want either bend the 2 ends up at right angles; or roll them halfway up the outside; or roll them up inside, so that they form two connecting swirls (D). Place on pastry sheet, each *palmier* 3 inches from neighbour in every direction – they will spread out to more than double in the oven.

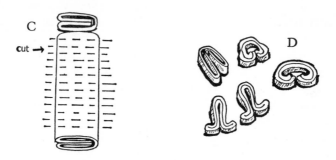

Cover and chill 30 minutes at least; dough must relax or the *palmier* designs will lose their shape during baking. Preheat oven to 450°F., Mark 8, and set rack in upper-middle level in time for next step.

2. Baking: oven has been preheated to 450°F., Mark 8

(Bake one sheet at a time.) Set in upper-middle level of pre-heated oven and bake for about 5 minutes, until when you lift a biscuit with your spatula, the bottom has begun to caramelize. Remove from oven, close oven door, and rapidly turn the biscuits over. Sprinkle tops of each with a dusting of sugar, and return to oven for 3 to 4 minutes more, or until sugar topping has caramelized nicely – but keep an eye on them, because they burn quickly. Remove one by one to a rack, where the *palmiers* will crisp as they cool.

Note: The baking will take a little experimenting on your part, and timing will differ if biscuits are thinner one time, thicker another. Your object is to have the pastry cook through, making a crisp, attractively shaped biscuit with a caramel sheen.

(†) *Palmiers* will stay crisp for several days in dry weather when stored airtight; otherwise keep them in a warming oven or freeze them.

Eight French Cakes

Pain d'Épices
[Spice Cake – Spice Bread – Honey Bread]

Pain d'épices is the French equivalent of gingerbread, but is made with honey, rye flour, and mixed spices rather than from molasses, white flour, and ginger. Every country in Europe seems to have a honey bread, and each region in France has its own special formula. Dijon, for instance, cures the flour and honey mixture for several months in wooden tubs before the final blending and baking. Montbard stores the baked breads for a month before serving, and Rheims mixes raw bread dough into the honey and rye. Some recipes call for glacéed fruits, some for brown sugar, eggs, white flour, or ground nuts. Potash was the original leavening agent, and bakers often add carbonate of ammonia for a lighter loaf; householders use bicarbonate of soda. Here is a delicious home recipe that is easy to make by hand, and even easier in a heavy-duty mixer with flat beater. Serve *pain d'épices* with butter for breakfast or tea.

A NOTE ON THE RYE FLOUR

The rye flour called for here is ordinary rye flour for general bread making. If you happen to have the so-called rye meal, which is heavier and coarser, use half rye meal and half plain white flour; otherwise your *pain d'épices* will not rise properly.

[For 1 large or 2 small loaves]

1. The batter

1 lb. honey
8 oz. sugar
¼ pt boiling water
A 5- to 6-pt mixing bowl, or the bowl of a heavy-duty electric mixer

¼ tsp. salt
1 tbl. bicarbonate of soda
About 1 lb. rye flour (see note on rye flour preceding step 1)

Either with a large wooden spoon or in a heavy-duty mixer with flat beater, blend the honey, sugar, and boiling water until sugar has dissolved. Stir in the salt, soda, and ¾ pound of the flour. Beat in as much of the remaining flour as will go in, to make a heavy, sticky dough but one you can still manipulate. Beat thoroughly and vigorously (4 to 5 minutes of beating, if you are using a mixer, will improve texture).

3 oz. ground blanched almonds (pulverize them in an electric blender)
1 tsp. almond extract
3 tbl. dark rum
4 tsp. ground aniseed (pulverize in an electric blender)
½ tsp. ground cinnamon
½ tsp. ground cloves
½ tsp. ground mace
8 oz. glacéed fruit rinsed in boiling water, drained and cut into ⅛-in.
   pieces (orange peel, lemon peel, and citron)

Then add the rest of the ingredients listed. (If you are using a mixer, let the machine run at slow speed while the additions go in.)

2. Baking and storing: baking time 1 to 1¼ hours

A 3½-pt bread tin or two 1½- to 2-pt tins, heavily buttered and bottom lined with buttered waxed paper

Turn the mixture into the tin or tins. Dip your fingers in cold water and smooth top of batter. Tins should be half to two-thirds filled. Bake in middle level of preheated 325°F., Mark 3 oven. Batter will rise to fill tin and top will probably crack slightly; it is best not to open oven door for 45 minutes or to touch anything for fear of releasing the soda-engendered gases that are pushing the batter up. Small tins will take 50 to 60 minutes; the large one, about 1¼ hours. The spice bread is done when a skewer plunged to bottom of tin comes out clean, and when bread begins to show faint lines of shrinkage from edges of tin.

Let cool in tin for 10 to 15 minutes, then unmould on a rack. Immediately peel paper off bottom and gently turn the bread puffed-side up. When cold, in about 2 hours, wrap airtight in plastic. *Pain d'épices* improves in flavour when aged, so do not serve it for at least a day; a wait of several days is actually preferable. It will keep for several weeks under refrigeration, or may be frozen for several months.

Le Quatre Quarts
[Pound Cake – Yellow Butter Cake]

The French name for this cake, *Le Quatre Quarts*, or 'Four Quarters', comes from its original proportions, which are *un quart de livre*, a quarter pound each, of its four ingredients – eggs, sugar, flour, and butter. The English liked the formula so much that they used a pound of everything – hence, of course, pound cake. Of the several methods for making pound cake, we find by far the best one results from beating the eggs and sugar in an electric mixer until they double in volume and have enough body so that they keep that volume when the flour is rapidly blended in, followed by the softly creamed butter; the batter should look like a rich mayonnaise as you turn it into the pan. Besides beating the eggs, which presents no problem when you do it electrically, your other important object is to cream the butter so that it is soft enough to mix easily and rapidly into the batter without deflating it, yet has enough body so that it remains in suspension throughout the mixture rather than sinking to the bottom of the pan like melted butter.

[*For a 1½-pint tin, such as a round, 8- by 1½-inch tin*]

1. Preliminaries

A 1½-pt cake tin, buttered and floured
6 oz. butter
A small saucepan or bowl
A wire whisk

Preheat oven to 350°F., Mark 4, and set rack in middle level. Prepare the cake tin. Either beat room-temperature butter into a smooth cream, or cut chilled butter into ½-inch slices and beat over low heat until it begins to soften and continue beating until it is a mayonnaise-like cream. If it softens too much, beat over a bowl filled with ice and water. Butter must be like a heavy mayonnaise. Set aside.

2. The cake batter

3 large eggs
8 oz. sugar
The grated rind of 1 lemon or orange
An electric mixer and large bowl

Blend the eggs and sugar with the lemon or orange peel for a minute at low speed to mix, then increase speed to high and beat for 4 to 5 minutes or more, until mixture is pale, fluffy, doubled in volume, and looks like whipped cream. If you are using a mixer on a stand, measure the flour while the eggs are beating.

6 oz. plain flour
A sieve or sifter set on waxed paper
The creamy mayonnaise-like butter
2 rubber spatulas

Measure out the flour and sieve or sift on to the paper. Beat the eggs and sugar again for a moment if they have lost their body or volume. Turn speed to low and gradually sprinkle in the flour as you mix. Do this rapidly, and do not try for a perfect blending at this point; the operation should not take more than 15 to 20 seconds (for a mixer on a stand – longer for a hand-held model).

Still at low speed, and using 1 spatula to remove the butter from its bowl, and a second to dislodge it from the first, rapidly incorporate the butter into the egg mixture, taking no more than 15 to 20 seconds (with a mixer on a stand), and, again, not trying for a perfect blend.

Remove bowl from stand, if you have that kind of mixer, and rapidly cut down through batter and out to side with rubber spatula, rotating bowl and repeating the movement 2 or 3 times to complete the blending. Turn batter into prepared tin; run it up to rim all around with spatula, and bang tin lightly on table to deflate any bubbles.

3. Baking: about 40 minutes at 350°F., Mark 4

Immediately set tin in middle level of preheated oven and bake for about 40 minutes, until a skewer or toothpick plunged down into top centre of cake comes out clean. Cake will have risen slightly over top of tin, top will have browned nicely, and cake will feel lightly springy when pressed. Cool 10 minutes in tin, then unmould on to a rack; if you wish to serve it plain, immediately reverse it on to another rack so its puffed side will be uppermost.

4. Serving

The *Quatre Quarts* may be served as it is, sprinkled with powdered sugar. Or fill and ice it with anything you wish. Below is a quick and simple filling.

Crème au Citron, Crème à l'Orange
[Lemon- or Orange-cream Filling]

[Enough for an 8- to 9-inch cake]

6 oz icing sugar
1 tbl. lemon juice or concentrated frozen orange juice
The grated rind of one lemon or orange
1 tbl. hot water
1 egg
1 oz. butter
1 tbl. cornflour
A small saucepan and a wire whisk

Beat all ingredients together over moderately high heat until mixture thickens and comes to the boil. Continue beating over low heat for 2 minutes until starch cooks and cream looks translucent.

2 to 3 oz. unsalted butter
Pinch of salt

Remove from heat and beat in butter, as much as you wish up to 3 ounces. Salt very lightly, to taste. Filling will thicken as it cools. May be refrigerated for several days, or frozen for several months.

Split cake in half, and, if you wish, sprinkle the inside of each half with drops of rum or of orange liqueur. Spread filling on bottom half and re-form the cake. You may paint the cake with warm apricot glaze and brush chopped nuts around the circumference, or simply sprinkle the top with icing sugar.

Le Cake
[Rich Yellow Loaf Cake with Rum, Currants, and Cherries]

A French *cake* is always baked in a *moule à cake* – meaning a loaf tin – and a French *cake* always has fruits in it. It is not at all a fruit cake in the English sense of solid fruit held together with batter; it is, rather, a slightly modified pound-cake formula flavoured with rum and currants, and baked with a layer of glacéed cherries in the centre. Serve it with tea or with fruit desserts; it keeps well for several days under refrigeration, or it may be frozen.

A NOTE ON FRUITS FALLING TO BOTTOM OF CAKES DURING BAKING

We struggled for years trying to devise some system to prevent fruits from sinking to the bottom of the cake during baking. Finally, we realized that we were using plain flour and our batter was too light. As soon as we switched to strong plain flour our troubles were over. To make doubly sure, we also suggest dusting the fruits with a combination of flour and baking powder.

[*For a 2½-pint tin, approximately 10 inches long and 3½ inches deep*]

1. Preliminaries

A 2½-pt tin, bottom lined with waxed paper, interior of tin buttered and floured
6 oz. butter in a small saucepan or bowl
A wire whisk
4 oz., or about 30, glacéed cherries, on a plate
5 oz. strong plain flour

A rubber spatula
1 tsp. baking powder
A square of waxed paper
4 oz. currants, on a plate
A fine-meshed sieve

Preheat oven to 350°F., Mark 4, and set rack in middle level. Prepare the cake tin. Cream the butter (over heat if necessary, then over cold water) to a smooth mayonnaise-like consistency. Wash cherries in very hot water to remove preservatives, dry on paper towels, and cut each cherry in half. Measure out the flour. Mix the baking powder and a tablespoon of the flour on waxed paper, then sprinkle over the currants, tossing and stirring to coat them. Because currants and cherries are to remain separate, turn currants into sieve placed over cherries and shake off the baking powder and flour on to cherries. Return currants to their plate, coat cherries with mixture, and sieve cherries over the bowl of flour; return cherries to their plate.

2. The cake batter

2 large eggs
2 egg yolks
8 oz. sugar
3 tbl. dark Jamaican rum
An electric mixer, and large bowl on stand, or 5- to 6-pt mixing bowl

Beat the eggs, yolks, sugar, and rum at moderate speed to blend, then increase to high speed and beat 5 to 6 minutes or more, until mixture is thick, pale yellow, creamy, and the consistency of lightly whipped cream. You must beat long enough for it to thicken this way, or the batter will be too light to support the fruit.

Turn flour out on to waxed paper. At slow mixing speed, gradually sprinkle the flour into the egg mixture, taking 15 to 20 seconds but not trying for a perfect blend at this point; eggs must not be deflated by over-mixing.

The creamy mayonnaise-like butter
2 rubber spatulas

Still at low speed, and using 1 spatula to remove the butter from its bowl and a second to dislodge it from the first, rapidly incorporate the butter into the egg mixture, taking no more than 15 to 20 seconds and, again, not trying for a perfect blend.

The floured currants

Remove bowl from stand, if using that kind of mixer. Rapidly fold currants into batter with a rubber spatula, as you complete the blending.

The prepared cake tin
The floured cherries

Turn half of the batter immediately into the tin. Rapidly spread the cherries on top, and cover with the rest of the batter, running it up to rim of tin on all sides with rubber spatula. Tin will be two-thirds to three-quarters full. Immediately proceed to the baking.

3. Baking: about 1 hour at 350°F., Mark 4

Set in the middle level of the preheated oven and bake for about an hour. Cake is done when it has risen to fill the tin, is lightly browned, and a skewer plunged through the cake comes out clean. The top will crack, which is normal and there will be very slight lines of shrinkage from tin in several areas. Let cake cool in tin for 10 minutes, then run a sharp, thin knife between sides of tin and cake; unmould on to a rack. Immediately peel paper off cake if it has adhered, and turn cake right-side up.

4. Serving and storing

Serve as it is with tea or with fresh fruit desserts, slicing cake crosswise like a loaf of bread. To store, wrap airtight and refrigerate or freeze, but bring to room temperature before serving for best flavour and texture.

Le Génoise Électrique
[Light, Yellow, Whole-egg Cake, for Layered Cakes
and *Petits Fours*]

Génoise is one of the basic French cakes used for *petits fours* and
fancy filled cakes. The classic method is to beat whole eggs and
sugar over hot water until the mixture is warm and thick,
then to beat it at room temperature until it is cool and even
thicker. An electric mixer will accomplish almost the same
thickness of batter, and works perfectly well when you are
adding only a small amount of butter, as in the following
recipe. Typical of the best French cakes, there is no baking
powder here, meaning that you must fold the flour and butter
into the cake batter with such speed and delicacy that you do
not deflate it, and the cake will rise as it should in the oven.
Typically again, this is a low-lying cake of $1\frac{1}{2}$ inches that is
usually split in half for filling and icing. If you like a high
layered cake, make two of them for 4 layers. Use any shape of
tin you wish; a square or rectangular tin is easiest for *petits
fours*.

[*For a $1\frac{1}{4}$-pint tin, such as a round one 8 by $1\frac{1}{4}$ inches*]

1. The cake batter

2 oz. butter in a small saucepan
An 8- by $1\frac{1}{2}$-in. round cake tin, bottom lined with waxed paper,
    interior of tin buttered and floured
$2\frac{1}{2}$ oz. cake flour
A sieve or sifter
A 12-in. square of waxed paper

Preheat oven to 350°F., Mark 4, and set rack in middle level.
Melt butter and set aside. Prepare cake tin; measure flour and
sift or sieve on to waxed paper.

3 large eggs
4 oz. sugar
$1\frac{1}{2}$ tsp. vanilla extract
The grated rind of 1 lemon
A pinch of salt
An electric mixer with large bowl
A rubber spatula

Beat eggs, sugar, vanilla, lemon rind, and salt for 5 to 10 minutes or more depending on efficiency of mixer, until very thick, pale yellow and mixture forms a definite and slowly dissolving ribbon when a bit is lifted and falls back on surface.

Then remove bowl from stand, if you have that kind of mixer, and with one hand, sift on a quarter of the flour and rapidly cut down through batter and out to side with rubber spatula, rotating bowl and repeating the movement quickly 6 to 8 times, until flour is almost incorporated. Sprinkle on half the remaining flour, and when almost incorporated, fold in a third of the tepid melted butter; continue alternating butter and flour until all (except milky residue at bottom of butter pan) is incorporated. Do not overmix: batter must retain its original volume.

Immediately turn batter into prepared tin running it up to the edge all around with spatula. Bang lightly on table, and place at once in preheated oven.

2. Baking and cooling: baking time 25 to 30 minutes at 350°F., Mark 4

Bake for 25 to 30 minutes. Cake is done when top is spongy if pressed, and when cake shows a hairline of shrinkage from tin at one or two places around the edge.

When done, remove cake from oven and let cool 10 minutes in tin. Then reverse on to a rack, and in a few minutes the cake will drop out of the tin. Peel paper off bottom of cake if it has adhered.

When cool, in 1½ to 2 hours, if you are not going to fill and ice the cake, wrap it airtight (it dries out easily), and refrigerate for several days, or freeze for several months.

3. Filling and icing suggestions

Fill and ice the *génoise* in any manner you wish; besides the Mocha butter cream and chocolate fondant suggested below, see the list of possibilities on pages 660–62.

Crème au Beurre à la Meringue Italienne
[Meringue Butter-cream Filling and Icing]

½ the recipe for *meringue italienne* (sugar syrup whipped into beaten egg whites), step 1, page 557

An electric mixer
8 to 10 oz. unsalted butter in a bowl
2 tbl. rum or kirsch
1 tbl. instant coffee dissolved in 2 tbl. boiling water, and cooled

When the meringue mixture has been beaten until cool with the electric mixer, it is ready to receive the butter. Cut up butter, if cold, and beat over heat for a moment until it starts to melt; continue beating with electric mixer or wooden spoon until butter is soft and fluffy. (If by chance you have heated butter too much, beat over cold water to reconstitute it.)

By dollops, beat the equivalent of $\frac{1}{2}$ pound of the butter into the meringue, then beat in the rum or kirsch and droplets of coffee until butter cream is a light coffee colour. If butter cream turns grainy after addition of liquids, beat in more of the butter by spoonfuls to smooth it out again. Cover and chill, until of easy spreading consistency.

(†) Butter cream may be frozen; when thawed, beat in more softened butter to smooth it, along with a little more liqueur if you feel it necessary.

Icing the cake

The cool *génoise* cake
A long, sharp thin knife for splitting the cake
A cake rack set over a pizza tray or baking sheet
2 tbl. rum or kirsch
The chilled butter cream (beaten to a smooth consistency)
A flexible-blade spatula
A 2-pt measure of hot water

(Illustrated directions for splitting, filling, and icing cakes are in Volume I, pages 718–21.) Cake is to be iced upside down, meaning that the part that was at the bottom of the tin is considered to be the top of the cake; this is because sides must slant slightly outwards for fondant to cover them easily, later. Cut a tiny wedge up side of cake to guide you in re-forming it. Slice cake in half, making 2 layers; turn them cut-side up and sprinkle with rum or kirsch.

Spread about a third of the butter cream on bottom layer of cake, and replace top layer, lining it up with wedge. Being sure butter cream is smooth, spread all but 4 tablespoons over top and sides of cake. Even icing with spatula dipped in hot water, making sides as smooth as possible; retain or even exaggerate their outward slant towards bottom of cake. Set in freezer or refrigerate for about $\frac{1}{2}$ hour, until icing is well set. (Smooth again with spatula dipped in hot water if necessary.)

3 cups chocolate-flavoured fondant, page 660
A flexible-blade spatula
The reserved butter cream, chilled
A paper decoating cone, page 662

When icing has set, and with cake on its rack set over a tray to catch drips, heat fondant just enough for it to be liquefied and of easy pouring consistency. Pour all of it at once over the top of the cake, rapidly spreading it, if necessary, with spatula so that it falls evenly over the sides. It sets very quickly, and can be touched only when liquid.

When set, in a few minutes, pack chilled but smooth and malleable butter cream into paper cone and squeeze out whatever decorative motif your creative spirit suggests to you.

Store cake in refrigerator, but remove to room temperature for 20 to 30 minutes before serving so that fondant will regain its bloom.

Gâteau aux Noix
Le Saint-André
[Walnut Cake]

The *Saint-André* is a delicious walnut-filled creation that can be either a dessert or a cake (see following recipes).

[*For a 9- by 1½-inch cake*]

1. Preliminaries: preheat oven to 350°F., Mark 4

A 2½-pt cake tin (9 by 1½ ins. if round), bottom lined with waxed paper, tin buttered and floured
4 oz. walnuts, either whole or chopped

3 tbl. sugar
An electric blender
A sheet of waxed paper
1½ oz. plain flour
A sieve
A rubber spatula
2 oz. soft butter in a 2-pt bowl
A wooden spoon

Prepare cake tin. Grind half the nuts with half the sugar in the blender, turn out on to the waxed paper; grind the rest of the nuts and sugar, and add to the first half. Sieve the flour over the nuts and mix well with rubber spatula, smoothing out any lumps in the mixture. Soften the butter in the bowl and beat to a creamy mayonnaise-like consistency. Set aside.

2. The cake batter

4 oz. sugar
3 large eggs
2 tbl. kirsch
Pinch of salt
An electric mixer and 5- to 6-pt bowl
The softened butter
A rubber spatula
The ground walnuts
The prepared cake tin

Beat the sugar and eggs with the kirsch and salt for a moment at low speed to blend, then increase speed to high and beat several minutes (7 to 8 with a hand-held machine) until mixture is pale, fluffy, doubled in volume, and holds in soft peaks. Remove bowl from stand. Scoop a 2-spoonful dollop of egg mixture into the softened butter and mix with rubber spatula; set aside. Sprinkle a third of the ground nuts over the egg mixture and delicately fold them in with a rubber spatula, being careful to deflate the eggs as little as possible. When almost incorporated, add the same amount again, fold, and sprinkle on the remainder. When that is almost incorporated, add the creamy butter and rapidly fold in. Turn batter into cake tin, which will be about two thirds filled. Tilt tin to run batter up to rim all around, bang lightly on table, and set immediately in middle level of preheated 350°F., Mark 4 oven.

3. Baking: about 30 minutes at 350°F., Mark 4

In about 20 minutes the cake will have risen to the top of the
tin; in another 10 minutes it will have sunk slightly, and will
show a very faint line of shrinkage at points around edge of
tin, indicating that the cake is done. Remove from oven, and
let cool 10 minutes. Run a knife around cake, and reverse on to
a rack; in 5 minutes or so, cake will drop out of tin. Peel paper
off bottom of cake in a few minutes, when it has loosened.

(†) When cold, wrap airtight and refrigerate or freeze.

To Serve the *Saint-André* as a Dessert

¾ pt *crème Chantilly* (lightly whipped cream, page 588) flavoured with
  vanilla or liqueur, and sweetened with icing sugar
Either: chopped walnuts or caramelized walnuts, page 553;
Or: grated or shaved chocolate and the chocolate sauce on page 563

Transfer the *Saint-André* to a serving dish, spread *crème Chantilly* over it, reserving some to pass in a bowl. Decorate top of
cake with walnuts or chocolate. Pass chocolate sauce separately.

Le Saint-André aux Abricots
[Walnut Cake with Apricot Filling, Glazed with Fondant]

This way of serving the *Saint-André* (page 638) as a cake is very
attractive. The cake is split and filled with apricots, re-formed
and glazed with apricot; ground caramelized walnuts, *pralin
aux noix*, are brushed against the sides; white fondant is spread
over the top with incrustations of caramelized walnuts.

[*For the 9- by 1½-inch walnut cake, page 638, serving 6 to 8*]

½ package (½ tbl.) unflavoured powdered gelatine softened in a small
  saucepan with 2 tbl. kirsch
The ½ pt apricot filling, page 660

Heat softened gelatine mixture until gelatine has completely
dissolved, then stir into apricot filling. Cut a tiny wedge in side
of cake, then slice in half, making 2 layers. When apricot filling
is cold and has set enough for spreading, spoon it over bottom
layer of cake; replace top layer, lining it up with wedge.

5 oz. apricot jam (preserves) forced through a sieve into a small saucepan
2 tbl. sugar
A wooden spoon
About half the quantity of ground caramelized walnuts given on page
      553, or chopped walnuts

Bring strained apricot jam and sugar to the boil, stirring, for
several minutes until last drops to fall from spoon are sticky.
Paint top and sides of cake with the glaze. When glaze has set
slightly, brush ground caramelized walnuts or chopped walnuts against sides of cake all round. (This technique is illustrated on page 655.)

About 6 tbl. kirsch-flavoured white fondant, page 657
About 1 dozen caramelized walnut halves (more if you wish), page 553

Heat fondant over hot water until smooth and of spreading
consistency; rapidly spread as even a layer as possible over top
of cake. While fondant is still quite soft, press the walnuts into
it, arranging them around the edge of the cake or in any manner you wish. (If fondant on top of cake has hardened, melt a
little more and brush on bottom of walnuts as you stick them
on the cake.)

(†) Cake will keep several days when covered airtight in the
refrigerator, or it may be frozen for several weeks, at least.

La Charlotte Africaine

[Chocolate Dessert or Layer-cake Made from Left-over Cake]

When you find yourself with left-over wedding cake, pound
cake, sponge cake, or even shop-bought cake of a reasonably
home-made quality, use it again to make another cake. Pound
cake is particularly good for this; if you have sponge cake, you
may wish to enrich the mixture with a little butter. This recipe
is easy to make with the electric mixer when you follow the
sequences outlined here. The cake is baked in a dish or tin 4 to
5 inches deep, like a French *charlotte* mould; treat it as a dessert
with whipped cream and chocolate sauce, or as a cake with
filling and icing.

[*For a 6-inch cake 3 to 4 inches high, serving 8 to 10*]

1. The cake batter

The cake tin: a 3-pt *charlotte* mould or cylindrical baking dish 4 to 5 ins.
  deep
¼ oz. soft butter
A round of waxed paper
2 tbl. flour
8 oz. good plain chocolate
A 3-pt saucepan
¼ pt milk
A wooden spoon
8 oz. pound cake, wedding cake, sponge cake, sponge fingers, or other
  left-over white or yellow cake

Preheat oven to 350°F., Mark 4, for step 2. Prepare cake tin by smearing butter inside, fitting round of paper in bottom, buttering that, rolling flour around interior and knocking out excess. Break chocolate into saucepan, add the milk, and stir with a wooden spoon over moderate heat until chocolate is melted and smooth. Remove any icing or filling from left-over cake, and shred cake into crumbs; stir into the chocolate mixture.

An electric mixer with small bowl
4 egg whites at room temperature
Pinch of salt
¼ tsp. cream of tartar
3 tbl. sugar

Being sure beaters and bowl are clean and dry, beat egg whites at moderate speed until foamy; beat in salt and cream of tartar. Gradually increase speed to fast, beating until soft peaks are formed. A tablespoon at a time, and beating 30 seconds between spoonfuls, beat in the sugar, and continue beating at high speed until stiff peaks are formed. Proceed immediately to next paragraph.

The mixer with large bowl
4 egg yolks
4 oz. sugar
2 tbl. dark rum or orange liqueur
The tepid chocolate mixture from first paragraph
Optional: 1½ to 2 oz. soft butter

With the same electric mixer blades but in a different bowl, proceed at once to the egg yolks. Gradually beat the sugar into the yolks and continue beating until mixture is thick and pale yellow, and a bit lifted in the beaters falls back on the surface in a slowly dissolving ribbon. Beat in the rum or liqueur and the chocolate mixture, continuing for 30 seconds or so to make sure the batter is smooth and free of lumps. Beat in optional butter if you are using sponge cake or sponge fingers, and proceed immediately to next paragraph.

A rubber spatula
The beaten egg whites
The prepared cake tin

With spatula, stir a quarter of the egg whites into the batter to lighten it; scoop the rest of the egg whites on top and delicately fold in. Turn batter into prepared tin, tilt tin in all directions to run batter up to rim all around. (Tin will be two-thirds to three-quarters filled.) Set at once in middle level of preheated oven.

2. Baking: oven has been preheated to 350°F., Mark 4

Bake for about an hour. Cake is done when it has risen almost to rim of tin; the top will crack, and a cake tester or skewer plunged down through a crack in the centre will come out dry, with a few crumbs but no liquid adhering. Let cake cool for 20 minutes. To unmould, run a thin flexible knife around cake; turn a serving plate upside down over tin, reverse the two, and give a sharp downward jerk to unmould cake on to plate.

(†) If you are not serving or icing immediately, let cake cool; wipe out cake tin and reverse over cake, then slip it into a plastic bag and refrigerate. Cake will keep 3 or 4 days, or may be frozen for a month or more.

To Serve the *Charlotte Africaine* as a Dessert

Slice into 2 or 3 layers, fill and ice with *crème Chantilly* (lightly beaten and sweetened cream), page 588, or the *Chantilly meringuée*, page 562, and pass chocolate sauce separately.

To Serve the *Charlotte Africaine* as a Cake

Slice into 2 or 3 layers, and follow any of the suggestions on pages 660–62, such as butter-cream filling with chocolate icing.

Le Glorieux
[A Very Rich, Very Light Chocolate Cake]

This dark and delicious cousin of the *Quatre Quarts* is made with cornflour instead of flour, but again the secret of a full, light cake lies in how rapidly and delicately you fold the cornflour and finally the chocolate and butter into the egg mixture. Here we have suggested a 2-layer cake: the batter is divided and cooked in 2 tins; one still-warm cake goes upon the other with chocolate filling in between. You may ice the cake with more chocolate, with white meringue icing, or, if it is a dessert, with whipped cream.

[For 2 small cakes or 1 large one, serving 12 to 16]

1. Preliminaries

7 oz. good plain chocolate
2 oz. unsweetened baking chocolate
3 tbl. orange liqueur
The grated rind of 1 orange
½ lb. butter
Two 1½-pt cake tins (such as round ones 8 by 1½ ins.), bottom lined with
    waxed paper, tins buttered and floured

Preheat oven to 350°F., Mark 4, and place rack in middle level. Break up chocolate and melt with orange liqueur and orange rind over hot water (directions are on page 646); it must be perfectly smooth and creamy. Cut the butter into ¼-inch slices and beat piece by piece into the chocolate, again making sure mixture is perfectly smooth and creamy. (A hand-held electric mixer is useful here.) If consistency is too liquid – it should be like a heavy mayonnaise – beat over iced water. Set aside.

2. The cake batter

5 large eggs
½ lb. sugar
1 tsp. vanilla extract

An electric mixer and 5- to 6-pt bowl (be sure mixer blades and bowl
   are clean and dry)

Beat the eggs and sugar for a moment at low speed to blend,
then increase speed to high, add vanilla, and beat several
minutes (7 to 8 with a hand-held machine) until mixture is pale,
fluffy, doubled in volume, and holds in soft peaks.

4 oz. cornflour
A sieve or sifter set over waxed paper
The chocolate-butter mixture
A rubber spatula

Just as you are ready to blend the various batter elements
together, sift the cornflour on to the paper, check on the
chocolate-butter to be sure it is a smooth, thick cream, and
give the eggs and sugar a few turns of the beater if they have
lost their body.

   At slow mixing speed, gradually sprinkle the cornflour into
the egg mixture, taking 15 to 20 seconds to incorporate it but
not trying for a perfect blend; you must not deflate the beaten
eggs. Remove bowl from stand, if you have that kind of
mixer. Fold a large gob of egg mixture into chocolate-butter
to lighten it. Then, a large gob at a time, start folding chocolate-butter into eggs, rapidly cutting down through batter and
out to side with rubber spatula, rotating bowl, and repeating
movement 2 or 3 times. When almost incorporated, add another gob, and continue until all is used. Immediately turn the
batter into the prepared tins. Rapidly push batter up sides of
tins all around, and bang lightly on table to deflate possible
bubbles. Tins should be about two-thirds filled. Place at once in
middle level of preheated oven, leaving at least 2 inches of
space between tins as well as walls and door of oven.

3. Baking and filling

Bake for 25 to 30 minutes. Cakes should remain slightly moist,
in the French manner, and are done when a skewer or toothpick plunged into centre comes out looking oily, with a few
speckles of chocolate clinging to it. Cake will usually rise $\frac{1}{4}$ to
$\frac{1}{2}$ inch above rim of tins. Cool for 10 minutes. Top of cakes
will crack and flake slightly, which is normal. Make the following filling while cakes are cooling.

(*a*) *The chocolate filling* (glaçage au chocolat)*:*

3 oz. good plain chocolate
½ oz. unsweetened baking chocolate
3 tbl. orange liqueur
2 to 2½ oz. unsalted butter, cut into ¼-in. slices

Melt the chocolate in the liqueur over hot water. When perfectly smooth and creamy, beat in the butter piece by piece. If mixture is too soft for easy spreading, beat over iced water until the consistency of mayonnaise.

(*b*) *Filling the cake:*

A cake rack
A baking sheet

When cakes have cooled for 10 minutes, run a knife around edge of one to loosen it from the pan and unmould on to cake rack. Peel off waxed paper.

Spread top with filling. Immediately unmould second cake on to one end of baking sheet. Line up cake on sheet exactly with cake on rack, then slide the one upon the other. Peel paper off top of second cake. If sides are uneven, trim with a knife.

(†) If not to be iced or served immediately, cover airtight as soon as cake is cool or it will dry out. Cake may be frozen at this point; thaw for several hours at room temperature.

4. Icing and serving

To serve the cake as a dessert or with tea, spread lightly whipped cream, sweetened and flavoured with vanilla or orange liqueur, around and over the cake (*crème Chantilly*, page 588, or the *Chantilly meringuée*, page 562), and decorate with shaved or grated chocolate.

Or use the plain Italian meringue (hot sugar syrup whipped into stiffly beaten egg whites, page 557), or the meringue butter cream on page 636.

Or while the cake is still warm, spread on the same chocolate and butter mixture that you used for the filling, or use one of the chocolate butter creams listed in Volume I, pages 727–30.

*Le Succès
Le Progrès
La Dacquoise
[Meringue–nut Layer Cake with Butter-cream
Icing and Filling]

This particularly delicious type of cake rarely appears outside
France, yet it is far easier to make than a layer cake, and in-
finitely more elegant. Light yet rich, every mouthful is a poem.
This is the kind of pastry you will see in the very best French
pastry shops, and it is one that you can duplicate or even improve upon because you need not skimp on ingredients or
quality.

To describe the cake, it is layers of baked meringue mounted
one upon the other, like an ordinary layer cake, with filling in
between. The meringue layers, *fonds à Succès*, are composed of
egg whites and sugar beaten in a machine like any meringue,
but when it forms stiff peaks ground almonds are folded in.
The meringue is then spread out in disc shapes, heart shapes
like our illustrations, or whatever other shapes you wish, and
baked, like all meringues, in a very slow oven. The taste and
texture of this mixture is, of course, far more interesting than
plain meringue and just as easy to make.

HISTORICAL AND PHILOLOGICAL NOTES

While the cooked discs of meringue are called *fonds*, meaning
foundations or layers, and *fonds à Succès* when the cake is titled

Le Succès, you will see the terms *fonds à Progrès, fonds parisiens, Dacquoise, broyage suisse,* and *gâteau japonais* in French recipe books and elsewhere. Some authorities consider the *Succès* as containing almonds, and the *Progrès* almonds and filberts (*noisettes,* hazelnuts), while the *Dacquoise* is either formula plus cornflour and butter; other recipes make no distinctions. *Broyage* obviously comes from *broyer,* to grind, and refers to the ground nuts in the meringue; *gâteau japonais* appears to be British for meringue–nut layer cake.

There are various opinions, also, on what should fill and what should ice a *Succès* versus a *Progrès* or a *Dacquoise*. Since no one agrees on anything you are quite safe in doing whatever you wish. In addition to the icing and filling in the following recipe, other suggestions are at the end of it, on page 656.

MANUFACTURING NOTE

An electric mixer, even the small hand-held type, makes both the meringue and the butter cream fast and simple to do. Form the meringue discs with a spatula if you have no large canvas pastry bag, but the bag usually makes neater shapes. Non-stick baking sheets are especially recommended for meringues, or non-stick baking paper. If your baking sheets are not large enough to hold three 8-inch discs, make 4 smaller discs and a 4- rather than a 3-layer cake. (A discussion on beating egg whites is in Appendix 2, page 685, and illustrated directions for beating and folding egg whites are in Volume I, pages 178–82.) You will need toasted almonds and almond *pralin* (caramelized almonds), and do read the recipe through before you plan to make the cake so there will be no surprise ingredients or timings.

A NOTE ON NUTS – FILBERTS

You may use either ground blanched almonds or half and half ground almonds and ground filberts (hazelnuts, *noisettes*) in the following recipe. Filberts are not as easily available here as in France, and the ready-shelled packaged nuts turn rancid rapidly; shelled or ground filberts should be stored in the freezer, as should ground almonds.

To prepare shelled filberts for cooking, first eat a few to be sure they are fresh and fine, then spread the nuts on a baking sheet and dry them out in a 350°F., Mark 4 oven for about 15 minutes, until skins begin to flake off and nut flesh has browned very lightly. Remove from oven, rub nuts a small handful at a time between paper towels to remove as much skin as will easily come off. Grind the nuts in batches in an electric blender.

If you use half ground filberts and half ground blanched almonds rather than almonds alone for the meringues in the following recipe, call your cake *Le Progrès* rather than *Le Succès*.

[*For an 8-inch cake, serving 8 to 10*]

1. Preliminaries

$\frac{1}{2}$ to 1 oz. soft butter
2 large baking sheets 14 by 16 ins. (non-stick if possible)
1 oz. flour
A marker, such as an 8-in. round pot lid, a cake tin, a heart, or whatever shape you wish your cake to be
A rubber spatula
6 oz. ground blanched almonds (may be ground in an electric blender)
$\frac{1}{2}$ lb. sugar (caster recommended)
A double thickness of waxed paper about 10 by 12 ins.
1 level tbl. plus $1\frac{1}{2}$ level tsp. unsifted cornflour
A fine-meshed sieve
A canvas pastry bag 12 to 14 ins. long with round metal tube opening $\frac{3}{8}$ in. in diameter

Preheat oven to 250°F., Mark $\frac{1}{2}$. Rub soft butter over top of baking sheets, covering surface completely. Roll flour all over buttered surface and knock off excess. Make three 8-inch rings or other shapes on baking sheets by drawing around marker with point of rubber spatula. Measure the almonds and sugar on to waxed paper, and work with fingers to remove any lumps. Sieve over this the cornflour, and mix in with rubber spatula; set aside. Assemble the pastry bag. (Note that you will need *pralin* – ground caramelized almonds, page 551 – for the butter cream in step 5, and toasted almonds for the sides of the assembled cake, step 6; toast the almonds for both after the meringues have baked, and the *pralin* takes but a few minutes.)

2. The meringue–almond mixture (*pâte à Succès*)

6 egg whites at room temperature
A clean, dry bowl and clean, dry electric-mixer blades
⅛ tsp. salt
¼ tsp. cream of tartar
3 tbl. sugar
1½ tsp. vanilla extract
⅛ tsp. almond extract
The almond–sugar–cornflour mixture from step 1
The assembled pastry bag

Place egg whites in bowl and start beating at moderately slow speed for 1 to 2 minutes, until they are foamy. Beat in the salt and cream of tartar; gradually increase speed to fast, taking a minute or so, until egg whites form soft peaks. Continuing at fast speed, gradually beat in the 3 tablespoons of sugar, and continue until egg whites form stiff, upstanding peaks. Beat in the vanilla and the almond extracts.

If you are using a standing mixer, remove bowl from stand; the rest of this operation continues rapidly by hand and your object here is to deflate the egg whites as little as possible – they must continue to hold their volume so that you can form the meringue shapes for baking. Sprinkle 2 tablespoons of the almond–sugar–cornflour mixture over the beaten egg whites; cutting and folding with rubber spatula, delicately blend the two together, rapidly rotating bowl with one hand as you fold with the other. When almost blended, sprinkle on more of the mixture, rapidly fold in, and continue with the rest until all is used; reach all over bottom and sides of bowl with the final addition. The whole blending process should take less than a minute; scoop the meringue into the pastry bag, all of it or as much as will fit in easily.

3. Forming the 3 meringue discs (*les fonds à Succès*)

Squeeze out a line of meringue the width of your thumb and ½ inch high all around inner side of line marked on your baking sheet (A). Continue around and around until you have filled the entire space with meringue (B). Smooth top of meringue lightly with a spatula (C). Immediately make the 2 other meringue shapes in the same manner, using the other baking sheet for the third meringue.

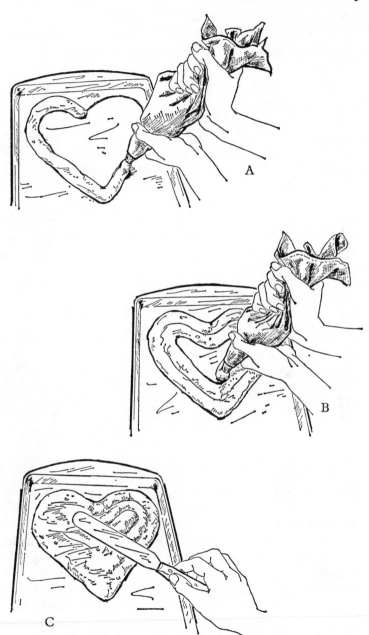

A

B

C

4. Baking: about 40 minutes at 250°F., Mark ½

Set baking sheets on the upper-middle and lower-middle levels of preheated oven. The meringues are actually to dry out rather than bake; they will not puff up, and they will not change shape, but they will colour lightly during baking. They are done as soon as you can gently push them loose from the baking surface, in 30 to 40 minutes. As soon as they are done, slip them carefully with a spatula on to cake racks to cool. They bend a little when still hot from the oven, but rapidly crisp as they cool; they are fragile and break easily, but a crack or break is not a disaster because the meringues are to be covered with icing and filling.

5. Butter cream for icing and filling (*crème au beurre à l'anglaise*)

8 oz. sugar
6 egg yolks
A wire whisk or hand-held electric beater
A heavy-bottomed enamelled or stainless saucepan, 3- to 4-pt size
¼ pt hot milk
A wooden spoon
12 to 14 oz. chilled unsalted butter
1 tsp. vanilla extract
3 tbl. kirsch, dark rum, or strong coffee

Make a *crème anglaise* (custard sauce) as follows: gradually beat sugar into egg yolks and continue beating for several minutes until mixture is thick and pale yellow. In a thin stream of droplets beat in the hot milk, and set mixture over moderate heat. Stir slowly with wooden spoon, reaching all over bottom of pan, for 4 to 5 minutes or until sauce thickens enough to film spoon with a creamy layer – do not let it come to simmer, but you must heat it to the point where it thickens. Immediately remove from heat and beat vigorously for 1 minute to cool slightly.

If you wish to continue with an electric mixer on a stand, scrape the custard into the mixer bowl; otherwise proceed with hand-held electric beater (or with a wire whisk). Cut the ¾ pound of chilled butter into ¼-inch slices and add a piece or two at a time, beating vigorously as butter melts and is absorbed; when all the butter has gone in, cream should be cool, smooth, and glossy, like a thick mayonnaise. Beat in the vanilla and kirsch. (If mixture turns grainy, soften rest of butter by beating it or working with fingers, and beat in successive tablespoons until butter cream smooths out.)

(a) For the icing:

2 oz. unsweetened baking chocolate, melted

Remove a quarter of the butter cream to a small bowl, stir the smooth melted chocolate into it, and reserve for icing top of cake, end of next step. Chocolate butter cream must be perfectly smooth and free of lumps when it covers top of cake: beat well, if necessary, before using.

(b) For the filling:

Half the quantity of almond *pralin* (ground caramelized almonds) given on page 551

Stir the *pralin* into the remaining butter cream; this will be the filling. *Pralin* butter cream must have enough body to hold its shape as a filling; chill if necessary.

6. Assembling the cake

A tray or baking sheet to set cake rack on
A flexible-blade steel spatula
6 oz. flaked, shaved, slivered, or chopped blanched almonds, toasted

One by one, place meringues on a cutting surface, set the marker you used in step 1 on top, and trim meringues with a small, sharp knife. This is so that edges will line up properly when circumference of cake is iced. Return 1 meringue to cake rack set over tray.

Spread a third of the *pralin* butter cream over the meringue on the cake rack (D). Centre second meringue on top of first (E), and spread with half the remaining *pralin* butter cream. Cover with the final meringue. Spread remaining *pralin* butter cream evenly around the edges of the cake with a spatula (F).

Note: You may prefer to spread almonds around sides of cake (following illustration) before icing the top; proceed in either order you wish, whichever seems easier for you. Spread

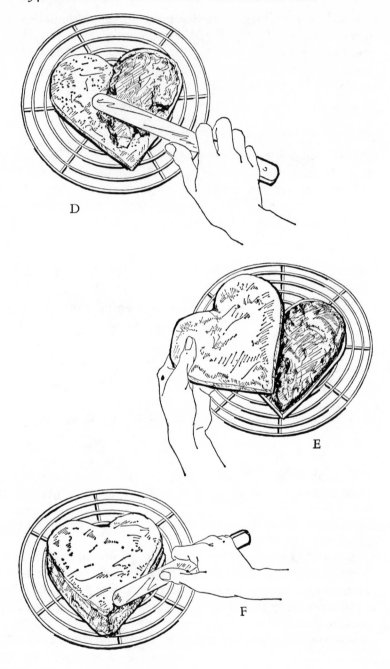

D

E

F

the chocolate-flavoured butter cream as evenly as possible on top of cake with a spatula (G). Either balancing cake on the palm of one hand or leaving on rack, whichever you prefer, brush almonds against sides of cake all around (H).

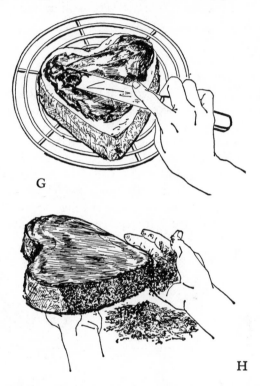

G

H

The cake is now finished unless you wish to make fancy rosettes, swags, or other decorations on top with chocolate butter cream pushed through a pastry bag; French *pâtissiers* often write the name *Le Succès* on top of the cake in butter cream or white icing.

7. Serving – after at least 2 hours of refrigeration

Transfer cake to a serving dish, and cover with a large bowl or a plastic dome; refrigerate. Cake should be chilled at least 2 hours to firm the butter cream. To serve, cut into serving slices as you would any layer cake.

(†) *Le Succès* will keep perfectly for several days under refrigeration. It may be frozen, but the butter cream will probably lose its creamy smoothness; it is best to freeze discs and
butter cream separately, then assemble before serving, beating
more softened butter into thawed cream, if necessary, to reconstitute it.

Other fillings for *Le Succès*

A complete list of icings and fillings is on pages 660–62, including recipes from both volumes. Other butter creams that
are popular with this cake are Mocha-flavoured butter cream
with *pralin* plus Mocha-coloured fondant, and chocolate butter
cream with chocolate icing. Other ideas are the *mousse au
chocolat* used for the *Saint-Cyr* on page 556, which stands up
well enough when chilled and need not be frozen, and the
other and richer mousse with butter in Volume I, page 644,
into either one of which you could fold *pralin*. The almond
and strawberry mixture for *charlotte Malakoff* could be deliciously adapted, as well as the chocolate variation following
it (Volume I, pages 646–8).

Brésiliens
[Individual Meringue–Almond Cakes – *Petits Fours*]

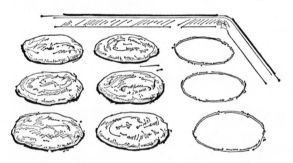

Rather than a large cake, you may prefer individual servings;
mark whatever shapes you like on buttered and floured baking
sheets, fill with the meringue mixture, and bake as directed in
step 4, page 652.

Fill, ice and decorate as described in the master recipe, step 6, page 653, but you will need only 2 layers – one for the top, and one for the bottom.

Icings, Fillings, and a Paper Decorating Cone

Fondant
[Sugar Icing]

For cakes, *petits fours*, Napoleons, candied fruits, and sweets.

White fondant is to the *pâtissier* what the racket is to a tennis player. It is ready in an instant to be warmed briefly over hot water, flavoured with a dash of vanilla, liqueur, or chocolate, and to be poured over a cake. It makes a beautifully smooth covering that hardens just enough to form a protective layer, but remains just the right texture for eating. Commercial pastry chefs can buy it ready-made in a tin or jar, and so may French householders. It is easy to make yourself, however, and really one of nature's wonders, because it consists only of sugar syrup boiled to the soft-ball stage, cooled to tepid, then kneaded for several minutes until it miraculously turns from clear and limpid to snowy white. It keeps for months, even years, and is always ready to become an immediate icing.

Although we have only called for fondant a few times in the book, it is so useful to have on hand, and really so easy and such fun to make, that we felt it should be in your repertoire.

[*For about 2 cups*]

1. The sugar syrup

A marble surface 18 by 24 ins., or a Swiss-roll tin or large metal tray
3 tbl. white corn syrup or ¼ tsp. cream of tartar
½ pt water
A heavy-bottomed 3-pt saucepan
1¼ lb. sugar (pure cane sugar, or crushed sugar lumps)

A cover for the pan
Optional: a sugar thermometer
A 2-pt measure with $\frac{3}{4}$ pt cold water and 2 ice cubes
A metal spoon (not for stirring, only for testing sugar)

Syrup is to be poured on to marble, or into a tin or tray, which should be ready before you begin. Dissolve the corn syrup or cream of tartar (or glucose) with a bit of the water in the saucepan; pour in the rest of the water, and the sugar. Set over moderately high heat. Swirl pan slowly by its handle, but do not stir sugar with a spoon while liquid is coming to the boil. Continue swirling for a moment when liquid boils and changes from cloudy to perfectly clear. Cover pan, raise heat to high, and boil for several minutes until bubbles have thickened slightly. Uncover, insert sugar thermometer if you are using one, and continue boiling for a few minutes to the soft-ball stage, 238°F.: drops of syrup hold their shape softly when formed into a ball in the cold water. *Note:* If you do not boil the syrup to the soft-ball stage, your fondant will be too soft: if you boil to the hard-ball stage, your fondant will be hard to knead and difficult to melt when you want to use it.

2. Cooling the syrup; about 10 minutes

Immediately pour the syrup on to the marble or into the tin or tray. Let cool about 10 minutes, until barely tepid but not quite cold to the touch; when you press it lightly you can see the surface wrinkle.

3. Kneading the syrup into fondant: 5 to 10 minutes

A pastry scraper, a painter's spatula, or a short, stout metal pancake turner
Useful but not essential: 2 tbl. ready-made fondant

As soon as syrup is ready, start kneading it vigorously with scraper, spatula, or turner: push it up into a mass, spread it out again, and repeat the movement for 5 minutes or more. After several minutes of kneading, the syrup will begin to whiten (if you happen to have some ready-made fondant, add it at this point, and the syrup will quickly turn to fondant); as you continue to knead, it will gradually turn into a crumbly snow-white mass, and finally stiffen so that you can no longer knead it. It is now, officially and actually, fondant. Do not be discouraged, however, if it takes longer than 5 to 8 minutes, or even 10 minutes, to turn to fondant; go off and leave it for 5 minutes; come back and knead it again – it will eventually turn (you might have started to knead it before it was quite ready for you).

4. Curing and storing fondant

A 1½-pt screw-topped jar or a metal bowl with cover
Several thicknesses of well-washed cheesecloth about 6 ins. square

Although you may use the fondant immediately, it will have better texture and sheen – or bloom, as the professionals say – if you let it rest at least 12 hours. Pack it into the jar or bowl, top with the dampened cheesecloth, cover airtight, and refrigerate. As long as the top is damp, fondant will keep for months and months.

5. How to use fondant

2 cups fondant in 3-pt pan
1 to 2 tbl. kirsch, rum, orange liqueur, or strong coffee; or 1 tsp. vanilla
    and a tbl. or so of water
A larger pan of simmering water
A wooden spoon

Combine the fondant and liqueur, coffee, or vanilla and water in the saucepan and set in larger pan of simmering water. Stir thoroughly, reaching all over pan, as fondant slowly softens and turns into a perfectly smooth, glossy cream that coats the spoon fairly heavily.

Use immediately, either pouring it directly over a cake set on a rack over a tray, spreading it rapidly over whatever surface you are icing, or dipping *petits fours* or sweets into it. It sets rapidly, and you must work quickly to obtain a smooth surface.

Storing melted fondant

Store like fresh fondant. Unless you are turning it into chocolate fondant, it will have more sheen and bloom if you mix it with fresh fondant before using again.

Coloured Fondant

Use strong coffee for Mocha or tan fondant, stirring it in by droplets to get the shade you wish; stir 4 to 6 ounces melted chocolate into the melted fondant for brown or chocolate fondant; use drops of food colouring for pastel shades.

Confit d'Abricots en Sirop

[Apricot Filling or Sauce Using Tinned Apricots]

This deliciously simple filling or sauce is made with diced tinned apricots lightly caramelized in their own syrup and flavoured with kirsch or lemon. Serve it with custard desserts, such as the *Pélerin* on page 583, or as a filling for tarts like the *jalousie* on page 600, spoon it over the apricot sorbet on page 544, or fold in a little gelatine and walnuts or sliced almonds and use as a cake filling as suggested for the *Saint-André* on page 640.

[*For about ¼ pint*]

A 1-lb. tin of peeled apricots in heavy syrup
A small, heavy saucepan
2½ oz. sugar
1 tbl. lemon juice and the grated rind of ½ lemon
1 tbl. kirsch or cognac

Drain the apricot syrup into the saucepan and bring to the simmer with the sugar. When sugar has dissolved completely, boil the syrup rapidly until last drops to fall from spoon are thick and sticky (230°F.). Cut apricot flesh into ⅜-inch dice. Fold them into the syrup and add the lemon juice and rind. Boil slowly for 5 minutes. Remove from heat and fold in the kirsch or cognac.

List of Icings and Fillings

Apricot filling or sauce

Confit d'abricots en sirop, above (diced tinned apricots boiled in their own syrup, liqueur flavouring; with gelatine added as cake filling, page 640, *Le Saint-André*).

Baked meringue decorations

Meringue italienne, page 557 (*Le Saint-Cyr*, steps 1 and 2) (boiling sugar syrup whipped into beaten egg whites, formed into meringues, and baked).

Butter cream with custard base

Crème au beurre à l'anglaise, page 652 (*Le Succès*), and Volume I, page 729 (cooked custard sauce with butter and flavouring beaten in).

Butter cream with egg-yolk and sugar-syrup base

Crème au beurre au sucre cuit, Volume I, pages 727–9 (boiling sugar syrup beaten into egg yolks, mixture poached over hot water, beaten until cool, then butter and flavouring beaten in).

Butter cream with Italian meringue base

Crème au beurre à la meringue italienne, page 636 (boiling sugar syrup beaten into egg whites, beaten until cool, then butter and flavouring beaten in).

Fondant

Page 657 (sugar syrup boiled to the soft-ball stage, cooled, then kneaded until it turns snowy white; flavoured with liqueur or chocolate).

Ground caramelized almonds

Pralin aux amandes, page 551 (*Le Kilimanjaro*, step 1) (same as *pralin aux noix*, but with almonds).

Ground caramelized walnuts and caramelized walnut halves

Pralin aux noix, page 553 (*pralinée aux noix*, step 1) (walnuts stirred into caramel syrup and ground when cold; or walnuts dipped into caramel syrup and used for decorations).

Meringued whipped cream icing or filling

Chantilly meringuée, page 562 (*meringue italienne* combined with whipped cream).

Orange or lemon butter-cream icing or filling

Crème au beurre à l'orange, or *au citron*, Volume I, pages 720–22 (eggs, yolks, flavouring, and butter stirred together over heat to thicken into a simple filling; more butter beaten in to turn it into a butter cream). See also another version of the filling, *crème au citron*, page 631; this may also be turned into a butter cream in the same way.

Simple butter cream with icing sugar

Crème au beurre, ménagère, Volume I, page 727 (egg yolks beaten with icing sugar, flavouring, and butter – uncooked).

Soft chocolate icing

Glaçage au chocolat, page 646 (*Le Glorieux*, step 3), and Volume I, page 730 (melted chocolate and butter, with or without liqueur flavouring).

White meringue icing

Meringue italienne, page 557 (*Le Saint-Cyr*, step 1) (boiling sugar syrup whipped into beaten egg whites).

Comment Faire un Cornet en Papier
[How to Make a Paper Decorating Cone]

Cut heavy freezer paper or bond paper into a right-angle triangle whose short sides (A and B) are approximately 12 and 15 inches long. Hold the hypotenuse side of the triangle (C) with your left hand, thumb on top and opposite the point of the right angle (X). With your right hand, curl the longer end of the hypotenuse (Z) around towards your left, bringing its

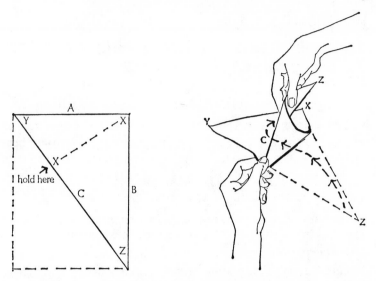

underside against the top of the right angle (x). You now have formed a cone with the right side of the paper. Curl the other end of the hypotenuse (Y) towards your right, around the outside of the first cone, bringing its point (Y) to the back of

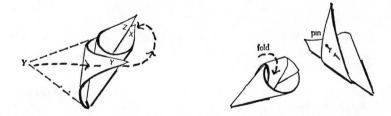

the right angle (x). You have now completed the cone; slide points back and forth at top, to close tip of cone at other end. Secure cone either by bending points x, y, and z down inside, or by using a straight pin. Cut tip of cone with scissors to make any size of opening you wish.

Appendix One
List of Stuffings for Meats
and Vegetables

STUFFINGS WITH MUSHROOMS

Mushroom *duxelles* and spinach (*farce Viroflay*): for stuffed lamb and veal (in the stuffed shoulder of lamb recipe, page 271).

Mushroom *duxelles* with onions, cream cheese, and parsley: for stuffed vegetables (in the stuffed aubergine recipe, Volume I, page 537).

Mushrooms, giblets, breadcrumbs, and cream cheese: for chicken, veal, and stuffed vegetables (in the roast chicken section, Volume I, page 274).

Mushrooms, onions, and ham: for stuffed lamb, veal, or chicken, and for stuffed vegetables (in the lamb section, Volume I, page 366).

Mushrooms and kidneys; mushrooms and chicken livers; mushrooms and ground lamb; mushrooms and forcemeat: see following section.

STUFFINGS WITH MEAT

Chicken giblets, herbs, crumbs, and cream cheese: for veal, chicken, turkey, and stuffed vegetables (in the roast chicken recipe, Volume I, page 266). The same, with mushrooms (Volume I, page 274).

Chicken-liver mixture for stuffings, sausages, and *pâtés* (in the *pâté* section, page 429).

Chicken livers, mushrooms, rice, and puréed cooked garlic (*farce évocation d'Albuféra*): for chicken, turkey, veal, and stuffed vegetables (in the poached chicken section, page 369).

Chicken livers, rice, *foie gras,* and truffles (*farce à la d'Albuféra*): for chicken, turkey, and veal (in the poached chicken section, page 367).

Foie gras and prunes: for stuffed duck, goose, or turkey (in the stuffed goose recipe, Volume I, page 309).

Foie gras and truffles: for fillet of beef, veal, or chicken (in the fillet of beef recipe, Volume I, page 329).

Forcemeat and mushrooms (*farce normande aux boudins blancs*): for chicken, turkey, or veal (in the poached chicken section, page 371).

Kidneys and mushrooms: for stuffed lamb or veal (in the lamb section, page 266).

Kidneys, rice, and herbs: for lamb or veal (in the stuffed lamb section, Volume I, page 365).

Minced braised beef and chard: for stuffed vegetables, as a meat loaf, or as sausages (in the sausage section, *les tous nus*, page 407).

Minced braised beef, ham, onions, and herbs: for stuffed vegetables, or as a meat loaf (in the stuffed cabbage section, page 506).

Minced lamb, aubergines, mushrooms, and herbs: for stuffed lamb, stuffed vegetables, and as a meat loaf (the *moussaka* recipe, Volume I, page 377).

Minced lamb, olives, and onions: for stuffed lamb and stuffed vegetables (in the lamb section, Volume I, page 366).

Minced lamb, salmon, anchovies, and onions: for stuffed lamb and stuffed vegetables (in the lamb section, Volume I, page 367).

Minced left-over veal, turkey, or pork with onions and herbs: for stuffed vegetables or as a meat loaf (in the aubergine section, page 471).

Minced pork, onions, herbs and breadcrumbs (*farce de porc*): for stuffed meats and vegetables (in the stuffed lamb section, Volume I, page 365).

Minced pork with ham, truffles, and *foie gras*: for stuffed veal and chicken, or for use as a *pâté* mixture (in the veal section, *veau en feuilletons*, page 302).

Sausage and apple: for duck, goose, and pork (in the roast duck recipe, Volume I, page 300).

Sausage and chestnuts: for duck, goose, turkey, and pork (in the roast goose recipe, Volume I, page 311).

Sausage, ham, and rice: for meats and stuffed vegetables (in the stuffed cabbage recipe, page 498).

Sausage, ham, greens, and breadcrumbs: for meats and stuffed vegetables (in the beef roll recipe, page 223).

Sausage, rice, and apricots (*farce Trébizonde*): for duck, goose, pork, and turkey (in the suckling pig recipe, page 310).

Veal, ham, rice, and chard or spinach: for stuffed veal or lamb (in the breast of veal recipe, page 299).

STUFFINGS WITHOUT EITHER MEAT OR MUSHROOMS

Almonds, cheese, and breadcrumbs: for stuffed onions, or courgettes (in the stuffed courgettes recipe, page 491).

Aubergines, peppers, onions, tomatoes, and herbs: for stuffing cold vegetables (in the vegetable chapter, page 463).

Chopped olives, pimentos, and herbs: for *paupiettes* of meat (in the beef roll recipe, page 227).

Chopped peppers, onions, and mustard breadcrumbs: for *paupiettes* of meat (in the beef roll recipe, page 226).

Garlic and herbs: for *paupiettes* of meat, and as a flavouring for boned red meats (in the lamb section, Volume I, page 364).

Rice and chopped peppers, tomato topping: for stuffed vegetables (in the stuffed courgette recipe, page 493).

Rice, garlic, and herbs: for stuffed meats and vegetables (in the beef roll recipe, page 228).

Rice, onions, and cheese: for stuffed vegetables (in the stuffed onion recipe, page 495).

Appendix Two
Kitchen Equipment

The following pages contain an illustrated round-up of some kitchen equipment (*batterie de cuisine*) we find useful, so that you will see it all in one place rather than scattered throughout two volumes.

Some of these implements are standard American or English, others are professional American or English, still others can be found in kitchen shops or mail-order catalogues. As always, we advise you to look for solid, practical, professional equipment designed by people in the cooking business who sell to chefs. If you have trouble locating good equipment in your area, ask your butcher or the owner and chef of the best restaurant in town.

FRYING PANS

For browning meats and vegetables and for general sautéing, the heavy-duty professional frying pan with its long handle and sloping 2-inch sides is the best shape. Cast-aluminium models (A and D) come either with plain or non-stick interiors. The French *poêle* (B) is of *tôle épaisse* (very thick sheet metal); one with a bottom diameter of 7 to 7½ inches is ideal for omelettes. The oval cast-iron pan (E), *poêle à poissons*, is as useful for browning roasts as it is for sautéing fish. The short-handled cast-iron pan (C) is also good in the oven, and is the pan to use for *pommes Anna*; the same shape can be found with an enamelled surface, making it ideal for cooking in white wine, or for storing and serving stews or sautés.

You should have at least three sizes of frying pans – a large one 11 inches across its top diameter, a medium, or 10-inch, pan, and a smaller 7- to 8-inch pan for single servings and *crêpes*. You will probably end up with many more, some of one material, some of another, and each your pet for certain techniques.

SAUTÉ PANS

The straight-sided frying pan (sauté pan) known as a *sautoir* in French is useful for fried chicken and for chicken sautés and fricassees, beef stews, fish stews, and numerous vegetable dishes. Because the cooking usually takes place on top of the stove, it must be of heavy material. The traditional shape (A and B) is typical of the copper *sautoir* and of the professional cast aluminium; the sides are $2\frac{1}{4}$ to $2\frac{1}{2}$ inches high. The deep pan (C) is of cast iron; this is a fine cooking utensil, but remove foods from it as soon as they are done to prevent discolouration.

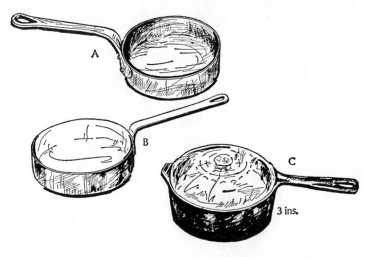

SAUCEPANS, COVERS, AND COLANDERS

You will need saucepans (*casseroles*) for sauces and saucepans for general boiling and simmering. When you are cooking with white wine or egg yolks, use a non-staining material like lined copper, stainless steel, flameproof ceramic or glass, or the familiar French enamelled cast iron with wooden handle (A).

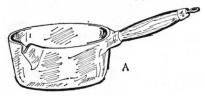

For boiling potatoes, pasta, and their like, cast aluminium is fine although you will have to scour it from time to time. The professional shape (B-1) is well designed; 2½, 3½, 7 and 10 pints (B-2) will give you a reasonable range of pan sizes.

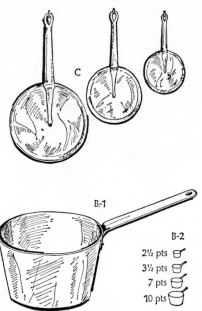

C

B-1

B-2

2½ pts
3½ pts
7 pts
10 pts

Rather than having a special cover for each pot, a series of long-handled covers allows one to fit several sizes of saucepans (c).

Soup pots (*marmites*) are essential for *pot-au-feu*, soups, *bouillabaisse* lobsters, green beans *à la française*, and spinach. A 12-pint pan and another of 25- to 40-pint capacity would meet most of your needs. One of them might be the two-handled type (E or F), and another the preserving pan type with bucket handle (H). A French earthen-

D

E

ware *marmite* (G) is attractive for soups and stews that are cooked and served in the same pot.

A large sturdy colander is a must; buy one 10 to 11 inches across the op diameter and 5 to 6 inches high, with feet (D).

CASSEROLES AND BRAISING PANS

Casseroles (*cocottes*) can double as saucepans or roasters, and are essential for stews and braises. Enamelled ironware is always good because it will go on the stove or into the oven (A, B, C) and foods will not discolour in it; the oval shape is the best if you are limited in

space or budget. The French *daubière* (G) is in lined copper. Earthenware casseroles (D, E, F) are wonderful for cooking and serving because they spread and retain heat. The attractive copper *cocotte* (H) was designed for the famous potato dish, *pommes Anna*, page 517, but may be used as a casserole or as two separate baking dishes.

GRATIN DISHES AND ROASTING PANS

Flameproof dishes about 2 inches deep are used for baking, gratinée-ing, roasting, and serving, and you should have a reasonable number of sizes. Enamelled iron *gratin* dishes (*plats à gratin*) (A and E) are either oval or round, and come from scrambled-egg size up to 13 to 14 inches long and 9 inches wide. Earthenware *gratin* dishes (B) are always attractive for serving. A nest of aluminium dishes (F) is conveniently stored and long lasting. Rectangular enamelled iron (C) can be plain or with non-stick interior, and will double for roasting or gratinéeing. Be sure to have a rack (D) that will fit into your large roasting pan so that legs of lamb can be raised out of their juices.

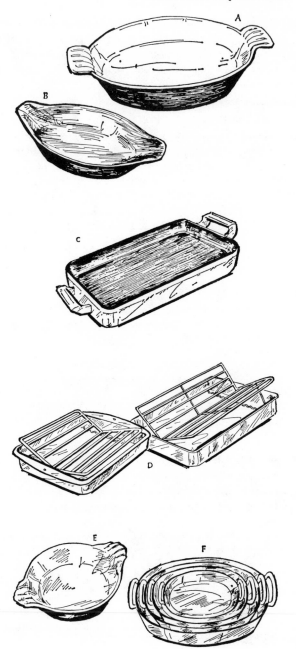

IMPLEMENTS – KNIVES

Very sharp knives are the mark of the serious cook, and continual use of the butcher's steel will keep them razor sharp. Carbon steel knives are preferred by most chefs, but there are stainless knives that will sharpen easily too.

The central hoard

The straight-edged, wedge-shaped cook's knife (C, D, E, F, G, H) is the all-purpose shape for chopping, slicing, paring, and general cutting; you will need at least three, from the 2- to 3-inch blade for paring and small minces to the 10- to 12-inch blade for chopping and rapid slicing. Curved blades (A and B) are good for paring. A professional butcher's steel (J) with blade 10 to 12 inches long is the best sharpening equipment. A larding needle (I) is indispensable for larding meat.

Slicers, carvers, and boners

Slicing, carving, and boning knives have curved blades. Here is the slicing scimitar (K), and two other slicing shapes (L and M). The stubby knife (P) and its longer companion (O) are boning knives, as is the very

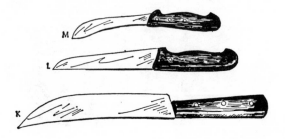

thin knife known as a chicken sticker (Q) with its short blade; the
longer-bladed version (N) is a Norwegian herring filleter, which is
also useful for slicing off pork rinds and for cutting thin sheets of
pork fat.

Serrated sawers

Serrated knives include the curved grapefruit knife (A), the bread
knife (B), the all-purpose slicer (C), the frozen-food cutter (D), the
ham slicer, which also does smoked salmon (E), and the vicious-look-
ing French meat slicer (F), which is, in addition, very good with slab
bacon.

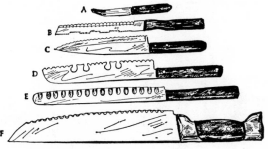

Choppers and rockers

Traditional chef's knives (J and K) are for general chopping, as
illustrated in Volume I, page 45. The Japanese version (I) works

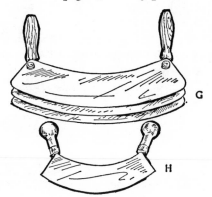

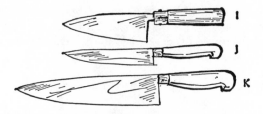

equally well. The two rockers (G and H) are marvellous for mushrooms and parsley, particularly the 3-bladed professional model.

BASHERS, BLUDGEONS, AND BLUNT INSTRUMENTS

For whacking up turkey carcasses, chopping bones, and flattening cutlets, here is a choice of weapons. The meat tenderizer with its cast-aluminium head has waffled sides for tenderizing (A) and smooth sides for flattening cutlets; you can also use it as a hammer, although the rubber-headed hammer that you can buy at any good hardware

shop (F) is less noisy. The French cleaver, *feuille à fendre* (D), or an ordinary hatchet (E) are for whacking carcasses or bones, and a hammer helps. The French cleaver-tenderizer, *batte à côtelettes* (B), is a useful instrument, and the wooden British basher (C) is for flattening cutlets that are held between sheets of waxed paper.

SCISSOR ACTION

Heavy shears for cutting fish fins, gristle, and rib cages are the serrated French pair (A) and the heavy utility model (F), also French. Poultry

shears with their curved blades (B) are useful on occasion, as are the
sharp-pointed lobster shears (C). General purpose stainless kitchen
scissors with take-apart blades (E) can go into the dishwasher. The
scissor-action cherry or olive stoner (D) is invaluable when you have
those jobs to do.

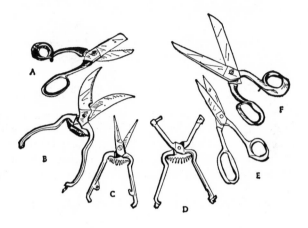

FOUR PAIRS OF SPOONS

You can rarely have enough spoons, and all sizes are needed. Large
models of tough non-metallic composition (A and B) are essential for
stirring in non-stick pans. Large stainless-steel spoons (E and F) have
hundreds of uses, as do the smaller spoons (C and D). The sturdy ice-
cream spoon (H) does its job well, as does the scoop (G).

EIGHT FORKS

For testing meat and artichokes, for lifting, carving, and spearing, you need a number of sharp-pronged forks like the large chef's model (H) for enormous roasts and giant birds, and general-purpose forks (E and G), as well as something like the slender Danish three-pronged pickle fork (D). A wooden fork (F) is useful for stirring braised rice, and a salad fork (C), combined with spoon, does many a neat job of tossing. The table fork (B) is constantly on call for beating eggs, pricking pastry, general lifting, and stirring, while the small two-pronged fork (A) comes in for pokings and turnings.

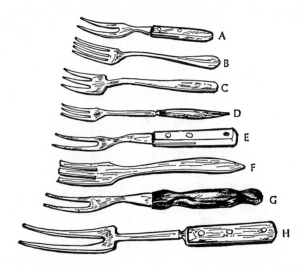

TURNOVER TOOLS – SPATULAS

Flexible-blade spatulas scrape fragile biscuits off baking sheets, spread icings over cakes, and slide *quiches* on to plates; the 12-inch blade (c) and 8-inch (B) are useful sizes. The palette knife (A) is marvellous for delicate liftings and spreadings. Pancake turners of non-metallic composition (D) are essential when you cook in non-stick pans, and stainless all-purpose models (E, F, H) are standard equipment. The very wide turner (G) does many a lifting job, such as getting asparagus out of hot water.

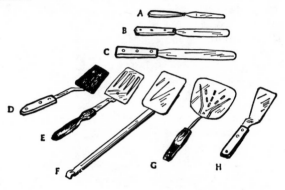

RETRIEVERS

Metal tongs (A and C) are for lifting and turning meats on a barbecue or in a pan, as well as for retrieving items from boiling oil. The Japanese wooden tongs (B) do many chores and are especially great

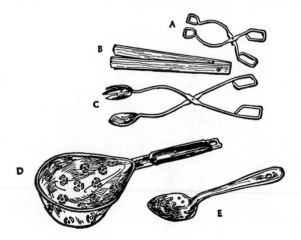

for turning bacon in the pan. Life would be hard without the perforated spoon (E), and if you become addicted to the great Italian
scoop (D) you will never boil brussels sprouts without it by your side.

WOODEN SPOONS, SPATULAS, AND CHOPSTICKS

Why stir it with a wooden spoon? Because it blends the flour and
butter *roux* without racket, and it scrapes the coagulated roasting
juices into the deglazing sauce with more quiet efficiency than metal
against metal. Actually, the French bowl-less wooden spatula (I, G, F),
or the Japanese wooden spatula (H), or the non-stick spatula implements (C and D) are far more useful for every stirring, scraping,
mixing, and beating job than the wooden spoon (A and B). Do not
forget wooden chopsticks (E); they will beat the eggs for the omelette,
lift the green bean out of the boiling pot for testing, and turn the
bacon.

GADGETS AND MISCELLANY

Opening, prying, and poking operations will be easier on fingers and
tempers when you have something like (A) or (C) for screw-topped
jars, or the all-purpose-everything item (B). The French tool (G) is
for tins and general prying, while the box-opener–hammer–hatchet
instrument (D) is useful anywhere. Ice picks, both the single-pointed
(F) and the 5-pronged (E), are multi-purpose musts. Citrus zesters
(H and J) are good for bar as well as kitchen, and the potato ballers
(I and K) are useful for fruits and vegetables alike.

For grating, puréeing, and grinding, some hand-operated gadgets
do a better job than the electric blender or mixer. Use 4-sided grater
(L) when you want to grate orange rind or you need coarsely grated
cheese, or a few slices of carrot; look for one in stainless steel. When

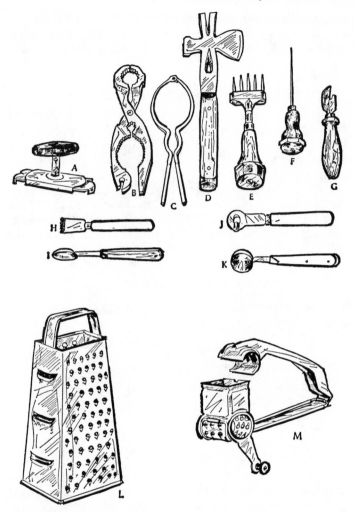

grated cheese is to be spread over the *sauce mornay*, hold the little French rotary grater (M) right over the *gratin* dish. The table model (N) is for great mounds of cheese if you do not have a grating attachment for your electric mixer.

Again, in spite of the marvels of the electric blender, you do need an efficient food mill for apple-sauce, puréeing soups, turnips, artichoke hearts, and tinned Italian plum tomatoes. The French model (O), with removable discs and folding rubber-padded feet is still the best, in our opinion. One with a top diameter of 9 inches is the standard size; if you are having more than one, the 7-inch size is handy for small jobs like sieving hard-boiled egg yolks.

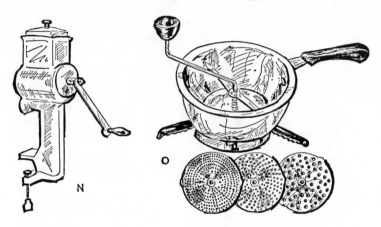

The old-fashioned potato masher (P) is not to be ignored, nor is the rectangular-headed garlic press (Q). Beware of faulty designs, however, especially in garlic presses. These should take a quite large,

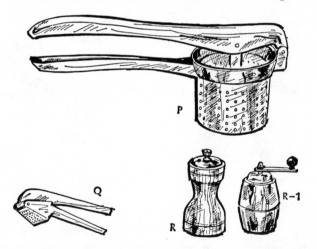

whole, unpeeled clove of garlic; the point is that you do not have to peel the garlic. The rectangular head allows a reasonably large clove to be puréed, and the holes should be just the right diameter for the press to do its work easily; if the one you buy does not perform as you think it should, take it back and demand a refund. Get yourself a good peppermill for the kitchen; the French Peugeot models (R and R-I) are always reliable.

Public performances are long when the flame lies low; chafing-dish heat elements are for cooking, and must provide proper heat. Unless you want the efficient gas-operated model (T), look for the kind that will hold a whole can of solidified alcohol (s) and that has an opening which will give you a large heat source.

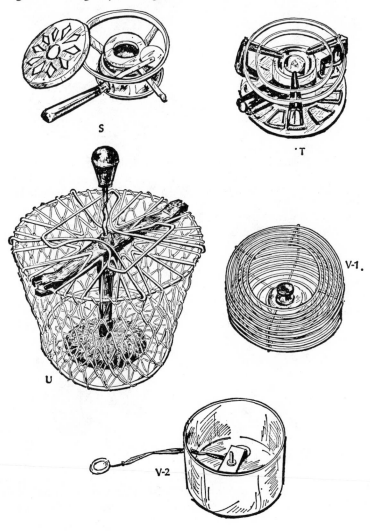

The French salad basket (U) also comes with a rotary ratchet-gadget that spins salad greens dry in a jiffy. The basket for the Swiss model (v-1) fits into a container (v-2) which catches all the splattering water as the lettuce leaves whirl inside it.

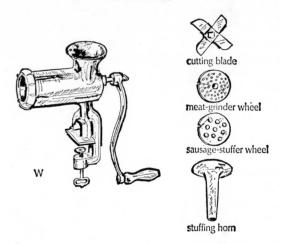

cutting blade

meat-grinder wheel

sausage-stuffer wheel

stuffing horn

W

If you do not have a mincer attachment for your electric mixer, buy yourself a sturdy table model (w), always picking the large size for quick and easy operation. Many mincers come with the sausage-stuffing horn you will need for the *charcuterie* recipes illustrated on pages 379–82.

THE PASTRY BAG

From squeezing out cream puffs to making meringue cakes and potato borders, nothing will do the work as easily nor with as pro-

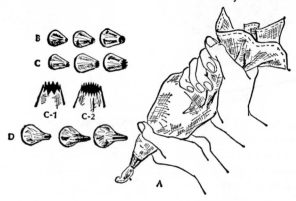

B

C

C-1   C-2

D

A

fessional a look as the pastry bag (A) with its collection of inter-changeable metal tubes. Buy the big professional, washable, canvas bags, 12, 14, and 16 inches long; in comparison with your other kitchen equipment, these are inexpensive, and so are the metal tubes. For a start, get 2 or 3 tubes with plain round openings varying from $\frac{1}{4}$ to $\frac{3}{4}$ inch in diameter (B), and a cannelated group of the same dimensions (C). Among the latter, the widely spaced teeth (C-1) are for rough masses like *pommes duchesse*, while the fine teeth (C-2) are for icings. Ribbon tubes, both plain and cannelated (D), are used particularly for such decorations as the meringues for the *Saint-Cyr* on page 556; one of each, $\frac{3}{4}$ inch wide, should be sufficient.

BEATING EGG WHITES

You are far more likely to welcome soufflés, meringues, cakes, and baked Alaskas – or even to encourage them – when you have the proper egg-white beating equipment. We urge you to consider the type of heavy-duty electric mixer illustrated here (A). Its large revolv-

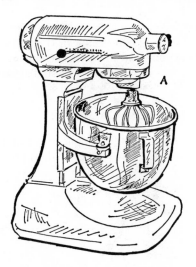

A

A-1

ing whisk (A-1) also rotates around the bowl, beating egg whites so easily it will never again occur to you to think of them as a problem. In fact, this is a replica of the large industrial machines designed by professionals for professionals; to have a home model available is a tremendous help to all of us.

While you are at it, buy an extra bowl and an extra whisk, to save you the chore of washing and drying in a single recipe like the *Saint-Cyr* on page 556, which calls for a butter and chocolate mixture as

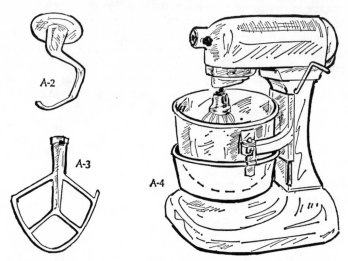

A-2

A-3

A-4

well as for beaten egg whites. The straight-sided bowl, in addition, is just the right shape for raising yeast dough. The dough hook (A-2) works very well for kneading French bread or *brioche* dough, while the flat beater (A-3) will do the whole operation for a pastry dough from working the butter into the flour to blending in the cold water; when you are doubling or tripling pastry recipes, or blending large

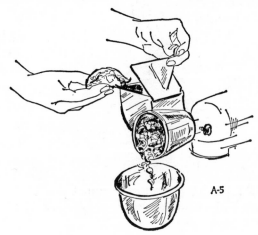

A-5

batches of sausage meat, the heavy-duty action and ample bowl do the work with ease and speed. The bowl or jack attachment that holds either hot water or ice around the main mixing bowl (A-4) quickly warms the eggs and sugar as you beat them into a foaming mass, or chills the fish *quenelle* mixture so that you can beat in the maximum amount of cream. The set of rotary graters, slicers, and shredders (A-5) makes fast work of lots of cheese to grate, potatoes or onions to slice, or even mushroom *duxelles*.

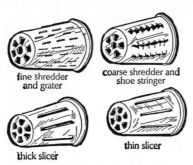

fine shredder
and grater

coarse shredder and
shoe stringer

thick slicer

thin slicer

Whether you beat egg whites by machine or by hand, the theory and practice are the same. Have them at room temperature: they tend to coagulate and fleck when chilled. Start beating rather slowly until they begin to foam, add a pinch of salt and, if you are not using unlined copper, a scant $\frac{1}{4}$ teaspoon of cream of tartar for each 4 egg whites. Gradually speed the beating action to fast as you circulate the beater all around the bowl, keeping the whole mass in motion, and beating in as much air as possible to increase the volume of the egg whites by sevenfold at least, and until they form the peak illustrated here (B).

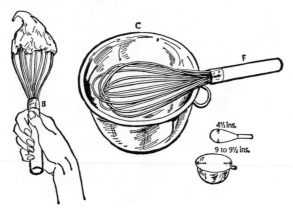

4½ ins.

9 to 9½ ins.

The unlined copper bowl (c) is chic, expensive, and looks pretty hanging by its ring on the kitchen wall; it works marvellously well. A small stainless bowl (D) held in one hand, and electric beater

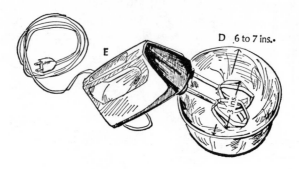

held in the other (E), and cream of tartar work very well too. The important point for each is the beater–bowl relationship. Use the largest whisk that will fit into a copper bowl (F) or the smallest stainless bowl that will function with your hand-held electric beater; in each case, this is so that you can keep the whole egg mass in continuous motion.

TEMPERATURE CHANGES

Great-grandmother used to calculate how hot her oven was by the time it took to brown a piece of white paper; taffy was done when the sugar syrup formed a hard ball in a glass of water; and if she missed on the roast she claimed she had got out of the wrong side of the bed that morning. Meat thermometers take the guess out of roasting; standard types are the stainless model (D) and the dial type (c). A thermometer for deep-fat frying (A) can double for sweet making, but if you do much sugar work you will want a sugar thermometer too. Accurate oven thermometers are essential for any serious cooking. The stainless-steel type (B) is to be had in most stores. When you are warned not to let the *crème anglaise* come near the boil or you may scramble the egg yolks, yet sternly reminded that you still must heat them enough to thicken the sauce, this stainless-steel temperature spoon (E) will tell you when 160°F. and the danger point have arrived; since its temperature dial registers from 50°to 400°F., you can also use the spoon for sugar boiling and deep-fat frying.

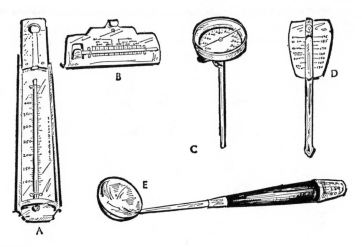

TINS

Round cake tins (A)

1. Top diameter 8 inches; $1\frac{1}{2}$ inches deep. 2. Top diameter 9 inches; $1\frac{1}{2}$ inches deep.

French tins (*moules à biscuits, moule à manqué*): 1. Top diameter $8\frac{1}{2}$ inches; $1\frac{1}{2}$ inches deep. 2. Top diameter 9 inches; 2 inches deep.

Square cake tins (B)

1. Measured across the top, 8 inches by 8 inches; 2 inches deep.
2. Measured across the top, 9 inches by 9 inches; $1\frac{1}{2}$ inches deep.
3. Measured across the top, 9 inches by 9 inches; 2 inches deep.

French tins (*moule à manqué carré*): 1. Measured across the top, $7\frac{3}{4}$ inches by $7\frac{3}{4}$ inches; $1\frac{1}{2}$ inches deep. 2. Measured across the top, 9 inches by 9 inches; $1\frac{1}{2}$ inches deep.

Pizza trays, round biscuit trays (C)

Inside diameter, 12 to 14 inches; $\frac{3}{4}$ inch deep.

French tin (*tourtière*): various sizes, usually in black iron (*tôle noire*).

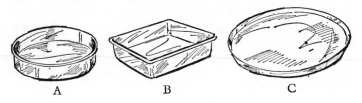

Swiss-roll tin, baking tin (D)

Measured across the top, $15\frac{1}{2}$ inches by $11\frac{1}{2}$ inches; 1 inch deep.

French tin (*caisse à biscuits, caisse à génoise*): many sizes, from 8 inches by 12 inches up to bakery dimensions.

Baking sheets (E)

From 9 inches by 14 inches to 14 inches by 17 inches for home ovens.

French baking sheets (*plaques à pâtisserie, plaques à bords évasés, plaques à pinces*): in *tôle noire* or in aluminium, various sizes from 12 to 14 inches on up.

Pie plates (F)

1. Top diameter 8 inches; $1\frac{1}{4}$ inches deep. 2. Top diameter 9 inches; $1\frac{1}{2}$ inches deep. 3. Top diameter 11 inches; $1\frac{1}{4}$ inches deep.

There is no French equivalent.

Bread tin, meat-loaf tin, angel-loaf tin (G)

Measurements vary according to individual manufacturers. Bread tins are usually $7\frac{3}{4}$ inches by 4 inches, and $2\frac{1}{4}$ inches deep, or $9\frac{1}{4}$ inches by $5\frac{1}{4}$ inches, and $2\frac{3}{4}$ inches deep. Angel-loaf tins are usually 13 inches or 16 inches long.

French tins (*moules à cake, moules à biscottes, moules à pain de mie* (covered)) come in a variety of sizes.

PASTRY: ROLLING, SCRAPING, AND GLAZING

If you are going into *quiches, pâtés en croûte,* and especially into the fascinating realm of French puff pastry, pages 164–211, get yourself a slab of marble; its coolness helps prevent the dough from softening, and its smooth surface is easy to scrape clean. A piece that can slide in and out of your refrigerator will be a miraculous help to pastry-making in hot weather. You can usually find ready-cut polished marble in furniture stores; you can sometimes pick up an old marble

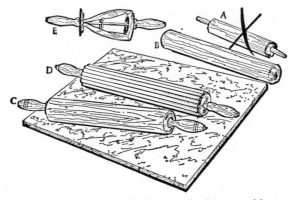

table-top or bureau-top in a junk shop; or look up marble suppliers in the telephone directory. The minimum size to consider is $\frac{3}{4}$ inch thick and the size of your refrigerator shelf.

One or two professionally designed rolling pins with rolling surfaces 16 to 18 inches long are essential for any pastry work – the silly toy pin (A), still sold to débutante cooks, makes hard work of any rolling operation. The French boxwood pin, *rouleau à pâtisserie en buis* (B), which is 18 inches long and 2 inches in diameter, or its Italian equivalent, both without handles, are as useful for rolling as

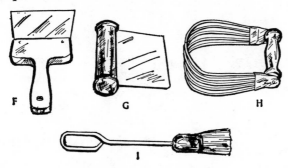

they are for beating chilled pastry into rolling shape. The fine professional American pin (C), made of polished hardwood with ball-bearing handles, is heavy enough to do half the work for you, and the French cannelated pin (D), *le Tutove*, is especially designed to spread out the layers of butter inside the puff pastry or croissant dough as you roll. The rotary croissant cutter (E) then finishes the operation.

For scraping pastry off the work surface, and also for cutting and chopping dough, the hardware-shop paint scraper (F) does almost as good a job as the French pastry scraper, *coupe-pâte* (G). The pastry blender (H), with its multiple chopping blades, cuts the butter into the flour when you are making pie dough by hand – it prevents the hot-finger syndrome that causes cardboard pastry.

Several pastry brushes (I) are needed, for glazing the tart with beaten egg as well as for general basting; be sure to buy ones designed for pastry or for basting, since cheap brushes leave bad tastes and drop hairs.

SMALL MOULDS (*PETITS MOULES*) FOR TARTLETS, *BRIOCHES, PETITS FOURS*

These should be in tinned metal, *fer-blanc*, which is less likely to cause sticking problems than aluminium; if you have to scrub them after baking, warm them briefly and rub lightly with oiled paper towelling

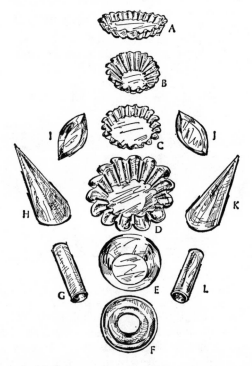

to keep the moulds from rusting or sticking. Buy at least a dozen of whatever models you choose, so that you can form and bake as many at once as possible. Tartlet moulds (A, C, E, I, J) are usually $\frac{1}{2}$ inch deep and from $1\frac{1}{2}$ to 3 inches in diameter or length. Individual *brioches* are usually baked in the round fluted moulds (B and D), although these moulds can serve for tartlets and entrée pastries too. Baby *savarins* are formed and baked in the ring mould (F), while *cornets* and *rouleaux* are formed around the metal horns (H and K) and tubes (G and L).

CUTTERS (*DÉCOUPOIRS; EMPORTE-PIÈCES*)

If you are going into serious pastry work, sets of round and oval cutters neatly packed in tin boxes make storage and retrieval no problem at all. Oval cutters come plain (*unis*) (I) or fluted (*cannelés*) (D–H), with the smallest in the set being $1\frac{5}{8}$ inches long and the largest $4\frac{3}{4}$ inches. Sets of plain (J) and fluted round cutters (K–O) go from $\frac{5}{8}$ inch to 4 inches in diameter. The tiny cutters in the foreground, *découpoirs à truffes* (P–X), make designs in truffle slices, egg whites, and other small decorative elements for aspics and pastries. Something like the ravioli wheel (B), the large Italian wheel (A), or the pastry wheel (C) is always useful for pie doughs, puff pastries, and general dough cutting.

When you must prick the sheet of dough for Napoleons, page 605, all over at $\frac{1}{4}$-inch intervals, a fork takes quite a number of minutes while

the roller pricker (Y), which doubles as a meat-tenderizer, covers the area in a few passes; its cast-aluminium head is 2 inches in diameter and its sturdy wooden handle is 4 inches long.

FLAN RINGS AND *VOL-AU-VENT* CUTTERS

Flan rings, *formes sans fond* (G, H, J, K, and I), come in all sizes and many shapes; they are designed especially for making the free-standing tart shells, pie shells, and *quiches* illustrated in Volume I, pages 162–5. A set of graduated *vol-au-vent* cutters (A–F) comprises 12 discs slightly

raised to provide a finger hold in the centre; discs range in size from 4 to 10½ inches in diameter. They are invaluable not only for cutting the *vol-au-vent* on page 187, but also for making circles in floured pastry sheets, like the biscuit cups on page 548, or for any other circular cutting or marking operations, like the free-standing tart shells on page 159.

SOUFFLÉ DISHES AND BAKING DISHES

When you are instructed to 'bake the dessert in 2½-pint cylindrical mould or dish, such as a *charlotte*, 4 inches deep', A, D, and E are the dishes to use. The French *charlotte* moulds (A and D) are the most useful baking dishes you can have in your kitchen, because you can bake in

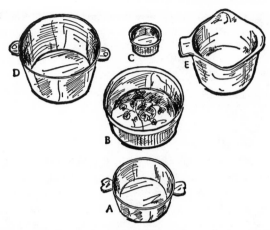

them, mould in them, caramelize them, heat them on top of the stove as well as in the oven, and you can serve from a napkin-wrapped *charlotte* mould. Be sure you buy the all-purpose type in tin-washed metal, *tôle étamée*; there are some models in flimsy aluminium that are good only for cold desserts. The flameproof ceramic baking and soufflé dish (E) is excellent too, and a little deeper than the *charlottes*. French ovenproof white soufflé dishes (B and C) are attractive for baking and serving; for soufflés, tie a paper collar around them to hold the puff, as illustrated in Volume I, page 182.

PÂTÉ MOULDS

Although you can make do with other methods, the traditional hinged mould for *pâtés* is comforting to own, decorative to look at,

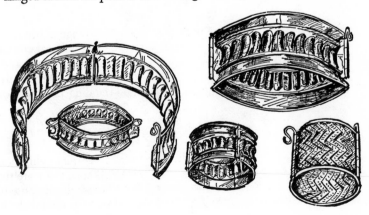

and will produce the beautiful finished product illustrated on pages 433–9. These are of *tôle étamée*, tin-washed metal, and come in many sizes, shapes, and patterns. A 2-litre (3½-pint) size is the most useful when you are buying only one. If you do not know how much a particular mould will hold, set it on a large piece of heavy foil or brown paper, fill with dried beans or rice, remove mould, and measure the beans or rice.

MISCELLANEOUS SMALL MOULDS

Eggs form themselves most happily in aspic when the mould is oval; the *moules à dariole ovales* (B and C) come with plain or fancy bottoms.

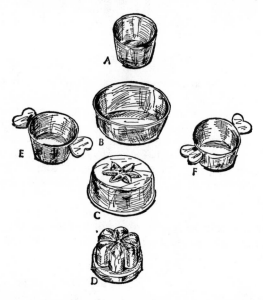

Babas are baked in tiny *charlotte* moulds (E and F) or the *dariole ronde* (A); these are useful also for individual servings of aspic, and for small soufflés and custards. The miniature fluted mould (D) is for fancy aspics.

MOULDS FOR BAKING, FOR ASPICS, AND FOR FROZEN DESSERTS

Although the *Kougloff* and *trois frères* moulds (A and D) are designed for cakes, and the ice-cream moulds (E and F) for *bombes glacées*, all of the models pictured here are useful for aspics, and all, with the obvious

exception of the fish (B), would do for frozen desserts and Bavarian creams. Use a simple pattern for frozen desserts (C and G); beware of too complicated a design or you may have terrible difficulties unmoulding; the pattern in H is about as far as you can go. Although more modern materials are available, we like *tôle étamée*, tin-washed metal, for both baking and aspics because it seasons well – meaning it seems to present few sticking problems. Tin-lined copper for aspics is pretty to look at if you do not mind the initial expense and subsequent cleaning.

WINE GLASSES

If space is a problem, you need only one type of wine glass for claret, Burgundy, Rhine wine, champagne, or Chianti – the tulip-

shaped glass (A); fill it slightly less than half full to give room for swirling and sniffing. Equally serviceable is the shorter glass (B). If you are going to serve both a red and a white wine at a meal, use a larger glass (A) for the red wine in proportion to the one for the white wine (B); the white wine glass is usually placed on the outside. All of these are inexpensive and should be available in any wine shop or department store, as well as in all the restaurant and hotel supply stores. For prestigious clarets and Burgundies, the large-bowled glass (F) is amusing; a normal serving of 3 ounces looks small in it but develops its fullest bouquet. If you like to see all the champagne bubbles, hollow-stemmed crystal (E) is what to look for, although some connoisseurs sniff at wide-mouthed glasses for that noble brew. Cut-crystal sherry glasses (C) will start off any gathering in an elegant manner, and the brandy snifter (D) will release after-dinner esters.

CORKSCREWS AND BOTTLE-OPENERS

The reasonably priced barman's corkscrew and bottle-cap opener (A) is designed for professionals. The flange on the left rests on the neck of the bottle to give you leverage, while the knife blade on the right,

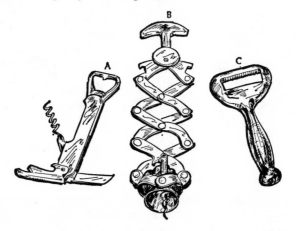

extended for display here but folded into the body of the opener when not in use, is for cutting the lead-foil cap off the wine bottle. The familiar French zig-zag (B) does a good job of leverage when corks are stubborn, and the heavy bottle-cap opener (C) is highly efficient.

Appendix Three
Temperature Equivalents for Oven Thermostat Markings

Fahrenheit	Gas Mark	Centigrade	Heat of Oven
225°F.	$\frac{1}{4}$	110°C.	Very cool
250°F.	$\frac{1}{2}$	130°C.	Very cool
275°F.	1	140°C.	Cool
300°F.	2	150°C.	Cool
325°F.	3	170°C.	Moderate
350°F.	4	180°C.	Moderate
375°F.	5	190°C.	Fairly hot
400°F.	6	200°C.	Fairly hot
425°F.	7	220°C.	Hot
450°F.	8	230°C.	Very hot
475°F.	9	240°C.	Very hot

Appendix Four
Table of Measures

U.S. cups	Fluid U.S. ounces	British terms (approx.)	Fluid British ounces	Metric terms (approx.)	Milli-litres
1 tsp.	$\frac{1}{6}$ oz.	1 tsp.	$\frac{1}{6}$ oz.	1 tsp.	5
1 tbl.	$\frac{1}{2}$ oz.	1 tbl.	$\frac{1}{2}$ oz.	1 tbl.	15
$\frac{1}{4}$ cup	2 oz.	4 tbl.	2 oz.	$\frac{1}{2}$ dl	59
$\frac{1}{3}$ cup	$2\frac{2}{3}$ oz.	5 tbl.	$2\frac{4}{5}$ oz.	$\frac{3}{4}$ dl	79
$\frac{1}{2}$ cup	4 oz.	$\frac{1}{5}$ pt	4 oz.	1 dl	119
$\frac{2}{3}$ cup	$5\frac{1}{3}$ oz.	$\frac{1}{4}$ pt	5 oz.	$1\frac{1}{2}$ dl	157
$\frac{3}{4}$ cup	6 oz.	6 oz.	6 oz.	$1\frac{3}{4}$ dl	178
1 cup	8 oz.	8 oz.	8 oz.	$\frac{1}{4}$ l	237
$1\frac{1}{4}$ cups	10 oz.	$\frac{1}{2}$ pt	10 oz.	3 dl	296
$1\frac{1}{3}$ cups	$10\frac{2}{3}$ oz.	$\frac{1}{2}$ pt	11 oz.	$3\frac{1}{4}$ dl	325
$1\frac{1}{2}$ cups	12 oz.	12 oz.	12 oz.	$3\frac{1}{2}$ dl	355
$1\frac{2}{3}$ cups	$13\frac{1}{3}$ oz.	13 oz.	13 oz.	$3\frac{3}{4}$ dl	385
$1\frac{3}{4}$ cups	14 oz.	$\frac{3}{4}$ pt	14 oz.	4 dl	414
2 cups (1 pt)	16 oz.	$\frac{3}{4}$ pt	16 oz.	$4\frac{3}{4}$ dl	475
$2\frac{1}{2}$ cups	20 oz.	1 pt	21 oz.	6 dl	592
3 cups	24 oz.	$1\frac{1}{5}$ pt	25 oz.	$\frac{3}{4}$ l	710
4 cups (1 qt)	32 oz.	$1\frac{1}{2}$ pt	$33\frac{1}{3}$ oz.	1 l	946
6 cups ($1\frac{1}{2}$ qt)	48 oz.	$2\frac{1}{2}$ pts	$49\frac{1}{2}$ oz.	$1\frac{1}{2}$ l	1420
8 cups (2 qt)	64 oz.	$3\frac{1}{4}$ pts	66 oz.	2 l	1893
$2\frac{1}{2}$ qts	80 oz.	4 pts	83 oz.	$2\frac{1}{2}$ l	2366
3 qts	96 oz.	5 pts	99 oz.	$2\frac{3}{4}$ l	2839
4 qts	128 oz.	$6\frac{1}{2}$ pts	133 oz.	$3\frac{3}{4}$ l	3785

Notes

1. British and metric terms are approximate. Fluid ounces and milli-litres are exact. For home cooking exact measures are not usually necessary. All spoon measurements in this book should be regarded as level spoonfuls.

2. 1000 ml = 100 cl = 10 dl = 1 l.

Index

Page references are to this volume (II) and to Volume I (I).

Page references are to this volume (II) and to Volume I (I).

Page references are to this volume (II) and to Volume I (I).

Page references are to this volume (II) and to Volume I (I).

Page references are to this volume (II) and to Volume I (I).

choux brocoli: *see* broccoli
choux de Bruxelles: *see* brussels
    sprouts
clafouti(s), (I) 699–702
  apple (aux pommes), (I) 701; (II)
    567
    rum, and currants (normande),
      (II) 567
  blackberry (aux mûres), (I) 701
  cherry, (I) 699
    with liqueur (à la liqueur), (I) 700
    or pear, with almonds (à la
      Bourdaloue), (I) 702
  pear (aux poires), (I) 700, 702
  plum (aux pruneaux; aux prunes),
    (I) 701; (II) 569
  see also suggestions for other fruits,
    (II) 570
clarification of meat stocks, (I) 130
clarified butter, (I) 34–5
coat a spoon (definition of), (I) 30
cochon de lait: *see* pork, suckling pig
cockerel, (I) 256
cocktail appetizers: *see* appetizers
cognac
  for cooking, (I) 51
  for jellied stocks and aspics, (I) 133
cold
  buffet, (I) 574–617
  dishes, list of, (I) 615–17
  see also chicken, cold; soups, cold;
    etc.
compote of fruit
  peaches, poached in syrup, (I) 672
  pears poached in red wine, (I) 685;
    (II) 574
concombres: *see* cucumbers
cone, paper decorating, to make, (II)
  662
confit d'oie: *see* goose, preserved
conversion formulas, (II) 699
coq au vin, (I) 287
coq en pâte, (II) 372
coquilles Saint-Jacques, (I) 238–40
  bouillabaisse, (II) 66
  see also scallops

cornet en papier, to make, (II) 662
cornets, puff pastry (II) 198–203, 610
cornflour
  for soufflé sauce base (I) 655, 660
  thickening for brown sauce, (I) 89
couper en dès (to dice), (I) 31
COURGETTES
general information, (II) 477–9
  to blanch whole, (II) 478–9
  to buy and store, (II) 477
  to grate and salt, (II) 483–4
  peeling, blanching, salting, (II)
    478
  weights and measures, (II) 478
  in aubergine casserole (ratatouille),
    (I) 539
  baked: *see below* gratinéed
  blanched, whole; recipes, (II)
    479–83
  in cream
    grated (râpées à la crème), (II)
      485
    pieces, with tarragon (étuvées à
      la crème), (II) 481
  with garlic, parsley, and béchamel
    (en persillade, gratinées),
    (II) 483
  grated
    in cream (râpées à la crème), (II)
      485
    moulded custard of, with cheese
      (timbale), (II) 488
    in olive oil and garlic (râpées,
      sautées à la provençale), (II)
      486
    sautéed (râpées, sautées), (II) 484
    with spinach (aux épinards), (II)
      486
  gratinéed (baked)
    with cheese (à la milanaise), (II)
      481
    with cheese sauce (mornay), (II)
      483
    with garlic, parsley, and
      béchamel (persillade), (II)
      483

Page references are to this volume (II) and to Volume I (I).

Page references are to this volume (II) and to Volume I (I).

ENTRÉES AND LUNCHEON DISHES,
  vol-au-vent
    with chicken filling (garniture de
      volaille, financière), (II) 211
    with seafood filling (garniture
      dieppoise; aux fruits de
      mer), (II) 210
    with sweetbread filling (ris de
      veau à la financière), (II) 208
entremets: see desserts
épices, pain d', (II) 627
épices fines, for sausages, (II) 385
épinards: see spinach
equipment: see kitchen equipment
escabèche, (I) 592
escalopes de veau: see veal, scallops
espagnole sauce base, (I) 85
étuver (to braise), (I) 29

Fahrenheit–Centigrade conversions,
  (I) 42–3; (II) 699
faire sauter (to toss), (I) 33
farces: see pâtés and terrines;
      sausages; stuffings
farina (semoule de blé)
  semolina gnocchi, (I) 205
  for thickening soup, (II) 40
farine: see flour
fat
  fat back, (I) 603; (II) 386
  goose, (I) 307–8; (II) 417–20
  pork, (I) 603; (II) 385, 423, 435
  removal of, (I) 30
  to render, (II) 418
  for sautéing, (I) 32–3
  see also larding; pork, fat
fennel (fenouil)
  cold, à la grecque, (I) 576
  garnish for soup, (II) 48
feuilletée, pâte: see pastry, puff
filberts (noisettes)
  meringue layer, for cake (le
      Progrès), (II) 648
  to prepare, (II) 649
fillet
  of beef: see beef, fillet

fillet – contd
  of fish: see fish fillets
  mignon, (I) 317, 323
  steaks, (I) 317, 322–6
FILLINGS
  aubergine, for hard-boiled eggs or
      tomatoes, (II) 466
  for cake; see cake fillings; see also
      list, (II) 660–62
  cheese, for appetizers, entrées,
      pastries, (I) 224–6; (II) 201
  chicken
    cream (fondue de volaille), (I) 226
    for vol-au-vent (garniture de
      volaille), (II) 211
  for crêpes, (I) 693–8
  for croquettes, (I) 226
  for desserts: see desserts, fillings
  seafood
    cream (fondue de crustacés), (I)
      225
    for vol-au-vent (garniture aux
      fruits de mer), (II) 210
  stuffings: see stuffings and list, (II)
      664–6
  sweetbread, for vol-au-vent (ris de
      veau à la financière), (II) 208
  turkey (fondue de volaille), (I) 226
financière, à la (garniture)
  with chicken, quenelles, etc., (II)
      211
  with sweetbreads, etc., (II) 208
fines herbes, (I) 37
FISH (poisson), (I) 229–54; (II) 71–83
  general information, (I) 229; (II) 71–2
    buying, (I) 229
    fish for bouillabaisse, (I) 68
    fish for poached fillets, (I) 230
    fish for quenelles, (I) 206–7
    fish for stews and soups, (II) 71–2
  bouillabaisse, (I) 70
    fish for, (I) 68
  fillets (filets)
    poached in white wine (pochés
      au vin blanc), (I) 230–39
    stuffed (de sole farcis), (I) 238

Page references are to this volume (II) and to Volume I (I).

Page references are to this volume (II) and to Volume I (I).

Page references are to this volume (II) and to Volume I (I).

Page references are to this volume (II) and to Volume I (I).

Page references are to this volume (II) and to Volume I (I).

Page references are to this volume (II) and to Volume I (I).

Page references are to this volume (II) and to Volume I (I).

roux – *contd*
  for brown sauce, (I) 87; (II) 232
  for cheese sauce, (II) 453
  for white sauce, (I) 74
rum (rhum)
  in apple aspic, (I) 669
  babas, (I) 704
  in butter creams, (I) 727–30
  cake, caramel custard, flambée
    (charlotte jamaïque en
    flammes), (II) 589
  for cooking, (I) 51
  soufflé, with macaroons (soufflé
    démoulé aux macarons), (I)
    662
  syrup for babas, (I) 705
rye flour, in spice cake (pain
  d'épices), (II) 627

sabayon sauce, for pears, (II) 575
Saint-André, le, (II) 638, 640
Saint-Cyr, le, glacé, (II) 556
Saint-Jacques en bouillabaisse, les,
  (II) 66
Saint-Jacques, velouté de, (II) 67
salad(s) (salades), (I) 579–81
  combination (niçoise), (I) 579
  mussel (de moules), (I) 250
  potato (de pommes de terre), (I)
    578–81
  rice for (riz au blanc), (I) 570
  rice and beetroot (à la d'Argenson),
    (I) 581
  sweet pepper (de poivrons,
    provençale), (II) 539
salmon (saumon)
  gratin (aux fruits de mer), (I) 176
  mousse, (I) 600
  quenelles, (I) 211
  soufflé, (I) 187–8
  in stuffing for lamb (farce
    mentonnaise), (I) 367
  timbales, (I) 196
salt
  cure of goose, (II) 418
  cure of pork, (II) 410

salt – *contd*
  spiced, for charcuterie (sel épicé),
    (II) 384–5
SAUCE(s), (I) 73–124
  note: sauces for desserts listed
    separately
  general information, (I) 73
  aïoli, (I) 111; (II) 81
    for chicken (bouillabaisse), (II)
      355
    for fish stew (bourride), (II) 81
  alsacienne; de Sorges, (I) 112–13
  anchovy (aux anchois), (I) 85
    with garlic for beef stew
     (provençale), (I) 352
  aurore, (I) 81
  bâtarde, (I) 84
  béarnaise, (I) 104
    with meat-glaze flavouring
     (Colbert), (I) 105
    with tomato flavouring
     (Choron), (I) 104
  béchamel, (I) 74–83
    with aubergines, (II) 460
  bercy
    with fish fillets, (I) 231
    with steak, (I) 320
  bonne femme, (I) 238
  bordelaise, (I) 95, 321, 453
  bourguignonne, (I) 95
  brandy, (I) 321
  brown (brunes), (I) 85–96
  butter (beurre)
    brown (noir; noisette), (I) 117
     for calf's brains, (I) 447
     for chicken breasts (noisette),
      (I) 295
    cold flavoured, (I) 118–124
    lemon (au citron), (I) 117
    white (blanc; nantais), (I) 117
  caper (aux câpres), (I) 85
  Chantilly, (I) 102
  chasseur, (I) 93, 399
  chaud-froid
    blanche neige, (I) 124
    for chicken, (II) 349

SAUCE(S) – *contd*
  cheese with wine and garlic
    (fondue de fromage), (I)
    124, 137
  Chivry, (I) 81
  Choron, (I) 104
  Colbert, (I) 105
  cream (crème; suprême), (I) 78, 79,
    292–4, 492
    and mushroom, for ham, (I) 423
    and mustard, for liver, (I) 438
    sour (vinaigrette à la crème),
      with dill, (I) 114
    and white wine, for chicken
      fricassee, (I) 282
  curry
    brown (brune au cari), (I) 92
    white (au cari), (I) 82, 285; (II)
      328
  deglazing, (I) 94–5, 279, 295
  diable, (I) 90
  dieppoise, (I) 236
  dill, (I) 114
  duxelles, (I) 93
  egg yolk
    (parisienne; allemande), (I) 79
    see also below hollandaise;
      mayonnaise
  espagnole (sauce base), (I) 85
  game (poivrade), (I) 89
  garlic (à l'ail)
    and anchovy for beef stew, (I)
      352
    and basil (pistou), (I) 64; (II)
      217–18, 464–6, 483
    and egg yolks for chicken, (I) 280
    for lamb, (I) 362–3
    mayonnaise (aïoli), (I) 111; (II)
      81, 355
    and pepper (rouille) for fish
      soup, (I) 70
  herbal
    brown (aux fines herbes), (I) 91
    hollandaise, (I) 102
    mayonnaise, (I) 109, 110, 112
    white wine (Chivry), (I) 81

SAUCE(S) – *contd*
  hollandaise, (I) 97–105
    electric blender or liquidizer, (I)
      100
    hand-made, (I) 98–9
    mock (bâtarde; au beurre), (I) 84
    variations, (I) 101–5
  italienne, (I) 95, 444
  jus lié, (I) 89
  Madeira (madère), (I) 93, 323, 325
    brown, with truffles (Périgueux),
      (I) 94
    with mushrooms, (I) 551
    for tongue, (II) 324
  maltaise, (I) 103
  marchand de vins, (I) 321
  marrow (moelle), (I) 37, 320–21,
    453
  matelote, (I) 449
  mayonnaise, (I) 105–13
    electric blender or liquidizer, (I)
      108
    hand-made, (I) 106–7
    remedy for turned, (I) 107
    variations, (I) 108–13
  mornay, (I) 80, 216
    for broccoli, (II) 453
    for poached chicken, (II) 347
  mousseline, (I) 103
    sabayon, (I) 103, 190
  mushroom (duxelles), (I) 93
    brown (à l'italienne), (I) 95, 444
    and cream, (I) 422
    with tomatoes (chasseur), (I) 93,
      399
  mustard (moutarde), (I) 85, 115
    brown (Robert), (I) 91
    with cream (à la normande), (I)
      413
    for liver, (I) 438
    with pearl onions and currants
      for tongue (à l'aigre-douce),
      (II) 321
    with tomatoes and cream
      (Nénette), (I) 419
  Nantua, (I) 238

Page references are to this volume (II) and to Volume I (I).

Page references are to this volume (II) and to Volume I (I).

Page references are to this volume (II) and to Volume I (I).

sweets
  chocolate truffles (les truffes aux
    chocolat), (II) 617
  walnut and almond puffs (les
    croquets Denison), (II) 618
Swiss chard: *see* chard
syrup (sugar)
  for butter-cream filling, (I) 727-8
  caramel, (I) 623: (II) 590
  for fondant, (II) 657
  for fruit poaching, (I) 672-3,
    685-6
  kirsch, for savarins, (I) 707
  rum, for babas, (I) 705

tables
  chicken types, (I) 256
  of equivalents (American, French,
    British), (I) 39-43; (II) 700
  soufflés, ingredients proportions, (I)
    183
  temperature conversion, (I) 43; (II)
    699
  timetables for roasting: *see*
    chicken; duck; etc.
tarragon (estragon)
  butter (beurre d'), (I) 121
    with meat glaze (Colbert), (I)
      121
  chicken
    in aspic, (I) 587
    casserole-poached, (II) 357
    casserole-roasted, (I) 272
    fricasseed, (I) 286
  sauce: *see* sauces, tarragon
TART(S) FOR DESSERT (tartes
    sucrées), (I) 675-92; (II)
    593-602
  almond (Pithiviers), (II) 611
  apple (aux pommes), (I) 678; (II)
    597
    with custard (normande), (I) 680
    upside-down (des Demoiselles
      Tatin), (I) 681
  apricot (aux abricots), (I) 682
  variations, (I) 683-4

TART(S) FOR DESSERT – *contd*
  cherry (aux cerises, flambée), (I)
    686-7
  cream cheese (au fromage frais), (I)
    691
    and prune (et aux pruneaux), (I)
      691
  custard fillings for, (I) 629-31
  fruits, various, in puff pastry, (II)
    599, 602
  jam (jalousie), (II) 600-602
  lemon (au citron), (I) 688-91
    with almonds (et aux amandes),
      (I) 690
    soufflé, (I) 688
  lime soufflé (aux limettes), (I)
    688
  pastry dough for, (I) 675-7; (II)
    162-3
    puff pastry, (II) 174-80
  pastry shells for, (I) 677
    puff pastry, (II) 593-7
  peach (aux pêches), (I) 682
  pear (aux poires), (I) 681; (II)
    597
    and almond (à la Bourdaloue),
      (I) 685
  pineapple (à l'ananas), (I) 688
  puff pastry (pâte feuilletée)
    almond (Pithiviers), (II) 611
    apple or pear (aux pommes ou
      aux poires), (II) 597
    other fruits, (II) 599, 602
    peekaboo with jam or fruit
      (jalousie), (II) 600-602
    shells for fruit (abaisses en
      feuilletage pour, aux fruits),
      (II) 593-7
  strawberry (aux fraises), (I) 683
TART(S) FOR ENTRÉE
  moulds for, (I) 162-3; (II) 694
  onion, (I) 171
  pastry dough for, (I) 159-62; (II)
    156-8, 162-3
  pastry shells for, (I) 162-6; (II)
    159-62

Page references are to this volume (II) and to Volume I (I),

Page references are to this volume (II) and to Volume I (I).

turnip(s) – *contd*
purée, with rice (purée Freneuse),
(II) 532
purée of swedes (la purée,
châteaux en Suède), (II) 533
sautéed in butter (petits, sautés, en
garniture), (II) 534
soup, green (potage Untel), (II)
41–3
turnovers
with Roquefort cheese (petits
chaussons au Roquefort),
(I) 227–8
pastry dough for, (I) 159–62; (II)
156–8, 162–3, 166–73

unmoulding, directions for
aspics, (I) 597–8
cakes, (I) 713–14
desserts, (I) 626
utensils: *see* kitchen equipment

vanilla (vanille), (I) 626
ice cream, with chocolate sauce
(Chantilly glacée, au
chocolat), (II) 563
other sauces and flavourings, (II)
564
in sauce or filling (crème anglaise;
crème pâtissière), (I) 627–30
soufflé, (I) 656, 660
variations follow recipe: symbol*
before recipe title
VEAL (veau), (I) 380–406; (II) 282–308
general information, (I) 380–88; (II)
282–3, 289–90
cuts for
chops, (I) 400; (II) 283
ossobuco, (II) 294
patties, (I) 402
roasting, (I) 380
scallops, (I) 395
steaks, (I) 402; (II) 283
stewing, (I) 392; (II) 289–90
quality, (I) 380
timing for roasts, (I) 381

VEAL – *contd*
blanquette, (I) 389, 392
boudin blanc (sausage), (II) 371, 387
brains: *see* brains
braised
baked in pastry (feuilletons, en
croûte), (II) 306
sliced and stuffed (en
feuilletons), (II) 302
breast (poitrine de)
general information, (II) 296–8
to bone, (II) 297–8
to buy, (II) 296–7
stuffed, braised (farcie), (II) 298–
302
stuffings for
chard or spinach, (II) 299
other stuffings, (II) 302, 664–6
chops and steaks (côtes de;
rouelles), (I) 400–402; (II)
283–9
braised
gratinéed with cheese (au
fromage), (II) 285
with herbs (aux herbes), (I)
400
variations, (I) 402
with mushrooms and cream
(braisées aux champignons),
(II) 286
with potatoes (Champvallon,
gratinées), (II) 287
in wine (dans leur jus), (II) 283
variations (pistou, bonne
femme, etc.), (II) 289
cold, (I) 616
kidneys: *see* kidneys, veal and lamb
knuckle with beans (cassoulet), (I)
437
left-over
in aubergine and tomato
casserole, (II) 470
for patties, (I) 406
loaf (pain de), (I) 406
marinades, (I) 387–8, 605; (II) 303
pâtés: *see* pâtés and terrines

Page references are to this volume (II) and to Volume I (I).

Page references are to this volume (II) and to Volume I (I).